PHAIDON
BOOK OF THE
BALLET

PHAIDON
BOOK OF THE
BALLET

With a Preface by Rudolf Nureyev

PUBLISHER'S NOTE

For nearly four hundred years the history of ballet has continued without a break, pursuing a clear internal logic throughout that time though manners and audiences might change, and aims and expressive quality might vary. The overall production of theatrical dance has been immense, one might almost say infinite, since it is certain that no institution or scholar of the dance, no team of historians, could ever make a definitive list of all the ballets performed in every land during those centuries. Thus, for this book a choice has had to be made and, as with all choices, it must arise from a judgment of value which, however carefully weighed and considered, finally depends on the cultural education and sensibility of the selector. Our constant aim has been to record crucial moments in the long history of the dance and to present a panorama that includes those ballets no longer in today's repertory, but which nonetheless had a definite influence on the evolution of the art that has achieved such glory and wide acclaim in our time. Historians, critics, musicologists, choreographers, designers, museum and theatre directors, photographers have all contributed to this volume, and to all of them we profer our sincere thanks. If this book has succeeded in bringing a wider audience to the ballet, and in conveying a better understanding of the immense amount of historical assimilation, problems, research, and devotion that lies behind every ballet production, our common endeavour will have been well rewarded.

The following have contributed to this book: Alfio Agostini (AA), Silvia Berti (SB), Michele Buzzi (MB), Pietro Caputo (PC), Carla Maria Casanova (CMC), Paolo Fenoglio (PF), Angelo Foletto (AF), Moira Hodgson (MH), Olive Ordish (OO), Paolo Pacca (PP), Mario Pasi (MP), Giovanni Secondo (GS), Maria Simone Mongiardino (MSM).

ERRATA

p.9   Line 4: for 'larmoyant' read 'lachrymose'.
p.24   Line 39: for 'Bolshoi' read 'Kirov'.
p.32   Line 2: after Fonteyn add Kenneth MacMillan.
p.36   3 lines from bottom: for '*Quinta*' read Fifth Symphony.
p.233   Col 1, line 8: add (8) Rudolf Nureyev. Designed by Ezio Frigerio. London Colliseum, June 1977. London Festival Ballet with Rudolf Nureyev as Romeo and Patricia Ruanne as Juliet.
p.322   Col 2: Under Nureyev Rudolf add 'Raymonda, 154' and 'Romeo and Juliet 233'.

Editor-in-chief: Riccardo Mezzanotte
Editors and Picture Researchers: Francesca Agostini, Ada Jorio
Layout: Bruno Lando

Originally published in Italy under the title *Il Balletto: Repertorio del teatro di danza dal 1581*

Translated from the Italian by Olive Ordish

This edition published in 1981 by
Phaidon Press Limited,
Littlegate House, St Ebbe's Street, Oxford, OX1 1SQ

Copyright © 1979 by Arnoldo Mondadori. Editore. S.p.A., Milano
English Translation copyright © 1980 by Arnoldo Mondadori Editore, S.p.A., Milano

Printed and bound in Italy
by Officine Grafiche,
Arnoldo Mondadori Editore, Verona
ISBN 0 7148 2192 6

Ballet is still relatively young. Its history is short – it celebrates its 300th anniversary this year – but it is odd and interesting. Like a Cinderella fable in reverse, it tells the story of an art born in the ballrooms of princes which has gradually stolen into the hearts and firesides of ordinary people. Conceived in Italy and born in France, it grew up in Russia and its descendants flourish today in every continent in the world.

During the last twenty years its popularity has spread enormously – an 'explosion' in which I have been lucky enough to take part: dance today is no longer a minority art of interest only to a few specialists. At the same time it has become the subject of serious research of the kind applied to music, painting or drama. A knowledge of the past is essential if we are to take an intelligent view of the present and the future.

This book should be, then, a useful help to the enjoyment of today's performances as well as a fascinating glimpse of past achievements. The idea of presenting the ballets chronologically, instead of in the more usual alphabetical order, is excellent; besides a reference list, we get a survey of the whole growth of the art. At the time of writing this, I have no idea how the scheme will work out – some ballets have been revived and revised so often that they have become virtually timeless; but the general scheme seems to me logical and practical.

One of the lessons I have learnt from my own career – often giving me some amusement – is the way in which tastes differ from country to country. A ballet which gives me a big success in one place will be coolly received in another. Working as I do with many companies in many countries I have become rather objective about this; I recognise that everybody has his own preferences and prejudices and has a right to them. This book is being compiled in Milan and will obviously reflect a view of ballet as seen from Italy. This is bound to differ in some ways from the values applied in, say, London or New York; some favourite works and choreographers may be missing, while unfamiliar names will loom unusually large.

This seems to me a valuable corrective. Ballet is too wide-ranging an art to be contained in any single framework. Italy, is, after all, where it began, and I wish this book – its latest offspring – every success.

RUDOLF NUREYEV

While dancing is as old as mankind itself, it is customary to credit the birth of ballet to the performance in 1581 of the *Ballet Comique de la Reine* at the Palais du Petit Bourbon. It was not, of course, the first ballet in history – understood as a choreographic display of characters in a theatrical ambience – but the earliest of which we have records, or which is generally accepted as such in its unity of dance, music, and action illustrating a definite subject – in this case the story of Circe.

At that point in time, in a clearly defined center of power, two streams of tradition flowed into one: on one hand the dances that had grown up with the spirit of the people, and on the other the culture of a society that was turning back to classicism by way of mythology. It was the culmination of a long historical course of events which had started in the primitive "collective unconscious" and evolved through a continuous series of mutations and adaptations. Like all forms of theater, ballet developed in step with society and was its mirror. From time to time it took on the features of the dominant culture – today we might say that of the people – or interpreted the views of the opposition, neither of which remains the same for long. It has been a protracted journey from the diversion of a royal court to the modern philosophical ballet; progress has been slow and has not always followed a straight line. Ballet would not be what it is today had it not, as time went on, adopted new values without which it would have remained a mere spectacle of movement.

Those values, the importance of which grew until they became indispensable, could be dramatic, literary, musical, visual, or political. Modern dance and ballet are conscious participants in a total culture inasmuch as they see themselves as the voice of the present. And we have no choice but to refer to our own times.

In little more than half a century the society in which we live has broken away from all past experience, firmly maintaining that some of it can never be brought back to life. Next to traditional forms it has set very new and often opposite ones. The relationship between producer and consumer in the arts has radically altered, while freedom of expression has grown beyond all bounds. The greater participation of the ordinary citizen in public life, whether in representative or "popular" democracy, and the increasing spread of education, have brought with them a wealth of new ideas and an extraordinary widening of subject-matter. These call for ever deeper study and more intense, broader sharing of emotion that can be stimulated by a "message." When a ballet involves tens of thousands of people (as with Beethoven's *Ninth Symphony* when choreographed by Maurice Béjart), one cannot avoid drawing conclusions or refuse to look the phenomenon in the face.

Maia Plisetskaia in Carmen Suite. *Choreography by Alberto Alonso.*

7

Without entering into the question of this ballet's quality, let us examine its components:

– the transposition to a modern key of Beethoven's idea of the Absolute, with an accent on the theme joy–freedom–universality;

– the interpretation of that theme through the teaching of Frederick Nietzsche and, in particular, the "Dionysiac";

– the discovery that the Beethovenian theme and the Dionysiac element are connected with the idea of love and youth;

– the acceptance of the idea of going beyond romantic individualism and the heroic myth;

– the consequent recognition of their harmonious fusion in the collective unconscious;

– the use of different choreographic canons.

Within this framework *Ninth Symphony* appears as a ballet that involves the audience in an open-ended dialogue, at the same time interpreting a trend of thought (the challenge of youth) some years ahead of its time. This challenge is not presented on the level of rebellion or slogans, but as the need to supersede old situations and institutions. The "new happiness" – a favourite topic during these years – is dealt with by philosophical means and becomes a theatrical event (by way of Beethoven–Schiller–Nietzsche–oriental philosophy–socialism), replacing the principle of alienation and asserting – and there were many examples in the 1970s – the right to a policy of diversity.

Another basic characteristic of contemporary ballet is the breaking down of barriers between different modes of expression. Classical ballet, modern dance, the language of the body, oriental dancing, all can exist side by side, both silence and words can be brought into play; the choice is almost limitless. That such innovations are no longer greeted with cries of outrage is a measure of the art's progress in harmony with the liberation of culture and custom.

Obviously ballet is above all a choreographic activity; but no one could believe today that its value can be measured solely on that level. The concepts of beauty, harmony, and pleasure are as old as those of escapism, relaxation, and purity applied to music. It is certainly possible to evaluate a work of art outside its historical context and without considering its motivation, but that implies the acceptance of several important limitations.

One can admire the Beethoven of the *Ninth Symphony*, written in 1824, in a direct and simple way. But to grasp it, to understand why it was composed in that exact form at that particular time, one must know something of the composer's life, his opinions, his philosophy, and his education; investigate the composer-society relationship, discover why he took up so new and different a position in the face of the established work of his contemporaries.

Again, if we are not familiar with the arts at the turn of the nineteenth century, and the tragedy that overshadowed Europe, it will be difficult to understand the music of Gustav Mahler, which foresaw the split between man and nature, mourned the loss of love, and told us why we must fear death.

We must ask ourselves, moreover, whether it is possible to see and hear Alban Berg's *Wozzeck* without relating it to the horrors of World War I (although it is not mentioned in the opera) and poverty, and without looking critically at the idea of authority.

Also, when we consider that most famous of romantic ballets, *Giselle*, created in 1841, we shall remain blinkered if we fail to recognize in the music of Adam and the choreography of Perrot-Coralli (and much more besides) the preoccupations of a fanciful literature, the dawn of a new feminine ideal, an echo of larmoyant pathos, the thematic parallel with contemporary opera (love, grief, betrayal, madness), and the negation of logic according to the principles of the romantic liberation. It is its inner meaning and, of course, the artistic qualities of its presentation which have enabled *Giselle* to survive, a work that cannot be reduced to the formula uniting the almost melodramatic mime of the first act with a second act that is pure *ballet blanc*.

In our century the romantic ideal of womanhood (pure, fragile, sinless, a spirit ready for heaven) which sent Théophile Gautier into ecstasies is no longer considered historically true and is therefore unacceptable. That explains the new interest in the part of Prince Albrecht, one that Lifar chose for himself, not solely from motives of ambition or exhibitionism. The trend persists, and for the same reason. Of course the ballerina's part remains the central point of Adam's ballet, but it is projected in a more credible and rational light.

Since we now possess new critical standards, the same as those we apply to opera and drama, we are able to confront the phenomenon of ballet in its entirety. It is an entity growing from the contemporary world; its ever-increasing popularity a sign of its vitality and modernity. The universality of its language makes it easy to understand at all levels. Withered branches (such as the conventions of eighteenth-century mime) have fallen away and been replaced by a more fundamental form of gestural expression. We could say that the new thrust of ballet partially coincided with the crisis of the written word. The declaration of principles pronounced by Mikhail Fokine in 1904 and demonstrated in his work of the next ten years remains valid to this day. When Fokine maintained that "music is not a mere accompaniment to rhythmic steps but an organic part of the dance" and that "the quality of choreographic inspiration is determined by the quality of the music," he was stating one of the important truths of our age. Fokine also said that dancing was interpretation, not gymnastics, and that it was no longer possible to construct ballets out of a series of "dance numbers" and *entrées*. "Star turns" were irrelevant; for him ballet was a unity of movement, sound, and vision. The artists should subdue their personalities to the ballet and the mood of its music, not vice versa. We can imagine his contempt for those eighteenth-century composers whose poor and affected music was intended only to show off the skill of the prima ballerina.

These things were said in Russia – the Imperial Russia of 1904 – and forecast the revolution that swept through ballet under the patronage of Sergei Diaghilev, thanks to the active support of musical geniuses, especially the young Stravinsky (whose best-known works of that period were *Firebird* and *Petrouchka*). Ten years later the same Fokine laid down five essential points for the new ballet. We shall see what they were; but it must be said at once that in 1904 Fokine's ideas were not accepted in the Imperial Ballet, and that after 1914 he found himself superseded and set aside by new choreographic talent rising in the world of the *Ballets Russes*, from Nijinsky to Massine and from Nijinska to Balanchine. His mind looked ahead, but his heart turned towards the past.

The famous five points or principles can be summarized as follows: a) nothing according to pattern or ready-made; b) dance and mime at the service of dramatic expression, never used as mere *divertissement*; c) no conventional gestures unless required by the style of the ballet; expression involves the whole body; d) no purely ornamental grouping but a significant spatial relationship between group and individual; e) ballet has free and creative associations with the other arts and, in particular, should use music that has truth and quality and is not merely of accompaniment standard.

Creativity, the discovery of the body, the union of the arts, the rejection of the conventional: these were ideas destined to grow and triumph in the years to come. The first wave of ballet "reform" was put in motion by Sergei Diaghilev, a professional impresario and a man of immense culture and intuition. Diaghilev gathered around him an extraordinary group of artists whom he spurred and inspired to create a whole new repertoire. Modern ballet was born in those days as music, painting, and dance joined forces under that visionary banner.

Through Diaghilev, Fokine's ideas found their practical expression: a company of star dancers centered on Tamara Karsavina and Vaslav Nijinsky; a company of brilliant personalities pivoting on the strange gentleman who adored top hats and monocles. There were Massine and Balanchine, Sokolova and the aged Cecchetti, Bolm and Bronislava Nijinska. . . Musicians such as Stravinsky, Prokofiev and Satie; painters such as Alexandre Benois, Bakst, Picasso, and Rouault. Let us turn to the last London appearance of the Russian Ballet at Covent Garden in 1929. The program included *Le Bal* by Balanchine–Rieti–De Chirico, *The Prodigal Son* by Balanchine–Prokofiev–Rouault, and *Aurora's Wedding* (a part of *The Sleeping Beauty*) by Petipa–Tchaikovsky–Bakst. Among the performers was Serge Lifar who, after the company had been dispersed, dominated the French ballet scene for a long and fruitful period.

The cream of Russian and European creativity had gathered around the figure of Diaghilev, including young dancers in the process of being "groomed for stardom." When he died, his pupils, like the twelve apostles, were scattered to the four corners of the earth, bringing a life and continuity to ballet that we are only beginning fully to appreciate today.

The great movement of the *Ballets Russes* (in which it is hard to rank one participant above another, unless it be Vaslav Nijinsky, a strange character who left the scene quite young in 1919 and spent the rest of his life in a gentle state of mental alienation) gave birth to the most important events in the world of dance during our century. Besides the achievements of Lifar in Paris, there was the pioneer work of Ninette de Valois in England, Massine's activity in Europe, and Balanchine's great work of creating a national ballet in America. It is no exaggeration to say that ballet all over the world, even in Russia during the early Soviet period, was profoundly influenced by Diaghilev's actions, and that all the greatest exponents of dance were either members of his company or referred to its ideas.

Diaghilev had recruited into his company the best dancers of the day: Nijinsky, Karsavina, and many others had left the Imperial Ballet to follow him in his marvellous adventure. The enormous wealth of talent that came together in the early twentieth century gave rise to a renewal of the arts so radical as to deserve the title of a second Renaissance.

A succession of ballet creations curved away from the late romantic tradition

Swan Lake, *the American Ballet Theater production.*

10

until, aided by works of genius, they established the restoration of a classicism which was free of all the dross of romanticism (the Apollonian ideal) to release a whole new range of experiment. Always some new technical solution was found to deal with each existential problem as it arose. The repertory of Diaghilev's Russian Ballet still survives almost in its entirety, which is something of a miracle. Ballets such as *L'Après-midi d'un Faune*, *Daphnis and Chloë*, *Firebird*, *Les Noces*, *Parade*, *Les Biches*, *Petrouchka*, *The Prodigal Son*, *Pulcinella*, *Apollon Musagète*, *The Rite of Spring*, *Sheherazade*, together with the revived classics, were a part of the era's highest culture. In particular, they grafted onto the static world of the old ballet an exuberant new growth of vitality, innovation, and discovery. *Petrouchka* chased away the old fairy-tale conventions; the pagan mob trampled down the dainty ladies' wigs and fans.

From that moment there was no stopping the stream of ideas, confrontations, challenges, bombshells, violence, and rage. The ideal of a free association of talents producing a maximum of creativity spread like an oil stain, demonstrating the advantages of autonomy and independence and, at the same time, the usefulness of wisely administered subsidies. It should, however, be borne in mind that ballet has progressed only when it has been understood (as so many great men from Noverre to Fokine have tried to tell us) that music must be an integral part and the life blood of the dance, not just its accompaniment. A thousand miles stretch between *The Corsair* and *Agon*; from *Raymonda* to *Molière Imaginaire* the distance is lunar.

Those who believe only in formal values and claim that ballet must preserve an absolute purity (but what purity?) are stuck fast in a reactionary position, as are those who consider it absurd to employ a stage director for opera: there is no need for a tenor to understand the music, they consider, and innovations in staging are dangerous. On the other hand, since advanced ballet has shattered the romantic image, which exalted the soloists at the expense of the whole, it is hardly surprising if the plasticity of the group is often seen as the sum total of the body's expressive power. When Balanchine said that Béjart was a sculptor, he seized upon a significant innovation in modern ballet. But had not Balanchine himself, when he imposed the most drastic simplification on the costumes in his ballets (for reasons of expense as much as anything), opened the way – far more than the advocates of "free-style dance" or the cult of ancient Greece – to the revaluation of the body, physical beauty, and muscular harmony? The long, long legs of his ballerinas and the strong, if epicene, youths of Béjart's company are in line with the aesthetic taste (purity, essence, the rejection of everything counterfeit) which leads to the neoclassical and thence to abstract dance.

Nothing unusual there. Music, too, had followed that path of clarification and fining down, only to regain at last a worldly, if not positively showy, character. Between the art nouveau "cinema" of Mahler and the concise definition of Webern a whole new conception of culture and western civilization had intervened. But after Webern was there not a tendency to return to richness of sound, the social game, the dangers of allegory, in the works of Stockhausen, Berio, Cage?

In ballet the romantic period was assailed by the barbarian hordes and thrown to the ground by the tribe of Diaghilev. Then the search for a better order of things, accompanied by a loss of confidence in the aborted revolution, replaced degenerate prettiness with a statuesque Olympian beauty, and the prince who met the forces of evil with gods and goddesses and echoes from a mythical past. This new flight from reality was met with an anger that expressed itself in a very modern and subversive hardness, stated with an audacity (as, for instance, in Bartók) that finally led to total liberation. Plot or no plot, past, present, diversion, anguish, torture, madness, revolt, abstraction, imitation – everything was admissible, even a reinterpretation of the classics which demystified them and turned their meanings upside down.

Today the creation of a ballet demands not only an extensive knowledge of the world but also a considerable work of analysis. The modern choreographer's learning must be wide and scholarly, his sources of reference up-to-date and exhaustive. He is no longer dealing with the fairy-tale world of the past, or, if he is, it is in order to question and reinterpret it. His object today is to discover the true face of the life we live. If he has not the natural and intellectual ability to interpret it, his work will have neither success nor duration.

Dancing is as old as mankind; or, at least, as old as man's earliest forms of association. The village, the tribe, those groups we class as "primitive," gave birth to the act of dancing, spontaneously translating the important events of their existence into bodily movements performed to vital rhythms. In these circumstances the dance is a social and public event and has nothing to do with spectacle. The earliest forms of dancing are very simple, moving in a circle being the most usual. That type is found among the most diverse peoples in the early stages of their development and at widely separated periods of time (civilization, if we can call it that, is no respecter of synchronization). Motives for dancing are of various kinds, connected at first with people's feelings and their relations with nature and the mysteries of life and the universe, later becoming a ritual to be repeated at very definite seasons or for special needs.

Primitive dance is the expression of a group, of tribal man, and is not at first subjected to any rules or discipline. Only when it takes on the character of a ceremony does it demand codified actions. The group is the important element, but from it, sooner or later, will emerge – always spontaneously at first – someone who can do something better than the others. For example, if a boy can leap and caper with exceptional skill, his performance will automatically become a "solo number" inserted into the ritual. Then others will attempt to vie with him. In the folk dances that are being revived in the present day (as by the Igor Moisseiev Company, for example) the basic formula of the primitive village or tribal ceremony shows through quite clearly, even under the guise of a sophisticated performance.

The group evolves simple dances, the soloist gives a display: that situation is part of collective life. Ten thousand years ago, and still today in parts of Africa, Australia, and South America, dancing expressed in movement the primal creative urges. It was the first step towards the conquest of the world. The process by which it developed through imitation is obvious. It is interesting to note, however, that one of the easiest and most natural models is the animal, the only thing that moves of its own volition, a creature that can frighten, give pleasure, fight, be trapped and hunted, and finally give rise to songs and dances vaunting heroic exploits.

Soon the hidden world of magic and religion takes possession of the dance.

Powers beyond man's control are substituted for real and visible powers. These divinities are to be propitiated and praised, while evil forces must continually be kept at bay. Procreation, too, the mysterious phenomenon of reproduction, had a magical and religious significance. In times past the concept of fertility was not scientific but a matter of faith.

The civilizations of Greece and Rome have left us some exact information about their dances and how they were performed (leaving aside the biblical references to David and Salome). At that time, not only their ritual importance but also their commercialization was increasing. The dance became a marketable commodity, a property, and began to have a creative relation with music. The accompaniment was no longer "savage" rhythms but the playing of the first "civilized" instruments. Women acquired grace of movement to the dulcet sounds of flute and lyre. There were choreographic entertainments for the rich and powerful; as for the "people," their objectives changed, but not their rites. After the mysteries of nature, after the gods, after the one God, came the absolute monarch, the god on earth. While Salome may have been the first prima ballerina in history, it was Louis XIV who started the theatrical activity which seemed so new but was, in fact, none other than the projection, in a secular context, of the ancient ritual that had already become part of the theater some two thousand years before the birth of Christ.

Life is danced, or rather what is felt about life and the processes of living is danced. Primitive society is not organized and knows no logic: the unknown prevails and every representative art is dominated by a simple relationship with the fear and exaltation of nature. In mythology good and evil are clearly pigeonholed, and the people of ancient civilizations had very distinct mental landmarks whereby to orientate themselves. When things went well for them, there were rites and mysteries to be performed, but there were also joyous hedonistic occasions to be celebrated. In the classical age, when beauty was discovered and glorified, and harmony invented, Jove and Apollo, the thunder and the song, coexisted.

This sort of society, which gave rise to the most varied theatrical entertainments (and dancing, of course) was an island of civilization in a sea of barbarism, but still kept its primitive, irrational faith in fear-ridden and erotic rites. Christianity did away with that system, repudiated its brutal sexuality, and initiated a mystical society that promised to all those who suffered on this earth the reward of a very different, moralistic Olympus. The elevation of otherworldly values implied the negation of worldliness. From there it was but a short step to the equating of pleasure with sin. Even dancing was a sin. It survived only as clandestine folk ritual or as religious procession. God was in heaven; on earth was only death. The primal fear assumed a new disguise.

So it was not mere chance that when pleasure came back into fashion during the Renaissance it took the form of a revival of classicism. The society that sprang from the ashes of the Middle Ages was organized, with a new faith in logic and able to construct for itself a durable framework. Satan left the stage; Apollo entered. Chivalry and idealism left the field to the practice of realism, and the ruling classes celebrated their festivals with ever greater magnificence. Science abetted technical ability in putting ingenious machinery at their service. The fashionable adjective was "big"; monastic culture had invaded the courts

Rudolf Nureyev and Carla Fracci in The Nutcracker *by Tchaikovsky.*

and palaces and turned humanist.

With repetition and familiarity the festivals moved into the theater and became public performances; what had been spontaneous became organized. Necessity produced professionals, professionalism necessitated rules, the learning of which called for special training, for schools. Tradition and imitation were no longer enough: the casual figures of folk dances had to be codified for professional use and elevated to a higher artistic plane. The return of mythological plots with their secondary pastoral subplots was not fortuitous: it was the expression of a society of new gods who, like their ancient prototypes, disposed of absolute power (though now deprived of mystery). Louis XIV wished to be known as the Sun King for political reasons; he did not choose to dance the part of Apollo purely for his own pleasure. The high priests of art in the Parisian Olympus were Beauchamp, Lully, and Molière. By the seventeenth century, thanks to its political power, Paris had taken over the themes invented by the Italian noblemen. Dancing had become ballet. The modern era had begun.

Just as Bona Sforza introduced green vegetables to Poland, so Catherine de' Medici brought the masque dance to Paris. That lady may have lacked sensitivity and gentleness, but she did have an aristocratic feeling for festival and theater. To her reign belongs the protoballet, *Le Ballet Comique de la Reine*, dated 1581. However, it was under Louis XIV that ballet (dance as a public performance) came into its own. If the court masques of the Renaissance took as their dominant theme the glorification of the king's or prince's authority, with Louis XIV the idea was magnified into the identification of power with divinity. The display of absolute authority in the person of the leading character, before whom even people of rank had to bow the knee, carried a political message. It was the indication of a total centralism that used cultural symbols to raise the monarch above all others. The dancing prince, a picture that would have filled his warlike predecessors with horror, held no shock for his contemporaries. The King of France did not stop at that, but made every effort to bring the system to perfection, founding the *Académie Royale de Danse* (1661) and the *Académie Royale de Musique* (1669), otherwise the Opéra.

A boy prodigy, Louis XIV appeared in the *Ballet de la Nuit* by Lully–Beauchamp–Clément at the age of fourteen. It was in 1654, a date to be remembered, like that of the birth of Molière's *comédie-ballet*, a weapon of art and polemics aimed at any possible opposition from aristocracy or high bourgeoisie.

Monsieur Pierre Beauchamp, a leading dancer himself in his day, naturally the "first," was of enormous importance to the history of ballet. It was under his direction that ballet became French, and because of him that so many ballet terms are still in the French language, just as musical ones are mainly Italian. If it is true that power makes history – in every sense – then the court of France at that time had every right to dictate the rules. The names of the leading personalities of the period are symbolic and are still used as technical references. The word *ballon*, for example, meaning the capacity of elevation, of leaping from the ground and performing steps in the air, is derived from the name of Jean Balon or Ballon, principal dancer at the Opéra from 1691 to 1710 and celebrated for his amazing lightness. But Monsieur Balon's stage costumes were not very suitable for displaying athletic prowess. They were elegant, overloaded, ornate: even the clothes of dancers reflected the baroque opulence and stately pomp of the age.

With their faces hidden by masks, the dancers directed by Lully and Beauchamp had undoubtedly borrowed a great deal from Italian pantomime, but its conventions were modified by ever greater technical variations and improvements. Beauchamp felt the time had come to put some order into his branch of art. Accordingly he invented the first system of dance notation, listing and labelling the main movements and attitudes. It is unquestionably to him (although Arbeau first implemented them at the end of the sixteenth century) that we owe the five basic foot positions, which Balanchine considers to be the foundation of the whole vocabulary of classical ballet. History owes Beauchamp yet another bold innovation. In 1681 professional dancers performed on the stage of the Opéra for the first time. It was in *Le Triomphe de l'Amour* by Lully, and the professionals in question were Mesdames Lafontaine, called the Queen of the Dance, Roland, Lepeintre, and Fernon. Creator of the *style noble*, Beauchamp has become legendary as a trainer of leading dancers to a level that has endowed them with glamour ever since. At a time when men were considered indisputably the superior sex, and women, owing to their dresses, had to limit themselves to displaying nothing more than a modest grace, he invented the great ballerina. After "Queen" Lafontaine came Subligny, and after her, Prévost, whose charm is recalled in Raoux's famous portrait of her posing in a position that is nearly an attitude. All in all, it was an age of virtuosi in playing musical instruments, dancing, composing, and thinking in terms of theater. One cannot imagine a more complete artist than Lully, the Florentine turned Frenchman.

Connected with opera on one side and with comedy on the other, ballet had not yet come of age, far less become an independent art in the modern sense. During the eighteenth century, dancing, either in the spirit of the piece or not, was invariably introduced at suitable moments in the action of the play or opera. The stage direction "enter the dancers" signified an interlude and gave rise to the term *entrées*. Molière's comedy-ballet was a step forward in the concept of a festival or ball in high society or at court, while the works of Lully and Rameau were a tribute to the spectacular and prodigious nature of an aristocratic culture. When Louis XIV died, the world, with a sigh of relief, relinquished the absolute authority of a power based on the ancient Roman pattern. There was an explosive liberation of customs and manners, and the quest for total pleasure set in. The majestic forms of baroque gave way to the frivolous and cynical rococo. One might say that it was the beginning of the desanctification of a power which until then had been as much an article of faith as religion. Aristocratic society accepted the decadence which was eventually to prove its ruin, and seemed amused by it. The court still went through its now obsolete rituals, but a new exotic element was making itself felt, bringing with it aesthetic pleasure and a novel elegance. Exploration and discovery were opening up the world: the Americas were now accessible and China itself was not as far away as it had been.

Rameau's *Indes Galantes* (1735) was the seminal starting point of a type of production and a taste that spread over Europe like wildfire. Even apart from the grand spectacular effects recorded in the chronicles (the taste for marvels exemplified by wrecks and volcanic eruptions), there are a number of interesting features: firstly, the inclusion of critical thought expressed in the contrast between the happy, hospitable New World and old, violent, war-torn Europe; secondly, the exploitation of brilliant and very varied dance techniques to afford the greatest possible pleasure. From the personalization of performances which is inseparable from professionalism and theatrical programming, there emerged a definitive "star system." There was the case of Louis Dupré, described by Noverre as a "beautiful and perfectly organized machine," imposing and splendid in his richly baroque array. An immortal exponent of the *danse noble*, Dupré was still able to fascinate as acute an observer as Casanova when he was over fifty years old. A body like Dupré's would be the joy of a modern choreographer.

The career of a professional dancer demanded ever higher standards of achievement. Hitherto court dancing had been *terre à terre* or *danse basse*, that is to say that one or other of the two feet always remained on the ground. When, in about 1730, *danse haute*, in which both feet might leave the ground at once in a hop or leap, was introduced, an almost revolutionary change was set under way. Apart from the quarrels between the Lullyists and Rameauists on that very subject, it must be emphasized that the transition from court dances – in large or small rooms with the audience seated around – to dances in a theater, with the public in front and on a lower level, automatically led to new techniques, as well as the concealment of a certain amount that had been visible before. The chief effect of having spectators in the stalls was that leaps and feats of physical virtuosity were what excited the most admiration and amazement. It was no longer enough to move from one stately attitude to another. There must be something more, something different. Almost as in the tribal dances of primitive people, he who could make three skips, where the average was only two, became a star.

That situation meant the final separation of amateur and professional. Thenceforward it was impossible for courtiers to take part in a performance that required so exacting a period of training. The various bravura pieces became part of the repertory to be bequeathed to future generations of dancers. One of the practical consequences of the new *en l'air* style was a lightening of the cumbersome stage costumes, and especially the shortening of skirts. When the celebrated Marie Anne Cupis de Camargo performed her *entrechat-quatre*, crossing her feet four times while still in the air, it was essential for the audience to be able to see and appreciate the step. Moreover, it is impossible to leap high when weighed down with heavy materials, heavy ornaments, large headdresses, or full wigs. Unlike Camargo, Marie Sallé, another famous dancer, gave grace and expression priority over skill, and excelled in mime. In those formative years of ballet, London and Paris were rivals, each presenting a number of creations that were destined to go down in history. About the middle of the century, however, things changed and new needs arose. Camargo and Dupré both retired in 1751; Sallé died in 1756. Virtuosity triumphed and the Italians arrived on the scene: for example, Barbara Campanini and Gaetano Vestris, father of Auguste, master of all talents in the nineteenth century. With this new passing generation, the foibles of the age were transferred to ballet. The caprices of Gaetano Vestris would make a book in themselves. But the great event that completed the reshuffling in that fateful year of 1751 was the promotion of Jean-Georges Noverre to *premier danseur* of the Opéra. Noverre was the herald of advanced ideas, and his book *Lettres sur la Danse et sur les Ballets*, published in Stuttgart and Lyons in 1760, was his basic testimony. Naturally there were other contemporary innovators, such as Hilverding and Angiolini, who contributed to the evolution of dancing, but Noverre was the guiding spirit, the master to whom we must first and always refer.

One may wonder why so much of his activity took place outside Paris, especially in Germany. History will help us to understand. France was in decline, entering the troubled years that preceded the revolution; other powers great and small were imitating her past grandeur to the tune of millions.

If Noverre was able to stage lavish productions in Stuttgart, it was because the Duke of Württemberg financed the enterprise generously by hiring out his mercenary armies to the kingdom of France. Vienna's star was in the ascendant, and with it that of Milan. Two dates should be recorded: in 1761 *Don Juan* appeared, with music by Gluck and choreography by Angiolini; 1763 saw the first production of *Medea and Jason* by Noverre, to music by Rodolphe. They both carried the banner of the ballet of action with plot, logical progression, and cultural relevance. Gluck destroyed the convention of the virtuoso singer. Noverre suppressed the virtuoso dancer. Their intention was to replace the tyranny of the interpretive artist by the rule of the creator.

Gluck and Noverre collaborated in *Orfeo* and *Alceste*. Intelligence and reason, they maintained, should govern the life of man; the truth about facts and feelings should no longer be concealed. Frivolity, perfumes, illusions of the past must be set aside; Europe must observe herself clear-eyed. Anticipating Mozart and the revolution of 1789, they were eager for truth. The masks fell from the faces of the dancers (from that of Gaetano Vestris in *Jason* first of all) and the ruling class. Reduced to little people, full of vices and virtues like the rest of mankind, aristocratic society was only too glad to hand the baton to the middle classes. Noverre the reformer was for expression above all and banished everything that was its negation: away with useless ornament and virtuosity as an end in themselves. Ballet should be a picture alive with passion, situations, activities, manners, and sensibility. Philosophers, writers, musicians were in agreement. The idea of faithfulness to the artist's conception (from Gluck to Diderot) emerged; also, for the first time, the courage to display the shape and beauty of the dancer's body. There was no stopping the reforming spirit: ballet companies sprang up almost everywhere and the repertory grew richer. The *ballet d'action* incorporated the old virtuosos with the new talents and the encyclopedists defined ballet as "an action expounded by dancing." By this time the die was cast. It remained only to ensure that librettos and texts got rid of the fearless heroes of myth and legend and turned to real life with real people in place of tailors' dummies. Novelists, playwrights, and authors of comic opera had already done so; only "serious" opera, patron of ballet, hung back.

In 1786 Jean Dauberval gave us *La Fille Mal Gardée* with an entirely non-aristocratic plot, characters, and dancing – a danced comedy. A new world was revealed, peopled by peasants who were peasants, squires who were squires, ambitious mothers, and sentimental daughters. The good and sincere triumphed, not the powerful. There was little time for argument or thinking of the ballet's

Following pages: A moment in the ballet Héliogabale. *Choreography by Maurice Béjart.*

future, for it was not long before decisions were made by gunfire, repression, and the guillotine. The France of the Louis kings disappeared; men like Charles Didelot took refuge in Czarist Russia, foreshadowing its future as the home of ballet. When the great Napoleonic adventure was over, the Restoration, though without cultural support, imposed some provisional order in the arts — an order in which at least the theater flourished. But defeated France had lost its preeminence in ballet. That now passed to Italy and especially to the Scala in Milan, thanks to Viganò, who carried on Noverre's reforms, and to the great Carlo Blasis, whose *Code of Terpsichore*, published in London in 1829, established the basic terms of classical ballet.

While the French Revolution had deconsecrated the past, the Bonapartist dictatorship had the good sense to restore it, preparing the way for a return to classical antiquity. But trends of thought can be stronger than Holy Alliances: people had tasted the liberty of being individuals, and critical individuals at that. Rejecting official restraints, they pursued in private what was frowned on in public. Romanticism freed the passions and emotions and established a new relationship with nature. While striving for truth, it provided a passport to dreams, rejecting old politics and promoting early ideals of justice, abandoning reason and delighting in ghosts. An enemy of vulgarity and naturalism, the romantic spirit in ballet exalted feminine purity and innocence, accepted the power of magic, and believed in the redeeming quality of death. Everything had to be on a grand scale: love, heroism, and sacrifice. The romantics yearned for a world of the spirit and, not finding it on earth, looked for it elsewhere. That, too, was escapism, setting against earthly unhappiness the unattainable mystery of an extraterrestial bliss. To this were added conflicts of class and hopeless love affairs. The ethereal quality expressed by dancing on points (Maria Taglioni being its perfect exponent), and extreme simplification of dress (the "sylphide" style suggesting weightless creatures of air), emphasized the romantic ballet's detachment from the earth and its love for the supernatural. The settings of these so-called *ballets blancs* made full use of the moon, the mysteries of nature, and deserted places where unhappy spirits roamed; but at the same time ballets could be romantic-exotic, romantic-sentimental, or romantic-diabolical. The most enduring fruit of this era was the elevation of the prima ballerina into an apotheosis of grace. Taglioni, Elssler, Grisi, Cerrito, and Grahn fascinated the public, while ballet achieved a new eminence through the contributions of genuine musicians. The outstanding example is Adam, the composer of the score of *Giselle*, the most famous, the best-loved, and probably the most frequently performed of all ballets during the first half of the nineteenth century.

The *maîtres de ballet* of the period followed their fortunes in France once again, putting themselves at the service of the great ballerinas, who were, however, not French. The dancers toured about, their public grew enormously, schools of dance spread everywhere. From the west they extended northwards to Denmark with Bournonville, and towards the east in a continuous diaspora towards the theaters of Imperial Russia. And there a very negative phase took over, in which everything centered on the great interpreters and their partners; music was mere accompaniment and librettos became trivial. While romanticism was burning up its last energies in a Europe that was seeking its separate national identities, the great classical tradition emigrated to St. Petersburg, where Italian and French ballet masters perpetuated a hallowed style in optimum conditions of organization and calm – even political calm.

But let us turn back for a moment to *Giselle*, produced at the Paris Opéra in 1841 with Carlotta Grisi and Lucien Petipa in the leading roles. Why *Giselle* at just that time? Not only, it seems, because it is a famous ballet that has remained in the repertory or because its music is of a superior class to that of comparable productions of its day. Other qualities were needed to account for its importance. It was the work that most perfectly exemplified and brought to a conclusion the sentiments of the second romantic generation. *Giselle* had ancestors of worth and high lineage. The librettist, Théophile Gautier, the poet and writer who perhaps contributed more than any other to the growth of nineteenth-century ballet, had been inspired by a German legend included in Heine's *Deutschland, ein Wintermärchen*. The French poet wrote to his German colleague: "In your beautiful book I found a fascinating passage ... elves in white robes ... snow-coloured spirits who danced without pity ... delectable apparitions that you glimpsed in the Harz mountains or on the banks of a river in the misty night or under the moon. ..."

Here Gautier gives us all the ingredients of the romantic dream: the moon at night, magic, spells, mysteries of nature, morbid cruelty, the sense of yearning, and destruction.

That purely unearthly element, however, was not considered in 1840 as material sufficient in itself to make a theatrical entertainment. As had happened with *La Sylphide*, but in much more conventional terms, Gautier and his collaborator Saint-Georges balanced fantasy with realism, using formulas that had already been successful in opera. Thus the country girl Giselle, who believes in the love of a handsome unknown (really a somewhat scoundrelly prince) and has been deceived, goes mad and dies, as is quite usual in opera librettos. Then the scene changes to the supernatural world of the "wilis," white-clad spirits without mercy – or with just enough to grant that, if the prince can withstand the challenge of the fatal dance until dawn, the spell will be broken.

The plot satisfies so many demands of the drama of sentiment: pity for the poor, deceived girl, tears for her death, the Damocles' sword of the punishment for betrayal; salvation through love, acceptance of difference in class, and the separation of two worlds. It is not heroic romance, but the romance of pathos; one does not hope, one weeps. Its vision of the world is almost mystical, even if its paradise is not inhabited by angels.

In this masterpiece, literature, music, and theatrical technique were perfectly fused to produce an immortal choreographic creation, the marvellous flowering of a school of dance that had reached its zenith. The names of the choreographers, Coralli and Perrot (although Marius Petipa's later improvements must not be forgotten), still figure deservedly in the program, to testify to a work that could not be any different or better or more faithful to the text.

The dancer of the ballet's title role was Carlotta Grisi: Gautier raved about her; Perrot, who had discovered her in Italy, was infatuated. The girl, with her big blue eyes and sweet, delicate face, followed Taglioni and Elssler in the hearts of the Parisians. It was said that her feet had incredible points of steel: she could balance on one point with the stillness of a statue. In *La Péri* she threw herself with utter fearlessness from a height of two meters into the arms of her partner,

Lucien Petipa. She could be a comédienne or a romantic ballerina; for Giselle she was perfect. There are countless witnesses to her complete artistry and versatility, her ability to make one laugh or cry. But the other side of the coin was the eclipse of the male dancer, who was reduced to a repetition of sterile mannerisms as a mere assistant of the ballerina.

It was a long time before a miracle like *Giselle* came again. Except for *Coppelia* (Delibes and Saint-Léon, 1870), pre-Tchaikovsky productions fluctuated between the exotic, the fantastic, and the popular. The repertory ranged from the black romanticism of Hoffman, through fiction and adventure, to folk dances. It was the age of the musical potboiler, while on the interpretive side the Italian school still reigned supreme. The decadent romanticism of the latter half of the century was beaten back by the forces of scientific positivism. It was in Imperial Russia, the least modern state in Europe, the state in which a powerful court and brutal aristocracy were still dominant, that the old classical ballet found its last refuge, thanks to the importation of the best French choreographers and Italian dancers, as well as the most fashionable composers. The high season of romantic ballet ended in the 1850s. It made a sudden and brief recovery in Russia during the last decade of the same century as a consequence of the momentous meeting between Marius Petipa, his colleague Ivanov, and Piotr Ilyich Tchaikovsky. With the latter's three major ballets, *Swan Lake*, *The Sleeping Beauty*, and *The Nutcracker*, three highly important results were achieved:
– the ultimate perfecting of classical choreography;
– the definitive acceptance of the composer's vital role;
– the birth of the Russian school.
The effects of these events were revolutionary, because they imposed a complete revision of dance-theater relationships, reaffirmed a better way of thinking in the theater, and opened the way to all sorts of reforms and innovations such as the reinstatement of the male dancer, a concern for fresh cultural contributions, and bringing scenarios more up-to-date. Composers of the Minkus, Pugni, and Drigo type sank into the twilight, eclipsed by the rising sun of Tchaikovsky with his genius and his gift for inventing melodies comparable to those of Delibes (who in 1876 composed the music for *Sylvia*). In Italy the spectacular Manzotti-Marenco ballets bore witness to an utter decadence of artistic values and qualities. In Russia Tchaikovsky's *Swan Lake* was ahead of its time: in 1877 it was a failure, although in 1890 and 1892 it triumphed. Why?

In the first place, *Swan Lake* was a qualitative leap forward, leaving all previous productions behind. Created by a famous composer of the Maryinsky Theater (now the Bolshoi) in St. Petersburg, the ballet revealed itself as a threat to the supreme authority of the *maîtres de ballet*. The music had not only to be danced but also interpreted; it served ideas as well as personalities. Nevertheless, the production was still closely tied to the past and the romantic dream, with its two contrasted planes of reality and fantasy and with its legendary, magical elements.

Although the plot might be said to have been fashionable, the composer's intentions were probably defeated by the forces in the field. Without going into detail concerning the first performance, choreographed by the unknown Riesinger, it is enough to mention that a large part of the music was omitted to make room for "numbers" taken out of other ballets to show off the soloists. The initial failure of *Swan Lake* is a classic example of misunderstanding. When it was revived in 1895 with new choreography by Petipa and Ivanov, the whole richness and balance of its content were made manifest. Besides the leading role of Odette-Odile with its multiple and contrasting themes, there was at last a part for the chief male dancer, stripped of all the usual tired clichés, a characterization no longer anonymous. The classical, the brilliant, even the popular, were abundantly present; the music was symphonically conceived with its famous echo of *Lohengrin* presaging the play's atmosphere. In short, the world of ballet was at last confronted with a musical and theatrical genius, a genuine man of culture. There was no turning back.

Prince Siegfried is already a modern man who wants to make his own choices in life, but finds himself caught against his will in a deadly emotional trap. The lady in the case has a dual aspect in which the purity of early romanticism is contrasted with seduction in the service of the forces of evil. Rothbart, magician or emblem of a barbaric power, schemes to destroy the happiness of an apparently contented court. The ballet is perfectly planned and is never far from greatness throughout its length. In regard to choreography *Swan Lake* is an unsurpassable model of the classical style, and as such has become the high point of every repertory. Petipa's and Ivanov's basic work has been subjected to an infinite number of "revisions," but they have left its heart intact. For a ballerina, the part of Odette-Odile, the white swan and the black, represents the peak of her career; for a *corps de ballet*, *Swan Lake* is a test of maturity; for Tchaikovsky's successors, an inescapable standard of excellence.

Tchaikovsky's trilogy, which includes, as already mentioned, *The Sleeping Beauty* and *The Nutcracker*, was not only the final culmination of a splendid era. It also looked forward into a future that turned away from fairy stories, but could not manage without the principles of the classical style. It was in particular *The Nutcracker*, derived from a story by Hoffmann, that demonstrated both musically and culturally the need for a renewal. Hoffmann's text is more than a "story," because it concerns itself with psychology and demythologizes the picture of a childish world enclosed in family tenderness, to afford a glimpse into a future capable of being blissful and terrible at the same time.

The music Tchaikovsky composed for *The Nutcracker* was certainly far more beautiful and important than that for *The Sleeping Beauty* or *Swan Lake*, so much so that it exists in its own right in the suites that have been drawn from it. The ballet's dramatic sense, each dancer representing a recognizable character, shows a growing taste for entertainments with some regard for logic and credibility. After the brilliant but superficial shows of the preceding twenty years, ballet had regained its self-respect side by side with the other forms of theater and, what was more essential, attracted the attention of first-rate composers. The time was approaching when, as the great theorists of the past had hoped, all the arts would collaborate. But in the meantime two important circumstances intervened: the decline of opera, unable to continue in the same vein in the new intellectual climate (which we shall examine later), and the fall of the great monarchies with the values they represented. The antiromantic movement, grown strong on the ruins of its predecessors, would seek new forms of expression and a combination of original talents, remote and abstruse, rejecting all "bourgeois" harmony and throwing to the winds all the respectability on which the nineteenth century had fed.

An Italian, Pierina Legnani, first danced the leading role in *Swan Lake*, but the time was drawing near when all the great ballerinas would be Russian, products of an institution (the Imperial Russian Ballet and its school) that had gathered to itself the best choreographers and teachers of Europe. But it was fated that the fruit of that flowering of artists (Anna Pavlova is the first name that springs to mind) should come to full maturity abroad. Obviously the Russia of the Czars could not be open to artistic innovation, and it was, without any shadow of doubt, the last bastion of conservatism, to say no worse. The new kinds of art championed by the "free-style" movements were challenging a regime based on absolute authority.

The abortive revolution of 1905, the defeated armies, the terrible World War I, and the subsequent victory of the Bolsheviks under Lenin are facts of history; but the earliest mass emigration of Russian artists preceded all those political events and, in the case of ballet, centered on the figure of Diaghilev, impresario, aesthete, the man who knew how to impress tired, decadent Europe with the irresistible strength of the Russian creators and artists. That strength spread from the public to the private sector, then became international, concentrating all the most vital talents around the center of the new and modern. Ballet returned to Paris, making it once more the world's artistic capital.

Paris underwent experiences unknown in the rest of Europe, witnessing movements such as impressionism and symbolism. In this atmosphere there developed an attitude to cultures which was open and receptive and a manner of behaviour which was certainly freer than elsewhere. The city possessed the beauty and weight of a matchless past, its people were easy and tolerant, and its poor areas offered young talent a refuge and the most stimulating of environments. A pleiad of poets and painters (and then composers) had given France once again the fascination she had lost after the end of the Empire. The landscape surrounding the city, the rapport with the provinces, the fascination of a language still used internationally – all made Paris the model to be emulated, the place to seek one's fortune, the launching pad for the young. Certainly in the old French capital there was more freedom than elsewhere and with this freedom came a taste for the daring and the pleasure of unrestricted enjoyment. If we remember Victorian moralism, Prussian coarseness, Viennese bigotry, Czarist restrictions, it is easy to understand the reasons for certain choices and certain loves.

In addition, Paris offered an internationalism (as it always has) unknown elsewhere. Writers and artists from abroad felt at home in the city, as happened with Chopin and Liszt, then with Picasso and Apollinaire, then with the American generation of Gertrude Stein and Ernest Hemingway.

When in 1907 Diaghilev organized a series of concerts in Paris, featuring Russian music, his trump cards were Feodor Chaliapine, Rimsky-Korsakov, Scriabin, and Rachmaninov, a constellation of geniuses. Soon new stars from the Maryinsky, such as Vaslav Nijinsky and Karsavina, would appear above the horizon, while the bombshell of Stravinsky's music lay ready to explode over Europe. In 1909 Diaghilev brought his private company, the *Ballets Russes*, to Paris to dance *Le Pavillon d'Armide* and *Prince Igor*. His choreographer was Fokine, able at last to realize his theories of ballet, while his company consisted of the pick of the St. Petersburg dancers. Diaghilev's greatest talent among many, however, was that of being an impresario capable of enriching his enterprise with all the new art and talent that was springing to life in Europe: Vaslav Nijinsky, in his all too short career, brought the idea of the great male dancer back to life; Massine and Balanchine reformed choreography; Benois, Goncharova, and Bakst created a new conception of stage decor; dancers of enormous accomplishment so impressed the public that for decades afterwards it was almost impossible to think of a ballerina who was not Russian (various dancers from other nations were forced to Russianize their names).

Diaghilev, father of modern ballet, the man to whom all those who came after were in debt, "caused" the creation of masterpieces that could vie in their success with the great classics. It is enough to think of *Firebird* (1910), *Petrouchka* (1911), *L'Après-midi d'un Faune* (1912), *The Rite of Spring* (1913), and *Parade* (1917), all first produced in Paris. The iconoclastic force of these productions, the controversy to which they gave rise, the charge of innovation they carried, were all part of this new growth of ballet. It had left the calm hinterland of the fairy tale to enter vehemently into life, march with the avant-garde, take up the challenges thrown at bourgeois art by all those who saw the future as a paradise of creative freedom, as the glorious time when all respectability, convention, old usages, and false realism would be thrown into the sea. Although Diaghilev could not abandon the past, he made the present grow and interpreted it. He was capable of putting on *Apollon Musagète* (Stravinsky–Balanchine–Bauchant; principal dancer: Lifar) in 1928, almost a neoclassical manifesto, while European culture was retiring behind the barricades to dream anew of a spiritual order far from the "barbarians"; then, in the next year, of producing *The Prodigal Son* (Prokoviev–Balanchine–Rouault) along expressionist lines. At his death in that same year, 1929, the company dispersed, but such was its dominion over the dance that its members led the field for decades in every part of the world. It is no exaggeration to say that all the "greats" of the dancing world – even Ninette de Valois and Martha Graham – had passed through Diaghilev's sieve. Only Italy, for obvious political reasons, and because the last phase of opera (Puccini, Mascagni) was in progress there, stayed outside the movement. In any case, fascism did not care for dancing, which played no part in its antiquated populism, nor in the brutish interpretation of the culture of ancient Rome and her Caesars.

World War I and the Russian Revolution confirmed the artistic leadership of Paris, but during the 1930s a shift took place towards America. The trend was furthered by the deteriorating political situation brought about by the rising dictatorships and the comparative wealth of the American public. London and Paris held out as long as possible, and finally succeeded in saving the great European spirit from Nazism. Meanwhile the great talents of music and dance emigrated in droves to the United States, giving life to a new dominant culture. The movement coincided with Soviet Russia's return to tradition and orthodoxy and the death of high German culture, which had developed, among other things, new kinds of nonacademic dancing and made a fundamental contribution to the style known as free or modern dance. It would be wrong, at this point, not to acknowledge the influence of Isadora Duncan and her "Greek" dancing. Her role as innovator was to survive better than her ideas. The long avenue opened up by Duncan (who abandoned the traditional ballet dress and shoes and encouraged improvisation) led directly to expression by the whole body, and thence, even if unintentionally, to abstraction and the destruction of realism. It is not by chance that she, who was attached to revolutionary Russia and the Russian poet Essenin, has recently been reinstated in various ways, even though her aesthetic theories have been downgraded by the more austere schools of modern dance.

Experiments in dance techniques unrelated to classical ballet (and thus antiromantic in their nature) could arise from quasi-religious or primitive-historical motives, as with Ruth St. Denis in America, or they could have their basis in an independent ideal of instinctive creativity inspired by nature, art, Greek divinities, or pre-Renaissance painting, as in the case of Isadora Duncan. That American dancer's spirituality, manifested in very free terms, expressed itself as a lyricism straining to rediscover the beauty that was Greece. Dressed in the simplest of garments, or even naked, she was a paradigm of artistic nobility. As to the religious message of Ruth St. Denis and her husband Ted Shawn (who together founded the Denishawn School), it went no further than a contemplation of the past and a taste for the exotic (moreover, the tone was distinctly sermonizing): but they started barefoot dancing, which has gone on ever since.

Interest in this type of dancing increased with the arrival of German *Freitanz* and the eurhythmics of Dèlcroze. But it was the desire to plunge more deeply into life that was the reason for young people like Martha Graham and Doris Humphrey breaking away. The former, especially, gave a primary impulse to modern dancing with her school and her ability to create a new technique, thus realizing the dream of a dance theater that was typically American, not merely in attitude but as part of the native culture.

At about the same time, however, another great personality was building up his theories in Europe: Rudolf Laban, born in Bratislava in 1879, was opposed to the slightly inhuman grace of classical ballet. It was he who launched the ideas, even before 1914, of the investigation of movement and the total coordination of physical expression and bodily movement in relation to psychological motivation. Like a scientist, Laban studied the dynamics and reactions of the human body and invented classifications worthy of an anthropologist. He was the originator of the dance of the expressionist period, now linked with the names of Mary Wigman and Kurt Jooss, whose reign in Germany was all too short, but was, in a strange way, resurrected in the balletic partnership of Bartók–Milloss.

Free-style dance, now known as modern dance, was an abjuration of academic ballet, perfectly in tune with the twentieth-century aesthetic movements that were sweeping through every sector of the arts. But the divorce was not final. On the contrary, in recent years the two forms of dancing have enriched one another and, in the latest choreographic creations, can be said to have joined forces. Their relationship can be summed up as follows: academic dance is the indispensable alphabet; modern dance completes the classical expressive dialogue.

Let us turn back for a moment. The antiromantic protesters of the first two decades of this century, with their iconoclastic manifestos, really believed they could change the world through thought and put forward alternative values com-

Jorge Donn as the Sun King in Molière Imaginaire *by Maurice Béjart.*

28

pletely opposite to those of the past. The movement's revolutionary spirit demanded the destruction of the language used hitherto, decreed the end of all illusions and faith in the past. The avant-garde, aware of the vital energy radiating from the civilization of the machine age, while laying new stress on human protest and the inherent creative power of the masses, also trained its sights on targets of political emancipation. Alas, the World War shattered their hopes of scientific humanitarianism and socialist brotherhood, even while the world revolution they had set their hearts on was starting in St. Petersburg.

The reality presented by the early 1920s was very different from the dreams of the night before. In a few years the old order would come back in force and deviations would be frowned on.

The rebirth of an exaggerated nationalism, soon expressed in violence against progressive ideas, filled writers and artists with a sort of distrust that made them retreat into positions of disengagement.

During the 1930s the last continental strongholds of revolutionary art were dismantled: in both Germany and the Soviet Union, though in different circumstances, the forces of self-preservation favoured trends that would maintain the reigning government in power. Brecht's exile and Maiakovsky's suicide were two events emblematic of that ebbtide. The strangulation of the Spanish republic put the seal on a policy that involved the complicity, in an incredible version of *realpolitik*, of European democracies and fascism (and the Soviet Union, which was in full cultural retreat, could not but send arms).

In a situation of extreme danger and unease, artists and intellectuals (except those who went into exile to continue the fight against persecution — and, of course, except for the collaborators) set their own standards in opposition to the brutal ones that surrounded them. They found them in a return to harmonies of the past and a cult of reason far removed from their own time. They could not turn back to romanticism and so leap back to the eighteenth century; they could only carry the antirealist, abstract argument to its conclusion by using elitist techniques that had nothing in common with the empty, illustrative art favoured by the totalitarian powers. Taking refuge from the vulgar, lower middle-class vogue for Nibelung myths, parochial collectivism, or the mock-Roman, yet rejecting faith in the masses and primitive values, many artists abandoned the barricades and retreated into ivory towers.

On one side was neoclassicism, on the other abstract art; in addition came the survival of past cultures. In general, the present day was rejected. An illuminating example was that of Stravinsky, a composer who, though apolitical, was more sensitive to the flow of events than almost any other. The composer of ballets such as *Petrouchka* and *The Rite of Spring* (and of *The Soldier's Story*) produced (and Balanchine was his echo) such works as *Apollon Musagète*, *Pulcinella*, and *Le Baiser de la Fée*. The return to the past was almost glaring. *Apollon*, especially, became a clear manifesto, since it was a complete revision of principles, promoting in no uncertain terms the ideal of a superior harmony quite detached from "modern times" or relevance to the present. There was a return to eighteenth-century musical forms, a revival of the works of past composers, not too radically revised. Tchaikovsky took pride of place and, by the same token, ballet was to be purged of overmuch action. Soon it was devoid of any plot at all. The modernized school of Balanchine was proving the most influential in the field of ballet at that time. Sets and costumes were by necessity reduced to a minimum, even the classical forms (witness the tutu, now a mere symbol of its former self). At the same time heroes and characters from antiquity came back into circulation, even some gods supposed to be forgotten. Also, important music, not originally written for dancing, was gradually appropriated for ballet. Indeed, in recent times it has become more or less the standard choice.

The important balletic events of the interwar period were:
– the birth of the American school fathered by Balanchine, and the growth in the United States of modern dance, partly due to exiles from Europe;
– the rise of the English ballet as heir of the prerevolutionary Russian school, with additional artistic contributions of its own;
– the reign of Serge Lifar at the Paris Opéra, the last bastion of the great avant-garde period; also known for the revival of the great romantic ballets (a new *Giselle*) and the space given to European neoclassicism;
– the return of Soviet arts to traditionalism at the expense of the revolutionary works of the 1920s and early 1930s.

The prevailing tone was one of positive optimism well suited to the old traditional values. These four sets of circumstances were to develop, in their various ways, a new and impressive stage in the history of the dance. Let us see how.

Balanchine, a Russian like Fokine, Massine, and Lifar, would have been able to stay in Europe, in Paris, or anywhere else. After the final performance of Diaghilev's *Ballets Russes* (1929), his company dispersed and found opportunities of employment in several different directions, but especially with the *Ballets Russes de Monte Carlo*, founded in 1932 by René Blum and Colonel de Basil. However, in 1933 the Georgian choreographer went to New York and with Lincoln Kirstein and others started the School of American Ballet, the nucleus of the subsequent American Ballet, later the New York City Ballet.

The best talents in American dancing gathered around Balanchine. Established at the Metropolitan Opera House in 1935, the American Ballet Company began to create new generations of artists, attracting the attention of the best directors and composers of America. In the shadow of Stravinsky, a United States ballet tradition began to flourish, a rich amalgam of tradition and national themes. In Balanchine's shadow arose the star of Jerome Robbins. Within a few years the American ballet became the most important in the west; after the war it even set out on the conquest of Europe.

Balanchine brought the ballerina back into the limelight, actually creating a new physical type: long legs, supreme elegance, an extended line, an almost asexual beauty. His creations radiated an ideal of purity. All around him grew up new dance ventures, some weakened by a too insistent Americanism, others possessed by a modern view of art that finally caught up with existential themes. The names of Graham, Dollar, de Mille, Nikolais, Cunningham, Feld, Ailey, Neumeier, Joffrey, and Lang are only a few among the largest constellation of choreographers ever produced in so short a time.

Developments in English ballet were no less important. Revived by Ninette de Valois and Marie Rambert in the 1920s and early 1930s, it evolved a distinctive school rich in intelligence and humour. Several celebrated companies such as Ballet Rambert and the Vic-Wells, later the Royal Ballet (with its Royal

Academy of Dancing), emerged, graced by such dancers as Anton Dolin, Alicia Markova, Margot Fonteyn, and by choreographers such as Ashton, Tudor, Helpmann, and Cranko. Some went overseas to inspire new companies abroad. William Walton and Vaughan Williams were among the well-known composers who wrote music for ballet at that time, while Oliver Messel contributed his own version of baroque magnificence to stage decor. When Nureyev arrived from Russia, British ballet reached a peak of splendour, and in the 1960s the partnership of Fonteyn and Nureyev was rated the best in the world, while new stars, such as Anthony Dowell, Lynn Seymour, and Antoinette Sibley were already visible above the horizon.

Generally speaking, all this achievement was in the classical tradition. It was not until the 1960s that modern dance took a firm hold, at first under strongly American influence, but later developing its own strength. Ballet Rambert went over to modern dance in 1966; in the following year Robert Cohan founded the London Contemporary Dance Theatre and its school. Other modern dance companies sprang up in various parts of the country. The two traditions existed side by side, rivals, but growing nearer to one another.

The spirit of France emerged almost intact from the ordeal of war. At all levels the arts began to flourish anew in a spirit of genuine creative liberty. The decadence and structural weakness of the Opéra had not hindered French ballet from expressing itself effectively, either by continuing to develop its inheritance from the past (Lifar–Cocteau) or through the initiative of impresarios (de Cuevas), with the collaboration of the new avant-garde artists. In these circumstances, new personalities, outside the establishment, emerged: men such as Roland Petit and Maurice Béjart, who prescribed a third way, somewhere between the American school and the Russo-Soviet tradition. New musical forms were introduced to ballet, especially by Béjart; concrete music and advanced compositions came from Xenakis and Boulez; and so on. Philosophy, social awareness, even political protest, found their way into the theater of the dance.

From existentialism to oriental philosophy, ballet seemed to be leaning on books. The novel, ideology, the theater, even the spoken word began to play their parts, helping to interpret the role of man in society, of human behaviour and alienation. Classical and contemporary dance, once opposed, now grew close, reinventing the past and exploring the future, upsetting established modes and manners. Béjart, who had established his headquarters in Brussels, was looking for new venues in which to stage his productions and found them in circuses and sports stadia. The French regained their taste for plot and action in which they could involve themselves. In that they broke away from the Americans, who rejected any story on principle, though later – with great reserve – they began to come around to the idea.

Unlike Balanchine, Béjart paid most attention to the male dancer, also creating an unmistakeable type, ascetic and strong, often of an ambiguous beauty, very modern and sometimes in the 1968 mould – the year, that is to say, when youth all over the world declared its total difference from all its predecessors. Dance techniques had by that time reached a stage of high perfection, and the world had completely changed.

The most extraordinary case, however, is that of the Soviet Union. It was

An incident from the ballet Requiem, Malédictions et Lumières. *Choreography by Joseph Russillo.*

Russia which had taken the lead in ballet at the end of the nineteenth century and produced in Tchaikovsky's three ballets all that was best in academic dance, combining French and Italian influences (for the great contribution of Cecchetti at that point cannot be ignored). It was Diaghilev with his Russian company who had ushered in the new era. Russians were the best interpreters, composers, choreographers, and designers for ballet. The revolution and the civil war that followed it drenched the country in blood, obliging those artists to work abroad, while in the new state contrary artistic trends came to the fore, encouraged by a culture that was libertarian and antiromantic – often to the point of a complete break with the past. In those circumstances the dominant figure, as we know, was Maiakovsky, while Duncan was preferred to Petipa. There was a growing need for a theater and ballet in line with the country's revolutionary situation. But the position of the Imperial theaters, deprived of their stars, was extremely difficult; moreover, the old ballet, now looked on as an aristocratic art, was completely out of fashion.

The enlightened cultural policy of Lunacharsky, the Minister of Arts, sought to remedy the breakdown and at least, during the 1920s, kept in some sort of touch with the exiles. The Stravinsky of *Petrouchka* and *Firebird* was replaced in 1920–1921 by Leontiev and Lopukhov, and some of the avant-garde trends of that time were apparent in ballet as in the theater. Machines, sport, athleticism, the spoken word, and singing were used in an expressionist way. However, the classics survived and the public continued to love them.

A proof of the Soviet authorities' open mind on the subject during the 1920s was their attempt to engage Diaghilev as director of state theaters, and their collaboration with him in *Pas d'Acier*, a constructivist ballet to music by Prokofiev. Diaghilev's death and the hardening of Soviet policy are separate events, but they lie at the root of a change of course in Russia, which, it must be remembered, had some parallel in the western world. The antiexpressionist, antimodern reaction resulted in a return to the past, seen as a symbol of political order and contentment and dominated by a fear of change, there as elsewhere.

Ballet was increasing in popularity all over the Soviet Union; new and efficient companies and schools sprang up. But in spite of the contribution of such composers as Shostakovich, Glier, Asaviev, and Katchaturian, their creations were never up to the level of the rest of the world (and their decor was sadly behind the times). An exception was Prokofiev. In any case, it was the Petipa style that prevailed, sometimes adulterated by a touch of expressionism, or with a little folk dancing to please the popular taste.

The strange contradiction in Soviet ballet was the wealth of schools and dancers accompanied by a scarcity of choreographers and innovation. During the 1930s the country became intensely inward-looking and finished by repudiating its own best period, preferring the cult of the classics quite devoid of any modern art. This isolation led to a considerable backwardness in all forms of artistic production.

Fortunately, an unexpected event occurred in 1933: Sergei Prokofiev returned to his native land. The great musician had left Russia in 1921 with the approval of Lunacharsky and had started a fine career as pianist and composer in France and America. Working in ballet, he had provided Diaghilev with modernistic scores for *Chout*, *Ala and Lolly*, *Pas d'Acier*, and *The Prodigal Son*. His music was permeated with violence, irony, a sense of the grotesque, and great melodic invention. Together with Stravinsky and the early Shostakovich, he had put life into the etiolated body of twentieth-century music.

Disappointed with America and oppressed by the need to earn his living by giving concerts, Prokofiev decided to return (in the historically ominous year in which Hitler seized power in Germany) so as to be able to compose music under a state guarantee, freed from the rules of impresarios and commerce. The importance of his return was immense and coincided with the last great period of art in his homeland. It is enough to mention his collaboration with the film director Eisenstein, and the wealth of symphonic and chamber music produced in those years under the dual guidance of stylistic continuity and adherence (often wrung from him) to the demands of the regime.

The most conspicuous people in the field of ballet at that time were the choreographer Lavrovsky and the ballerina Ulanova. The most crying need was the invigoration of the current repertory, just as the chief ambition was to make the Russian ballet worthy of its great antecedents.

Like Tchaikovsky, Prokofiev composed the music for a triad of full-length ballets with one eye on the theater and the other on the fairy tale (both directed towards the state morality). Unlike Tchaikovsky, however, he put drama first, especially in *Romeo and Juliet*, which, after initial misunderstanding and difficulties, became enormously popular. Besides demonstrating that music is the decisive element for the durability of a ballet, he restored the concept of theatricality, and so revived the creative spirit of the state companies. The other two ballets, *Cinderella* and *The Stone Flower*, were also launched in difficult circumstances (the war, the crisis, postponements), but remained as milestones along the path of a highly mechanized conservatism which, in the end, proved unproductive, judging from the modest quality of *Spartacus*, or the spectacle as an end in itself that was *Ivan the Terrible*, a posthumous tribute to Prokofiev by the choreographer Grigorovich. More interesting to our eyes are the ballets staged away from the famous theaters, particularly those produced at the Malegot in Leningrad by the young Oleg Vinogradov, who insinuated a vein of spirituality into his last creations, such as *Jaroslavna*.

Nevertheless, the Soviet Union presented the postwar world with a vast array of dancers, male and female, who gave an impressive picture of the growth of their academic school. Galina Ulanova made a sensation when she first danced in the west, but so also did the competence of the whole company, the precision of the execution, the talent of the men, and the romantic grace of the girls. During the 1950s and 1960s the Russian – now Soviet – ballet companies were received with enthusiasm, but they presented only the great classics. Nonetheless, there was a noble rivalry between them and the Russian ballet in exile, that of George Balanchine.

But there was something amiss in that great organization shut off from new experience. The exchanges and tours abroad revealed a new world to the Russian dancers and gave rise to severe tensions. When Rudolf Nureyev, the young star of the Kirov, decided to stay in the west, he triggered off a chain reaction of discontent. It was a big event for European ballet, which was immediately invigorated and stimulated by it, especially in England and Italy. Moreover, it was a symptom of the need for change in the Soviet Union which should have been enacted twenty years earlier to prevent the exodus. Other valuable dancers, such as Barishnikov and Makarova, followed their colleague's example. The moment of truth had come to the state theaters, and there is every likelihood that in the next few years the enormous artistic potential of the country will explode, giving life to a grand new phase of creativity, and ready to absorb the European and American heritage now so predominant and far in advance.

So we come back to our point of departure: ballet has taken to itself everything the arts have to offer; it is no longer merely part of a production but master in its own house. It seems to me that in the story of its progress one important point tends to be forgotten: the universality and immediacy of its language. There is no need for intermediaries or interpreters, and that in an age that has seen the gradual decline of words as a means of communication and expression. Today ballet is an art complete in itself, but above all it is a modern art in the fullest sense of the word, because it puts its essential components on an equal plane. To speak of ballet solely in terms of choreography is pure formalism, or merely an exercise in pleasure, like speaking of opera only in regard to singing, or theater only in regard to elocution. In ballet choreographic, musical, visual, and ideal values are inseparable; the widest freedom of expressive and technical choice is essential. That leads naturally to the recognition of a new type of artist, one we might describe as versatile, insofar as he or she is an expert not only in pure dance but also in music, mime, and the spoken word. This may be a return to the glories of the past, to the concept of the many-sided artist, the Renaissance man. A new standard of excellence makes itself felt, to the considerable confusion of traditional critical opinion.

One result of the enriched vocabulary of balletic language is the huge number of new creations produced in the last few years, a productivity unequalled in the other theater arts. New "titles" can be counted in their hundreds, and every company, public or private, large or small, continues to enlarge and renew its repertory. On the other hand, the classic ballets of the nineteenth and twentieth centuries are continually revived, and by that we mean not only *Swan Lake* and *The Nutcracker*, but also *Petrouchka* and *The Rite of Spring*.

The original *Rite* arranged by Nijinsky has since undergone countless reinterpretations, not merely simple variations on a theme but new versions from the ground up. The pagan rite has emerged beyond the boundaries of primordial Russia to become the symbol of a wider human dimension. There is a significant difference between Béjart's panic and his Africanized vision and the forest mysteries evoked by Neumeier; while Pina Bausch and Glen Tetley stand at opposite ends of the spectrum, both symbolically and aesthetically.

Some new creations, especially those in the vanguard, spread abroad like the proverbial oil stain; others, however, are indissolubly linked with the companies that produced them. In either case, something new is performed every season, for choice something that stands out because it exploits some novel idea for the first time.

The importance of being able to compose dances to any type of music can never be sufficiently stressed. When in 1933 Massine composed choreography to Tchaikovsky's *Quinta* (*Les Présages*), he opened up a new vista that was later to seem self-evident. It meant the end of "accompaniment" music and the need to explore great compositions or to reinvent through them. Since our heritage of

Ballerina Merle Park curtsies to the audience after a performance of The Nutcracker.

music is vast, it is clear that the opportunities of interpreting it with dance movement are equally enormous.

And yet the passing on and diffusion of ballets is faced with one great difficulty: the choreography cannot be written and handed down like an orchestral score. Of many ballets of the past nothing now remains to us but pic res, a few instructions, and a description or two.

The problem is how to record all the movements of all the participants clearly and completely. Whatever method is used must be capable of universal application. Another important question is authors' rights for the choreographer, who should be protected by copyright. Balanchine refers to the importance of the Dance Notation Bureau, founded in New York in 1940, which has made the preservation of many dances and ballets possible, and hence also their reproduction with a high degree of fidelity. However, one gets the impression that everyone is working for himself according to his own system, with a strong dash of empiricism thrown in. Of the several systems of notation, the one established by Rudolf Laban is probably the most useful and exact.

The vocabulary of mime, abundantly codified in the past, is used less and less in modern ballet, although plenty of it can be seen in ballets such as *Giselle*, *Coppelia*, *Swan Lake*, and *The Sleeping Beauty*. As a key to understanding the plot or meaning, traditional mime has been replaced by more contemporary expressive attitudes. It is no longer obligatory to indicate love by placing two hands over the heart or to shake one's fists above one's head to show rage.

Whereas in opera the libretto and score provide a firm substructure (the stage direction in this context being secondary), in ballet the plot and music can be expressed only by the choreography. And that aspect can be conveyed by the director or his assistant alone. Now, fortunately, we have a new aid at our disposal, namely the cinema, which can record the performance on stage and also the work of preparation.

Steps and positions, which have no significance in themselves, acquire meaning and value in the context of their choreographic order in the ballet. Like words in a sentence, their relation to each other is infinitely variable.

Just because ballet steps are not words lined up formalistically in a sentence, the more dedicated dancers must study their parts in depth. An interesting kind of logical dialogue is developing, with subject-matter continually renewed and values perennially reassessed. Today, fortunately for us, we are confronted with the problems of our own lives and the concerns of contemporary society. Ballet has assimilated, precisely because it is a young art performed by young people, the ferment of the younger generation and the desire for liberation that does not concern the peoples of the Third World alone. In some cases ballet has become so highly sophisticated that it demands of its audience a literary philosophy which is both profound and diversified.

During recent years, for instance, two of Maurice Béjart's creations have almost brutally thrown the glove in the face of the old world of ballet. We are referring to *Notre Faust* and *Molière Imaginaire*, which extend the ideas of Petrarch's splendid *I Trionfi*. The *Molière* ballet is a prodigious spectacle of dancing, singing, and speaking, reversing the Molièrian concept of *comédie-ballet* to introduce the idea of *ballet-comédie*. It presupposes a complete knowledge of Jean-Baptiste Poquelin's texts, but it does not confine itself to a historical evocation of the character. On the contrary, it becomes a moral essay insofar as it judges, and in judging interprets. *Molière Imaginaire* is a production to be remembered, because it marks the beginning of a new aesthetic creed, and because it shows with the greatest clarity the need to be involved in life, to discuss, but not to repudiate history and books.

Equally important is the idea of *Notre Faust*, an extraordinary revisiting of Goethe's work by a man who lives intensely in the present. In this creation, too, there is some speaking and the dramatic content is very important – but without a deep knowledge of the history, philosophy, and literature of yesterday and today the ballet could not have been created. The same goes for *I Trionfi*, created in the Boboli Gardens in Florence with the most complete understanding of a high moment in Italian poetry. Psychology, psychoanalysis, oriental philosophy, libertarianism, and the spirit of the 1960s are not for Béjart vehicles of deconsecration but matters for critical reflection, as are also the themes of alienation, consumerism, spirituality, and politics. A revival of Stravinsky's principal ballets has been another of Béjart's achievements, rendered possible by his company's organized structure (*corps de ballet*, a creative finishing school), ruled by an iron discipline and possessing interchangable soloists.

Béjart's *Ballet du XXme Siècle*, established at the Théatre de la Monnaie de Bruxelles, is in a very favourable situation. It enjoys the security of state support combined with independence and a free relationship with the dancers. The New York City Ballet, in spite of grants and private funds, leads a hand-to-mouth existence, never certain of its future. Balanchine, too, although his headquarters are at the Lincoln Center and he has the backing of the great American theater public, admits to a perpetual shortage of funds.

Most of the major European ballet companies are subsidized by the state. But it is only when they are able to retain autonomy (in production and administration) and are not linked to the opera that they can be productive and profitable. Such is the case with the Royal Ballet and to some extent with the smaller companies in Great Britain and West Germany, but they still have financial problems. Another essential condition is the free circulation of artists, especially in countries where ballet is not in a very strong position. It is not good for companies to be too hidebound by their organizations as is the case at the Paris Opéra and with various Italian opera managements (even the Milan Scala), where ballet is in a subordinate position, with no independent productions of its own and consequently not of the highest quality.

As to the state ballets of the "Peoples' Republics," the numerous schools, and the many dancers that graduate from them after superlative training, find insufficient outlet in a repertory so lacking in all that is free and modern. In East Germany the next few years may show us more promising developments, as interest in modern choreography is growing rapidly there. The same seems to be true of the Hungarian school, which even exports dancers to West Germany and lends soloists to Béjart's company. Polish ballet has experimented with a few avant-garde works and has developed an interesting theater of mime. The ballet companies of the remaining Iron Curtain countries, however, are in practice little more than provincial branches of the Bolshoi and Soviet conservatism (the young Leningrad group does not yet enjoy the same official protection); Yugoslavia, as one might expect, stands between east and west, between nationalism and internationalism.

Outside Europe, Japan and Cuba present the most interesting phenomena: the Asiatics study in New York, London, and Moscow, reproducing the techniques learnt with the precision of clockwork; the Cubans, between America and Russia, have produced their own school of ballet, which combines national culture with the academic and with modern dance. In mainland China, ballet exists in a world apart: with the ancient national tradition, academic techniques often reach a very high standard, but are subjugated to naive moralistic and revolutionary propaganda.

The Scandinavian countries, such as Denmark and Sweden, certainly cannot be ignored. In the former the old Royal Ballet has kept its importance and its repertory, but does not reject more advanced ideas. In the nineteenth century, Copenhagen rivalled Paris and London and staged key productions still danced today (it is enough to mention the name Bournonville). In the latter the leading personality of dance has been Birgit Cullberg, whose company inspired many of the most far-reaching movements of dance reform in Europe (Béjart is to some extent in her debt), with a repertory which is both interesting and stimulating. Modern dance flourishes in Holland (van Manen and van Dantzijg are distinguished choreographers), while in Belgium Béjart's success has sparked off various dance enterprises in other parts of the country. In liberated Spain Antonio Gadés continues his activities while waiting for the organization of a national company – and with that we enter the field of ballet based on folklore, which is popular in the Third World and Latin America, as well as, of course, in socialist countries, but is outside the scope of this book.

Obviously, the most powerful countries are those who export the most. Thus Europe is invaded by American choreographers and dancers, just as once she was invaded by the Russians (now it is the dissidents that come). At the moment a new generation of choreographers is emerging, pupils of Balanchine, Béjart, Graham, and other pioneers. If a world without frontiers ever materializes, we shall see a wonderful flowering of ballet. Meanwhile, a promising new situation (of which we cannot as yet measure the consequences or importance) is the communication between Béjart and the Soviet Union for which Maia Plisetskaia has fought so persistently. It has already been of help to Vladimir Vassiliev in the new *Petrouchka* and to the Vassiliev–Maximova partnership in *Romeo and Juliet* danced to Berlioz's music. Furthermore, the great ballet master Messerer is giving the *Ballet du XXme Siècle* classes in academic dancing. And so it is a world in movement, continuously evolving along the lines we have described, and hoping to win an ever greater share in theatrical activity and an ever greater interest among the public.

A galaxy of new names waits at the gate, young dancers, choreographers, musicians, and designers eager to carry forward the work of their predecessors. And so we see, paraded before us, four centuries of ballet represented by historical pictures and genuine photographs – from the court to the stage, from the salons of aristocrats to the open air, from books to real life.

The subject-matter of this book is the global repertory of ballets, with special reference to two basic points: the description and historical facts concerning productions that had a special significance in their time, and an idea of their theatrical presentation. We include ballets that are no longer performed, together with others that still remain with us.

Naturally, we have had to select, and the result can be no more than an anthology of the outstanding events in ballet history. Our selection has been based on relevance to the present day, musical and artistic values, and the most lasting choreographic influences. A large section is devoted to ballet before the romantic period of the nineteenth century in Europe, but it is to what followed and what is in progress now that we want particularly to draw the reader's attention.

To make a choice also implies, logically, to exclude, but with discrimination. It is not our intention to record all the ballets that have ever been, but to provide points of reference, a series of landmarks as complete as possible, concerned with what ballet has been and what it is today. When opportune we also deal with the music that accompanies and sustains it.

From all this there arises indirectly a story with recognizable characters, a story indissolubly linked with the theater, certainly, but filing past in the background are all the dreams and fears of our age, the ascents and the declines, the retreats and the new discoveries.

We beg the reader who sees a performance of dancing not to stop at the outward facts, the immediate picture, the uncomplicated memory, but always to look into the state of the culture that produced it. Let him penetrate behind the scenes and ask himself all the possible "whys," remembering above all that ballet is not a happy island in an immutable world, and that what he has witnessed has its parallels in music, painting, drama, literature, poetry, and philosophy. Our approach must be free of prejudice, looking towards the future, but not above the fray; rejecting rhetoric, affectation, and ignorance, trusting in intelligence rather than contrivance, loving exploration and everything that is alive and lively. To be attracted, today as yesterday, by the red badge of courage – that is the interpretative key we offer our readers.

Mario Pasi

The ballroom of the Petit Bourbon palace in Paris at the beginning of the Ballet Comique de la Reine, *performed on October 15, 1581. Action and dance took place in the center of the hall, two sides of which were taken up by scenery. Opposite: the* entrée *of the mermaids in the same ballet.*

Catalogue of Ballets

BALLET COMIQUE DE LA REINE

A choreographic, dramatic, and scenic display consisting of a prologue, two parts, and a grand ballet finale. Choreography by Baltazarini di Belgioioso (Balthasar de Beaujoyeulx). Verse by La Chesnaye. Music by L. de Beaulieu, Salmon, Beaujoyeulx, and others. Scenes and costumes by Jacques Patin. Performed in Paris, 1581. Performers: Mlle. de Saint-Mesme (Circe), M. de la Roche (The Nobleman; actor), M. de Beaulieu (Glaucus), Mlle. de Beaulieu (Thetis), Mlles. de Vitry, de Surgères, de Lavernay, d'Estavay (Nymphs), M. de Jutigny (Pan), M. du Pont (Mercury), the Queen of France and the Princess of Lorraine (two Naiads), members of the court of Henri III of France.

SYNOPSIS. The action is supposed to take place in the garden of Circe's palace, the scene being set at one end of a large rectangular hall, the King and his court seated at the other. Prologue: a nobleman, prisoner of the enchantress Circe, escapes from the palace and stops in front of the King, whom he asks for help in a long *tirade* full of allegorical meaning. Part One: enter three mermaids and a triton dancing and singing, while a large fountain bearing naiads, tritons, and singers is drawn forward by three seahorses. Twelve naiads recite verses to the King under the guidance of Glaucus and Thetis, who sing a duet, accompanied by the chorus and orchestra hidden in the topmost gallery of the room. Ten costumed violinists enter playing an *entrée de ballet*, which is then danced by twelve naiads with twelve pages

as partners. Now Circe appears and immobilizes everyone with her magic wand; even Mercury, chosen by the gods to defeat her, falls victim to her spell. In the first act finale the interior of the park is revealed, inhabited by men changed into beasts by Circe, at whose feet now lies the unconscious Mercury. Part Two: eight satyrs playing flutes join the dryads in a song of homage to the King. On one side the grotto of Pan appears. The nymph Opi begs the god to free the wood of enchantment. After the entrance of the Four Virtues, Minerva appears in a large allegorical chariot and turns to the King to recite a long speech (*tirade*) which is followed by a chorus of six voices. Invoked by the goddess, Jove descends from the skies. Pan with his eight satyrs joins him, and all advance towards Circe's palace. The infuriated enchantress, amid the cries of her animals, takes the field against her assailants, but is vanquished by Jove's thunderbolt. Gods and goddesses, satyrs and nymphs, pay homage to the King, delivering Circe to him in chains. A complicated *entrée* danced by the dryads advancing from the garden background is followed by a last solo sung by Jove. Then the naiads, led by the Queen, perform the *grand ballet* finale, danced by the whole court and made up of forty measures in geometrical patterns, circles, squares, triangles, and so on, at the center or head of which is always the Queen. She, after the company has made its deep bows and curtsies before the throne, ceremoniously proffers a gift to the King, a gesture repeated by all the ladies who have danced in the ballet to all the gentlemen of the court.

A design by Bernardo Buontalenti for one of the dance interludes in The Fair Pilgrim (La Pellegrina).
The choreography of these interludes was by Emilio d'Cavalieri, Giovanni Bardi, and others.

■ This sumptuous court spectacle is widely held to be the beginning of ballet, or rather of modern theatrical dance. We can accept that convention only to a certain degree. In fact, ballet, in the true sense of a form of theater that has separated from drama and opera to acquire its own artistic independence, did not arise before the mid-eighteenth century; moreover, the roots of modern choreographic theater, broadly speaking, go back to the aristocratic displays of the early Italian Renaissance, in which mime, dancing, music, song, and recitation were combined to provide "interludes" at feasts and court entertainments. Indeed, they sometimes constituted entertainments in their own right, as at the celebrated "choreographic banquet" arranged by Bergonzio Botta in 1489, in which, perhaps for the first time, the danced diversions were all related to a single subject. From these multiple, direct forebears, the *Ballet Comique de la Reine* was born, commissioned by the widowed Queen Catherine de Medici, mother of Henri III of France, for the wedding celebrations of the Duke de Joyeuse and the King's sister-in-law, Mlle. de Vaudemont. Baltazarini di Belgioioso, Italian by birth and training, was highly esteemed at the court of France, where he was appointed violinist, choreographer, and Master of the Revels from 1555, when he joined the retinue of the Marshal de Brissac as a member of his much admired orchestra. However, Beaujoyeulx — as Belgioioso had quickly been rechristened in France — also cast his mind back to a type of dance spectacle already familiar in Italy for more than a hundred years. He reorganized the elements of those entertainments, added a few touches from the French theater and court, and thus created his masterpiece, the model of a type of production that was in many ways new and destined to develop and change in France for many decades as the *ballet de cour*, an entertainment composed of dancing, music, poetry, and lavish scenery, costumes, and stage machinery. In his important preface to the *Ballet Comique de la Reine*, published in 1582, Belgioioso seems perfectly aware of his creation's originality and explains that he called the ballet *comique* because it was in dramatized form and so allied to comedy. In what concerns the relation between dance and music, he gives priority to the former, thus revealing what is really ori-

Another of Bernardo Buontalenti's drawings for an interlude in La Pellegrina.
The work was performed in Florence on May 2, 1589.

ginal in his conception, namely an enrichment of the choreographic content, which thus becomes the cornerstone of the production and permits it to be defined as a ballet. Nevertheless, the long poetic speeches, the vocal arias and choruses, and last but not least the technically ingenious scenery, take up a large part of the work, as can be seen from the not very musically interesting score, only a third of which was used for dancing. The formal scheme of the *Ballet de Circé*, as the *Ballet Comique* was sometimes called, became the model for all subsequent court ballets. First came the spoken prologue expounding the theme of the entertainment, then followed a series of *entrées* consisting of mime, dances, recitation, solo and choral singing, and instrumental music through which the action was unfolded. The entertainment finished with the *grand ballet*, in which the whole court took part, dancing in carefully rehearsed geometrical arrangements. Several thousand spectators, middle-class as well as aristocratic, crowded into the grand hall of the Petit Bourbon Palace to see the first and only performance of *Circé*. It lasted almost six hours and cost an enormous sum; echoes of its magnificence made a great impression on contemporary society. Note that, as was characteristic of court ballets and earlier forms of dance spectacle, the scenic arrangement was quasi-theatrical: action and dancing took place in the center of the hall, one side being occupied by the scenery and the other three by the audience seated on raised platforms and galleries. The reason for the dance figures so often being geometrical in design was that they were intended to be viewed from above.   A.A.

INTERLUDES FROM "THE FAIR PILGRIM" *(La Pellegrina)*
Six interludes of dancing and music from the play by Girolamo Bargagli. Choreography by Emilio de Cavalieri, Giovanni Bardi, and others. Verses by Ottavio Rinuccini and Giovanbattista Strozzi. Music by Luca Marenzio, Emilio de Cavalieri, Jacopo Peri, Giulio Caccini, Cristofano Malvezzi, Antonio Archilei, and Giovanni Bardi. Settings and scenic machines by Bernardo Buontalenti. Performed at Florence on May 2,

1589, on the occasion of the wedding of Ferdinando de'Medici and Christine of Lorraine. Forty-one participants, including dancers and singers, among them Luca Marenzio (Saturn), Jacopo Peri (Venus), Giulio Caccini, Emilio de Cavalieri, Vittoria Archilei, Lucia and Margherita Caccini.

SYNOPSIS. First interlude: *Harmony of the Spheres:* spirits descend from the clouds to pay homage to the happy pair. Second interlude: *The Rivalry between the Muses and the Pierides:* speeches, madrigals, and dances by the mythological characters in competition with one another. Third interlude: *Apollo's Pythian Combat:* the god defeats the Python, who has been terrorizing the inhabitants of Delos, in a lively mime followed by a dance of victory. Fourth interlude: *The Land of Demons.* Fifth interlude: *The Song of Arion,* with dances by naiads and tritons. Sixth interlude: *The Descent of Apollo and Bacchus together with Rhythm and Harmony:* a song of praise to the bridal pair is followed by a dance "in oriental style." The entertainment finishes in a grand ball.

■ Theatrical dance in the late Italian Renaissance and early baroque period existed as interludes of song and dance interpolated in spoken plays or in the budding opera. In the former case especially it was relatively independent since, although not as yet an entertainment in itself, it was definitely separated from the rest of the play and so had no spoken content, as did the court ballets of France. A famous and significant example was the interludes between the acts of *La Pellegrina* by Girolamo Bargagli, the whole making up a long and splendid entertainment put on by Count Bardi and some of the more important members of his council, among whom was Emilio de Cavalieri, choreographer, dancer, and composer. He and Count Bardi are credited with a major part of the choreographic invention. The subject-matter of the interludes was entirely divorced from the dramatic plot and merely provided a pretext for mythologizing and lauding the classics-loving Florentine councillors by means of song and dance, the second of which showed a surprisingly mature sense of theater. While the choreography is still of the "extended ballroom" type, with changing geometrical patterns, the abundance of leaping steps compared to "base dancing" produces a certain dynamic quality even in the ensemble numbers, while in the solo parts the mime and dance almost work as drama. An example is provided by the third interlude, in which Apollo's fight with Python is shown in five separate phases (inspired by ancient classical sources) and with lively choreographical expressiveness: in a sense, it is a complete "ballet of action" two centuries before that category was theoretically defined. The description of these interludes left to us by Cristofano Malvezzi shows quite clearly that the dances were performed on a raised platform, and so were designed to be seen from the front – a far cry from the scenic viewpoint of the French court ballet and earlier Italian displays of that kind. The new conception of ballet was decidedly theatrical. A.A.

BALLET OF THE KNIGHTS OF FRANCE AND BÉARN *(Ballet des Chevaliers Français et Béarnais) Story by Catherine de Parthenay. Pau, August 23, 1592.*

SYNOPSIS. The starting point of this "ballet drama" is the traditional rivalry between the French and Béarnese knights, but mingled with it are mythological episodes and characters such as Cupid, Mercury, and nymphs.

■ Performed at Pau, the capital of Béarn, the ballet can be interpreted as a mannered celebration of concord with the French and an invitation to put aside the old rivalry and zealously serve the royal family, some members of which were present at the entertainment. With plenty of spoken passages, it adopts the program of the court ballet typified by the *Ballet Comique de la Reine* of 1581. Thus it is composed of a prologue followed by a sequence of *entrées* of dancers, singers, and reciters, and finishes with a *grand ballet.* P.P.

THE BALLET OF CHESS *(Ballet des Échecs) A danced masque, probably from an idea by Henry of Savoy, Duke of Nemours. Paris, Carnival, 1607. Danced by members of Henri IV's court.*

SYNOPSIS. After a short prologue some of the masquers spread out a large canvas chessboard. Two men in Spanish costume enter dancing and sit on either side of the board to represent the players. The remaining masquers, court ladies among them, then enter disguised as chessmen and dance through a game of chess.

■ Of all the forms taken by the court ballet, the danced masque is the furthest from true theatrical dancing and most like a mere court amusement. It remained popular throughout the reign of Henri IV, though with the comparative austerity imposed on the court by the minister Sully. The complicated staging of the "dramatic" ballet was given up and the entertainment dwindled into a game danced in fancy dress, vaguely composed around some theme, but without any coherent action. After an instrumental overture, there came *entrées* by various personages – clowns, stereotypes, allegorical and fantastic characters (chessmen in the case of the ballet chosen as an example, one of the more dignified of its kind), and after them the inevitable *grand ballet* finale. The choreography of the solo parts was fairly free, ranging from mime to *danse noble* or acrobatic feats, while ensemble dances were strictly a matter of geometrical patterning. If the names of the choreographers, composers, and designers have failed to come down to us, it is probably because they were collective enterprises without any imprint of creative talent. The interest of the danced masque is purely historical inasmuch as its combination with dramatic and operatic ballet gave rise to the *ballet à entrées,* the final form of the true court ballet. A.A.

THE MASKE OF BEAUTY

Choreography and designs by Inigo Jones. Subject by Ben Jonson. London, January 10, 1608.

SYNOPSIS. The goddesses with their trains parade with songs, declamation, and dancing, for an award of beauty.

■ In England the maske or masque, originating in the early sixteenth century, became a true form of theater, gradually gaining in quality and sophistication during the first half of the seventeenth century. Partly inspired by the French *ballet de cour*, they were at first court entertainments in which masked participants entered, sometimes even on horseback or on allegorically decorated carts, and invited all those present to join in the dancing. Masques, already enjoyed by the English monarchs Henry VIII, Edward VI, and Elizabeth I, rose to a peak of splendour during the reign of James I, when they had the advantage of plot and poetry by the playwright Ben Jonson and lighting, scenery, and costumes by Inigo Jones. The creators of various works of this kind, they collaborated for nearly twenty years, producing a great number of lavish entertainments, the best known of which are *The Maske of Beauty*, *The Maske of Blackness*, and *The Maske of Hymen*. They were productions made up of song, spoken verse, and dancing, requiring resplendent costumes and scenic apparatus of great ingenuity. The collaboration ceased abruptly in 1629 when their last maske, *The New Inn*, failed dismally, and Jonson put all the blame for the failure on the shoulders of Inigo Jones.   P.P.

THE BALLET OF THE DISDAINFUL LADIES (*Il Ballo delle Ingrate*)

Ballet-opera in one act. Music by Claudio Monteverdi. Libretto by Ottavio Rinuccini. Choreography attributed to Isacchino Ebreo. Performed at Mantua Teatro della Commedia, on June 4, 1608, during the wedding festivities of Francesco Gonzaga and Margherita of Savoy.

SYNOPSIS. Cupid accompanies his mother Venus to the mouth of a great cavern "inside which swirl globes of blazing fire, while countless infernal monsters pass in and out," where they seek an interview with Pluto. Venus and Cupid plead with the King of the Underworld to allow the ladies who in life have been unkind to their lovers to come into the light of day for a little while to show "every proud soul, what torment cruel beauty can bring." Pluto consents, and from the shadows of Hell "leads forth the condemned band of Disdainful Ladies who must perform the ballet." Cupid and Venus make way for the disdainful ones, who go through a dance expressing deep sorrow, regret, and repentance. Following an admonition by Pluto, "the Disdainful Ladies, beginning a second dance with movements full of grief and despair, and with a thousand intertwinings and a thousand variations..." pass back into the infernal regions, after a sad farewell to life sung by one of their number.

■ This was Monteverdi's third work for the festival at the court of Mantua in 1608. Following *Arianna* and the *Idropica* by Guarini, the *Ballo delle Ingrate* was, according to some, a "ballet in the French manner," such as Monteverdi must have seen during his visit to France. While not denying the possibility of some influence of that nature – which would in any case be a re-importation (see *Ballet Comique de la Reine*, page 43) – any such connection seems superficial, suggested, perhaps, only by the dancers descending from the stage to the floor to perform the ballet. That procedure, however, had been practiced for a long time, and in this case was more likely to have been suggested by the interest in the theater of ancient Greece so prevalent among the Florentine councillors of state. Be that as it may, the coherence and expressive density of the *Ballo delle Ingrate* was due not only to the genius of Monteverdi, but also to the polished poetic invention of Ottavio Rinuccini, which places the work well above and beyond any French ballet of the time. The name of the choreographer who devised the dances included in the entertainment, as well as the pastoral ballet that followed it, presumably to cheer the audience up after witnessing the sad fate of the disdainful ladies, is unknown. Reyna supposes it to have been Isacchino Ebreo, for many years ballet master at the Mantuan court, but for reasons of chronology that seems unlikely. In any case, we know nothing of the choreography itself, although a few hints in the libretto suggest that it consisted of dances in the style and with the technical accomplishment of the most advanced *danse noble*, possibly mixed with mime of intense dramatic significance. There is no doubt, however, that the dancing, while remaining an integral part of the production, was little considered in comparison with those theoretical and literary elements that were leading not to ballet as a separate branch of theatrical art, but towards the dawning splendours of opera. A.A.

THE MUSIC. Although nothing remains to us of Monteverdi's first collaboration with the poet Ottavio Rinuccini except *Arianna*'s sublime "Lament," we still have the *Ballo delle Ingrate (The Disdainful Ladies)* of the same date – 1608. It seems likely that Monteverdi valued the composition highly, and the printed edition (published thirty years later, in 1638, by Vincenti at Venice, by which time the work had already been repeated in Vienna) has evidently been revised and rearranged. Some of the compositional characteristics, coloratura passages, and vocal ranges (especially in Pluto's part) are in a style definitely later than 1608 and more nearly related to the madrigals published in the same volume. The curious counter-morality of the plot is reflected in the music, which in the first part is essentially discursive and somewhat conventional. The systematic alternation of recitative and dialogue between Cupid and Venus, or the goddess and Pluto, never amounts to the genuinely melodic. However, the tuneful musical cues do provide a first indication of the characters' personalities. Cupid is given the less original score, while Venus's music has gracefully noble inflections and is sometimes humanly frivolous. Pluto, on the other hand, in the powerful, regal, almost caricatured accents of the vocal composition, seems to follow the generally panegyrical tone of the narration (we are far removed from the austere and more serious eloquence of Pluto's part in *Orfeo*). The musical atmosphere begins to rise with the duet between Venus and Cupid, *"Ecco ver noi l'addolorate squadre"* ("See coming towards us the sorrowful band"), in which pity for the unhappy souls has inspired Monteverdi to compose a passage of harmonious beauty. More complex (being made up of two recitatives followed by two arias of equal length and finishing with a chorus for four female voices), the final "lament" is one of those moving elegies which rank among the loftiest achievements of Monteverdi's genius. The instrumental arrangement for the *Ballet of the Disdainful Ladies* is particularly interesting: "five violas da braccio, harpsichord, and archlute, which instruments may be doubled if the size of the location requires it." But still more significant is the way in which these instruments were used to obtain the essential expressive and narrative character. For example, the subdued tones appropriate to the dance of the unfortunate ladies is achieved by splitting up the elements of the orchestra: they never play all at once, and the second violin becomes silent when the tenor viol begins. Another sure dramatic effect is the progressive reduction of sound that marks the conclusion of the play. Beginning with all the instruments playing together, it ends with the sad song of a single disdainful lady accompanied by one archlute only; she is answered by a last chorus unsupported by any instrument at all.   A.F.

BALLET OF THE FAIR TURKS *(Ballo di Donne Turche)*

Operatic ballet in one act. Choreography by Santino Comesari. Music by Marco da Gagliano. Libretto by Alessandro Ginori. Masque costumes designed by Jacopo Ligozzi. Florence, Pitti Palace, February 26, 1615. Performers: sixteen Florentine gentlemen.

SYNOPSIS. From a rich vessel arrived in Florence ten Turkish ladies disembark, accompanied by six Turks. "Brought into the presence of Their Serene Highnesses," they beg for the freedom of their husbands, enslaved by the "ever conquering army" of Tuscany. After a disconsolate dance by eight of the ladies, their respective husbands appear, declaring themselves to have already been released by the generous Prince. They are happily reunited, and there follows the *grand ballet* in which the said Prince and all his court finally join.

■ It is to Santino Comesari, ballet master at the Medici court in the early seventeenth century, that we owe the choreography of *The Ballet of the Fair Turks together with their consorts, freed from slavery. Danced in the royal palace of Pitti before Their Royal Highnesses of Tuscany* (so runs the title of the libretto by Alessandro Ginori, printed by Cosimo Giunti at Florence in 1614).

The Cardinal's Palace Theater. In the foreground are Louis XIII, the Queen, and Cardinal de Richelieu.

Among numerous such entertainments performed at the time, this one stands out through its music by Marco Zenobi da Gagliano, a celebrated contrapuntist and a distinguished man of the theater belonging to the generation that succeeded the Cameratisti. His contemporaries considered his work "amazing, because, to the same strains four different dances can be performed, namely the courante, the canary, the galliard, and the Italian lute dance." In this work Comesari succeeded in bestowing an organic vitality on the choreographic style then fashionable in Italian courts. A slender plot served as pretext for an entertainment in costume, song, and dance, the orchestral part of which consisted in a sequence of courtly and character dances linked by short passages of mime.   A.A.

THYRSIS AND CLORE (Tirsi e Clori)

A pastoral dance with voices and instruments, in one act. Music by Claudio Monteverdi. Libretto possibly by Alessandro Striggio. The Court Theater of Mantua, April 1616.

SYNOPSIS. There is no real plot. The nymph Clore and the shepherd Thyrsis converse briefly, exchanging frequent invitations to joy and the dance that are immediately taken up by the chorus. The long, danced *divertissement* is of a pastoral nature.

■ Designed, according to the theatrical usage current in the late sixteenth and early seventeenth centuries, as an interlude of dance and music during a long and varied court entertainment, *Thyrsis and Clore* was composed by Monteverdi, already in the employ of the Venetian republic but still attached to the Gonzagas' court, for the Mantuan spring festival of 1616. The name of the choreographer is unknown. Every Italian court had one or two masters of ballet, and the arrangement of the dances for an entertainment was entrusted to the chief ballet master so much as a matter of course that it was not always thought necessary to mention him by name. In this case the choreography was designed to match the style of the choral music, which was pastoral in nature, and consisted of stately court dances for the ensembles and livelier, more skipping passages for the solo dances. The author of the poetic text, notable for the deftness of its rhythms, recitatives, and choruses, is also uncertain. Probably it was Alessandro Striggio, who produced several works in Mantua at that time, but it could have been Ercole Marliani or some other writer about the Mantuan court. One should note the influence exercised by the music on this and other lyric compositions in which the verses were written to the music. Very interesting in relation to the entertainment as a whole is a letter of practical instructions sent by Monteverdi in November 1615, possibly to Striggio: ". . . see that the musicians are arranged in a crescent shape with an archlute and a harpsichord at the corners, one sounding the base for Clore, the other the base for Thyrsis, and that these, too, should have lutes in their hands to pluck as they sing and to play in time to the dancing. After they have finished their dialogue six other voices join the

Three pictures from the Ballet of Renaud's Deliverance, *in which Louis XIII took part, dressed as a fire demon.*

Above: An entrée *with the figure of Armida in the centre.*

chorus, making eight voices in all, also eight violas da braccio with double-bass and spinet harp . . . all keeping time to the melody, with the agreement of the ballet master." The score of this fine work, with its exquisite vocal construction enhanced by a musical accompaniment rich in tonal effects, was published by Monteverdi in his *Seventh Book of Madrigals*.

OTHER VERSIONS. Aurel Milloss. Sets and costumes by Gino Sensani. Florence, Teatro Comunale, May 9, 1951 (XIV May Music Festival of Florence). Principal interpreters: Yvette Chauviré, Vladimir Skouratoff, Xenia Palley, Violette Verdy, Deryk Mendel. This was the first and only choreographic production of the piece since the time of Monteverdi (when it was performed several times, especially at Venice). In this otherwise strictly accurate version Milloss has added slight dramatic quality to the allegorical action by inserting in the score two of Monteverdi's madrigals relevant to the subject of Thyrsis and Clore, in which a new theme is developed from Clore's sadness at losing her loved one, sweet memories of the past, and finally the happy reunion, celebrated with joyous dancing. Outwardly the style of the dancing is seventeenth-century pastoral, but the complex choreographical architecture, corresponding to the counterpoint of the score, reveals that every movement develops from its own interior need for expression.   A.A.

Above: Scene showing Armida's palace destroyed and musicians celebrating Renaud's triumph.

THE BALLET OF RENAUD'S DELIVERANCE
(Ballet de la Délivrance de Renaud)

A court ballet-opera in one act with grand ballet finale. Choreography by M. de Belleville. Music by Pierre Guédron, Gabriel Bataille, Antoine Boësset and Jacques Mauduit. Libretto and general plan by Durand (from an episode in Gerusalemme Liberata *by Torquato Tasso). Scene, machine, and costume designs by Tomaso Francini. Paris, Louvre, January 29, 1617. Performers: the Duc de Luynes (Rinaldo), Marais (Armide), King Louis XIII (Fire Demon), M. De Belleville (Demon), and numerous members of the French court.*

SYNOPSIS. Renaud, bewitched by Armide, rests among trees guarded by dancing demons who bring him to a cave. Two knights arrive to rescue him, but the scene is changed by magic into Armide's garden, adorned with enchanted fountains. Using their magic wands, the two knights drive off first a nymph and then six monsters sent out to destroy them. They find Renaud lost in a happy dream and, showing him the unworthiness of his situation as reflected in an enchanted shield, free him from the spell. Armide hastens thither with her suite of demons to win back her lover, but is again defeated by new magic and metamorphoses. A sorcerer hermit finally announces to Renaud's soldiers, who emerge from a nearby wood, that their captain has been set free. Once more the scene changes, and everyone joins in the *grand ballet*.

■ The above is a perfect example of a court ballet of the operatic type, a development of the *ballet comique* (or *dramatique*) and a great advance on the artistically impoverished ballet-masque so popular during the reign of Henri IV. The pastoral or knightly plot, unfolded by mime and sung recitative, serves as a pretext for a number of dance *entrées*, serious or comic, and finishes with the traditional *grand ballet* executed by all the nobly born, sumptuously clad masked dancers. In this new type of entertainment, the ballet-opera which became established after the *Ballet d'Alcine* in 1610, the dancing was no longer continually interrupted by long poetic *tirades* as in the *ballet dramatique* (see *Ballet Comique de la Reine*, page 43) but took place at the same time as the singing. This shows the Italian influence due to the artists summoned to the French court by Marie de Medici, among whom were Giulio Caccini and Ottavio Rinuccini. M. de Belleville was probably the creator of the purely choreographic part of *Renaud's Deliverance*, the ballet as a whole having been conceived by the poet Durand and characterized by astonishing stage effects, the work of Tomaso Francini, who devised, among other things, four complete changes of scene. It should be noted that the stage set up by Francini in the grand salon of the Louvre, Louis XIII's favourite palace, was *à l'Italien*, that is, entirely frontal, so that the dances took place on the stage instead of in the middle of the room as hitherto. King Louis XIII sometimes danced in *entrées* beside his favourite, the Duc de Luynes, who took the part of Renaud, while the famous dancer Marais played Armide *en travesti* according to the custom prevailing after 1600, in which

Entrée du herault & des tambours

20

Ballet of the Fairies of St Germain Forest. Entrée *of the herald and drums.*

women might dance only in the final *grand ballet* and not in the *entrées* connected with the plot.   A.A.

THE FIGHT BETWEEN TANCREDI
AND CLORINDA (*Il Combattimento di Tancredi e Clorinda*)
A staged madrigal. Music by Claudio Monteverdi. Text taken from Gerusalemme Liberata *by Torquato Tasso. Venice, the house of Count Girolamo Mocenigo di San Stae; Carnival, 1624.*

SYNOPSIS. In front of Jerusalem, besieged by the Crusaders, the brave Christian warrior Tancredi meets Clorinda, the Moslem heroine secretly loved by him, but does not recognise her dressed in black and rusty armour, so challenges her to a duel. The fatal battle begins. Clorinda is wounded and asks for baptism. Tancredi fetches the baptismal water from a nearby stream. When he lifts the helmet he sees the face of his dying loved one, but as if transfigured "in the act dying happy," and is just in time to hear her last words of love and forgiveness.

■ Claudio Monteverdi composed the music of *The Fight between Tancredi and Clorinda* to the text of verses 52 to 62 and 64 to 68 of the twelfth canto of Tasso's poem. A ballet-opera, or martial and amorous madrigal – as the author defined it – it was commissioned by the Mocenigo family, and performed "in the presence of all the nobility, who were so affected with pity that they were near to tears, and applauded. . . ." To the two main characters Monteverdi added a third: Testo, the poet himself, who narrates and comments on the action. The plot was further unfolded by the singers reciting from Tasso's book while the dancers mimed the scene on the stage. In the orchestra were four violas, a double bass, and a harpsichord. The composition was included in *Martial and Amorous Madrigals with some short pieces for the Theater*, published in Venice in 1638. P.P.

BALLET OF THE FAIRIES OF ST. GERMAIN
FOREST (*Ballet des Fées des Forêts de Saint-Germain*)
A court ballet (with entrées) *in five parts. Subject and choreographical invention by Henri de Savoie, Duc de Nemours. Paris, Louvre, February 11, 1625. Performers; Marais (the fairy Guillemine), M. de Liancourt (the fairy Jacqueline), M. la Barre, M. Picot, M. Delfin, etc., and noblemen of Louis XIII's court, among them the King himself.*

SYNOPSIS. Five fairies from the forest of Saint-

Ballet of the Fairies of St Germain Forest. Entrée *of the "Esperducattes."*

Germain come into the presence of the court, and each of them presents an allegorico-burlesque display inspired by her particular dominion, e.g., Guillemine, Spirit of Music, is followed by an enormous dummy representing Music and by bizarre musicians; Gillette, Fairy of Gamblers; Jacqueline, Fairy of the Mad, who brings in her train "*des Embambouinez, des Demy-Foux, des Fantasques et des Esperducattes*"; Alizon, Fairy of the Quarrelsome Peasants, the Head Bashers, and the Physicians; finally Macette, the Spirit of the Dance, who, after various *entrées* by her followers, conducts the *grand ballet* finale.

■ This entertainment, one among countless theatrical displays staged during the reign of Louis XIII, marks the triumph of the *ballet à entrées* over the *ballet mélodramatique* (see the *Ballet of Renaud's Deliverance*, page 51). In the first examples of the genre these dancing "entrances" were quite without dramatic content, even though they had a much higher artistic and theatrical quality than the earlier "masquerades." The music, songs, book, and scenery were far from remarkable, while the dancing, too, had entirely lost its expressiveness, being reduced to a mere pretext for showing off the technical skill of the professional dancers and noble dilettantes, all masked in accordance with the theatrical convention of the time, and all

fantastically attired. The choreography of this "fairy ballet" was probably the work of M. De Belleville, director of ballets at the court of Louis XIII for many years. It was, however, the Duc de Nemours, an eminent courtier almost fanatical about ballet, who was responsible for the general idea. Among the dancers were celebrities of the time, such as Marais and La Barre.   A.A.

BALLET OF THE HEIRESS OF BILBAO (*La Douairière de Billebahaut*)
A court ballet. Music by Antoine Boësset, François Richard, Paul Auger. Libretto by René Bordier, Claude de l'Estoile, Charles Sorel, Théophile de Viau, Imbert, Honorat de Bueil. Paris, Louvre, February 1626. Performers: Marais, Louis XIII, professional singers and dancers, and members of the court.

SYNOPSIS. America, Asia, Europe, and Africa send their representatives to the grand ball in honour of the heiress's engagement. Her bethrothed bears the symbolic name of Fanfan de Sotteville, probably to stress that he is a fool. The arrival of the delegations from the four corners of the world serves as a pretext for a varied ballet, preceded as always by a spoken prologue and divided into a long series of *entrées*. The festival ends with the usual *grand ballet* finale.

A court ballet with *entrées*, having a strongly comical element not greatly counterbalanced by the rest of the action. It was among the first of its kind to use professional dancers to replace the gentlemen of the court in the solo numbers. Louis XIII, however, was among the performers. The ballet was so successful and gave so much pleasure to the King that it was repeated at the Hôtel de Ville only a few days after its first performance and attracted more than four thousand spectators.   P.P.

THE SPIRITS OF THE MOUNTAIN *(Ballet des Montagnards)*
Court ballet in five parts. Subject, choreography, and probably music by Filippo d'Agliè. Paris, August 21, 1631.

SYNOPSIS. The prologue is spoken by Rumour, "carrier of gossip," a figure of fun. Then follow the entrances of the spirits of the mountain winds, noises, lights, and shadows. The light-footed spirits of the first element carry windmills and bellows. Echo leads the dance of the mountain noises wearing sleigh bells. Falsehood, masked and limping, introduces the mountain lights, bearing lanterns, and then comes the shadows of the mountain, led by Sleep. Lastly, True Report presents the best mountain dwellers of all, those of the Alps, richly clad spirits who open the *grand ballet*.

■ Between 1624 and his death in 1667 Count Filippo d'Agliè di San Martino, courtier, man of letters, musician, and above all choreographer, created a large number of ballets for the Turin court of the Princes of Savoy, the only one in Italy where the more or less French type of *ballet de cour* was cultivated. This *Ballet of the Spirits of the Mountain*, considered his masterpiece, was created in Paris at the request of the Cardinal Maurice of Savoy, who was in France on a diplomatic mission, in order to rebut the Parisian courtiers' pretensions to superiority over the "mountain folk" of Piedmont and show them the refined and magnificent standards of Savoyard entertainments. We have little exact information about d'Agliè's choreography, except that it was highly praised by Ménestrier, who described it in 1669 as "the most brilliant in the world for its infinity of ingenious invention." We can surmise that the elegance of the entertainment as a whole was balanced by a mature choreographic technique inherited from the celebrated school of Milan to which tradition d'Agliè was certainly indebted. The form of these entertainments was that of the typical court ballet, divided, as in this case, into a series of *entrées*. There is no doubt that, in the work of this strange Italian choreographer-courtier, the genre found the maximum artistic worth attainable within its limits.   A.A.

THE WEDDING OF THE GODS *(Le Nozze degli Dei)*
A fable in music and dance, by Giovanni Carlo Coppola. Choreography by Agnolo Ricci. Staged by Alfonso Parigi. Florence, Pitti Palace, July 8, 1637.

■ The wedding of Ferdinand II of Tuscany with Vittoria della Rovere of Urbino was celebrated in Florence on July 5, 1637, and followed by two weeks of "feasting, plays, equestrian ballets, horse races, and other amusements." The central artistic event in this "festival of the Arno" was the musical fable by the young cleric Giovanni Carlo Coppola (a sizable edition of which was printed in the same year). The entertainment combined singing, acting, and dancing, but it was the last that really mattered and that was the work of Agnolo Ricci, one of the most important Italian choreographers in the first half of the seventeenth century and chief ballet master at the Medici court for several decades. Alfonso Parigi staged the production in the open in the courtyard of the Pitti Palace, in contrast to the usual custom of performing such light musical pieces inside the palace. The *"Description of the Festival at Florence in honour of the Royal Marriage, etc. . . ."* by *Ferdinando de Bardi*, tells us about the *Wedding of the Gods*. "The dances were a great success, because of their exquisite quality, variety, and the number of noble gentlemen taking part, while the suitability of the music was a delight . . . . Finally, the costumes, rich beyond belief but appropriate to the characters, the frequent changes of scenery, the machines at work almost continuously to show us what wonders they can perform nowadays, all lift this production well above the average."   A.A.

BALLET OF THE PROSPERITY OF THE ARMS OF FRANCE *(Ballet de la Prosperité des Armes de France)*
A court ballet (with entrées*) in five acts. Choreography probably by M. de Belleville. Theme by Cardinal Richelieu. Scenery and scenic effects by Georges Buffequin. Paris, Théâtre du Palais Cardinal, February 7, 1641. Performers: Daniel Mallet, M. de la Force, "le sieur Cordelin" and his company, nobles of the court of France.*

SYNOPSIS. A sort of allegorical celebration of French military successes under the government of the cardinal and statesman Richelieu. There were numerous scene changes, from a wood into Inferno, snow-clad Alps and sea, etc. The entrances represented French victories at Arras, Casale, on the Alps, and so on.

■ Commissioned and conceived by the same Cardinal Richelieu to be performed in the private theater at his residence, this sumptuous piece of self-glorification was professedly in honour of the reigning pair, Louis XIII and Anne of Austria. The *Ballet de la Prosperité des Armes de France* is a mature example of the *ballet à entrées*. Compared with the first productions of its kind (see the ballet of *The Fairies of St. Germain Forest*, page 52), the dramatic theme is more substantial and the stage design more relevant. Moreover, the entertainment has returned to the "Italian style," in which the entire action takes place on the stage before an audience seated in a room, a scheme already introduced several decades earlier by Francini, but abandoned again for

Ballet of the Heiress of Bilbao. *Entry of the Grand Turk and his train.*

masquerades and *ballets à entrées* which occupied the whole hall, as in the original court ballets.   A.A.

TOBACCO (Il Tabacco)

Court ballet (with entrées*) in five parts. Choreography, libretto, and music by Filippo d'Agliè. Turin, Royal Palace, Carnival, 1650.*

SYNOPSIS. In the opening scene natives of Tobago Island sing the praises of their precious weed. The numerous *entrées* that follow present scenes connected with the use of tobacco, from ancient ritual sacrifices to modern smokers of all nations, the whole concluding with the *grand ballet.*

■ An authoritative commentator of the period, classifying the prolific choreographic output of Count Filippo d'Agliè di San Martino, placed *Tobacco*, a fantastic court ballet inspired by the recent legalization of smoking, among the "ingenious ballets." Creator of all the different components of his productions, from dances and music to words and the often strange scenic effects, d'Agliè was still remembered a century later as "perhaps the most fertile genius of theatrical and courtly inventions that has ever existed" (Cahusac, 1755). A.A.

ROYAL BALLET OF NIGHT (Ballet Royal de la Nuit)

Court ballet in four parts with forty-three entrées *in all. Choreography by Pierre Beauchamp, Jean-Baptiste Lully, and others. Music by Jean de Camberfort and Jean-Baptiste Lully. Subject by Clément. Verses by Isaac de Benserade. Scenery and mechanical stage effects by Giacomo Torelli. Paris, Salle du Petit Bourbon, February 23, 1653. Performers: Beauchamp, Lully, Lambert, Robichon, Mollier, etc., King Louis XIV, and many courtiers of the highest rank.*

SYNOPSIS. The ballet's intention is to show everything that happens in Paris between dusk and dawn. Part One: prologue by Night is followed by fourteen *entrées*, pastoral, mythological, allegorical, and grotesque, related to events of the evening hours from six to nine o'clock. Part Two: from nine to midnight amusements reign, plays and balls, shown in six *entrées* portraying Ardenti, Roger and Bradamante, Angelica and Medoro, Janus, Ganymede, Hebe, Bacchus, the wedding of Thetis, episodes from Plautus's comedies, etc.; Venus presides with "Games, Laughter, Hymen and the rest of her suite." Part Three: in thirteen *entrées*. Cupid conducts Diana, goddess of the moon, to the shepherd Endymion, while peasants and astrologers, alarmed at the eclipse, invoke her help. The spirits of Darkness favour the hour of the sabbath, peopled by demons,

Ballet Royal de la Nuit. *Louis XIV in his costume as the Sun King. Enthusiast of dance, the King loved to appear in the numerous ballets presented at court.*

Opposite: Louis XIV dressed as Apollo.

witches, and werewolves. The scene ends with a nighttime fire. Part Four: in ten *entrées*. Sleep and Silence evoke Dreams. The Four Elements appear and introduce the Furies, adventurers, a devotee of Juno, a coward, poets, philosophers, lovers, and other representatives of the four Temperaments. Day begins to dawn; Aurora arrives in a superb chariot driven by the Sun, who disperses the clouds and promises the greatest day on earth. All join in the *grand ballet* that concludes the entertainment.

■ A mature and polished example of the court ballet, and a masterpiece of its kind, comprising within a flexible framework of fantasy every possible variation on its theme, the *Ballet of Night* brings together the three great names of the history of dance in the second half of the seventeenth century. Above all, King Louis XIV, an enthusiastic promotor and protector of the dance, who, from the part he played in this very ballet at the age of fourteen, adopted the title of the Sun King. Then there was Jean-Baptiste Lully, made court composer that same year, who took part in the ballet as well as composing some of the music and choreography, and was destined to become the protagonist and absolute dictator of the musical theater in France for several decades. Finally, we have Pierre Beauchamp, dancer and part-choreographer of the *Ballet of Night*, subsequently founding father of the French academic tradition of dancing, a celebrated choreographer and the collaborator of Molière and Lully. Other contributions to the success of the ballet were the delicate poetic inventiveness of Isaac de Benserade, a gifted librettist head and shoulders above previous writers of French court ballets, and the magnificence of the stage design. It was one of the last valid productions of this type of balletlike entertainment, though the genre was to linger on in stereotyped versions for another twenty years, gradually giving way to more differentiated and artistically conscious forms of musical theater.   A.A.

THE MUSIC. Giovanni Battista Lulli, whose name was Frenchified to Jean-Baptiste Lully, was a key figure in an age of intellectual change and discovery. An artist of wide interests and great versatility, he was able to take his place at the court of France as a master musician of the highest order, capable of exactly interpreting the King's demands and at the same time improving relations with the theater in its dramatic and satirical forms. The name of Lully shines in the artistic firmament of the seventeenth century because of his superior mastery of composition which, united with a gift for organization and an intuitive political sense, guided the passage of music from diversion to creative art. He is considered to be the creater of French opera: an expert in declamation, he raised the importance of accompanied recitative and improved orchestral playing and the interpretation of songs, giving special weight to dramatic content. His love for the theater brought him into close collaboration with Molière, when together they gave life to the high form of entertainment known as *comédie-ballet*, one of the historic and aesthetic points of reference of the period. It was a new genre, consisting of a series of diversions interconnected and unified by an overriding comedy of manners that endowed it with great narrative homogeneity. Undoubtedly Molière's texts were on a higher plane of literary greatness, but it is also true that Lully's music was the best possible accompaniment to them. He was a partner and no mere auxiliary. There were twelve comedies and pastoral plays in which the two great artists collaborated, including famous pieces such as *Le Bourgeois Gentilhomme* and *Monsieur de Pourceaugnac*. With Lully's compositions, the Italian influence on French music became even more marked. It is also interesting to note how the heroic or mythological themes were giving way to, or at best coexisting with, more realistic, true-to-life subjects. The "New Man" was weighed up against historical characters; an element of social criticism emerged, and, moving out of the theater, remained as an eternal testimony to a new way of thinking and being of which the moral force survives to this day.   A.F.

Apollon — *Le Roy*

THE LAVENDER BALLET (Il Gridelino or Ballet du Gris de Lin)

Choreography, subject-matter, and music by Filippo d'Agliè. Turin, 1653. Among the performers, besides d'Agliè himself, were the Princes of the House of Savoy.

SYNOPSIS. Cupid, blindfolded, grieves at being deprived of the sight of all that is beautiful, and calls on Light to help him. Iris, personification of the rainbow, appears, summoned by Juno. To please the god of love, who wishes for the universe to be made still more beautiful, she displays all her colours. Cupid chooses lavender, that subtle mixture of pink and grey – today we think of lilac or pale violet – that happened to be not only the symbolic colour of "true and constant love," but also the Queen's favourite shade. Therefore Cupid decreed that flowers, plants, feathers, and ornaments should all turn lavender.

■ By the time Filippo d'Agliè had presented the ballet *Il Gridelino* at the court of Savoy (it was repeated in Paris not long afterwards under the name of *Le Gris de Lin*, at the request of Anne of Austria, Louis XIII's Queen), he already had some twenty works to his credit. Greatly admired by his contemporaries, who saw in him an artist "of remarkable poetic, allegorical, and moral gifts," Filippo d'Agliè counts among the most distinguished creators of court ballets. This dignified artist-courtier is considered to be one of the last effective interpreters of a type of entertainment that was increasingly becoming a stereotype of tedious adulation.   P.P.

THE BORES (Les Fâcheux)

A ballet-comedy in three acts and a prologue. Text by Molière, ballet scenario by Molière and Pierre Beauchamp. Music and choreography by Pierre Beauchamp. Scenery by Giacomo Torelli from Charles le Brun. Vaux-de-Vicômte, August 17, 1661.

SYNOPSIS. Plot is almost nonexistent. A mildly amorous theme gives Molière a pretext to bring onstage an irresistible collection of thoroughly tiresome characters: the idiotic singing dancer, the duelling addict, the idle theorist on matters of gallantry, the nobleman who *will* tell boring stories of his prowess at the hunt, the silly and petulant would-be scholar. The choreographical diversions come at the end of the acts. The prologue is immediately followed by a dance of naiads, dryads, and fauns; the first act finishes with dancers playing a kind of cricket; the second with dances by bowls players, sharpshooters, and cobblers; the third and last ends with Swiss guards armed with halberds dispersing a crowd of masqueraders, symbols of the tiresome people who have been pestering the central character.

■ *Les Fâcheux* was the first example of ballet-comedy in theatrical history. How this type of entertainment, destined to become a true genre, came into existence, was told by no less a person than Molière himself in an explanatory introduction addressed to Louis XIV. "The

idea," he wrote, "was to combine a comedy with ballet. But since we had only a small group of skilled dancers, we were forced to divide up the ballet *entrées*. Thus we decided to send on the dancers during the intervals of the play, giving the actors time to change and reappear in different costumes. To avoid breaking the play's narrative thread, we tried our best to connect the dancing with the play so that they formed a unity. However, we had not much time to spare and, moreover, as the overall plan was not the work of a single individual, some parts of the ballet were less relevant to the play than others. Be that as it may, it is a form of entertainment new to our theater, though not perhaps without precedent in antiquity, and, as long as everyone enjoys it, it may serve as a point of departure for other works, capable of being composed at greater leisure." So that was the origin of *comédie-ballet*. *The Bores* was commissioned from Molière by Superintendent Fouquet for a court festival which was to last two days. Molière conceived, wrote, and rehearsed the entertainment in two weeks. At its first performance it was an enormous success. Except for a few people around the court who felt that they had been included among the bores, everyone enjoyed it. The King enjoyed it most of all, to the point where he asked Molière to add a couple of scenes, indicating some of his courtiers who might well serve as models. *The Bores* pleased Molière's "victims" rather less. They consoled themselves by swelling the already crowded ranks of the playwright's embittered enemies.   P.P.

THE MAGNIFICENT LOVERS (Les Amants Magnifiques)

Ballet-comedy. Text by Molière. Ballet scenario by Isaac de Benserade. Choreography by Pierre Beauchamp. Music by Jean-Baptiste Lully. St Germain-en-Laye, February 4, 1670.

SYNOPSIS. "The King, who in all he undertakes aims only at the superlative, proposes to offer the court a diversion that will include everything the theater has to offer. To realize this great project and to write such an abundance of good things, he has chosen as a subject the love of two rival princes. During a visit to the Vale of Tempe, where the yearly Games are being celebrated, they compete with one another in devising every festivity imaginable to delight a young princess and her mother." This situation provided a narrative framework for the ballet-comedy of the now highly successful trio, Lully–Molière–Beauchamp, as recorded in the introduction to the original libretto. The ballet proper consisted of five *entrées* displaying separately and together gods of the earth and water, nymphs, tritons, clowns, statues, priests and priestesses, acrobats, slaves, and men and women dressed as Greek warriors.

■ It seems that the plot was suggested to Molière by Louis XIV himself. Indeed, the King was intended to play two parts: Neptune at the beginning of the ballet and Apollo at the end. Whether he ever did so in fact is uncertain. Some maintain that he was dissuaded against taking part, or ever again appearing on the ballet stage, by some of Racine's lines in *Britannicus*, supposedly alluding to His Majesty, referring to a character who was pleased *"à disputer des prix indignes de ses mains / à se donner lui même en spectacle aux Romains"* ("to compete for prizes unworthy of his hand, and show himself to make a Roman holiday"). It is highly improbable, however, that Racine, a cautious and astute tactician at court, would have risked alluding to his munificent patron in such an unflattering way. More probably Louis XIV gave up the stage because his incipient corpulence was becoming difficult to conceal, and contented himself thenceforth with inspiring, suggesting, or imposing subjects for his sumptuous *divertissements*. *Les Amants Magnifiques* was a tremendous success, especially the complicated stage machinery. The court begged for an immediate repeat performance, and on September 7 of the same year the production was put on again with an even richer choreographic content.　　　　　　　　　P.P.

THE WOULD-BE GENTLEMAN (*Le Bourgeois Gentilhomme*) including the *Ballet of Nations*

A ballet-comedy in five acts with a ballet finale. Text by Molière. Choreography by Pierre Beauchamp. Music by Jean-Baptiste Lully. Chambord, October 14, 1670. Dancers of the entrées *and final ballet: Messieurs Beauchamp, Dolivet, La Pierre, Favier, Mayeu, Chicanneau, and other members of the* Académie Royale de Danse.

SYNOPSIS. The subject of Molière's comedy is well known. The main character is a newly rich personage of humble origin who longs to be accepted as a member of the aristocracy, and whose simple vanity is exploited and mocked by everyone. There were five balletic diversions: an interlude or *entrée* at the end of each of the first four acts, and a true ballet (unlike the others, it had no connection with the story) at the conclusion of the play. *Entrée I:* four male dancers, led by the dancing master, demonstrate to Monsieur Jourdain "a little sample of the most beautiful steps and movements with which a dance can be varied." *Entrée II:* four tailor's apprentices express in dance their delight at M. Jourdain's generosity. *Entrée III:* the six waiters who have served the meal offered by M. Jourdain to Dorimène and Dorante dance as if to introduce the entertainment one imagines is being prepared in the next room. *Entrée IV:* the dance of the false Turks after M. Jourdain's Turkish investiture. *Finale: The Ballet of Nations* in six danced and sung *entrées:* a man distributes the ballet scenarios, interrupted by three importunate persons and by numerous dancers in various national costumes.

■ After its first performance at the Château de Chambord, where the King and his court were staying at the time, the piece was repeated barely a month later at the theater of the Palais Royal in Paris for the benefit of the citizens. The danced part of Molière's famous ballet-comedy was unusually long, so much so that the ballet scenario of the interludes and finale was published separately from the book of the play. The success of the choreographic portion is confirmed by the fact that the "Turkish ceremony" ending the fourth act, and the *Ballet of Nations* finale, with a few changes and additions, were made into a *Ballet of Ballets*, which was performed in the following year. Both date and title are significant, for *Ballet of Ballets* was the last of the true *ballets de cour*, while *Psyche*, presented in the same year, ended the tradition of the *comédie-ballet*, and with it the collaboration of Lully, Beauchamp, and Molière. Incidently, it was also in 1671 that the first French opera, *Pomone* by Cambert and Perrin, was produced, and that the *Académie Royale de Danse*, founded in 1661, became the *Académie Royale de Musique et de Danse*. The *Bourgeois Gentilhomme* can be considered the masterpiece among ballet-comedies, a formula renewing the combination of danced interludes and drama first attempted more than a century earlier, though with a very different balance of scenic, choreographic, musical, and acted elements and, especially, without the superior organic unity of development that Molière and his two collaborators were able to achieve. Here the union of play and ballet was no mere theoretical proposition but an effectively coherent realization in which one of the two elements seemed to flow naturally from the other. In spite of its short life (only ten years from *Les Fâcheux* in 1661 and *Psyche*), the genre has some historical importance, for Lully progressed from ballet-comedy to ballet-opera, a basic formula of the French musical theater for more than a century.　　　　　　　　　A.A.

PSYCHE (*Psyché*)

A ballet-comedy in five acts. Text by Molière. Music by Jean-Baptiste Lully. Choreography by Pierre Beauchamp. Ballet scenario by Corneille and Philippe Quinault. Paris, Palais des Tuileries, January 17, 1671.

SYNOPSIS. A fairly conventional rendering of the legend of Cupid and Psyche, freely drawn from Apuleius and somewhat influenced by La Fontaine. Venus hates Psyche because she attracts too much admiration and courtship and is too indifferent to love. She charges her son Cupid to wound her "with all the arrows of his vengeance." The play opens sadly with an oracle decreeing the banishment of Psyche. Then Cupid abducts her and falls in love with her. Their happiness turns to despair when they are forced to part. We see the fury of Venus. The final outcome is a happy one, for Cupid and Psyche meet again in heaven through the mediation of all-powerful Jove.

■ The danced episodes show, among many other marvels, Venus descending from the skies and returning thither "by means of astounding machinery" (the prologue); the dance of the mourners, emphasizing general grief at the sad fate foretold for Psyche (first act); six Cyclops and four Fates dance in the palace of columns and lapis lazuli built by Vulcan as a love-nest for Cupid and Psyche (second act); four of Cupid's henchmen dance with four Zephyrs to celebrate the

The Triumph of Love (Le Triomphe de l'Amour).
Engraving by Jean Bérain.
Opposite: Jean-Baptiste Lully in a stage costume.

of court ballet with its pastorally set prologue and danced interludes, and arranged the dramatic composition in concert with Quinault. The scenic effects were achieved by means of highly complicated machinery and equipment. The action was unfolded in a formal manner that called for music and recitatives modelled on the austere rhythms of French declamation. Public taste, prepared for more serious works by Racine's first successes (*Andromaque* was written in 1667), was prepared to welcome the change, and the production met with instant acclaim. Lully seized his opportunity. Taking advantage of Molière's recent death and the King's pleasure at the success of *Cadmus and Hermione*, the Florentine composer got rid of the French comedians at the Palais Royal and quietly put himself into their place, thus exerting a decisive influence on the French theater and preparing the way for serious opera. From 1673 until his death in 1687, Lully produced a new opera or ballet-opera every year.

C.M.C.

THE TRIUMPH OF LOVE (*Le Triomphe de l'Amour*) *Court ballet in one act with twenty* entrées. *Choreography by Pierre Beauchamp and Louis Pécourt. Music by Jean-Baptiste Lully. Scenario by Philippe Quinault and Isaac de Benserade. Scenery and machines by Vigarani. Costumes by Jean Bérain. First performance: St. Germain-en-Laye, January 21, 1681. The cast included the Dauphin of France, his wife the Princess of Bavaria, important members of Louis XIV's court and of the Princess's train, and dancers of the Académie Royale, among them Beauchamp, Pécourt, Fabre, and Favier.*

SYNOPSIS. The scene is a magnificently decorated hall in which the arrival of Cupid in triumph is awaited. Appearing in the twenty *entrées* that ensue are Venus, Neptune, Diana, Mercury, the Graces, Flora and Zephyr, naiads, dryads, fauns, Pleasures, and the peoples of all the world, who join in praising the power of Love. The triumphal arrival of Cupid is followed by a sort of apotheosis in which Jupiter appears, enthroned among the clouds and surrounded by all the others, to celebrate the glory of Love.

■ As has already been stated, the history of the *ballet de cour* can be considered as ending with the *Ballet des Ballets* in 1671. *The Triumph of Love*, produced ten years later, was a special case of more or less conscious revival, an exercise in nostalgia for a form of entertainment that had vanished from the French court – and thus vanished altogether – after the Sun King had retired from dancing in it himself, thus depriving it of a large part of its reason for existence. The recent wedding of the Dauphin with Princess Marie Anne Christine of Bavaria was the pretext for this solitary revival. Experts now occupied with other pursuits were recalled: the librettist Quinault collaborated with the old poet Benserade, who wrote the verses for the leading characters, and had lost none of his skill in witty topical allusions; dances were arranged by Pierre Beauchamp with his

mutual passion of the lovers (third act); eight Furies dance frenziedly amidst flaming ruins and raging torrents (fourth act); the spectacle ends with a *grand ballet* during which gods and goddesses descend from the clouds (by the astounding machinery) and one by one join in the dance.

It was above all the amazing stage effects and spectacular choral dancing that caused the tremendous success enjoyed for decades by this work, which marked the end of ballet-comedy and finished the collaboration between Molière and Lully. After the arrival of opera in France (with Cambert and Perrin's *Pomone*), the latter turned to tragic opera, presages of which are already discernible in *Psyche*.

P.P.

CADMUS AND HERMIONE (*Cadmus et Hermione*) *A balletic tragedy. Choreography by Pierre Beauchamp. Libretto by Philippe Quinault. Music by Jean-Baptiste Lully. Paris, April 27, 1673.*

■ *Cadmus and Hermione* is the first example of a tragedy danced to music. It was a matter of redeeming ballet from its customary sickly pastoral context and treating it instead as the almost natural outcome of a determined situation in the framework of classical tragedy. Lully entrusted the choreography to Beauchamp, who still to some extent clung to the traditions

Academistes de Chiron.   LeRoy, Mrs Fainetot
Bontemps: Cabou. Les Srs Mollier. Bruneau. Langlois.
Baptiste, le Vacher, Beauchamp, deForge, et Dolinet.

pupil and successor, Pécourt, while the music was composed by Lully, now taken up with tragic opera. In this work, however, a new sense of theatrical form has been grafted onto the now sterile root of court ballet, especially in regard to the choreography, while the structure and range of the sung part might nearly justify *The Triumph of Love's* inclusion in the category of ballet-opera. There is another reason, too, why this entertainment marked a new era in dance history. The diversity and difficulty of the steps required called for professional dancers. Therefore, after its first performance at court, in which so many princes and aristocrats took part, *The Triumph* was repeated on March 16 of the same year at the Palais Royal theater, in a reduced version with scenery by Rivani instead of Vigarani, and danced entirely by members of the Académie Royale de Musique et de Danse, among whom was Mlle. Lafontaine in the principal female role. For the first time a woman danced on the stage of a public theater, where, until then, feminine parts had been danced by men disguised as women. The long ascent of the female principal in ballet had begun.

OTHER VERSIONS. Léo Staats. Paris, Opéra, 1925. Principal dancer: Janine Schwarz.   A.A.

PERSEUS (Persée)
Ballet-opera in a prologue and five acts, from the tragedy by Quinault. Music by Jean-Baptiste Lully. Choreography probably by Pierre Beauchamp. Paris, Académie Royale de Musique et de Danse (Opéra), April 17, 1682.

■ The importance of *Perseus* to ballet history lies in its having been considered worth reviving almost a hundred years after its first performance, that is to say in 1771, when the dancing took decided precedence over the tragic content. Another innovation dates back to the occasion. The ballet was performed at Versailles on the day after the wedding of the future Louis XVI and Marie Antoinette, danced by the ballerinas Marie-Madeleine Guimard, Sophie Arnould, and Victoire-Anne Dervieux, and by the superlative Vestris (of whom it was said that, when dancing, he touched the ground "only out of politeness to his fellow-dancers"). On this occasion Mlle. Dervieux, a radiant beauty of eighteen, already famous for her scandalous behaviour and highly placed lovers, appeared for the first time in the modern theater's history "nude," which meant only that she did not wear a flesh-coloured "body stocking" beneath her "Grecian" garment.   C.M.C.

THE TEMPLE OF PEACE (Le Temple de la Paix)
Ballet-opera in six acts. Choreography probably by Pierre Beauchamp. Libretto by Philippe Quinault. Music by Jean-Baptiste Lully. Fontainebleau, October 20, 1685.

■ *The Temple of Peace* was repeated in Paris, at the Académie Royale, in November of the same year. The

mythological pastoral plot included a great many scenes of shepherds and shepherdesses. It was one of Lully's last works (1685 was also the year in which he composed the *divertissement Idylle sur la Paix*) and precedes his masterpiece *Armide* by only a year.   C.M.C.

THE FAIRY QUEEN
An operatic masque in three acts. Music by Henry Purcell. Libretto by Ezekiah Settle, after Shakespeare. London, Dorset Gardens Theatre, April 1692.

SYNOPSIS. The plot is taken from *A Midsummer Night's Dream*, but contains many characters not in the original play, turning it into a gallimaufry of persons and incidents among which the Shakespearian episodes form only a part.

■ The opera, one of Purcell's most ambitious works, consists of a succession of arias, choruses, spoken scenes, and dances. From a choreographic point of view, it resembled a series of masques, sometimes mere diversions, but often coherent with the stage action. P.P.

THE MUSIC. A musician without antecedents, a composer without followers, Purcell was an isolated figure in the pre-Handelian musical panorama of England. Although English theatrical conditions were not favourable to true opera, Purcell's presence was particularly significant in this context, because he brought to fruition the synthesis between the art of Italian opera and the rich flowering of English instrumental music. The greater part of the music he composed for the theater consisted of short pieces complete in themselves and capable of being used separately. *The Fairy Queen* was a free adaptation (very free, of necessity, since Shakespeare's play had no surviving musical content) devised in 1692 from *A Midsummer Night's Dream*. It required complicated scenic apparatus and, to facilitate the elaborate scene changes, was divided into a succession of musical interludes made up of various songs, duets, choruses, and dances. The classical formulas were changed and reshaped with evocative power and audacious compositional skill. The polished variations of the concluding chaconne have a positively Handelian potency. His highly personal use of ground bass gives the instrumental texture a typically veiled and shadowy colour accentuated by his resort to archaic and strangely solemn polyphonic moduli. Descriptive passages such as the "Monkey Dance" or "Hark! the Echoing Air" also achieve strangely modern effects, but it is above all the glorious melodies that shine through and illuminate the whole score.   A.F.

GALLANTRY IN EUROPE (L'Europe Galante)
Ballet-opera in four acts and a prologue. Music by André Campra. Choreography by Louis Pécourt. Libretto by Houdart de la Motte. Paris, Académie Royale de Musique et de Danse (Opéra), October 24, 1697.

SYNOPSIS. Presented on the stage are the varying ways in which love is manifested in Europe, i.e., in Italy, Spain, Turkey, and France. The librettist remarks: "We have chosen the countries with the most contrasting and the most theatrically rewarding characters .... We have adhered to the generally accepted ideas about these peoples. The Frenchman is represented as voluble, indiscreet, and gallant, the Spaniard as devout and fanciful, the Italian as jealous, astute, and violent." The author's picture of the Turk, haughty and authoritarian, is rather vaguer.

■ Among Campra's many theatrical works, *L'Europe Galante* is the one that best epitomizes what was new in spoken, sung, and danced entertainment. The balletic episodes were now more closely integrated with the plot; they no longer merely underlined it in an allegorical manner, but formed part of the action. Even the dancing "told a tale." The mythological personages had gone; it was the characters in the play itself who danced and gave life to the choreographic action.   P.P.

VENETIAN FESTIVAL *(Les Fêtes Venitiennes)*
Ballet-opera in five acts and a prologue. Choreography by Louis Pécourt. Music by André Campra. Libretto by Antoine Danchet. Paris, Académie Royale de Musique et de Danse (Opéra), June 17, 1710.

A typical ballerina's costume of the first half of the eighteenth century, for a ballet-opera by Jean-Philippe Rameau.

SYNOPSIS. In the prologue Folly and Reason confront one another and dispute as to which shall have dominion over the city. Folly wins and with that the parties, serenades, and games are given free rein. The prologue ends in an acrobatic display. The first act is devoted to a water festival; the second to a grand carnival ball; the third to the fortune tellers of St. Mark's Square; the fourth to a play; the fifth to the definitive triumph of Folly.

■ This ballet-opera by André Campra is permeated with a fine vein of satire and neglects mythological themes in favour of contemporary ones, especially that of the Venice Carnival, which always occupied a great deal of space in newspapers all over Europe. True to the principle that claimed "to please the public, one must lengthen the dances and shorten the dancers' dresses," Campra made a great success with *Venetian Festival*, due above all to the spectacular and magnificent ballet *entrées*.   P.P.

THE LOVES OF MARS AND VENUS
A ballet with story in six scenes. Choreography and scenario by John Weaver. Music by Symonds and Firbank. London, Drury Lane Theatre, March 2, 1717. Principal dancers: Louis Dupré (Mars), Hester Santlow (Venus), John Weaver (Vulcan).

■ *The Loves of Mars and Venus* is remembered as one of the first attempts at mimed ballet. Its creator, John Weaver, was not only a dancer and choreographer, but also a theorist of dance. A champion of dramatic dancing, he held that ballet should be true to nature, represent genuine characters and passions, and eschew the mechanical and all merely virtuoso and spectacular artifices.

OTHER VERSIONS. Skeaping. Scenery by D. Walker. Lincoln, Theatre Royal, January 30, 1969, Royal Ballet.   P.P.

THE JUDGMENT OF PARIS
Ballet-mime. Choreography and scenario by John Weaver, from the text by William Congreve. Music by Mr. Seedo. London, Drury Lane Theatre, February 6, 1733.

■ *The Judgment of Paris* was conceived as a dramatic entertainment in song and dance inspired by ancient Greek and Roman models. Weaver, dancer, choreographer, teacher and, theorist, was, in fact, aiming at a revival of Roman pantomime and the true expression of character and human emotion. Thus he was a pioneer of dramatic dance at a time when the fashion was for ballets that were empty of feeling and intended solely for amusement. However, *The Judgment of Paris*, Weaver's last work, was not one of his best, because it compromised in order to please public taste. John Weaver found it impossible to stick to his ideals completely, owing to the competition provided by John Rich, who was staging grandiose pantomimes at Drury Lane that could hardly fail to please the public.   C.M.C.

THE GALLANT INDIES *(Les Indes Galantes)*

A ballet-opera in a prologue and three acts. Music by Jean-Philippe Rameau. Libretto by Louis Fuzelier. Choreography probably by Michel Blondy. Scenery by Servandoni. Paris, Académie Royale de Musique et de Danse (Opéra), August 23, 1735. Principal performers: Mlle. Rabon, Louis Dupré, David Dumoulin, M. le Breton, M. Javellier, Marie Sallé.

SYNOPSIS. The lightly treated subject is of a "gallant" nature and in the exotic taste of the period. It is divided into a prologue, in which Love decides to leave war-torn Europe and seek his adepts in more distant lands, and three acts or *entrées* quite independent of one another. Act I: *The Incas of Peru*: a Peruvian maiden leaves her people to fly with a Spanish officer during a spectacular volcanic eruption. Act II: *The Generous Turk*: two lovers, separated by various misfortunes, are reunited thanks to the magnanimous Grand Turk. Act III: *The Persian Festival*: Prince Tacmas surprises his favourite Zaira with the page Ali, but Fatma, in love with the Prince, resolves the situation, so that the play ends with two happy couples. The epilogue shows the victory of Love over the goddess of war, Bellona.

■ A fourth *entrée*, called *The Savages*, was added for the 1736 revival of this ballet-opera, which was an attempt on Rameau's part to associate himself with the style of Lully, especially in the arrangement of the "scenes" (the spoken and recitative passages), in order to appease the Lullyist conservatives who were his detractors. An aristocratic diversion and, at the same time, a manifestation of the French taste for spectacle, *Les Indes Galantes* is one of the masterpieces of ballet-opera. It retrieved that harmony between the diverse components of choreography, drama, and music which had been lost since Lully's day in a farrago of entertainments devoid of any dramatic thread, consisting of an unrelated series of sung, declaimed, or danced scenes. The style of the *fête galante*, on the other hand, was marked by a certain aristocratic and upper-class taste in contrast to the solemn ceremoniousness of the court ballet, and was used here in a balanced theatrical whole in which the dancing already had a mature representative function. Admittedly, in this case the subject had little unity, being a series of amorous episodes weakly linked by their exotic background, but Rameau was soon to achieve greater narrative unity with important results in tragic ballet-opera (see *Castor and Pollux*, page 65). The choreography of *Les Indes Galantes* was probably arranged by Michel Blondy, who was ballet master at the Académie Royale de Musique et de Danse at the time, and was designed for dancers of advanced technical ability. In addition to a free composition of academic steps and positions already familiar, he adapted various courtly and popular dances such as the gavotte, the *loure*, and the jig, as well as the *rigaudon*, the *bourrée*, the *musette*, and English country dancing.

OTHER VERSIONS. The magnificent revival produced at the Paris Opera House on June 18, 1952, was repeated several times. The different acts were entrusted to various choreographers and designers. Prologue: choreography by Albert Aveline, decor by Dupont and Arbus. Act I: choreography by Aveline, decor by Wakhevitch. Act II: choreography by Serge Lifar, decor by Carzou. Act III: choreography by Harald Lander, decor by Fost and Moulène. Act IV: choreography by Lifar, decor by Chapelain-Midy. Principal dancers: Nina Vyroubova, Liane Daydé, Lycette Darsonval, Serge Lifar, Max Bozzoni, Michel Renault, etc.   A.A.

THE MUSIC. Rameau's deep musical knowledge, applied to the now accepted stylistic elements established by Lully, enabled him nevertheless to advance to a more modern and original type of composition even though its instrumental density made it hard at first to understand. The transformation of spoken passages into recitative had allowed Lully to introduce a new sort of opera. Rameau continued in the same direction, giving Lully's recitative a singing quality in place of simple accompanied declamation. The melodies, too, though not

A costume design for a character in Les Indes Galantes *(mid-eighteenth century) by J. P. Rameau.*

reaching the perfection of contemporary Italian and German arias and often adhering to the rondeau form of their predecessors, had already achieved a new range of melodic expression.

For the overture, however, he adopted the classical model (lento, allegro, lento) but omitted the central fugue and substituted a freer, more descriptive movement. This was the first time an overture expressed musical anticipation of the situations and sentiments to be illustrated in the course of the opera. After *Hippolyte et Aricie*, Rameau also tried to establish himself with the ballet-opera. *Les Indes Galantes* was the result. It was the composer's first major success. This work, made up of a prologue and three acts, is still performed today. The libretto is by Fuzelier and is ideal for the narrative and descriptive opportunities it offers the musician. The opera is important above all from the choreographic and symphonic point of view. A *suite* has been taken which illustrates the high level of instrumental expression and new cadences. Other fundamental scores are *Castor and Pollux*, 1737, libretto by Bernard, *Les Fêtes d'Hébé* and *Dardanus*, 1739, and others which followed annually (scenarios by Voltaire, L. de Cahusac, P. J. Bernard, and J. F. Marmontel). The year 1760, with *Les Surprises de l'Amour* and *Les Paladins*, marked the end of Rameau's output, which had amounted to thirty-three complete works, not all of which have come down to us, and collaboration on five comedies by Alexis Piron for which the music was composed in 1623–1626.   A.F.

CASTOR AND POLLUX (Castor et Pollux)

Ballet-opera in five acts. Music by Jean-Philippe Rameau. Libretto by Bernard. Choreography probably by Michel Blondy. Paris, Académie Royale de Musique et de Danse (Opéra), October 24, 1737.

SYNOPSIS. Act I: in the palace of the King of Sparta preparations are being made for the wedding of Telaira and Pollux, the immortal twin of the mortal Castor. But since Castor loves and is loved by Telaira, Pollux sacrifices his own happiness to secure that of the lovers. The marriage is celebrated with dancing. Suddenly, however, the rejoicings are interrupted by the arrival of an enemy army led by the jealous Phoebe. A mortal wound fells Castor to the ground. Act II: Castor's funeral. The grieving Telaira offers to yield up her husband to her rival, Phoebe, if only she will bring him back to life. Pollux, now the victor, suggests pleading with his father Zeus to bring his beloved brother back to the world of light. There follows a dance of victory by athletes and gladiators, joined by the women. Act III: in the temple of Zeus, the father of the gods appears to Pollux who pleads for Castor's life. Hebe and the Graces dance around Pollux, reminding him of the delights of his immortality, to dissuade him from his design of descending into Hades to take his brother's place. He steals away, however, to fulfill his purpose. Act IV: Pollux, guided by Mercury, reaches the Underworld, while Phoebe, powerless to prevent him, throws herself into the abyss. Demons perform a dance to drive

Eighteenth-century sketch of a character from Castor and Pollux *by Jean-Philippe Rameau.*

Pollux back, followed by a dance of Happy Shades seeking to enchant him. Castor rediscovered, Pollux sends him back to the light and his bride, but Castor will accept the sacrifice for no longer than one day. Act V: in Sparta Castor is reunited with Telaira amid popular rejoicing, but soon he decides to return to his fate and give his brother back his immortality. At this point Zeus descends from the clouds, bringing Pollux from the Elysian fields, and grants the light of divinity to both the twins. The heavens open to celebrate the virtue and happiness of Castor, Telaira, and Pollux, while the Celestial Choir sings their praises and the Hours and Planets dance. The whole company joins in a balletic *divertissement* to end the opera.

■ An excellent example of the tragic ballet-opera (or even tragic ballet), *Castor and Pollux* enjoyed an extraordinary success, as testified by numerous revivals all through the century, danced by the brightest stars of the Opéra, from Gaetano Vestris to Maximilien Gardel. The organic unity of the various formal and expressive elements, already achieved by Rameau in his development of the ballet-opera form (see *Les Indes Galantes*, p. 64) was here also attained in the coherence of the dramatic construction, the work of the librettist Bernard, a poet of great renown in his time, whom Voltaire admired and nicknamed Gentil-Bernard. In addition to the choreography being an essential part of the drama there is no doubt that this work as a whole constitutes a final stage in the separation of ballet from opera, due to a growing awareness of their potential independence. Indeed, while the emphasis here is still on the music and lyrics, that is to say the operatic element, it was only a few years before the birth of the *ballet d'action*, in other words, ballet as a self-sufficient theatrical form.

OTHER VERSIONS. Nicola Guerra. Staged by Jacques Drésa and Maurice Moulène. Paris, Opéra, March 21, 1918, and revived several times. Principal dancers: Aida Boni, Anna Johnsson, Albert Aveline.

A.A.

THE FESTIVAL OF HEBE (*Les Fêtes d'Hébé* or *Les Talents Lyriques*)

Ballet in a prologue and three entrées. *Music by Jean-Philippe Rameau. Scenario by Gauthier de Montorge. Choreography probably by Michel Blondy. Paris, Académie Royale de Musique et de Danse (Opéra), May 21, 1739.*

SYNOPSIS. The three *entrées* are dedicated respectively to poetry, music, and the dance. Although in pastoral vein, the ballet is not without dramatic force, and the second episode takes place in an atmosphere of agonizing suspense heavy with sad foreboding. The music accompanying these *ballets figurés* is among Rameau's most personal creations.

■ Associated with the *Fêtes de Hébé* was an important new arrival, who made her first appearance in Paris on July 14, 1739. It was a ballerina from Parma, Barbara Campanini, known as "La Barbarina," who was to win the hearts of the Opéra audience, eclipsing even the celebrated Sallé, then at the height of her fame. La Barbarina, who was eighteen years old at the time, was joined in Paris by her master and partner, the Neapolitan dancer Antonio Rinaldi from Fossano. She owed her renown above all to her perfect *entrechat-huit*. Frivolous and fickle, she lost her reputation through scandalous love affairs and theatrical quarrels, finally leaving Paris for England.

C.M.C.

PYGMALION (*Pygmalion*)

Ballet-opera. Music by Jean-Philippe Rameau, libretto by Houdart de la Motte, revised by Ballot de Sauvot. Choreography probably by Antoine Bondieri de Laval. Paris, Académie Royale de Musique et de Danse (Opéra), August 27, 1748.

■ It was from this year in the musical evolution of

Jean-Georges Noverre, dancer and great eighteenth-century choreographer, from an engraving by Saunders.

ballet-opera that a new type of panoramic overture came into fashion, introducing the principal characters and the main features of the plot. The device was used in *Pygmalion*, *Zoroastre* (1749), and *Acanthe et Cephise* (1751).

C.M.C.

CHINESE FESTIVAL (*Les Fêtes Chinoises*)

Music by Jean-Philippe Rameau. Choreography by Jean-Georges Noverre. Costumes by Louis Bouquet. Paris, Opéra-Comique, July 1, 1754.

SYNOPSIS. The scenario consists of a series of exotic incidents from Chinese folklore, then greatly in fashion.

■ This was Jean-Georges Noverre's first major success, although in later years he repudiated this early work. Although it was not until 1754 that *Les Fêtes Chinoises* really seized the public imagination, it had been composed and presented, probably in a less finished form, in Paris in 1749, in Marseilles, and perhaps Strasbourg, in 1751, and in Lyons in 1751 or 1752. This Noverre ballet still belongs to the tradition of André Campra productions, that is to say, of exuberant, fantastic spectacles full of artifice, ingenuity, and mechanical devices, usually of immense length (lasting up to ten hours). Noverre's innovations will be discussed later. It was in 1755 that he began to give serious thought to the theory of ballet. In 1760 he published his *Letters on Dancing and Ballet*, which became the seminal and definitive guide to the subject. *Les Fêtes Chinoises* enjoyed so much success in Paris that the company was invited to appear in the ballet at the Drury Lane Theatre in London. There it was not well received by the public, probably not so much for artistic reasons as because of the tension between the two countries on the eve of the Seven Years' War. Repeat performances were abruptly cancelled, and Noverre returned to France with the sole consolation that the actor David Garrick, who had invited him to London, described him as "the Shakespeare of the Dance."   P.P.

THE TOILET OF VENUS or LOVE'S RUSES (La Toilette de Vénus or Les Ruses de l'Amour)

A ballet d'action in three acts. Choreography by Jean-Georges Noverre. Lyons, 1757.

SYNOPSIS. There is no real plot. The entertainment is more a series of choreographic variations on the mythological themes so popular in the theater of that time. The ballet opens with Venus intent on using every artifice to increase her beauty, after which the goddess is dressed while nymphs and the Graces make up garlands of flowers for her. The allegorical characters representing sports and pleasures wait on the goddess and dance around her. There follows a series of *entrées* on the subjects of seduction, jealousy, frivolity, and betrayal. Then comes the courtship of the nymphs by some fauns, during which the twelve fauns fight for the favours of six nymphs. The departure of fauns and nymphs towards a neighbouring copse keeps all, as Noverre remarked, within the bounds of propriety.

■ The same Noverre referred to this, his first really significant creation, as a "warm and friendly ballet." His earlier works had been bound by tradition. Now, made bold by the production's success, he began to delve into the significance of this type of entertainment. Three years later, in 1760, he was to write his famous *Letters on Dancing and Ballet*, the most deeply thought out theoretical text of his time. What Noverre was aiming for was an "expressive form of dancing continually in action," free of all the clutter and falsity that tended to make it ridiculous. Away, then, with "hideous masks, absurd wigs, clumsy panniers." It was necessary to concentrate on the action and movement. All that was superfluous to the general significance of the ballet must be discarded. Every part of the performance should be coordinated to express the theme of ballet. Considered the most incisive reformer of his age, comparable only to Angiolini, Noverre created over 150 ballets.   P.P.

DON JUAN or THE STONE GUEST (Don Juan or Le Festin de Pierre)

Mime ballet in three acts. Choreography by Gasparo Angiolini. Scenario by Gasparo Angiolini and partly by Molière. Music by Christoph Willibald Gluck. Stage design by Giulio Quaglio. Vienna Burgtheater, October 17, 1761. Principal dancers: Gasparo Angiolini (Don Juan); the ballerinas Pagani, Clerc, and Reggiano; the male dancers Dupré, Turchi, and Viganò.

SYNOPSIS. Act I: Don Juan sings a serenade to Donna Elvira, daughter of the Commendatore, and is allowed into the house. Surprised by the Commendatore, Don Juan fights and kills him. Donna Elvira laments brokenheartedly over her father's body, but follows her seducer. Act II: festivities in Don Juan's palace, during which the libertine leaves Elvira's side to pay court to other women. The Commendatore's statue enters the hall and, left alone with the central character, all the guests having fled in terror, invites him to return the visit. Donna Elvira pleads in vain with Don Juan not to fulfill his pledge. Act III: Don Juan keeps his appointment in front of the Commendatore's funerary monument. Upon refusing to honour his obligation to Elvira, Don Juan is surrounded by spirits and furies and swallowed in the burning chasm that opens beneath him.

■ It was in Vienna, one of the centers of European ballet in the mid-eighteenth century, rich in a choreographic tradition already veering towards the expressive pantomimic style of Hilverding's work, that Gasparo presented *Don Juan*, his masterpiece, the first complete balletic mime in the history of dance and thus the first true ballet in the modern sense of the word. This achievement took place against a background of general reform in the musical theater, in which Vienna played a central part, largely owing to a group of artists and writers. Outstanding among them were Gluck, Ranieri de'Calzabigi, and, last but not least, Gasparo Angiolini. The three names were united in the creation of *Don Juan*, for which Gluck composed the music in close collaboration with the Italian choreographer, while Calzabigi wrote the dissertation published on the occasion of the ballet's first performance, a sort of manifesto of ballet-mime of the greatest aesthetic interest, expounding Angiolini's ideas of theatrical dance. As in his operas Gluck aimed at the sung interpretation of a drama, so Angiolini had put his own choreographic theories into practice, achieving in *Don Juan* (a year before Gluck's *Orpheus and Eurydice*) a "ballet of action" far removed from the mere meaningless diversions fashionable at the time. The reformation of ballet, which became an independent form of theater, thus preceded that of opera and even contributed to the latter's development. Indeed, dancing played an essential narrative part in Gluck's operas. Moreover, in Angiolini's view, the expressive unity of dramatic danced mime required that the "new" music should correspond closely to the action. In the above-mentioned dissertation introducing the scenario of *Don Juan*, Angiolini describes his creation as a "ballet-mime in the taste of the antique world," for which the pantomime "consisted in the art of portraying the customs, passions, and deeds of gods, heroes, and men by means of bodily movements, attitudes, and gestures performed in rhythm with the music and capable of conveying the desired meaning. These movements and gestures should compose a kind of interconnected discourse, so to speak, a sort of visual recitation made easier for the audience to grasp by the accompanying music ..." It should be noted, however, that mime as conceived by Angiolini was always of a dancing character. Yet the

Scene from Don Juan. *Choreography by Aurel M. Milloss, inspired by Gasparo Angiolini's original. Milan, Scala, May 11, 1977.*

needs of expressive mime in no way repudiated the academic standards of pure dance or *danse noble*, but rather integrated them with conscious historical accuracy into a new dramatic dimension. On this point Angiolini was opposed to Noverre, the other great theorist of eighteenth-century ballet, in that he supported "limited" mime, that is to say mime fused with the dancing and in rhythm with the music, rather than "walked through" as in the works of the French choreographer. Another subject of argument between the two masters was the use of synopses in ballet programs. Angiolini was against them, maintaining that the dance itself should be able to convey any theatrical plot or emotion without outside explanations "humiliating to the art." This artistic principle governed the creation of *Don Juan*, the dramatic impact of which won the unstinted applause of contemporary audiences, although Angiolini himself said of it in later years that in it "theory outstripped practice." The literary source of the scenario was *Don Juan ou le Festin de Pierre* by Molière, but in adapting it to ballet form Angiolini also drew on *El Burlador de Sevilla* by Tirso de Molina, stressing the intrinsically tragic aspect of the story, so that the end result is to some extent new and original. It is interesting to observe how a number of elements from the Angiolinian script (as also some in Bertati's libretto *Il Convitato di Pietra* by Cazzaniga) were adopted by Da Ponte and Mozart for *Don Giovanni*. It is impossible, of course, to reconstruct the choreography. We can gather only a vague idea of it from purely literary references to the plasticity and relevance of the dancing

and the expressive intensity of the lyrically orchestrated danced mime. Proof of this ballet's lasting vitality and historical and artistic value is provided by its numerous modern versions. It is not by chance that one of them was produced by the most distinguished reformer of ballet in our century, Michel Fokine. For fidelity to the spirit and choreographical-theatrical ideas of Angiolini, however, none have surpassed the various productions of *Don Juan* staged by Aurel Milloss, the most recent of which, in 1977, used Gluck's score in its entirety, yet seems in its choreographic style and fresh dramatic invention like a free re-creation, bringing to Angiolini's masterpiece new life and meticulous sense of history.

OTHER VERSIONS. 1) Vincenzo Galeotti (after Angiolini). Copenhagen, Theater Royal, October 29, 1781. 2) Charles le Picq (after Angiolini, but called *Il Convitato di Pietra*). London, King's Theatre, March 12, 1785. 3) Rudolf Laban. Berlin, 1925. 4) Michael Fokine (scenario by Fokine and E. Allatini). London, Alhambra Theatre, June 25, 1936, Ballets Russes de Monte Carlo. 5) Otto Krüger. Düsseldorf, Deutsche Oper am Rhein Ballet, January 27, 1958. 6) Leonide Massine. Scenario by Massine from Molière, title *Don Giovanni*. Milan, Scala Theater, March 7, 1959. 7) Erich Walter. Wiesbaden, May 1963, Wuppertal Opera Ballet. 8) John Neumeier. Music by Gluck and T. L. de Victoria. Frankfurt, Städtliche Bühnen, November 25, 1972. 9) Aurel M. Milloss (freely adapted from Angiolini). Augsburg, Tanzbühne Theater, September 23, 1933; then Düsseldorf, Städtliche Tanzbühne, May 28,

1935 (under the title *Don Juans Ende*); then Florence, June 1951; and finally Milan, Scala Theater, May 11, 1977.   A.A.

THE MUSIC. For the first time, in Gluck's *Don Juan*, music, subject, and choreography have fused to constitute the first example of a modern ballet and the point of departure for Gluck's musical reform. With *Don Juan* the action is conveyed through music which is harmonious, instrumental, and rhythmic. The acts are characterized by different tonalities – the six pieces of the first in D major or minor – and the character of Don Juan by a recurring motif in a *stile galante*. The musical numbers are written in the closed form typical of the period. The story is told in music which does not attempt to be realistic. The overture is brilliant, in one tempo, *allegro*, taken up *con brio* by the strings to which the brass give a sonorous reply. After the entrance of Don Juan and the musicians, the elegant introductory movement of serenade is immediately contrasted with an *allegro maestoso* (the unsheathing of the sword), an *allegro furioso* (the duel), an *allegretto risoluto* (the fall of the Commendatore), and the *moderato risoluto* (the joy of the victor Don Juan). All the musical numbers of the other scenes culminating with the famous "Dance of the Furies" follow this scheme. The turbulent and raging character of this piece provides an unusual dramatic and instrumental climax. Gluck further used this extract inserting it in the opera *Orpheus* in Paris in 1774. It was obvious that its influence would be felt by other composers. Boccherini, in his Symphony in D minor, *La casa del diavolo*, 1771, borrowed from Gluck's ballet in the last movement.   A.F.

PSYCHE AND CUPID (*Psyché et l'Amour*)
Ballet d'action. *Choreography and scenario by Jean-Georges Noverre. Scenic design by Giovan Battista Colomba. Costumes by Louis René Bouquet. Stuttgart, February 11, 1762.*

■ This production, together with *Medea and Jason* and *The Death of Hercules*, performed in the same year, formed a triad of Noverre's first true mime-ballets. (The great tragic ballets were to appear in Vienna in 1767.) The date of *Psyche and Cupid's* first performance is important, since it is central to the controversy as to whether Noverre or Angiolini was the original creator of the new form of ballet born from the fusion of dance and mime. Noverre laid claim to the distinction with his *Lettres sur la Danse et sur le Ballet* (Lyons, 1760), which constitutes, even if not devoid of errors and inexactitudes, the most complete manifesto of the new school of ballet. It is to Angiolini, however, that we owe the earliest great dance-mime production, *Don Juan*, in 1761. Although first performed a year later than the publication of the *Lettres* it must be said that Angiolini was putting the theories of ballet reform into practice at a time when Noverre was still producing ballets devoid of dramatic content and even pandering to the eighteenth-century taste for *divertissements*. Thus, while Noverre can justly lay claim to being the earliest theorist

Gaetano Vestris, called "dieu de la danse" (as was also Louis Dupré) in female costume, from a drawing in the Opéra Library, Paris.

of the *ballet d'action*, Angiolini must be granted priority for his realization of the "grand pantomime," an idea that was in any case in the air at that time, and went back to Angiolini's master, Hilverding. Noverre had a great success with his *Psyche and Cupid* at London's Covent Garden Theatre in 1797, after he had gone through a number of disastrous experiences during the French Revolution.   C.M.C.

CUPID AND PSYCHE (*Amour et Psyché*)
Mime-ballet in four acts. Choreography and subject by Franz Anton Hilverding. Music by Vincenzo Manfredini. Moscow, October 20, 1762.

SYNOPSIS. The ballet deals with the well-known theme of Cupid and Psyche, adapted to a purely danced and mimed interpretation.

■ Little but the title remains to bear witness to the creative talents of Franz Anton Hilverding, who worked mainly in Vienna from 1742 onwards except for a six-year sojourn in St. Petersburg, during which time he produced the ballet *Amour et Psyché*. A work of his maturity, it probably represented its creator's fully developed aesthetic aim, namely the synthesis of "danced ballet" and "mimed ballet" (pure dance and dance expressing action) in order to create true "dramatic mime," in which the whole action could be danced, divided into acts, and arranged to form a strictly logical dramatic construction. This conception makes Hilverding the real pioneer of the *ballet d'action*, twenty years before Angiolini and Noverre declared their aesthetic theories. In the famous "quarrel" between the two, the former referred explicitly to the work of his master, Hilverding, as the earliest example of putting such theories of fundamental reform into action.   A.A.

MEDEA AND JASON (*Medée et Jason*)

A tragic ballet of action. Choreography and scenario by Jean-Georges Noverre. Music by Jean-Joseph Rodolphe. Scenic design by Giovan Battista Colomba. Costumes by Louis Bouquet. Stuttgart, Court Theater, February 11, 1763. Principal dancers: Mme. Nency (Medea) and Mlle. Toscanini (Creusa), Gaetano Vestris (Jason), Angiolo Vestris, Charles le Picq, Lepi.

SYNOPSIS. With a few modifications, the story follows the classical tragedy in which Medea, betrayed by Jason, avenges herself on him by killing her own children, as well as her rival, whom she murders by means of deadly gifts. She then flees away on a winged chariot, to the fury of Jason and the people of Corinth.

■ By the time Noverre had created this ballet, his first true masterpiece, his theories of theatrical dance as formulated in *Lettres sur la Danse* (1760) had come to full maturity and made his name one of the most renowned in the history of ballet. Noverre was indeed one of the chief choreographers of his time, but his principal merit was to guide theatrical dance, in the light of his theories, towards a new dramatic and expressive conception of ballet, one already foreseen by John Weaver in England, introduced by Sallé in France, and, most important of all, brought to fruition in Hilverding's and Angiolini's *ballets d'action*, but never before confirmed with such clear-cut resonance throughout Europe as by Noverre. The diffusion of balletic ideas was signally forwarded by the famous polemics between the two masters, in which the adversaries took opposing stands regarding the relation between mime and dance, and as to the ideal content of ballets. They were, in fact, both arguing from the same basic conception of ballet as a complete and independent art form with definite and logically developed subject-matter expressed by means of classical dance techniques combined with dramatic mime. Inspired, as it was, by the later eighteenth-century aesthetic feeling for naturalism and freely expressed emotion, this fundamental movement of reform was entirely opposed to the gallant, mannered superficiality of rococo ballet then dominant in France. Both choreographers were against these displays without dramatic significance, and condemned all the theatrical conventions now judged to be absurd, above all the formalized costumes, the star ballerina system, and the overemphasis on virtuosity. Through the theory and practice of the two great reformers, the *ballet d'action* had become a self-sufficient theatrical form based on a variously composed blend of dance, mime, and gesture. From that time onwards the term "ballet" assumed its full, precise, and modern meaning. Noverre's first chance of really putting his ideas into practice, after a

number of unresolved creative efforts, came in 1761 when he was invited to direct the ballet company at Stuttgart financed by the Grand Duke Charles Eugene of Württemberg. Both Noverre and the dance were to owe much to that extravagant balletomane. During the six years he spent in Stuttgart, the Frenchman was able to create some of his masterworks and to earn a reputation as the greatest choreographer of his time, partly owing to the first-rate organization placed at his disposal and to the remarkable dancers whom he trained or influenced, among them the already celebrated Gaetano Vestris, as well as Angiolo Vestris, Jean Dauberval, Charles le Picq, Mlle. Nency, and the two Toscaninis. In the first of the great tragic ballets, *Medea and Jason*, the leading male part was performed by Gaetano Vestris, principal dancer at the Paris Opéra and often a guest at Stuttgart. Although trained in the artificial academic style, he was able to reveal an unsuspected aptitude for the affecting gesture as well as a technical versatility and interpretive talent for which Noverre himself declared him to be superior to the great Dupré from whom Vestris had inherited the title "*dieu de la danse*." Deeply impressed by Noverre's masterpiece, Vestris revived it at the Burgtheater in Vienna in 1767, then again in 1770 at the Paris Opéra in a shortened version performed as an intermezzo in an opera by La Borde, with music by that composer. In 1775 the ballet was presented at the Opéra again, this time uncut and with the original music by Rodolphe, to herald Noverre's return in the following year. The principal dancers were Anne Heinel, Marie-Madeleine Guimard, and Gaetano Vestris. The production was summarized in the *Mercure de France* as follows: "The inconstancy of Jason, who deserts Medea to marry Creusa, his new passions, Medea's scorn, the efforts she makes to reawaken her faithless husband's love by showing him their children; the jealous woman's fury, her enchantments, Jason and Creusa's wedding banquet, the cunning Medea's feigned reconciliation with her rival and the envenomed gifts she proffers her, Creusa's torments and death; Jason's despair and rage, the infuriated Medea flying off in a chariot drawn by dragons; the killing of her children, whom she slays before their father's eyes; a rain of fire and the burning of the palace: the spectacle and all these dire events produce a stupendous effect ... so potent is the art of mime. . . ." The preceding revival of 1770, danced by Marie Allard, Guimard, and Vestris, marked a small but significant revolution in ballet costume, made necessary by the new ideas. The masks that traditionally covered the dancers' faces were abandoned after Gaetano Vestris had appeared without one in the part of Jason.

OTHER VERSIONS. 1) Noverre, with Charles le Picq. Venice, Teatro San Benedetto, 1771; later at the Bolshoi Theater in St. Petersburg, May 7, 1791. 2) Noverre, with Gaetano Vestris (also in the revival mentioned above). London, King's Theatre, March 29, 1781. 3) Noverre, with Dominique Le Fèvre. Scenery by Pietro Gonzaga, costumes by Francesco Motta and Giovanni Mazza. Milan, Scala Theater, September 21, 1788 (under the title *Giasone e Medea*).   A.A.

Medea and Jason *from an English print of 1781. It was given in London with choreography by Gaetano Vestris, who reproduced Noverre's original.*

SEMIRAMIS *(Semiramide)*
Ballet-opera in three acts, from the tragedy by Voltaire. Music by Christoph Willibald Gluck. Choreography by Gasparo Angiolini. Vienna, January 31, 1765. Prima ballerina: Mme. Nency.

SYNOPSIS. Queen Semiramis dreams of the ghost of Ninus, her husband, whose death she herself had procured. The spirit threatens revenge and swears that she will be killed by her own son. The Queen, though shaken, continues in her intention of choosing a new husband. In spite of the High Priest's pronouncement that it is against the will of the gods, and although terrifying supernatural events occur, she decides to marry Ninyas, son of Ninus. During the wedding feast the late Assyrian King's ghost appears once more and commands Semiramis to shut herself into a tomb and Ninyas to kill her there. Ninyas does so, but, horrified to learn that he has murdered his mother-wife, attempts suicide.

■ This subject was much to the taste of the age and was exploited for numerous theatrical pieces. Angiolini's version was effective yet balanced. Among the many works of reference available (Zeno, Metastasio, Calderon, Crébillon) he chose as inspiration Voltaire's tragedy written in 1748, perhaps the least blood-curdling version. His success was remarkable. A contemporary witness, Ranieri dei Calzabigi, says: "A sublime success ... the spectacle's effect was greater than I could have imagined. The tragedy itself, so often played at the same theater by excellent actors, has never so gripped the attention or torn the heart with pity .... The actress-ballerina who played Semiramis made one weep and tremble. . . ." The written scenario was preceded by a *Dissertation on the Mimed Dance of the Ancients*, an important programmatic text in which Angiolini advocated the great artistic potentiality of the

danced dramas of antiquity, which it was his intention to revive with *Semiramide*, the archetype of the mimed tragic ballet.   P.P.

THE DEPARTURE OF AENEAS or DIDO ABANDONED *(Le Départ d'Enée* or *La Didon Abandonée)*
Heroic ballet in three acts. Choreography, music, and scenario by Gasparo Angiolini. St. Petersburg, Court Theater, September 26, 1766. Principal dancers: Santina Aubri (Dido), Gasparo Angiolini (Aeneas).

■ Gasparo Angiolini came to St. Petersburg as ballet master to the court of Catherine the Great in 1766, the same year in which he wrote and staged *Dido Abandoned*. He was preceded by a high reputation as dancer, choreographer, theorist of the ballet, and tenacious adversary in argument of that other distinguished contemporary choreographer, Jean-Georges Noverre. In his *Dido Abandoned* he followed Pietro Metastasio's tragedy, to which he adhered with absolute fidelity. From it he fashioned a very simple ballet, stark and without frills. He stripped the dances of all stage tricks, limiting the choreography to a functionalism that conceded little to ingenious but unnecessary inventions. Pietro Metastasio himself was pleased with the result and wrote to Angiolini, saying, "It is now forty years since my poor Dido first deafened the audiences of Europe with her laments, but until now not one of your celebrated colleagues has known how to make such miraculous use of the play as you have done." Angiolini's work, which was one of his first and most notable advances in the direction of the *ballet d'action*, won immediate success. Quickly revived, it had within a short time been shown in all the major theaters of Europe.   P.P.

THE ORPHAN OF CHINA *(L'Orphelin de la Chine)*
Ballet in four parts. Choreography and scenario (taken from Voltaire) by Gasparo Angiolini. Music by Christoph Willibald Gluck. Vienna, April 1, 1774.

■ Referring to the above production in Vienna, R. Haas records the opinion of a spectator in these words: "Cabaret music. Mime as chilly as death. No dancing!" Be that as it may, on September 24, 1777, Angiolini presented *The Orphan of China* at St. Petersburg with his own music, and this time a French diplomat (the Chevalier de Corberon), who was in the audience, remarked: "The music is heavenly. It is entirely Angiolini's." This fact was at the center of an argument between Angiolini and Ivan Perfilievitch Yelegin, the director of the Imperial Theater. The latter complained that Angiolini, like other Italian artists such as Lolli and Paisiello, tried to get out of the clause contracting him to compose the accompanying music as well as produce the ballets assigned to him. *"Il commença par faire les siens et il n'exigea pas de musique"* ("At first he did his own and required no music"), the Russian impresario wrote to Grigori

Potemkin, but then "[Angiolini] *sur douze programmes de Noverre il ne consentit qu'a écrire la musique d'un seul . . .*" ("out of twelve programs by Noverre he agreed to compose the music for only one . . ."), which was hardly surprising, since the rivalry between the two choreographers was already in full swing. After this argument Angiolini (who had, after all, composed the music of many of his own ballets, and used some of Paisiello's) quitted Russia once more, leaving the field to another Italian, Giuseppe Canziani.   C.M.C.

THE AGE OF INNOCENCE or THE ROSE GARDEN OF SALENCY (*La Prima Età dell'Innocenza* or *La Rosaia di Salency*)
Ballet d'action. *Music by Louis Baillou. Scenario and choreography by Jean-Georges Noverre. Milan, The Grand Ducal Theater, 1775. Principal dancers: C. Villeneuve, E. Dupré, S. Gallet.*

■ This was Noverre's most interesting creation in the course of his two-year stay in Milan (1774–1776), when he was the chief choreographer to the Grand Ducal Theater, one of the posts held by him during the long period he spent in the service of the Austrian Imperial family. While not particularly deeply worked out or significant, it belongs among Noverre's most mature choreographic works. The *ballet d'action* was by this time a definite and accepted genre.   A.A.

THE SPIRIT SEEKER (*La Chercheuse d'Esprit*)
Ballet in one act. *Choreography by Maximilien Gardel. Scenario and music by Charles Simon Favart. Choisy and Fontainebleau. November 1777, in the presence of the court.*

■ The ballet was performed again in Paris on March 1, 1778, the principal parts being danced by Marie-Madeleine Guimard and Pierre Gabriel Gardel, Maximilien's brother, a dancer and choreographer. *La Chercheuse d'Esprit* was one of Maximilien Gardel's greatest successes and also one of his best on the artistic level. A choreographer and dancer sympathetic to Noverre's reforms, he followed him as *maître de ballet* at the Opéra in 1781. Nevertheless, if we are to believe contemporary evidence, Gardel not only lacked Noverre's choreographic genius; he never even approached it. Friedrich Melchior Grimm, student of French artistic life before the revolution, wrote of him: "Neither much invention, nor much wit, nor very interesting."   C.M.C.

TRIFLES (*Les Petits Riens*)
Ballet in three episodes. *Scenario and choreography by Jean-Georges Noverre. Music by Wolfgang Amadeus Mozart and others. Paris, Académie Royale de Musique et de Danse (Opéra), June 11, 1778. Principal dancers: Marie Allard, Marie-Madeleine Guimard, Jean Dauberval, Auguste Vestris.*

Original sketch for a scene in The Orphan of China. *Choreography and scenario by Gasparo Angiolini, music by C. W. Gluck; it opened in Vienna on April 1, 1774.*

Sketches of characters from the ballet Les Petits Riens *to music by W. A. Mozart, given for the first time on June 11, 1778 at the Paris Opéra.*

SYNOPSIS. First episode: jokes and pranks by Cupid, who is finally trapped in a cage by the people he has tricked. Second episode: game of blindman's buff in a pastoral setting. Third episode: Cupid at his tricks again; he introduces to two shepherdesses a third, disguised as a shepherd. However, the two simple maids see through the deception when they notice her breasts. (The order of the episodes is uncertain.)

■ This title, not perhaps one of the most important among Noverre's ballets, is recorded because it marks the sole collaboration between two of the greatest artistic geniuses of that age, Noverre and Mozart. During his third visit to Paris, in the spring of 1778, the composer, then twenty-two, met the famous choreographer, chief ballet master at the Académie Royale, who commissioned him to write part of the music for a light mime ballet of charming, delicate frivolity, composed of *"petits riens,"* to be shown at the Opéra on the following June 11 as an intermezzo in Piccinni's opera *The False Twins.* The score consisted of some twenty numbers: an overture and twelve short pieces by Mozart together with other collected items described by the Salzburg musician in a letter to his father as "wretched old French airs." After a few performances that met with considerable success during that season, Noverre's ballet was forgotten. All that now remains of it is Mozart's score, found a hundred years later and inserted into Köchel's catalogue as No. 10. But we do not know

the order they came in nor to which parts of the ballet they corresponded. The scenario being lost, even the above synopsis is known only from a few scattered allusions contained in a report published in the *Journal de Paris* the day after the first performance. Obviously nothing remains of the choreography, though it must undoubtedly have been in the *ballet d'action* style of mixed mime and pure dance that Noverre had brought to perfection by then. It appears he created at least three ballets called *Les Petits Riens*, probably all with similar subjects: the first in 1767 to music by Gluck, repeated in a revised version the following year; the second, the one here described, in 1778; the third in 1781 with music by Barthélémon.

OTHER VERSIONS. Numerous choreographers in our own century have attempted to revive the ballet as a suite of dances based on Mozart's music, but without reference to Noverre's original version. Among them: Isadora Duncan; Mariquita, 1912; Boris Romanoff, 1922; Hans Storck, 1927; Frederick Ashton, London, Mercury Theatre, March 10, 1928; Ninette de Valois, London, Old Vic Theatre, December 13, 1928; Erika Hanka, Vienna, 1946; Ruth Page, Chicago, 1946; R. Lunnon, Oslo, 1956; etc. The only choreographer inspired by Noverre's original production was Aurel Milloss, first at Augsburg in 1933, then in a new version at Düsseldorf in 1935 (which won Laban's praise for its "Noverrian manner"), and in a definitive production at the Teatro Quirino in Rome on November 19, 1945, with scenery and costumes by Dario Cecchi, the principal dancers being Olga Amati, Mariantonietta Pontani, and Ugo Dell'Ara. Milloss limited his subject-matter to that of Noverre's first episode, the pranks and punishment of Cupid, with a few references to the other two episodes. The new ballet consisted entirely of pure dancing, and in the strict musicality of its chor-eographic development bore the unmistakeable imprint of Milloss. Nevertheless, its fidelity to Noverre's style and his theories of theatrical dance make it a work of almost scholarly historic reconstruction, as close as can be achieved to the original Noverrian conception. A.A.

THE MUSIC. When the music of *Les Petits Riens* is considered by itself and without preconceptions it must be admitted that the composition is far from ineffectual, nor is it without excellent passages in which Mozart's creative vivacity seems subdued to a charming discur-sive flexibility. The overture, using the full classical orchestra typical of Mozartian music (strings, wind instruments, and drums), is assured and already very accomplished in its tone values, impressing more by its brilliance than by its modest use of counterpoint and having little in common with the typical first movement of a sonata. All sorts of expressive devices and original combinations are brought into use (for example, in the third piece the flute is echoed by a second flute or piccolo; the fifth provides the oboe with a graceful solo passage). The writing is particularly light and charming, with a feeling for typically French gallantry which reveals a less familiar side of the twenty-two-year-old composer's inventiveness. In the pastoral *Pantomime* (perhaps the most attractive part of the score), the lively passages for strings are furnished with every sort of embellishment, while the graceful, inviting progression is redolent of a Parisian salon. The sequence of the pieces is as follows: Overture, Largo, Gavotte, Andantino, Allegro, Larghetto, Gavotte Allegro, Adagio, (Allegro?), graceful Gavotte, Pantomime, Passepied, Gavotte, Andante. A.F.

PAFIUS AND MIRRA (Pafio e Mirra)
Ballet in one act. Choreography by Claudio le Grand. Scenario by Mattia Verazi. Music by Antonio Salieri. Scenery by Fabrizio Galliari. Costumes by Motta and Mazza. Milan, Scala Theater, August 3, 1778. Principal dancers: Caterina Curtz (Mirra), Claudio le Grand (Pafius), Anna Agostini, Francesca Bracci, Terrades Tommasini, Gregorio Grisostomo, Vincenzo Bardella, Antonio Crespi.

SYNOPSIS. The scene is a big amphitheater in Cyprus, where captives are to be thrown to the wild beasts. Pafius descends into the arena to fight the wild beasts alone in order to save his fellow-prisoners from slavery. His beloved, Mirra, tries to follow him, but is held back. During the fight a lion is about to leap on Pafius when Mirra throws herself into the ring to stand as a shield between man and beast. The people, moved at the heroic gesture, burst into the arena, overwhelm the lion, and set

the lovers free with all their fellow-victims.

■ Presented after the first act of Salieri's *Europa Riconosciuta*, this ballet is remembered chiefly for having been the first ever performed at the Scala, on the night of the new theater's inauguration, together with *Apollo Placato*, which ended the evening's entertain-ment. The music, now lost, was also by Antonio Salieri, then the master of music to the Imperial Austrian court and thus the natural choice for the opening perfor-mance of what already appeared to be one of the most important theaters of the Empire. The scenario by the Abbé Mattia Verazi is of scant interest, as was well noted by contemporary observers, who, on the other hand, were enthusiastic about the choreography of Claudio le Grand. Although a minor figure in the pan-orama of the age, he appears to have been a reliable pro-fessional in the world of dance, who knew how to exploit, within the limits of a scholastic and con-ventional compositional technique, both his French experience and his knowledge of the Italian academic tradition of which, up to the Renaissance, Milan had been the center of growth and diffusion. The two chief parts in *Pafius and Mirra* were performed by Le Grand and Caterina Curtz, "leading serious dancers" amid a host of "*demi-caractère*" and "grotesque" dancers, according to the classification then in use. Monaldi described Caterina Curtz and Giustina Campioni (principal dancer in the second ballet of the evening) as "figures of secondary importance in regard to art, but with the advantage of a seductive charm." All the same, their technical skill must have been considerable, as Rovani's critical remark demonstrates: "The whole art of ballet seems to have been reduced to leaping. It's not a matter of dancing any more, but of seeing who can jump highest. The one that gets nearest to the stage ceiling is reckoned the best dancer." The leap and *entrechat*, one of the most dazzling technical feats of academic dance, were already fairly advanced, though still lacking the artistic distinction conferred on them by Carlo Blasis a few decades later. A.A.

APOLLO PLACATED (Apollo Placato)
Ballet in one act. Choreography by Giuseppe Canziani. Music by Luigi de Baillu and Antonio Salieri. Scenario by Mattia Verazi. Scenery by the brothers Galliari. Costumes by Francesco Motta and Giovanni Mazza. Milan, Scala Theater, August 3, 1778. Principal dancer: Giuseppe Canziani.

SYNOPSIS. Phaethon, ambitious but dangerous driver of the sun chariot, threatens to send the entire universe into the flames. Providentially the great Jupiter intervenes with one of his thunderbolts, hurling the rash charioteer from the heights into the abyss of the deep. Apollo, in despair at the death of his son, vows to avenge him by extinguishing forever the light of the world. However, moved by the prayers of his fellow-gods, he relents and agrees to obey the supreme ruler's command by restoring to mortals the daylight they so very much long for.

■ Performed on the opening night of the Scala Theater of Milan, together with the opera *Europa Riconosciuta* by Antonio Salieri, and another ballet (*Pafius and Mirra*), it was the last item on the program, of which Pietro Verri remarked: "The entertainment, although sumptuous, gradually becomes boring, because there is nothing in it to touch the heart."   P.P.

THE DEATH OF CLEOPATRA *(La Morte di Cleopatra)*

Tragic mime-ballet in four acts. Choreography, scenario, and music by Gasparo Angiolini. Scenery by Pietro Gonzaga and Francesco Caccianiga. Costumes by Motta and Mazza. Milan, Scala Theater, August 5, 1780 (autumn season). Principal dancers: Paolo Franchi (Mark Antony), Carolina Pitrot (Cleopatra), Luigi Bardotti, Vittoria and Rosa Pelosini, Giuseppe Costantini.

■ Together with *The Death of Cleopatra*, on August 21 of the same year, and also at the Scala, Angiolini presented a light mime-ballet called *L'Amore e l'Azzardo* (Love and Chance) composed by himself and referred to in the *Gazzetta Enciclopedica*. Pietro Verri was moved by *The Death of Cleopatra*, of which he wrote to his brother after its first performance: ". . . a beautiful mime-ballet . . . a big, imposing and moving spectacle. The dancers are first-rate. The last scene in the underworld . . . is a splendid affair. Characters excellently drawn. Octavius false, cold, ambitious; Antony brave, open-hearted, impetuous in his passion; Cleopatra voluptuous, passionate, and untrustworthy." In replying, his brother Alessandro Verri referred to the Angiolini and Noverre controversy: "The genius of our Italian must surely be superior to that of the Frenchman, since the latter can only make himself understood with the help of a printed program, while the former leaves the matter to the audience. Nogère or Noverre or whatever he's called is not being too successful in Paris. . . ." And again: "Noverre seems to be stirred by ideas he cannot bring to fruition, and his programs are eloquent witnesses to his folly, for they show that he is unable to make what he is supposed to be representing clear in any other way. Angiolini is a poet, he has a heart and judgment. If he were an expert dancer and had a taste for costume design and the noble gift of bestowing elegance on all the minor performers, he would be perfect, especially as he composed the music and the one song. They say that, given a theme, he will improvise on his violin, and that he can be a veritable fount of new ideas." In the course of the following season at the Scala in 1781 Angiolini presented seven more new ballets.   C.M.C.

THE CONVALESCENT IN LOVE *(Il Convalescente Innamorato)*

Comic ballet by Francesco Clerico. Venice, San Samuele Theater, 1784.

■ After its first performance in Venice in 1784, *The Convalescent in Love* was shown at the Scala during the carnival season of 1790, together with *The Death of Hercules (La Morte d'Ercole)*, *The Proud Mistress Scorned (La superba innamorata a suo dispetto)* (September 26, 1789), and *The Fall of Troy (La Caduta di Troia)*, all by the same Clerico. The principal dancers were: Francesco Clerico, Rosa Clerico Panzari, Nicola Angiolini and Antonia Tommasini.

According to Ritorni, it was "like one of those comic ballets written for the theater of antiquity, not, as so often, an extravagant burlesque full of superficial drollery but a rational comedy and really delightful." Ritorni also mentions "a very pleasing contradance of doctors administering medicine to the invalid."   C.M.C.

THE WHIMS OF CUPID *(Amors og Balletmesterens Luner)*

Ballet in one act. Subject and choreography by Vincenzo Galeotti. Music by Jens Lolle. Copenhagen, Theater Royal, October 31, 1786.

SYNOPSIS. Numerous couples in different national costumes present themselves in Cupid's temple to be united. The god, however, first stipulates that they must be blindfolded and then mixes the couples up higgledy-piggledy. A series of *pas de deux* ensues before the confusion is cleared up, and the affair ends in a merry celebration.

■ An important point in the long and honourable tradition of Danish dancing is marked by this work of Vincenzo Galeotti (the pseudonym of V. Tomasselli), Florentine dancer and choreographer trained by Noverre at Stuttgart and later by Gasparo Angiolini in Venice, who finally settled in Copenhagen in 1775 as principal ballet master and choreographer to the Royal Danish Ballet. Though a pupil of both reformers, he was decidedly on Angiolini's side, acknowledging him as his ideal master. During his forty years' activity in Denmark he presented many of Angiolini's ballets, as well as numerous creations of his own. Galeotti was quickly recognized as a talented interpreter of the more advanced school of Italian choreography and, at the same time, as the founder of Danish ballet, until then a trifling and lackluster enterprise. His ballets were praised for their coherent dramatic construction, and still more for the rich inventiveness of the choreography, which could express every emotion and event in terms of dance in accordance with Angiolini's aesthetic creed. During Galeotti's long reign in Copenhagen his choreographic productions varied in character and followed diverse trends, but never lost the unmistakable stamp of their creator. *The Whims of Cupid*, a light, sentimental ballet with a faintly ironical gaiety that falls halfway between mythology and a comedy of character, forms a jumping-off place for imaginative and cleverly constructed choreography. In spite of being a minor work when compared to the dramatic choreography of Galeotti's more serious ballets, it has always enjoyed a lively success, from its opening night up to the present time. It has remained in the repertory of the

Anonymous eighteenth-century water colours representing two "Negro" characters. Paris, Opéra Library.

Royal Danish Ballet throughout, and thus kept a certain faithfulness to the original. Since 1942 it has been danced in the choreographically reconstructed version by Harald Lander, with sets and costumes by Ove Christian Pedersen. It is the oldest ballet to have survived up to our own day.

OTHER VERSIONS. Harald Lander (after Vincenzo Galeotti). Sets and costumes by Chapelain-Midy. Paris, Opéra, February 27, 1952.   A.A.

AGAMEMNON'S RETURN *(Il Ritorno di Agamennone)*
Tragic ballet in five acts. Choreography by Francesco Clerico. Venice, San Benedetto Theater, Carnival, 1789. Principal dancers: Francesco Clerico (Agamemnon), Giovanna Baccelli (Clytemnestra), L. Panzieri (Orestes), Rosa Clerico Panzieri (Cassandra).

SYNOPSIS. Agamemnon, conqueror of Troy, returns to his own land, bringing with him Cassandra. The prophetess only has to see Clytemnestra's face to know her evil plans. Protests from the Queen and conflict with Aegisthus, the Queen's lover, follow. Cassandra takes refuge in Apollo's temple. There, when joined by Agamemnon, she utters fearful prophecies, but is naturally not believed. Next comes the scene of the royal feast and then of the murder of Agamemnon in his apartments. Cassandra warns Electra to send her brother Orestes to safety. Aegisthus intervenes, consign-ing the prophetess to the soldiers. Clytemnestra, amid popular uproar, nominates Aegisthus as King while Electra remembers Orestes's rights. Cassandra commits suicide, foretelling Orestes's vengeance.

■ The only notices we have of this ballet are by Ritorni, who wrote: "... there follow warlike dances of great beauty," and, referring to Cassandra's interpretation in the second act, "a magnificent monologue vividly performed by Rosa Clerico, sister of the composer, one of those actresses formed by nature for the expression of sublime passion." And again he writes of Cassandra's death: "As she falls, strange events occur. The coffin is wrapped in dense, swirling mist from which emerge various symbolic apparitions, last of all the semblance of Orestes armed with the avenging dagger. It was all beautifully done, everything in the drama was heroic, but perhaps the soliloquy and duet in the second act stood out even more grandly than the rest." *Agamemnon's Return* was repeated at the Scala under the title *Agamennone* in the autumn season of 1801.
                                                                C.M.C.

THE WAYWARD DAUGHTER, NAUGHTY LISETTE *(La Fille Mal Gardée)*
Ballet in two acts and three scenes. Scenario and choreography by Jean Dauberval. Composer unknown. Bordeaux, Grand Theater, July 1, 1789. Revived in 1828 at the Paris Opéra with music by Louis Joseph Ferdinand Hérold.

SYNOPSIS. Act I. Scene 1: Madame Simone (in some versions Marcellina) is a rich landowner who employs a number of peasants in her fields. Her daughter, Lise, is in love with a handsome peasant, Colas (or sometimes Colin). But he is poor, of course, and that doesn't suit the mother at all. Colas, sent away by Simone, asks Lise to meet him in the fields, and she accepts. Meanwhile Thomas (or Michaud), a rich, landed proprietor, arrives with his silly son Alain in tow. Thomas asks for the hand of Lise for his son, and the widow Simone, aware of the wealth to be bestowed on the young man as his marriage portion, gives her consent. Lise does not agree and neither does Alain, although, being very timid, he is content to be ruled by their parents' wishes. Scene II: everyone is in the fields at harvest time. The characters become more definite. While Lise and Colas fall ever deeper in love, Alain plays the fool childishly and Simone flirts with Thomas. A sudden storm scatters all the harvesters. Act II: Simone, still determined to force Lise into a marriage with Alain, gives her a wedding veil and teaches her a nuptial dance. Lise, knowing that Colas is nearby, pretends to consent to her mother's wish, and manages to get him into the house while the widow leaves the room for a moment. When she comes back he hides in the bedroom (or, in another version, in a barn). Simone coaxes her daughter to try on a wedding dress, but at that moment Thomas and Alain arrive, so that Lise is hustled into the bedroom in her petticoats. The wedding having been fixed, Madame Simone gives Alain the key to the bedroom. When he opens the door, however, he finds Lise and Colas in each other's arms. General confusion. In the end all comes right for the young couple, who are united in marriage with Simone's blessing and to the fury of Thomas. Alain, for his part, continues his childish diversions. The marriage plans naturally lead to a fourth scene in front of or inside the church.

■ After nearly two centuries *La Fille Mal Gardée* is still in today's repertory. It is the most famous ballet of the past, and, after Galeotti's *I Capricci di Cupido*, the oldest. But that is not the only claim to distinction of Dauberval's ballet. For the first time the plot is modern and the characters ordinary people. The story of Lise and Colas, lovers separated by difference of class but united by their love, was in tune with the times in 1789, the first year of the French Revolution. *La Fille Mal Gardée*, in its subject-matter, is in line with the sentimental literature of the eighteenth century and contains some elements of *opera buffa*. Its freshness of plot and lively scenario enabled the ballet to survive into the romantic period. The facile, anonymous musical accompaniment of the first version was subsequently arranged by a composer of light music, Ferdinand Hérold, in 1827 into the score that has been used for numerous later productions all over Europe. Another,

From La Fille Mal Gardée, *created by Jean Dauberval in 1789. This illustration is from a version with choreography by Frederick Ashton presented at Covent Garden Opera House in London in 1960.*

less important, musical accompaniment was contributed by Hiertel in 1864. The two most interesting versions now in the international repertory are those by the English choreographer Frederick Ashton and the Russian Oleg Vinogradov. But we must not forget that *La Fille Mal Gardée* was also produced in St. Petersburg by Petipa in 1885.

OTHER VERSIONS. 1) Bronislava Nijinska and Dimitri Romanoff. Scenery and costumes by Sergei Soudelkin. First performance: New York, Center Theater, January 19, 1960, Ballet Theater Company. Music by Hiertel. 2) Frederick Ashton. Scenery and costumes by Osbert Lancaster. London, Covent Garden, January 29, 1960. Royal Ballet Company. Principal dancers: Nadia Nerina, David Blair, Stanley Holden, Alexander Grant. Music by Hérold. 3) Oleg Vinogradov. Scenery by Sotnikov. Costumes by Ratner. First performance: Leningrad, Little Theater, 1970, Malegott-Ballet. Music by Hérold. M.P.

THE MUSIC. Louis Joseph Ferdinand Hérold, who was born in Paris in 1791 and died prematurely in 1833, was the accomplished composer of a large number of opera and ballet scores, usually very successful. Remembered in particular is the romantic opera *Zampa*, the only one by him that has remained in the repertory

and the pages of musical anthologies. An eclectic composer of some brilliance but little depth, in this ballet Hérold achieved a model of charm and elegance, underlining the comic and moralistic character of the story without ever sinking to the facile or hackneyed. M.F.

OFFERING TO LIBERTY (*Offrande à la Liberté*)
Ballet d'action. *Choreography by Pierre Gardel. Music by Rouget de Lisle. Paris, October 2, 1792.*

■ This ballet was designed by Pierre Gardel, *maître de ballet* of the Paris Opéra, to testify to his personal allegiance to the revolutionary ideals. Performed as an intermezzo, the ballet was a choreographic transposition of the *Marseillaise*. P.P.

FLORA AND ZEPHYR (*Flore et Zéphire*)
Ballet divertissement *in one act. Choreography and scenario by Charles-Louis Didelot. Music by Cesare Bossi. Scenery, costumes, and machinery by Liparotti. London, King's Theatre, July 7, 1796. Principal dancers: Mme. Hilligsberg (Cleonice, a nymph), Mme. Rose (Flora, a nymph), Mlle. Parisot and Mme. Bossi (shepherdesses),⟩ C. L. Didelot (Zephyr), Menage (Cupid), Miss Hill (a cherub).*

SYNOPSIS. Zephyr, in love with Flora, descends from the sky and begs Cupid to shoot an arrow into his loved one's heart to win it for him when she comes as usual to the copse. But then his eyes fall on the beautiful Cleonice asleep in the field and the inconstant Zephyr immediately becomes infatuated with her. When Cleonice awakes she makes fun of him, then, to commemorate their meeting, draws a picture of them both on the wall of a temple. Cupid warns Zephyr that Flora is approaching and flies to fetch her. Cleonice, too, departs into the sky together with Cupid, cherubs, and winged spirits.

■ The ballet continues along these lines, with dancers taking off into the air at every opportunity. *Flore et Zéphire* is, in fact, said to be the first ballet to have used silent, invisible wires to give the illusion of winged dancers, typical characters in the romantic ballets that were to come into fashion a few years later (*La Sylphide, Les Wilis*).

Didelot's masterpiece, it raised him to the ranks of the great choreographers and earned him an invitation from Czar Paul I to settle in Russia as dancer, ballet master, and professor of dancing (1801–1811). The first Russian performance of *Flore et Zéphire* took place at St. Petersburg at the Hermitage Theater in January 1808, with Danilova and Duport in the leading parts. After this triumphant success Didelot set his heart on presenting the ballet in Paris, which he finally did on December 12, 1815, after a long delay caused by the intrigues of the jealous Gardel, all-powerful ruler of the Opéra. The memorable first night was reported in the *Journal des Debats* as follows: "The mere names of the

Auguste Vestris, son of Gaetano, from an engraving published in London in 1781.

Nineteenth-century print of two characters from Flore et Zéphire *by C. L. Didelot.*

cast give us a taste of the pleasures to come. Albert, in his guise of Cupid, is today's best possible interpreter of the part. The two Mesdemoiselles Gosselin (senior and junior) dance Flora and Venus.... Didelot's Zephyr appears in the center of the stage as if by magic, brushes the meadow with the tips of his wings, hovers in space for a few minutes, then lands in the treetops before disappearing into the clouds as if it were the most natural thing in the world. Presented with such a sensational new experience, the audience could not control its enthusiasm. The applause continued far into the interval and redoubled when Zephyr swooped down on to the stage in the same manner as he had left it and then flew away again with Flora in his arms. That new feat sent the crowd's ecstasy soaring to the stars." This happy outcome amply repaid Didelot for all the anxiety and vexation he had suffered. Louis XVIII, who was present on the occasion, immediately granted him the sum of 2,000 francs, but since Gardel had made him agree to bear all the costs of the production himself, and since those came to 2,400 francs, poor Didelot still had to pay for it out of his own pocket. Because of this scurvy treatment he gave up all idea of remaining at the Opéra and decided to return to Russia. There his training produced dancers of the caliber of Danilova, Istomina, Likhutina, Zubova, and Teleshova. He had a fundamental influence on the development of Russian ballet. On June 3, 1830, *Flore et Zéphire* was revived at the King's Theatre in London, in which Maria Taglioni made her debut in England. C.M.C.

GENERAL COLLI IN ROME or THE BALLET OF THE POPE (*Il Generale Colli in Roma* or *Il Ballo del Papa*)

Mime-ballet in five acts. Choreography by Dominique Le Fèvre. Music by Pontelibero. Scenario by Solfi. Scenery by Landriani. Costumes by Motta and Mazza. Milan, Scala Theater, February 25, 1797. Principal dancers: Giuditta Bolla (Princess of Santa Croce), Lorenzo Coleoni (Cardinal Busca), Luigi Corticelli (Senator Rezzonico), Raimondo Fidanza (General Colli), Paolo Franchi (head of the Dominicans), Dominique Le Fèvre (Pius VI).

■ This *succès de scandale* was the most famous production of the 1797 season at the Scala, and not only there. There were eleven repeat performances. The intention of the promoters, wrote Luigi Rossi in *Ballo alla Scala*, was to announce the birth of the Age of Reason, a message underlined by the dedication to "the People of Milan" in the scenario's heading. Citizen Le Fèvre not only composed the choreography but also danced the part of Pius VI. Angiolini (who had been invited to stage the ballet, but declined) felt that it would be highly embarrassing to represent a pope "performing pirouettes on the stage." Le Fèvre, on the other hand, not only accepted but, dressed in papal robes, indulged in all sorts of personal fantasies. The height of improbability was reached in the fifth act when, still according to Rossi, Pope Pius, in spite of overtures from General Ludovico Colli. sent by Austria to fight the French, embraces the cause of France and exchanges his papal crown for a Phrygian cap, then breaks into a *farandole* that leads into the grand finale with its *carmagnole* and its performance of the *Marseillaise*, as staged a few years earlier in Paris under the title *Offrande à la Liberté*. The sacrilegious tone of the ballet was evident even in the second-act *divertissement*, in which the *corps de ballet* danced before the pope, displaying their charms in a fairly explicit manner. *The Ballet of the Pope*, which was received with enthusiasm by the populace, chiefly, perhaps, because they were let in free, marked the admission of politics into the Scala. To prevent what they feared would be a dangerous anti-government precedent (the mime satirized Pope Pius's anti-French policy), the Austrians, who were back in Milan, had all copies of the scenario burnt, hoping thereby to destroy its memory. However, in its 1901 Christmas issue, dedicated to the Scala, *L'Illustrazione Italiana*'s cover showed a scene by the artist E. Matania from *The Ballet of the Pope*. C.M.C.

DANCE MANIA (*Dansomanie*)

Mime-ballet in two acts. Choreography by Pierre Gardel. Music by Etienne Nicholas Méhul. Paris, Opéra, June 14, 1800.

Sketch of Salvatore Fiume in a scene from The Creatures of Prometheus *in the 1952 Scala version, with choreography by Aurel M. Milloss inspired by Salvatore Viganò's original of 1801.*

■ This ballet inaugurated the return of splendour and elegance to the Opéra stage after the austerities of the revolution. Though purely an entertainment and still clinging to the old traditions, *Dansomanie* did offer one novelty: the introduction of the waltz to the Opéra. On this occasion Gardel, choreographer and leading dancer, performed a minuet with exquisite grace, inspiring Berchoux to write, *"Gardel, le grand Gardel des danseurs révéré / Vieilli dans les ballets et choréographie / Brillant d'un triple éclat dans la* Dansomanie / *Beau dans le menuet et presqu'égal aux dieux / Qu'il anime à la danse et du geste et des yeux /."* ("Gardel, the great Gardel by fellow-dancers praised, matures in ballets and choreography. In *Dansomanie* he with three-fold luster shines, glorious in minuet, near equal to the gods he plays in dance, in gesture and in telling glance").

Excelling in many arts, Gardel was also an accomplished solo violinist. His appearance in *Dansomanie* was quite an event, because as early as 1795 failing health had caused him to give up dancing except on very exceptional occasions. Two years after *Dansomanie* opened, Gardel, now at the peak of his authority in the ballet world, was nominated director of the School of Dance, having succeeded his brother Maximilian as *maître de ballet* some years earlier. He held the post for forty years, passing unharmed through the revolution, the Napoleonic era, and the restoration. He was overseeing the production of *Dansomanie* in Vienna in 1806 when Filippo Taglioni took his first steps as a choreographer.   C.M.C.

LAGERTHA

Ballet in three acts. Choreography and scenario (after C. Prahn) by Vincenzo Galeotti. Music by Claus Schall. Copenhagen, Theater Royal, January 30, 1801.

■ In 1801, the year *Lagertha* was composed, Vincenzo

Galeotti was ballet master at Copenhagen's Theater Royal, where he passed the final and most important part of his teaching and choreographical career (see *Amors og Balletmesterens Luner*, page 75). *Lagertha* introduced a new element into ballet history. For the first time, ballet concerned itself with a theme from Nordic folklore. The protagonists of *Lagertha* were traditional folk heroes. Its invention was not fortuitous, but the foreshadowing of subject-matter that was to fascinate several choreographers of the romantic period. The choreographer of *Lagertha* was inspired by a poem by Christen Prahn. The first performance was greeted with rapturous acclaim. There were many revivals in a number of different theaters, the last taking place in 1821, after which it gradually sank into oblivion.   P.P.

THE CREATURES OF PROMETHEUS *(Die Geschöpfe des Prometheus)*
Heroic-allegorical ballet in two acts. Choreography and scenario by Salvatore Viganò. Music by Ludwig von Beethoven. Scenic design by Plasser. Vienna, Hoftheater, March 28, 1801. Principal dancers: Maria Casentini and Salvatore Viganò (the Creatures), Cesari (Prometheus), Ferdinando Gioja (Bacchus), Aichinger

Salvatore Fiume from an engraving by G. Scotto.

(Pan), Mlle. Brendi (Terpsichore), Mlle. Cesari (Thalia), Mlle. Renth (Melpomene).

SYNOPSIS. With lightning snatched from the sky, Prometheus the Titan imbues with life the creatures he has fashioned from the primeval clay. They come alive but without feelings or reason. They resist all Prometheus's attempts to make them human, stubbornly remaining inert as vegetables. The disappointed Titan is about to destroy his handiwork when the god Pan holds him and persuades him to bring his creations to Parnassus and submit them to the enlightening influence of the Arts. On Parnassus Apollo greets Prometheus and presides over the education of his creatures. This is carried out by members of his train in various episodes featuring Amphion, Orion, Orpheus, Melpomene, Thalia, Terpsichore, Pan, and finally Bacchus, who leads the dance celebrating the triumph of the Arts, by whom Man has been infused with the beauty of life and nobility of spirit.

■ In this ballet by Salvatore Viganò the art of theatrical dance reached one of the happiest occasions and culminating points in its history. Viganò's conception of "danced drama" and its perfect if ephemeral execution constitute the complete and logical solution of Angiolini's and Noverre's theoretical problems regarding the relations between dramatic action, mime, dance, and music in ballet. The principles and practice of the *ballet d'action* were taught to Viganò during his youthful apprenticeship to the great Dauberval, who had inherited them from Noverre, together with some of the

Maria Medina, Spanish dancer, wife of the choreographer and dancer Salvatore Viganò.

grace and technical brilliance of the French school, which was all the master required. Viganò, on the other hand, had from the beginning focused his attention on the expressive element and the need for dramatic coherence and continuity in the *ballet d'action*. Following where Angiolini had led, he gradually but systematically perfected in his own work a formal and expressive synthesis of mime and dance, turning it into an original and unified choreographical language capable of unfolding a coherent dramatic, lyrical, or allegorical plot, while representing with "poetic truth" the passions and feelings of the characters concerned. Little by little, from *ballet d'action* to *grand ballet*, Viganò brought this language to a high pitch of precision and flexibility in the service of his astonishing theatrical imagination. The results he achieved were of outstanding excellence both visually and musically. He was a man of vast literary and theatrical culture; a musician himself, probably encouraged by his uncle, Luigi Boccherini, he nearly always used music of high quality for his ballets, though it was usually adapted from the works of past or present composers. He was also very interested in stage design, and during his time at the Scala employed Alessandro Sanquirico, the most eminent scenic designer of the day, on his permanent staff. During Salvatore Viganò's thirty years of creative life, ending only with his death in 1821, *The Creatures of Prometheus* was considered his first genuine masterpiece. The subject was after his own heart, a grand heroic myth treated as an allegory of the human condition and capable of universal application. In 1813, while working at the Scala, he returned to the same theme in his *Prometheus* (see page 86), a work of his full maturity and a much altered and amplified version of the Viennese *Creatures*. In the "little Prometheus" (as Ritorni called this work in his *Commentaries* of 1838, translating *Die Geschöpfe des Prometheus* as "The People of Prometheus"), Beethoven's score, the only one he wrote for ballet, complied faithfully with Viganò's requirements, but must surely, with its severely symphonic construction, have had, in its turn, a restraining influence on the choreography. Notwithstanding the scenic simplicity of *Creatures* when compared to the spectacular staging at the Scala, Viganò's choreographic style was already evident in the complex and flowing movements of the groups, which, like those of the solo parts, were pure, though expressive, dance. On the whole, Viganò's poetic translation of action into ballet was appreciated by the Viennese public of 1801, although the time was not yet ripe for such a fundamental innovation, and *The Creatures of Prometheus* gave rise to a certain amount of misunderstanding and criticism. After twenty-eight performances during its first year and the following one, the ballet was never revived. Among the artists who must have known it and felt its influence were Gaetano Gioja (see *Caesar in Egypt*, page 84) and his brother Ferdinando, who was one of the dancers in its first showing. In our own century most of the ballets bearing the name *The Creatures of Prometheus* have had nothing in common with the original except Beethoven's music, since neither Viganò's scenario nor, of course, his choreography have survived. However, Serge Lifar's version, staged at the

Paris Opéra in 1929, was not without importance, mainly for the quality of the dancers, among whom, as well as Spessitzeva and Peretti, was Lifar himself in the part of Prometheus, made the central character in a plot fairly distant from the original one. It was this creation that marked the beginning of the great dancer's career at the Opéra, where he was to remain the ruling spirit for thirty years. Aurel Milloss, however, in his version of Viganò's ballet, created at Augsburg in 1933, managed to maintain a perfect balance between creative originality and pedantic faithfulness to the original. After its first production, the ballet was perfected in the course of numerous revivals, among them a notable one in 1952 at the Scala in Milan. Of all the later versions of this danced drama, only Milloss's production can be considered an authentic interpretation of Viganò's artistic and choreographic principles.

OTHER VERSIONS. 1) Nicola Guerra (story by Sándor Bródy). Budapest, Opera House, 1913. 2) Serge Lifar (his own scenario, based on the studies of M. Léna and J. Chantavoine). Scenic design by F. Quelvée. Paris, Opéra, December 30, 1929. Principal dancers: Olga Spessitzeva, Suzanne Lorcia, Serge Lifar, Serge Peretti. 3) Aurel M. Milloss (after Viganò). Scenic design by B. Klein. Augsburg, Municipal Dance Theater, September 23, 1933; later Rome Opera, December 19, 1940; Milan, Scala, December 31, 1952 (scenic design by Salvatore Fiume, danced by Olga Amati, Giulio Perugini, Ugo dell'Ara); Florence, May Music Festival, 1956 (scenic design by Franco Laurenti); Vienna, State Opera House, December 2, 1963; etc. 4) Erich Walter. Düsseldorf, Deutsche Oper am Rhein, 1966. 5) Frederick Ashton (own scenario). Scenic design by Ottowerner Meyer. Bonn, City Theater, June 6, 1970. Touring section of the Royal Ballet.

THE MUSIC. When he was composing the eighteen numbers that make up *The Creatures of Prometheus*, the myth of Prometheus was never far from Beethoven's mind. Nevertheless, there is no lack of lightness and vivacity, especially in the overture which starts with a splendidly theatrical seventh chord, developed throughout the rest of the movement, forming a close-knit and elegant instrumental *divertissement* in which the lively themes are taken up by the woodwinds. Beethoven's concern with the underlying philosophical content results in a particularly sensitive score in which the vaguely neoclassical academicism of the form is offset by the sumptuous and brilliant writing. It would be superfluous to run through all the numbers here, but a few of the most effective passages should be noted. One of these is the accompaniment to the serene world of Parnassus, musically evoked in *No. 5* (Adagio, Andante almost Allegretto) in which the harp is first heard interpolated with the woodwind (for practically the only time in all Beethoven's works); while in the second part of the same number a dreamy melodic theme is allotted to the cello. Still more notable is the finale: the apotheosis is accompanied by a heroic theme very dear to Beethoven's heart. Present for the first time in a contradanse for orchestra, this unmistakable motif can be heard again in the *Variations, Op. 35* for piano and in the last movement of the *Third Symphony*, where it becomes the fulcrum and point of departure for all the ensuing contrapuntal development.   A.A.

ACHILLES AT SCYROS *(Achille à Scyros)*
Ballet in three acts. Choreography by Pierre Gardel. Music by Luigi Cherubini. Paris, Opéra, December 18, 1804.

SYNOPSIS. Achilles, disguised in women's clothing, is in hiding at the court of Lycomedes, King of Scyros, when Greek ships arrive under the captaincy of Ulysses, with the apparent aim of asking the King, his friend, for reinforcements of men and ships. The Greeks bring gifts, feminine articles for the women, arms for the men. Achilles, forgetting his female disguise, leaps on the weapons and is thus unmasked. Ulysses persuades him to return to his own country and fight. Deidameia, daughter of Lycomedes and loved by Achilles, tries to detain him, but the King urges him to resume his manly dress and regain his dignity. First, however, the marriage of the two young lovers is celebrated.

■ The story of this ballet was taken from Metastasio's opera of the same name and turned into a pastiche ballet by Gardel. It is the only one for which Cherubini composed the music, and is an academic work, episodic but suffused with the noble ideals of neoclassical grandeur characteristic of all works by Gardel the younger (brother of the more celebrated Maximilien), a typical choreographer of the Napoleonic era.   C.M.C.

ACIS AND GALATEA *(Acis et Galathée)*
Pantomime (or mime) ballet in one act. Choreography by Louis Antoine Duport. Music by Henri Durondeau and Luigi Gianella. Paris, Opéra, May 10, 1805.

SYNOPSIS. The story tells of the hopeless love between Acis and Galatea. Galatea, one of the Nereids, is promised to the Cyclops Polyphemus, but prefers the more attractive Acis, by whom she is courted. The infuriated Polyphemus crushes his rival under a rock. Acis's flowing blood is transformed into the Sicilian

Sketch of Alessandro Sanquirico in a scene from The Walnut Tree of Benevento, *performed at the Scala, Milan, on April 25, 1812, with choreography by Salvatore Viganò.*

river named after him. Galatea returns to her sister Nereids.

■ *Acis and Galatea* was the first ballet designed by Duport, inspired perhaps by his rivalry with Auguste Vestris, choreographer as well as dancer. In 1804 the two men were both performing in *Achilles at Scyros*, Vestris as Achilles, Duport as Ajax. The latter wanted to invent his own variations to prove his worth as a choreographer. After that he composed several ballets for the Opéra while still pursuing his career as a dancer, but in fact remained much inferior to his rival, both as choreographer and dancer. The ballet was revived at Vienna's Court Opera House in 1812, under the title of *Acis und Galathea, oder Der Riese Polifem.*   C.M.C.

ACHILLES IN SCYROS (Achille in Sciro)
Ballet in four acts. Choreography by Pietro Angiolini. Music by A. Rolla and Baiglin. Story from Pietro Metastasio. Scenic design by Pasquale Canna. Milan, Scala, May 1806. Principal dancers: Fortunata Angiolini, Armando Vestris, Teresa Brugnoli.

SYNOPSIS. See *Achilles at Scyros*, page 83.

■ At least thirty-two operas of the same name were written (by Pergolesi, Paisiello, and Jommelli among others) between 1663 and 1837. Together with *Hippolytus and Aricia* (1811), this mime-*ballet d'action* (according to the principles of Gasparo Angiolini) was one of Angiolini's son's greatest successes. It was composed for the Scala while he was chief choreographer at the great Milan theater.   C.M.C.

THE TWO CREOLES (Les Deux Créoles)
Pantomime (or mime) ballet in three acts. Choreography and scenario by Jean Aumer. Music by Jean Durondeau. Paris, Théâtre de la Porte St. Martin, June 28, 1806. Principal dancers: Madame Quériau (Théodore), Mlle. Caroline (Zoë), M. Lefèbre (de la Martinière), Mlle. Aline (Mme. de Sénange), Madame Descuillé (Marianne), M. Robillon (Dominguo).

SYNOPSIS. On a sugar plantation in the Île de France (now the island of Mauritius), Zoë and Théodore, much in love, are teasing one another. A black slave enters with her child; they are in flight from a cruel master. The two creoles give her food and hide her. The slave master is in search of his slave. When he finds the fugitive, he wants to take her with him, but finally yields her up to the pair. A letter arrives from an aunt, calling Zoë back to France. The two lovers decide to get married at once so that they will not be parted. When they get to the church, however, the Governor appears with an order to take Zoë with him. The young couple are parted and the girl is put on a ship bound for France. Once at sea, the ship runs into trouble. Théodore plunges into the waves to rescue Zoë, but the vessel catches fire and sinks. While the crowd mourns their death, the lovers emerge from the water and are carried to safety. The Governor

now consents to their wedding and even offers his castle for the celebration of the marriage feast.

■ *The Two Creoles* was the second ballet inspired by Bênardin de Saint-Pierre's novel *Paul et Virginie*, the first, created by Gardel at the Paris Opéra, having been performed three days earlier. Geoffroy, an ardent admirer of Gardel, writing in the *Journal de l'Empire*, severely criticized Aumer's production. Although the subject was the same, he wrote, "the play, choreography, style, and dancers have nothing in common." According to Geoffroy, *The Two Creoles* was a "mere parody, almost a burlesque, of *Paul et Virginie*." The critic of the *Courrier des Spectacles* had a different opinion: "It presents episodes so full of emotion and such varied scenes that, with the exception of three or four steps, it should be no less successful than the famous ballet *Jenny* ... The author has left no stone unturned to make it interesting ..." Aumer's ballet was performed in the Court Theater of Vienna on July 20, 1809, under the title *Paul und Virginie oder Die Zwei Kreolen.*   C.M.C.

THE STRELETSY REVOLT (Gli Strelizzi)
Mime-ballet in six acts. Choreography and scenario by Salvatore Viganò. Music by various composers. Scenic design by Alessandro Sanquirico. Venice, La Fenice Theater, Carnival, 1809. Principal dancers: Salvatore Viganò (Czar Peter I of Russia), Amalia Muzzarelli Cesari (Elizabeth).

SYNOPSIS. Inspired by an episode from Russian history, the ballet presents the so-called Streletsy Revolt of 1697. The Streletsy faction, a powerful military group backed by the Princess Sophia, tries to dethrone Czar Peter I. The final bloodbath, which seemed inevitable after the Emperor had discovered and suppressed the conspiracy, is avoided, thanks to the intercession of Peter I's mistress, Elizabeth. The episode ends without bloodshed in the exile of the conspirators.

■ This very complex dance drama alternates crowd scenes (among others, a soldiers' dance in the first act) with long *pas de deux*, the most successful being that between the Czar and Elizabeth in the third act. *The Streletsy Revolt* was composed during Viganò's less productive period (in 1809 he created only one other ballet: *Hippothoön* (*Ipotoo*) for Padua). After his establishment in Milan (1812), however, his creative abilities developed (see *Prometheus*, page 86).   C.M.C.

CAESAR IN EGYPT (Cesare in Egitto)
Heroic-tragic mime-ballet in five acts. Choreography and scenario by Gaetano Gioja. Music by various composers. Scenery by Paolo Landriani. Costumes by Giacomo Pregliasco. Milan, Scala, August 18, 1809. Principal dancers: Giovanni Coralli (Julius Caesar), Teresa Coralli (Cleopatra), Gaetana Abrami (Ptolemy), Giuseppe Paracca, Francesco Venturi, Paolo Brugnoli, etc.

PROMETEO

BALLO MITOLOGICO

INVENTATO E POSTO SULLE SCENE

DEL R. TEATRO ALLA SCALA

DA

SALVATORE VIGANÒ

nella primavera dell'anno 1813.

MILANO

Dalla Società Tipografica de'CLASSICI ITALIANI
Contrada del Cappuccio.

Frontispiece from the scenario of Prometheus *created by Salvatore Viganò to music by Beethoven, Mozart, Haydn, Weigl, and others.*

great Viganò described *Caesar* as "the prince of heroic ballets," adding that none of his own works could be compared to it. That was excessive modesty: even contemporary opinion was aware of how much Gioja owed to the creator and unsurpassed master of danced drama, whose works (see *The Creatures of Prometheus*, page 81) had undoubtedly influenced him. And it was indeed his "danced dramas" that brought Gioja fame. Most of his ballets – over two hundred in all – were of that type, even if he did not invariably achieve the noble concentration and synthesis of expressive components proper to the style of Viganò. The work in question, however, was a shining example of Gioja's art and of the genre "grand tragic-heroic pantomime ballet" (as *Caesar in Egypt* was originally described), in which the blending of choreography, drama, and music – some of the last being composed by the choreographer himself – the proportion between solo and group dancing, the fusion of dance and mime, spurning mere technical virtuosity and banal gesture, the clarity of dramatic action and the seeking after true emotion, all combined to form a work of great dramatic density, artistically pure, yet unfailing in its effect on the public of that time. Although, as can be seen from their subjects – tragic, heroic, epic, historical, or mythological – Gioja's major works still conformed to the neoclassical ideal, there were already hints of a dramatic mood and sensibility more typical of the romantic era, especially in his later creations (see *Gabriella di Vergy*, page 91). The way in which the two opposing trends of the time were beginning to mingle is illustrated by the fact that *Caesar in Egypt*, the classical masterpiece of the "Sophocles of the Choreographic Art" (as Gioja was called) had as its protagonist Giovanni (Jean) Coralli, who thirty years later was the choreographer of *Giselle*, the archetype of romantic ballets. A.A.

SYNOPSIS. The involved and complicated plot is based on "historical information taken from Plutarch and other authoritative writers" and exalts the virtues of Caesar in all his military, political, and amorous activities. From "the day of Pharsaglia that sealed Pompey's fate," the scene moves to the court of Cleopatra. She is contending for power with her brother Ptolemy, who eventually loses his life. The fatal Queen, after appearing as "Venus surrounded by Graces, Cherubs, Nymphs and Bacchantes," is captured by her enemies. She is freed at last when Alexandria is conquered. The walls of her prison collapse to reveal a spectacular scene of the city rejoicing at the entry of the Roman army. The grand finale shows the triumph of Caesar and Cleopatra.

■ Gaetano Gioja, one of the greatest Italian choreographers of the early nineteenth century, is remembered above all for his *Caesar in Egypt*, first shown at the San Carlo Theater in Naples in 1807, then expanded and perfected two years later for the Scala at Milan. There it was recognized as its creator's masterpiece. Napoleon Bonaparte himself, present at the first performance, took it on himself to interpret the crowd's emotion and enthusiasm by expressing his admiration to Gioja. The

THE WALNUT TREE OF BENEVENTO (*Il Noce di Benevento*)
Ballet in four acts. Choreography and scenario by Salvatore Viganò. Music by Franz Xavier Süssmayr. Scenery by Alessandro Sanquirico. Costumes by Giacomo Pregliasco. Milan, Scala, April 25, 1812. Principal dancers: Annette Begrand, Antonio Chiarini, Giovanni Coralli. Teresa Coralli.

SYNOPSIS. Scene: a forest with a huge tree center stage. It is the Benevento walnut tree, where, according to legend, the women are transported by night at certain seasons to a congress of demonic spirits. The ballet opens with a sabbath of witches and evil spirits. Dorilla, who has accompanied her husband Robert on a hunting expedition, but is now lost and exhausted, falls asleep beneath the tree. Two witches (spirits of Good and Evil) seek to take possession of her. Sorceries of every kind supervene (the second act takes place in the belly of a stag to which Dorilla has been transported) with continual symbolic references. After many vicissitudes, the spell is broken and husband and wife are reunited. The ballet concludes with a joyful scene of merrymaking, feasting and dancing.

■ The ballet was created at about the same time as *The Daughter of Air (La Figlia dell'Aria)* and *Isthmian Games (Giochi Istmici)*, during the early 1800s, probably when Viganò was so creatively active in Vienna (see *The Creatures of Prometheus*, page 81), and revived in a much more finished form during his first year at the Scala. The "moral" printed on the libretto's flyleaf advises us that, "Outwardly we see the fate in store for foolish people who let themselves be led astray by false appearances or doubtful motives," and adds, "The name of the ballet should really be *The Battle between Reason and Error*." Paganini, who saw the ballet, was so impressed by the oboe solo accompanying the entry of the witches that he reproduced it, more or less, in his variations for violin called *The Witches (La Streghe)*.   C.M.C.

PROMETHEUS (Prometeo)

Mime-ballet ("choreodrama") in six acts. Choreography and scenario by Salvatore Viganò. Music by Ludwig von Beethoven, Wolfgang Amadeus Mozart, Franz Josef Haydn, Joseph Weigl, and Salvatore Viganò. Scenery by Pasquale Canna. Costumes and machinery by Giacomo Pregliasco. Milan, Scala, May 22, 1813. Principal dancers: Antonietta Pallerini (Eone), Gaetana Abrami (Lino), Luigi Costa (Prometheus), Giuseppe Villa (Jove), Giuseppe Paccini (Minerva), Giovanni Bianchi (Mercury), Francesco Venturi (Vulcan), Giuseppe Bertelli (Hercules), M. Chouchous (Mars), Amalia Brugnoli (Cupid), Margarita Bianchi, Celeste Viganò, Antonia Millier, Anna Silel, etc.

SYNOPSIS. Act I: Prometheus, surrounded by a chorus of the Virtues, the Arts, and the Muses, contemplates from on high the wilderness where primitive, brutelike human beings are lumbering about. Planning to educate them, the Titan descends to earth, but he is sorely disappointed when he witnesses the ferocious way in which they fight for the apple he has offered them as an example of agriculture. He invokes Minerva, then flies away in her winged chariot. Act II: in a sky thronged with supernatural apparitions, a heavenly procession precedes Apollo in his sun chariot. Prometheus ignites a piece of Minerva's spear in the immortal flame. For this act of sacrilege he is hurled from his chariot by a thunderbolt from the infuriated Jove. Act III: he falls to earth and is trampled underfoot by the witless humans. However, sparks scattered from the divine firebrand he carries with him generate bevies of cherubs who, by their magic, instill the brutish men with reason. Now they can distinguish and recognize what surrounds them. Prometheus is saved by his favourites, Eone and Lino, and, to complete the regeneration of mankind, leads everyone to the Temple of Virtue. Act IV: from Vulcan's forge, Cupid, envious of Prometheus's achievements, obtains an arrow with which to trouble men and women. Mercury enters with an order from Jove that the divine smith should forge a chain of immense strength to restrain the Titan. Though at first unwilling, Vulcan obeys and gives his handiwork to the Cyclops, who prepare Prometheus's punishment. Act V: Virtue

Nicola Molinari dressed as the sultan in the ballet La Schiava Sultana.

welcomes the men and women to her temple, where a conclave of Muses, Graces, Sciences, and Arts undertakes to instruct them. Cupid surreptitiously pricks Eone with his dart. Immediately she falls in love with Lino, who, however, is interested only in his zither until the divine boy presses against Lino's chest a handkerchief soaked with the woman's tears. The two lovers plead with Prometheus, and he, indignant with Cupid, summons Hymen to bless the union the mischievous god has already made inevitable. Then the Cyclops emerge from underground to seize the Titan and take him down with them, while Virtue implores Mars to beg for mercy from the father of the gods. Act VI: the Cyclops drag Prometheus to the Caucasian mountains and there chain him to a rock, driving a diamond nail into his breast. A thunderclap announces the appearance of a vulture, who swoops to devour the hero's heart. A festive procession enters, but when the people see their benefactor's plight they are horrified and implore Hercules to help him. Hercules climbs the mountain, slays the vulture, and sets Prometheus free. Minerva and Hygeia descend from the clouds to heal his wounds and bring with them Jove's pardon. Jove himself appears in glory, surrounded by his court of gods, and Immortality flies down to crown the Titan Prometheus while the people express their happiness in joyful dances.

Antonia Pallerini in the costume of Gabriella di Vergy in the ballet of that name.

■ "I consider myself fortunate to have seen with my own eyes the *Prometheus* of which the masses and those who have only heard of it have formed such a false idea. They suppose it to be a mere show of ingenious machinery and sensational spectacle. On the contrary, while some of the portrayals of the gods are not above criticism, it is a moral drama and, spectacular though it is, its true value lies in the sublime and astonishing expression of poetic ideas and dramatic situations." With those words, taken from his *Commentaries on the Life and Dramatic Ballets of Salvatore Viganò* (1838), Carlo Ritorni recognized the artistic essence of the magnificent entertainments that characterized the peak of Viganò's ballet career, beginning in 1813, when he was appointed choreographer at the Scala in Milan, and ending only at his death in 1821 (leaving aside his beginnings at La Scala in 1811–1812). "Expenses, the building of the machinery, the research, the spectacle – all were on a huge scale" (Ritorni). The long and meticulous preparation of the production, probably largely because of the astounding scenic effects, resulted in an immediate and enormous success, as testified by the famous monologue in *Giovannin Bongee* by Carlo Porta, and the comment in one of Monaldi's historical works that it aroused "popular emotion such as has not been evoked, perhaps, by any other splendid theatrical spectacle." Ugo Foscolo and Andrea Appiani, among others, echoed the enthusiasm of Stendhal, who in numerous of his writings expressed unstinted admiration for Viganò and his *Prometheus*. For these and other observers at least, the true artistic content of his works, lying above and beyond the striking scenic effects, did not go unappreciated. The *ballet d'action* or mime-drama was already superseded in *Prometheus*, a true choreographic drama expressed entirely in terms of dance both in the unfolding of the action and in the characterization, which Viganò in his major works so successfully integrated with the scenic tradition of grand neoclassical ballet. Of course there were some who deplored the passing of the brilliant formality of French academic dance and reproached Viganò for an excessive use of mime (Rossini among them), without understanding that it was no longer a question of "walking through the mime" in the Noverre manner, but of mime expressed purely in dance and in time to the music, or, to put it differently, dance that was "expressive" throughout, part and parcel of the dramatic action. Even before he reached Milan, Viganò had been aiming at the stylistic synthesis which he finally realized in *Prometheus* at the Scala. It was not by chance that he returned to the same theme of Aeschylean tragedy that had inspired his earlier masterpiece (see *The Creatures of Prometheus*, page 81), but expanded it into the universality of moral content, expressed in mythological allegory, that was more congenial to his artistic ideals. He also lengthened the ballet so that it became necessary to supplement Beethoven's original score with music by himself and other composers. The ballet's success must also have been partly due to the quality of the performers, tirelessly rehearsed by the choreographer. The special stars were the popular Antonia Pallerini and Gaetana Abrami (*en travesti*) and the vigorous dancer-mime Luigi Costa. There were numerous repeat performances during the year. For the autumn season the scenery was redesigned by Pablo Landriani, and the cast was joined by Filippo Taglioni (Mars), later a central figure in romantic ballet. There were no more revivals after the first year. Essentially classical, yet with hints of a budding romanticism, the genre of "choreodrama" was the offspring of a specific moment and an irreplaceable personality. It died with its creator. Various reconstructions by second-rate imitators followed, one of them (faithful only to the scenario) being staged by Augusto Huss at the Scala in 1844.

OTHER VERSIONS. 1) Augusto Huss (Viganò's scenario). Music by Anton Roht and others. Scenery by A. Merlo, G. Fontana, and G. Boccaccio. Milan, Scala, August 20, 1844. 2) Ninette de Valois (her own scenario). Music by Beethoven, arranged by Constant Lambert. Scenery by J. Banting. London, Sadler's Wells Theatre, October 13, 1936. 3) Elsa Marianne von Rosen (her own scenario). Music by Beethoven. Stockholm. Theater Royal, May 3, 1958.   A.A.

On this and the next page are illustrations made for the Traîté élémentaire, théorique et pratique de l'Art de la Danse *by Carlo Blasis.*

NINA or DRIVEN MAD BY LOVE (La Folle par Amour)

Mime-ballet in two acts. Choreography and scenario by Louis Milon. Music by Louis Persius. Paris, Opéra, November 23, 1813.

SYNOPSIS. The story of the unhappy love between the eponymous Nina and her lover Germeuil.

■ As well as having a number of antecedents in the history of ballet, the subject was more particularly derived from Paisiello's opera *Nina o la Pazza per Amore.* Milon is considered the precursor of romantic ballet. P.P.

OTHELLO (Otello)

Tragic ballet in five acts. Choreography and scenario by Salvatore Viganò. Music by various composers. Scenery by Alessandro Sanquirico. Milan, Scala, February 6, 1818. Principal dancers: Antonia Pallerini (Desdemona), Nicola Molinari (Othello), Giuseppe Bocci (Iago), Maria Bocci (Emilia), Filippo Ciotti (Cassio), Pietro Trigambi (Rodrigo), Girolamo Pallerini (Montano), Carlo Bianciardi (Doge), Carlo Nichli (Brabantio).

SYNOPSIS. Othello obtains from Brabantio the hand of his daughter Desdemona, who returns his love. Appointed Governor of Cyprus, Othello has aroused the envy of Rodrigo and Iago. The latter instills the jealous Moor with doubts about the relationship between Desdemona and the young officer Cassio. He adds fuel to the flames by inciting Cassio to fight and then advising him to ask Desdemona to intercede with Othello for his pardon. Her plans in Cassio's favour, together with a handkerchief slyly stolen from her apartment and shown by Iago to Othello as proof of her infidelity, send the Moor into a fever of jealousy. He publicly insults his wife in front of an official delegation just arrived from Venice, and that night, a prey to madness, he strangles her in her bed. When he learns, too late, of her innocence, Othello runs himself through with his sword.

■ *Othello*, (like *Coriolanus, Mirra,* and *La Vestale*) is a danced tragedy. The ballet, throwing off the shackles of academic formula, enters the sphere of drama with psychological value; the rhythm of movement and gesture melts into the music and the tragic pathos has a "speed and effectiveness that Shakespeare himself could not attain" (Stendhal). Again, Stendhal makes an interesting comparison between Rossini's *Othello* and the ballet version by Viganò: "Viganò shows a greater genius than Rossini in audaciously opening the ballet with a *Furlana*. In the second act he once more holds the palm through the serene majesty of the palace scene: an aristocratic reception held in the gardens at night, during which Othello's jealousy steadily grows. In this way we reach the fifth act of Viganò's ballet without yet being sated with violence and strong emotion, so that the sudden acceleration of the tragedy moves us to tears. I have rarely seen a member of the audience weeping at Rossini's *Othello*" (Stendhal, *Vie de Rossini*, 1823). The ballet *Othello* was a spectacular production as both the subject and contemporary taste demanded, with much crowd work and superb sets by Alessandro Sanquirico, who designed most of the scenery for Viganò's creations. C.M.C.

THE VESTAL VIRGIN (La Vestale)

Tragic ballet in five acts. Choreography and scenario by Salvatore Viganò. Music by various composers. Scenery by Alessandro Sanquirico. Milan, Scala, June 9, 1818. Principal dancers: Antonia Pallerini (Emilia), Nicola Molinari (Decius).

This treatise, published in Milan in 1820, with others written by Carlo Blasis, form a synthesis of two centuries' development of academic dance.

SYNOPSIS. During the festival in honour of Ceres, Decius, son of the consul Murena, falls in love with Emilia, one of the Vestal Virgins. At first she meets his advances "with maidenly reserve, then with ill-concealed tenderness as her ardour matches his." It is a hopeless love. Emilia will not yield. She flees, she prays, and she implores her goddess for help. "The poor girl implores him not to persist with a suit that must prove fatal, but is then too weak to resist further and falls into his arms." They are discovered and Emilia is condemned to burial alive. In attempting to save her, Decius hurls himself on the high priest, but is transfixed and killed by a soldier of the guard. He dies invoking Emilia's name.

■ When Salvatore Viganò, as chief choreographer at Milan's Scala Theater, produced *The Vestal Virgin*, he had just followed the immensely successful *Prometheus* with a series of minor works. Then he created three tragic ballets: *Othello, Daedalus,* and *The Vestal Virgin.* All three were triumphs. The critics debated long as to which was the best. The judges could not agree but the majority voted for *The Vestal Virgin.* Public, critics, and many of the intellectuals were enthusiastic. "Salvatore Viganò," wrote the "Milanese" Stendhal, "has transcended all other forms of expression. His instinctive art has enabled him to discover the true nature of the dance: romantic above all." That was the first use of the word "romantic" in relation to ballet. The subject of *La Vestale* may have been taken from the opera of the same name by Spontini, which had been performed at various European theaters, but not yet at the Scala. P.P.

THE FALSE LORD (*Il Finto Feudatario*)
Ballet in one act. Choreography and scenario by Carlo Blasis. Music by Francesco Antonio Blasis. Scenery by Alessandro Sanquirico. Costumes by Rossetti and Majoli. Milan, Scala, April 12, 1819. Principal dancers:
Adelaide Grassi (Luisa), Giuseppe Villa (Fritz), Girolamo Pallerini (Maturino), Giuseppe Bocci (the Mayor), Filippo Ciotti (the Vassal), Giovanni Francolini (Frank).

SYNOPSIS. The original story was as follows: "The scene is a village in the Tyrol. Young Fritz and the stupid Maturino are rivals for the hand of Luisa, niece of the Mayor. She would like to accept Fritz, but her uncle wants to leave the decision to their feudal overlord, who is momentarily expected. Frank, the lord's servant, arrives in the village, and silly Maturino takes him for his master. Frank decides to amuse himself by continuing the deception for a while, but when the real lord arrives his fraud is discovered. The lord grants Luisa her Fritz and forgives his servant's innocent trick."

■ Performed as the closing *divertissement* of an evening's program at La Scala, comprising the opera *Il Falegname di Livonia* by Giovanni Pacini and the ballet *Bianca, o sia il Perdono per Sorpresa* by Salvatore Viganò (with front-rank dancers such as Pallerini, Molinari, and Bocci), *The False Lord* had no success. Nor were most of the numerous ballets created by Carlo Blasis after this first one any better received. They have all fallen into oblivion, and perhaps none of them would be worth mentioning here, were it not that their creator's name is one of the most important in the history of ballet. His activities as a theorist, expressed mainly in the *Traité élémentaire, théoretique et pratique de l'Art de la Danse* of 1820 and the *Code of Terpsichore* in 1828, but also in many other of his writings, were the summary and consummation of more than two centuries of technical, theoretical, artistic, and dramatic development in academic dance. The *danse d'école* of French tradition, born from the matrix of Italy in the seventeenth century, but becoming ever more confined in a sterile mannerism since the foundation of the

Académie Royale de Danse (1661), found in Blasis's systematization and, in a sense, definitive codification at once a purification and an enrichment. His noble synthesis of its ideal components and universal extension established his work as the grammar and stylistic bible of the art of dancing at a peak of its historical and international evolution. A man of encyclopedic culture, Carlo Blasis saw dance in the theater as a union of all the other arts, striving towards that classical ideal of Apollonian perfection of form which he identified as spiritual beauty. At his school of "beldanzare" (corresponding to the operatic belcanto of the period) during his long, intensive, and celebrated teaching years, he trained almost all the dancers that embodied the dream of the romantic ballerina, as well as those who spread his doctrines abroad in the course of the nineteenth century and later, beginning with Giovanni Lepri and the great master of ballet Cecchetti. In this sense especially, the work of Carlo Blasis forms a link between classicism and romanticism. Moreover, some of his creations, including the otherwise not very significant The False Lord, come close in spirit to the romantic ballet.   A.A.

THE TITANS (I Titani)

Epic ballet in six acts. Choreography and scenario by Salvatore Viganò. Music by Ayblinger and Viganò. Scenery by Alessandro Sanquirico. Milan, Scala, October 11, 1819. Principal dancers: Luigi Sidini (Jove), Nicola Molinari (Hyperion), Maria Bocci (Theia), Antonia Pallerini (Selene), Adelaide Grassini (Helios), Teresa Oliviera (Eone), Giovanni Bianchi (Nereus).

SYNOPSIS. In a clearing scattered with trees and spring flowers, girls and boys dance hand in hand with cherubs. The next scene shows a grim and savage place where Atlas lives with the Titans and Cyclops. They plan to sow discord among the mortals and offer Theia vessels full of strife and trouble to scatter in the world of men. Carried to earth and opened, the vessels pour forth every sort of calamity. When discord reigns supreme, the Titans emerge from their cavern and make war against mankind. Then, piling the mountains on top of one another to form a ladder to heaven, they attack great Jove himself. But their ambitious revolt cannot succeed. The enraged god hurls his thunderbolts at them and drives them down to the depths of the earth from whence they came.

■ The Titans was almost the last of the more than forty ballets created by Viganò. It remained unequalled in its class. The first act especially, representing the golden age of innocence, was realized with such poetic feeling, harmony of movement, and overall beauty that the curtain fell to a veritable hurricane of applause. This epic ballet was Viganò's personal creation and illustrated the natural evolution of his genius. It was the culminating point of the series of tragic ballets (Mirra, 1817, Othello and The Vestal Virgin, 1818) belonging to the same category of ballet, presented at La Scala from Prometheus in 1813 (see page 86) onwards. The conversion of mime to dance and vice versa was a

Sketch by Alessandro Sanquirico for a scene from the ballet Gabriella di Vergy *in the revised version of 1822, the choreography of which was altered and expanded by its original creator, Gaetano Gioia. On the opposite page is another set design by Sanquirico for the ballet* The Titans, *produced at the Scala, Milan, on October 11, 1819, with choreography and scenario by Salvatore Viganò.*

reversal of academic tradition so fundamental as to call for new working methods and dancers with new characteristics. Henceforth choreography took much longer to prepare and required countless rehearsals; anonymous dancers were snatched from the *corps de ballet* and rose to the heights of stardom, among them Nicola Molinari, Luigi Costa, Celeste Viganò, and, above all, Antonia Pallerini. It was also the time when the true Scala *corps de ballet* came into existence, dancers in a group, yet imbued with the values of soloists. It was indeed the exceptional standard of interpretative skill required by this sort of "dance drama" that prevented it becoming a school. Although Viganò's heritage passed on to his brother Giulio and Louis Henry, the noble yet fragile genre was not strong enough, without his presence, to survive into the future.   C.M.C.

GABRIELLA DI VERGY

Tragic mime-ballet in five acts. Choreography and scenario by Gaetano Gioja. Music by Romani and Brambilla. Scenery by Luigi Facchinelli. Florence, Imperial Regio Teatro della Pergola, autumn 1819. Principal dancers: Francesca Rolandi Pezzoli (Gabriella), Luigi Costa (Fayel), Ferdinando Gioja (Rodolphe de Courcy), Gaetano Gherini (Philippe Auguste).

SYNOPSIS. The scene is laid in a castle in medieval France. Gabriella di Vergy is to marry the Count Fayel for political reasons, but still grieves for her true love, Rodolphe de Courcy, her former betrothed and a poet. King Philippe Auguste arrives to take part in the wedding festivities. A member of his suite soon makes himself known as Rodolphe. The King wishes him to marry Emma, and Gabriella herself urges him to obey, although her heart is breaking. A moving scene shows "the unfolding of the two lovers' passion and acceptance of sacrifice." Count Fayel discovers them together and, believing his wife unfaithful, throws her into prison and challenges Rodolphe to a duel. Gabriella, in prison, learns of her lover's death: her desperation increases the insensate jealousy of Fayel, who serves up to his consort the heart of her murdered love. Gabriella dies of sorrow. Too late the King and Emma arrive to bear witness to her virtue. Fayel acknowledges his error and kills himself, falling on the dead body of his wife.

■ In the long series of Gaetano Gioja's sumptuous ballets influenced by Viganò's "dance drama" in the true spirit of neoclassicism (see *Caesar in Egypt*, page 84), *Gabriella di Vergy* was the first to show a marked romantic element. It is already evident in the medieval and melodramatic subject-matter and in the character of the protagonist, a true sentimental heroine, torn between passion and virtue. The treatment of the theme, though not renouncing the grand ensemble numbers, aims above all to stress the more emotionally expressive passages. In his preface to the scenario, Gioja shows himself quite conscious of that aspect when he writes, among other things, "The difficulty of introducing opportunities for dancing in such a story was nearly enough to dissuade me from using it at all. After careful consideration, however, I yielded to its inherent interest and pathos." The thought given to the expressive element is shown by various insertions in the text: thus, of the scene where Rodolphe is recognized by Gabriella in the presence of Fayel, the King, and Emma, he writes, "Emotions swell in the hearts of all those present, in each according to the respective character." The portrayal of these emotions was naturally conveyed by means of dramatic mime, but always within the convention of pure and dignified dance.

In the course of the next few years *Gabriella di Vergy* was frequently revived in the major theaters of Italy, produced by Gaetano Gioja himself, by his brother Ferdinando, or by others, up to the end of the century. A particularly important occasion was the production at the Scala on August 24, 1822, in a version revised and amplified by Gioja himself, with new scenery by Alessandro Sanquirico, the most distinguished theatrical designer of the day. The title role was danced by the much acclaimed Antonia Pallerini, Viganò's favourite interpreter, supported by some of the most famous La Scala dancers of the time: Nicola Molinari as Fayel, Giuseppe Villa (Rodolphe), the powerful mime Giuseppe Bocci (Philippe Auguste), Maria Bocci (Emma, now renamed Almeida), Pietro Trigambi (Alberico).

A.A.

Amalia Brugnoli, the first ballerina to dance "on point," here seen with her husband Paolo Samengo.

CINDERELLA (Cendrillon)

Fairy-tale ballet in three acts. Choreography and scenario by François Decombe, called Albert. Music by Fernando Sor. London, King's Theatre, March 26, 1822. Principal dancer: Maria Mercandotti.

SYNOPSIS. This was the first ballet of any importance based on the fairy tale by Perrault which, between the late nineteenth century and now, has undergone such varying fortunes as a subject for ballet (see *Cinderella*, pages 149, and 246).

■ The choreographer, Albert, was first dancer at the Opéra from 1817 to 1835 and one of its choreographers until 1842. The music was written by the Catalan, Sor, remembered less as a composer than as one of the most distinguished guitarists of his time. P.P.

THE PRISONER OF THE CAUCASUS or THE SHADE OF THE BETROTHED (Il Prigioniero del Caucaso or L'Ombra della Fidanzata)

Ballet in four acts. Choreography by Charles Didelot. Music by Catterino Cavos. Scenario by Charles Didelot, after Pushkin. St. Petersburg, Bolshoi Theater, January 27, 1823. Principal dancers: Avdotia Istomina and Nicholas Goltz.

SYNOPSIS. The story is of the love between a Russian prisoner (Rostislav) and a Circassian girl (Kzelkia). The plot thickens with the arrival of Rostislav's promised bride, also a prisoner. At first the wild Kzelkia is ready to kill her rival, but humane impulses prevail and she even helps the affianced pair to escape. While crossing a river during their flight, however, the girl is drowned. Her spirit appears to Rostislav, telling him to give her

ring as a token of love to the Circassian maid. At the wedding celebrations of Rostislav and Kzelkia, Tartars and Circassians make peace with their Russian foes.

■ In its adaptation to ballet form, Pushkin's story has undergone certain changes, both as to historical content (the final reconciliation between Tartars, Circassians, and Russians) and in the plot (Didelot adds another female character, Rostislav's Russian fiancée). All sorts of special technical resources were brought into use, including the sight of an eagle swooping down from the skies to carry off a baby from the Circassian camp (Act I), and the ghost of the bethrothed girl (Act III). *The Prisoner of the Caucasus* was one of the last of the twenty ballets created by Didelot at St. Petersburg. The homage he paid to Pushkin by seeking inspiration in one of his literary works was repaid by the great admiration the poet felt for French choreography. Didelot's favourite pupil, Adam Glouchkovsky, revived the ballet in 1827 with his wife, Tatiana, dancing the part of Kzelkia. There were later revivals; the last, which was the work of George Skibine with the Marquis de Cuevas Ballet Company, made use of – and helped to pay for – the fabulously expensive *Prince Goudal*, produced in 1944.

OTHER VERSIONS. 1) Adam Glouchkovsky. St. Petersburg, 1827. 2) Leonid Lavrovsky (scenario by Lavrovsky, N. D. Volkov, and E. S. Zilberstein). Music by Boris Asaviev. Scenery by B. M. Khodazevich. Leningrad, Maly Theater, April 14, 1938. 3) Rostislav Zakharov. Moscow Open Air Theater, August 17,

1938. 4) George Skibine. Music by Aram Khachaturian. Scenery by Dobuzjinsky. Paris, Théâtre de l'Empire, December 4, 1951. Principal dancers: Marjorie Tallchief, George Skibine, Grand Ballet du Marquis de Cuevas.   C.M.C.

THE FAIRY AND THE KNIGHT (La Fée et le Chevalier)
Choreography and scenario by Armand Vestris, Vienna, Court Theater, 1823. Principal dancers: Amalia Brugnoli, Armand Vestris.

■ Little but the title remains of this ballet created by Armand Vestris, the very moderately talented son of the famous Auguste, while he was *maître de ballet* in Vienna. *The Fairy and the Knight*, however, has its place in ballet history because it seems to have been the first appearance in a theater of a technical innovation, introduced by Amalia Brugnoli in the leading part, one that was destined to typify the romantic ballerina and become a permanent and indispensable part of female academic dance: dancing on point. Whether Brugnoli actually invented the device can no longer be determined. It seems to have sprung spontaneously and impersonally from the ballet of the period, and to have been adopted almost simultaneously by Amalia Brugnoli, the Milanese pupil of Carlo Blasis, by the Russian Istomina, and by the French Gosselin, receiving its ultimate blessing from Maria Taglioni in *La Sylphide* (see page 97). Taglioni herself gave Brugnoli the credit for the innovation, writing in her memoirs that in this ballet by the younger Vestris she "created a new style: she performed extraordinary feats dancing on the tips of her toes."   A.A.

THE CORSAIR (Il Corsaro)
Mime-ballet in five acts. Choreography and scenario (after Byron) by Giovanni Galzerani. Music by various composers. Scenery by Alessandro Sanquirico. Milan, Scala, August 16, 1826. Principal dancers: Nicola Molinari (Corrado), Antonia Pallerini (Gulnara), Giuditta Bencini (Medora), Pietro Trigambi (Seyd Pasha).

SYNOPSIS. On an island inhabited by a fierce band of pirates the wedding of the chieftain, Corrado, with Medora is being celebrated. The hero's joy is brief, however. Soon he has to leave his bride in tears and go to sea with his men. The scene shifts to the seraglio of the despotic Seyd Pasha, whose brightest jewel is his favourite, Gulnara. Their dalliance is interrupted by the invasion of the sea robbers, who devastate the palace, sparing only the women; at Corrado's side is Gulnara, who has fallen violently in love with him. Seyd counterattacks, defeating the pirates and imprisoning Corrado. Gulnara stabs the Pasha in his sleep and creeps surreptitiously into Corrado's gloomy cell. The two fly together to the pirates' island, where they land after fighting their way through stormy seas. In the meantime, Medora, believing Corrado dead, has died from sorrow. The

Maria Taglioni in the costume of Zoloë in Le Dieu et la Bayadère, *created by her father Filippo in 1830.*

pirate chief, holding her dead body in his arms, repulses Gulnara and rushes away from his companions to throw himself from the highest cliff. "A scene of horror!"

■ Drawn from Byron's poem of the same name, the fiery, impassioned story of *The Corsair* betrays the romantic sensibility which, in Giovanni Galzerani, was so unexpectedly superimposed on his turgid, neo-classical conception of dance drama, causing this fertile choreographer to be classed – not without justification – as a none too original imitator of Viganò and Gioja. Faithfulness to the choreo-dramatic ideals of his two revered masters was indeed the guiding principle of Galzerani's work, which comprised some eighty ballets (or "mimed actions") between 1815 and 1852. *The Corsair* was considered his masterpiece and survived more than twenty triumphant years and countless revivals at the Scala and elsewhere. In choosing this Byronic theme for his ballet, Galzerani predated by many years the French choreographers Albert and Mazilier (see *Le Corsaire*, page 123).   A.A.

DONA INES DE CASTRO (Ines di Castro)
Mime-ballet in five acts. Choreography and scenario by Antonio Cortesi. Music by Antonio Cortesi and others. Scenery by Alessandro Sanquirico. Turin, Theater Royal, March 20, 1827.

SYNOPSIS. The scene is Lisbon in the fourteenth century. King Alphonso intends his son, Don Pedro, to marry Bianca, Princess of Navarre. The young Prince, however, is already secretly married to Ines de Castro.

Maria Taglioni and her brother Paolo painted by Gabriel Lepaulle in the costumes of the Sylphide and James, characters in the ballet La Sylphide, *choreographed by their father Filippo Taglioni.*

When his secret is revealed, the King, offended and enraged, puts both of them in prison. Donna Bianca and the Spanish Ambassador demand that Ines be condemned to death, but the King now has pity on her. Some courtiers, enemies of Don Pedro, disobey the King's command and seize Ines to do away with her just as Alphonso goes to his son's cell to embrace and pardon him. When a friend, accompanied by Ines's rescued children, brings news of the treacherous act, father and son set off in pursuit of the villains. They surprise them near a cave, their daggers dripping with the blood of Ines, who dies in her husband's arms, mourned by the King. Don Pedro wreaks fearful vengeance on all the assassins.

■ The plot of the ballet, always considered Antonio Cortesi's masterpiece although one of his earlier works, was taken from a traditional Portuguese story often used in literature and the theater. The original source was an episode from *The Chronicle of Peter the First* by Fernão Lopes (1443), elevated to a poem, *Stanzas for the death of Inés de Castro* by Garcia de Resende (1516), and then used as a major literary theme in *A Castro* by Antonio Ferreira (1558); it is referred to again in A. H. de la Motte's tragedy *Ines de Castro*. A source nearer to Cortesi's own time was an opera by Nicola Antonio Zingarelli with a libretto by A. Gasperini, performed in Milan in 1798. Still in the operatic field, and under the same title, *Ines de Castro*, the subject was treated yet again by Giuseppe Persiani and his librettist Salvatore Cammarano (Naples, 1835). In spite of the overwhelmingly romantic subject matter, this ballet cannot be classed unequivocally as a romantic one. It was still hard for an Italian choreographer not to fall between two stools, having partly lost Viganò's synthesis of dance and mime, but not yet being ready to cast off his heritage entirely and create a completely new model capable of comparison with the victorious romantic ballet based on the French academic style of dancing. The separation of the danced episodes from those expressed exclusively in mime had already been noted by contemporary critics. An English commentator who saw *Ines de Castro* in London in 1833, while praising the musicality of the mime passages, deplored the violence of expression in Cortesi's "mute tragedy." In Italy his numerous ballets were very successful, especially *Ines*, which was repeated in various theaters for many years. There was a particularly brilliant revival at La Scala in 1831, with new scenery by Alessandro Sanquirico, and with Antonietta Pallerini, Herberlé, Rouzier, and Giuseppe Bocci as the principal dancers. Among contemporary Italian choreographers (not counting Filippo Taglioni, who worked abroad) Antonio Cortesi ranked as one of the most sympathetic to international romantic ballet, as can be seen from his freely adapted versions of *Sylphide* and *Giselle* (see pages 97 and 105; also *Beatrice of Ghent*, page 115). In modern times the story of Ines has inspired a ballet otherwise unconnected with Cortesi's creation. It was called *Doña Inès de Castro*, choreographed by Ana Ricarda to music by Joaquin Serra and performed by the Marquis de Cuevas Ballet Company on March 1,

Rudolf Nureyev in the part of James in a recent (1977) version of La Sylphide.

1952 at the Cannes Municipal Theater. Sets and costumes were by Celia Hubbard; Rosella Hightower, Ana Ricarda, and George Skibine danced the principal parts.

A.A.

THE SLEEPWALKER or A NEW LORD COMES (La Somnambule *or* L'Arrivée d'un Nouveau Seigneur) Mime-ballet in three acts. Choreography by Jean Pierre Aumer. Scenario by Eugène Scribe. Music by L. J. F. Hérold. Scenery by Pierre Ciceri. Costumes by Lecomte. Paris, Opéra, September 19, 1827. Principal dancers: Ferdinand alias Jean la Brunière (Edmond), Pauline Montessu (Thérèse), Louise Elie (Thérèse's adoptive mother), Amélie Legallois (Gertrude), Louis Montjoie (Saint-Rambert), Louis Mérante (a notary).

SYNOPSIS. The young Thérèse, promised in marriage to Edmond, is inexplicably found in the room of the noble Saint-Rambert, dressed only in her nightgown. Edmond, unconvinced by her protestations of innocence, turns his attentions to their seductive hostess Gertrude. But while Saint-Rambert tries to explain matters, Thérèse exonerates herself by being seen walking fast asleep along the parapet of the mill house. When she awakes her betrothed is waiting for her with open arms.

■ *La Somnambule* inspired two other theatrical works, the musical comedy *La Villageoise Somnambule* (Paris, Théatre des Variéteés, October 1827) and the most famous opera of the time, Bellini's *La Sonnambula* (Milan, Teatro Carcano, March 1831). The eminently romantic story alternated scenes of pastoral prettiness with others of intense emotion and proved to be the perfect subject for a ballet. In the title role (a fiercely contested part, Pauline Montessu, although tiny and not considered a great dramatic actress, showed herself to be not only highly technically proficient, but also capable of great emotional expressiveness. The part later entered the repertory of several great dancers, especially Pauline Leroux in the 1835 revival and Carolina Rosati in 1857. The subject has been used again quite recently in a new ballet by Balanchine (see page 246).   C.M.C.

THE SLEEPING BEAUTY (La Belle au Bois Dormant)
Mime-ballet in three acts. Choreography by Jean Pierre Aumer. Scenario by Eugène Scribe. Music by L. J. F. Hérold. Scenery by Pierre Ciceri. Machinery by Constant. Costumes by Lecomte. Paris, Opéra, April 27, 1829. Principal dancers: Lisa Noblet (Princess Isotta), Louis Montjoie (Prince Gannelore), Amélie Legallois (Arthur), Pauline Montessu (Fairy Nabote), Louise Elie (an old woman), Ferdinand alias Jean la Brunière (Gerard), Maria Taglioni (a Naiad).

SYNOPSIS. Freely adapted by Scribe from Perrault's famous fairy tale, the ballet was commissioned by the Opéra at the same time as *Manon Lescaut*, to follow up the success of *La Somnambule* (*The Sleepwalker*), all having texts by Scribe.

■ The public received *The Sleeping Beauty* with delight, but the critics' verdict was very different. They found it "long, slow, and deadly boring." Only the appearance of Maria (now more often called "Marie") Taglioni in the third act redeemed the ballet in their eyes. She was immensely admired, especially in the "magic dance" that Aumer had composed to show off her special quality of airy lightness. Whatever was thought of the choreography, the scenic design and ingenious machinery were a great success. The music did not come off quite so well (it must have been Hérold's last score for ballet). Its best moments were passages borrowed from Weber's *Oberon* and Rossini's *La Pietra di Paragone* (*The Touchstone*). It was in *Sleeping Beauty* that Nathalie Fitzjames, destined to become one of the brightest stars of romantic ballet, made her debut at the age of ten in the part of Cupid. A ballet of the same name, with choreography by Gardel and music by Carafa, had already been staged at the Opéra in 1825. The most epoch-making version of the story as a ballet was the Petipa–Tchaikovsky–Vsevolozhsky production of 1890 (see *The Sleeping Beauty* page 144).

C.M.C.

OCTAVIUS IN EGYPT (Ottaviano in Egitto)
Grand ballet in six acts. Choreography by Giovanni Galzerani. Music by various composers. Scenery by Alessandro Sanquirico. Costumes by Rosa Carvi. Milan, Scala, September 1, 1829. Principal dancers: Paolo Samengo and Amalia Samengo Brugnoli (primi ballerini), Giuditta Bencini-Molinari (Octavian), Giuseppe Bocci (Eros), Maria Bocci (Charmian), Giovanni Casati (Domitian), Maria Conti (Cleopatra), Antonio Ramacini (Mark Antony), Pietro Trigambi (Octavius Caesar).

SYNOPSIS. *Octavius* belongs to the grandiose and complex school of "mimic action" inspired by history (the best-known model of that type being Gioja's *Caesar in Egypt*, see page 84) and legend (*Francesca da Rimini*, 1825; *Buondelmonte*, 1827; *Bajazet*, 1829), and was written during the same years as Galzerani's masterpiece, *The Corsair*, taken from Byron's poem of that name (see page 93).

■ The ballet, which was very successful, was presented together with Bellini's *Bianca e Ferdinando* at Milan, the first performance of either work. *Octavius* – not to be confused with *Octavia in Egypt* also by Galzerani – was privileged in having in its cast the two leading dancers Samengo and Brugnoli, who performed purely virtuoso *divertissements* such as were often inserted into the main action in those days. Brugnoli, it will be remembered, is officially recognized as the inventor of dancing on point, as is acknowledged by Taglioni herself in her memoirs (see *The Fairy and the Knight*, page 93).   C.M.C

THE GOD AND THE BAYADERE (Le Dieu et la Bayadère)
Ballet-opera in two acts. Choreography of the danced episodes by Filippo Taglioni. Music by Daniel Auber. Scenario by Eugène Scribe. Paris, Opéra, October 13, 1830. Principal dancers: Maria Taglioni (Zoloë), Lise Noblet (Fatma), Adolphe Nourrit, tenor (the Unknown), Laure Cinti-Damoreau, soprano (Ninka), M. Levasseur (Olifur).

SYNOPSIS. The story begins with the arrival of a group of *bayaderes* (Hindu dancing girls) who sing and dance to delight the powerful judge Olifur. Various intrigues thwart the love of one of them, Zoloë, for the Unknown; to get him she competes with Fatma, another *bayadere*. Finally Zoloë is condemned to burn at the stake, but the Unknown reveals himself as the god Brahma and carries the *bayadere* with him to paradise.

■ The ballet-opera, a typically French fusion of the two forms, was popular at the Paris Opéra until far into the nineteenth century. *The God and the Bayadere*, to music by Auber, was inspired by one of Goethe's ballads.

This nineteenth-century engraving shows a scene from La Sylphide, *in which James follows the sylph into a dense wood.*

Eugène Scribe, a leading figure in the history of ballet, wrote the scenario of the danced part, which was fairly long and of artistic merit. In the ballet scenes of this opera, the choreographer, Filippo Taglioni, one of the most important exponents of dance in the romantic period, was already experimenting with the ideas and style that were to characterize the creations of his prime, or even romantic, ballet as a whole: an exotic, fairy-tale subject (in other examples often pseudo-medieval or pastoral); strange love affairs with supernatural beings; and so on, in the theatrical, musical, and literary taste of the period. Often these fantasies were expressed through a female *corps de ballet* portraying some imaginary state of existence (the *bayaderes*, though still human, were soon to be succeeded by sylphides, peris, wilis, and enchanted swans), and, above all, in the idealization of the ballerina, floating on the tips of her toes, a figure of ethereal lyricism. *The God and the Bayadere* was a personal triumph for Maria Taglioni, as were all the ballets designed by Filippo Taglioni to display his daughter's luminous artistic personality.   A.A.

THE SYLPHIDE (La Sylphide)
Ballet in two acts. Choreography by Filippo Taglioni.

Music by Jean Schneitzhoeffer. Scenario by Adolphe Nourrit. Scenery by Pierre Ciceri. Costumes by Eugène Lami. Paris, Opéra, March 12, 1832. Principal dancers: Maria Taglioni (the Sylphide), Joseph Mazilier (James), Lise Noblet (Effie), Mme. Elie (Madge), M. Elie (Gurn).

SYNOPSIS. The story is set in a Scottish village and the nearby wood. Act I: James is sleeping in an armchair by the fireside at dawn on the day of his wedding to Effie. Near him a winged spirit, a Sylphide, appears, gazes at him with love, and finally wakes him with a kiss. James tries to grasp the vision that has long been disturbing his dreams, but she vanishes, dancing. Effie, her mother, and some neighbours arrive to prepare the wedding; with them is Gurn, Effie's disappointed suitor. Madge, an old witch roughly sent away by James and succoured by Effie and Gurn, prophesies that the girl, who is not loved by her betrothed, will marry Gurn. Left alone, James sees the Sylphide again. This time, before fleeing, she confesses her love for him and invites him to follow her. Gurn has witnessed the scene and runs to call Effie, so that she shall see her betrothed's infidelity. Her ethereal rival is cowering in the big chair, but James hides her with his cloak. When Gurn whips it away the

Maria Taglioni, once more dressed as the Sylphide, from a nineteenth-century English print.

armchair appears to be empty. During the festivities the Sylphide moves among the dancers, visible only to James who pursues her in vain. Finally she plucks from his hand the wedding ring intended for Effie and flies to the forest. James rushes from the feast, leaving Effie in tears. Gurn then leads the dismayed guests in search of the vanished bridegroom. Act II: the witch Madge is in a dark cave, weaving magic spells by night, surrounded by her demon familiars. Into her cauldron she dips a filmy scarf. The scene is now a dense forest through which sylphs lightly flit. James enters followed by the Sylphide, with whom he is now desperately in love, even though she continually evades him, although showing tender feelings towards him. Meanwhile, Gurn, Effie, and the others have given up the hopeless search. James returns still baffled, and the witch makes her appearance to give him the scarf with which he can hold his elusive love. When the Sylphide approaches him again, he succeeds by trickery in encircling her with the magic scarf. Immediately her wings fall to the ground and she dies in the arms of her despairing lover. A procession of sylphs descends; they pick up their dead sister and carry her to the treetops. James, overcome, falls to the ground. In the distance we hear sounds from the marriage feast of Gurn and Effie, while the witch exults over her revenge.

■ Romantic ballet, already foreshadowed in the style and subject matter of many ballets, especially in France during the second and third decades of the nineteenth century, found its first complete realization in Filippo Taglioni's *The Sylphide*, in the leading character of its story, and in the perfect incarnation of that character in the person of its original interpreter, Maria Taglioni. Her stage personality may be said to have been made for the part of the Sylphide. The scenario, suggested to Taglioni by the tenor Adolphe Nourrit, was inspired, though much altered, by the novel *Trilby ou le Lutin d'Arguail*, written in 1822 by Charles-Emmanuel Nodier. It was a rich source of theatrically romantic fantasies centered round the hopeless and fatal love between a human being and a supernatural creature. In Taglioni's creation the theme acquires additional poetic and psychological overtones in the ambiguous personality of James, oscillating between his normal love for Effie and the obsessive fascination for an enchanted romance, the pursuit of a fatally alluring and elusive dream destined to a tragic end. Although the dramatic gist of the ballet takes place inside James's head, it is the Sylphide who is its artistic and choreographic heart. To express this inhumanly romantic ideal of womanhood, Maria Taglioni adopted the technico-stylistic device of dancing on point. Although she was not its inventor, it was through her dancing in *The Sylphide* that its use and significance were definitively established. As Alberto Testa wrote in his *Discorso sulla Danza e sul Balletto*, "In using her points Taglioni came into her own and reached the sublime. Others, perhaps technically more accomplished than she, may have used the method to achieve a dazzling virtuosity, but with Taglioni it became a means of expression through which she delineated and brought to life a whole personality. The extraordinary *aplombs* of which we hear so much from the critics and journalists of the period were, in truth, so many punctuation marks in the choreography, instants in which the fragile creature seemed to hang in the air.... Then again that tenuous attachment to the ground, supported only on the point of the toe, in an evanescent arabesque from which threads could be drawn to infinity, became the exact expression of a character, a sentiment, a situation." The *corps de ballet* in the second act, representing insubstantial feminine beings clad in moonlit tutus, was the prototype of the *ballet blanc*, a choreographic convention destined to survive and develop until almost our own time, although the mechanisms that enabled them to fly belong to an entirely obsolete theatrical taste. On the other hand, the romantic, white, semitransparent tutu reaching to just below the knee, designed by Lami for *La Sylphide*, has become a permanent type of ballet costume, often accompanied by the headdress Taglioni favoured. Filippo Taglioni's masterpiece was revived many times by its creator, always starring his daughter Maria – at London's Covent Garden Theatre on July 26, 1832, at the Theater Royal of Berlin in the same year, at the Bolshoi Theater in St. Petersburg on September 6, 1837, and at the Milan Scala on May 29, 1841. It was reproduced by Paolo Taglioni at the New York Park Theater on May 22, 1839, but after a last revival at the Paris Opéra in 1860 the original version of the ballet was abandoned until the present time, which has seen one or two attempts at a reconstruction (see below). *The Sylphide* which has been passed down to us is not the result of unbroken tradition and is, in essence, a different ballet, created by Auguste Bournonville at the Theater Royal in Copenhagen in 1836 and afterwards included in the repertory of the Royal Danish Ballet. Bournonville, who had seen Taglioni's ballet in Paris two years earlier, recreated it for Denmark's principal theater, where he was ballet master and chief dancer. He based it on the same scenario (although he used Herman Løvenskjold's music in place of Schneitzhoeffer's), but designed it to suit his own choreographic style, which was characterized by a crystalline clarity, a noble expressiveness, elegance, and an absolute technical perfectionism applied to every step and position. Various versions of the work have entered the repertory of the world's major ballet companies and been performed by the most famous dancers of our century. Today *The Sylphide* is an established ballet "classic."

OTHER VERSIONS. 1) Antoine Titus (after F. Taglioni). St. Petersburg, Bolshoi Theater, May 28, 1835. 2) August Bournonville. Music by Herman Løvenskjold. Scenery by Christian F. Christensen. Copenhagen, Theater Royal, November 28, 1836. Danced by Lucile Grahn, Auguste Bournonville. 3) Antonio Cortesi (after F. Taglioni). Genoa, Carlo Felice Theater, spring 1837; Florence, Pergola, autumn 1837; Venice, La Fenice Theater, Carnival, 1838; Turin, Regio Theater, Carnival, 1839; Milan, Scala, January 27, 1841. Scenery by B. Cavallotti and D. Menozzi. Principal dancers: Fanny Cerrito and Francesco Merante. 4) Federico Massini. Music by B. Borio and G. Garignani. Milan, Teatro della Cannobiana, 1860. 5) Marius Petipa (freely adapted from F. Taglioni). Music by Schneitzhoeffer and R. Drigo. Scenery by H. Levot and M. I. Bocharov. St. Petersburg, Maryinsky Theater, January 19, 1892. 6) Victor Gsovsky (after F. Taglioni, reconstructed by Boris Kochno and Roland Petit). Music by Schneitzhoeffer. Scenery by A. Serebriakoff. Costumes by C. Bérard. Paris, Théâtre des Champs Elysées, June 15, 1946. Danced by Nina Virubova and Roland Petit, Ballet des Champs Elysées. 7) Harald Lander (after A. Bournonville). Music by Løvenskjold. Scenery and costumes by Bernard Daydé. Paris, Théâtre de l'Empire, December 9, 1953. Danced by Rosella Hightower and Serge Golovine, Grand Ballet du Marquis de Cuevas; later at the Scala, Milan, January 18, 1962. Danced by Carla Fracci and Mario Pistoni; later in San Antonio, Texas, November 11, 1964. Music by Edgar Cosma after Løvenskjold. Danced by Toni Lander and Royes Fernandez, American Ballet Theater, and New York State Theater, May 20, 1967. Danced by Carla Fracci and Erik Bruhn, American Ballet Theater. 8) Elsa Marianne von Rosen (after Bournonville, from the reconstruction by Ellen Price de Plane). Scenery by A. Fridericia, Sweden, Växiö Theater, February 2, 1960. Danced by E. M. von Rosen, Scandinavian Ballet; later at London's Sadler's Wells Theatre, July 20, 1960. Danced by E. M. von Rosen and Flemming Flindt, Ballet Rambert; later in Washington, October 3, 1969. Danced by Margot Fonteyn, National Ballet of Washington. 9) Erik Bruhn (after A. Bournonville). Scenery by R. Prévost, Toronto, O'Keefe Center, December 31, 1964. Danced by Lois Smith and Erik Bruhn, National Ballet

Fanny Elssler dancing the cachuca *in* The Devil to Pay *created by Jean Coralli.*

of Canada; later in Rome, Opera House, March 24, 1966. Danced by Carla Fracci and Rudolf Nureyev; later at the Theater Royal, Stockholm, June 3, 1968. Danced by G. Andersson and N. Haggbom; later at the New York State Theater, July 7, 1971. Danced by Carla Fracci and Ted Kivitt, American Ballet Theater. 10) Hans Brenaa and Flemming Flindt (after A. Bournonville). Scenery by S. Frandsen. Costumes by H. Bloch. Copenhagen, Theater Royal, August 15, 1967. Royal Danish Ballet. 11) Pierre Lacotte (after F. Taglioni, literal reconstruction). Music by J. Schneitzhoeffer (interspersed with fragments from *L'Ombre* by Ludwig Maurer). Scenery by Marie-Claire Musson (after P. Ciceri). Costumes by Michel Fresnay (after E. Lami). French Television, January 1, 1972. Danced by Ghislaine Thesmar, Michaël Denard, Ballet de l'Opéra de Paris; later at the Paris Opéra, June 7, 1972. Danced by Noella Pontois, Cyril Atanassoff.   A.A.

THE REVOLT IN THE SERAGLIO (*La Révolte au Sérail*)
Fanciful ballet in three acts and four scenes. Choreography by Filippo Taglioni. Music by Théodore Labarre. Scenery by Ciceri, Léger, Feuchères, Despléchin. Costumes by Lormier, Duponchel. Paris, Opéra, December 4, 1833. Principal dancers: Louis Montjoie (Maometto, Sultan of Granada), Joseph Mazilier (Ismael), Maria Taglioni (Zulma), François Simon (Myssauf, Head Eunuch), Pauline Leroux (Zeir, a page), Louise Elie (Mina), Amélie Legallois (Female

Spirit), Jean-Baptiste Desplaces (an Imam).

SYNOPSIS. Ismael, on his return from Granada, where he has defeated the Spanish, finds that his beloved, Zulma, has become the favourite of the Sultan, Maometto. When the Sultan offers to grant him any wish he may have, Ismael asks that the slaves should be freed. Maometto accepts and signs an edict, but then repents his decision and revokes it in order to retain Zulma. She, braving his anger, confesses that she loves another. Zulma incites the slaves to rebellion, and by means of a talisman conjures up magic weapons. Having established their camp, the women are at drill when they hear that the Sultan is prepared to negotiate. Maometto pretends to grant their demand for liberty, but by a trick disarms the women and imprisons them. Zulma, to save Ismael's life, is forced to accept the Sultan as her husband. Ismael, outraged, throws the magic amulet Zulma had given him to the ground. She quickly picks it up and brandishes it in the air. With a clap of thunder the scene changes to the Garden of Life, where the Spirit of Women commands the Sultan to free the two lovers and treat all the women in his kingdom with justice.

■ The original title was *La Révolte des Femmes*, changed at the last moment, just before the curtain went up, to *Révolte au Sérail*. There was not even time to correct the printed program. It was the first and only ballet to deal with the emancipation of women and caused quite a stir in England. The cost of this spectacular ballet was enormous, matched, however, by its triumphant success, which was even greater than that of *Robert le Diable*. It remained in the repertory of the Opéra from 1833 to 1840, with a total of eighty-one performances; above all it was a triumph for Maria Taglioni. A certain weakness in the choreography did not, in this case, matter very much, since the public flocked to see the prima ballerina and Perrot dance a *pas de deux* together in the first act. Perrot was compared to Vestris and treated as if he played the lead, much to the annoyance of Taglioni, who remonstrated vociferously, suggesting that it was due to a hired *claque* in the audience. The leader of the *claque* replied that it had been "impossible to control the public's enthusiasm or stop a spontaneous ovation in favour of Perrot" (Ivor Guest). In November 1835, the part of Zulma was taken over with great success by Pauline Leroux when Taglioni left the boards for a certain time, complaining of a mysterious injury to her knee (*mal au genou*, which later became a proverbial saying): in reality the dancer was expecting her first child. Nine years later, on December 14, 1844, at the Drury Lane Theatre in London, *The Revolt in the Seraglio* was the scene of an appalling tragedy. During the performance the organza dress of a young and promising English dancer, Clara Webster, suddenly caught fire. She was horribly burnt and died after two days of agony. C.M.C.

THE ISLE OF PIRATES (*L'Île des Pirates*)
Mime-ballet in four acts. Choreography by Louis Henry, music by Carlini, Gide (Rossini, Beethoven).

Scenario by Adolphe Nourrit and L. Henry. Sets by Feuchères, Desplechin, Séchan (first and second acts), Philastre, Cambon (third and fourth acts). Costumes by Lami. Paris, Opéra, August 12, 1835. Principal dancers: Louis Montjoie (Akbar), Amélie Legallois (Marquise Isabella), Fanny Elssler (Matilde), Joseph Mazilier (Octavio), Teresa Elssler (Rosalie).

SYNOPSIS. The pirate Akbar, posing as a rich foreigner, is courting Matilde, but he is unmasked by Octavio, in love with the same lady. The pirate takes flight, carrying Matilde and her sister with him. Octavio follows them and fights a duel with Akbar for possession of Matilde. There is a quarrel among the pirates and finally, when a ship arrives to set the prisoners free, Akbar dies by his own hand.

■ It appears that this ballet, with which Henry made his debut at the Opéra, was his 127th production. The plot was not very interesting and the public received it coldly, in spite of the well-known dancers taking part. Henry, although French by birth, had lived in Italy for many years, which did not impress Opéra circles very favourably. Nor was he popular with the *corps de ballet*, who resented his iron discipline. Disappointed with the Paris reception of his *Isle of Pirates*, he returned to Naples, where he resided and worked for the San Carlo Theater. He was still living there when an epidemic of cholera broke out at the end of 1836. Contracting the infection from his daughter, he died a few days after her. In spite of its initial failure, *The Isle of Pirates* continued to play to large houses at the Opéra, chiefly, it seems, because of its spectacular scenery, which was very varied and a novelty to the Parisian audience. C.M.C.

THE DEVIL ON TWO STICKS (*Le Diable Boiteux*)
Mime-ballet in three acts. Choreography by Jean Coralli. Music by Casimir Gide. Scenario by Burat de Gurgy and Jean Coralli. Scenery and costumes by Feuchères, Séchan, Diéterle, Philastre, and Cambon. Paris, Opéra, June 1, 1836. Principal dancers: Fanny Elssler (Florinda), Joseph Mazilier (Cleophas), Jean Coralli (the Barber), Mlles. Legallois and Leroux, Mme. Barrez, Montjoie, Chatillon, etc.

SYNOPSIS. A complicated fantastic comedy set among alchemists' laboratories, drawingrooms, gardens, squares, and theaters in an imaginary Spain. Its chief character is the young student Cleophas, who is accompanied everywhere by a strange imp, Asmodeus, lame but possessing extraordinary magic powers, whom he once freed from an alchemist's alembic. In gratitude the demon has put himself at his liberator's service. They have various adventures in the course of which we meet, among others, Donna Dorothea and her brother Captain Bellaspada, the noble Don Gil, the young girl Pasquita, and, above all, Florinda, who ends a feast by dancing a sensational *cachuca*. The final scene shows the union of Cleophas and Pasquita amid feasting and dancing, while the little lame devil vanishes, loaded with gratitude from his young friend.

Maria Taglioni and Joseph Mazilier in La Fille du Danube, *a ballet by Filippo Taglioni.*

■ This was one of the first creations of any importance by the Frenchman (originally Italian) Jean Coralli Perracini, one of the greatest choreographers of the nineteenth century, who was ballet master at the Paris Opéra from 1831 to 1850. The story was taken from a book by La Sage and was typical of the sort of ballet most appreciated by French audiences at that time: fantastic and involved situations, numerous scenes, duels, transvestism, gallantry, love affairs, magic, sumptuous feasts, ballets within ballets, lovely dancers, and grotesque figures, all in an atmosphere of merriment and theatrical diversion, culminating in the obligatory grand finale. Only a talented choreographer of fertile invention like Coralli could make a successful ballet out of such a hodgepodge of ill-assorted components. His style of choreography, according to his successor Saint-Léon, was "essentially French, that is to say delicate, refined, and poetic." Nevertheless, in *Le Diable Boiteux* Coralli's Italian heritage is clearly in evidence, with its brilliance, sharp characterization, and technical virtuosity. Not for nothing was it the vehicle of Fanny Elssler's first big success. Théophile Gautier described Elssler as "the pagan ballerina," in contrast to the spiritual "Christian" Taglioni, referring especially to her *tacqueté* style (consisting of very rapid, tiny steps, *pas de bourrée*, etc. on point) and gift for *demi-caractère*, i.e., the introduction of characteristic national dances into the context of academic dance. Such was the *cachuca*, a

Spanish dance performed by the character Florinda in the last scene of the second act of *The Devil on Two Sticks*, which won Elssler instant fame and typified the ballerina's exuberant temperament throughout her career. Indeed, Fanny Elssler made it her party piece, often dancing it as a separate number, so that her name became as closely associated with it as was Taglioni's with *The Sylphide*. In pictures of the period the two rivals were nearly always portrayed in the costumes of the respective roles (as in the celebrated statuettes by Jean-Auguste Barre). Nevertheless, in the London revival of *The Devil on Two Sticks* in December 1836, Pauline Duvernay, the star of Drury Lane, danced the *cachuca* with such success that she too adopted it as her specialty   A.A.

THE DAUGHTER OF THE DANUBE (*La Fille du Danube*)

Ballet in two acts and four scenes. Choreography by Filippo Taglioni. Music by Adolphe Adam. Scenario by Eugène Desmarès. Scenery by Ciceri, Despléchin, Diéterle, Feuchères, Séchan. Paris, Opéra, September 21, 1836. Principal dancers: Maria Taglioni (Fleur-de-champ, Daughter of the Danube), Joseph Mazilier (Rudolph), Amélie Legallois (the Nymph of the Danube), Louis Montjoie (Baron Willibald), Pauline Leroux (the Girl), Germain Quériau (the Officer).

SYNOPSIS. The Daughter of the Danube is a foundling discovered as a baby on the bank of the river, carried to safety and entrusted to the care of the Nymph of the Danube. The girl, renamed Fleur-de-champ, grows up to fall in love with Rudolph, squire of the Baron Willibald. The Baron, however, chooses the foundling out of all the girls in the village to be his wife. Fleur-de-champ refuses him, throws her bouquet of flowers as a token of love to Rudolph, then leaps out of the window and is drowned in the Danube. The young squire goes out of his mind from grief and to cure him the Baron proposes that he should marry a girl who greatly resembles Fleur-de-champ. Rudolph will have none of it, and he too throws himself into the river. There he passes the test to which he has been subjected and recognizes Fleur-de-champ thanks to the nosegay of flowers. The Nymph of the Danube then brings the two lovers back to life.

■ Desmarès wrote the book of the ballet in 1835, but its production was delayed because of Taglioni's pregnancy (she gave birth to a baby girl, Eugénie-Marie-Edwige, on March 30, 1836). The public impatiently awaited the famous ballerina's return to the stage, fearing she might have lost her quality of ethereal lightness. Instead, tackling her new role, she returned before the Parisian audience in a performance of *The Sylphide*, the personification of evanescence. It was on August 10 and proved to be an evening of triumph. Now her new role, the Daughter of the Danube, would be an undoubted success. The critic Janin – as unquestioning, as devoted an admirer of Taglioni as was Gautier at that time of Fanny Elssler – called this ballet the sequel to *The Sylphide*, and praised it to the skies. Not all the

Maria Taglioni in her father's ballet La Gitana *set to music by Schmidt and Auber.*

Fanny Elssler dancing the cracovienne *from the ballet* The Gypsy *choreographed by Joseph Mazilier to music by F. Bénoist, A. Thomas, and T. Marliani.*

critics held the same opinion: the majority of them judged it severely, especially in regard to the choreography, though they all agreed in admiring the galop in the first act, the music for which was by the young Adam, who was commissioned by Desmarès, his former school friend. Three years earlier Adam had composed the music for the ballet in *Faust*, a score which he later reutilized in part for *Giselle*. *The Daughter of the Danube* remained in the repertory of the Opéra from 1836 to 1844 and was danced on thirty-six occasions in all. In 1837 it was danced in London, where it met with enormous success from the critics as well as the general public. In the same year the production went to St. Petersburg on the first Russian tour undertaken by the Taglionis, father and daughter. C.M.C.

THE GYPSY (La Gitana)

Ballet in a prologue, three acts, and five scenes. Choreography and scenario by Filippo Taglioni. Music by Schmidt and Auber. St. Petersburg, Bolshoi Theater, November 23, 1838. Principal dancers: Maria Taglioni (Lauretta), N. O. Goltz (Ivan). Frédéric, Shelikhov I, Artemiev, Spiridinov, Fleury, Reutova, Teleshova II, Bertrand, Samoilova, Shiriaeva, Apollonskja.

SYNOPSIS. The prologue shows the kidnapping by gypsies of Lauretta, daughter of the Duke of Medina-Celi, on their arrival at his castle in Madrid. The first and second acts are set in Russia. Ivan, the son of the Governor of the city of Novgorod, falls in love with a young gypsy girl he has met at the oriental fair. Curious as to her origin, he follows the girl — unknown to her — to the encampment, and eventually asks to join the gypsies himself rather than lose her. The two confess their mutual love. In the last act the scene moves back to Madrid. During a feast at the Duke's castle, the counterfeit gypsy Ivan is taken by surprise in the gardens. He is soon followed by the girl, who has fled from her gypsy master. It is the very place in which she was kidnapped years ago and she suddenly recalls the events of the prologue and remembers her identity. There are great rejoicings at the return of the Duke's lost daughter and for her wedding to Ivan, whose noble lineage is now revealed.

■ The ballet of *La Gitana* was produced by Filippo Taglioni during his first visit to Russia with his daughter Maria. The tour has remained famous: from the first day onwards hundreds of people stood for hours at the stage door just to see "the divine being" pass by. Immediately after the first performance, Taglioni's dancing had become legendary in Russia too. There was hardly anything that was not named after her, from the cut of her clothes to her hair style, from desserts to coffee and chef's specialties. "Fanaticism for the dancer during her successive tours of the Czarist capital reached unprecedented heights. She was loaded with fabulous jewels by princes and grand-dukes. A circle of balletomanes obtained a pair of her ballet shoes and reverently ate them at a sumptuous banquet ..." (L. Rossi, *History of the Ballet*). In the following year *La Gitana* was repeated in London with equally great success. As *The Times* reported, it was one of the most beautiful ballets ever produced, and no adjective was adequate enough to do justice to Taglioni's incomparable art. In 1839, one year after the first night of *Gitana*, Mazilier made his first venture into choreography by countering it with his *Gypsy*, created for Taglioni's great rival, Fanny Elssler. Taglioni's lover, Eugène Desmarès, wrote to the director of the theatrical journal *"Vert-Vert"* that *Gypsy* was a pale copy of *La Gitana* and that the *cracovienne* danced by Elssler which had made such a sensation was simply a *pas* already danced by Taglioni in London during the previous summer. The rivalry between the two ballerinas — or rather between their respective admirers — broke out more fiercely than ever. C.M.C.

THE GYPSY *(La Gipsy)*

Mime-ballet in three acts and five scenes. Choreography by Joseph Mazilier. Music by F. Bénoist, A. Thomas, T. Marliani. Scenario by H. Vernoy de Saint-Georges and Mazilier. Scenery by Philastre and Cambon. Costumes by Paul Lormier. Paris, Opéra, January 28, 1839. Principal dancers: Joseph Mazilier (Stenio), Fanny Elssler (Sara Campbell), Thérèse Elssler (Mab), Montjoie (Lord Campbell).

SYNOPSIS. Act I: the Royalist Lord Campbell celebrates the accession to the throne of Charles II with a hunting party. His vain and foolish nephew Narcissus offers to watch over Campbell's only daughter, Sara. Meanwhile Stenio, a Roundhead fugitive, enters and asks some gypsies encamped in the neighbourhood to let him take refuge in their caravan, disguised as a gypsy. When the pursuing soldiers have gone, a ferocious boar charges at Sara, wounding her in the arm. The cowardly Narcissus has fled but she is saved by Stenio. He refuses any reward and, not wishing to drink the health of King Charles, he leaves again. Trousse-Diable, head of the gypsy band, insults Lord Campbell, kidnaps the little Sara, and flees with her. Act II: Sara, who has grown up among the gypsies, is now eighteen. Narcissus reappears and is robbed by the gypsies. Trousse-Diable takes a miniature from him. Sara falls in love with Stenio, who has returned and revealed to her the secret of his noble birth, thus rousing the jealousy of Mab, Queen of the Gypsies, who is also enamoured of Stenio. Mab is, however, forced to celebrate their union, which is marked by a grand ball at which Lord Campbell and Narcissus are present. Sara, to whom Mab has given the stolen miniature in revenge, is imprisoned for theft. Act III: pronounced guilty by Lord Campbell, Sara attempts to kill herself with a dagger. The gesture reveals the scar on her arm, enabling her father to recognize her. At the ball given in her honour, Stenio reappears, still in love with

Sara. Mab enters and tells the irate peer of his daughter's love for the rebel. When Stenio repulses the Gypsy Queen, she kills him with a pistol shot. The despairing Sara, in true gypsy revenge, stabs Mab to death.

■ Drawn from Cervantes's *Novelas Exemplares*, the first ballet by Mazilier (originally Guilio Mazarini) was created in opposition to *La Gitana* by F. Taglioni, which had opened in St. Petersburg the previous year. Each act of *The Gypsy* had a different composer, one of them being Ambroise Thomas. Fanny Elssler, dressed in frogged jacket and booted and spurred, danced the famous *pas de la cracovienne*, destined to be a popular success comparable to that of her *cachuca* in *Le Diable Boiteux*. The whole ballet earned her and her sister Thérèse a high reputation as dramatic actresses. The London production opened with equally dazzling success on June 24, 1839. G.S.

Maria Taglioni and Antonio Guerra in the ballet L'Ombre. *The famous ballerina is captured, in this coloured lithograph by J. Bouvier, dancing the* pas de fleurs, *in which she gave proof of her extraordinary lightness.*

Costume of Giselle, a part first danced by Carlotta Grisi in the ballet of that name.

Costume for Albrecht, designed for Lucien Petipa in the ballet Giselle.

THE TARANTULA *(La Tarentule)*

Mime-ballet in two acts and three scenes. Choreography by Jean Coralli. Music by Casimir Gide. Scenario by Eugène Scribe and Jean Coralli. Scenery by Léon Feuchères, Charles Séchan, Jules Diéterle, Edouard Despléchin. Costumes by Paul Lormier. Paris, Opéra, June 24, 1839. Principal dancers: Fanny Elssler (Lauretta), Joseph Mazilier (Luigi), Jean-Baptiste Barrez (Dr. Omeopatica), Caroline Forster (Clorinde).

SYNOPSIS. The love between Luigi and Lauretta is opposed by her mother on the grounds that the young man is not rich enough. The mother sees things very differently, however, when Clorinde, a great lady, gives Luigi a generous reward for saving her from being ambushed by bandits. The wedding feast is in preparation when Luigi is bitten by a tarantula. Dr. Omeopatica, who has been called in to treat him, asks for the hand of Lauretta in exchange for his services. In despair, she consents; but when the wedding eve arrives she pretends that she, too, has been bitten by a tarantula, and this time, of course, the doctor's treatment has no effect and Lauretta is carried away in a funeral procession. Meanwhile Luigi has gone to find his benefactress who turns out to be the wife of the doctor, whom he thought had been killed by bandits. Discovering that the wedding between Lauretta and the homeopath has not yet taken place, the couple are reunited and all ends happily.

■ *The Tarantula* is a typical example of a romantic ballet enlivened by elements of folklore, and in which the down-to-earth is harnessed with the airy-fairy. The mixture was boldly conceived, especially by Coralli, to exploit the versatile talents of the great dancers of his day. *The Tarantula*, together with *Le Diable Boiteux* (also designed for Elssler, in 1836), *Giselle* (in collaboration with Perrot, 1841), and *La Péri*, 1843 (both the two last for Carlotta Grisi), was among the major works created by Coralli when he was chief choreographer at the Opéra in Paris from 1831 to 1846. The ballet was repeated in London in 1843, but with a slightly revised scenario, as it was not considered suitable to show a funeral on the stage. For Elssler *The Tarantula* offered another opportunity of underlining her rivalry with the "divine Maria." The critics averred that if Taglioni was "pure poetry," Elssler was "intelligence in action." It was also a personal success for Caroline Forster, who inspired the novelist Taxile Delord to insert the following peculiar conversation in his book *La Lune de Miel*: "I prefer la Forster. Do you know her?" "Who is she?" "A ballet dancer at the Opéra, an Englishwoman who knows how to dance. It's extraordinary." Revived in St. Petersburg ten years later (December 1849), *The Tarantula* was danced by Elssler, Prinkhunova, Richard, and Perrot. The ballet's text was drawn from an old Italian tale; its score by Gide was the last work of the composer's career, except for the music for *Ozaï* in 1847.   C.M.C.

THE SHADE (L'Ombre)

Ballet in three acts. Choreography by Filippo Taglioni. Music by Maurer. Sets by Fedorov, Serkov, Shenian, and Roller. Costumes by Mathieu. St. Petersburg, Bolshoi Theater, November 22, 1839. Principal dancer: Maria Taglioni.

SYNOPSIS. The shade of the title is the ghost of a murdered woman. Her lover remembers her and thinks of her constantly. The young woman, who died by inhaling the poisoned scent from a bouquet of flowers, dances as if suspended in the air, hardly touching the ground.

■ *The Shade*, a typical romantic *ballet blanc* of inspired fantasy, was one of Taglioni's most astounding creations. It was designed for the farewell performance of the 1839 St. Petersburg season, and was repeated there, danced once more by Taglioni, before her final departure from Russia. It had become a tradition that during the last week of the season Taglioni should perform one of her major successes each evening in turn. On the evening devoted to *L'Ombre* the enthusiasm rose to delirium. The dancer was called before the curtain thirty times. She bade farewell to the audience in seven languages (she spoke them all well), weeping with emotion. The *corps de ballet* had filled her dressing room with flowers until it looked like a conservatory. "It took three years," wrote Levinson, "even to begin to forget her. The sale of her furniture came as the epilogue to her triumph. Buyers contended eagerly for every memento of the Sylphide. With tears in their eyes, her most fanatical admirers sent the bidding sky-high for a pair of those slippers she had worn like wings." That simile became famous when Victor Hugo dedicated a book to Taglioni with the words *"à vos pieds, à vos ailes"* ("to your feet, to your wings"). The particular appeal of this ballet lay in the dissolving transformations and phantasmagoric effects of mist and waterfall. In the first act – as can be seen in the interesting series of lithographs depicting nine scenes from *The Shade* – there was the celebrated mirror scene in which reflections were so arranged as to project onto the glass apparitions that mimicked the dancers' action. The highlight of the choreography, however, was the *pas de l'Ombre* that was later introduced into other ballets, as it was in *Ondine*, one of Cerrito's greatest roles (London, 1843). When first shown in Paris in June 1844, Maria Taglioni still danced the leading part, but this time it was her farewell appearance at the Opéra (there had already been one the year before, on March 29, 1843, to mark the end of her undisputed reign of twenty-one years there). This time it was to be final, and Alfred de Musset commemorated the occasion with a nostalgic verse: *"Si vous ne voulez plus danser / Si vous ne faites que passer / Sur ce grand théâtre si sombre / Ne courez pas après votre ombre / Et tâchez de nous la laisser"* ("If you will dance no more, if you only pass by on this great somber stage, do not pursue your shadow, but leave it behind for us"). In contrast, Théophile Gautier, for the first time (he was to regret it later), wrote an adverse criticism of the dancer who had once been his great idol, comparing her to a graceful bird whose wings had got wet. The motive behind this inexplicable change lay – as the critic himself admitted – in his new passion for the fiery personality of Elssler, whom, however, he soon abandoned to devote himself definitively to Carlotta Grisi. Under the Italian title *L'Ombra*, the ballet finally reached the Scala at Milan in time for the 1846 carnival season. It was now in two parts and four scenes, with the same choreography by Filippo Taglioni, but to music by Viviani; the leading parts were danced by Maria Taglioni and Effisio Catte.　　　C.M.C.

GISELLE

Ballet in two acts. Choreography by Jean Coralli and Jules Perrot. Music by Adolphe Adam. Scenario by Jules Henri Vernoy di Saint-Georges and Théophile Gautier. Sets by Pierre Ciceri. Costumes by Paul Lormier. Paris, Opéra, June 28, 1841. Principal dancers: Carlotta Grisi (Giselle), Lucien Petipa (Albrecht), Adèle Dumilâtre (Myrtha), M. Simon (Hilarion).

SYNOPSIS. Act I: in a medieval Rhineland village the gamekeeper Hilarion loves Giselle and is furiously jealous of Loys, whose rough peasant guise conceals the identity of the Duke Albrecht. The latter now comes to meet Giselle after hiding his sword and sending his equerry away. The girl comes out of her house and accepts the courtship of Albrecht-Loys, who swears eternal love to console her for the answer "he loves me not" pronounced by the petals she has plucked from a daisy. Hilarion enters and declares his love for Giselle. Refused by her and driven off by Albrecht, he threatens revenge. The peasants dance to celebrate the wine harvest and Giselle joins in with enthusiasm in spite of her mother's fears and warning story of girls that have died after dancing on their wedding eve and become wilis, white phantoms who haunt the woods by moonlight. The festival is interrupted to greet the Prince of Kurland and his daughter Bathilde, who are returning with their attendants from the hunt. Giselle dances for the Princess, who gives her a necklace and then leaves with the others so that the rustic festivities can continue. When Albrecht arrives, Hilarion unmasks him, showing the sword he has found, then sounds his horn to recall the noble huntsmen and Princess Bathilde, who is betrothed to Albrecht. With feigned detachment, the young Duke ignores the presence of Giselle and offers his arm to Bathilde, indicating that his only wish was to divert himself with the country dances. Giselle, crushed and heartbroken at the deception, goes mad and expresses the anguish of her disoriented mind by insensate dancing to the consternation of all those present. She ends by grasping her lover's sword and, plunging it in her heart, falls dead in her mother's arms in front of the astonished and finally despairing Albrecht. Act II: at midnight, by Giselle's grave among the trees, Hilarion wanders, mortally afraid. Myrtha, ghostly Queen of the Wilis, appears and with a twig scatters the petals of every white flower in the forest, thus summoning her court of female phantoms. The wilis stream in to welcome their new companion, Giselle,

The night scene from Giselle *performed at the Bolshoi Theater in Moscow in the version dating back to 1944 and still in*

who appears, veiled, above her tomb and bows to the Queen before joining in their dance. On hearing the approach of human footsteps the wilis vanish. It is the mourning Albrecht, come to lay lilies on the grave of the girl he has learned to love too late. Suddenly he sees the hovering white image of Giselle and follows the hallucination into the wood. Hilarion reenters and is immediately surrounded by wilis who force him into a frenzied dance until he drops dead from exhaustion. When Albrecht returns, Myrtha condemns him to the same fate, which awaits all those who fall into the pitiless power of the wilis. Giselle, however, protects him as he clings to the cross, and implores the frigid Queen for mercy, but in vain. Although condemned to dance until exhaustion takes his life, Albrecht is sustained by Giselle's desperate love until the first light of dawn dispels the ghostly band. Giselle, after turning her lover's face towards light and life, follows her companions into the realm of shadows.

■ The absolute masterpiece of romantic dance theater, a marvellous synthesis of its every quality of style, technique, and dramatic feeling, *Giselle* still remains an indispensable keywork in ballet repertory all over the world. The ballet was born in 1841 from the collabora-

tion of some of the major talents of contemporary choreography. Its original idea came from Théophile Gautier, critic, writer, and poet, who played a formative role in defining the ideas behind French romantic ballet. Literally ravished by the art and personality of Carlotta Grisi, he discovered a theme fitting for her in a popular legend recorded in Heine's *Germany*, and with the help of Jules Henri Vernoy de Saint-Georges, a playwright with authority in the field of musical theater, fashioned it into a ballet scenario. Jean Coralli, chief choreographer at the Paris Opéra, created the choreography as a whole, but allowed Grisi's friend, Jules Perrot, to design the prima ballerina's solo dances. In fact the collaboration went further than that, even though it was only much later that, thanks to Serge Lifar, Perrot was recognized as part-author of the ballet. The music was commissioned from Adolphe Adam, whose score closely followed the choreography and emotional content of the ballet. Not least among those who helped to inspire this work was the protagonist herself, Carlotta Grisi, a young Italian dancer discovered by Perrot and immediately recognized as a bright new star, uniting in her person the contrasting artistic gifts of Taglioni and Elssler. At her side, in the role of Albrecht, the brilliant Lucien Petipa established his position as the leading male dancer

use. The choreography was recreated by L. Lavrovsky.

of the Opéra. Finally, Pierre Ciceri, a consummate professional of romantic stage design, perfectly represented in his "realism in fantasy" a certain theatrical taste of his epoch. *Giselle*'s most direct predecessor was obviously Filippo Taglioni's *The Sylphide* (see page 97). One similarity, more clearly defined in *Giselle*, is their construction on two successive planes, expressing two complementary aspects of the romantic sensibility. The first act is on the realistic level, though admittedly one of sentimental and fairy-tale medieval rusticity; the second deals with the supernatural, the other-worldly myth of magic symbolism. The plot thus provides a dramatic framework of high inspirational value and perfect structural balance to support that which is essential to the ballet and endows its vaguely sentimental atmosphere with artistic unity: the dance design or choreography. And the choreography of *Giselle* is romantic ballet at the highest point of its maturity. The academic style, already well established and codified, is rigidly adhered to where it concerns purity of line and the balanced composition of steps and figures, but never manifests itself in mere virtuosity. The dancing is always intimately linked to the dramatic development, to the point where the whole of the action, including mime passages, is expressed in dance, with no self-contained "numbers," so that an essential continuity is maintained throughout the narrative, dramatic, and lyrical episodes, and even the *divertissements* of the ballet. Also interesting is the challenge, represented by the part of Albrecht, to the complete dominance of the ballerina in the French romantic tradition (the role's importance has been underlined in more recent times by Serge Lifar's interpretation in 1932). The central role, however, remains the complex one of Giselle, ranging from laughing candour, through growing dread, to the tragedy of madness and death, and finally to a fragile spirituality still sorrowing for a lost love. Each phase is paralleled on the technico-stylistic level in which the brilliant variations of the "earthly" character and the restrained yet incisive mime of the first act are followed by the "aerial" effects and pure lyricism of the *ballet blanc* in the second. Nearly all the greatest ballerinas from Carlotta Grisi onwards have found in Giselle one of their most demanding and rewarding parts. It will suffice to list among them Lucile Grahn (1843), Fanny Cerrito (1843), Fanny Elssler (1843), Amalia Ferraris (1859), Carolina Rosati (1862), Ekaterina Vazem (1878), Emma Bessone (1887), Olga Preobrajenska (1899), Carlotta Zambelli (1901), Anna Pavlova (1903), Tamara Karsavina (1910), Olga Spessivtzeva (1924),

In the role of Aglaë, Maria Taglioni dances with a faun, played by Turchetto. From a contemporary print.

Galina Ulanova (1932), Alicia Markova (1934), Margot Fonteyn (1937), Tamara Toumanova (1939), Yvette Chauviré (1944), Svetlana Beriosova (1956), Carla Fracci (1959), Ekaterina Maximova (1960), Natalia Makarova (1961), Natalia Bessmertnova (1965), Merle Park (1967), Gelsey Kirkland (1975), Elisabetta Terabust (1976). The ballet has not passed down through an unbroken tradition. From time to time it has undergone phases of reconstruction that have purified it of accumulated accretions and established its choreography more firmly. The tradition started with the productions which Jules Perrot, emphasizing his own creative imprint, supervised in London as early as 1842, and in St. Petersburg in 1856. In the Russian capital he collaborated with Marius Petipa, who in 1884 made his own reconstruction of the ballet. This version became the model for later revivals in Russia and for Fokine's production for the *Ballets Russes* in Paris in 1910. Finally, Nicholas Sergeyev, working for the Paris Opéra in 1924, reproduced as faithfully as possible Petipa's version as danced at the old Maryinsky Theater in St. Petersburg. This was the rendition on which, more or less, all the innumerable subsequent productions of *Giselle* in Europe and America were based.

OTHER VERSIONS. 1) Jules Perrot and André Deshayes (from the original). London, Her Majesty's Theatre, March 12, 1842. Danced by Carlotta Grisi and Jules Perrot. 2) Antonio Cortesi. Music by N. Bajetti. Milan, Scala, January 17, 1843. Danced by Fanny Cerrito and Francesco Merante. 3) Marius Petipa (after Perrot). St. Petersburg, Maryinsky Theater, February 5, 1884. Danced by Maria N. Gorshenkova. 4) Michael Fokine (from the original). Paris, Opéra, June 18, 1910. Danced by Tamara Karsavina and Vaslav Nijinsky,

Diaghilev's *Ballets Russes*. 5) Nicholas Sergeyev (after Petipa). Paris, Opéra, November 26, 1924. Danced by Olga Spessivtzeva and Albert Aveline. 6) Serge Lifar (after Sergeyev). Paris, Opéra, March 11, 1932. Danced by Olga Spessivtzeva and Serge Lifar.   A.A.

THE MUSIC. It is said that the music for *Giselle* was composed in a single week. That confirms the composer's reputation for speed (in less than thirty years he completed, among other works, forty-one *opéras-comiques* and thirteen ballets), but does not diminish the value of the score. Both public and critics who attended the first night on June 28, 1841, at the Opéra, greeted *Giselle* as a triumph. Nor was the composer of the music forgotten. Two weeks later a whole page of *La France Musicale* was devoted to it. Escudier, the journal's director, put his name to a long and circumstantial musical analysis of the score, which he praised especially for its "elegance, the freshness and variety of the melodies, the vigour and novelty of the harmonic combinations, and the vivacity that pervades the musical texture from start to finish." The characteristic that most distinguishes this from the average ballet score of the period is its absolute originality (the only borrowings are eight bars taken from a song by Loïse Puget and another three from the Huntsmen's Chorus in Weber's *Euryanthe*). *Giselle* was also the first balletic work to introduce a leitmotiv as narrative device. Adam's exquisite professionalism illuminates every passage, lending added strength to the rich flow of his melody. Brilliant, when not heartrending (and influenced by Cherubini's symphonic sturdiness, as Escudier had already noted), the first part of the score as it approaches the dramatic climax – the mad scene – turns to a music of tragic density which ultimately dissolves into the lunar, evocative accompaniment of the second act. As often happened at that time, the score underwent alterations. For example, when Adam sold it to the publisher Meissonier it still lacked the short suite later interpolated and known as the "Dance of the Grape-pickers" which was written by Johann Friedrich Burgmüller, composer of, among other things, *La Péri*, another of Carlotta Grisi's triumphs.   A.F.

AGLAË or LOVE'S PUPIL *(Aglaë or L'Elève d'Amour)*
Ballet-divertissement in one act. Choreography and scenario by Filippo Taglioni. Music by Johann Friedrich Keller. London, Her Majesty's Theatre, July 8, 1841. Principal dancers: Maria Taglioni (Aglaë), Mathieu (faun), Albert (the Youth).

SYNOPSIS. Step by step a little Cupid is teaching Aglaë the art of dancing, but the pupil soon surpasses her small instructor and with grace and skill completes the gestures outlined by him. A faun, who has been watching the lesson, falls in love with Aglaë and inveigles her into a virtuoso *pas de deux*. But the girl loves another and the jealous faun tries to destroy their happiness. A group of girls immobilizes him by swiftly enlacing him with nooses of creeper.

This is romantic ballet of the lighter type. The slight theme was artistically realized, without scenic display but with elegant choreography flawlessly performed. Beaumont quotes a passage maintaining that Taglioni had never danced more brilliantly and that her main motive was to prove herself more than a rival to Fanny Cerrito, whose style was much more vivacious. It seems as if she had suddenly perceived the threat to her supremacy and, while she danced with her accustomed grace, she also engaged in a veritable *tour de force* with a lively energy equal to that of her young rival. It is interesting to observe how outward appearance was made to illustrate the type of character. For instance, the journals suggested that as soon as the audience saw the faun's black beard they knew he would not get the girl, whereas the appearance of the clean-shaven youth in his white tunic left them in no doubt that he would be the lucky suitor. Taglioni revived *Aglaë* in Russia during her tour there in 1842.   C.M.C.

NAPOLI or THE FISHERMAN AND HIS BRIDE
(Napoli or Fiskeren og hans Brud)
Romantic ballet in three acts. Choreography and scenario by August Bournonville. Music by Holger Simon Paulli, Edvard Helsted, Niels Wilhelm Gade, and Christian Lumbye. Scenery by Christensen. Copenhagen, Theater Royal, March 29, 1842. Royal Danish Ballet. Principal dancers: Caroline Fjeldsted (Teresina), August Bournonville (Gennaro), Stromboe (Golfo).

SYNOPSIS. Act I: a little square by the bay of Santa Lucia at Naples. Courted in vain by Giacomo and Peppo, pedlars of spaghetti and lemonade, the charming Teresina loves only Gennaro the fisherman. On his return from fishing, he denies rumours of his infidelity and gives her an engagement ring. To be alone they put out to sea, but a dreadful storm breaks out and Teresina is swept out of the boat by a huge wave. Gennaro comes safe to shore but is accused by the widow Veronica of letting her daughter drown. Comforted, however, by Brother Ambrogio, who gives him a picture of the Madonna, he embarks once more to search for his promised bride. Act II: the Blue Grotto in the Isle of Capri. Teresina, who has been rescued by two nereids is conducted into the presence of Golfo, the spirit of the sea. The sea god falls in love with her. When she refuses him he turns her into a nereid, wiping out all memory of her mortal life. Genarro arrives at the grotto in search of his bride, but she fails to recognize him. However, the Madonna's picture restores Teresina's memory and human form and soothes the wrath of Golfo, who heaps her with gifts. Act III: the Sanctuary of Monte Vergine near Naples. Gennaro reappears with Teresina and her mother among the pilgrims making their way to the Madonna of the Mount. The young man is accused of witchcraft for having brought a dead girl back to life. Brother Ambrogio then explains that the miracle could only have been performed through the power of the Holy Virgin, moved by Gennaro's fidelity. The wedding follows, concluding with a spirited tarantella.

Ib Andersen in the third act of Napoli, *the ballet by August Bournonville, at the Theater Royal, Copenhagen, 1975.*

Carlotta Grisi dancing the pas de songe *from the first act of* La Péri, *one of that ballet's most successful moments.*

■ *Napoli* was Bournonville's masterpiece. He was also Denmark's favourite dancer and the first to play the part of Gennaro. A faithful reflection of Neapolitan folklore, the ballet was inspired by his travels in Italy and can be considered the prototype of the Danish *ballet d'action* based more on real life than on supernatural fantasy. Though character dances and academic technique are perfectly blended, they are never thought of as an end in themselves, but always subordinated to a warm and poetic Mediterranean fervour. One recalls Bournonville's words, "I have danced above all to express the joy of living and to radiate happiness." Produced only one year after *Giselle*, *Napoli* is nearly always danced to the same choreography as it was 137 years ago, and has now been performed over 800 times. The *petits rats* of the Royal Danish Ballet habitually make their first appearance on the stage throwing flowers at Gennaro and Teresina's wedding cart. Sometimes the third act is given as a separate item, containing as it does the liveliest dances and variations, among them the celebrated tarantella.

Carlotta Grisi in La Péri *depicted in her famous "cascade," landing in the arms of Lucien Petipa, who took the part of Achmet.*

OTHER VERSIONS. 1) Harold Lander (condensed into one act). Sets and costumes by Osbert Lancaster. London, Festival Hall, August 30, 1954. Danced by Toni Lander, Oleg Briansky, London's Festival Ballet. 2) Erik Bruhn (*divertissement* made from the third act only). London, Covent Garden, May 3, 1962. Danced by Sibley, Park, Seymour, Parkinson, Lawrence, Usher, Bennett, the Royal Ballet. 3) Elsa Marianne von Rosen (original version in three acts). Gotheborg, Stora Theater, 1971. Danced by Evdokimova, Beaumont.

G.S.

THE BEAUTY OF GHENT (*La Jolie Fille de Gand*)
Ballet in three acts. Choreography by Albert. Music by Adolphe Adam. Scenario by J. H. Vernoy de Saint-Georges and Albert. Scenery by Pierre Luc Ciceri, Philastre, and Cambon, Paris, Opéra, June 22, 1842. Principal dancers: Albert Decombe (Marquis de San Lucar), Joseph Mazilier (Cesarius), Eugène Coralli (Zefiro, dancing master), Georges Elie (Bustamente, friend of San Lucar), Lucien Petipa (Bénédict), Germain Quériau (Count Leonardo), Louise Fitzjames (Diana, prima ballerina of the Fenice Theater), Carlotta Grisi (Beatrice, daughter of Cesarius), Maria Jacob (Julia), Adèle Dumilâtre (Agnese).

SYNOPSIS. On the eve of her wedding to Bénédict, Beatrice is courted by the Marquis of San Lucar. After becoming his mistress she lives in his splendid palace in Venice, where her father comes to beg her, in vain, to return home. Meanwhile the Marquis has been persuaded by a friend to play cards with him. He gambles away not only all he possesses but also Beatrice, whom he has wagered against his adversary's entire fortune. When she learns the truth, Beatrice flees, appalled, and goes back to Ghent, where she finds her sister about to marry Bénédict and her father dead from sorrow. Torn with remorse, she throws herself from a cliff. At that point she wakes up in her bedroom and realizes that it has all been a dream. Her wedding to Bénédict takes place after all.

■ This mime-ballet – derived from the play *Victorine, or The Night brings Counsel*, performed in Paris in 1831 – was the most extravagant entertainment ever produced at the Opéra. However, the expenses were amply covered during the six years that the ballet remained in the repertory. It was Albert's greatest creative success. In consenting to do the choreography, he, for the first time, abandoned his well-known principle of never designing a ballet unless he himself had written the story (which was why he had refused a commission, offered a few years earlier, of composing the choreography of *La Somnambule*, which was then passed on to Aumer). Originally, the title part of *La Jolie Fille de Gand* was to have been created by Pauline Leroux. Illness forced her to give it up and Carlotta Grisi stepped into her shoes, revealing a dramatic talent hitherto unsuspected. The Dance of Diana the Huntress in the ball scene won her an ovation. Indeed, the whole cast of that first production was exceptional. In 1843, still in Paris, the title role was taken by Adèle Dumilâtre who, in 1848, chose the same role for her farewell performance. It was on the same occasion that Louis Mérante made his debut. Tatiana Smirnova, who in 1844 danced a solo from *La Sylphide* which had been interpolated in Albert's ballet, was the first Russian prima ballerina to appear before the Parisian public. Her style was directly derived from Taglioni, who had a school in St. Petersburg. *La Jolie Fille de Gand* was first produced in London in 1844 when it was performed at Drury Lane Theatre under the title *The Beauty of Ghent* with Albert and Louise Fleury as principal dancers.

C.M.C.

ALMA or THE DAUGHTER OF FIRE (*Alma* or *La Fille de Feu*)
Ballet in four scenes. Choreography by Fanny Cerrito and Jules Perrot. Music by Giovanni Costa. Scenario by

A. J. J. Deshayes. Scenery by W. Grieve. London, Her Majesty's Theatre, June 23, 1842. Principal dancers: Jules Perrot (Belphegor), M. Desplaces (Emazor), Fanny Cerrito (Alma).

SYNOPSIS. Alma is a girl fashioned from rock by the demon Belphegor and destined to enchant all men. Her life will last as long as she succeeds in resisting the passions she herself evokes. If she falls in love, she will turn to stone. The spirit of evil plans to tempt her to her destruction. Transported to France during a festival, Alma is courted by the young Emazor and consents to stay in his apartments provided he does not claim her love. Belphegor, alarmed, begs her to leave the city. To free herself from her admirers, the girl gives each one of them an appointment in the same place at the same time. When they have all assembled and are about to cross swords, Emazor hastens in to announce that he has seen Alma with her lover. The rivals rush off to find her but are stopped by a curtain of flame that only Emazor succeeds in passing through without fear. The action moves to Granada where Alma, now a prisoner, is offered as a prize at a tourney. Lara and Emazor fight a duel and the latter is revealed as a Moroccan Prince exiled from Granada. Winner of the tourney, he puts himself at the head of his troops, defeats the Spaniards, and is proclaimed King. Immediately he offers to share the throne with Alma. Once more Belphegor appears, hoping to save his creation from danger, but Alma, choosing love above life, accepts Emazor and his throne. Suddenly the earth trembles and she turns to stone. The despairing Emazor destroys the crown he cannot share with his beloved.

■ *Alma* was one of the faithful standbys of the heyday of romantic ballet. For the first time the name of Perrot (the famous dancer, known as *"l'Aérien"* or "the male Taglioni") appeared on the posters as choreographer. It was the *pas de fascination* from Alma, arranged and danced by Perrot, that won him the post of chief choreographer at Her Majesty's Theatre in London. The ballet, created for London, was later rearranged by Perrot on several occasions: for Paris, Milan, and St. Petersburg. For Fanny Cerrito, too, *Alma* was a turning point. In it the ballerina (as she had already done in Paolo Taglioni's *Gitana* of 1839) "veered away from the repertory of *ballets blancs* towards compositions more in keeping with her personality" (Rossi). This new vein aroused enormous enthusiasm: the *pas de trois* from *Alma*, in particular, engendered a veritable fanaticism dubbed "Cerritomania." *The Times* wrote that the components of this ballet had been put together as if to strain each participant to his or her utmost capacity to produce a work perfect in all its parts.   C.M.C.

THE PERI (La Péri)
Fantasy ballet in two acts. Choreography by Jean Coralli. Music by Burgmüller. Scenario by Théophile Gautier and Jean Coralli. Sets (Act I) by Séchan, Diéterle, and Despléchin; (Act II) Philastre and Cambon. Costumes by Mirilhat and Lormier. Paris,

Opéra, July 17, 1843. Principal dancers: Carlotta Grisi (the Peri, then Leila), Lucien Petipa (Achmet), J. B. Barret (Roucem), Coralli (slave), Delphine Marquet (Nourmahal, favourite).

SYNOPSIS. Prince Achmet, weary of the pleasures of the harem, orders opium and dreams that he finds himself in the garden of the peris, legendary inhabitants of the oriental paradise. Here he meets their Queen, who gives him a talisman. He has only to kiss it for her to reappear before him. The Peri, however, does not relish the thought that she is loved only through her magic, so enters the body of a runaway slave (Leila) who was killed while seeking refuge in the palace. The Prince finds Leila so extraordinarily like the Peri that he falls in love with her, arousing the jealousy of his former favourite, Nourmahal. The Pasha, the owner of the slave, thinking she is still alive, claims her back. When Achmet refuses, the Pasha has him thrown into prison. There the Peri, appearing in her own form, puts him to the test by pleading with him in vain to renounce Leila. The Pasha condemns him to be thrown from a high window, but the prison walls dissolve and we see Achmet ascending to paradise hand in hand with the Peri-Leila.

■ In the summer of 1842 the Opéra acquired a new director, Pillet, who was little interested in ballet, being infatuated with the singer Rosina Stolz. In his view the chief importance of the season lay in producing successful operas. Carlotta Grisi's triumph, however, forced him to include ballets in his program. *La Péri* enjoyed a success little less than that of *Giselle* and had the good fortune to enrich the contempory imagination with new figures of romance and faerie which appealed to its taste for passionate southern and oriental romanticism. At the same time, new technical elements were being added to ballet through the so-called Spanish steps and the combination of Elssler's *tacqueté* style with the *balloné* style of Taglioni. The two best-known numbers from *La Péri* are the Dream Dance (Act I) and the Dance of the Bee (Act II). In writing of the first, Théophile Gautier, after having recorded Grisi's triumph, describes the leap, a high fall compared to a preciptious cascade and "destined to become as famous as that of Niagara ... with which the Peri falls from the clouds into the arms of her lover, not only a perilous *tour de force*, but one so full of grace as to suggest a fluttering feather rather than a human being dropping from a platform." It appears that in performing this daring feat she risked her life every night. The Drury Lane audience, fearing she might come to harm through some imperfection of equipment, advised her to discontinue the risky procedure. One cynical spectator, however, defied their delicate feelings by attending every performance because "sooner or later one of them was bound to prove fatal, and he would not miss it for the world." *The Peri* opened in London in September 1843, under the direction of Jean Coralli's son, Eugène. In the following year, 1844, the ballet was produced in St. Petersburg by Fréderic, with Andreyanova in the principal part. In 1846 it was revived at the Paris Opéra in an altered

A nineteenth-century lithograph of Fanny Cerrito wearing the costume of the vivandière *in the eponymous ballet.*

version without the second act, although that had included one of the best numbers in the ballet, the Dance of the Bee, which had been devised by Théophile Gautier, based on a sensuous dance he had seen in Egypt. Introduced in a *ballet blanc*, it showed Grisi at her delicate and graceful best portraying the Peri's attempts to drive away a bee by waving her scarf.

C.M.C.

ESMERALDA

Ballet in three acts. Choreography and scenario by Jules Perrot. Music by Cesare Pugni. Sets by William Grieve, costumes by Mme. Copère. Machinery by D. Sloman. London, Her Majesty's Theatre, March 9, 1844. Principal dancers: Carlotta Grisi (Esmeralda), Jules Perrot (Pierre Gringoire), Arthur Saint-Léon (Febo), Louis François Gosselin (Claude Frollo), Antoine Coulon (Quasimodo), Adelaide Frassi (Fleur-de-Lys), Mme. Copère (Aloisa).

SYNOPSIS. The poet Gringoire is captured by robbers and taken to their lair, the "Court of Miracles." There he is condemned to be hanged for the crime of having no money in his pockets. He will be reprieved only if some woman among those present will consent to marry him. The young Esmeralda, moved to pity, consents to the

bargain, but Claude Frollo, enamoured of her, plans to possess her that very night. The gang who have taken them prisoner together with Quasimodo are foiled by the arrival of the officer Febo. Love between him and Esmeralda springs up immediately, although he is engaged to marry Fleur-de-Lys. Esmeralda interrupts the wedding ceremony by dancing in with her husband, Gringoire. Forgetting all prudence, Esmeralda and Febo run towards each other and dance together to the despair of the bride and the fury of the guests. Leaving the crowd, they declare their mutual love. Frollo, who has been watching unseen, throws himself on Febo and strikes him to the ground. Esmeralda is accused of his murder and condemned to death, but just as the gallows are being erected Febo appears, Frollo's blow not having proved mortal after all. Reunited with Esmeralda, he shows the crowd who is the real villian.

■ The story is that of *Notre Dame de Paris* by Victor Hugo, somewhat altered and without the final catastrophe. The ballet was reasonably successful and Carlotta Grisi was pronounced the perfect personification of Esmeralda, combining the innocent gaiety of Cerrito, the sparkling coquetry of Elssler, and the ineffable poetry of Taglioni. A year after the London opening, Grisi introduced two of the variations from *Esmeralda* into Mazilier's *Diable à Quatre*. Another great Esmeralda, especially for her superlative dramatic interpretation, was Fanny Elssler, prima ballerina of the ballet's first night in St. Petersburg on December 21, 1848. Her partners were Didier (Quasimodo), Perrot (Gringoire), and Goltz (Frollo). Elssler chose the part again for her farewell performance at Moscow's Bolshoi Theater in March 1851. Beaumont tells an anecdote passed on to him by Prince Engalytchev, who was an eyewitness on that occasion: so many bouquets – over three hundred – were thrown on the stage at the end of the first act that she used them in place of a sofa in the second. In this final act she used to write her lover's name, Febo, on a wall with chalk, instead of composing it with letters according to the established tradition. But that evening the ballerina wrote in Cyrillic characters "Mockba" (Moscow), which set off an ovation that never seemed to end. *Esmeralda* followed the same vein of historical romantic dance that had given rise to *La Sylphide* (see page 97) and *Giselle* (see page 105). It was almost half a century before that vein was exhausted, for it lasted into the Second Empire up to the death of Saint-Léon, one of the leading figures in this last phase of romantic ballet. In spite of the great interpretative opportunities it offered, *Esmeralda* made little impression in France, Italy, and England. On the other hand, when it reached Russia it was immediately included in the repertory. Among the distinguished ballerinas who danced the name part were, besides Fanny Elssler, Marie S. Petipa, Carolina Rosati, Nadejda Bogdanova, Claudina Cucchi, Eugenia Sokolova, Virginia Zucchi, and Matilda Kschessinskaya.

OTHER VERSIONS. 1) Arthur Saint-Léon (after Perrot). Berlin, Theater Royal, January 19, 1847. 2) Hippolyte Monplaisir (after Perrot). New York, Park

Theater, September 18, 1847. 3) Domenico Ronzani (after Perrot). Scenery by Filippo Peroni and Luigi Vimercati. Milan, Scala Theater, January 31, 1854. Principal dancers: Caroline Pochini, Effisio Catte, Domenico Rossi. 4) Ferdinando Pratesi (after Perrot). Milan, Canobbiana Theater, spring 1865. 5) Marius Petipa (after Perrot). St. Petersburg, Bolshoi Theater, December 17, 1886; then at the Maryinsky Theater, November 21, 1899. 6) Agrippina Vaganova (after Perrot). Scenery by V. Khodasevich. Leningrad, Kirov Theater, April 3, 1935. 7) Nicholas Beriozoff (from the original). Scenery by Nicola Benois. London, Festival Hall, July 15, 1954. Principal dancers: Nathalie Krassovska, John Gilpin, Anton Dolin, London Festival Ballet.   C.M.C.

THE MUSIC. Cesare Pugni was born in Genoa on May 31, 1802, but studied at Milan from 1815 to 1822 with two distinguished musicians of the time, Antonio Rollo and Bonifazio Asioli. Pugni made his debut as a composer at the Scala in 1826 with his opera *Elerz e Zulmida*. He became a cymbalist in the orchestra of the same theater and, on the death of Vincenzo Lavigna, was appointed its musical director. Afterwards he moved to Paris (where he became director of the Paganini Institute). There he met the great choreographers of the time and started an artistic collaboration that was to be one of the most fertile in the history of ballet. In 1851 he took up residence in St. Petersburg to become official composer of ballet music at the Maryinsky Theater. He died in the Russian city on January 26, 1870. Pugni is known above all for his enormous output of musical works, including more than three hundred ballets, a dozen operas, over forty masses, other polyphonic works, and a few symphonies, among which was the *Sinfonia a canone* so highly praised by Meyerbeer. This extremely prolific composer was very popular with the public, his ballets being so easy to listen to and understand. He also found no difficulty in adapting his music to suit all sorts of choreographic needs and many different performers. His versatility and facility in composition undoubtedly helped him in his international career, even when they set limits to his artistic achievement. His time in Paris with Perrot was marked by an extraordinarily intense activity even more evident when he reached Her Majesty's Theatre in London. There Pugni presented some of the most renowned ballets of the nineteenth century, such as *Esmeralda* and the *Pas de Quatre* (in 1844 and 1845 respectively) which still find their place in some modern repertories. He also worked with Saint-Léon, Paolo Taglioni, Marius Petipa, and some of the greatest dancers of the century. Some of his ballets already well known in western Europe were transferred to St. Petersburg, but he also composed some new ballet music for that city.   A.F.

LA VIVANDIÈRE

Mime-ballet in one act. Choreography and scenario by Arthur Saint-Léon. Music by Cesare Pugni. Scenery by Despléchin, Séchan, and Dièterle. London, Her Majesty's Theatre, May 23, 1844. Principal dancers:

Maria Taglioni, Carlotta Grisi, Lucile Grahn, and Fanny Cerrito in the Pas de Quatre *by Jules Perrot.*

Fanny Cerrito (Kathi), Quérian (Bibermann), Saint-Léon (Hans), Berthier (Mayor), Fusch (Baron).

SYNOPSIS. In a little Hungarian village the inhabitants are celebrating the return of the soldiers from the war, and of Kathi, who has just given up her place as vivandière in the Baron of Grindberg's regiment. Hans, son of the innkeeper, is in love with Kathi and asks his father to consent to their marriage. He is opposed in this by two married men, the Mayor and the Baron, who are after the girl themselves. They convince the innkeeper that Kathi is no fit match for his son because of her poverty. While successfuly getting rid of Hans, the trick has made their wives suspicious. Mayor and Baron protest that the ladies have no cause for jealousy and receive from them a locket and a ring respectively as tokens of reconciliation. Meanwhile Kathi has wheedled a promise from the innkeeper that he will consent to the marriage if she can obtain a dowery. One after the other the two husbands pay court to her and by leading them on she manages to get hold of their wives' gifts. In exchange for their return she demands the dowry she needs. Thus tricked, the Mayor and Baron agree to her conditions, Hans is cured of his jealousy, and all ends happily with the wedding.

■ Although attributed to Saint-Léon, the choreography was in fact by Fanny Cerrito. With the exception of Maria-Taglioni and her ballet *Papillon*, she was the only woman choreographer before Mariquita, the inventive creator of *Gemma*. *La Vivandière* owed its success above all to four still renowned dances designed for Cerrito and her partner Saint-Léon: *Pas de la vivandière*, *Pas de six*, *Pas de l'inconstance*, but especially the redowa, a gay and at one time popular Bohemian dance in three-quarter time, very like a mazurka, which came into fashion as a ballroom dance in France towards the middle of the eighteenth century.

G.S.

BEATRICE OF GHENT or A DREAM (*Beatrice di Gand* or *Un Sogno*)

Mime-ballet in three parts. Choreography and scenario (after J. H. Vernoy de Saint-Georges) by Antonio Cortesi. Music by Adolphe Adam and others. Scenery by A. Merlo, G. Fontana, and G. Boccaccio. Milan, Scala Theater, March 7, 1845. Principal dancers: Fanny Elssler (Beatrice), Maria A. Fuoco (Agnese), Adèle Monplaisir (Giulia), Marguerite Wuthier (Diana), Gaspare Pratesi (San Lucar), Effisio Catte (Zeffiro), Ippolito Monplaisir (Benedetto).

SYNOPSIS. Beatrice, promised in marriage to Benedetto, is courted by the Marquis of San Lucar. Having absconded with him, she finds herself in a palace and later in a theater, where her father comes to curse her. There the Marquis, gaming with dice, uses her as a stake and loses. Already in the hands of the winner, Beatrice becomes frantic. Then she awakes in her own bedroom. It has all been a warning dream. The girl has come to her senses, and when the Marquis enters to claim her in reality she repulses him and leaves to marry her good Benedetto.

■ Antonio Cortesi, a choreographer inescapably linked with the now dying Italian tradition of danced drama in the classical pantomime style (see *Dona Ines de Castro*, page 93), nevertheless displayed a certain, if purely external, adherence to the international romantic school of choreography in his free rendering on the Italian stage of several ballets that were undeniably romantic. Thus, after reviving *La Sylphide* and *Giselle* (1843), he put on *Beatrice of Ghent*, its plot only slightly altered from the one used by Jules Henry Vernoy de Saint-Georges for Albert's *La Jolie Fille de Gand* (see page 111). The style of dancing, however, was typical of Cortesi: it was less a ballet than a succession of mimed dances, in which the expressive naturalness of the "Italian" dancers interpreted the action, in contrast to the academic roles of the ballerinas trained in the "French methods." One of the latter, although relatively more "expressive" than her rivals in the part, was the great star Fanny Elssler, adored in Milan as elsewhere until the end of 1848, when she became the object of anti-Austrian demonstrations. Like all Cortesi's ballets, *Beatrice* was frequently performed in various Italian theaters during the author's lifetime, after which it was abandoned forever. A.A.

PAS DE QUATRE

Ballet divertissement. Choreography by Jules Perrot. Music by Cesare Pugni. London, Her Majesty's Theatre, July 12, 1845. Danced by Maria Taglioni, Fanny Cerrito, Lucile Grahn, and Carlotta Grisi.

SYNOPSIS. A composition of pure dance, devoid of plot, for four "romantic ballerinas" clad in long, white tutus. It begins with a static tableau of the four dancers, who then draw apart with mutual curtseys of homage. Each in turn executes a solo in front of the others and then stands still again (in the original production the order was: variation by Grahn, variation by Grisi, waltz by Cerrito, and lastly a solo by Taglioni). Finally they all join in a *pas de quatre* that ends in the famous configuration for posterity in A. Chalon's well-known lithograph in which the ballerina who is "first among equals" is being crowned by her three partners.

■ Maria Taglioni, already a legend when *Pas de Quatre* opened in London, was crowned with a wreath of white roses by her colleague Fanny Cerrito during the public ovation that followed the short ballet which so clearly celebrated the elitist idea of the romantic prima ballerina. The project of presenting a combined performance by the four leading female dancers of the time (excluding a fifth, Fanny Elssler, Taglioni's implacable rival) was the inspiration of Benjamin Lumley, director of Her Majesty's Theatre. He brought it to fruition with the help of the choreographer, Jules Perrot. One can imagine what delicate tact was needed to maintain cooperation between four such famous and touchy stars: Maria Taglioni, the legendary Sylphide (see page 98) and archetype of the romantic ballerina; Carlotta Grisi, the expressive and versatile Giselle (see page 106); Lucile Grahn, elegant personification of the pure Bournonville style; Fanny Cerrito, darling of the London public for her personal charm no less than for her radiant academic accomplishment. Apart from displaying the talents of these dancers, each of whom was allotted a part exactly suited to her style and technique, Jules Perrot's choreography was recognized as

Margrete Schanne, Alicia Markova, Yvette Chauviré, and Carla Fracci in a revival of Pas de Quatre *at Nervi, 1957.*

the pure essence of romantic dance. It made imaginative use of the French academic technique, now codified under universally accepted terms, and blended it with the Italian influence derived from Carlo Blasis's theoretical work. Perrot revived the *divertissement* at the Scala, Milan, in 1846 (with Taglioni, Carolina Rosati, Sofia Fuoco, and Carolina Vente), and in London again in 1847 (Taglioni, Grisi, Cerrito, and Carolina Rosati). In 1936 Keith Lester pioneered what was to be a new series of revivals featuring all the most famous contemporary ballerinas.

OTHER VERSIONS. 1) Keith Lester (after Perrot). Music by Pugni, reorchestrated by L. Lucas. Markova-Dolin Ballet, 1936. Danced by Molly Lake, Diana Gould, Kathleen Crofton, Prudence Hyman. 2) Anton Dolin (after Perrot). New York, Majestic Theater, February 16, 1941. Danced by Nana Gollner, Katia Sergava, Alicia Alonso, Nina Stroganova; New York again, 1948. Danced by Alicia Markova, Mia Slavenska, Nathalie Krassovska, Alexandra Danilova; then Monte Carlo, 1951. Danced by Alicia Markova, Tatiana Riabouchinska, Paula Hinton, Noël Rossana; then Nervi, 1957. Danced by Alicia Markova, Yvette Chauviré, Carla Fracci, Margrete Schanne; then Leningrad, 1966. Danced by Natalia Makarova, Gabriela Komleva, Natalia Bolshakova, Nina Gruzdeva, etc.

A.A.

THE DEVIL TO PAY (*Le Diable à Quatre*)
Mime-ballet in two acts. Choreography by Joseph Mazilier. Music by Adolphe Adam. Scenario by De Leuven and Mazilier from C. Coppey's farce The Devil to Pay *or* The Wives Metamorphosed. *Sets by Ciceri, Despléchin, Séchan, Diéterle. Costumes by Paul Lormier. Paris, Opéra, August 11, 1845. Principal dancers: Carlotta Grisi (Mazourka), Joseph Mazilier (Mazourki), Lucien Petipa (Count Polinski), M. Coralli Jr. (Dancing Master).*

SYNOPSIS. The story is set in Poland and concerns the comic-dramatic adventures of two couples: a Count and Countess and two peasants, Mazourki and Mazourka. During a tenants' ball at the castle the Countess, irritated by the festivities, breaks a blind fiddler's violin. He happens to be a magician and punishes the lady by exchanging her identity for one day with that of Mazourka. The Countess's caprices are soon quelled by Mazourki's rough ways, while up at the castle the servants are bewildered by Mazourka's merry and amiable manners. After a series of amusing incidents and misunderstandings, the lady's punishment comes to an end. She is restored to her high degree, but promises to be less haughty in future, while Mazourka resolves to treat her compliant and devoted husband with more regard.

■ The entertainment was a tremendous success and the critics pronounced it a good idea to have introduced a popular theme into ballet. The mime elements used by Mazilier were, of course, derived from Italy. Mazilier, a

Playbill from the Scala Theater during Carnival, 1847.

highly esteemed dancer, started his choreographic career with *The Gypsy* (composed for Fanny Elssler as an answer to Taglioni's *Gitana*). Because of his versatility, it was said that he could invent a ballet during the day and dance every night. If he had a fault as a choreographer, it was in arranging group movements. A Russian critic considered him definitely inferior to Perrot, especially for ensembles. During a rehearsal, Grisi was injured by a nail that pierced her shoe and she was forced to leave the stage for some time. Her replacement, Adelina Plunkett, first in the role of the Countess and later in that of Mazourka, was most unfairly criticized for the audicity of risking comparison with Grisi in one of her best parts. The outstanding dances in the ballet are the mazurka based on a theme by Glinka, and the grand finale Adagio solo. There were four operatic versions of *Le Diable à Quatre* made between 1686 and 1809.

C.M.C.

CATHARINA or THE BANDIT'S DAUGHTER
(Catarina or La Fille du Bandit)
Ballet in three acts and five scenes. Choreography and scenario by Jules Perrot. Music by Cesare Pugni. Scenery by Charles Marshall. London, Her Majesty's Theatre, March 3, 1846. Principal dancers: Lucile Grahn (Catarina), Jules Perrot (Diavolino), Louis Gosselin (Salvator Rosa).

SYNOPSIS. Act I: the painter Salvator Rosa, captured by bandits of the Abruzzo, falls in love with Catarina, their chief, who in turn is loved by her lieutenant, Diavolino. Though entreated by the artist and an officer who offer her safe conduct, Catarina refuses to lay down her arms. Far from it; she performs a warlike dance with the bandits, the *pas stratégique*, miming a battle. When the regular troops arrive, Salvator Rosa falls wounded while defending his beloved Catarina. She is saved by Diavolino, who persuades her to escape with him. The other bandits are taken prisoner. The two fugitives seek asylum in a Roman tavern, where they disguise themselves as servants. Then the Duke of Collalbano, Salvator Rosa, and his affianced bride, Florida, arrive. Recognized by the painter, the fugitives are once more helped to escape from the soldiers, after a vain attempt, in complicity with the bandits' friends, to free the prisoners while the guards' attention is distracted by a lively *saltarello*. Act II: having taken refuge in the studio which Salvator is allowed to occupy in the ducal palace, Catarina discovers there a portrait of herself. When the Duke, the artist, and Florida visit the studio she has no alternative but to pass herself off as a model. Salvator lets her stay concealed there, but the jealous Florida has recognized her rival and reveals the hiding place to her pursuers, so that Catarina is captured. Act III: the judges condemn Catarina to death, but she is saved by the painter who, disguised as a father confessor, helps her to escape through a window. Diavolino, although awaiting her, is contemplating the murder of his rival. He and the girl put on masks and mix with the carnival crowd but are once more discovered and imprisoned. While Catarina is pardoned by the Duke and reunited with Salvator Rosa, Diavolini escapes yet again, and vanishes, masked, among the merrymakers.

■ Many of Perrot's ballets were based on realistic plots. *Catarina* emphasized that romanticism was a revolutionary movement, especially after the fall of Napoleon had divested the mythological ballet of its former popularity. It also demonstrated how much the triumphs of the Opéra owed their origins to the rhythmic pantomime of the Porte-Saint-Martin, where Perrot himself had worked as "mime, dancer, and monkey." The ballet's popularity grew rapidly because of the fascination and humanity of the unconventional characters who were imbued with the essence of the original story, and of the incomparable elegance of the mass movements. Founded on the contrast between feminine grace and military precision, this work was one of the greatest triumphs of both Lucile Grahn and Fanny Elssler, the second of whom danced the title part

Marie Taglioni, niece and namesake of the famous ballerina, in Thea, *a ballet created by Paolo Taglioni.*

at the Milan Scala in January 1847, and in St. Petersburg in November 1849. It was repeated with equal success by Sofia Fuoco at the Scala in 1853 and danced in St. Petersburg in 1886 by Claudina Cucchi, who personally trained the *corps de ballet* in military drill and exercises with firearms.   G.S.

THEA or THE FLOWER FAIRY *(Théa or La Fée aux Fleurs)*
Ballet in one act and two scenes. Choreography and scenario by Paolo Taglioni. Music by Cesare Pugni. Sets by Charles Marshall. Machines by D. Sloman. Costumes by Bradley and Whales. London, Her Majesty's Theatre, March 17, 1847. Principal dancers: Carolina Rosati (Thea, the favourite), Marie Taglioni Jr. (the Flower Fairy), Paolo Taglioni (Prince Hussein).

SYNOPSIS. In a Baghdad garden the favourite, Thea, looks fondly at Prince Hussein. He, however, is tired of the dances of odalisques and contemplates only the flowers that surround him. With the help of the Flower Fairy, Thea is transformed into a rose bush, and the Prince promises to marry the flower that succeeds in making him fall in love with it. The fairy plunges him into a deep sleep while the flowers turn into dancing girls. Hussein awakes and runs towards the rose, the object of his dreams, and makes her his wife.

■ The ballet was praised for its perfect balance between action and *divertissement*. It recalled the splendours of

Fanny Cerrito wearing Fatma's gypsy costume in La Fille de Marbre *by Arthur Saint-Léon.*

Eugène Coralli, who played the part of Doctor Matheus in Le Violon du Diable, *from a contemporary lithograph.*

Coralia (there the scene had been aquatic, here it was floral); to equal the success of *Thea* one would have to go back to Perrot's famous *Alma*. The choreographer, Paolo Taglioni, not only took part as a dancer but also introduced his daughter Marie (niece of her "divine" namesake), who was barely fourteen. After this debut the young ballerina proved a creditable substitute for her celebrated aunt in the last of Perrot's London *divertissements*: *The Four Seasons* (June 1848), in which she took the role of Winter in partnership with Carlotta Grisi (Summer), Carolina Rosati (Autumn), and Fanny Cerrito (Spring). In *Thea* the same Carolina Rosati, pupil of Carlo Blasis at the Scala, achieved a memorable success.
C.M.C.

THE ELEMENTS (Les Éléments)

Divertissement. *Choreography and scenario by Jules Perrot. Music by Bajetti. London, Her Majesty's Theatre, June 26, 1847. Principal dancers: Carlotta Grisi (Fire), Fanny Cerrito (Air), Carolina Rosati (Water), Cassan, James, Thevenot, Honoré (Earth).*

SYNOPSIS. As its name suggests, the *divertissement* takes the Four Elements as its characters and moves them in an ornamental garden among trees, leaves, fountains, clouds, nymphs, woodland creatures, and naiads. After the nymphs have made their entrance one by one, begins the adagio in which the *corps de ballet* takes part, arranged in picturesque groups, each differentiated by the colour of the element it represents. There follows a series of brilliant variations performed by each of the three leading characters in turn.

■ *The Elements* was one of the major attractions of the London stage in 1847. To bring together all the greatest dance personalities of the era in a single ballet was the achievement of Perrot, also responsible for the famous *Pas de Quatre* of 1845 (Taglioni, Cerrito, Grisi, Grahn), *Le Judgement de Paris* or *Pas des Déesses* of 1846 (Taglioni, Cerrito, Grahn, Saint-Léon), and *The Four Seasons* of 1848 (Grisi, Rosati, Taglioni, Cerrito). He was an excellent dancer himself (his famous elevation and the almost feminine perfection of his legs, unfortunately accompanied by an excessive width of chest and a decidedly ugly face, caused Bournonville to describe him as "a sylph with bat's wings"). Without doubt, Jules Perrot was highly gifted as a choreographer, especially in his ability to bring out the best in every dancer with whom he worked. In exalting the beauty of pure dance, he also brought the star system of nineteenth-century ballet to its peak. Divisive influence is always at work in the theater, as Carlotta Grisi's letter to the critic Fiorentino concerning this very *divertissement* makes abundantly clear: "the *pas de quatre* from *Les Éléments* . . . seems to me one of the best dances arranged by Perrot. Each of us has a separate entrance, and the scene in which Water enters to extinguish Fire is short but extremely graceful. My entry, as if in flames, is very effective, and so quickly done that no one can tell how I arrived on the stage. After that I have some splendid variations that win me an immediate ovation.

Thanks to this dance, if I have misunderstood what people have told me, it is I who have achieved the greatest success of the three." It was through Carlotta Grisi (he met her in Naples in 1834 and became her lover, her master, and finally her husband) that Jules Perrot created a new style, combining the "aerial" attributes of Maria Taglioni with the "earthy" quality of Fanny Elssler.   C.M.C.

THE MARBLE MAIDEN (La Fille de Marbre)

Mime-ballet in two acts and three scenes. Choreography and scenario by Arthur Saint-Léon. Music by Cesare Pugni. Sets by C. A. Cambon and J. Thierry. Costumes by P. Lormier. Paris, Opéra, October 20, 1847. Principal dancers: Fanny Cerrito (Fatma), Arthus Saint-Léon (Manasses), H. Desplaces (Alyatar), Quérian (Belphagor).

SYNOPSIS. The sculptor Manasses descends with Satan into the Kingdom of Fire ruled by Belphagor, whom he implores, in exchange for his soul, to breathe life into the female statue he has made, a figure so beautiful that he has fallen in love with it. Belphagor grants his wish, but only on condition the transformed woman remains insensible to human love. If she loves, she will turn to marble once more. Thus Fatma comes to life. A Moroccan Prince, Alyatar, asleep in Seville, sees her in a dream. When he awakens, Satan promises to make him acquainted with the girl of his dream. The meeting takes place amid the music and dancing of the Seville Fair. Fatma, conducted by Manasses, appears dressed as a gypsy dancer, thus contravening the Governor's edict. She is obliged to escape on board a boat, but the enamoured Alyatar swims after her. In the palace of Alhambra the King of Spain becomes infatuated with Fatma, but the Moors, led by Alyatar, defeat him and put him to rout. The victorious Prince offers marriage and his throne to Fatma, who has now fallen in love

with him, thus breaking the pact with the Lord of Hades. The moment she chooses human love rather than immortality the furious Belphagor changes her back into a marble statue. Satan takes possession of the appalled Manasses.

■ Arthur Saint-Léon, graceful dancer of notable technique, violinist, composer, inventor of an ingenious system of dance notation called *"Stenochorégraphie"* (in which the whole notation of the *Pas de six* from *La Vivandière* is still extant) was the future composer of the immortal *Coppelia*. He started his ballet career in Paris with *La Fille de Marbre*, there to launch his wonderful wife, Fanny Cerrito, then at the peak of the feminine charm and expressive virtuosity that had already conquered London. The ballet showed a remarkable resemblance to *Alma ou La Fille de Feu* by Jules Perrot which had opened on June 23, 1842, at Her Majesty's Theatre in London, produced by the choreographer and with the same Fanny Cerrito making a great hit with the *Pas de fascination* and the *Pas de trois*.   G.S.

THE DEVIL'S VIOLIN (Le Violon du Diable)

Mime-ballet in two acts and six scenes. Choreography and scenario by Arthur Saint-Léon. Music by Cesare Pugni. Scenery by Despléchin-Thierry. Paris, Opéra, January 19, 1849. Principal dancers: Fanny Cerrito (Hélène de Vardeck), Arthur Saint-Léon (Urbain), Eugène Coralli (Doctor Matheus), A. Fuchs (Saint-Ybars).

SYNOPSIS. Urbain, a young violinist, is deeply in love with the beautiful Hélène de Vardeck, but she prefers her suitor Saint-Ybars. The sinister Doctor Matheus offers Urbain the power to play his violin so irresistibly as to win the heart of his beloved, but in return he asks for the player's soul. Urbain refuses and the doctor breaks his magic instrument. Everything works out for

Lis Jeppesen, Arne Bech, and Annemarie Dybdal in a recent Danish version (1978) of Konservatoriet *(The Conservatory).*

New Danish version of Konservatoriet, *1978, again: Thomas Berentzen, Ib Andersen, Vibeke Roland, Ann Kristin Hauge, and Mette-Ida Kirk.*

A scene from The Holy Fair at Bruges, *a ballet created by August Bournonville in 1851, here danced by the Royal Danish Ballet during their 1966–1967 season.*

the best through the intervention of a holy man, the violinist's friend and master, who provides him with another violin, possessing beneficent powers no less effective than the evil forces of the first. When it is discovered that Urbain is not only a distinguished violinist but also a youth of noble lineage, his marriage with Hélène is approved, and the ballet ends with a quite independent *divertissement* based on a theme concerning hothouse flowers which transport their gardener to the land of roses, where he marries their Queen.

■ *Le Violon du Diable* was a revival of *Tartini il Violonista* produced at the Fenice Theater in Venice on February 29, 1848. The posters of the Venetian entertainment mentioned the ballet as "taken from an opera by Gavarini and written by Arthur Saint-Léon, with music by Saint-Léon and Felis, except the second act music composed by Cesare Pugni." At the Paris opening, however, subject and choreography were attributed exclusively to Saint-Léon, and the music exclusively to Cesare Pugni. We know that Saint-Léon was not only the best dancer of his time after Perrot (his elevation and *ballon* were exceptional) but also a virtuoso violinist of the school of Paganini. In his review written in 1847 of *La Fille de Marbre* (adapted by Saint-Léon from *Alma*), Théophile Gautier made the first suggestion: "Saint-Léon, as well as being a dancer and choreographer, is an excellent violinist, according to what people say who have heard him. Surely it must be possible to find a subject that will show off his talents as both dancer and musician." The result was, of course, *Le Violon du Diable*, in which Saint-Léon played the part of the violinist Urbain. The ballet was well received but gave rise to some spiteful comments: Coralli, it was said, "is a bit plump for a devil. If he had not taken care to have little horns peeping out of his wig, and thrown in a terrifying glare from time to time, he might have been

taken for an abbé . . .", and "Fanny Cerrito exhibits her rare and diverse qualities, but is perhaps not dramatic enough; at her first appearance one might describe her as a cold and pallid statue revolving on a marble pedestal. Elssler would have made a memorable interpretation of the part!" Fortunately, the critic finally relents: "In the last *pas de deux* with her husband (Saint-Léon had married Cerrito in 1845, but they were separated five years later), all Cerrito's gestures were of the utmost tenderness. It would be difficult to find more grace, freshness, lightness, or elevation."
C.M.C.

THE CONSERVATORY (*Konservatoriet*)
Ballet in one act. Choreography by August Bournonville. Music by H. S. Paulli. Copenhagen, Theater Royal, May 6, 1849. Royal Danish Ballet.

SYNOPSIS. In an early nineteenth-century academy of dancing in Paris, a ballet master, assisted by a violinist, is conducting a lively class of young dancers of both sexes. During the lesson various comic and sentimental episodes alternate with teaching passages and steps in the academic style of the period.

■ This short work without any definite plot, somewhere between a *divertissement*, a little comedy, and a demonstration of pure academic dance, was probably drawn by Bournonville from one of his earlier and much longer ballets, entitled *Proposal of Marriage through a Newspaper*, a not very interesting affair in which two young ladies, in the course of their adventures in Paris, find themselves in a ballet school. Removed from its narrative context, *Konservatoriet* became a homage to the school of the great Auguste Vestris, whose pupil Bournonville had been in his youth, and to the French academic style which constituted the essence of the choreographic language used by Bournonville for his Danish ballet company, based though it was on lines laid down by Galeotti (see *Amor*, page 141). In the austere and independent atmosphere of the Royal Danish Ballet in Copenhagen, this school of dancing, born in Italy and developed in France, underwent a process of purification and technico-expressive stylization that bore the personal imprint of the Danish master. It was remarkable for its joyous but balanced clarity, richness of invention, and luminous romantic lyricism devoid of gloomy introspection. Technically it could be recognized by the polished perfection of every step, the graceful *port de bras*, ease and lightness of *ballon*, and its frequent use of the "half point." Dramatic action was expressed entirely in dance; virtuosity for its own sake was frowned on. Finally, the Danish school restored the importance of the male dancer's role, enriching it both technically and expressively. Bournonville's style has been preserved almost intact in Danish ballet up to the present day, thanks to a strict and, so to speak, impermeable tradition of training and performance. His most important influence on world ballet, however, has been through his pupil, Christian Johannson, who taught in St. Petersburg, and thus contributed, together with the French and Italians, to the Russian school that eventually produced the Diaghilev Ballet. *Konservatoriet* is a perfect example of Bournonville's style and remains a permanent item in the Royal Danish Ballet's repertory, thanks to the efforts of Hans Beck (1861–1952), heir and custodian of the tradition, and of his pupil Harald Lander (1905–1971). To Hans Brenaa we owe the reconstruction of the ballet for various other international companies. A.A.

THE JOYS OF WINTER or THE SKATERS (Les Plaisirs de l'Hiver or Les Patineurs)

Divertissement *ballet in one act and two scenes. Choreography and subject by Paolo Taglioni. Music by*

Margot Fonteyn and Rudolf Nureyev in Le Corsaire, *Scala Theater, Milan, September 1966.*

The second act of Le Corsaire *(1856) by Joseph Mazilier, from a contemporary illustration.*

Cesare Pugni. London, Her Majesty's Theatre, July 10, 1849. Principal dancer: Carolina Rosati.

SYNOPSIS. A succession of scenes without any continuity of plot: the opening scene of a Polish wedding among the flowers of a winter garden is followed by one on a frozen lake at sunrise. A multitude of skaters disport themselves; gentlemen pass by on sledges, young men slide down the snowy slopes.

■ *Les Plaisirs de l'Hiver* (also called *Les Patineurs)* opened during a particularly torrid summer; so much so that when the curtain rose on a scene of snow and frozen fountains it had a delightfully refreshing effect on the audience. The music heightened the atmosphere with its onomatopoeic suggestions of the scraping of skates over ice. According to *The Times*, "the *divertissement* rises above the ordinary thanks to its very personal character. It is not complicated, but the sports of a Hungarian winter [sic, in place of Polish] are displayed with considerable grace. The dancers wear skates with little wheels underneath. The same device was used in a pantomime at Covent Garden last year, but the idea of *Les Patineurs* elaborated with a great variety of groups and steps is Paolo Taglioni's." *The Times* also criticized the lighting: "whereas in the ballet *Electra* everything was dark and the turning on of the electric light had an interesting effect, for the skaters, who need to be seen clearly, the electricity was disagreeably dazzling and did not go well with the scene as a whole." One of Paolo Taglioni's distinguishing characteristics was the use he made of the newest inventions in staging his ballets. The comedy dances in *Les Patineurs* were particularly appreciated: the Shiverers' Dance, the Dance of the Hussars, and the Grand Skaters' Quadrille (solos intermingled with *entrées* and interludes by the ensemble). In the final scene, the best skater (the dancer Charles) performs a brilliant sequence of pirouettes. Then the sun sinks and the skaters, arranged in groups of great charm, leave the stage in their horse-drawn sledges. On February 16, 1937, at the Sadler's Wells Theatre in London, the ballet was reconstructed under the title *Les Patineurs*, with choreography by Frederick Ashton and music by Meyerbeer. C.M.C.

THE HOLY FAIR AT BRUGES or THE THREE GIFTS *(Kermessen i Brügge* or *De Tre Gaver)*

Romantic ballet in three acts. Choreography and scenario by August Bournonville. Music by Holger Simon Paulli. Scenery by Jacques Noël. Copenhagen, Royal Opera House, April 4, 1851. Royal Danish Ballet. Principal dancers: Svend Erik Jensen, Paul Wessel, Fredbjorn Bjornsson (the three brothers).

SYNOPSIS. Inspired by paintings by Jan Steen and David Teniers depicting the Holy Fair at Bruges, the plot unfolds in Flanders towards the end of the seventeenth century. On the eve of a feast day three brothers save Eleonora, the beautiful daughter of the alchemist Mirewelt, from attack. The grateful magician rewards each of them with a gift. Geert receives a lady-killing ring, Adrian an invincible sword, and Carelis a violin that compels all who hear it to dance. After some extraordinary adventures, Geert, Adrian, and Mirewelt are accused of witchcraft and condemned to be burned at the stake. But Carelis saves them by making everyone dance to the sound of his playing until the judges and the populace are forced to grant a pardon. Carelis also wins the gratitude and love of Eleonora. Geert and Adrian return to their fiancées. The magic violin is deposited in the Town Hall, to be taken out only once a year when *kermesse* time comes around again to bring joy and gaiety to the inhabitants of the old Flemish capital.

■ Heir to the classical traditions of Pierre Gardel and Jean-Georges Noverre transmitted through his teachers Vincenzo Galeotti and Auguste Vestris, Bournonville was the only choreographer of his time to restore the masculine element in ballet to its true place. He refused to accept the secondary rank assigned to men in French ballet, and thereby achieved in his productions a perfect balance between male and female dancing. Men were given important parts and solos, arousing the interest and admiration of a public that had grown accustomed to bestowing extravagant praise on the ballerinas, as was the way in the romantic ballet then predominant in Europe, but none on their partners. It was otherwise in *Kermesse in Bruges*, in which Bournonville made exten-

Carolina Rosati in the costume of Medora in Le Corsaire, *created by Joseph Mazilier in 1856.*

sive use of the "high half point," and of *battements, grand-jetés*, and leaping elevations. The ballet has survived the wear and tear of time intact, and is still to be seen in the theaters of its land of origin.

OTHER VERSIONS. Hans Brenaa and Flemming Flindt (after Bournonville). Copenhagen, Royal Opera House, Danish Royal Ballet, October 23, 1966. G.S.

GEMMA

Ballet in two acts and five scenes. Choreography by Fanny Cerrito. Music by Nicolò Gabrielli. Scenario by Théophile Gautier and Fanny Cerrito. Sets by Rubé and Nolau. Costumes by Lormier. Paris, Opéra, May 31, 1854. Principal dancers: Fanny Cerrito (Gemma), Louis Mérante (Marquis of Santa Croce), Lucien Petipa (Massimo).

SYNOPSIS. The events take place in southern Italy in the seventeenth century. During the preparations for a grand ball, the Countess Gemma is thinking of the man she loves, the painter Massimo, who is just finishing her portrait. Enter the Marquis of Santa Croce, a rake endowed with magic powers and enamoured of Gemma who, however, does not return his love. Nevertheless he forces her to accept him. Later, when he leaves the ball, he makes her follow him. Soon Gemma is a prisoner in his castle and it is her wedding day. She manages to escape through a window and takes refuge in Massimo's house. When the Marquis comes to find her there, she succeeds in evading him by posing as her own portrait. However, while at a village wedding in the mountains, she falls into Santa Croce's power once more. The furious Massimo challenges the Marquis, who, in the ensuing duel, falls into a torrent. At last Gemma and Massimo, freed from the Marquis's evil machinations, can be united.

■ *Gemma* was the last of the six ballets arranged by Fanny Cerrito, now nearing the end of her splendid career as a dancer. She first proved herself as a choreographer in 1842 when she collaborated with Jules Perrot on *Alma* in London. The first ballet she devised by herself was *Rosida* (1845) to music by Pugni. Cerrito shared the leading roles of this ballet with Arthur Saint-Léon, for years her chief partner and choreographer, and, after 1845, her husband. *Gemma* was performed no more than seven times, because Cerrito left the Opéra, but its first night was a triumphal success, not only for her but also for Gautier and Count Gabrielle, the young Italian composer. The choreography was admired above all for the brilliance of some of its separate parts such as the *pas de deux* danced by Louise Taglioni and Beauchet, the Abruzzian dance, and the Mirror Scene (although that device was not new to ballet). Here the reflected image of Fanny Cerrito was impersonated by Pauline Mercier, a blonde sixteen-year-old of particular charm. The manipulation of crowd scenes in which often more than a hundred people took part was also impressive. Gautier (one must remember that he was coauthor of the scenario) wrote: "A choreographer must be at once poet, painter, musician, and strategist to be able to discipline and maneuver those crowds: qualities seldom united in a single person. Fanny Cerrito has attacked this formidable task with a skill that will surprise even those who were already convinced of her talent." In spite of that, this long ballet did contain some tedious passages and Cerrito shone above all as a dancer. In the scene in Massimo's studio, adapted from Perrot's *Le Délire d'un Peintre*, her poses reminded Gautier of Canova's *Amore e Psiche*. In *Gemma* Cerrito also displayed her remarkable gifts as a mime, and the same was true of Mérante, who was well to the fore in the part of Santa Croce. One dissenting voice amid the general praise was that of *Figaro*, which has left us an interesting account of the occasion: "Its success has been exaggerated and the enthusiasm has touched on the absurd. The auditorium was filled with dancers' mothers, and a colleague counted forty-four bouquets thrown from those boxes. One was even thrown to the revered Ferdinand Prévost, whose only duty was to come in front of the proscenium and announce the names of the authors."   C.M.C.

SHAKESPEARE or A MIDSUMMER NIGHT'S DREAM (*Shakespeare* or *Il Sogno di una Notte di Mezza Estate*)
Ballet in three parts. Choreography and scenario (after Rosier and de Leuven) by Giovanni Casati. Music by Paolo Giorza. Scenic designer unnamed. Costumes by G. Zamperoni. Milan, Scala, January 27, 1855. Principal dancers: Effisio Catte (Shakespeare), Claudina Cucchi (Miss Olivia), Assunta Razzanelli (Elizabeth of England), Federico Ghedini (Falstaff), Pietro Trigambi (Geremia).

SYNOPSIS. The great English poet, neglecting his genius and given over to a life of dissipation, is brought out of a tavern by Queen Elizabeth in masked disguise. She wants to save him from himself. In the course of a very complicated plot which includes the Queen's lady-in-waiting Olivia, her jealous fiancé Latimer, the bombastic Falstaff, the young couple Nell and Tom, and various other characters, the poet is recalled to his true self by a pageant arranged by the Queen in her garden. It shows him his own poetic creations: Romeo and Juliet, Othello, and Macbeth. All the complications are smoothed out as in a dream and Shakespeare recognizes in the Queen the lady he has come to love and who can offer him only friendship and protection in return. A grand ball at court is given in honour of the poet.

■ The poet and playwright, seen through the rosy haze of romanticism, inspired numerous novels. It was to this minor pseudo-historical and moralizing branch of literature that Giovanni Casati turned for the scenario of his ballet. Though its early performances were notably successful, partly owing to the excellence of the dancers, the ballet later fell into oblivion like all the other ballets in his long and fertile career at the Scala. Dancer, ballet master at the Scala school of dancing between 1868 and 1883, choreographer, and composer of many ballet scores, Giovanni Casati adhered to the Italian tradition which led from the danced dramas of Viganò to the academicism of Carlo Blasis (whose pupil he was), and culminated in the "grand Scala ballets" of Manzotti. He can be considered a transitional choreographer, but did at least link up the early and the final stages of nineteenth-century Italian ballet with remarkable stylistic wealth and artistic dignity. Among the cast of the original production was Claudina Cucchi. It was the first real success of one of the leading Italian stars of the most splendid period in Russian ballet history. A.A.

THE CORSAIR (*Le Corsaire*)
Mime-ballet in three acts. Choreography by Joseph Mazilier. Music by Adolphe Adam. Scenario by Jules Henri Vernoy de Saint-Georges and Joseph Mazilier (after Byron). Scenery by Edouard Despléchin, Charles Cambon, Joseph Thierry, and Martin. Costumes by Albert. Machinery by Sacré. Paris, Opéra, January 23, 1856. Principal dancers: Carolina Rosati (Medora), Domenico Segarelli (Conrad), Claudina Cucchi (Gulnare), Louise Marquet (Zulmea), M. Dauty (Saïd Pasha).

SYNOPSIS. Medora, a young Greek girl, is sold to Saïd Pasha by the slave dealer Isaac, who cannot resist the high price offered. The pirate Conrad seizes Medora and declares his love in his subterranean palace. Birbanto, Conrad's next-in-command, is jealous of his chief and sends Medora back to Isaac, who conducts her once more to the Pasha. Conrad, arriving with his men in disguise, is recognized, captured, and condemned to death. To save his life, Medora pretends to consent to marriage with Saïd Pasha while secretly plotting escape with the slave Gulnare. The latter impersonates the Greek girl during the ceremony so that the wedding ring is placed on her finger. That evening Medora, taking back her own identity, dances before the Pasha after having induced him to lay down his pistols and sword. Conrad enters and takes Medora away, while Gulnare, showing the ring, declares herself to be the Pasha's lawful wife. The ship on which Conrad and Medora are escaping meets a terrible storm and is sunk. The two lovers, however, are miraculously saved by landing on a rocky island.

■ Among the many ballets inspired by Byron's famous poem, starting with Galzerani's version in 1826 (see *The Corsair*, page 93), the most important is undoubtedly Mazilier's *Le Corsaire*, partly because it is the only one that continued to be revived from time to time up to the beginning of the present century. Also worthy of mention is *Le Corsaire* choreographed by Albert to music by Bochsa, produced on June 29, 1837 at the King's Theatre in London, with Herminie Elssler, Pauline Duvernay, and Albert himself in the principal parts (revived at Drury Lane in 1844 with Clara Webster in the lead). There is no doubt, however, as to the superior quality of Vernoy de Saint-Georges's scenario and the score by Adam (the composer's last, for he died later the same year) for the ballet arranged by Joseph Mazilier, one of the most distinguished choreographers of the period and chief *maître de ballet* at the Paris Opéra between 1853 and 1859, the years of his fullest and most fertile creativity. His choreographic style was strictly academic but in touch with his own epoch. The solo parts were infused with an intense dramatic expressiveness, perhaps because of his own bent as a character dancer. In these solos and in the *pas de deux* he showed a wealth of imagination and inventiveness, though he was less interested in the grouping of the ensemble, compensating for that weakness with splendid spectacle and technical ingenuity. *Le Corsaire*'s extraordinary success was due, on the one hand, to the variations assigned to the prima ballerina (in the seduction scene, the fan dance, and the dance of the odalisques) danced by Carolina Rosati, a product of Carlo Blasis's Milanese school, as was also Amalia Ferraris, with whom she shared her triumphs at the Opéra after 1856; and on the other hand, to the spectacular shipwreck scene that ended the ballet with a crowning glory of theatrical effects. Among the dancers on the opening night was Claudina Cucchi at the beginning of her great international career. *Le Corsaire* arrived in Russia, where it was to become a favourite with the leading ballerinas for decades, as a revival by

Jules Perrot in 1858 at the Bolshoi Theater in St. Petersburg. On the basis of that version Marius Petipa produced one of his own with musical additions by Cesare Pugni and Léo Delibes in 1868, Adèle Grantzow dancing the principal role. Petipa revived the ballet again at the Maryinsky Theater in St. Petersburg on January 13, 1899 for the *prima ballerina assoluta* Pierina Legnani, later adapting it to his own style of choreography and adding a *pas de deux* to music by Riccardo Drigo. This famous classical *pas de deux*, a pure gem of academic technique, subdivided in the traditional way into adagio for two, solo variations, and coda, survives to this day as a separate item detached from its parent ballet, from which, however, it has taken its name. It is danced throughout the world as one of the most testing trials of virtuosity possible for two dancers. Among the celebrated dancers who have recently performed it are Margot Fonteyn and Rudolf Nureyev, Ekaterina Maximova and Vladimir Vassiliev, and, lastly, Gelsey Kirkland with Mikhail Baryshnikov. A.A.

MARCO SPADA or THE BANDIT'S DAUGHTER
(Marco Spada or La Fille du Bandit)
Mime-ballet in three acts and six scenes. Choreography by Joseph Mazilier. Music by Daniel Auber. Scenario by Eugène Scribe. Sets by Cambon and Thierry (scenes 1, 4, 5), Despléchin (scene 2). Nolau and Rubé (scene 3). Machinery by Sacré. Costumes by Albert and Lormier. Paris, Opéra, April 1, 1857. Principal dancers: Segarelli (Marco Spada), Carolina Rosati (Angela, his daughter), Louis Mérante (Pepinelli, Captain of Dragoons), Amalia Ferraris (Marchesa Sampietri), Lucien Petipa (Count Federici), Eugène Coralli (Genario).

SYNOPSIS. The Governor of Rome, his daughter the Marchesa Sampietro, and a Captain of Dragoons, Pepinelli, are driven by a storm to take shelter in a house, little knowing it to be the hideout of Marco Spada, the bandit chief. The Governor, who is giving a grand ball the next day, invites the unrecognized bandit and his daughter Angela, once loved by Count Federici, now the promised husband of the Marchesa Sampietro. During the festivities Federici renews his professions of love to Angela, but the girl proudly replies that she prefers to share the perilous life of her father. Disappointed, the Count decides to marry the Marchesa without delay. While she is preparing for her wedding, Marco Spada's gang break into her room and abduct her, taking all her jewels and also the big chest in which is hidden Pepinelli, who is in love with the lady and has taken this desperate step to persuade her against the marriage. In the bandits' retreat, the Marchesa and Pepinelli are quickly united in matrimony by Spada, who hopes thus to eliminate his daughter's rival. The bandit chief then leads his men against the Dragoons, but is fatally wounded. Before drawing his last breath he declares that Angela is not really his daughter, but of noble birth, thus making it possible for her to marry Federici.

■ The ballet was taken from the comic opera of the

Scene from the first act of Far from Denmark (Fjernt fra Danmark) *by August Bournonville, with Vivi Flindt (in the hammock) in a production at the Copenhagen Theater Royal, October 1973.*

same name staged at the Opéra Comique in December 1852. The critics of the day were fairly unanimous in the opinion that the chief interest of the choreography lay in the "duel" between Carolina Rosati and Amalia Ferraris, and that supposition gave rise to some interesting remarks on the qualities of the two rivals. The contrast between the styles of Ferraris and Rosati was not unlike that which had divided the Opéra into two opposing factions in the time of Taglioni and Elssler. "The Ferraris is like a feather floating between two wafts of breeze. Never have we seen such graceful dancing on point." And again, from the critic Saint-Victor: "The competition between the two dancers is a duel between wings and feet, between spirit and flesh, between a weightless elf and a sturdy bacchante." He added that no one after Taglioni had been capable of such elevation, *ballon*, and *parcours*, and that "the adagio of her *grand pas* in the ball scene contained attitudes and *développements* of incredible audacity. . . . Her final dance was executed with such perfection that it alone sufficed to prove Signora Ferraris's incomparability as a ballerina." The famous Florentine critic showed some proof of impartiality, however, when he wrote of

Carolina Rosati, whose style, like Elssler's, could be defined as down to earth, that in the mask dance she triumphed with a sequence of *ronds de jambe de retour* "so radiant, so exquisitely polished, unexpected, spontaneous, and resplendent as to defy description." It was said that even if Rosati had lost her legs, she could still have danced with her smile and the toss of her head. Apart from this historical contest and the spectacular scenic design of the last act, the ballet was not of great interest. The music was a medley of themes from *Fra Diavolo, La Barcarola, L'Enfant Prodigue,* and other operas. Choreographically, too, even the best moments did not attain the inventiveness of *Le Corsaire*, and it was said that, except in the dance of the two ballerinas, Mazilier had not stretched his imagination, which proved that the Opéra once again needed new talent. Nevertheless, *Marco Spada* could be considered a financial success, even though dogged by an extraordinary run of bad luck: a wing of the scenery fell at the feet of a dancer; the bandits' cave could not be lowered to the stage at the right moment, and the Dragoons were obliged to improvise a mime while waiting for the scenery to be set up by hand (to the mirth of the

Emma Livry dancing in Le Papillon, *the only ballet choreographed by Maria Taglioni, from a contemporary engraving preserved in the Library of the Paris Opéra.*

audience); an unfortunate extra, set on fire by a bengal light, fell head first from above to the stage and remained unconscious for two hours. Finally Rosati caught a chill that prevented her from dancing for a week. The *corps de ballet*, alarmed by this series of catastrophes, hastened to acquire amulets and other objects calculated to avert the evil eye, and wore them for all subsequent performances. *Marco Spada* was one of those ballets that stretched the powers of the head machinist to the utmost. It was an extremely responsible post – as the fame of Sacré, head machinist at the Opéra from 1847 to 1872 bears witness. Complicated problems had to be resolved and bold inventions devised, for which the machinist was held accountable. The most famous examples of the craft were the collapse of the cave in *Jovita* (1853), the wreck in *Le Corsaire* (1856), and the two-level set in *Marco Spada*.   C.M.C.

SACOUNTALA

Mime-ballet in two acts. Choreography by Lucien Petipa. Music by Ernest Reyer. Scenario by Théophile Gautier. Sets by Martin (first act), Nolau and Rubé (second act). Costumes by Albert. Paris, Opéra, July 14, 1858. Principal dancers: Amalia Ferraris (Sacountala), Lucien Petipa (Dushmata, King of India), Louis François Mérante (Madhava, favourite), Eugène Coralli
(Durwasa, fakir), Louise Marquet (Hamsati, favourite), Mlle. Aline (Gautami, priestess).

SYNOPSIS. King Dushmata, hunting in the forest, comes upon a holy place, lays down his arms, and prays. When a group of girls arrives he hides himself. One of them (Sacountala) enchants him so that he emerges from his hiding place and declares his love, offering her a ring as pledge. A fakir, outraged by such amorous exchanges in a sacred spot, plucks the ring from her finger and throws her into the river. The girl survives and comes to the King in his palace, but he, owing the the fakir's curse, fails to recognize her and, urged on by the favourite, Hamsati, orders Sacountala to be burned. Just then a fisherman arrives at the palace with the ring he has found inside a fish. Immediately the King's memory is restored and preparations are made for his marriage to Sacountala.

■ *Sacountala* was based on the well-known story of the same name by the fourth-century Indian poet Kalidasa. In 1858 Joseph Mazilier was still chief *maître de ballet* at the Opéra but, now in his sixties, he felt the task of composing a new full-length ballet to be too exhausting, so passed it on to Lucien Petipa, who was second in command. *Sacountala* was the third ballet produced at the Opéra for Amalia Ferraris (following *Les Elfes*,

1856 and *Marco Spada*, 1857, both by Mazilier). Her performance won enthusiastic approval. The ballet was revised after the public dress rehearsal by the addition of several scenes not included in the scenario. Although he had not been consulted, Gautier approved of the changes. The music has a distinctly oriental flavour, although never sinking to a slavish imitation of eastern music.   C.M.C.

CLEOPATRA

Ballet in five acts. Choreography by Giuseppe Rota. Music by Paolo Giorza. Scenery by Peroni. Costumes by Mazzini. Milan, Scala, February 26, 1859. Principal dancers: Teodoro Charansonney, Carolina Pochini, Ettore Poggialesi (all bearing the rank of primi ballerini assoluti); Assunta Razzanelli (Cleopatra), Effisio Catte (Antony), Federico Ghedini (Octavius), Luigi Donesi (ancient Egyptian), Agostino Panni (Diomedes), Antonio Franzago (Proculeius), Luigi Radice (Canidius), Giuseppe Bocci, Pietro Trigambi (Cleopatra's ministers), Cristina Hochelmann, Rachele Conti, Giovannina Adamoli (Cleopatra's maids); a quintette danced in the third act by: Charansonney and Poggialesi and the "hermit's pupils," Hochelman, Conti, and Adamoli.

SYNOPSIS. A court banquet attended by Cleopatra and Mark Antony is interrupted by a messenger bearing a declaration of war from Octavius Caesar. Cleopatra, ambitious and greedy for power, abandons Antony and orders the Egyptian army to combine with that of the Roman invader. Dying, Antony curses the woman who has betrayed him. Octavius enters Alexandria in triumph. Cleopatra exercises all her power of fascination to seduce him, but in vain. He takes the Queen prisoner to Rome. Cleopatra, unable to bear the shame, kills herself by means of an asp's bite. The ballet ends with the funeral obsequies of the fatal Queen.

■ In 1859, with *Cleopatra*, Giuseppe Rota reached the peak of his fame. At first a dancer, Rota made a precocious debut as a choreographer after a short professional apprenticeship, and staged a considerable number of ballets in various Italian towns (his definitive field of action was Milan, first at the Cannobiana Theater and then at the Scala) and at the Opéra in Paris (where he produced *La Maschera* in 1864). It was in one of his ballets, *Il Giuocatore*, at the Carlo Felice Theater in Genoa in 1855, that Enrico Cecchetti made his first professional appearance at the age of only five. In Rota's choreography the perfect balance of Carlo Blasis's ideal ballet was upset by the inflated emotions of that particular moment of Italian history just after the Risorgimento, which led to the positivist euphoria of Manzotti. Poised between two different epochs, Rota's productions were characterized by empressive mimed action and spectacularly grouped crowd scenes. In *Cleopatra*, the fifth act (the Queen's funeral) was added to enable the choreographer to present a meticulous reproduction of ancient Egyptian rites, in which the deceased were subjected to a sort of trial to decide

The interior of the Opéra during a performance in honour of Czar Alexander II. Paris, 1867.

whether they were worthy of ceremonial entombment. The star of *Cleopatra* was Carolina Pochini, even though her name does not figure among the leading characters. It was the custom then to interlard a ballet with solos and *pas de deux* in the nature of academic *divertissements*, no matter how irrelevant to the plot, performed by famous dancers, and these were the main attraction of the evening's entertainment.   C.M.C.

FAR FROM DENMARK or A COSTUME BALL ON BOARD SHIP *(Fjernt fra Danmark or Et Kostumebal on Bord)*
Light comedy-ballet in two acts. Choreography and scenario by August Bournonville. Music by Hans Christian Lumbye, Joseph Glaeser, Louis Gottschalk, Edouard Dupuy, Andreas Lincke. Sets and costumes by Ferdinand Christensen, Troels Lund, Edward Lehmann. Copenhagen, Theater Royal Opera House, April 20, 1860. Royal Danish Ballet.

SYNOPSIS. Act I: a Danish ship on a cruise in the southern Atlantic drops anchor in an Argentine port. On the verandah of the Danish Consul's house by the sea the ship's ceremonial gunfire can be heard. While the coloured servants enliven the evening with their dancing, a romantic intrigue proceeds between a naval officer, the Consul's daughter, and one of her suitors. Act II:

everything depends on the grand masquerade ball given on board the ship, during which the sailors, in the national dress of various countries, perform dances typical of their lands of origin. The formal opening dance from Spain is followed by livelier ones characteristic of the Eskimo, Chinese, and American Indian sailors. Thus, once again, Bournonville contrived to give his enthusiastic soloists a chance to display their skill and spirit.

■ A mature work, this ballet also provided the change of background that so appealed to Bournonville, with his deep interest in foreign and exotic places. During his travels all over Europe he collected ethnic and folk dance patterns and, by filtering them through his masterly critical sense, produced results of the highest choreographic value, always dramatically motivated. He raised the traditional to the level of art. The authentic face of every nation represented was transmuted through his personal style "in harmony with the past ideals of Noverre and the future ones of Fokine." Inspired by the world cruises then popular in Danish high society, *Far from Denmark* has always remained in the repertory of its native land, being performed in its entirety. Abroad, however, it is usually known only by its second act, very popular because of the long and lively character dances it contains.   G.S.

THE BUTTERFLY *(Le Papillon)*
Mime-ballet in two acts and four scenes. Choreography by Maria Taglioni. Music by Jacques Offenbach. Scenario by Maria Taglioni and Vernoy de Saint-Georges. Sets by Cambon, Thierry, Despléchin, Nolan, Rubé, and Martin. Paris, Opéra, November 26, 1860. Principal dancers: Emma Livry (Farfalla), Louise Marquet (the enchantress Hamza), Louis Mérante (Djalma), Berthier (Patimate).

SYNOPSIS. Act I: the ancient sorceress Hamza is making up in front of a mirror in the hopes of rejuvenating herself sufficiently to attract Prince Djalma, whose kiss could give her back her youth and beauty. She catches the beautiful Farfalla mimicking her and tries to strike the girl with her crutch, but misses her and injures her own servant Patimate. At that moment Djalma enters, and instead of paying court to her, kisses Farfalla, while his guardian reveals his suspicion that it is Hamza who once kidnapped the daughter of the Emir. When the spiteful sorceress falls asleep, Farfalla tickles her with a flower, fluttering around her like the insect whose name she bears ("Farfalla" being the Italian word for butterfly). Some ladies of the court amuse themselves by chasing the gaily coloured insects, and so Farfalla falls into their net and is passed on to the prince. In the act of pinning her down, he recognizes the girl and allows her to fly away with the swarm. She is soon recaptured by Hamza, but Patimate sets her free and traps his mistress in the net instead, sending the old witch to the Emir as the kidnapper of his daughter. Act II: under threat, Hamza makes Farfalla reappear and restores her to the Emir, who affiances her to Djalma.

The sorceress, however, succeeds in coming between the two just as they are about to embrace, thus receiving the kiss which by its magic will give her back her youthful charms. When the Prince still repulses her, she sends him to sleep in an enchanted garden and turns Farfalla into a butterfly once more. Djalma awakes to find Farfalla fluttering about him. He grasps the creature and conceals her. The wedding procession approaches preceded by a torch carrier. Attracted by the light, the butterfly is caught in the flames; her wings are singed and she falls, changed back to her womanly form, into the Prince's arms. The spell is broken and Hamza is turned into a statue.

■ This, the only ballet choreographed by Maria Taglioni, was the first to have a score composed by Offenbach. It was also the triumph of the unfortunate Emma Livry, who was to die at the age of twenty only a few months later, on July 26, 1863, from burns sustained during a rehearsal of *La Muta di Portici*, when her tutu caught fire from a proscenium light. She was a thin, rather plain girl, whose success was due to her technical and artistic gifts alone. The critics wrote of her that "her steps would have left no imprint on the flowers." Commenting on her favourite pupil's admirable performance, Taglioni said, "It is true that I never saw myself dance, but I must have danced like her!" She gave poor Emma a photograph bearing the famous inscription: "Make the public forget me, but do not forget me yourself."   G.S.

THE DAUGHTER OF PHARAOH *(Dotch Faraona)*
Ballet in three acts and seven scenes, with prologue and epilogue. Choreography by Marius Petipa. Scenario by Vernoy de Saint-Georges and Marius Petipa. Music by Cesare Pugni. Scenery by Roller and Wagner. Costumes by Kelwer and Stolyakov. St. Petersburg, Maryinsky Theater, January 18, 1862. Principal dancers: Marius Petipa (Lord Wilson and Ta-Hor), Carolina Rosati (Aspicia, Pharaoh's daughter), M. T. A. Stukalkin (John Bull and Passifont), M. N. O. Goltz (Pharaoh).

SYNOPSIS. Prologue: in an oasis of the Egyptian desert Lord Wilson and his manservant John Bull, who have joined a caravan of Armenian merchants, are forced by a dust storm to take refuge with the others in a pyramid, where the guardian of the monument shows Wilson the mummy of the Pharaoh's favourite daughter. Under the influence of opium given them by the merchants, Wilson and Bull fall into a hallucinatory dream. The young Aspicia, rising from her sarcophagus, calls her retinue back to life and, placing her hand on the young lord's heart, vanishes in a cloud. Act I: Wilson and Bull, reincarnated under the influence of the drug into the ancient Egyptians Ta-Hor and Passifont, save Aspicia from the jaws of a lion. Ta-Hor,

Ekaterina Maximova and Vladimir Vassiliev in a scene from Don Kikhot, *in the version by Alexander Gorski, produced at the Opéra in 1977.*

refusing any reward, declares his love to her, but she is already promised in marriage to the King of Nubia. Aspicia, however, prefers to flee with Ta-Hor, thus rousing her father's anger. The disappointed suitor sets off in pursuit of them. Act II: discovered hiding in a fisherman's hut by the Nubian King, Aspicia proves as insensible to his protestations of love as to his threats, and throws herself into the Nile to escape him. She sinks down to the underwater realm, where the Ruler of the Waters gives a feast in her honour, inviting all the world's important rivers. The King of the Nile grants her the power of rising to the surface on a shell. Act III: Ta-Hor, taken captive, is sent before Pharaoh, who decrees that unless he brings back the Princess, he will die by a serpent's bite. Aspicia reappears, accuses the King of Nubia, and, on the threat of letting herself be bitten by the snake, secures Ta-Hor's freedom. Consent to their marriage now won, she ascends to Osiris's heaven with him. Epilogue: the stage darkens; we are back in the interior of the pyramid. Wilson, Bull, and the merchants wake from their drug-induced sleep, while the mummies and statues are once more inanimate.

■ The resounding success of this ballet (which lasted four hours and employed eighty dancers), inspired by Théophile Gautier's *Le Roman de la Momie*, was prepared in only six weeks for Carolina Rosati's farewell performance. It won Petipa the position of *maître de ballet* at the Maryinsky Theater and tempted other great ballerinas, including Marie Petipa, Vazem, Zucchi, Tchessinskaya, and Pavlova, to undertake the heroine's role, each contributing her own interpretation of the part.   G.S.

FLICK AND FLOCK (Flick e Flock)
A "grand fantastic ballet" in two parts. Choreography and scenario by Paolo Taglioni. Music by A. Hertel. Scenery by Peroni. Costumes by Zamperoni. Milan, Scala, February 13, 1862. Principal dancers: Amina Boschetti (Nella, Princess Topaz, and Nereid), Effisio Catte (Flick), Teodoro Gasperini (Flock), Regina Banderali (Queen of the Gnomes, Amphitrite).

SYNOPSIS. Flick, son of an alchemist who died some time before, decides to search for his father's treasure in order to pay his debts and save his fiancée Nella from the designs of the powerful burgomaster. He is accompanied by his friend Flock. They enter a secret passage leading to the Kingdom of the Gnomes, where Flick is condemned to be tortured, in spite of the pleas of Princess Topaz. However, the Statue of Destiny comes to life and orders that the two young men should be sent in search of a magic ring instead. After being wrecked, they find themselves in Amphitrite's palace under the sea, inhabited by nereids. Flick and Flock watch fantastic evocations of spirits by the Genie of Truth. Finally Flick asks the Genie to tell his fortune and is shown a vision of his native land and his friends and family. Amphitrite sends up a mighty column of water that carries the two friends to the surface and they are soon back in the house of Nella and her sad old grandmother, to whom they bring an elixir of youth. A messenger arrives to conduct Flick and Nella to the Temple of Fortune, where their marriage is celebrated with great splendour.

■ The bizarre adventures of Paolo Taglioni's two heroes became suddenly popular and the ballet enjoyed unusual success as testified by the hundred and more repeat performances in 1862 and the following three years. Specially appreciated was the dance in the grand finale, performed by a group of girl dancers wearing military jackets and *bersagliere* plumed hats with their plain tutus. This patriotic display was received with immense enthusiasm and marked the culminating point of a succession of stunningly showy scenes such as were expected in the Italian *grand ballet* of the later nineteenth century. Paolo Taglioni, one of the few good choreographers then active in Italian ballet, knew how to give such superficial theatrical effects a certain artistic dignity, due chiefly to the imagination and richness of his own choreographic style, derived as much from the French tradition as from the Italian. It was not fortuitous that the dancers in his ballets were among the most strictly academic, albeit with the expressiveness of the Italian school. One of them was Amina Boschetti, the heroine of *Flick and Flock*, a dancer who combined a lively dramatic personality with the impeccable technique learned in the school of Carlo Blasis.   A.A.

THE SPRING (La Source)
Ballet in three acts and four scenes. Choreography by Arthur Saint-Léon. Music by Léon Minkus (first and fourth scene) and Léo Delibes (second and third scene). Scenario by Charles Nuitter and Arthur Saint-Léon. Sets by Despléchin, Lavastre, Rubé, Chaperon. Costumes by Loumier and Albert. Paris, Opéra, November 12, 1866. Principal dancers: Guglielmina Salvioni (Naila), Eugénie Fiocre (Nouredda), Louis Mérante (Djemil), L. Marquet (Morgab).

SYNOPSIS. Act I: Naila, the spirit of a spring in a mythical Persia, is protected by the hunter Djemil, who prevents the gypsy Morgab from polluting the stream with poisonous plants. Djemil falls in love with Nouredda and picks a beautiful flower from a preciptious crag for her sake, refusing a reward but daring to lift her veil to see her lovely face. To punish the offence, her brother ties him up with rushes and condemns him to die of thirst beside the spring. Naila sends the waters of the stream over Djemil's bonds and sets him free, and although she reproaches him for having picked her magic flower, promises to help him win his loved one. Act II: accompanied by Morgab, Nouredda arrives at the palace of the Khan, her promised husband. They are joined by Djemil who, with his enchanted flower, conjures up a spring from which Naila emerges. As soon as he sees her, the Khan prefers her to Nouredda. The rejected girl swears to avenge herself with the help of Morgab. Act III: once more Djemil offers his love to Nouredda, but her brother interrupts them and tries to kill him. He is again saved

Liliana Cosi and Paolo Bortoluzzi in Coppelia *at the Scala during the 1974–1975 season.*

by Naila, who bids him flee with Nouredda, although the water spirit, desolate that her love is unrequited, warns him that Nouredda does not care for him. He begs her to use the magic flower to make the girl fall in love with him, and Naila, well knowing that her life is bound up with that of the flower, sacrifices herself by hanging it over Nouredda's heart, which at last warms towards Djemil. Naila grows pale and slowly dies as the jet of water from the spring ceases to flow.

■ Originally the ballet was designed for Adèle Grantzowa, but as she hurt her foot during rehearsals and was then detained in St. Petersburg for the Czarevitch's wedding celebrations, Lucian Petipa and Charles Nuitter passed the title part on to Guglielmina Salvioni, an accomplished but limited soloist. From Russia Arthur Saint-Léon sent the choreographic directions by letter to Paris. The "contralto" Salvioni could not have

been a great success, for Saint-Léon could not wait to replace her with the "soprano" Grantzowa, renowned for her *retraites sur les pointes*. However, it was Eugènie Fiocre in the part of Nouredda who made the most distinct success, especially in the Guzla dance. She was also the first dancer to be painted by Degas, who was in the audience. The third Naila was the Italian Angelina Fioretti, who danced the part on December 23, 1867.

OTHER VERSIONS. Arthur Saint-Léon arranged a new version entitled *The Lily* for Adèle Grantzowa, who performed it at St. Petersburg in 1869. Produced in Italy under the title *La Sorgente*, and at the Viennese court as *Naila* in 1878, *The Spring* has also had several more recent revivals: by A. Koppini at St. Petersburg in 1902, by N. Sergeyev as a farewell evening for Agrippina Vaganova at St. Petersburg in 1916, and again, with choreography by Vaganova and Ponomaryov, at Leningrad in 1925. Léo Staats used the ballet's music (in an arrangement by H. Busser) for dances in his *soirée de fête* at the Paris Opéra in 1928. Separate versions of the *pas de deux* were arranged by Cranko for Stuttgart in 1964 and by Balanchine for the New York City Ballet in 1968.   G.S.

DON QUIXOTE *(Don Kikhot)*
Ballet in a prologue and four acts. Choreography and scenario by Marius Petipa. Music by Ludwig Minkus. Sets and costumes by Pavel Isakov, Fiodor Shenyan, and Changuine. Moscow, Bolshoi Theater, December 14, 1869. Principal dancers: Anna Sobeshanskaja (Kitri), Sergei Sokolov (Basil), Gillert (Don Quixote), Pavlova (Juana), Espinosa (Sancho Panza).

SYNOPSIS. Prologue: Don Quixote, obsessed by stories of medieval chivalry, tells his servant Sancho Panza of his decision to become a knight errant and improvises a suit of armour. Act I: in a Barcelona marketplace, Kitri is forced by her innkeeper father to accept the offer of the rich Gamache and turn away Basil, the man she loves. Don Quixote arrives at the inn astride his horse Rosinante and believes he recognizes in Kitri his loved and idealized lady Dulcinea. Act II: Don Quixote challenges Gamache to a duel but is mocked and chased away. Basil pretends to kill himself and begs Kitri's father with his last breath to grant him his daughter's hand in marriage. The dying man's request being granted, he throws off the pretence and is happily united with his Kitri. Among the windmills Don Quixote pays homage to the King of the Gypsies and joins in the dances the latter has organized to make fun of him. Afterwards he attacks the marionettes of a travelling puppet-show as if they were enemy soldiers and charges at the windmills, taking them to be hostile giants. Act III: wounded in the combat, the Knight of the Doleful Countenance seeks shelter in a forest with Sancho, and they fall asleep. He dreams he is in Dulcinea's garden, inhabited by fantastic beings, where he fights a gigantic spider. A last, emerging the victor, he sees his adored lady. But the dream fades away. Now Don Quixote falls in with the Duke and his train and is invited to the castle. Act IV: in the Duke's castle grand festivities are held in honour of Don Quixote, who is challenged to a duel and crushingly defeated by the Knight of the Silver Moon, who in reality is none other than the deluded Knight's old friend Carrasco. He extracts a promise from the Don to sheathe his sword for at least a year. Bitterly disappointed, but faithful to his word, Don Quixote lays down his arms and returns home.

■ Other choreographers before Petipa had been inspired by Cervantes's famous character, among the best known being Jean-Georges Noverre (*Dom Quichotte*, music by Josef Starzer, Vienna, 1786), Louis Milon (*Les Noces de Gamache*, Paris, 1801), Charles Louis Didelot (*Don Kikhot*, St. Petersburg, 1809), Salvatore Taglioni (*Don Chisciotte*, Turin, 1844), and Paolo Taglioni (*Don Quixote*, Berlin, 1850). The only ballet on the subject to

have established itself in choreographic literature, however, is Marius Petipa's *Don Kikhot*, revived by its originator at the Bolshoi Theater in St. Petersburg on November 9, 1871, the principal dancers being Alexandra Vergina and Lev Ivanov. It has been passed down to the modern Soviet repertory via the reconstructions by Alexander Gorski in 1900 and Rostislav Zakharoff in 1940. Created early in the most fertile and mature period of Petipa's Russian career, this work reveals in the *pas d'action* forwarding the narrative the influence of his master Perrot and, at the same time, his own predilection for pure academic dance, in a series of exquisite interludes entirely unconnected to the plot. The richness and technical perfection of the attitudes and steps, the fantastic variety of the *enchaînements*, both in the academic passages and in the highly stylized "character" dances (of folk origin), combine to make up the high value of Petipa's ballets belonging to this creative phase. It is no accident that *pas de deux* from this and his other major ballets have been borrowed to be used as separate bravura pieces in the repertory of virtuoso dancers. The *grand pas de deux* from *Don Quixote* is now usually performed in the revised version established by Anatole Oboukhov.

OTHER VERSIONS. 1) Alexander Gorski (full-length ballet, scenario altered and reduced to three acts). Moscow, Bolshoi Theater, December 6, 1900; later at the Maryinsky Theater in St. Petersburg on January 20, 1902; revived at the Bolshoi Theater, Moscow, on February 10, 1940, by Rostislav Zakharov; this version was reproduced by Witol Borkowski at the Liverpool Empire Theatre on June 28, 1962 (Ballet Rambert); then at the London Coliseum, July 1, 1970 (Festival Ballet). 2) Laurent Novikov (abbreviated version), 1924, for Anna Pavlova's company. 3) Georges Gué. Helsinki, March 6, 1958. Danced by Doris Laine, Klaus Salin, National Ballet of Finland. 4) Rudolf Nureyev. Vienna State Opera House, December 1, 1966. Danced by Ully Wührer, Michael Birkmeyer, Konstantin Zajetz. 5) Using C. Gerhard's scenario and music, Ninette de Valois put on her own version of *Don Quixote* at Covent Garden Opera House in London, February 20, 1950. Danced by Margot Fonteyn, Alexander Grant, and Robert Helpmann. 6) George Balanchine (*Don Quixote*) to music by Nicholas Nabokov. New York, State Theater, May 27, 1965. Principal dancers: Suzanne Farrel, Deni Lamont, George Balanchine, New York City Ballet.   A.A.

THE MUSIC. Ludwig Minkus, a Russo-Austrian composer, was born in Vienna in 1827 and completed his musical studies there, although he spent most of his later life in Russia. He began his career as a composer of ballet music in Paris in April 1846, with *Paquita*, written in collaboration with Deldevez; later he worked on the score of *La Source* with Delibes, which opened with scant success on November 12, 1866. Meanwhile *The Union of Tethis and Peleus*, one of his mythological ballets, played at the open-air theater on Olga Island in Russia to celebrate the visit of the German monarch to Czar Alexander II in August 1857, was enormously successful, partly owing to its magnificent staging. After this impressive achievement, Minkus moved to Russia in 1869 and worked with Petipa, first in Moscow, where he wrote *Don Quixote* (which remains one of his best-known works and is still in the repertory of the National Soviet Ballet), and later in St. Petersburg. In that city he became a solo violinist as well as inspector of the Maryinsky Theater's musical section between 1861 and 1872, after which he more or less stepped into Cesare Pugni's place and composed ballet music for the same theater. He kept that position until 1886. In 1872 Gedeonov commissioned Cui, Borodin, Mussorgsky, and Rimsky-Korsakov to write the music for the opera *Mlada*, but left all the ballet music to Minkus, showing the high esteem in which that composer was held. The project was abandoned, however. Minkus's reputation received a blow in the years that followed through the opinions of Vsevolozhsky, who was appointed director of the state theaters and gave Tchaikovsky his chance. Minkus's music fulfilled all the technical needs of the ballet of those days, but had no further pretensions. Contemporary critics were already referring to his superficiality, composed of "smoothly flowing tunes and commonplace rhythms."   A.F.

COPPELIA, or THE GIRL WITH ENAMEL EYES
(Coppélia, or La Fille aux Yeux d'Émail)
Mime-ballet in two acts and three scenes. Choreography by Arthur Saint-Léon. Music by Léo Delibes. Scenario by Charles Nuitter and Arthur Saint-Léon. Sets by Charles Cambon, Edouard Despléchin, and Jean-Baptiste Lavastre. Costumes by Paul Lormier. Paris Opéra, May 25, 1870. Principal dancers: Giuseppina Bozzacchi (Swanilda), Eugénie Fiocre (Franz), François Dauty (Coppelius).

SYNOPSIS. Act I: in the village square of a Galician village the young Swanilda enters and dances in front of the house of Doctor Coppelius the toymaker. She tries to attract the attention of Coppelia, standing as always, still and serious in the window, a strange girl whom the inhabitants suppose to be the old magician-craftsman's daughter. Franz is fascinated by her, although he is engaged to Swanilda, who now watches him enter and throw a kiss towards the window. The jealous girl jokes teasingly with the lad before dancing with her friends. Soon all are joining in a czardas. When the square is empty again Coppelius comes out of his house and goes off, absent-mindedly dropping the key. Swanilda and her friends find it and, filled with curiosity, enter the house. Coppelius returns, anxiously looking for his key, then, seeing his door open, dashes into the house. Franz, thinking the doctor far away, also gets into the house through a window. Act II: the girls enter the old man's workshop on tiptoe. There they see Coppelia seated in a corner. Swanilda advances shyly towards her and discovers to her joy that the figure is only a mechanical doll. Meanwhile the others are amusing themselves by turning on all the automatons with which the workshop is filled. Coppelius bursts furiously into the room and all the intruders run away. Only Swanilda has not been able to reach the door in time; she hides in Coppelia's corner, taking the place of the doll. Franz arrives and, surprised by the indignant magician, confesses that he loves his "daughter" Coppelia and would like to marry her. Feigning friendliness, Coppelius offers his guest a sleeping-draught. When Franz falls senseless to the ground, the doctor carries him to the side of his precious doll (really Swanilda) and calls on his magic arts to transfer the young man's life to the supposedly inanimate creature whom he loves as if it really were his daughter. Swanilda falls in with the plan and pretends to progress gradually from mechanical movements to a radiant human vitality. To the amazed delight of the old man, she performs two brilliant dances (Spanish and Scottish) until, tired of the joke, she capriciously turns the workshop upside down and wakes Franz, then shows the doctor the real Coppelia in a corner. The two young people go off happily together, while Coppelius sadly embraces his cold automaton. In the village square the marriage of Swanilda and Franz is celebrated with a long series of festive dances, interrupted only by the wedding ceremony and one last, short appearance of the misanthropic Coppelius.

■ *Coppelia* belongs to the select company of nineteenth-century ballets that have survived down to our own day without a break in continuity and still have their place as a main feature in the programs of every ballet theater and company. The plot, taken by the archivist of the Opéra, Charles Nuitter, from E. T. A. Hoffman's story *Der Sandmann*, introduced into ballet the world of automatons, dolls, and marionettes that was to produce so many thematic offshoots, culminating in the disturbing element of humanity in the puppet *Petrushka*. Little of Hoffmann's Gothic romanticism is left in Saint-Léon's ballet, a lively comedy in which the more dramatic element is concentrated in the strange character of Coppelius, and thus confined to the first scene of Act II. It casts no shadow on the joyous clarity of the amiable fairy tale with a happy ending, which is the archetype of Second Empire ballet (in its last phase). *Coppelia* was, in fact, the last ballet produced at the Opéra before the Franco-Prussian War forced that theater to close its doors, and marked the end of an epoch for ballet as for much else. The choreographer Saint-Léon died three months after the first performance of this, his masterpiece, and the following November saw the death from smallpox during the siege of Paris of the first interpreter of Swanilda's part, Giuseppina Bozzacchi, on her seventeenth birthday. After the premature death of this young ballerina, discovered by Saint-Léon at Madame Dominique's school of dancing and acclaimed in her one and only professional role, the Opéra ballet fell on evil days, partly, no doubt, due to the loss of so many leading personalities. Amalia Ferraris and Carolina Rosati had left, Emma Livry's brief reign had come to a tragic end, Adèle Grantzow had proved an unsatisfactory substitute; Mazilier had died and now Saint-Léon himself. All the same, in *Coppelia* the Opéra acquired a "classic," for it has stayed in the repertory from its first revival in 1870 (danced by Léontine Beaugrand) until today, and the

The Kingdom of the Shades, *a version of* La Bayadère *confined to the fourth act of the ballet and arranged by Rudolf Nureyev. Here the Royal Ballet ensemble.*

original version has been kept to with unusual faithfulness. Traditionally the part of Franz was entrusted to a ballerina in travesty, as it was to Eugénie Fiocre who partnered Giuseppina Bozzacchi in the first performance. An essential ingredient of *Coppelia* was – an unprecedented circumstance in nineteenth-century ballet – the music by Léo Delibes, a composer still undervalued today. He appears as Tchaikovsky's only predecessor in the musical renaissance of modern ballet. Saint-Léon's choreography, on the other hand, revealed the loss of stylistic coherence and unity of development in the late romantic French ballet. In the three scenes of *Coppelia*, the fragmentation of the action, both narrative and academic, of the first, the mime of the fantastic *ballet d'action* of the second, and the exquisite but irrelevant solo

and ensemble *divertissements* of the third, are so many adaptations of various preexisting forms that fail to fuse into a new, organic whole. Still, within those limits, which in fact reflected the general creative malaise affecting the ballet of the period, Saint Léon was able to give his masterpiece all the freshness and fascination of his delicate, imaginative, and inventive choreography, especially in the academic solo parts enlivened with the national and folk overtones of the many character dances (mazurka, czardas, gig, bolero, etc.) interspersed throughout the ballet.

OTHER VERSIONS. 1) Marius Petipa. St. Petersburg, Bolshoi Theater, November 25, 1884. Danced by Barbara Nikitina. 2) Enrico Cecchetti and Lev Ivanov.

St. Petersburg, Maryinsky Theater, January 26, 1894. Reconstructed by Nicholas Sergeyev. London, Sadler's Wells Theatre, March 21, 1933. Danced by Lydia Lopokova, Stanley Judson, Hedley Briggs. 3) Giorgio Saracco. Milan, Scala, January 26, 1896. Danced by Carlotta Brianza, Vittorio de Vincenti. 4) Hans Beck and Glasemann. Copenhagen, Theater Royal, December 27, 1896. Danced by Valborg Borchsenius, Hans Beck. Revived by Harald Lander at the same theater, September 8, 1934. Danced by Margot Lander; then at Festival Hall, London, August 31, 1956. Danced by Belinda Wright, John Gilpin. 5) Nicholas Zvereff. Monte Carlo, 1936. Danced by Vera Nemchinova, Ballets de René Blum. 6) Aurel Milloss. Milan, August 14, 1946. Danced by Emilia Clerici, Ugo Dell'Ara, Aurel Milloss, Scala Ballet. 7) Michel Descombey. Paris, Opéra, June 26, 1966. Danced by Claude Bessy, Cyril Atanassoff. 8) Enrique Martinez. New York, Brooklyn Academy, December 24, 1968. Danced by Carla Fracci, Erik Bruhn, American Ballet Theater; then Milan, Scala, May 12, 1973. Danced by Carla Fracci, Niels Kehlet, Enrique Martinez. 9) George Balanchine and Alexandra Danilova. Saratoga, Performing Arts Center, July 17, 1974. Danced by Patricia McBride, Helgi Tomasson, Shaun O'Brien, New York City Ballet. 10) Roland Petit. Ballets de Marseille.   A.A.

CAMARGO

Ballet in three acts and five scenes. Choreography by Marius Petipa. Music by Ludwig Minkus. Scenario by Jules Henri Vernoy de Saint-Georges and Marius Petipa. Sets by Andrei Roller. Costumes by Evgenij Ponomarov. St. Petersburg, Maryinsky Theater, December 17, 1872. Principal dancers: Adèle Grantzow (Marie Camargo), Simskaya II (Madeleine Camargo), Nicholas Goltz (Camargo père), Paul Gerdt (Vestris), Lev Ivanov (Comte de Melun).

SYNOPSIS. Vestris arrives at the Camargos' house accompanied by a violinist to give a dancing lesson to Marie Camargo (the famous eighteenth-century dancer-to-be). The violinist, who is really the Comte de Melun under an assumed name, is fascinated by Marie although he is engaged to be married to her sister Madeleine. The two men invite the sisters to a grand masked ball at St. Germain, and after some hesitation, the girls accept. Marie takes part in it as a professional dancer, and Melun takes advantage of the general confusion to seize her and carry her to his palace. Returned home, Marie considers how to avenge herself and her sister for the Count's conduct. At a party given by the Duc de Mayenne she strips the mask from the last of the innumerable ladies Melun is insolently courting in the presence of her husband. The Comte de Melun is obliged to keep his word and marry Madeleine, while Marie declares she will dedicate her life to the dance. At a grand ball at Versailles Marie is the outstanding success of the evening.

■ The ballet is based on a true incident that occurred in 1728 when the two sisters were being courted by the Comte de Melun. The occurrence, transferred to the stage, was greeted with enormous enthusiasm by both critics and public, thanks in part to the superb performance of Grantzow (or, in Russian, Grantzova). A historic event connected with *Camargo* took place on January 28, 1901, when Pierina Legnani chose the title role for her farewell evening, and gave a performance that has remained famous in the annals of the Maryinsky Theater. An earlier ballet entitled *Camargo* was created by Hippolyte Monplaisir (scenario and choreography) with music by Costantino dall'Argine, at the Scala on January 11, 1868; it was revived by Marzagora, still at the Scala, for the Carnival of the same year, and at the Regio in Turin during the 1871 Carnival.

OTHER VERSIONS. Lev Ivanov. Music by Ludwig Minkus. Scenery by Oreste Allegri. St. Petersburg, Maryinsky Theater, January 28, 1901.   C.M.C.

PIETRO MICCA

Historical ballet in eight scenes. Choreography by Luigi Manzotti. Music by Giovanni Chitti. Sets by Magnani.

Sketch of a costume for Sieba, *a ballet created by Luigi Manzotti to music by Romualdo Marenco.*

Costumes by Zamperoni. Rome, Aliberti Theater, January 20, 1875. Principal dancers: Francesco Baratti (Raffaele, Count della Torre), Carlo Coppi (Vittorio Amadeo II of Aosta), Antonio Coppini (Alberto), Luigi Manzotti (Pietro Micca), Filomena Pratesi (Maria, his wife).

SYNOPSIS. Pietro Micca is recruiting volunteers to come to the defense of Turin, which is threatened by the French. Raffaele della Torre, disguised as a hermit, preaches that disaster will befall anyone who joins in the resistance. Unable to curb the patriots' enthusiasm, della Torre tries to delay them, preceding them along the way and plotting against their advance. His conspiracy is thwarted by Pietro Micca, who manages to get hold of some incriminating documents. The hero, together with his friends, lays the mines which will prove fatal to the French in the cellars of the citadel. Pressed by the speed of events, Micca sends his companions to safety, but remains behind to light the fuse, sacrificing his own life beneath the ruins that will bury him, the traitor della Torre, and all the French. The last scene shows the triumph of King Vittorio Amadeo II as he takes the oath on the hill of Superga.

■ "Luigi Manzotti's creative development reflected the changing taste of Italy, turning from the passions of the Risorgimento to a new middle-class and industrial civilization. Starting from the inspired patriotic epic of *Pietro Micca*, the most celebrated Italian choreographer of the last decades of the nineteenth century descended to the mediocre hedonism typical of the *Belle Époque* in the form of his ballet *Sport*" (Rossi, *Il Ballo alla Scala*). Manzotti started his career as choreographer at the Scala (his debut as a dancer had taken place three years earlier in *Bianca di Nevers* by Ferdinando Pratesi), while still continuing to dance. The part of Pietro Micca became his showpiece, and was the role he chose for his farewell to the public in 1881, in a version of the ballet put on for the *Esposizione Nazionale* and staged at the Arena in Milan in spectacular style, with fireworks and a charge by ballerinas dressed as *bersaglieri* and accompanied by sixty-four drums.
C.M.C.

SYLVIA or DIANA'S NYMPH (*Sylvia* or *La Nymphe de Diane*)

Ballet in three acts. Choreography by Louis Mérante. Music by Léo Delibes. Scenario by Jules Barbier and Baron de Reinach. Sets by Jules Chéret, Alfred Rubé, and Philippe M. Chaperon. Costumes by Eugène Lacoste. Paris, Opéra, June 14, 1876. Principal dancers: Rita Sangalli (Sylvia), Louis Mérante (Aminta), Marco Magri (Orione), Marie Sanlaville (Eros), Louise Marquet (Diana).

SYNOPSIS. Act I: beside the statue of Eros in a sacred wood, the nightly games of fauns, dryads, and wood nymphs are interrupted by the arrival of Aminta, a young shepherd in love with Sylvia, a nymph dedicated to Diana, whom he has seen on a previous night. Hiding when the nymphs appear, he is discovered and dragged to the feet of Sylvia herself. She, disdainful of his love, shoots an arrow at the figure of Eros, but wounds instead the young man who has taken refuge behind it. The statue comes to life and pierces the nymph with one of his golden arrows. The dark hunter Orion abducts Sylvia when she returns alone to gaze tenderly at the fallen Aminta. After she has gone he is cured by a magician and sets off on the track of the abductor. The shepherds recognize the sorcerer as Eros and worship him. Act II: in Orion's cave Sylvia repels Orion's advances but, seeing she is a prisoner with no way of escape, she consents to sit with him at a banquet and persuades him to drink while she performs a dance in honour of Bacchus. When the barbarous huntsman and his slaves fall into a drunken sleep, Sylvia invokes the god of love, sacrificing her weapons to him. As Eros appears to save her, the walls of the cavern dissolve. Act III: by the seashore, near a temple to Diana, Aminta wanders desperately among the revellers celebrating the rites of Bacchus and Silenus. A young pirate disembarks with his slaves, one of whom, after dancing voluptuously before Aminta, reveals herself to be Sylvia. The reunited lovers are attacked by the furious Orion and run towards Diana's temple. The brutal huntsman strikes at the temple door with his axe. Suddenly storm clouds darken the sky and a terrible roll of thunder announces the angry goddess, who appears on the threshold of her temple and transfixes Orion with an arrow from her bow. Then she turns on the young couple and accuses her nymph, who confesses that she is in love, of breaking her sacred vow. Holding a lamp aloft, the pirate rises up in front of Diana, who recognizes him as Eros, while a vision of Endymion in a shining cloud reminds the goddess that she too once loved. She pardons Sylvia and Aminta. The dark clouds vanish to reveal Diana's palace, where she with Eros by her side celebrates the union of the two lovers in a splendid apotheosis.

■ Inspired by Tasso's *Aminta*, the very plot of *Sylvia* with its mythological-pastoral ambience and its fragmentary action eked out with any excuse for bravura steps or sumptuous spectacle, reveals the decadence – on the level of creative choreography – of ballet at the Paris Opéra during the last decades of the nineteenth century. (Perhaps it could be said that the great tradition had taken refuge in Russia.) Nevertheless, Louis Mérante, though a much less gifted choreographer than his predecessor Saint-Léon, knew how to create a starring part for a prima ballerina, giving her every opportunity to shine in exhibitions of virtuosity in pure academic style. The first to dance the part of Sylvia was Rita Sangalli, who showed herself to be the new star so long awaited by the audience at the Opéra, where the ensemble kept faithfully to the French tradition but the prima ballerinas were generally Italian. The reign of Grisi, Cerrito, Sofia Fuoco, Rosati, and Ferraris lasted for many years, interrupted without great success by the German Adèle Grantzow and the impeccable French dancer Léontine Beaugrand, before returning to Italy with the single appearance of Giuseppina Bozzacchi (see

The Electricity scene from the ballet Excelsior *in a revival of that work by Luigi Manzotti given at the Scala in 1910.*

Coppelia, page 133. According to the historian Ivor Guest, *Sylvia* would have been swiftly forgotten if it had not been for the score, a real masterpiece of ballet music. It is probably the main reason the ballet has been revived several times in our own century in versions varying in completeness and faithfulness to Mérante's original. Delibes's music has also been used by Leonid Lavroski for the ballet *Fadetta*, drawn from a story by George Sand and presented at the Kirov Theater in Leningrad on March 21, 1934. George Balanchine created a short *Sylvia-Pas de Deux* to a fragment by Delibes, danced at the New York City Center by Maria Tallchief and André Eglevsky and still in the repertory of the New York City Ballet.

OTHER VERSIONS. 1) Giorgio Saracco (after Mérante). Milan, Scala, January 26, 1896. Danced by Carlotta Brianza, M. Garrony. 2) Lev Ivanov and Pavel Gerdt. St. Petersburg, Maryinsky Theater, December 2, 1901. Danced by Olga Preobrajenska. 3) Fred Farren (in one act). Scenario by C. Wilhelm. Music arranged by C. Clarke. London, Empire Theatre, May 18, 1911. Danced by Lydia Kyasht. 4) Serge Lifar. Paris Opéra, February 5, 1941. Danced by Lycette Darsonval, Serge Lifar. 5) Frederick Ashton. London, Covent Garden, September 3, 1952. Danced by Margot Fonteyn,

Michael Somes. One-act version at the same theater, December 18, 1967. Danced by Nadia Nerina, Gary Sherwood. A.A.

THE BAYADERE *(Bayaderka)*
Ballet in four acts. Choreography by Marius Petipa. Scenario by Sergei Khudekov. Music by Ludwig Minkus. Sets and costumes by I. Andreyev, M. Bocharov, P. Lambin, A. Roller, M. Shishkov, H. Wagner. St. Petersburg, Maryinsky Theater, January 23, 1877. Principal dancers: Ekaterina Vazem (Nikija), Pavel Gerdt (Solor), Lev Ivanov (the Rajah), Maria Gorshenkova (Aija), Maria M. Petipa (Gamsatti).

SYNOPSIS. Act I: in an Indian temple a young warrior, Solor, offers a tiger as a gift to the Rajah. He lingers in the temple, waiting for his beloved Nikija, the *bayadere*. She refuses the advances of a Brahmin, who threatens revenge, but consents to go with Solor, if he will swear fidelity to her. Act II: in his palace the Rajah offers Solor the hand of his daughter Gamsatti in marriage. Solor, fascinated by the girl's beauty and afraid of offending the ruler, forgets his vow and accepts. During the festivities that follow, the Brahmin tells the Rajah of Solor's promise to Nikija. Meanwhile, Nikija learns from Gamsatti the name of her future husband and protests in vain to her powerful rival. A slave suggests to Gamsatti that she should kill Nikija. Act III: during the wedding of Solor and Gamsatti, Nikija dances with the other *bayaderes*. The slave hands her a basket in which is concealed a poisonous snake that bites her. The Brahmin offers to save her on condition that he shall have her for himself, but the girl refuses and continues to dance until she drops lifeless. In despair at Nikija's death, Solor is sent to sleep by a fakir's spell. As in a dream, his spirit wanders in the kingdom of shadows, and there he finds his beloved *bayadere*, to be reunited to her forever.

■ Supernatural female creatures, such as sylphs, wilis, shades, water nymphs, and later swans, enjoyed great popularity in nineteenth-century ballet. They gave theatrical justification for using the *corps de ballet* in a sort of abstract choreography not tied to the human condition, and they appealed to the contemporary taste for idealized, fantasized womanhood. The *bayadere* (since *The God and the Bayadere*, see page 96), having a touch of the exotic as well, enjoyed special favour. This ballet was one of Marius Petipa's first genuine triumphs at the Imperial Theater of St. Petersburg, as well as an occasion of great acclamation for the superb dancing of Ekaterina Vazem, to whom the evening was dedicated. Serge Lifar wrote: "He [Petipa] knew how to profit from the ideas of Perrot, the dramatist of the dance, and, equally, from those of Saint-Léon, singer of the dancing *aria*, the solo, and after twenty years of collaboration with the two masters he created the Russian ballet which, at the end of the nineteenth century, was to lead the whole world. . . . Petipa trained successive generations of Russian dancers, enriched the art of dancing with new steps and movements, developed and extended academic technique, introducing elements of character, but he never opened up new paths. He reigned over a hothouse art [the Imperial Russian Ballet] and was mainly the guardian and preserver of academic traditions." *The Bayadere* has remained in the Soviet repertory, where, however, it is now presented in an altered and truncated edition (see *Other Versions* below). In the west it is now known chiefly in a version limited to the fourth act and entitled *The Kingdom of the Shades*, which consists of an ensemble for the female *corps de ballet*, a *pas de trois* for three Shades with a solo variation for each of the three ballerinas, then the entrance of Solor with a variation of vigorous virtuosity, followed by the meeting with Nikija and a wonderful *pas de deux* by the two reunited lovers in a world of unreality. This ballet holds the quintessence of Petipa's choreographic style: the slenderest of dramatic threads, hardly more than a romantic atmosphere, as the pretext for a crystalline composition of pure dance. The thirty-six Shades, in identical long white tutus, enter one after the other, executing an initial *arabesque penchée* in profile, followed by the same slow series of steps, creating the hypnotic impression of an endless flow in crescendo giving way to a choreographic counterpoint of enchanting perfection. It is one of the highest and most fertile

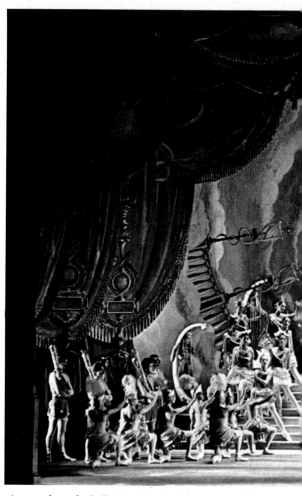

A scene from the ballet Excelsior *by Manzotti and Marenco.*

moments in Petipa's art, and its influence still reverberates in Balanchine's geometrical abstractions.

OTHER VERSIONS. 1) Alexander Gorski and Vasili Tikhomirov. Moscow, Bolshoi Theater, January 31, 1923. 2) Agrippina Vaganova. Leningrad, Kirov Theater, December 13, 1932. 3) Vladimir Ponomaryov. Leningrad, Kirov Theater, February 10, 1941. Principal dancers: Natalia Dudinskaya and Vachtang Chabukiani; then (fourth act only, entitled *Shadows*) Covent Garden, London, July 4, 1961, and the Metropolitan, New York, September 14, 1961. Principal dancers: Kaleria Fedicheva and Sergei Vikulov, Kirov Ballet. 4) Rudolf Nureyev (one act, entitled *Kingdom of the Shades*). Covent Garden, London, November 27, 1963. Danced by Margot Fonteyn, Rudolf Nureyev, Royal Ballet. 5) Natalia Makarova (one act). New York, July 1974. Danced by Cynthia Gregory, Ivan Nagy, American Ballet Theater; in 1977, Gelsey Kirkland, Mikhail Baryshnikov.   A.A.

Centre: Carla Fracci. Performance at the Scala, Milan, in September 1974, under the direction of Filippo Crivelli.

SIEBA or THE SWORD OF WOTAN (*Sieba* or *La Spada di Wodan*)
Ballet (choreographic story) in seven acts. Choreography and scenario by Luigi Manzotti. Music by Romualdo Marenco. Scenery by Alfredo Edel. Turin, Theater Royal, 1877.

SYNOPSIS. King Harold (Aroldo) of Thule is endangered by the conspiracy of his minister Kafur and his ally, the piratical mercenary Holerut. The god Wotan sends the young King a miraculous sword, brought to him by the valkyrie Sieba. The spiteful Surtur, a wicked god, enemy of Wotan, causes Sieba to fall in love with Harold and be loved by him in return, against the laws of the valkyries. On the battlefield the pirates capture the King as planned by Kafur, who steals the magic sword and takes command of the army. Meanwhile Sieba is condemned to the horrors of the Underworld to which the triumphant Surtur drives her. At last Wotan allows her return to the light, but still assigns her to life among mortals. Sieba, with the help of the boy Cadmo, a slave of the pirates, sets her beloved Harold free, thanks to the intervention of Wotan, who blows up a tempest that drowns the pirates but preserves the young slave and the two lovers. Thus King Harold is restored to his people and marries Sieba.

■ The use of a subject drawn from Germanic myth in a ballet (following in the wake of *The Goddess of Valhalla* by Pasquale Borri a few years earlier at the Scala) can certainly be attributed to the effect of Wagner's operas on the musical theater of the late nineteenth century. *Sieba* marked the beginning of the successful collaboration between Manzotti and the composer Romualdo Marenco, as well as the first appearance of the fantastic transformation scenes so typical of Manzotti's *"grand ballet"* (see *Excelsior*, page 140, and *Amor*, page 141). Most memorable among the many later productions supervised by the choreographer was the ballet's first revival at the Scala, Milan, on January 11, 1879, scenery by Carlo Ferrario, with Rosita Mauri, Bice Vergani (Aroldo), Carlo Coppi (Cadmo), Giuseppe Grezzi (Wotan), Francesco Baratti (Kafur).

OTHER VERSIONS. Giovanni Pratesi (after Manzotti). Milan, Scala, January 14, 1933. Danced by Attilia Radice, Placida Battaggi, Gennaro Corbo, Tony Corcione.   A.A.

EXCELSIOR

A historical, allegorical, spectacular ballet in six parts and eleven scenes. Choreography and scenario by Luigi Manzotti. Music by Romualdo Marenco. Sets and costumes by Alfredo Edel. Milan, Scala, January 11, 1881. Principal dancers: Bice Vergani, Carlo Montanara, Rosina Viale, Carlo Coppi, Angelo Cuccoli.

SYNOPSIS. Part I: *Obscurantism*: in Spain of the Inquisition the Spirit of Darkness holds enchained a beautiful woman, Light, Progress, Civilization. But the links of the chain break, Light triumphs, the personification of human genius appear, and Obscurantism retires defeated, cursing at so much radiance. *Light*: surrounded by riches and brilliance, the grandeurs of antiquity can be seen. Then the discoveries of the new era, the fruits of science, make their appearance: Steam Power, Telegraphy, the Suez Canal, the Mont Cenis tunnel. A new age enters in triumph and a happy future illuminates the path of humanity. Part II: *The First Steamboat*: a village on the River Weser. In the village inn the success of young Valentino, winner of the boat race, is being celebrated. He is challenged by his defeated rival. Obscurantism warns the contestants of the arrival of a steamboat, piloted by its inventor, Papin. "It is a work of the devil," he tells them. The boatmen destroy the vessel. Papin dies in the struggle, but Light proclaims his glory to the crowd. *New York*: over a stormy sea ploughs a great steamship. It is the development of Papin's invention. Obscurantism falls, overpowered. Part III: *Electricity*: we are in Alessandro Volta's laboratory in Como. He stands deep in thought beside his "pile." Though threatened by the Spirit of Darkness, Light protects him. At last a spark flashes out. It is victory. *Washington*: Obscurantism finds himself in Telegraph Square, dazzled by the light. A crowd of telegraph boys come out, guided by Civilization. The malevolent being steals away, cursing. Part IV: *The Simoon*: a caravan is crossing the desert when it is overtaken by the simoon, a terrible sandstorm. The unfortunate travellers are robbed by desert marauders and prepare to die in the darkness. The Spirit of Evil rejoices, but Light points to the horizon where a new route has opened, *the Suez Canal*. In place of the desert is a wide canal and the town of Ismailia where all European civilization is foregathered, brought together by Science. There are ships, tents, and people of every race dancing with joy. Part V: *The Ultimate Mining Operation*: the great work of the Mont Cenis tunnel is almost completed, and Evil lurks, seeking revenge. The engineers install the last charge, which will demolish the remaining rock dividing Italy from France. The detonation is awaited in an atmosphere of suspense. Then at last the barrier falls and workers and engineers of the two nations embrace one another. Now Obscurantism is truly defeated and Light condemns him to see the peoples united in universal happiness. The ground then opens up and the dark spirit is swallowed into its depths. Part VI: *The Apotheosis of Human Genius*: all dance joyfully to the glory of the present and the greater glory to come, in the guise of Science, Progress, Brotherhood, and Love.

■ *Excelsior*, performed 103 times during the year 1881, was one of the greatest successes of Italian ballet. It was a stupendous affair, crowded, colourful, full of ideas that would please and stimulate the general public. With its unlimited faith in scientific progress, it interpreted the optimism of the new classes who saw industry and fresh discoveries as the way to save humanity from its age-old ills. It had, moreover, a positive feeling of world brotherhood and internationalism, and, in its confrontation of light and darkness, pointed towards a new morality nourished with hope. Not at all a romantic ballet, practical and secular, *Excelsior* was the perfect product of the great reformist illusion, and a monument to human intelligence finally successful in bending the forces of nature to its will. In those years scientific discoveries still seemed miracles destined to change the course of events. Manzotti and Marenco, well aware of these tendencies, gave free rein to their imaginations in a grand display of stage effects and spectacle. Thus *Excelsior* is an entertainment closely related to its epoch, and though it may be accused of naiveté, it would be unjust not to consider it as an important document of late nineteenth-century Italian culture. It was admittedly the expression of an unsophisticated taste, the reflection of a certain decadence in regard to choreography; but its impact on the public was and remains extraordinary, as can be seen from the recent revivals after so many years of oblivion. Marenco's music is simple and suitable for dancing, sometimes inspired by folk dances such as the famous mazurka of the Weser, grown famous as the accompaniment to *"Bella se vuoi venire sull'omnibus."* *Excelsior* is a little masterpiece of fusion between various kinds of entertainment; choreographically Manzotti combined nineteenth-century tradition with the most lively of modernism. Perhaps the ballet could best be described as an agile elephant, highly decorated and very cinematographic (even though the cinema was not yet in existence).

OTHER VERSIONS. *Excelsior* was revived in 1883, 1888, 1894, 1909, and 1916, always with the same choreography (in 1916 in a new version by Renato Simoni at the Scala). On May 22, 1885, Carlo Coppi staged it at Her Majesty's Theatre in London. Between 1895 and 1956 it could be seen adapted for the marionettes of the *Teatro dei Piccoli*, with revivals at the Piccola Scala in 1969. In 1931 a "reproduction" by Giovanni Pratesi was put on at the San Carlo Theater in Naples in an atmosphere heavy with fascism, with updatings such as Marconi in the place of Volta and S.O.S. instead of Suez. Finally, on June 27, 1967, *Excelsior* was revived at the Communale in Florence for the *Maggio Musicale*, and enjoyed a successful run, including performances at the Scala and in Rome. The choreography was by Ugo Dell'Ara, the music rearranged by Fiorenzo Carpi, the sets and costumes designed by Giulio Coltellacci. Manzotti's prologue "To the Reader" was spoken by Alfredo Bianchini. Under the direction of Filippo Crivelli there were some departures from the original, such as the character of the freed slave in the Suez scene. Among the dancers were Ludmilla Tcherina, Ugo Dell'Ara, Carla Fracci, Attilio

Labis. The grand finale with the flags and uniforms of all the nations aroused immense enthusiasm, as did the sumptuous and ingenious staging.   M.P.

NAMOUNA

Ballet in two acts and three scenes. Choreography by Lucien Petipa. Music by Edouard Lalo. Scenario by Charles Nuitter and Lucien Petipa. Sets by Rubé, Chaperon, Lavastre. Costumes by Eugène Lacoste. Paris, Opéra, March 6, 1882. Principal dancers: Rita Sangalli (Namouna), Louis Mérante (Don Ottavio), M. Pluque (Adriani).

SYNOPSIS. Act I: in a casino in Corfu, Lord Adriani is playing dice with Count Ottavio. He wagers and loses all, including his ship and his favourite slave, Namouna. Ottavio, although tempted to keep her, offers Namouna his winnings and her liberty. Vexed, Namouna leaves the ruined Adriani. Ottavio is courting his bethrothed, Elena, with a serenade, but the vengeful Adriani insults both him and his musicians. The threatened duel is averted by the intervention of the veiled Namouna, who dances to attract people to the scene. Elena is annoyed by the attention Ottavia pays to the unknown girl.

Olga Spessivtzeva in The Sleeping Beauty, *London, 1921.*

Adriani, too, courts Namouna, but she repulses him in favour of Ottavio, against whom he is planning an ambush. Ottavio is saved by some sailors who take him on board. Act II: having arrived with Ottavio on the island of Ali the slave trader, Namouna makes herself known to her fellow-slaves and sets them free. The feast is interrupted by the pursuing Adriani, who with his crew of pirate oarsmen takes Ottavio prisoner. However, when the slave girls begin to dance the pirates are ensnared and disarmed, while Adriani himself is intoxicated by the charm of Namouna, who takes advantage of the situation by escaping with Ottavio. They set sail on the ship while the furious Adriani dies, stabbed by a slave girl.

■ In the past a preeminent partner for F. Elssler, C. Grisi, A. Ferraris, and C. Rosati, and already the collaborator of Verdi, Rossini, and Wagner in composing opera *divertissements*, Lucien Petipa was in addition a capable choreographer, responsible for the ballets *Sacountala, Graziosa, Le Roi d'Yvetot,* and *Namouna.* The last was created for Rita Sangalli, back from four years of triumph in America. She was a most accomplished dancer, a fascinating woman of the *Belle Époque*, and finally the author of a book, *Terpsichore.* Although as a whole *Namouna* was weak in dramatic construction and musically uneven, so that it was soon forgotten, the ballet provided Sangalli with a great success in her *pas de charmeuse* and flower dance; she also included a "pizzicato" adapted from the famous one in *Sylvia*, created for her in 1876 by Mérante-Delibes.

OTHER VERSIONS. 1) Lifar used Lalo's score for his *Suite en Blanc* (1943). 2) Choreography and scenario adaptation by Peter Wright. Music by Eduard Lalo. Decor by Peter Farmer. Stuttgart, Stuttgart Ballet, June 2, 1967. Danced by Keil, Cragun.   G.S.

AMOR

Ballet (choreographic poem) in two parts and sixteen scenes. Choreography and scenario by Luigi Manzotti. Music by Romualdo Marenco. Scenery by Giovanni Zuccarelli. Costumes by Alfredo Edel. Machines by Luigi Caprara. Milan, Scala, February 17, 1886. Principal dancers: Antonietta Bella, Ernestina Operti, Giuseppina Cecchetti, Enrico Cecchetti, Ettore Coppini, Carlo Coppi, Egidio Rossi, Francesco Magri.

SYNOPSIS. The ballet is a celebration of love as the "archetype of the Universe," by means of a long series of mythological, historical, and allegorical scenes ranging from the primitive Chaos, through various epochs in human history up to the Battle of Legnano, the triumph of liberty, and the conquests of modern civilization.

■ Inspired, according to the author's statement in his complicated scenario, by the "First Love" that appears at the beginning of the third canto of Dante's *Divine Comedy*, this colossal spectacle was the ultimate expres-

A scene from Act III of The Sleeping Beauty *performed at the Bolshoi Theater, Moscow, with choreography by Yuri Grigorovich.*

academic style. Consequently, if many aspects of Manzotti's choreography seem overornate, even elephantine, to our modern sensibilities, fed on synthetic ballets derived from Diaghilev, we must not ignore that in these original choreographical works Manzotti summed up all his experience of the great nineteenth-century tradition. In his creations we can discern the source not only of the mechanical precision of the Hoffman Girls ... but also of the feeling and movement of various scenes by Petipa, especially in *The Sleeping Beauty*, or even in certain marvellous diagonal moves in Fokine's ballets, to say nothing of the athleticism and acrobatics of Nijinska, Golejzovsky, Balanchine, or Lifar in his early manner" (*Enciclopedia dello Spettacolo*, see Manzotti). To give some idea of the magnitude of the spectacle, it will suffice to say that 600 dancers and extras took part in *Amor*, 200 scene workers and technicians, twelve horses, two oxen, and one elephant, and it required 350 square meters of scaffolding, 1,600 square meters of painted scenery, 3,000 costumes, and 8,000 diverse properties and pieces of equipment, among them two large steam generators, etc. The ballet met with enormous success that lasted throughout the forty-four repeat performances of the first run. Because it was so difficult to stage, however, it was revived only once (with another fifty performances) in 1902, still at the Scala, in a shortened version produced by Ettore Coppini.   A.A.

THE FAIRY DOLL (Die Puppenfee)

Pantomimic divertissement in one act. Choreography by Joseph Hassreiter. Music by Josef Bayer. Scenario by J. Hassreiter and F. Gaul. Scenery by Antonio Brioschi. Vienna, Court Opera, October 4, 1888. Principal dancer: Camilla Pagliero.

SYNOPSIS. Various customers enter a big toyshop. The shopkeeper is showing the family of an English millionaire his mechanical puppets: a Chinaman, a Tyrolean girl, a Spanish lady, a Japanese, a Moor, a Punchinello, a poet, a doorkeeper, and finally a fairy doll who fascinates the Englishman. He buys her and orders her to be sent. When midnight strikes the shop comes alive: all the dolls dance around their fairy queen. Disturbed by the sound, the shopkeeper and his assistant rush down to the shop, but find everything in order. The final scene shows the dolls dancing around the shopkeeper.

■ The ballet, which was revived several times in the ensuing years, always met with rapturous success. It arrived at the Scala on February 1, 1893, with Anita Puliti in the title role, and was revived there twice: in 1903 in a version choreographed by Achille Coppini, with Anita Grassi as the fairy; and in 1930 with Luisa Baldi, this time with choreography by Heinrich Kröller, "one of the rare standard-bearers of academic dance at a time when free expressionist dance was spreading across central Europe like wildfire" (Rossi). When the ballet was first performed, the composer, Josef Bayer, was on the crest of a wave, employed at the Vienna State Opera as director and composer of ballet music.

sion of Italian nineteenth-century *"grand ballet."* It rose above the creative and choreographic degeneration of Italian ballet in that period (degenerate in spite of the unsurpassable academic technique of the dancers) only in the magnificent crowd scenes of which Luigi Manzotti was a master. Nevertheless, as Gino Tani, with his acute sense of history, remarks: "Beyond the more obvious and spectacular aspects of Manzotti's work, it is only fair to acknowledge its essential and valid qualities: a sure instinct, breadth of vision, a sense of *multum in parvo*. ... History and art were brought to life on the stage in colossal, epic proportions by means of insights and inventions of bewildering audacity. The 'grand ballet' had everything. Besides the mime Coppi, the cast included Cecchetti, Operti, Geminazzi, Limido, Legnani, Cormani, Palladino; and between one crowd scene and the next, among the colourful 'dance numbers,' there were still *solos* and *pas de deux* in the purest

Ekaterina Maximova and Vladimir Vassiliev in The Nutcracker *at the Bolshoi Theater, Moscow.*

Massine's *La Boutique Fantasque* (page 187) was obviously derived from *Die Puppenfee*.   C.M.C.

THE SLEEPING BEAUTY (*Spiashchaia Krasavitsa* or *La Belle au Bois Dormant*)

Ballet in prologue and three acts. Choreography by Marius Petipa. Scenario by Ivan Vsevoloisky and Marius Petipa. Music by Piotr I. Tchaikovsky. Scenary by Ivan Andreev, Mikhail Bocharov, Konstantin Ivanov, Henrykh Levogt, and Matvei Shishkov. Costumes by Ivan Vsevoloisky. St. Petersburg, Maryinsky Theater, January 3, 1890. Principal dancers: Carlotta Brianza (Princess Aurora), Pavel Gerdt (Prince Desiré), Maria M. Petipa (the Lilac Fairy), Enrico Cecchetti (Carabosse and the Blue Bird), Varvara Nikitina (the Blue Fairy), F. I. Kshesinsky (King Florestan), Giuseppina Cecchetti (the Queen).

SYNOPSIS. Prologue: in the palace of King Florestan XXIV they are celebrating the christening of the new-born Princess Aurora. The six fairies invited each bring a gift and bestow a blessing on the cradle carried to them in royal procession. Suddenly the wicked witch Carabosse bursts in on them, followed by her demon train. She is offended not to have been invited to the christening by the Master of Ceremonies, Cantalbutte, and, in spite of his pleas for pardon, pronounces a curse on the baby: one day she will prick her finger on a spindle and die. The dismay of the royal parents and the court is somewhat relieved by the Lilac Fairy, who has left her gift for last, and now grants that the Princess will not die, but fall into a deep sleep from which she will be awoken only by the the kiss of love. Act I: sixteen years have gone by, during which every pin and thorn has been banished from the realm and the Princess has grown into a radiantly beautiful girl. At her birthday ball four Princes have arrived from various parts of the world to ask for her hand in marriage. She dances with each of them, but seems more pleased with the simple rose she carries than with any of her other splendid gifts. An old woman approaches and presents her with an object she has never seen before. It is a spindle, with which the princess pricks her finger and instantly falls into a heavy slumber. Throwing off the clothes of the supposed old woman, Carabosse appears triumphant amid the grieving court. The Lilac Fairy comes to keep her promise, and by her magic a thick forest grows up around the palace, while everybody in it falls asleep and the courtiers remain unconscious around the Princess's bed, just as the spell struck them. A hundred years pass by. Young Prince Desiré with his retinue makes a halt in a clearing in the forest, where they dance and play games. The Prince joins in at first, but then stands aside, overtaken by a pensive mood. The Lilac Fairy appears before him and shows him a vision of the Princess Aurora. Entranced, the young man tries to approach her, but the picture suddenly fades. He begs the fairy to lead him to the sleeping beauty and follows her to the entrance of the silent palace. Carabosse and her acolytes retreat, powerless to prevent the breaking of the spell. Through the petrified court the prince advances until he reaches the canopy beneath which Aurora sleeps. At his kiss she wakes, and with her wake all the others. The King and Queen bless the happy couple. Act III: Aurora's wedding is being celebrated in the grand ballroom of the palace. Taking part in the dancing are the courtiers, the fairies, the Princes, and a number of fairy-tale characters such as Puss-in-Boots and the White Cat, Red Riding Hood and the Wolf, the Bluebird and his companion. Last of all the bridal pair dance before proceeding to their wedding and happiness.

■ Of the three famous ballets for which Tchaikovsky composed the music – *Swan Lake, The Sleeping Beauty*, and *The Nutcracker* – the second (the first in the order of its definitive choreography; see *Swan Lake*, page 149) is the one that most truly interprets the ideal and establishes the style, formal structure, and character of classical ballet. It is true that this ballet belongs historically and conceptually to the late romantic period; that the score, though balanced, well-designed, and luminous like no other Tchaikovsky wrote, is not at all "classical" in the strict sense; and that the story by Vsevoloisky, taken from Perrault's *Mother Goose Tales*, was steeped in the decadent and sugary romanticism that survived especially in the late nineteenth-century theater of Imperial Russia. Nevertheless, Petipa's choreography, in bestowing an expressive reality on this pretty, conventional plot, turned what might have been just another *"grand ballet"* of the period into an unsurpassed model and masterpiece of classical ballet. With Petipa's successful career in Russia – due in some part to the presence of celebrated Italian ballerinas – academic dance found on Russian soil the ideal meeting place and synthesis of the French and Italian traditions. It was the golden age of its dance history, in which the apotheosis of pure technique fused with the absolute equilibrium of a style which, as Stravinsky wrote, "in its true essence, in the austerity of its forms, constitutes the triumph of order over the arbitrary." In this sense Petipa's ballet is the most essentially classic product in the history of theatrical dance. And it is *The Sleeping Beauty* that is the clearest realization of those ideals: a purely choreographic work composed in academic style at an extremely high technical level, supported by a slender dramatic substructure only just strong enough to give it rarefied overtones of feeling, and closely linked to a score of high musical quality that is yet based as a whole, and even in some detail, on the choreography. Thus the passages of mime necessary to the story do not disturb the ballet's atmosphere of theatrical abstraction but merely articulate the succession of passages of pure dance, ensemble or solo, lyrical or sparkling, moving or virtuoso. Preeminent among them, a paradigm of choreographical beauty, is the famous *Rose Adagio* danced by the prima ballerina in the first act, a triumph of academic technique with its superb, ceremonious reiteration of long-sustained "attitudes" on point between the brief "supports" of one or the other of the four cavaliers. Every pretence of story-telling vanishes in the third act, which is given over to the traditional finale of spectacular *divertissements*, a veritable feast of academic dance culminating in the glorious Bluebird *pas de deux* and to a still higher degree in the exquisitely pure *grand pas de deux classique* of Aurora and her Prince. The part of Beauty, first danced in 1890 by Carlotta Brianza, a great ballerina of the high Italian school, still offers the greatest challenge to all the most radiantly classical dancers, while the ballet as a whole, with its rich array of opportunities for soloists and *corps de ballet*, has always been one of the favourite works in the repertory of all the great ballet companies. Under the titles *La Belle au Bois Dormant, The Sleeping Beauty, Spiashchaia Krasavitsa, Dornröschen*, or *La Bella addormentata nel Bosco*, it has been preserved and revived all over the world in versions largely faithful to Petipa's original, transplanted to the west in the reconstruction composed by Sergeyev on the basis of Stepanov's choreographic notation. Presented in London by Diaghilev's Russian Ballet in 1921, this magnificent production (see *Other Versions* below) brought the world-famous company to the verge of financial disaster, but also revealed once and for all the merit and historical importance of *The Sleeping Beauty*, without which, according to Alexandre Benois, "ballet history in Russia, and indeed the whole world, would have followed another path. The Russian Ballet Company itself would never have seen the light if the *Beauty* had not aroused in us [the future founders] an irresistible enthusiasm, a sort of delirium." In 1922 Diaghilev presented a potted edition of the ballet, consisting of a suite of dances drawn almost entirely from the third act. Under the title *Le Mariage d'Aurore*, or *Les Noces d'Aurore*, or, in English, *Aurora's Wedding*, this version entered the repertory of several companies, but fortunately today the ballet is nearly always performed in its entirety.

OTHER VERSIONS. Principal productions of Petipa's original as a full-length ballet: 1) Giorgio Saracco. Milan, Scala Theater, March 11, 1896. Danced by Carlotta Brianza and Giorgio Saracco. 2) Alexander Gorski (slightly altered). Moscow, Bolshoi Theater, January 17, 1899; then at the Maryinsky Theater, St. Petersburg, February 16, 1914. 3) Nicholas Sergeyev. Reconstruction of the original from Stepanov's notation. Narrative scenes and a few dances choreographed by Bronislava Nijinska. Sets and costumes by Léon Bakst. London, Alhambra Theatre, November 2, 1921. Danced by Olga Spessivtzeva, Pierre Vladimirov, Serge Diaghilev's Ballets Russes. Then a one-act version – *Le Mariage d'Aurore* – sets by Alexandre Benois. Paris, Opéra, May 18, 1922. Danced by Vera Trefilova, Pierre Vladimirov, Diaghilev's Ballets Russes. 4) Fiodor Lopokov. Petrograd, Academic State Theater, October 8, 1922. 5) Asaf Messerer and Alexander Chekrygin. Moscow, Bolshoi Theater, December 20, 1936. 6) Nicholas Sergeyev (three revivals). London, Sadler's Wells Theatre, February 2, 1939, revived on February 20, 1946 in collaboration with Frederick Ashton to celebrate reopening of Covent Garden Opera House. Stage designs by Oliver Messel. Principal dancers in both productions: Margot Fonteyn and Robert Helpmann. 7) Nives Poli. Milan, Scala, January 24, 1940. Danced by Nives Poli, Dino Cavallo. 8) Konstantin Sergeyev.

Leningrad, Kirov Theater, March 25, 1952. 9) Mary Skeaping. Stockholm, January 13, 1955. Danced by Marianne von Rosen and Bjorn Holmgren, Royal Swedish Ballet. 10) Ninette de Valois (after N. Sergeyev, see 6). Copenhagen, Theater Royal, May 8, 1957. Royal Danish Ballet. 11) Nicholas Beriosov (after N. Sergeyev). Stuttgart, State Theater of Württemberg, December 21, 1957. 12) Robert Helpmann and Bronislava Nijinska (after N. Sergeyev). Paris, Théâtre des Champs-Élysées, October 27, 1960. Danced by Rosella Hightower, Nicolai Polajenko, International Ballet of the Marquis de Cuevas. 13) Vaslav Orlikovsky. Vienna State Opera, May 4, 1963. 14) Yuri Grigorovich. Moscow, Bolshoi Theater, December 7, 1963. 15) Rudolf Nureyev. Milan, Scala, September 22, 1966. Danced by Carla Fracci, Rudolf Nureyev. 16) Ben Stevenson and Beryl Grey. London, Festival Hall, August 24, 1967. Danced by Noëlla Pontois, John Gilpin, London Festival Ballet. 17) Kenneth MacMillan (after N. Sergeyev). Berlin, Deutsche Oper, October 8, 1967. Danced by Lynn Seymour, Rudolf Holz; then London, Covent Garden, March 15, 1973. Danced by Antoinette Sibley, Anthony Dowell, Royal Ballet. 18) Alicia Alonso. Paris, Opéra, December 31, 1974. Danced by Noëlla Pontois, Cyril Atanassoff.   A.A.

KALKABRINO

Fantastical ballet in three acts. Choreography by Marius Petipa. Music by Ludwig Minkus. Scenario by Modesto Tchaikovsky. St. Petersburg, Maryinsky Theater, February 13, 1891. Principal dancers: Carlotta Brianza (Marietta and Draginiatza), Pavel Gerdt (Kalkabrino), Nicholas Legat (Olivier), Enrico Cecchetti (Reuben).

SYNOPSIS. Act I: in a village of Provence, Marietta and Olivier are in love. A band of smugglers headed by Kalkabrino arrives in the village. The smuggler chief is bewitched by the country girl and wants to marry her against her will. Chased away by Olivier and cursed by a monk, he swears vengeance. Act II: in the forest the evil spirits are gloating over the thought of seizing Kalkabrino's soul, now lost beyond redemption through the friar's curse. The demon Malacorda causes Draginiatza to take on the likeness of Marietta. When Kalkabrino returns, he is fascinated and deceived by her resemblance to the girl he desires, and so seduces her with splendid gifts and takes her with him. Act III: in the smuggler's camp the wedding feast is being prepared, and the fiendish double appears in all her splendour of silk and jewels. At the height of the dancing, Draginiatza complains of the dim light, seizes a torch, and starts a terrible fire. While the other smugglers flee, terrorized by demons, Kalkabrino, magnetized by the treacherous beauty, embraces her passionately. Dawn breaks and Draginiatza, losing her resemblance to Marietta and appearing now as a ghastly hag, drags the smuggler chief to hell, but not before calling up the vision of Olivier's wedding to Marietta, blessed by the friar.

■ It is always extremely difficult to understand the exact

meaning intended by a ballet at the time of its creation. *Kalkabrino* is no exception to the rule. We only know that in this piece Petipa's choreography (typical of the academic structure he had created, with the advantage of always having the same *corps de ballet*, the same theater, and the same enlightened despotic power at his disposal) laid particular stress on the dual role of Marietta and Draginiatza danced by the star of the Scala, Carlotta Brianza. She met with the same overwhelming success as she had enjoyed the year before in the part of Princess Aurora in *The Sleeping Beauty*, displaying yet again that Italian virtuosity which the unquestioned mastery of Carlo Blasis had imposed on the stages of all the world. G.S.

ing themselves, until Clara falls asleep, clutching her present, and dreams. Magically the room grows larger and, at a sign from Drosselmeyer, the toys come alive. The tin soldiers parade, but suddenly an army of mice led by their King bursts out of the cellars and a battle begins, in which the toys, despite the Nutcracker's valour, are defeated. The Nutcracker stands alone, defying the mice, but the magician Drosselmeyer comes to the rescue, handing Clara a lighted candle with which she puts the mice to flight, while the Nutcracker turns into a handsome prince. Act II: the night sky clears to reveal a host of stars; snowflakes fall and Clara with her Prince embarks on a magic boat. In a kingdom of Christmas trees, candies, and cakes, Clara's party

The Nutcracker *in the version arranged by Rudolf Nureyev and danced for the first time in Stockholm on February 29, 1968. In the center Nureyev himself dressed as Drosselmeyer.*

THE NUTCRACKER (*Shchelkunchik* or *Casse-Noisette*)
Ballet in two acts. Choreography by Lev Ivanov. Music by Piotr Ilich Tchaikovsky. Scenario by Marius Petipa. Sets and costumes by M. Botcharov and K. Ivanov. St. Petersburg, Maryinsky Theater, December 5, 1892. Principal dancers: Antonietta Dell'Era, Pavel Gerdt, Olga Preobrajenska, Nicholas Legat.

SYNOPSIS. Act I: it is Christmas Eve (in the USSR always referred to as New Year's Eve); rich Mr Stahlbaum is giving a party for his children, Clara (or in the Soviet version, Masha, a Russian diminutive of Maria) and Fritz. Mr Drosselmeyer arrives bringing presents and amuses the children with mechanical dolls (in the USSR he is supposed to be a puppet master). To Clara he gives a nutcracker in the shape of a toy soldier. The spiteful Fritz breaks it, but Drosselmeyer mends it at once. The party goes on, grown-ups and children enjoy-

becomes a marvellous *divertissement* after the Prince has finally defeated the Mouse King in a duel. It has all been a dream, but Clara wakes up with her Nutcracker and remembers her wonderful adventure.

■ As is well known, the ballet was inspired by E. T. A. Hoffmann's story *The Nutcracker and the Mouse King* published in 1819 in the *Serapion Brethien*. In the original it is a fairy story not without "black" implications, wherein the fantasies of childhood blend with the dark side of the unconscious. Clara's dream expresses her wish to see in the grotesque toy a handsome Prince who will love her and take her with him. Then it is invaded by evil spirits (mice and bats) or by the nocturnal fears aroused in children by the threatening world of darkness. All the characters display a well-defined duplicity, starting with Drosselmeyer (a more refined relation of Dr. Coppelius, another of Hoffman's creations), who is at once the family friend who loves children and a conjuror of magic manifestations. If the figure of the Nutcracker-Prince whose transfiguration is caused by others' wishes for identification is fairly simply explained, the image of Clara lends itself to more complex inquiries. She is, in fact, a child expressing a desire to be a grown woman: her story is a premonition of what is to come, but it is made clear that it will not be easy or always pleasant to reach the fruits she wants to pluck. The world around her is indeed silly and frivolous and even unpleasant (her brother's spite), so that the only way to attain happiness, after overcoming fearful ordeals, is in dreams. This implication ends by distorting the Christmas fairy tale of Petipa's imagination, and leaves the way open for endless interpretations and modifications. Few ballets have been devised as impressively as this masterpiece by Tchaikovsky and Ivanov. Today, in spite of Soviet conservatism, it is the psychological approach of modern choreographers that prevails, even of those such as Nureyev and Baryshnikov, who have left their Russian motherland. Even on the choreographic level, the work of Petipa and Ivanov has evolved, and we are presented with an extraordinary range of refinements and imagination. It is enough to cite the opening party scene, the behaviour of the children (real ones), the characterization of the mechanical dolls, the fight between the tin soldiers and the mice, the brilliant *divertissement*, or the classic beauty of the *pas de deux*. Here Ivanov, the first important Russian choreographer, gave proof of exceptional maturity. He could evoke nursery creatures such as the Sugar Plum Fairy in dance or even on the plane of great theater. With *The Nutcracker* he revitalized the fairy-tale world with intelligence, eclipsing the inanities of contemporary ballet and opening a wide door to the modern world. The fortunes of *The Nutcracker* were certainly favoured by Tchaikovsky's score, which enjoys an independent existence as the *Casse-Noisette Suite*, and perfectly conveys the world of dream and fears through which Clara perceives the great experience of being a woman. Tchaikovsky had many petty annoyances to endure while creating the score under Petipa's direction, but in the end he was certainly satisfied with the composition: the *Suite*, first performed in March 1892, at a concert given by the Imperial Music Society, was received with much enthusiasm. The recently-invented celesta featured in the ballet's orchestration. And the administrator of the Imperial theaters, Vsevoloisky, felt he could look forward with confidence to the fate of the ballet which he had commissioned only two years earlier from the great master Petipa.

Pierina Legnani, above, as Odette/Odile in Swan Lake; *below, in* Cinderella.

OTHER VERSIONS. 1) Vassili Vainonen. Leningrad, Kirov Theater, 1934 (replacing the productions by Gorski and Lopokov in 1917 and 1929 respectively), with Galina Ulanova. Scenery by Dmitriev (the character of the fairy omitted). 2) Nicholas Sergeyev. London, Vic Wells Ballet, June 30, 1934. First reconstruction in the west of the original version, with Alicia Markova, Helpmann, and Elsa Lanchester. Sets and costumes by Hedley Briggs, Lydia Lopokova consultant. Subsequently interpreted by Margot Fonteyn and Robert Helpmann. Revised by Frederick Ashton in

1951 for Sadler's Wells, with Beriosova and Blair. 3) Boris Romanoff. Ballets Russes de Monte Carlo, 1936, new version presented in many parts of Europe. 4) Margherita Froman. Milan, Scala, February 19, 1938. Scenery by Alexandre Benois, with Nives Poli, Marzoni, and Amati. 5) William Christensen, San Francisco Ballet, 1944. 6) George Balanchine. New York, February 2, 1954. New York City Ballet. Sets by Horace Armistead. Costumes by Karinska. Masks by Vlady. Danced by Alberta Grant, Michael Arshanski, Paul Nickel, Maria Tallchief, Nicholas Magellane. This version, repeated at the New York State Theater on November 11, 1964, with scenery by Rouben Ter-Arutunian, went back to Hoffman's original story, dividing the ballet into two acts, the first seen in the real world, the second in a dream. Balanchine remained faithful to the original score and in general followed the main lines of the Maryinsky choreography, though with various innovations and scenic adaptations. This version still enjoys great success in America. 7) Alfred Rodrigues. London, 1956. Sets and costumes by James Bailey, with Margot Fonteyn and Michael Somes. 8) David Lichine. London, December 24, 1957. London Festival Ballet with Anton Dolin. Another version in 1968 by Jack Carter. 9) Yuri Grigorovich. Moscow, Bolshoi Theater, 1966. Faithful to Petipa's scenario and inspired by enthusiasm. Sets and costumes by Simon Virsaladze. 10) John Cranko. Stuttgart, 1967, with a greatly altered plot. It is supposed that Clara, now Lena, has fallen in love with a soldier, Corrado, and that she has been kidnapped by the mice, from whom Corrado succeeds in saving her. Drosselmeyer becomes a comic fairy in whose realm Corrado finally wins the girl. 11) Rudolf Nureyev. Stockholm, Theater Royal, February 29, 1968. Sets and costumes by Nicholas Georgiadis, with Nureyev himself doubling the parts of Drosselmeyer and the Prince. The Russian dancer underlines the mysterious side of the story, evoking nightmares and terrors and somewhat discounting the fairy-tale element. His *Nutcracker* was immediately included in the Royal Ballet repertory and has been reproduced in many theaters around the world, among them the Scala, where it was first performed on September 18, 1969. 12) Roland Petit. Paris, 1976. Ballets de Marseille, in a modern, whimsical version. 13) Mikhail Baryshnikov. Washington, Kennedy Center, December 21, 1976. American Ballet Theater. Sets by Boris Aronson. Costumes by Frank Thompson. Lighting by Jennifer Tipton. Principal dancers: Marianna Cherkassy, Alexander Minz and Mikhail Baryshnikov as Nutcracker and Prince. The former Kirov dancer stresses the magic powers of Drosselmeyer, creator of both Nutcracker and Prince, and shows Clara on the threshold of adolescence, well able to defend her dream in spite of Drosselmeyer's power. This psychological approach is extremely interesting and has won Baryshnikov a big success as choreographer as well as dancer. 14) Nicholas Beriozov. Turin, Theater Royal, September 27, 1978, with some alterations and the use of other music by Tchaikovsky. Principal dancers: Elizabeth Terabust and Patrice Bart. 15) Joseph Lazzini. Ballet Royal de Wallonie of Charleroi, 1978. Sets and costumes by Daniel Jassogne and Xenia Chriss, with the plot rearranged into four fantastic parts and a grand final *pas de deux*.

THE MUSIC. Tchaikovsky's score is one of the most brilliant and delightful ever composed for a ballet, and is written with extreme elegance. Famous pieces such as the Waltz of the Flowers, the Snowflake Waltz, and the melodies of the *divertissement* are equalled by the various symphonically conceived passages that accompany the party and battle scenes. The instrumental colour is always interesting, and the *pas de deux* in the penultimate scene magnificent. Sometimes a female chorus is used. Finally, one can hardly sufficiently praise the composer's ability to render all the ternary forms of the ballet acceptable and to enrich with ever varying rhythms a composition that has no mannered or imitative moments.   M.P.

THE MAGIC FLUTE (*Volshebnaia Fleita*)
One-act ballet. Choreography and scenario by Lev Ivanov. Music by Riccardo Drigo. St. Petersburg, Little Theater of the Imperial Ballet School, March 10, 1893. Principal dancers: S. Belinskaya (Lisa), M. Fokine (Luca), S. Legat (Marquis), C. Christerson (Oberon).

SYNOPSIS. Lisa, daughter of a rich landowner, loves Luca, disapproved of by her mother because of his poverty. The local Marquis comes down to the village to choose himself a bride. His eye falls on Lisa and he asks for her hand in marriage. In spite of maternal pressure, Lisa makes fun of him. Meanwhile Luca, waiting for Lisa, sees her mother turn away a poor begging hermit. Pitying his miserable state, Luca gives the old man his last few coins, receiving as a thanks offering an enchanted flute, the sound of which sets everyone dancing. The Marquis accuses Luca of witchcraft, and the judge, who himself has been forced to dance, condemns him to death. The hermit then reveals himself to be Oberon and saves the young man. He sends the Marquis packing and obliges the mother, in exchange for his pardon, to consent to the marriage of Luca.

■ The first public performance was at the Maryinsky Theater, St. Petersburg, on April 23, 1893 (Michael Fokine, Agrippina Vaganova, Sergei Legat). Unrelated to Mozart's opera of the same name, it was a new version of *The Enchanted Flute or the Unwilling Dancers*, a ballet by the Italian mime Fortunato Bernardelli, which he took to Moscow in 1818. Lev Ivanov, an excellent and very musical dancer and an underestimated choreographer of great talent, spent his whole career dominated by the powerful personalities of Perrot, Saint-Léon, and Petipa, who saw in him a dangerous rival, but did not fail to exploit his gentle, submissive character. They were in his debt for the originality of his spatial grouping, poetic imagination, and probably for unrecognized choreographic contributions to many of their works. *The Magic Flute* was retained in the repertory of Pavlova's company (Pavlova, Volinine, Cecchetti).   G.S.

CINDERELLA (Solyushka)

Imaginative ballet in three acts. Choreography by Marius Petipa, Lev Ivanov, Enrico Cecchetti. Scenario by Lydia Pashkova (from Perrault's fairy story). Music by Baron Fittinghof-Schell. Scenery by Levogt, Shishkov, Botcharov. St. Petersburg, Maryinsky Theater, December 1, 1893. Principal dancers: Pierina Legnani (Cinderella), Pavel Gerdt (Prince), Enrico Cecchetti (Pignerolle), Matilda Kschessinskaya II (Odette), M. Andersen (Aloisa).

SYNOPSIS. Act I: Cinderella, clad in rags, is forced to help her ugly and simpering sisters put on their sumptuous dresses for the grand court ball given by the Prince in his palace, which she is forbidden to attend. She is left alone. Soon, however, her fairy godmother appears, bringing beautiful clothes for the ball, a coach and servants, and takes her to the palace on one condition. She must leave on the stroke of midnight. Act II: when she arrives at the ball the Prince has eyes for no one else and prefers her to all the other guests. But, as midnight begins to chime, she remembers her promise and slips away, losing one of her little shoes. Finding it, the Prince proclaims that he will marry the girl to whom it belongs. Act III: Cinderella secretly returns to the garden to find what she has lost. Meanwhile the Prince invites all the beautiful ladies to try on the slipper, but it fits none of them. With the help of the fairy godmother, Cinderella is once more transformed into a lovely Princess and, having passed the test, is chosen by the Prince to be his bride.

■ Although in this ballet the dances were to some extent sacrificed to the splendour of the costumes, heavy and awkward as they were for the numerous academic, even semiacrobatic, steps Pierina Legnani, the first interpreter of the role, was called upon to dance, she succeeded admirably, amazing the audience by performing for the first time the famous thirty-two *ronds de jambe-fouettés* which, repeated later in the part of Odile in *Swan Lake*, were to become the crown of virtuosity and the future standard of comparison for every great ballerina. Legnani and Kschessinskaya were the only two dancers ever to be awarded the title of "prima ballerina assoluta" at the Maryinsky Theater. The original music and choreography of *Cinderella* have not stood the test of time and have been replaced everywhere by more recent choreography to go with Prokoviev's stupendous score written in 1945 for the same subject.

OTHER VERSIONS. 1) François Decombe Albert. Music by Fernando Sor. London, King's Theatre, March 26, 1822. Danced by Maria Mercandotti. 2) Fred Farren. Music by S. Jones. London, Empire Theatre, January 6, 1906. Danced by Adeline Genée. 3) Michael Fokine. Music by Frederick d'Erlanger. Sets and costumes by N. Goncharova. London, Covent Garden. Danced by Riabouchinska, Petroff, Ballet Russe Colonel de Basil.   G.S.

SWAN LAKE (Le Lac de Cygnes or Lebedinoe Ozero)

Ballet in four acts. Choreography by Marius Petipa and Lev Ivanov. Scenario by Vladimir Beghitchev and Vassili Geltzer. Music by Piotr Ilich Tchaikovsky. Scenery by Ivan Andreyev, Mikhail Bocharov, and Henryk Levogt. St. Petersburg, Maryinsky Theater, January 15, 1895. Principal dancers: Pierina Legnani (Odette-Odile), Pavel Gerdt (Siegfried), Giuseppina Cecchetti (the Queen Mother), P. A. Bulgakov (Rothbart).

SYNOPSIS. Act I: in his castle grounds, Prince Siegfried is celebrating his twenty-first birthday with his friends. The Queen Mother enters to chide him affectionately for his frivolity. She reminds him that the moment has come for him to choose a bride from among the girls invited to the court ball on the following day. When the Queen has gone, the dancing starts anew until the Prince, standing apart and overcome by a vague melancholy, sees some white swans fly across the sky and decides to leave with his friends to hunt them. Act II: beside the banks of a moonlit lake near the castle, a group of beautiful swan-maidens appears, rising from the water. The Prince has already aimed his bow when the Swan Queen presents herself. She tells Siegfried, entranced by her beauty, that she is the Princess Odette changed into a swan, like her companions, through a spell cast by the sorcerer Rothbart, from which she can be freed only by one who will swear eternal love to her. The happiness of the two young people, now deeply in love, is echoed in the dances of the swans, but in the distance Rothbart appears, menacing and ready to reclaim the bewitched creatures under his sway. Siegfried swears he loves Odette and invites her to the ball on the following night. Dawn breaks and she, with her companions turned back to swans, must follow the enchanter. Act III: in the castle ballroom the Queen Mother makes a majestic entrance and the Grand Master of Ceremonies opens the festivities. The young Prince dances with the six young ladies who are presented to him, but his thoughts are with Odette and, to his mother's disappointment, he refuses to choose one of them as his bride. The unexpected arrival of an unknown nobleman and his daughter is announced. It is the Baron Rothbart with one of his daughters, Odile, the seductive but evil double of Odette, in whom Siegfried fancies he recognizes his beloved. Meanwhile court *divertissements*, with various national dances, succeed one another until the Prince, enslaved by the magic fascination of the girl in black, dances with her and chooses her as his bride, publicly avowing his love for her. Their fatal trick successful, Rothbart and his daughter leave in triumph, while the wandering white spirit of Odette appears momentarily in the window. In despair, Siegfried rushes to the lake. Act IV: in the same place as their meeting, the swans dance sadly by the lake as they wait for Odette. She arrives in tears at the fate to which she is now condemned and falls to the ground among her companions. Siegfried, beside himself, finds her at last and lifts her tenderly, imploring forgiveness. Odette is dying. He takes her diadem and throws it in the lake, which rises to submerge the two lovers. Their spirits are seen to fly upwards towards the sky above the

Opposite: Maia Plisetskaia in Yuri Grigorovich's version of Swan Lake, *1956.*
Above: Natalia Bessmertnova and A. B. Godunov in a 1969 revival with the same choreography.

lake, now calm once more. (In other versions of the end, Rothbart stirs up the lake against Siegfried, who follows Odette into its waters; the two rise up again and then go towards a better world together. Or Siegfried challenges the magician and, in the fight that follows, throws him into the lake; the spell is broken, the swans turn back into girls, and the lovers set off towards happiness.)

■ This is one of the principal works in the classical repertory of all the ballet theaters and companies of the world. Earliest of Tchaikovsky's famous triad (see *The Sleeping Beauty*, page 144, and *The Nutcracker*, page 146), *Swan Lake* was in fact the last to be produced in its definitive form, almost twenty years after the composition of the music and the drafting of the scenario. The ballet was first staged on February 20, 1877 at Moscow's Bolshoi Theater, with choreography by Julius (or Wenzel) Reisinger, scenery by Changuine, Waltz, and Groppius, and with Pelageya M. Karpakova as the protagonist. Because of the banal choreography, it was a failure. Two further versions at the Bolshoi met with no better success. The first was on July 13, 1880, with the dancer Y. Kalmikova, the second on October 28, 1882, with Lydia Geiten, both choreographed by Joseph Hansen. Then eleven years passed before the director of the Maryinsky Theater, St. Petersburg, seeing the success of the other two ballets composed by Tchaikovsky, decided to revive *Swan Lake*, commissioning Marius Petipa, chief ballet master of the Imperial Ballet, to arrange the choreography. Petipa entrusted the task of making a preliminary version, reduced to the second act only, to his assistant Lev Ivanov. It was performed on February 17, 1894, at a memorial evening for the composer, who had died a few

Elena Riabynkina in the name part in Raymonda
by Marius Petipa to music by Alexander Glazunov.

months earlier. Later, Petipa tackled the whole ballet, overhauling the scenario and the score, in which he interpolated some fragments of Tchaikovsky's piano orchestrated by Richard Drigo, who included a few passages of his own composition (for the *grand pas de deux*). The choreography was a collaboration between Petipa and Ivanov: the style of the French master is discernible in the mime passages intermingled with *divertissements* in the first act, and in the pure academicism varied with character dances in the third, while it is to the Russian choreographer that we owe the delicate lyricism of the second and fourth acts. With this definitive realization of *Swan Lake* in 1895, Marius Petipa and Lev Ivanov achieved a classic of the theater of dance, a perfect mingling of academic choreographic composition and moonlit, late romantic poetry, formal clarity and disturbing psychological symbolism, dazzling virtuosity and expressive intensity, conventional drama and inner depth. At the time, the ballet's triumph was attributed above all to the great Italian dancer Pierina Legnani, a perfect interpreter of the dual role of Odette-Odile, immediately recognized as one of the most arduous in ballet repertory. From the dramatic point of view it required the dancer to represent the tremulous reserve and ecstatic surrender of the swan-maiden, then the provocative and magnetic fascination of Odette's evil double. On the strictly choreographic level this duality is matched by the romantic academic style of the two "white scenes" and the glittering virtuosity and academic skill of the third act, culminating in the thirty-two *fouettés* at the end of the *grand pas de deux*. Since Pierina Legnani, only ballerinas endowed with a strong personality and a wide technical-dramatic range have been able to perform this difficult part with the artistic excellence it demands: among them have been Anna Pavlova, Matilda Kschessinskaya, Olga Preobrajenska,

Olga Spessivtzeva, Alicia Markova, Galina Ulanova, Alexandra Danilova, Margot Fonteyn, Maia Plisetskaya, and Natalia Makarova. The choreography of *Swan Lake* has been preserved through an uninterrupted tradition. In Russia the line has run by way of Alexander Gorski's 1901 revival, which has remained in the repertory in a revised form by Asaf Messerer; in the rest of the world through Nicholas Sergeyev's conscientiously reconstructed version of 1934 on which nearly all the many subsequent productions have been modelled.

OTHER VERSIONS. We list below the chief revivals (or revisions) of Petipa and Ivanov's original production. 1) Alexander Gorski. Moscow, Bolshoi Theater, January 24, 1901; repeated by Asaf Messerer and Alexander Radunsky (choreography of fourth act by Messerer), *ibid*, 1956. Danced by Maia Plisetskaia; by Yuri Grigorovich, *ibid*, December 25, 1969. Danced by Natalia Bessmertnova. 2) Michael Fokine (in two acts). London, Hippodrome, May 16, 1910. Danced by Olga Preobrajenska. 3) Michael Mordkin. New York, Metropolitan Theater, December 19, 1911. Danced by Ekaterina Geltzer. 4) Serge Diaghilev's Ballets Russes (in one act). London, Covent Garden, November 30, 1911. Danced by Matilda Kschessinskaya. 5) Agrippina Vaganova. Leningrad, Kirov Theater, April 13, 1933. Danced by Galina Ulanova. 6) Nicholas Sergeyev. London, Sadler's Wells Theatre, November 20, 1934. Danced by Alicia Markova; then at the New Theatre, London, September 7, 1934. Danced by Margot Fonteyn. 7) Harald Lander. Copenhagen, Theater Royal, February 8, 1938. Danced by Margot Lander. 8) George Balanchine (in one act, with his own choreography). New York, City Center, November 20, 1951. Danced by Maria Tallchief. 9) Vladimir Bourmeister. Moscow, Stanislavsky-N. Dantchenko Theater, April 24, 1953. Danced by Violetta Bovt; then Paris, Opéra, December 21, 1960. Danced by Josette Amiel. 10) Frederick Ashton, Rudolf Nureyev, and Maria Fay. London, Covent Garden, December 12, 1963. Danced by Margot Fonteyn. 11) John Cranko. Stuttgart, State Theater, November 14, 1963. Danced by Marcia Haidée. 12) Rudolf Nureyev. Vienna, State Opera House, October 15, 1964. Danced by Ully Wührer, then by Margot Fonteyn and Rudolf Nureyev. A.A.

CAVALRY HALT (*La Halte de Cavalerie*)
Ballet in one act. Choreography and scenario by Marius Petipa. Music by Johan Armsheimer. Sets by Levogt. Costumes by Panomaryev. St. Petersburg, Maryinsky Theater. January 21, 1896. Principal dancers: Marie Petipa (Maria), Pierina Legnani (Teresa), Pavel Gerdt (Pierre).

SYNOPSIS. In an Austrian village, Pierre is undecided which to choose of two girls who love him, Teresa or Maria. Unknown to one another, each girl gives him a ribbon, one a blue, the other a red, as a pledge, and arranges to meet him. Unfortunately they both arrive at the same time and a quarrel starts, only interrupted by the arrival of a company of hussars. Teresa runs off, but Pierre is caught by them, tied up, and shut in a hut. The soldiers try to seduce Maria, but she succeeds in freeing Pierre, who escapes and soon returns with the peasants, indignant at the hussars' behaviour. The chivalrous colonel of the hussars, however, desists from making

■ Renowned to this day for having devised the classical foundations of ballet, Marius Petipa was indefatigable in the research of historical backgrounds and expert at providing a dramatic framework to support the con-

Above: Anna Pavlova, the famous Russian dancer who made her debut in St. Petersburg in 1899.

Left: Vaslav Nijinsky as the Slave in Le Pavillon d'Armide, *a ballet by Michael Fokine.*

tributions of composers and designers. Influenced by the style of Saint-Léon, he introduced a great variety of *divertissements* and *ballabili* and foresaw the great popularity of "balletized" national dances such as he used in *Swan Lake* and *The Sleeping Beauty* (in this case mostly performed by hussars and lancers). His last three miniature ballets, *Ruses d'Amour, Les Millions D'Arlequin,* and *Les Saisons,* were characterized by vivid, colourful dances of fantasy ranging in background from Arcadia to the *Commedia dell'Arte* and the bacchanale. Pierina Legnani created the leading role in *La Halte de Cavalerie;* she was succeeded by Anna Pavlova, who made her debut in it in 1899.   G.S.

SPORT

Ballet in four scenes. Choreography by Luigi Manzotti. Music by Romualdo Marenco. Scenery by Magni, Rota, L. Sala, and Songa. Costumes by Edel. Milan, Scala, February 10, 1897. Principal dancers: Cecilia Cerri (Florence Bernier), Łuisa Cristino (Lady Waldeck), Vittorio de Vincenti (the Jockey), Antonio Monti (the Marquis de Franckeville).

SYNOPSIS. An elegant sportsman, the Marquis de Franckeville, has seduced the actress Florence Bernier and also Lady Waldeck, wife of an American millionaire. The two rivals follow their lover all over the world, from his mountain climbing in the Alps to the skating championship in Canada, to the horse races at Longchamps and the Venetian regatta, always with mixed success. Nor is hunting, fishing, or even a futuristic invasion of cyclists missing.

■ *Sport* was the last of Manzotti's grand trilogy which started with *Amor* and had its apotheosis in *Excelsior* (1881). As "modern" and spectacular as the other two, *Sport* was intended as the celebration of every kind of athletic activity. Although the scenario concerned an eternal triangle, it was only an excuse for displays of skill by soloists and stupendous ensembles for the *corps de ballet*, whose costumes were very daring for that period. *Sport* has been seen as the ancestor of the precision maneuvers of the Hoffman Girls and their like, and even – more questionably – as an influence on Fokine's geometric groupings and on the styles of Golejzovsky, Nijinska, Balanchine, and Lifar. The ballet's popularity was enormous (forty-four performances in the first season), and was equally successful when revived in 1905 and 1906 under the direction of Achille Coppini.

C.M.C.

RAYMONDA

Ballet in three acts. Choreography by Marius Petipa. Music by Alexander Glazunov. Scenario by L. Paskova and M. Petipa. St. Petersburg, Maryinsky Theater, January 19, 1898. Principal dancers: Pierina Legnani (Raymonda), Sergei Legat (Jean de Brienne), Nicholas Legat (Beranger), Paul Gerdt (Abderaman).

SYNOPSIS. Act I: Raymonda, betrothed to Jean de Brienne, is celebrating her birthday. Her fiancé, who is expected the next day, sends some presents in advance, including an embroidered portrait of himself. First, however, a Saracen Knight, Abderaman (or Abderame) arrives and pays court to the lady. In the next scene Raymonda dreams that Jean comes down from his portrait to dance with her, only to find on waking that Abderaman is there to renew his amorous proposals. Act II: while the festivities continue, Raymonda is anxiously awaiting the arrival of her betrothed. Abderaman invites her to dance, then with his accomplices attempts to abduct her. At this moment Jean enters with his brother, the King of Hungary. A duel is fought between the two rivals and the Saracen falls. Act III: a feast at the castle to celebrate the wedding of the lovers.

Scene from a version of Les Sylphides *performed at*

■ In some of its scenes, and to some extent in its melodies and tone colour, this ballet pays clear homage to the Tchaikovskian tradition, especially to certain passages from *Swan Lake* and *The Sleeping Beauty*. The story serves as a pretext for an almost too profuse series of *divertissements* designed to show off the virtuosity and special gifts of the famous soloists. That explains its success at the turn of the century.

OTHER VERSIONS. This ballet has always been able to stimulate the acting ability of the great ballerinas. Thus, in Russia, where it is still danced, there was a production in 1900 directed by the choreographer Gorski at the Bolshoi Theater in Moscow. After the October Revolution it was often put on both at the Kirov in Leningrad and at the Bolshoi. The revival by L. Lavrovsky on October 13, 1945, gave Maia Plisetskaia her first success in a leading part. In Italy, *Raymonda* was performed for the first time at the Teatro Nuovo in Spoleto on July 10, 1964, with Petipa's choreography revised by Rudolf Nureyev, sets and costumes by Beni Montresor, and orchestral direction by Ashley Lawrence. With the Royal Ballet Company of London, the chief parts were taken by Nureyev and Doreen Wells (substituting for Margot Fonteyn, who was ill and could only dance in the last few performances). Nureyev and Fonteyn were together again when the detached third act of the ballet was danced at Nervi on June 28, 1968 (sets and costumes by Barry Kay). In May 1976, there was a version at the San Carlo Theater in Naples, with choreography by Loris Gai and direction by Beppe Menegatti. Principal dancers: Carla Fracci, Burton Taylor, and Bruce Marks.

Moscow's Bolshoi Theater, with choreography by A. Gorski and stage design by V. Ryndin.

THE MUSIC. The Tchaikovskian model inspired Glazunov to compose agreeable music, always easy to listen to, but also commonplace. Clearly it lacked the nobility or inner expressive force inherent in Tchaikovsky's music. All the same, there are particularly happy and very individual moments, such as the heroine's entrance and the first act waltz; also the Arab dance in the second act, and the finale, which achieve elegance of form, harmonic audacity, and a firm contrapuntal technique.   P.C.

THE TRIAL OF DAMIS (Ruses d'Amour)

Ballet in one act. Choreography and scenario by Marius Petipa. Music by Alexander Glazunov. St. Petersburg, Hermitage Theater, January 17, 1900. Principal dancers: Pierina Legnani (Isabella), Pavel Gerdt (the Marquis Damis), Giuseppina Cecchetti (the Duchess Lucinda).

SYNOPSIS. A rustic festival in the style of Watteau is being held in honour of the engagement between Isabella, daughter of the Duchess Lucinda, and the handsome but poor Damis. During the charming marionette show performed by strolling players, Isabella disguises herself as a maidservant, changing places with Marinette in order to test the love of her fiancé, who has not yet met her. Only when Damis, fascinated by the supposed maid, declares his wish to run away with her, leaving his fiancée in the lurch, as he thinks, does Isabella reveal her identity and consent to marry him, happy to know she is loved for herself and not for her wealth and pedigree.

■ The fourth from the last of Petipa's works (with Pierina Legnani one year from her retirement), this was the last to retain a certain freshness of invention before the catastrophic failure of *The Magic Looking-Glass* in 1903, a ballet that put an end to a career that had flowered under four Czars and was henceforth doomed to a melancholy decline. For Petipa, who because of disagreements with the Government Supervisor Teliakovsky had not had his contract renewed, fell victim to his own formulas, which had become too rigid and failed to change with the politico-theatrical times. A connecting link between Vestris and Diaghilev, he was the catalyst that fused the grace and elegance of the French school with the fire and brilliance of the Italian. His choreographic idiom and Fokine's postulates were soon to give birth to a new Russian school of dance.   G.S.

THE SEASONS (Vremena Goda)

Ballet in one act. Choreography and scenario by Marius Petipa. Music by Alexander Glazunov. Sets by Lambini. Costumes by Ponomaryev. St. Petersburg, Imperial Theater, February 21, 1900.

SYNOPSIS. The ballet unfolds in four scenes and is an evocation of the yearly phases of the natural world, represented by a number of episodes, some amorous, others idyllic, but all dominated by nature's cycle of winter sleep, awakening, blossoming, and then harvest moving towards sleep again.

THE MUSIC. It is one of Glazunov's most important works. As a pupil of Rimsky-Korsakov, he can be con-

sidered the last heir of the "Group of Five." The first
scene is characterized by a theme with variations ... [illegible faded text]

ARMIDA'S PAVILION (Le Pavillon d'Armide)

*Ballet in one act of three scenes. Choreography by
Michael Fokine. Music by Nikolai Tcherepnine.
Scenario, sets, and costumes by Alexander Benois. St.
Petersburg, Maryinsky Theater, November 25, 1907.
Principal dancers: Anna Pavlova (Armida), Pavel Gerdt
(the Viscount), Vaslav Nijinsky (the Slave).*

SYNOPSIS. Scene I: a fantastic hunting pavilion
belonging to a sorcerer-marquis contains as its chief
treasure a splendid Gobelins tapestry depicting the
garden of Armida. A young Viscount, surprised by a
storm when on his way to visit his fiancée, seeks refuge
there. As midnight strikes, the figure of Time surmounting the clock turns his hour glass upside down
and the Hours emerge to dance, while the figures in the
tapestry glow and mysteriously come to life. Scene II: in
the pavilion gardens, Armida appears with her train and
her favourite slave. The marquis-magician persuades her
to ensnare the Viscount who, bewitched by her fascination, dreams that he is René, her returned lover. The
orgiastic festivity that follows is enlivened by demons,
masked monsters, buffoons, and slaves seized from the
harem. After the bacchanale and before vanishing into
air, Armida leaves her gold-threaded scarf in the
Viscount's hands. Scene III: as the sun rises, the
Viscount awakes and remembers, but dismisses it all as
a dream until the Marquis shows him the scarf lying on
the floor by the clock. Then he sees that Armida in the
tapestry no longer wears her scarf. Reality or magic
trickery? A final mime scene between the magician and
the young man makes an unusual ending to the ballet.

■ In writing the scenario of this ballet Benois was inspired by Théophile Gautier's short story *Omphale*, and
perhaps influenced by *Coppelia* and *The Tales of Hoffman*. *Le Pavillon d'Armide* was the only ballet staged at
the Maryinsky Theater of St. Petersburg under the
patronage of the journal *Mir Isskustva*, which had
already backed a production devised by Benois to a
suite entitled *Promenade de Louis XVI dans le Parc de
Versailles*. Although with a seventeenth-century background, *Le Pavillon d'Armide* was not without its
Russian aura of "Turkishness," and it was in this ballet
that the astounding Nijinsky made his first sensational
apearance on the western scene.

OTHER VERSIONS. Originally staged by Fokine on
April 15–18, 1907, under the title *The Enchanted*

THE BLOOD-RED FLOWER or BEAUTY AND THE BEAST (Alenky Tsvetochek)

*Ballet-fantasy in six scenes. Choreography by Nicholas
Legat. Music by Thomas Hartmann. Scenario by Pavel
Marzhetsky (after Sergei Aksakhov). Sets and costumes
by Konstantin Korovin. St. Petersburg, Maryinsky
Theater, December 16, 1907. Principal dancers: Anna
Pavlova, Olga Preobrajenska, Vera Trefilova, Michael
Fokine, Alexis Bulgakov, Adolph Bolm, Paul Gerdt.*

■ Sometimes known by the title of Madame de Villeneuve's famous story *Beauty and the Beast*, this ballet is
considered one of the most important creative works of
Nicholas Legat, a major personality during the last
phase of the Imperial Russian Ballet, especially in his
teaching capacity. His pupils at the Imperial Ballet
School of the Maryinsky Theater, where he was
succeeded by Christian Johansson, were almost all

Tamara Karsavina, one of the ballerinas in Les Sylphides
when it was first performed in Paris in June 1909.

Russian dancers whose names soon became famous in Russia and the world, and some of whom appeared in this ballet. A typical ballet of its period, with its fantasy element upheld by strictly academic technique in numerous passages of dance linked by long mime scenes, *The Blood- red Flower* was a great success. It was revived at Moscow's Bolshoi Theater on January 1, 1911, with new choreography by Alexander Gorski, but with the same plot, music, and scenic design as the original by Legat.

OTHER VERSIONS. Various ballets based on the same story and called *Beauty and the Beast* have been produced: 1) Carlo Coppi. Music by Georges Jacobi. London, Alhambra Theatre, January 4, 1898. Principal dancers: Cecilia Cerri, Lytton Grey, Giuseppina Casaboni, Julie Seale, Egidio Rossi. 2) John Cranko. Music by Maurice Ravel (from *Ma Mère l'Oye*). *Pas de deux* London, Sadler's Wells Theatre, December 20, 1949. Danced by Patricia Miller and David Poole. 3) Lew Christensen. Music by Piotr Ilich Tchaikovsky, adapted by Earl Murray. San Francisco Opera House, May 23, 1958. San Francisco Ballet. 4) Peter Darrell. Music by Thea Musgrave. London, Sadler's Wells Theatre, November 19, 1969. Danced by Donna-Day Washington, T. Sakai, Scottish Theatre Ballet.   A.A.

THE DYING SWAN *(Le Cygne)*

A solo dance. Choreography by Michael Fokine. Music by Camille Saint-Saëns. St. Petersburg (Theater of the Circle of Nobility, 1905), Maryinsky Theater, December 22, 1907. Dancer: Anna Pavlova.

SYNOPSIS. In a lonely place a dying swan appears. After a short, sad dance she falls to the ground with folded wings.

■ This brief dance, created by Fokine for Anna Pavlova, was danced by the incomparable ballerina all through her career, becoming the symbol of her personality and interpretative art. Since her death it has been performed by the most celebrated stars. Quite simple in choreographic content, calling for no special virtuosity, it yet requires an impeccable academic technique so that every position and each slightest movement attain the visual perfection the piece demands, and at the same time vividly render the emotional tension of each passage and of the part as a whole. The ballerina enters an empty and nearly dark stage, followed by a single beam of light, and skims across as if in flight (with quick, little *pas de bourée suivis* on point), suggesting with her flowing *port de bras* the slow beating of great wings. She is a creature of pure and fragile beauty soon to die. Her brief appearance is suddenly suffused with pain culminating in one despairing moment of useless rebellion before she sorrowfully folds her wings and resigns herself to death, one last quiver passing through her prostrate form. Within the three minutes this dance takes to perform, Fokine, at the outset of his creative career, already understood how to deploy his in-novatory conception of dance, combining the purest academicism with a mime involving every part of the body in order to express the essence of the dramatic content. The music accompanying *The Dying Swan* is the well-known piece from Saint-Saën's *Carnival of the Animals*.   A.A.

JAVOTTE

Ballet in three acts. Choreography by Léo Staats. Scenario by Jean-Louis Cruze. Music by Camille Saint-Saëns. Scenery by Amable. Costumes by Pinchon. Paris, Opéra, February 5, 1909. Principal dancers: Carlotta Zambelli (Javotte), Léo Staats (Jean).

■ Although *Javotte* was originally created by Mariquita on December 3, 1896, at the Grand Theater in Lyons, the version here described is the one with which Léo Staats opened his fertile career as choreographer at the Paris Opéra. He was also a distinguished dancer who created the male lead of Jean and danced it during *Javotte*'s numerous revivals at the Opéra. After so many years of choreographic decadence at that theater, during which the principal male parts were practically always danced by women in travesty, it was a new beginning for men in ballet, that was soon to be stimulated by the coming of the Russian Ballet Company and confirmed by Serge Lifar's advent there in 1929. While the choreography of *Javotte* may not have borne the mark of genius, Staats had in this and his other works profited from an academic training of the first rank and, although it was weighed down with some now obsolete conventions, a style that restored to the art of ballet some of the dignity it had lost. The first night of *Javotte*, which it shared with the opera *Samson and Delilah* by the same composer, was also a personal success for Carlotta Zambelli, delightful and technically brilliant in the title role. The last of a long line of Italian stars at the Paris Opéra, she arrived there in 1894 at the age of nineteen, straight from the Scala at Milan, and remained as dancer and teacher until 1955, contributing a great deal, especially as instructor to French ballet during the reign of Lifar.   A.A.

LES SYLPHIDES

One-act ballet (a romantic reverie). Choreography by Michael Fokine. Music by Frédéric Chopin, orchestrated by Serge Taneyev, Anatole Liadov, Nicholas Tcherepnin, and Igor Stravinsky (from previous arrangements by Alexander Glazunov and Maurice Keller). Set and costumes by Alexandre Benois. Paris, Théâtre du Châtelet, June 2, 1909. Diaghilev's Russian Ballet Company. Principal dancers: Anna Pavlova, Vaslav Nijinsky, Tamara Karsavina, Alexandra Baldina.

SYNOPSIS. The ballet has no plot. It is composed of a suite of dances in the romantic ambience of a moonlit park. The sylphides, an ethereal evocation of eternal femininity (prima ballerina, two soloists, and a female corps de ballet in romantic white tutus) dance with the melancholy "poet" in search of the ideal. The dances are in the following order: 1) Prelude: the curtain rises on all the dancers posed motionless. 2) Nocturne: ensemble danced by the whole cast. 3) Waltz: solo variation performed by one of the soloists. 4) Mazurka: solo by the prima ballerina. 5) Mazurka: solo by the male dancer. 6) Prelude: solo by the other soloist. 7) Waltz *pas de deux* for the prima ballerina and the poet. 8) Grand waltz: final ensemble.

■ Michael Fokine, dancer and choreographer of innumerable works, was at his best in the stylization of historical, folk, and exotic forms of dance. This famous ballet was composed in his creative prime, which coincided with the early years of Diaghilev's Russian Ballet. *Les Sylphides*, inspired by the romantic ballet in atmosphere, costumes, and above all choreographic style – as well as in its title, clearly derived from Filippo Taglioni's *The Sylphide* – was prepared for the opening season of that company in Paris, and was the perfected version of Fokine's earlier works to the music of Chopin. The first, called *Chopiniana*, was presented at the Maryinsky Theater in St. Petersburg on February 10, 1907, and repeated there on March 8, 1908; the orchestration of the piano score (a polonaise, a nocturne, a mazurka, a tarantella, and a waltz) was by Alexander Glazunov, and a thin story line connected the series of academic and character dances. An altered version, danced by Olga Preobrajenska, Anna Pavlova, Tamara Karsavina, and Vaslav Nijinsky, was produced on April 6, and repeated, still at the Maryinsky, on February 19, 1909, under the title *Grand Pas sur la Musique de Chopin*, the additional music orchestrated by Maurice Keller. When Diaghilev included the ballet, together with others by Fokine, in his program at the Châtelet Theater, it finally became *Les Sylphides* (from a suggestion by Alexandre Benois) and all trace of plot was removed. The order of the music was established as follows: *Prelude*, op. 28, no. 7; *Nocturne*, op. 32, no. 2; *Waltz*, op. 70, no. 1; *Mazurka*, op. 33, no. 2; *Mazurka*, op. 76, no. 3; the opening *Prelude* repeated; *Waltz*, op. 64, no. 2, and, finally, the *Grande valse brillante*, op. 18, no. 1. Keeping closely to the spirit and letter of Chopin's music, Fokine created an exquisitely romantic choreography with the "intangible and poetic atmosphere of a dream" (Grigoriev). This he achieved above all by a continuous flow of movement, *pas d'élévation*, and grouping typical of romantic ballet, but supported by a highly evolved academic technique which, combined with the abstract expressiveness of the work as a whole, is instantly recognized as something modern and personal. The extraordinary interpretative gifts of Pavlova, Karsavina, and Nijinsky sealed the success of *Les Sylphides*, which long remained in the Russian Ballet Company's repertory. The numerous revivals of *Les Sylphides* through which the ballet has descended to our day have usually kept faithfully to the original, although there have been a few new versions (more than one arranged by Fokine himself), some entitled *Chopiniana* and some with scenery drawn from Corot's paintings.

OTHER VERSIONS (from Fokine's original). 1) Ivan Clustine (*Chopiniana*). London, Opera House, October 6, 1913. Anna Pavlova's *Ballet Russe*. 2) Vaslav Nijinsky. London, Palace Theatre, March 2, 1914. Nijinsky's Company. 3) Royal Danish Ballet (*Chopiniana*). Copenhagen, Theater Royal, October 14, 1925. 4) Tamara Karsavina. Hammersmith, Lyric Theatre, June 23, 1930. Ballet Rambert. 5) Alicia Markova. London, Sadler's Wells Theatre, March 8, 1932. Vic-Wells Ballet. 6) Alexander Chekrygin (*Chopiniana*). Moscow, Bolshoi Theater, January 24, 1932. 7) Michael Fokine (modifications). René Blum's Monte Carlo Ballet, 1936; then at New York Center Theater, January 11, 1940. Ballet Theater. 8) Alexandra Danilova (*Chopiniana*). New York State Theater, January 20, 1972. New York City Ballet.   A.A.

THE MUSIC. The music for *Les Sylphides* consists of a sequence of piano compositions by Chopin, orchestrated by Glazunov. As mentioned above, the score is arranged in the following order: in place of an overture comes the *Prelude*, op. 28, no. 7, played through twice (and repeated as the third number from the last). This piece was probably one of the first preludes composed by Chopin and is based on a kind of mazurka theme: a gentle andantino repeated twice with different harmonic climaxes. The next number is the *Nocturne*, op. 32, the one of B-flat major with the dramatic, pulsating middle section, particularly interesting in that it marks Chopin's transition to a more imaginative style of piano composition, and one more original in its technical solutions. Obviously, in a score arranged for ballet the pieces more directly allied to dancing could not be omitted. We refer to the waltzes, of which there are three in *Les Sylphides*. The first is very short (scarcely a hundred bars) in G-flat, op. 70, no. 1, memorable for the Schubertian flavour evident in the contrasting movements of theme and trio. The *Waltz*, op. 64, no. 2 and the *Grande valse brillante*, op. 18, no. 1 form the last two numbers of the ballet. The former, composed in 1847, is worthy of note for the elegance of its writing; the second for its clear articulation, which appears all the more personal for its deliberate divergence from the path of Viennese sentimentality. The principal theme arises from the same note repeated six times; in the coda, on the other hand, all the melodic motifs of the waltz are recalled, to wonderfully suggestive and masterly effect. Finally there is the *Mazurka*, op. 33, no. 2, belonging to a group of compositions that first saw the light in Paris, and in which a nostalgia for the atmosphere of the composer's native land was sublimated into brilliant and spontaneous expression.   A.F.

CLEOPATRA

One-act ballet. Choreography and scenario by Michael Fokine. Music by Anton Arensky, with some passages by Taneyev, Rimsky-Korsakov, Glinka, Moussorgsky, and Glazunov. Sets and costumes by Léon Bakst. Paris, Théâtre du Châtelet, June 2, 1909. Principal dancers: Ida Rubinstein (Cleopatra), Anna Pavlova (Ta-Hor),

Michael Fokine in the costume of Harlequin in Carnival, *a ballet of his own creation.*

Michael Fokine (Amun), Tamara Karsavina and Vaslav Nijinsky (slaves).

SYNOPSIS. The noble Amun, destined by the High Priest for marriage with the temple dancer Ta-Hor, falls desperately in love with Queen Cleopatra, who has just arrived with her ritual train of flautists and zither-players. He tries in vain to approach her. Writing his message of love on a scrap of parchment, he sends it flying on an arrow to the foot of the litter on which the enigmatic beauty voluptuously reclines. Having read his words, the Queen orders the guards, who have already seized Amun, to bring him before her. She is attracted by his splendid appearance and offers him a night of love in exchange for his life. The despairing Ta-Hor having been sent away, Amun falls in ecstasy into the arms of Cleopatra. After a lascivious bacchanale comes dawn, and the Queen, her fleeting passion appeased, tenders him the poisoned cup, paying no heed to his imploring looks. She observes his heartrending agony with cold detachment, then moves away with her retinue. The unhappy Ta-Hor finds Amun's lifeless body and tries in vain to revive it. Mad with grief, she falls on his corpse.

■ Originally this work was conceived by Ivanov, under the influence of the old ballet *La Fille de Pharaon* and of Isadora Duncan's revival of interest in classical antiquity. He never finished it, however, and it was first produced a year before the 1909 version, in St. Petersburg, by Fokine under the title *Une Nuit d'Egypte*. Together with *Les Sylphides* and *Le Pavillon d'Armide*, this ballet shared the enormous success that greeted the first Parisian season of Diaghilev's Russian Ballet, when that company was still mainly inspired by the national orthodoxy of the Imperial Russian Ballet and used only dancers from the same source, that is to say, a selection from the galaxy of stars created by Johansson, Cecchetti, Legat, and Petipa. Much of its success was due to the sumptuous scenery and exotic costumes designed by Bakst, and to the burning, enigmatic personality of Ida Rubinstein as Cleopatra, first seen emerging from a sarcophagus as a royal mummy, wrapped in twelve bandages embroidered with lotuses, dynastic symbols, and silver filigree, from which she was slowly unwound to reveal a body of sculptural beauty. Her powers of seduction and dramatic mime enabled the audience to overlook the lack of academic technique which prevented her from ever becoming a great dancer of undisputed merit.

OTHER VERSIONS. 1) Fokine. Original title: *Une Nuit d'Egypte (Egiptskie Notchi)*. Music by A. Arenski. Scenery by O. Allegri. Costumes by M. Zandin. St. Petersburg, Maryinsky Theater, March 21, 1908. Danced by Olga Preobrajenska, Anna Pavlova, Pavel Gerdt, Vaslav Nijinsky. 2) London version of 1918. After Fokine's Parisian production, with music from *Mlada, Russlan and Ludmilla, Kovancina,* and *Les Saisons*, but with sets and costumes by Robert and Sonia Delaunay, those designed by Bakst having been destroyed in a fire during the South American tour of 1917.   G.S.

SALAMMBÔ

Ballet in five acts and seven scenes. Choreography and scenario by Alexander Gorski. Music by Andrei Arends, with passages from A. Glazunov, V. Nebolsin, A. Tfasman. Scenery by Konstantin Korovine. Moscow, Bolshoi Theater, January 10, 1910. Principal dancers: Ekaterina Geltzer (Salammbô), Mikail Mordkin (Mâtho), Vladimir Riabtsev (Spendio)

SYNOPSIS. The story concerns the tragic fate of Salammbô, Princess of Carthage, and the Libyan Mâtho, after the uprising against the Carthaginians by their own mercenaries, turbulent and rebellious through not having been paid after the First Punic War. The curtain rises on the mercenaries feasting in the gardens of Hasdrubal, the father of Salammbô. At the height of the festivities, she makes her entrance, majestically descending a vertiginous stairway, clad in a red and black cloak, playing a lyre. Meanwhile Mâtho has penetrated the defenses of Carthage and succeeded in reaching the temple and taking away the veil of the goddess Tamit, which is believed to be closely associated with the fate of the city. Stealing into Salammbô's bedchamber, he shows her the veil, then flees, struck dumb by her beauty. In the battle that follows Hamilcar is defeated. The High Priest then persuades Salammbô, priestess of Tamit, to recover the precious veil. She goes to her enemy's tent and seduces him. During the love duet with Mâtho, who is in a state of intoxicated bliss, she manages to regain the talisman. Now fortune changes in Carthage's favour, but that does not prevent the mercenaries from besieging the city. By sacrificing young girls to the cruel god Moloch, Hasdrubal succeeds in breaking the siege and routing the rebels. Mâtho is taken prisoner and tortured. Unable to forget the night of love with her dear enemy, Salammbô cannot bear the horror and falls dead, prostrate with grief.

■ The ballet's intensely dramatic plot was based on Flaubert's novel of the same name. Under the influence of Stanislavsky's theories, Gorski applied his reforming zeal to the principles of Petipa, as he had already begun to do in *The Daughter of Gudula*. After six months of intensive work with Arends and Korovine, he had created a true "mime drama," stripped of tutus, symmetrical choreography, *divertissements*, and stereotyped variations to produce a unified drama with logically connected scenes. The *corps de ballet* took part in the action, dressed in sandals and long, stylized costumes suitable to the historical period. The new conception is well illustrated by Mâtho's adagio for Salammbô, a woman ardently desired, yet a superior being to be worshipped – very different, incidentally, from the impassive priestess described by Flaubert. The extraordinarily vivid mime, hieratic majesty, and impetuous passion of Geltzer's heroine, together with the generous humanity dramatically portrayed by Mordkin, ensured the great popularity that the ballet, in spite of adverse reviews, enjoyed for several years.   G.S.

CARNIVAL *(Le Carnaval)*

Mime-ballet in one act. Choreography by Michael Fokine. Music by Robert Schumann (Suite for piano, orchestrated by Glazunov, Rimsky-Korsakov, Liadov, Tcherepnine). Scenario by Léon Bakst and Michael Fokine. Set and costumes by Léon Bakst. St. Petersburg, Pavlova Hall, March 5, 1910 (benefit performance promoted by the journal Satyricon*). Principal dancers: Leonid Leontiev (Harlequin), Tamara Karsavina (Columbine), Vera Fokina (Chiarina), L. Schollar (Estrella), B. Nijinska (Papillon), V. Meyerhold*

Michael Fokine, choreographer of Scheherazade, *here seen with his wife Vera Fokina in a scene from the ballet.*
On the adjoining page: Ida Rubinstein as Zobeida in the same work, which was first danced at the
Paris Opéra in 1910 during Diaghilev's Russian Ballet Company's second season.

(Pierrot), A. Bekefi (Pantaloon), V. Kiselev (Florestan).
First performance in Berlin: Theater des Westens at
Charlottenburg, May 20, 1910. Diaghilev's Russian
Ballet Company. Lydia Lopokova (Columbine), Vaslav
Nijinsky (Harlequin), Enrico Cecchetti (Pantaloon).
The same cast danced in the first performance of the
ballet at the Paris Opéra on June 4, 1910, during the

second season of Diaghilev's Russian Ballet.

SYNOPSIS. The scene, representing the anteroom to a
ballroom, consists only of two divans striped in red,
green, and black, set against heavy, bright blue curtains.
In a gay and lively atmosphere of carnival festivity the
characters of the ballet, in lightly clowning mood, come

On this page, two costume designs by Léon Bakst for Firebird. *On the next page, a sketch by Alexander Golovine for the same ballet.*

and go, choose and change partners, whirl about one another, all with delicate precision and perfect timing. The ballet has no real plot. It is a gossamer confection made up of gallantry, coquetry, squabbles, passing courtship, and teasing rejections, woven around the central couple, Harlequin and Columbine, and a melancholy, white-faced Pierrot, longing for but unable to enter the life of the flirtation and sentimental skirmishing that forever eludes him, the metaphysical image of the disillusionments and frustrations of the human condition.

■ Fokine, drawing inspiration from Petipa's *Les Millions d'Arlequin*, had only three rehearsals in which to prepare this delicate, stylized pastiche, modelled on the sentimental, facetious romanticism of the 1840s, but seen through the slightly mocking eyes of a later age. Although the characters are drawn from the *Commedia dell'Arte*, they have been transformed into figures of Fokine's fervid, late-romantic imagination. The numerous and demanding *pas de deux, pas de trois, pas seuls*, and the dazzling *pirouettes à la seconde* allotted to the men raised the position of the male dancer to a new level, as can be seen from the parts of the lively, effervescent Harlequin and the pathetic, frustrated Pierrot. Hints of Schumann's autobiographical writings run through the ballet, his dual personality reflected in both the impetuous Florestan and the dreamy, solitary

Eusebius. In many of the ballet's revivals, these subtler implications have been ignored, so falsifying Fokine's masterpiece. *Le Carnaval* has been an inspiration to many artists, including Ordoño de Rosales, Charpentier Mio, and in particular Paul Scheurich, who has immortalized the characters in bronzes, bas-reliefs, and Meissen porcelain.

OTHER VERSIONS. 1) Fokine (considerably altered version). London, Coliseum, Serge Diaghilev's *Ballets Russes*, 1918. Danced by Lydia Lopokova and Stanislas Idzikowsky. 2) Evina. London, Sadler's Wells Ballet Theatre, October 24, 1933. Danced by S. Idzikowsky. 3) Bourmeister. Moscow, Stanislavsky Theater, 1946. 4) Eliot Feld's American Ballet Company, Brooklyn Academy of Music, October 24, 1969.   G.S.

THE MUSIC. The music used for *Carnival* is of complex origin, some pieces being taken from a series of Schumann's *Sehnsuchtwaltzer* composed in 1833 from an original motif of Schubert's, while others arise from free variations on a theme of four notes. The basic notes underlying *Scènes Mignonnes* are A, E-flat major (ES), C, and B natural (or H), thus forming the name Asch, the birthplace of Ernestine von Frichen, the girl the twenty-four-year-old composer was in love with. The twenty-two numbers of *Le Carnaval* are full of subtle biographical and literary references, confirming the essentially lyrical nature of the young Schumann's inspiration. The original roots of the waltz springing

from Schubert's melody are maintained in the predominantly ternary structure of *Le Carnaval*. In a few bars each character at the magic masked ball imagined by Schumann is vividly evoked, ever poised to turn from frivolity to sentimental confidences, from psychological outline to suggestively prophetic musical symbolism (it must not be forgotten that the fascinating stage directions were added by Schumann after the composition was completed). We recognize Pierrot, Columbine, Harlequin, Pantaloon, Chiarina (Clara Wieck), Estrella, Chopin, and Paganini (their styles of composition wonderfully caught), besides Schumann himself in his contrasting personalities of Eusebius and Florestan. At the end all the characters come together for the fascinating *Marche des Davidsbündler contre les Philistins*, in which one of Schumann's polemical hobbyhorses rears its head again (he was a keen supporter of the new in art against the conservatism and spiritual mediocrity represented by the "Philistines"), leading into the delightful epilogue. The *Scènes Mignonnes* are played in

the following order: Préambule, Pierrot, Arlequin, *Valse noble*, Eusebius, Florestan, Coquette, Replique, Sphinxes, Papillons, A.S.C.H.-S.C.H.A. (Lettres Dansantes), Chiarina, Chopin, Estrella, Reconnaissance, Pantalon et Colombine, Valse allemande, Paganini, Aveu, Promenade, Pause, Marche des Davidsbündler contre les Philistins.   A.F.

SCHEHERAZADE (Shéhérazade)

Dramatic ballet in one act. Choreography by Michael Fokine. Scenario by Léon Bakst (?). Music by Nikolai Rimsky-Korsakov. Scenery and costumes by Léon Bakst. Paris, Opéra, June 4, 1910. Serge Diaghilev's Russian Ballet. Principal dancers: Ida Rubinstein (Zobeida), Vaslav Nijinsky (Zobeida's favourite slave), Alexis Bulgakov (Shahryar), Basil Kissilev (Shah-Zeman), Enrico Cecchetti (the Chief Eunuch).

SYNOPSIS. The Sultan Shahryar leaves his harem on

163

the pretence that he is going hunting with his brother Zeman, who has hinted to him that his favourite, Zobeida, is unfaithful. No sooner has the Sultan departed than the ladies of the harem urge the Chief Eunuch to open the doors to the negro slaves. The most handsome among them, dressed in gold, is chosen by Zobeida, and together they become the central point of a frenzied orgy. As it rises to its climax they are interrupted by Shahryar's unexpected return. He orders a massacre from which no one escapes. Zobeida stabs herself with a dagger and falls at the feet of her lord.

■ This was the first true creation of the *Ballets Russes*, all the other ballets presented during that first Paris season of 1909 (with the exception of the dances from *Prince Igor*) being new versions of already existing works. The scenario of *Scheherazade*, which gave the first impetus to that dazzling spectacle of sensual exoticism, was probably suggested by Alexandre Benois, even though Diaghilev, in his usual casual manner, attributed its paternity to Bakst from some obscure idea of fairness. In any case, the ballet as a whole was something of a collective work by the whole company. The disturbing inner tensions of Michael Fokine's choreography, with its exciting, new treatment of the ensemble, were emphasized by the interpretations of the solo parts by Ida Rubinstein and Nijinsky, she with her sensuous beauty, he with his amazing technique and the magnetism of his stage personality. The audacious scenic designs of Léon Bakst were a sensation; they set a whole new fashion in lush and glowing interior decor, a veritable "Russian ballet style." *Scheherazade* was a tremendous success at its first showing and in the many repeat performances put on by Diaghilev's company up to 1924. In 1911 Bakst's scenery was supplemented with a drop curtain by Valentin Serov, designer of the famous manifesto for the Russian Ballet's first Paris season. Rimsky-Korsakov's symphonic *suite Scheherazade* was deprived of its third movement when Fokine used it for his ballet. Although the composer's original "program" was abandoned, the music perfectly matched the new story, and was later used for other versions of the ballet, none of which, however, could be compared with the original.   A.A.

THE MUSIC. Composed in 1888, the symphonic *suite Scheherazade* was thought of as a sort of free musical interpretation of some of the tales from *The Thousand and One Nights*. The score, full of exotic feeling and subtle suggestions, was undoubtedly Rimsky-Korsakov's symphonic masterpiece, a shining example of his unique instrumental genius. It set a standard, and was to be perpetuated and sublimated in the early scores of Stravinsky, as well as becoming an essential point of reference in the history of musical instrumentation. Besides possessing the thematic felicity and formal strength typical of the composer, *Scheherazade* is unique in the richness of its tone colour. With an orchestra that had not yet plumbed the depths of the impressionist composers, but could respond to the fundamentally classic, Rimsky-Korsakov opened up whole new vistas of atmospheric sound and colour. The

fanciful story underlying *Scheherazade* in no way hampers the musical inspiration, which seems always miraculously fresh and complete. The various episodes of the symphonic *suite* are spread over four closely connected movements; the unifying element leading from one to the other consists of solo violin passages (symbolizing Scheherazade telling stories to her menacing lord). This motif serves as an introduction to each of the four movements and recurs as a leitmotiv running through the sumptuous instrumental texture, which also includes other recurring themes, all subjected to a rigorous process of symphonic development.   A.F.

THE ORIENTALS (*Les Orientales*)
Five ballet sketches. Choreography by Michael Fokine. Music by Alexander Glazunov, Christian Sinding, Anton Arensky, Edvard Grieg, Alexander Borodin. Scenario by Serge Diaghilev. Scenery and costumes by Constantin Korovine and Léon Bakst. Paris, Opéra, June 25, 1910. Diaghilev's Russian Ballet. Principal dancers: Tamara Karsavina, Ekaterina Geltzer, Vera Fokina, Vaslav Nijinsky, Alexandre Volinine.

■ Set in the salon of a lavishly ornamented eastern palace, this entertainment had no definite subject, but consisted of a suite of five dances drawn from previous oriental ballets in the repertory of Diaghilev's company and slightly modified. Coming in the wake of *Scheherazade*, it kept the Parisians' more superficial fascination with the *Ballets Russes* at fever pitch, without stifling the essential originality of Fokine's choreographic style.   A.A.

FIREBIRD (*Shar Ptiza* or *L'Oiseau de Feu*)
Ballet in three scenes. Choreography by Michael Fokine. Music by Igor Stravinsky. Scenery and costumes by Golovine and Bakst. Paris, Opéra, June 25, 1910. Diaghilev's Russian Ballet. Principal dancers: Michael Fokine (Prince Ivan), Tamara Karsavina (the Firebird), Enrico Cecchetti (Kostchei).

SYNOPSIS. Scene I: in the enchanted garden of the magician Kostchei, there are trees bearing golden apples, and beautiful Princesses he has captured are imprisoned in the castle. Prince Ivan, who has climbed over the fence, catches sight of an extraordinary creature, the Firebird, who has been lured there by the apples. Ivan seizes the red- and gold-feathered being. Terrified, she pleads with him to let her go. To gain her freedom, the Firebird gives him one of her plumes, which has the power to protect him from the wizard's spells. Scene II: left alone as night falls, Ivan sees the captive Princesses steal from Kostchei's castle to play a game of ball with the golden fruit. At last the most beautiful among them timidly approaches the Prince and tells him of how the sorcerer captures travellers and turns them into stone. He has fallen in love with her but cannot prevent the maidens returning to the castle. The Princess begs him not to follow: it is too dangerous to defy Kostchei on his own ground. Scene III: Ivan is cast down, but bravely follows his beloved Princess farther into the garden. Alarms sound and a small army of monsters, Kostchei's guards, advance upon him. The enraged magician casts his spells at the Prince, but Ivan remembers the enchanted feather and waves it in his face. The Firebird returns and forces Kostchei and his creatures to dance until they fall exhausted, when she lulls them into a deep sleep. Knowing that the wizard keeps his soul hidden in a great egg, the Firebird orders Ivan to get hold of it. He throws it to the ground. The shell breaks, Kostchei dies, the castle vanishes, the Princesses are freed, and the two lovers can now be united forever. The ballet ends with an apotheosis celebrating their love and liberty.

■ This ballet, which occupies a fundamental place in the history of dance, was inspired by an old Russian fairy tale. It tells of a Czar whose garden contains trees with golden apples, but the precious fruit is regularly stolen from him by a bird of fire with golden feathers and eyes like oriental crystal. The Czar sends his sons to catch the thief, but it is the youngest, Ivan, who succeeds in snatching a feather from the magic bird. The plume is so magnificent it lights up the night. Now the Czar wants the bird itself and asks his sons to bring it to him. With the help of the "grey wolf" Ivan fulfills his father's wish. From this folk tale the ballet was born. Diaghilev offered the composition of the score to Anatole Liadov, a pupil of Rimsky-Korsakov, but he refused the task, whereupon the commission was given to the young Stravinsky, whose remarkable talents Diaghilev had already divined. He was prepared to gamble on the genius of a little-known composer, and he won the wager, for *Firebird* triumphed in its first Paris season in 1910 and entered the list of long-lived successes. The original story was changed to suit the times: the heroic Ivan was opposed by the wicked magician, while a love interest was introduced to the folk tale in the person of the beautiful Princess. One is perforce reminded of *Swan Lake*, or even of the dance-to-death in *Giselle*. The ballet owed much to the past but brought new life to the ancient myths, cauterizing the old story with the primordial force of the new music and an expressive violence that belonged to the twentieth century. One of the most fascinating qualities of *Firebird*, and its historical value, lies in its refurbishing of tradition and in the translation of its symbols — the Prince, the prisoner, the beautiful maiden, the mythological animal-woman, and the mysterious nocturnal atmosphere — to a new dimension. Prince Ivan passes from imaginative folklore, from the pantheistic innocence of the past, to total liberation from evil. Kostchei is a Bluebeard, keeper of monsters and cousin to Carabosse of *The Sleeping Beauty*. The connection with Tchaikovsky is still plain, as is also the love of colourful adventure typical of Rimsky-Korsakov, composer of *Le Coq d'Or*. It could be said that *Firebird* sounds the knell of the old tradition and heralds the primitive, pagan climate of *Rite of Spring* and the revolutionary folk feeling of *Petrouchka*. It is strange that with a point of departure so clearly derived from Rimsky-Korsakov, the score should have proved, if not avant-garde, at least a break-

ing off. The idea for the scenario is generally attributed to Fokine, but — if we are to believe Stravinsky — the whole ballet was a group effort, especially by Bakst, Benois père, Nijinsky, Diaghilev, and the composer himself. The great impresario's intention was to export a work that was Russian from top to bottom. The result certainly exceeded expectation, for to us it seems the starting point of "modern ballet." Fokine's choreography, which was later reproduced and revised many times, enriched the post-Petipian style with strong elements of folklore and mime. Many years later — in 1960 — Stravinsky told Robert Craft of considerable doubts and worries regarding his creation from the aesthetic angle, which is understandable in view of the Russian master's subsequent works.

OTHER VERSIONS. *Firebird* was revived by the Diaghilev Company in 1926 with sets and costumes by Goncharova (the original ones having been inadvertently destroyed), and was reproduced in Edinburgh on August 23, 1954, with the same designs, and with Margot Fonteyn, Michael Somes, Svetlana Beriosova, and Frederick Ashton in the cast. An important postwar production was performed at the New York City Center on November 29, 1949, by the New York City Ballet under George Balanchine, with scenery by Marc Chagall. The leading dancers were Maria Tallchief and Francisco Moncion. Balanchine's version is particularly elegant and dramatic; it has been modernized, but with imagination, and is not unmindful of the traditional legend. The finale, for instance, is "at Ivan's court," and shows the classical wedding apotheosis. In later revivals Balanchine's work has been extended by Jerome Robbins, with the idea of representing Chagall's picture in movement (New York State Theater, 1970). In the same year, John Neumeier produced a futuristic version of the ballet at Frankfurt, presenting it as science fiction: Kostchei is an enormous robot with a face in the shape of a television screen, while Ivan is a space hero. New choreography was arranged by Brian McDonald in 1972 for the Harkness Ballet at the Kennedy Center, New York.

THE MUSIC. While the score of *Firebird* is profoundly original, its spiritual fathers are Rimsky-Korsakov and Tchaikovsky, to whom the author owes, respectively, much of his tone colour and a number of formal devices. Nevertheless, the heritage of the past is overwhelmed by a highly personal work of antiromantic iconoclasm, which is naturally much more obvious in the *suites* he wrote in 1919 and 1945. The charming Russian melodies are broken into by violent explosions of sound, and it is these contrasts that make the music so new and unexpected (when one considers the *Lullaby* and the *Infernal Dance*). The ballet's final scene of apotheosis produces an effect of golden splendour, the exact opposite of the mysterious introduction so evocative of fear and nocturnal apparitions. Stravinsky maintained that *Firebird* belonged very much to its time, except that the folk music element was more vigorous than other comparable music of the period, even if not very original. It was a point of departure for subsequent musical exploration; but in the meanwhile he kept to approved methods of expression, using great skill and sometimes verging on impressionism. As in Stravinsky's other early works, the orchestration is vastly rich and full of marvellous devices – a style he was to abandon for the desiccation of neoclassicism and the rigours of experimental modernism.   M.P.

MOTHER GOOSE (Ma Mère l'Oye)

Ballet in one act and six scenes. Choreography by Jane Hugard. Music by Maurice Ravel (orchestration of the piano score for four hands). Scenario by Mmes. de Beaumont and d'Aulnoy (from Perrault's fairy tale). Scenery by M. Dresa. Paris, Théâtre des Arts, January 28, 1911. (Children's Ballet for Mimie and Jan Godebski.)

SYNOPSIS. Scene I: *Spinning-Wheel Dance*: a prelude similar to the one for *The Sleeping Beauty*. While playing, Princess Florina trips over the spindle of an old woman at her wheel. Through the spell of a wicked fairy the prick she receives sends her into a hundred-year sleep. Scene II: *The Sleeping Beauty's Pavane*: the old woman, who is really a good fairy, does all she can to ease the Princess's plight by filling her dreams with delightful visions. Two little blackamoors prepare for the coming entertainment by announcing the titles of the various episodes. Scene III: *Interlude of Beauty and the Beast*: Beauty is looking at herself in a mirror clumsily supported by the two little Moors. They let it fall so that it breaks and reveals the Beast concealed behind it. Beauty is at first horrified but is gradually won round by his moving avowal of love. When at last she consents to kiss him, the spell is broken and the Prince restored to

his own handsome form, which had been changed to that of a beast by a wicked enchantment. Scene IV: *Tom Thumb*: this is the well-known story of Tom Thumb and his brothers, lost in the forest and unable to find their way home, because while they were sleeping under the trees birds had eaten the trail of crumbs that Tom Thumb had laid, like Ariadne's thread, to guide them back. Scene V: *Laideronette, Empress of the Pagodas*: the inhabitants of the Pagodas, lighting the scene with their tiny lanterns, perform a dance with graceful curtseys, but the delightful court of exotic little people takes flight in terror when a messenger announces the coming of Laideronette accompanied by the terrible Green Serpent. Scene VI: *The Magic Garden*: a hunting horn proclaims the arrival of Prince Charming. Guided to the enchanted garden by love, he discovers the couch on which Florina sleeps and awakens her with a kiss. There is great rejoicing among all the characters.

■ The symphonic *suite Ma Mère l'Oye* has long overshadowed the ballet it once accompanied, and the original version does not survive. The choreography used today, sometimes with variations, is that arranged by Todd Bolender in 1933. It is no longer a children's ballet, but a human drama with psychoanalytical undertones. Now it is the painful search for her own identity of a woman, no longer young, who from the darkness of her couch sees on the lighted stage another self, returned to girlhood, live through the loneliness, dreams, illusions, and romantic loves of adolescence. All are transfigured in a dreamlike symbolism; visions are seen as if in a film obscured by drifting clouds, of a beaked bird-man, an evil Tom Thumb, and the unconscious cry of a suppressed eroticism in the form of a Chinese prince with the head of a lion.

Sketch by Alexandre Benois for the first and fourth scene of Petrouchka. *Opposite, from left to right: V. Nijinsky as Petrouchka, Tamara Karsavina, and Bronislava Nijinska, who both danced the Ballerina.*

OTHER VERSIONS. Choreography and scenario by Todd Bolender. Decor by A. Derain. New York. Central High School of Needle Trades Auditorium, October 31, 1943. Principal dancers: Mary Jane Shea, Francisco Moncion, Todd Bolender, Dick Beard, American Concert Ballet. Revised and modified version: New York, New York City Center, November 1, 1948. Principal dancers: Marie-Jeanne, F. Moncion, T. Bolender, B. Tompkins, New York City Ballet.   G.S.

THE SPIRIT OF THE ROSE (*Le Spectre de la Rose*) *Choreographic picture in one act. Choreography by Michael Fokine. Music by Carl Maria von Weber, orchestrated by Hector Berlioz. Idea suggested by Jean-Louis Vaudoyer (from Théophile Gautier). Set and costumes by Léon Bakst. Théâtre de Monte Carlo, April 19, 1911. Danced by Tamara Karsavina and Vaslav Nijinsky.*

SYNOPSIS. A young girl returns to her room after a ball, a rose clasped between her hands. She smells its fragrance with sensuous delight, then sinks into an armchair and falls asleep. In her dream the Spirit of the Rose leaps lightly through the window and circles around her before drawing her into an enchanted dance. Finally he brings her back to the armchair and with a sudden leap disappears whence he came. The girl awakes, pleasantly moved, and looks around her. She sees only the fallen rose on the ground, and tenderly picks it up.

■ The subject of this short, delicate ballet, presented with exceptional success during the first Monte Carlo season of Diaghilev's Russian Ballet, was suggested to Jean-Louis Vaudoyer by some verses from Théophile Gautier, the poet and leading spirit of French romantic ballet (see *Giselle*, page 105). The atmosphere of *Le Spectre de la Rose* is indeed one of romanticism seen through impressionist eyes. The exquisitely mid-nineteenth-century idea of a girl dreaming of her ideal, dehumanized but not to the point of losing all sensual allure, has in this ballet achieved a theatrical and choreographic form of finest essence and expressive stylistic abstraction. In this work for two dancers only, lasting no more than fifteen minutes and set in a scene of charming simplicity, Michael Fokine's choreography is composed in the purest, yet rich and mature, academic style, devoid of traditional pantomime and inessential technical virtuosity. In spite of its apparently abstract form, it is profoundly poetical and emotionally expressive. Another, more obvious novelty was the stress laid on the male dancer's role, almost at vanishing point (except in Denmark) since the early part of the nineteenth century until rescued by the reforms of Fokine and the *Ballets Russes*. The technically more demanding part in *Le Spectre de la Rose* is that of the Rose Spirit, especially the *grand jeté* with which he makes his entrance and exit. Vaslav Nijinsky endowed this ballet with his legendary fame, giving all who saw him in it a liberating sensation of almost hypnotic ecstasy. Claudel wrote: "He moved like a tiger: it was not a progress from one *aplomb* to the next of an inert load, but an elastic collaboration with weight, as that of a wing with the air, involving the whole muscular and nervous apparatus of the body, not a mere trunk or statue but a unified organism of power and movement." It was said of Nijinsky's extraordinary *ballon* that he seemed able to stay in the air, or resemble a figure painted on the backcloth, while Diaghilev maintained that he had seen women in the audience faint at the moment of his celebrated final leap. In this work, which it is wrong to call a *pas de deux*, the ballerina has a relatively easy part, technically speaking. In any case, Karsavina's interpretation was enchanting, especially in the true *pas de deux* at the heart of the ballet, which according to Grigoriev was "a kind of waltz so unreal as to seem truly the continuation of a dream." The Russian Ballet revived *Le Spectre de la Rose* several times, danced successively by Alexandre Gavrilov, Stanislas Idzikovsky, and Anton Dolin, and after them by many major dancers from Serge Lifar to Mikhail Baryshnikov (1975). After Fokine's time there were many reconstructions of the ballet by, among others, Anton Dolin (1932), Tamara Karsavina (1944), Roland Petit (1946), Maris Liepa (1966), etc. It is worth noting .that the music Fokine used for *Le Spectre de la Rose* was Carl Maria von Weber's *Invitation to the Waltz* (for piano), orchestrated by Berlioz in 1841 for a ballet created by Saint-Léon as an intermezzo at the first performance of the opera *Der Freischütz*.   A.A.

NARCISSUS (Narcisse)

One-act ballet (a mythological poem). Choreography by Michael Fokine. Scenario by André Bakst. Music by Nicholas Tcherepnine. Sets and costumes by Léon Bakst. Monte Carlo, April 26, 1911. Serge Diaghilev's Russian Ballet. Principal dancers: Tamara Karsavina, Bronislava Nijinska, Vaslav Nijinsky.

SYNOPSIS. Narcissus, entranced by his own image reflected in the water, ignores the enamoured nymph Echo. She and her companions call upon the goddess Nemesis to punish him for his scorn, and he is turned into a flower bending over the pool that mirrored him.

■ *Narcissus* was expressed in choreographic language of great subtlety and consistency. Fokine's art and the intellectual atmosphere of the *Ballets Russes* revealed a feeling for an ideal classical antiquity that went far beyond mythological references or the "Greek" tunics in which the dancers were clad. Karsavina's performance fascinated the audience, but now the role of the male dancer was beginning to attract equal attention. Vaslav Nijinsky and Michael Fokine danced the title part on alternate nights.   A.A.

PETROUCHKA

Ballet in one act and four scenes. Choreography by Michael Fokine. Music by Igor Stravinsky. Scenario by Stravinsky and Alexandre Benois. Sets and costumes by Alexandre Benois. Paris, Théâtre du Châtelet, June 13, 1911. Serge Diaghilev's Russian Ballet Company. Principal dancers: Vaslav Nijinsky (Petrouchka), Tamara Karsavina (the Ballerina), Alexander Orloff (the Moor), Enrico Cecchetti (the Old Showman).

SYNOPSIS. Scene I: the carnival fair in a St. Petersburg square in 1830. The people are enjoying all the fun of the wintry fair — peasants, soldiers, gypsies, gentlefolk, coachmen, and nurses. In the background is a curtained booth. The crowd jostles and laughs, peasants stamp to the strains of a concertina, a girl dances to a pathetic little tune on a barrel organ. Suddenly the merriment and fun are interrupted by the sound of drumbeats. A mysterious melody on a flute heralds the appearance of the Old Showman (or magician). The blue curtains open at last to disclose three compartments, each containing a puppet: in the center the Ballerina doll; on the left the splendidly clad Moor; on the right Petrouchka, the sad marionette. At a command from the Showman, the three puppets perform a mechanical little dance. The Moor and Petrouchka are in love with the Ballerina, who appears to prefer the Moor. The jealous Petrouchka grows angry and attacks his rival, upon which the Showman ends the performance, the crowds drift away, and the puppets collapse into immobility. Scene II: Petrouchka's room. Shut into his cell by the cruel Showman, the poor creature tries to escape. In despair, he protests against his master that he, too, has the right to feel. The door opens and the Ballerina enters. Petrouchka clumsily expresses his joy and love, but his awkward passionate avowals are beyond the doll's comprehension and she leaves him. Alone again, Petrouchka feels himself to be nothing but a clown with no chance in life. Scene III: the Moor's room. Although he, too, is a prisoner, he is quite content to loll upon his couch, playing with a coconut. The Ballerina enters and dances to excite his admiration. He tries to imitate her steps and then embraces her. They are interrupted by Petrouchka who bursts in and threatens his rival. The angry Moor chases him out with his scimitar and the poor clown escapes him with difficulty. The scene is a repetition of their dance in the square and Petrouchka is still the loser. Scene IV: meanwhile, outside in the square, the fair and the dancing go on, rising to a peak of festivity in the old Russian style; there is even a performing bear. All is brought to a sudden stop when Petrouchka suddenly rushes out of the booth followed by the Moor, who stabs him dead. The onlookers are horrified and believe it to be a real crime. The police arrive and question the Showman, but he shows them that the figure on the ground is only a cloth doll. Now the fair is over and all the merrymakers have gone. The Showman is dragging his inanimate puppet back to the tent when suddenly the ghost of Petrouchka emerges, appearing waist-high from its roof, a threatening, indomitable, and triumphant figure.

■ *Petrouchka* did not begin as a ballet. Having finished *Firebird* and not yet having started work on *The Rite of Spring*, Stravinsky was seized by the idea of writing a work for piano and orchestra, a sort of duel between the solo and the rest, ending in a victory for the ensemble. In Stravinsky's mind the piano part represented a puppet, Petrouchka, the immortal and unhappy hero of all fairs, the Russian Pierrot. On hearing the music, Diaghilev was so enthusiastic about it that he asked the composer to turn his musical picture into a ballet. Stravinsky, in collaboration with the artist and stage designer Alexandre Benois, got to work and produced the scenario described above. The ballet was seminal in the history of dance and proved immensely popular. The part of Petrouchka was played most impressively by the great Nijinsky: he was a puppet with a soul, capable of portraying the utter anguish of his desperation and unattainable desires. The drama of the marionette with the feelings of a man, but unable to express them, symbolizes an eternal conflict that goes beyond the surface plot and becomes an existential fact. But the importance of the ballet as a definitive break with the romantic tradition is intrinsic in both form and content. *Petrouchka* is, perhaps, the first truly tragic ballet constructed according to strict criteria of intellectual logic. The public of 1911 was transported by its modernity. The work was grafted on Russian tradition, but seen through surrealist eyes, and its search for truth was unswerving. The basic idea conceived by Diaghilev, Stravinsky, and company gave Fokine an ideal opportunity to apply his principles. On the expressive level the duality of moods permitted a violent contrast between popular and academic styles, between group folk dancing and classic dance movement. This ballet, moreover, made new demands on the dancer, requiring more than mere balletic skill: in fact, it required an unprecedented acting ability. Petrouchka is the ancestor of a long line of comfortless ballets in which we find the problems of the twentieth century reflected and anticipated: pain, war, insecurity, violence, relationships to power. Stravinsky's pioneering music was in perfect harmony with those principles, in his plaintive barrel-organ tune, the melodies so wrongly called vulgar, and the conciseness of his rhythms. The cultural leap from *Firebird*, in which Rimsky-Korsakov's influence is still so evident and the fairy-tale element so straightforward, is immense. The more brutal side of life, the acceptance of defeat, the attempt to probe the characters' psychology, are utterly opposed to the romantic image of heroism and fate. The triangular relationship between Petrouchka, the Ballerina, and the Moor, in the power of the ruthless Showman-Magician, is a debate between happiness and unhappiness, not to be resolved by the light of everyday commonsense, but only by the intellectual projection of consciousness (Petrouchka's ghost), the sign that the Master Magician's victory is only partial. Later, by extending the symbolism and adjusting the psychological content, this

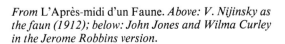
From L'Après-midi d'un Faune. *Above: V. Nijinsky as the faun (1912); below: John Jones and Wilma Curley in the Jerome Robbins version.*

quadrangular relationship was somewhat modified. Maurice Béjart recently reversed the situation from puppet-man to man-puppet, adding an extra psychological factor in the identification (by means of masks) of Petrouchka with his partners, the Ballerina and the Moor. In the numerous revivals of Fokine's original creation, his leading personage has gradually acquired ever subtler and more precise characteristics and become less mechanical and contrasted, in a process of humanization which verges on the themes of love, sorrow, and the liberation of feeling. If it is true, as we are told, that Vaslav Nijinsky was able to give the tragic puppet a soul (according to Stravinsky), we must also remember that the great Petrouchkas of more recent times, Rudolf Nureyev and Vladimir Vassiliev, have raised the characterization to heights then undreamed of. The interpretations by Massine, Robbins, and Woizikowsky are also worthy of note.

OTHER VERSIONS. 1) Michael Fokine. Royal Danish Ballet, 1925; then Ballet Theater, October 8, 1942; then Royal Ballet, March 26, 1957. Danced by Alexander Grant, Margot Fonteyn, Peter Clegg. 2) Léonide Massine. City Center, Joffrey Ballet, March 13, 1970. 3) Dimitri Romanoff and Yurek Lazovski. American Ballet, June 19, 1970. 4) Maurice Béjart. Ballet du XXme Siècle, January 19, 1978. Danced by Vladimir Vassiliev and Rita Poelvoorde.   M.P.

THE PERI (La Péri)

Ballet in two acts. Choreography and scenario by Ivan Clustine. Music by Paul Dukas. Sets and costumes by René Piot. Paris, Théâtre du Châtelet, April 22, 1912. Principal dancers: Natalia Truhanova, W. Bekefi.

SYNOPSIS. Prince Iskender, tired of earthly loves and burning with a restless spirit of adventure, goes in search of the flower of eternal youth, which he finds at last clasped in the hands of a sleeping Peri. He takes the flower, but lingers to admire her celestial beauty. When the fairy wakes he loses his heart to her and she dances seductively, determined to win back the talisman at any cost. Overcome by love, and renouncing immortality, the Prince returns the magic flower in exchange for a kiss. The Peri slowly vanishes, taken up to the crystal domain of her paradise, leaving Iskender to the fate of all mortal men.

■ In 1911 Diaghilev commissioned a score from Paul Dukas, with a view to reviving Coralli's famous *La Péri* with new choreography by Fokine and stage designs by Bakst for the current season of his Russian Ballet. Unfortunately, disagreements arose: Natalia Truhanova, recommended by Dukas for the title role, did not please Diaghilev, who thought her a mediocre dancer. The project was abandoned and taken up later by Clustine.

OTHER VERSIONS. 1) Léo Staats. Paris, Opéra, 1921. Danced by J. Bourgat; idem. 1931. Danced by Olga Spessivtseva, S. Peretti. 2) Frederick Ashton. Sets and costumes by William Chappell. London, Mercury Theatre, Ballet Club, February 16, 1931. Danced by Alicia Markova, F. Ashton. 3) Serge Lifar. Monte Carlo, Nouveau Ballet de Monte Carlo; later at the Opéra, Paris, February 25, 1948. Danced by Y. Chauviré. 4) F. Ashton. Sets by Ivor Hichens. Costumes by André Levasseur. London, Covent Garden, Sadler's Wells Ballet, February 15, 1956. Danced by Margot Fonteyn, Michael Somes. 5) G. Skibine. Paris, Opéra, December, 1966. Danced by C. Motte, J. P. Bonnefous. 6) P. Darrell. Sets by M. Fraser. London, London Festival Ballet, January 9, 1973. Danced by Samsova, Prokovsky.   G.S.

THE MUSIC. In *La Péri* Paul Dukas has succeeded in combining a solid symphonic structure in the German tradition, the sumptuous style of César Franck, and a Debussy-like impressionism, without losing the original orchestral eloquence that makes the thematic material so dense and varied. The score shows not only the composer's incomparable mastery of form and instrumental style, but also his intellectual grasp of the Wagnerian idea of the relation between music and dance so clearly seen in the second version of the bacchanale in *Tannhäuser*. Its affinity with the exoticism of Ravel's *Daphnis and Chloë* (produced in the same year, 1912) is clear from the first bars of the fanfare which precedes the actual ballet: constructed with rhythmic clarity and a command of subtly suggestive harmonies, it resembles some magical incantatory call. Almost immediately the work's two main themes emerge. The first, solemn and noble, is clearly intended to represent Iskender. It is forcefully articulated by the trumpets and oboes and embellished by brilliant arabesques from the violins, which sustain the motif to the final chords. The delineation of the seductive and irresistible Peri, on the other hand, is entrusted to a melodic line of emotional intensity played on the English horn, 'cello, and horns, calling up a febrile and voluptuous atmosphere infused with oriental colour. Practically speaking, the score is composed by using these two themes in various ways that serve to unify the whole, highly successful, work.
                    A.F.

THE BLUE GOD (Le Dieu Bleu)

A Hindu legend in one act. Choreography by Michael Fokine. Music by Reynaldo Hahn. Scenario by Jean Cocteau and Frédéric de Madrazo. Sets and costumes by Léon Bakst. Paris, Théâtre du Châtelet, May 13, 1912. Serge Diaghilev's Russian Ballet. Principal dancers: Tamara Karsavina (the Young Girl), Lydia Nelidova (the Goddess). Vaslav Nijinsky (the Blue God), Max Frohman (the Young Priest).

SYNOPSIS. A young Hindu is about to be consecrated as priest in the temple, but the solemn rite is violently interrupted by a girl who loves him and tries to hold him back. The High Priest condemns her to be thrown to the temple monsters and devoured. Her desperate prayers are answered by the Goddess and the Blue God, who intervene to save her from the monsters and then disappear, leaving the lovers in a glow of sanctified bliss.

Costume design by Léon Bakst for shepherdess in Daphnis and Chloë *by Michael Fokine.*

Vera Fokina and Michael Fokine in Daphnis and Chloë.

■ In composing the choreography of this ballet, Fokine was influenced by the Siamese dances he had seen in St. Petersburg years before. He also reproduced and stylized some recurring poses from Indian figurative art, which was enthusiastically studied for the occasion by the young Cocteau, Diaghilev himself, and above all by Léon Bakst, the stage designer. The designs and sketches for *Le Dieu Bleu* are among his best work. However, even Nijinsky's mysterious and magical fascination, the highly gifted Nelidova, and the ever enchanting Karsavina were not enough to save the ballet from relative failure. After a few performances it was abandoned.   A.A.

THAMAR

One-act ballet. Choreography by Michael Fokine. Scenario and stage designs by Léon Bakst. Music by Balakirev. Paris, Théâtre du Châtelet, May 20, 1912. Diaghilev's Russian Ballet. Principal dancers: Tamara Karsavina, Adolf Bolm.

SYNOPSIS. Thamar, Queen of Georgia, lies somnolent on her couch in a high turret. Her servants watch the road that passes below. When a stranger is seen they bring him into the castle. He is fascinated by Thamar, who leads him on and finally seduces him. Once she has subjugated him, the ruthless Queen has no further interest in the stranger. She stabs him, and her servants throw his body out of a window to the torrent below, as they have done with all her other lovers. Thamar returns to her couch, while the watchmen lie in wait for a new victim.

■ The ballet was very successful for a time, having something of the colour and sensuous appeal of *Scheherazade*, but has long dropped out of the repertory. Thamar was one of Karsavina's famous parts, and there is a well-known drawing of her in the costume by John Sargent. The dancer herself recalled that she found it hard to visualize the character until Diaghilev suggested to her that Thamar should have "a livid face with eyebrows in a single line," a feature that can be seen in the portrait.   O.O.

THE AFTERNOON OF A FAUN (*L'Après-midi d'un Faune*)
One-act ballet. Choreography by Vaslav Nijinsky. Music by Claude Debussy. Set and costumes by Léon Bakst. Paris, Théâtre du Châtelet, May 29, 1912. Diaghilev's Russian Ballet. Principal dancer: Vaslav Nijinsky.

SYNOPSIS. A faun is resting on a hillside in the heat of a summer afternoon; he plays on a reed flute and eats grapes. Seven nymphs appear, making their way towards a nearby pool. The faun has never seen such creatures and comes down to observe them. They in their turn are amazed. When he springs towards them they run away, terrified. They return and the faun tries to communicate with them, but they leave again, all except one who responds to his courtship. As soon as he tries to grasp her, however, she too runs off, letting fall her silk scarf. He picks it up, caresses it, imagines it is the nymph herself, and finally falls on the scarf as if in an act of love.

■ The literary source of *The Afternoon of a Faun* is the well-known poem by Stéphane Mallarmé (Those nymphs — I would fain wake them up again); the musican source is the still more famous *Prélude à l'après-midi d'un faune* by Debussy, one of the masterpieces of impressionism (1892). Its translation to dance was the work of Nijinsky, who for the first time was attempting creative choreography in a purely occidental context. Abandoning Fokine's theories, he sought to bring an archaic civilization back to life by reproducing figures and attitudes from Hellenic vases and bas-reliefs (angular, almost athletic bodies seen in profile), heedless of problems of theatrical propriety. The ballet is short and centered almost entirely on a single character, the faun, thus reversing the dancer-ballerina priority of the romantic school. Its allusion to a primordial sexuality could not fail to upset the public of the day and bordered on a scandal. Nijinsky portrayed the faun as innocently voluptuous and violent, putting his exceptional athletic prowess and strength to the service of a new technique: head and feet in profile, geometrical arm movements, a delirium of the senses suggested with a sly enchantment not uninfluenced by art nouveau, all combined to convey the spirit of Mallarmé's poem filtered through the veil of Debussy's music. During the years of *Petrouchka* and *Rite of Spring* (among Nijinsky's outstanding successes), the significance of the primordial values that Stravinsky evoked for Diaghilev was enriched by a potent new ingredient, the rediscovery of "myth," the same symbol that a few years later was to be one of the cornerstones of the neoclassical revival. After its first performance in Paris, *L'Après-midi d'un Faune* became a confirmed success and was danced by some of the greatest artists of the twentieth century on much the same lines as Nijinsky. The faun's piebald costume has hardly changed through the years.

OTHER VERSIONS. An interesting variation on the theme of love and dreams, to the same music by Debussy, was put on at the City Center of New York on May 14, 1953, by the New York City Ballet, with choreography by Jerome Robbins. In the hands of Balanchine's closest collaborator, *Afternoon of the Faun* became a long *pas de deux* (first danced by Tanaquil le Clercq and Francisco Moncion, scenery and lighting by Jean Rosenthal, costumes by Irene Sharaff). The setting is modern: a dance studio with mirrored walls. The young man lies asleep, a young girl comes in and practices at the bar. He wakes up and she runs away. In the end the young man goes back to his dreams; the illusion is over. Robbins has divested the episode of all reference to ancient Greece, but has followed the gist of the story on a human level. The choreography is a brilliant blend of the emotionally expressive and the classically academic. All the original ballet's dark sensuality and primeval sense of wonder has gone.   M.P.

DAPHNIS AND CHLOË *(Daphnis et Chloë)*
Dramatic ballet in three scenes. Choreography and scenario by Michael Fokine. Music by Maurice Ravel. Sets and costumes by Léon Bakst. Paris, Théâtre du

Vaslav Nijinsky in Jeux. *Drawing by M. Rap (from G. B. Donarini's collection).*

Châtelet, June 8, 1912. Serge Diaghilev's Russian Ballet. Principal dancers: Tamara Karsavina (Chloë), Vaslav Nijinsky (Daphnis), Adolf Bolm (Dorkon).

SYNOPSIS. Scene I: a sacred grove by the Mediterranean coast containing a grotto dedicated to the god Pan. With other young men and women, the shepherd Daphnis and the nymph Chloë dance in honour of the great Pan. They have been lovers from their earliest youth, but the others are slightly disbelieving. The girls flirt with Daphnis while Chloë, a little jealous, accepts the advances of another shepherd, Dorkon. Daphnis rebukes Dorkon, but is persuaded to settle the matter by a dancing match. He easily defeats his boorish rival and Chloë rewards him with a kiss before going off with her companions. Soon afterwards the beautiful Licania comes to tempt him, but in vain. Suddenly the noise of battle is heard; pirates have invaded the island and the defenseless girls take refuge in Pan's grotto. The pirate chieftain, Braxis, seizes Chloë and carries her off before Daphnis can intervene. The young shepherd is in despair and reproaches Pan for being indifferent to the profanation of his temple. Now comes a wonder: in a mysterious light the three stone statues of nymphs guarding the grotto come to life, begin to dance, and lead Daphnis to a great image of the god that fills the sky. The shepherd begs the god to save his beloved Chloë. Scene II: on another island, in the pirates' lair, Braxis orders Chloë to dance. Unwillingly she does so, then begs to be released, but the pirate, with a grin, refuses. At that moment a strange light illumines the sea, and the terrified pirates, ordered by Pan to relinquish the nymph, take flight. Scene III: we are once more in the sacred grove, where Daphnis is mourning the loss of Chloë. Dawn comes up, and his fellow-shepherds tell him that she has been set free by Pan, moved by the thought of his own love for the nymph Syrinx. The two young people act out the old legend for their companions and all ends in a joyous dance of love and happiness.

■ Diaghilev commissioned the score of *Daphnis and Chloë* from Ravel in 1911. It was an old idea of Fokine's which had been turned down by the Imperial Ballet, probably alarmed by his theories of ballet reform. In the event, two of Ravel's *Daphnis and Chloë* suites were already composed before the ballet was designed. The result, especially from the point of view of interpretation, was excellent, and it was a great success, although it was then that the rivalry between Nijinsky and Fokine started. The latter, feeling himself overshadowed, left the company for two years. His new interest in classical antiquity, seen almost in the terms of an adventure novel, encouraged Fokine – partly inspired by Isadora Duncan's work, according to Karsavina – to study certain forms of Hellenism as a contrast to western academicism. It could, indeed, be said that every ballet produced under Diaghilev's regime was a break with the past. *Daphnis and Chloë*, with its eighteenth-century sources, its use of the "theater within a theater" convention, and its typically Russian love of an adventure story, could hardly be considered innovat-

ory were it not for its somewhat experimental choreography and the ingenious modernity of Ravel's music, which was able to conjure up antiquity by means of descriptive impressionism. The legend is explored through the feelings of the human characters, but basically it is a fable showing how the gods tidy up the troubles and disorder created by men. The ballet in its original form was frequently repeated.

OTHER VERSIONS. 1) John Taras. Lincoln Center, May 22, 1975. Danced by Peter Martins, Nina Fedorova, Karin von Aroldingen. 2) Glen Tetley. Stuttgart, Württemberg State Theater. Danced by Richard Cragun, Marcia Haydée, Birgit Keil, Egon Madsen.   M.P.

THE MUSIC. "My intention was to compose a vast fresco, not ruled by historical accuracy but inspired by the Greece of my dreams, Greece as it was imagined by French artists of the late eighteenth century. The work is constructed in symphonic form according to a strict tonal plan, in which a certain number of themes are developed in such a way as to ensure the homogeneity of the score." Ravel's words are especially illuminating with regard to the criterion imposed for the composition of *Daphnis and Chloë*. "A choreographic symphony in three parts" was how the author defined his work, meaning with that definition to stress the music's independent viability, that it would survive whatever happened to the ballet, a view that was later confirmed by the two orchestral *suites* Ravel drew from the score which are now – especially the second – part of the regular concert repertory. Certainly in this work Ravel extended his fine tonal sensibility and original mastery of form to their limits. He regarded the score

quite consciously as a sort of distancing from the Debussian type of tone colour, from pure impressionism, while adopting, on the other hand, a compositional rationality that, without renouncing the evocative colour of musical images, aimed at a firmer construction, within clear thematic limits, that made it the residuary heir of the Wagnerian leitmotiv. The need to suggest an exotic atmosphere also affected the makeup of the orchestra, which included unusual instruments such as the aeoliphone (to imitate the rustling of leaves in the wind), and the transparent composition, leaving plenty of room for the tonal colour of flutes, harps, celestas, and the various percussion instruments. A flexible and delightful vocal chorus is frequently blended into the general sound and in one ethereal passage is used unaccompanied.   A.F.

THE SPIDER'S BANQUET *(Le Festin de l'Araignée)*
One-act ballet. Choreography by Léo Staats. Music by Albert Roussel. Scenario by Gilbert des Voisins. Set and costumes by Maxime Dethomas. Paris, Théâtre des Arts, April 3, 1913. Principal dancer: Sarah Djeli.

SYNOPSIS. A spider entices a butterfly and imprisons her in his web. Other insects also become trapped until a praying mantis manages to get free and interrupt the sanguinary spider's feast by killing him. This insect drama ends with the butterfly's funeral.

■ The author of this curious entertainment, Gilbert des Voisins (a descendant of Maria Taglioni), found his inspiration in a book by the naturalist Henri Fabre. The subtle impressionism of Roussel's music and Léo Staats' classical choreography made this one of the latter's

Dancers in ritual poses invented by V. Nijinsky for The Rite of Spring. *Opposite: Scene from the same ballet, performed by the Royal Winnipeg Ballet.*

most successful productions. The story was enacted without a trace of realism in an atmosphere of remarkable dramatic abstraction.

OTHER VERSIONS. 1) Albert Aveline. Paris, Opéra, May 1, 1939. Danced by Suzanne Lorcia and Solange Schwarz. 2) Andrée Howard. London, New Theatre, June 6, 1944. Danced by Celia Franca, Sadler's Wells Ballet. A.A.

GAMES *(Jeux)*

Ballet (choreographic scene) in one act. Choreography by Vaslav Nijinsky. Music by Claude Debussy. Subject by Léon Bakst and Vaslav Nijinsky. Set and costumes by Léon Bakst. Paris, Théâtre des Champs Elysées, May 15, 1913. Serge Diaghilev's Russian Ballet. Principal dancers: Tamara Karsavina, Ludmilla Schollar, Vaslav Nijinsky.

SYNOPSIS. Looking for a tennis ball that has been hit some way from the court, a young man meets two girls. He flirts sometimes with one, sometimes with the other, then nonchalantly goes back to his tennis.

■ To accompany the delicate but cold and abstract action and choreography of *Jeux*, Claude Debussy composed his only score for the *Ballets Russes* and one of his very few for ballet (Debussy's music *L'Après-midi d'un Faune* was composed as a concert piece before Nijinsky's ballet of the same name for which it was used). Gino Tani wrote: "While the atmosphere of *Jeux* is always impressionistic, its harmonic and structural texture goes far beyond other music of its period. More than in Debussy's other works, the composition seems free of the strain and dynamics of musical preparation and solutions, even of the laws of traditional harmony, through a neoimpressionism expressed in sound, which foreshadows the boldest innovations of our century.

Pierre Boulez maintains it to be the first source of post-Weberian harmony. This new and difficult form of musical expression was a challenge to Nijinsky no less than to his audience and explains the comparative failure not only of his choreography for this ballet but also for others that followed it. . . ." The second of Nijinsky's ballet creations, one year after the scandal of *L'Après-midi d'un Faune* and one month before that of *The Rite of Spring, Jeux* met with a cool reception that was never later repealed. Although he possessed an academic technique second to none and a sense of theater that amounted to genius, Nijinsky lacked the clarity of thought and the intellectual education necessary to transform inspiration into an artistically valid work. Moreover, in this as in his other choreographic works, he daringly – and perhaps unsystematically – combined purely academic dance steps with explicitly anticlassical movements and attitudes, which, although suitable enough for as modern a subject as *Jeux*, could not fail to upset the most respected critics of the era. It involved, to quote Gino Tani again, "a technique that André Levinson immediately described as 'a cold, rhythmic formalism' of the Dalcrozian school, which was soon to lead to the hard, tortuous, heavy, and brutal movements of *Rite of Spring*. And hence to a 'fatal incongruity' although these naive and realistic symbols undoubtedly conveyed 'some of the elements of contemporary life' and 'points of contact with the newest trends of painting, which sought for synthesis through geometrical simplicity.'" Although *Jeux* was dropped from the Russian Ballet repertory after its Parisian season of 1913, it has survived up to the present day in revised versions with new choreography.

OTHER VERSIONS. 1) Jean Börlin. Paris, Théâtre des Champs Elysées, October 25, 1920. Danced by Carina Ari, Jenny Hasselquist, Jean Börlin, Rolf de Maré's Ballet Suédois. 2) William Dollar. New York, Center Theater, April 23, 1950. Danced by Nora Kaye, Norma

Vance, Igor Youskevitch, American Ballet Theater. 3) John Taras. New York State Theater, April 28, 1966. Danced by Allegra Kent, Melissa Hayden, Edward Villella, New York City Ballet. 4) Aurel Milloss. Rome, Opera House, December 2, 1967. Danced by Elisabetta Terabust, Alfredo Rainò, Giancarlo Vantaggio. 5) Flemming Flindt. Paris, Opéra, April 12, 1973.   A.A.

THE MUSIC. Modern critics tend to regard the score of *Jeux* as the most convincing testimony of Debussy's instrumental genius. It has undergone an unexpected linguistic and stylistic evolution and become, in some respects, less facile. With *Jeux*, Debussy ceased to be the "French impressionist composer," conveying a naturalistic atmosphere through impressionistic musical sound. Here, under the influence of the *pointilliste* school, the music became intensely fragmented: an extreme thematic atomization which paradoxically permits the score to be classed as "cellular." Pierre Boulez states that Debussy was starting a more elastic aesthetic of composition "based on the idea of irreversible movement; to listen to it one must submit oneself to its development, because the constant evolution of the themes pushes all ideas of architectural symmetry aside." Equally innovatory is the importance of the instrumentation, which becomes a true orchestral function, anticipating to a certain extent the aesthetic and expressive forms of *Klangfarbmelodie* (tone colour melody). It is also highly significant that *Jeux*, so full of technical and expressive innovations, should have been Debussy's last symphonic score: clear evidence that the isolation in which the composer always worked affected his artistic choices and pushed him towards a rethinking of all the canons of musical composition, with a revolutionary stance that was radical, yet unobtrusive and little recognized,   A.F.

THE RITE OF SPRING *(Le Sacre du Printemps)*
Ballet in two parts. Choreography by Vaslav Nijinsky. Music and scenario by Igor Stravinsky. Sets and costumes by Nicholas Roerich. Paris, Théâtre des Champs Elysées, May 29, 1913. Serge Diaghilev's Russian Ballet. Principal dancers: Maria Piltz in the part of the Chosen Maiden.

SYNOPSIS. Part I: the adoration of the earth. Curtain-rise reveals young men and girls in two separate groups. The surroundings are primeval and dominated by the dark forces of nature. At first the dances are light-hearted but gradually they change to more savage ritual movements. The young men take possession of the girls and carry them off. A fight between two rival tribes ensues, until a wise old man succeeds in making peace between them. There is a stunned silence, after which the men throw themselves to the ground in worship, rise again, and go into an even more frenzied dance. Part II: the sacrifice. The young women stand around the Sage near a fire. One of them is to be chosen as a sacrifice to the earth. The Chosen One, after a first mystic dance, stands still and alone in the middle of the stage. The young members of the tribe gather around her and

dance in a crescendo of brutal excitement. Finally, the Chosen Maiden joins them. The dancing grows ever more violent and unbridled until it reaches a climax and she falls to the earth exhausted and dies. The men carry her to the sacred stone, and all fall prostrate. The rite is over.

■ It is well known that on its opening night the ballet was greeted with riotous disapproval; right from the beginning there were whistles and boos, soon countered by applause. The protests grew more noisy as the performance progressed until, during the Sacrificial Dance, pandemonium broke out. Bravely the company carried on to the end although it was almost impossible for them to hear the orchestra. While Nijinsky, in the wings, could only count the beats, the conductor, Pierre Monteux, continued as if nothing were happening. Diaghilev ordered the company to hold out to the end of the ballet at all costs. He stood up in his box and called out "*Je vous en prie, laissez achever le spectacle!*" One can only imagine how difficult it must have been for Maria Piltz to give her superb rendering of the utterly novel and

Léonide Massine as Joseph in the ballet
The Legend of Joseph *by Michael Fokine.*

Set by Natalia Goncharova for Le Coq d'Or. *The ballet, danced to music by Rimsky-Korsakov, was created by Michael Fokine.*

exhausting Sacrificial Dance. Conditions in the audience were indescribable; some spectators actually came to blows. Among the ballet's champions was Claude Debussy. What enraged the public, apart from the brutality of the subject and the violence of the music, was Vaslav Nijinsky's choreography, which sought to convey a feeling of the savagery and eroticism of primitive religious rites by turning all the conventions of academic ballet technique inside out. *The Rite* was the negation of romantic taste and style; it was a vision of prehistory intended to shock the complacency of the theater-going public. Also, it was still 1913, the war had not yet broken out, and the audience's world still seemed the best of all possible worlds. Russian barbarism – later accepted without difficulty – was an uncalled for anticipation of the western barbarism that was to prevail so soon afterwards. *The Rite of Spring* was in essence an epic ballet, founded not on an edifying story but on group emotions; its subtitle, *Scene from pagan Russia*, is a very revealing one. To that is added the visual concept of spring in Russia, an explosion of fertility, the season when the earth's face changes overnight. Such a potent natural phenomenon gives birth to superstitions and religious rites. In that tribal culture the sacrifice of a young virgin was a tribute to that force, the unknown god who cannot be seen but produces wonders. According to Dame Marie Rambert, who was Nijinsky's assistant during the production of *Rite*, the Russian choreographer-dancer imposed a whole series of unusual positions and movements on the company: feet turned inwards, arms twisted round; jumps, polyrhythmic steps

of terror and uncontrolled frenzy. What might seem powerful and expressive today struck the unprepared audience of 1913 as ugly and, what is worse, ridiculous. At that point in his short and tormented career Nijinsky, in spite of his looming mental disorder, and to the displeasure of many of his colleagues, was laying the foundations of ballet's renewal. When one relates them to his time and its customs, culture, and certainties, his vehement violation of the rules in *Rite of Spring* makes the great iconoclasms of more recent years seem positively *petit-bourgeois*.

OTHER VERSIONS. Rechoreographed by Léonide Massine, still for the *Ballets Russes* (Paris, Théâtre des Champs Elysées, 1920; principal dancer: Lydia Sokolova). In April 1930, Martha Graham danced in a new version of *Rite of Spring*, also by Massine, at the Philadelphia Academy of Music. Since World War II the ballet has been revised, reconstructed, and reinterpreted by many of the greatest choreographers of the rising generations. The most interesting version was produced by Maurice Béjart in December 1959, at the Théâtre de la Monnaie, with his Ballet du XXme Siècle de Bruxelles, using Duska Sifnios in the leading role. Later it was performed by Tania Bari, Jorge Donn, and Rudolf Nureyev. Béjart altered the original meaning of the plot by changing the sacrifice of a virgin into the ritual physical union of a chosen maid and young man, a symbol of the positive and triumphant arrival of spring. Béjart's *Rite* – judged by Balanchine to be the best interpretation of Stravinsky's ballet – captures the full essence of the primeval ambience and the vigour of mass grouping and movement, and is extraordinarily logical. Deprived of its folklore element, the ballet ends up as a hymn of praise to life and love, a universal sanctification of irresistible forces. In 1962 *Rite of Spring* was put on by Kenneth McMillan at Covent Garden, London, with the Royal Ballet; decor by Nolan; Monica Mason as the Chosen Maiden. Glen Tetley also created a different version in 1975 at the Munich Opera House, describing a winter sacrifice ending in the rebirth of mankind (the following year it was revived in New York with Martine van Hamel and Mikhail Baryshnikov in the leading roles). On December 9, 1972, Natalia Makarova danced *Rite* at the Scala, Milan, in a new version by John Taras, with sets and costumes by Marino Marini. M.P.

THE MUSIC. In this composition Stravinsky, for the first time, completely turned his back on conventional tonalism in a very personal way, solidifying his musical material into successive blocks of sound, justified by the accumulation of tone colour thus achieved. With *The Rite of Spring* we enter the world of contemporary music, for the rejection of order, symphonic logic, and "charm" in this score signal the end of an era. The conventional romantic concept of beauty was knocked sideways by the barbaric rhythm of a composition offered to the public not as a poetic outpouring or an expression of its author's intimate feelings, but as the product of a calculated artistic contemplation, an objective equation in which the composer sets in motion and regulates musical forces that are not an integral part of his nature. Blunt notes from the bassoon, thrusting themselves into the higher range of the orchestra, open *Rite* with a dreaming, quasi-oriental theme soon submerged in a throbbing orchestral hum that represents the earth bursting into flower. Then man enters the scene with the dance of welcome to spring, which provides the first surprising example of how Stravinsky's rhythms become a basic means of expression. The same pattern is further developed in the great final dance, constructed by a process described by Casella as "rhythmic rubato," which consists of bringing together beats of diverse values, progressively working up to an irresistible paroxysm of sound. A.F.

THE TRAGEDY OF SALOME (*La Tragédie de Salomé*)

One-act ballet. Choreography by Boris Romanoff. Music by Florent Schmitt. Scenario by Robert d'Humières. Sets and costumes by Serge Sudeikine. Paris, Théâtre des Champs Elysées, June 12, 1913. Serge Diaghilev's Russian Ballet. Principal dancer: Tamara Karsavina (Salome).

■ The somber and disturbing story of Salome, with some additions such as the decking of Salome with jewels by Herodias, the stripping of them by Herod, and the bleeding head of John the Baptist reemerging from the sea during a storm that demolishes the palace, made up the plot put together by Robert d'Humières for a

choreographic performance by the famous dancer Loïe Fuller at the Théâtre des Arts in Paris in 1907. Entitled *La Tragédie de Salomé* it was set to an interesting score by Florent Schmitt. Ivan Clustine used the same scenario for an identically named ballet presented in Paris at the Théâtre du Châtelet on April 22, 1912, with Natalia Truhanova in the title role. The following year it was the turn of the *Ballet Russes*, which produced *The Tragedy of Salome* with choreography by Boris Romanoff, the only work he did for Diaghilev's company apart from the dances for the opera *Le Rossignol*. The ballet, which opened two weeks after the *succés de scandale* of *The Rite of Spring*, was a failure. Serge Grigoriev summarized the situation as follows: "... the chief reasons were the confused scenario, and the poor staging and stage design, while the music and choreography were little better. ... Later we presented *Salome* in Monte Carlo (1914), but even there its success was so slight that it was immediately withdrawn from the program." Revived subsequently, with different choreography, the title long remained in the repertory of the Paris Opéra.

OTHER VERSIONS. 1) Nicola Guerra. Paris Opéra, April 1, 1919. Danced by Ida Rubinstein. 2) Albert Aveline. Paris, Opéra, July 7, 1944. Danced by Suzanne Lorcia; revived there on December 15, 1954. Danced by Lycette Darsonval. A.A.

THE LEGEND OF JOSEPH (*Die Josephlegende*)

One-act ballet. Choreography by Michael Fokine. Music by Richard Strauss. Scenario by Harry, Graf von Kessler, and Hugo von Hofmannsthal. Sets by José-Maria Sert. Costumes by Léon Bakst. Paris, Opéra, April 15, 1914. Serge Diaghilev's Russian Ballet. Principal dancers: Léonide Massine (Joseph), Maria Kousnetzova (Potiphar's wife), Alexis Bulgakov (Potiphar).

SYNOPSIS. The well-known biblical episode is set against the background of an opulent Renaissance court resembling the paintings of Veronese and Tintoretto at the height of the Venetian republic's glory. It is a conflict between two worlds, in which wealth and satiety are contrasted with the open simplicity and spontaneous feelings of the pastoral life led by Joseph and his family. The bored, corrupt wife of Potiphar burns with desire for the noble and pious Joseph. But his devotion has already turned heavenwards; his chastity stands firm against her lewd proposals, which fill him only with revulsion. Her pride and vanity deeply wounded, the vicious woman now wants only to debase the living symbol of her unappeased desires and vague remorse. She falsely accuses him of trying to rape her and has him thrown into prison. Steadfast under torture, Joseph is condemned to death, but an archangel comes down to save him and raise him up to a celestial apotheosis, while Potiphar's wife, more in baffled hatred than in repentance, strangles herself with her chain of pearls.

■ This ballet, taken away from Nijinsky after his break with Diaghilev, marked the highly praised debut of the

Jean Babilée in the title role of Till Eulenspiegel, *for which he designed new choreography in 1949.*

nineteen-year-old Léonide Massine with the *Ballets Russes.* The famous impresario had engaged him after seeing him dance the tarantella from *Swan Lake* in Moscow. Fokine modelled the character of Joseph more on Massine's Byzantine good looks than on his still immature virtuosity in classical dance, which was subsequently polished by Cecchetti. The ballet itself, however, was not so well received. There was too much mime and not enough dancing; moreover, Kousnetzova, more opera singer than dancer, was not equal to expressing the anguished spiritual darkness of the character she played.

OTHER VERSIONS. 1) Kröller. Berlin, State Opera, 1921, and Vienna State Opera, March 18, 1922. 2) Balanchine. Copenhagen, Theater Royal, Royal Danish Ballet, June 18, 1931. 3) M. Wallman. Milan, Scala, 1952. 4) Antony Tudor. Buenos Aires, Colon Theater, August 19, 1958. 5) H. Rosen, Munich State Opera House, 1958. G.S.

THE GOLDEN COCKEREL *(Le Coq d'Or)*
Ballet-opera in three acts. Choreography by Michael Fokine. Music by Nikolai Rimsky-Korsakov. Scenario by V. Bielski, rearranged by Alexandre Benois. Sets and costumes by Natalia Goncharova. Paris, Opéra, May 21, 1914. Principal dancers: Tamara Karsavina (Queen of Shemâkhan), Alexis Bulgakov (King Dodon), Enrico Cecchetti.

SYNOPSIS. An astrologer has presented old King Dodon with a golden cockerel that will warn him of any approaching danger. In return the King promises the magician to grant him anything he wishes. After a battle with his enemies, in which his two sons are killed, Dodon meets the Queen of Shemâkhan and wants to make her his bride. When the astrologer himself claims the lovely Queen as his reward, Dodon is so angry that he kills him. The cock avenges his master by striking the King dead, and then flies away.

■ Although described as a ballet-opera, this dance arrangement of a few bars of Rimsky-Korsakov's opera *Le Coq d'Or* devised by Benois, Diaghilev, and Fokine had little in common with the precisely defined form of theater that went under that name. As Serge Grigoriev, permanent stage director of the Russian Ballet, recalls, when Diaghilev and his friends were deploring the lack of acting talent among opera singers (with the exception of Chaliapin), Benois suggested that the singers should be hidden, while dancers or real actors should perform their parts. That idea gave birth to this peculiar ballet danced to vocal music (already provided with a dramatic text), in which the singers were ranged on either side of the stage while dancers "doubled" their parts in mime. The scenic design contributed largely to the signal success of the spectacle. "Natalia Goncharova's scenery sumptuously blended the influence of fauves, rayonists, and cubists to produce her extraordinarily vibrant and colourful sets, based on contrasting shades of scarlet and golden yellow. They evoked the rough, glowing potency of a boyard palace, the delicate, flowered splendour of a sultan's carpet, and paintings of old Russian cities bristling with gateways and towers flung together without sense of perspective. The design is on a grand scale with simplified lines of force" (*Les Ballets Russes de Serge Diaghilev*, Ville de Strasbourg, 1969). It was Goncharova's first work for the Russian Ballet.   A.A.

STENKA RAZIN

One-act ballet. Choreography by Michael Fokine. Music by Alexander Glazunov. St. Petersburg, Maryinsky Theater, 1915. Principal dancers: Vera Fokina, B. Romanov.

SYNOPSIS. The plot, laid in the old Russia of the Middle Ages and derived from a brief historical note, tells of a group of wretchedly poor peasants. Driven to desperation by the tyranny and abuses of the landlords, they revolt, form themselves into an armed band, and even engage the Imperial troops in battle. Led by a brave Cossack peasant, Stenka Razin, the rebels, in a series of heroic exploits, take the regular army by surprise, inflicting several serious defeats. However, a year later Stenka Razin himself is surprised and vanquished at Simbirskij. Severely wounded, he goes into hiding, but is betrayed, taken prisoner, and finally executed in Moscow.   P.C.

LOVE, THE MAGICIAN (*El Amor Brujo*)

Mime-ballet in one act. Choreography by Pastora Imperio. Music by Manuel de Falla. Scenario by Gregorio Martinez Sierra. Madrid, Lara Theater, April 15, 1915. Principal dancer: Pastora Imperio.

SYNOPSIS. Carmelo's courtship of the gypsy girl Candelas is disturbed by apparitions of the ghost of a young man who, until his untimely death, was engaged to Candelas. She does not dare to accept her new suitor until Carmelo persuades the young Lucia to entice the phantasm away while the two lovers kiss, thus putting an end to the spell.

■ This old folk tale was told to the playwright Gregorio Martinez Sierra by Rosaria "La Mejorana," mother of the famous Andalusian singer and dancer Pastora Imperio, who had asked Manuel de Falla to compose "a song and dance" for her. The original idea was amplified and turned into a true gypsy ballet with singing, in one act and two scenes. The music by Manuel de Falla was very personal, not unmindful of international movements, but rich in a disturbing, resonant sensuality and fierce and lingering rhythms that were truly Spanish in feeling and closely allied to the spirit and style in which Pastora Imperio composed her ballet. The poor reception extended to *El Amor Brujo* by the Madrid audience did not prevent its frequent revival in different balletic versions, principally, no doubt, because of the music. Perhaps the most authentically "folk" and yet stylistically and expressively finished version was that by the great Spanish dancer and choreographer Antonio

(Antonio Ruiz Soler), presented in London in 1955.

OTHER VERSIONS. 1) Adolf Bolm. Chicago, Eighth Theater, January 1, 1924. A. Bolm Ballet Intime. 2) La Argentina (Antonia Mercé). Paris, Trianon-Lyrique, 1925. Danced by La Argentina and Vincente Escudero. 3) Boris Romanoff. Monte Carlo, Opera House, April 23, 1932. Danced by Felia Dubrovska, Ballet de Monte Carlo. 4) La Argentinita (Encarnacion Lopez). Madrid, Teatro Español, 1933. 5) Leon Woizikowsky. Paris, 1935. 6) Vincente Escudero. New York, Radio City Music Hall, March 21, 1935. 7) Serge Lifar. Paris, Opéra, January 26, 1943. Danced by Teresina, Lycette Darsonval, Roland Petit, Serge Lifar. 8) Mariemma (Emma Martinez). Paris, Opéra-Comique, June 19, 1947. Danced by Mariemma, Manolo Vargas. 9) Margherita Wallmann. Milan, Scala, December 31, 1949. Danced by Luciana Novaro, Giulio Perugini. 10) Pilar Lopez. Madrid, Teatro Comedia, March 1955. 11) Ruth Page. Chicago, St. Alphonsus Theater, December 12, 1954. Ballet Guild of Chicago. 12) Antonio (Antonio Ruiz Soler). London, Saville Theatre, April 5, 1955. Danced by Rosita Segovia, Antonio, Ballet of Madrid. 13) Luciana Novaro. Milan, Scala, December 21, 1962. Danced by Elettra Morini, Antonio Gades.   A.A.

THE MUSIC. The sun-drenched freshness of the score comes largely from de Falla's determination to blend Andalusian music with that of the gypsies, both of which existed side by side in most of southern Spain. In fact it can be said that in *El Amor Brujo* the academic music of Europe was for the first time integrated with gypsy music. The makeup of the orchestra is extremely limited (a chamber orchestra with piano), but the resulting sound is anything but poor; on the contrary, it is stimulated by the search for unusual and expressive effects (it is remarkable how the sound of guitars and castanets is suggested simply by new techniques of orchestration). What makes this ballet a true masterwork, however, is the way in which de Falla uses folk melodies, in snatches or even whole, without ever lapsing into mere illustration of mannered decorativeness. After a very lively orchestral introduction giving a musical picture of Andalusia, there follows a passage redolent of mystery that brings the story to the gypsy camp. The solo passages on muted trumpet and oboe, creating an aura of mourning and suspense, give way to the rapid dance movements of the *Cancion del Amor dolido* (Song of Sad Love). In The Magic Circle, de Falla's brilliant, terse orchestration accompanies the scene where the gypsies are preparing the magic spells. The *Danza ritual del Fuego* (Ritual Fire Dance) is a savage, pagan dance with which the composer conjures up the atmosphere of ancient rites, an evocation of spirits that goes back to the dawn of civilization. The irresistible rhythmic and instrumental energy of the *Danza del Juego del Amor* (Dance of the Game of Love) melts enchantingly into the impassioned melody on the English horn that represents the "voice of destiny" in the last sung passage of the ballet.   A.F.

THE MIDNIGHT SUN *(Le Soleil de Minuit)*
One-act ballet. Choreography by Léonide Massine. Music by Nikolai Rimsky-Korsakov (from The Snow Maiden*). Set and costumes by Mikhail Larionov. Geneva, Grand Theater, December 20, 1915. Serge Diaghilev's Russian Ballet. Principal dancers: Léonide Massine (Midnight Sun), Nicholas Zverev (Bobyl).*

SYNOPSIS. A ballet without a plot, it is composed of a series of dances featuring characters drawn from Russian folklore: Midnight Sun, the Snow Maiden, Bobyl the simpleton, shepherds, shepherdesses, peasants, and clowns.

■ Since the outbreak of World War I, Diaghilev had been struggling to maintain the existence and unity of his company, and neither the military conscription of the dancers, difficulties of transport, nor the impossibility of communicating at all quickly with the artists and composers detained in various countries for lack of a passport, prevented him from achieving his objectives. At the time of Massine's return from Florence in August 1915, the company's headquarters were at Ouchy near Lausanne, where Stravinsky, Bakst, Larionov, and Goncharova were already assembled, soon to be joined by Zverev, Idzikowsky, the Chabelska sisters, Nemchinova, and the English dancer Hilda Munnings (who had changed her name to Lydia Sokolova). Diaghilev decided to abandon the production of *Liturgy*, a balletic version of the Mass, which had been suggested to Massine by the paintings in the Florentine galleries, especially Simone Martini's *Annunciation*. In its place he commissioned Massine to prepare a new ballet to the *suite* drawn from Rimsky-Korsakov's opera *The Snow Maiden*. Thus *Midnight Sun* was born, under the supervision of Larionov, probably assisted by Goncharova, who collaborated on the stage designs. Among other things, the ballet was remarkable for bringing three new artistic talents into the limelight: Massine, for his first choreographic work done for the *Ballets Russes*; Larionov, whose first stage designs they were for the company; and Ernest Ansermet, beginning his career as orchestral conductor. This happy multiple collaboration resulted in a great success with both public and critics. "You see," Diaghilev said to Svetlov, "bring me the talent and in the bat of an eyelid I produce a choreographer" (Buckle). What undoubtedly contributed to the triumph, in addition to the dancers brilliantly performing the wild, whirling dances, were the dazzling stage pictures by Larionov, a notable connoisseur of Russian folklore. His resplendent compositions in midnight blue, scarlet, and gold, and his stylized, serrated costume designs, bold but faithful to the spirit of popular Russian iconography, soon accustomed the general public to the new and revolutionary shapes and colours. A third factor in the success was the tunefulness of *The Snow Maiden* music. The ballet stayed in the repertory for several years and was produced at the Century Theater in New York on January 17, 1916; at the Costanzi Theater in Rome on April 9, 1917; at the Paris Opéra on December 29, 1917; at the Lyceum in

Watercolour costume sketch by Pablo Picasso for the Chinese Conjuror, a character in the ballet Parade.

Barcelona on January 15, 1918, and at the Coliseum in London on November 21, 1918.   G.S.

LAS MENIÑAS
Pavane. Subject and Choreography by Léonide Massine. Music by Gabriel Fauré. Set by Carlo Socrate. Costumes by José-Maria Sert. San Sebastian, Eugenia-Vittoria Theater, August 21, 1916. Serge Diaghilev's Russian Ballet. Principal dancers: Lydia Sokolova, Léonide Massine, Leon Woizikowsky.

■ A solemn, ceremonial evocation of old Spain in a pavane danced by the characters represented in Velasquez's famous painting. The ballet was rapturously received on its opening night in San Sebastian, appropriately attended by King Alphonso XIII, Diaghilev's patron. Nevertheless, *Las Meniñas*, although it went on several tours, does not hold a very important place among the productions of Diaghilev's Russian Ballet.
                                                            A.A.

TILL EULENSPIEGEL
Dramatic comedy ballet in one act. Choreography by Vaslav Nijinsky. Music by Richard Strauss. Scenario and sequence by Vaslav Nijinsky and Richard Strauss.

Sets and costumes by Robert Edmund Jones. New York, Manhattan Opera House, October 23, 1916. Serge Diaghilev's Russian Ballet (second company). Principal dancers: Vaslav Nijinsky (Till Eulenspiegel), Flora Revalles (Lady of the castle), Lydia Sokolova (Apple-seller).

SYNOPSIS. The ballet, derived from a medieval German legend *The Merry Pranks of Till Eulenspiegel* by Charles de Coster (*Ulenspiegel und Lamm Goedzak*), was inspired by Richard Strauss's symphonic poem of the same name. It recounts the tragi-comic adventures of an ineffable rogue who plays his mocking tricks in the crowded marketplace of old Brunswick. There he mingles with all sorts: merchants, farmers, the ragged poor, whining beggars, proud professors, none too religious clergymen, gentlewomen, and gowned doctors of the law. It is the pillars of this privileged society that our jovial hero selects as the victims of his frauds, for he combines a ferocious sense of satire with a fine irony and justifies his misdeeds by his own disillusioned morality. Behold him, then, in his tattered olive-green raiment, with his teasing smile beneath a tousled mop of hair, burst into the market square, knocking over the baker's breadbasket and the honey-seller's

bench so that the poor can gather up what is spilt. Another time, quick as lightning, he manages to tie up a group of unsuspecting citizens as if they were a bale of hay, then cut their bonds so that they fall backwards, legs in air, looking very ridiculous. But Till has disappeared as quickly as he came, and his victims can only hobble off to lay their complaints before the mayor. Disguised in the capacious hood of a holy man, Till preaches a provocative sermon to an audience of credulous matrons and men of law. To the poor who ask for alms he counsels renunciation of worldly goods, then with a grin throws off his hood, makes himself known, and scampers off. The spectators, much out of countenance, go to the mayor and demand justice. Love, too, comes in for its share of mockery. The Lady of the manor, on coming out of church, is greatly flattered by the attentions of a certain cavalier in plumed hat who bows before her with courtly ceremony. But when his green jerkin shows beneath his cloak the passers-by double up with laughter and Till vanishes before the Lady realizes she has been tricked. And so her admirers also go to denounce him. Long beards, huge spectacles, and mortarboards proclaim the identity of five learned professors of the university. An unknown sixth joins them and demolishes their arguments with a farrago of

Drop curtain for Parade *by Pablo Picasso, who also designed the scenery and costumes. Léonide Massine's ballet, with music by Erik Satie and scenario by Jean Cocteau, may not have met with great critical acclaim on its opening night, but was nevertheless epoch-making for its iconoclastic forms.*

Dario Fo and actors during a rehearsal of The Soldier's Story, *a ballet with narration, music, and dancing.*

nonsense. And the professors, too, go off to denounce him. As night falls Eulenspiegel is still at his tricks, singing at the top of his voice that everyone is equal and inviting the poor to join in the dance. The exultant crowd carries him shoulder-high in triumph. But his dance is considered revolutionary, so he is arrested by the guards and brought before the Inquisition. Till remains untroubled, but all his accusers appear and he is condemned to hang from the gallows; only the noose will wipe out that ironic smile. Just as the people are mourning his death he appears again in a flight of balloons. Till Eulenspiegel has cheated even death and, like Petrouchka, will remain immortal.

■ This was the only ballet produced by his company to which that leading spirit, Diaghilev, made no prior contribution, and which he never saw, for the original version was only performed a few times in the United States, where it had been conceived, planned, and rehearsed, and never elsewhere. Nijinsky, in fact, who had recently been released from a Hungarian internment camp through the good offices of Diaghilev, had made his complete artistic independence a condition of his return to the *Ballets Russes*. Having been granted the direction of Diaghilev's second company, which was working in America, and having given up an earlier project for a nonconformist ballet featuring pregnant women, Nijinsky, at the peak of his mature genius, created in *Till Eulenspiegel* his swan song. After that he slowly sank in the quicksand of a mental alienation

which was to decline into catatonic schizophrenia. Robert Edmund Jones, the stage designer, wrote that Nijinsky's energy, daring, laughter, and blazing imagination were a continual source of wonder and delight to him. Nijinsky would be a mischievous boy one moment, tender, pleading lover or sinister medieval imp the next. Everything in the ballet seemed free, virile, artless, and down-to-earth, the whole suffused with a smile of mockery. In *Till Eulenspiegel* Nijinsky's characterization surpassed even that in *Petrouchka*, both tragic myths of redemption, both symbols of the rebirth of ballet. It achieved catharsis through laughter and pity.

OTHER VERSIONS. 1) Leonid Jacobson. Leningrad, Kirov Theater, 1933. 2) V. Kratina. Berlin, Stadtoper, 1940. 3) Jean Babilée. Sets and costumes by Tom Keogh. Paris, Théâtre des Champs Elysées. November 9, 1949. Danced by Jean Babilée, Ballets des Champs Elysées. 4) George Balanchine. Sets and costumes by Esteban Frances, New York, City Center, November 14, 1951. Danced by Jerome Robbins, Brooks Jackson, Franck Hobi, Beatrice Tompkins, New York City Ballet.   G.S.

THE GOOD-HUMOURED LADIES (*Les Femmes de Bonne Humeur*)
Ballet or choreographic comedy in one act. Choreography by Léonide Massine. Music by Domenico Scarlatti, orchestrated by Vincenzo Tommasini. Story

by Goldoni. Sets and costumes by Léon Bakst. Rome, Costanzi Theater, April 12, 1917. Serge Diaghilev's Russian Ballet. Principal dancers: Lubov Tchernicheva (Costanza), Lydia Lopokova (Mariuccia), Giuseppina Cecchetti (the Marchesa Silvestra), Léonide Massine (Leonardo), Stanislas Idzikowsky (Battista), Enrico Cecchetti (the Marchese de Luca).

SYNOPSIS. In eighteenth-century Venice the frolicsome "good-humoured ladies" send Count Rinaldo a love letter signed by an unknown hand. Five of them present themselves, all masked and bearing the appointed sign of a pink rose. Bewildered, he is left at last with the old Marchesa Silvestra. Mariuccia, in love with Leonardo, organizes a little dinner party for her lover and his friend, soon joined by the old gallant, the Marchese de Luca. Together with the other ladies, they fool first the old gentleman, and then his sister Silvestra, to whom they present as a serious suitor the waiter Nicolo, disguised as a great lord. Thus follows a whole entanglement of jests and tomfoolery devised by the mischievous ladies, leaving unscathed only the charming but mournful Costanza.

■ Carlo Goldoni's *Le Donne di Buon Umore* furnished Léonide Massine with the subject-matter of his first important ballet, presented by Diaghilev's company during its Italian tour of 1917, and repeated in Paris, Monte Carlo, and London. It was rapturously received everywhere and became one of the Russian Ballet's major successes. Massine's talent as a choreographer already showed its characteristic strengths: a sharp and brilliant comic vein inspired by the theater of the people – in this case the *Commedia dell'Arte* – governed by his inimitable style of narrative mime perfectly integrated with academic dance. In *The Good-Humoured Ladies* his feeling for a particular historical period was supplemented by careful research into seventeenth- and eighteenth-century dance, which enriched Massine's choreographic vocabulary and provided him with points of departure perfectly attuned to the Scarlatti music selected, yet in no way inhibited his exuberant young imagination and irrepressible high spirits. At Diaghilev's behest, Bakst's scenery, originally designed to appear as if distorted in a convex mirror, was "normalized" and became a barely stylized view of an eighteenth-century Venetian square. Among the dancers appearing in the first performance, in addition to Massine himself, brilliant in a character part, the illustrious Lubov Tchernicheva, and all the chief ballerinas of Diaghilev's company, were the two Cecchettis as the old Marquis and Marchioness – Enrico, the company's ballet master and the grand old man of academic dance tuition in this century; Giuseppina Cecchetti, his wife. *The Good-Humoured Ladies* was revived by Massine in London on July 7, 1949, for the Marquis de Cuevas' Grand Ballet; then for the Royal Ballet on July 11, 1962 at Covent Garden Opera House, with Anya Linden, Antoinette Sibley, Lynn Seymour, Stanley Holden, and Bryan Shaw dancing the principal parts.

OTHER VERSIONS. Luciana Novaro. Sets and

costumes by Pierluigi Pizzi. Milan, Scala, February 21, 1960. Principal dancers: Carla Fracci, Elettra Morini, Carmen Puthod, Fiorella Cova, Roberto Fascilla, Mario Pistoni.   A.A.

PARADE

Realistic ballet in one act. Choreography by Léonide Massine. Music by Erik Satie. Scenario by Jean Cocteau. Drop curtain, set, and costumes by Pablo Picasso. Paris, Théâtre du Chatelet, May 18, 1917. Serge Diaghilev's Russian Ballet Company. Principal dancers: Léonide Massine (Chinese conjuror), Galina Chabelska (American girl), Lydia Lopokova (Acrobat), Nicholas Zverev (Acrobat), Leon Woizikowsky (the Manager in evening dress), M. Statkewicz (the Manager from New York), M. Oumansky and M. Nova (the Horse).

SYNOPSIS. There is no plot. We see a parade of performers from a small circus, each giving a foretaste of his "act" to lure the public inside. Two managers, one European, the other American, mime ceremonious invitations to the crowd gathered outside a booth on the outskirts of a town on a dismal Sunday afternoon. These gigantic walking caryatids are figures of pure Picassian fantasy. Inside the European construction is a dancer concealed in a series of intersecting cardboard strips and blocks surmounted by a very cubist head and neck and wearing a white shirtfront to go with the most unconventional of tailcoats; he represents the Parisian circus manager with cane and pipe. The manager from New York has a head and trunk modelled on a skyscraper, wears a cowboy shirt and riding-boots, and carries a megaphone in one hand, a placard bearing the word "Parade" in the other. They are sent off by the sudden entrance of the sardonic Chinese conjuror in a coat of scarlet and gold. Advancing with the rapid steps of an automaton, he jerks his pigtail to and fro, making an egg appear and disappear with dizzying unexpectedness. Then comes the turn of the saucy, sailor-suited American girl, who bounds across the stage in a convulsive way, then seems to be steering a motor car, mimes scenes from the silent cinema and from an imaginary shipwreck, referring no doubt to the Titanic disaster, and finally goes into a ragtime routine from the true age of jazz before she, too, leaves the scene. Now the ringmaster – a dummy – enters mounted on a pantomime horse worked by two hidden dancers. The parade ends with a pair of acrobats who perform somersaults and flying leaps before disappearing into the wings. The melancholy finale shows all the "artistes" vainly renewing their invitation to the apathetic spectators, who drift away, quite satisfied at having seen so much of the show for nothing. The fall of the drop curtain marks the end of a drama of isolation.

■ The historical and artistic significance of *Parade* was far greater than one might suppose from its unenthusiastic reception by critics and public when it opened during the darkest days of World War I. Among other things, and in spite of consciences torn between fervent patriotism and defeatist resignation, there was a revival of interest in the humourous and music-hall aspect of the circus, the Dada manifesto was arousing keen discussion, while nascent fauvism, futurism, and surrealism were bubbling in the literary and artistic circles of Montparnasse. Apollinaire made it a tenet of faith ("*Parade* is the spirit of today"). Sensitive as an insect's antenna to the most imperceptible precursory vibrations of modernity, and thrust with each success more powerfully towards the avant-garde, Diaghilev ceased to employ the talents of Bakst and Benois after 1917, amazing operators of "the magic lantern for grown-up children" though they were. With *Parade*, his Russian Ballet Company shed its Slavonic soul in favour of an internationalism with a French flavour, becoming a veritable manifesto of cubism in the theater. Spurred on by the demon of novelty and the terror of losing his public if he did not continually entice it with the latest formula, the Diaghilev of 1917 sought to scandalize the audience with cubism and brash new music of the Parisian school, just as he had done in 1913 with *Rite of Spring*, restoring confidence afterwards by staging lush productions of Russian theater. Convinced of cubism's genuine value, he employed the genius of Picasso, whose theatrical designs were as violent and provocative as his contemporary painting. People were not yet ready to accept the new message, nor were they any more appreciative of the tapping typewriters, screaming sirens, thudding dynamos, and airplane noises Cocteau envisaged for Satie's score. In such unsettled and warweary times, an art of schism ceased to astonish and aroused only negative feelings. It was "a challenge to good taste and good sense," declared the critic Louis Schneider. Georges Seurat's painting *La Parade* of 1887 provided Jean Cocteau with the inspiration for his scenario. John Berger considered the entertainment to be a "bourgeois palliative" for the French defeats of 1917; later Lincoln Kirstein saw it as a metaphor of the creative spirit represented by the unctuous imperturbability of the Chinese conjuror. *Parade* was the first ballet to bring jazz into the theater, to discover the "decorative" music of a Satie, more cabaretic than symphonic in style, and to usher in the trend-setting reign of Cocteau, who was to express further disillusion and gloom in *Le Coq et l'Arlequin* and *Féerie*. *Parade* was revived at the Théâtre de la Monnaie in 1964 by the *Ballet du XXme Siècle*; at the New York City Center on March 22, 1973, by the Joffrey Ballet; at the London Coliseum on May 22, 1974, by the London Festival Ballet. John Taras also worked out a new choreography but was unable to complete his project for lack of permission to use the musical score.   G.S.

THE MUSIC. Satie, accepting that this score was to become a mere musical background to a host of noises from everyday life, developed the original idea in his own characteristic way. The noises, which were to give the impression of a bustling fair and convey nostalgia for its atmosphere, were in effect deliberately "composed" by Satie and inserted in a simple, rational score which brings out only the "poorer" elements of the traditional orchestra (enriched by everyday "instru-

ments" such as a typewriter, a pistol, a ship's siren, a Morse transmitter, etc.) and shuns the more agreeable instrumental combinations. On the surface *Parade* is a static work, but it is in that very quality that its dramatic intensity and provocation lie. In regard to melody, the work is akin to his three short piano pieces of 1912–1915, while the three ballet numbers are enclosed in a kind of double frame. The inner one, preceding the first episode and following the last, is of a disjointed, dehumanized character, the music of the managers. The outer frame, on the other hand, consists of a fugue which opens the score with the exposition and closes it with the "coda." The symmetrical consistency of the stylistic elements is seen in both the recurring alternation of binary and ternary rhythms and in the meticulous maintenance of a uniform and relentless tempo (of 76 beats, varying from time to time, per minute), accompanying the three episodes which follow one another without any link of continuity. A little before Debussy's death, Satie, as if accepting a personal challenge, launched the new musical movement in Paris, opening the doors to the aesthetic claims of "The Six" with a score that carried poverty and indignant realism like a banner.   A.F.

THE SOLDIER'S STORY (*L'Histoire du Soldat*)

Narrative ballet in five scenes, read, played, and danced. Choreography by Ludmilla Pitoëff. Music by Igor Stravinsky. Text by Charles F. Ramuz. Sets and costumes by René Auberjonois. Lausanne, September 28, 1918. Principal dancers: Gabriel Rossel, Georges Pitoëff, and Ludmilla Pitoëff.

SYNOPSIS. Scene I: a wood. The soldier is on his way home from the wars. He carries with him the portrait of his sweetheart and his fiddle. Seated on the bank of a stream he begins to play. The devil, disguised as an old gentleman, arrives on the scene and asks for his violin. The soldier, doubtful at first, finally consents; in return he receives a book said by the old man to be of great value. It will make him rich, he claims, so it's a good bargain. The devil asks the soldier to teach him how to play the instrument, and the persuades him to return to his village. Scene II: the village. The soldier, whose name is Joseph, has come home, but without his being aware of it many years have gone by and the young man gets a cold welcome. His sweetheart is married, with two children, and his mother wants nothing to do with him. The devil reappears, this time dressed as a cattle dealer. Joseph is angry, but the devil merely counsels him to follow the directions in the book. As a result the soldier grows rich, but he is not happy; he can only make money. Scene III: in his office Joseph is consulting his book. This time the devil appears as a poor old woman and shows him the violin. When the soldier asks to buy it back, the crone replies that first he must prove he can play it. In spite of his best efforts, Joseph can draw no sound from the instrument. When the old woman leaves him he destroys the book. Scene IV: Joseph begins a new life in a new land. It has just been announced that the King's daughter is afflicted

Set by Pablo Picasso for The Three-Cornered Hat, *a ballet by Massine with music by de Falla.*

with an unknown and mortal illness and that the King will give the Princess in marriage to anyone who can cure her. Persuaded to play cards with the devil, Joseph succeeds in winning back his violin and finds that he can now make it play again. By playing it before the Princess he brings about a miraculous cure. The devil returns and asks for the instrument back, but Joseph makes him dance to his fiddling until he falls to the ground exhausted. The two carry the diabolical creature outside and rejoice in their love. Though foiled on this occasion, the devil plans revenge: the soldier will be safe only as long as he stays within the boundaries of the Princess's country. Should he stray beyond them he will fall into the devil's power again. Some time later the Princess asks her husband to take her on a visit to his native land. He accepts, although he knows the outcome will be fatal. Scene V: as soon as the frontier is crossed the devil reappears, playing the bewitched violin. From now on the soldier will be his slave; the Princess calls him back in vain. The adventure is over.

■ A formidable example of the ballet of mixed media, *The Soldier's Story* is a brilliant mixture of dancing and the spoken word, which carry on the story alternately. The music, very modern and extremely beautiful, is entrusted to seven players; various famous actors have undertaken the speaking part. At other times it has been done by such theatrical celebrities as George Strehler, or even dancers such as Rudolf Nureyev. The Narrator conveys the dramatic plot, drawn from an old Russian fairy tale with a moral, but it is Stravinsky's music that finally plays the leading part. Elements of Russian peasant culture (the violin, the magic book, the superstition) dominate the story, as well as familiar fairy-tale ingredients (the sick Princess, the devil's disguises). The

original moral ("one can't change one's station in life with impunity") has become a modern parable, harsh, but basically not without pity for the sufferings involved in World War I, which apart from the diabolical element, Ramuz and Stravinsky saw as representing the human condition in general. Later even this Stravinskian work was destined to be completely derussified, its sources wiped out to make way for a less dated and thus more original reinterpretation. The boldest attempt of that kind was made in 1972 (first performance on January 7th at the New York City Center) by Eliot Feld with the American Ballet. He changed the story radically, basing his plot on the corruption caused by war, and the resulting crimes and disasters. The soldier is no longer the victim of the devil but of rogues and prostitutes, demons from the infamous brood produced and maintained by war. In introducing the theme of sexuality into the soldier's story, Feld pursued a policy of schism which extended to all the aspects of his theater.   M.P.

THE MUSIC. The circumstances that led to the choice of instruments used in the score of *The Soldier's Story* (clarinet, bassoon, violin, double bass, cornet, trombone, and percussion), and certain elements that influenced its composition, are well-known. Ernest Ansermet, it must be remembered, had brought back with him from America a collection of piano parts and records of the jazz music he had heard there and Stravinsky undoubtedly noted its essentially rhythmic and percussive qualities, which we can see in *Histoire*, as in *Ragtime for 11 instruments* and *Piano Ragmusic*. In addition to eleven pieces of music for the ballet action, he composed five shorter ones to link up the episodes. His inspiration came from many different sources: Bach chorales and Swiss bands, Argentine tangos and Viennese waltzes, American ragtime and Russian folk songs. None of these varied elements, however, disturbs the homogeneity of the brilliant and stylistically unexceptionable composition. From the skillful use of his six instruments he draws glowing colour and atmosphere, evoked with the greatest economy of means (to mention only that the orchestra is able to supply the sharps and flats characteristic of each family of instruments). The heterogenous thematic material is organized around the leading instrument, the violin, the musical personality of which is clearly of Russian origin. Its sound, nevertheless, is heard with decreasing frequency until in the devil's Dance of Triumph the last word is left with the percussion alone. The score of *The Soldier's Story* gradually sheds its more traditional connotations as it advances further into the theatrical narration, from the scathing irony of some of its scenes to the architectural austerity of others, losing its surface glitter and turning back to pure rhythm, the primal basis of all Stravinsky's expressive art.   A.F.

AUTUMN LEAVES

Poetic ballet in one act. Choreography and subject by Anna Pavlova. Music by Frédéric Chopin. Set by C. Corovine. Río de Janeiro, 1918. Principal dancers:

Anna Pavlova (the Chrysanthemum), Alexander Volin-ine (a young poet), Hubert Stowitts (the Autumn Wind).

SYNOPSIS. In a garden, a beautiful Chrysanthemum has been uprooted by the Autumn Wind. A young poet gently picks it up, but the Wind, rising again, snatches it from his hands. Once more the youth rescues the flower and lays it carefully on a mossy bank. While he reads a book, the Wind returns and whirls the Chrysanthemum about among the turbulent autumn leaves, finally abandoning it to die in the heat of the sun. Seeing that his efforts to revive the flower are in vain, the poet leaves the garden with his betrothed, who has come to meet him there.

■ This was the only ballet choreographed by Anna Pavlova (although she ventured on a few *divertissements*). Interested more in the perfecting of existing classical technique than in inventing new forms and steps, Pavlova created an exquisite ballet, taking great pains with the work as a whole, illumined, as it was, by her own beautiful performance (the Chrysanthemum was one of her greatest successes) and that of Volinine, who had succeeded Mordkin as her official partner. The *corps de ballet* represented the autumn leaves.   C.M.C.

First sketch by Pablo Picasso for the set of Léonide Massine's ballet Pulcinella, *created in 1920.*

THE FANTASTIC TOYSHOP (*La Boutique Fantasque*)

One-act ballet. Choreography and plot by Léonide Massine. Music by Ottorino Respighi (from Gioacchino Rossini). Set and costumes by André Derain. London, Alhambra Theatre, June 5, 1919. Diaghilev's Russian Ballet. Principal dancers: Lydia Lopokova, Léonide Massine, Lydia Sokolova, Stanislas Idzikovsky, Leon Woizikovsky, Enrico Cecchetti.

SYNOPSIS. The scene is the shop of a manufacturer of mechanical dolls at Nice in about 1865. Various customers – English, American, and Russian tourists – enter. The shopkeeper displays his best creations, among them dolls who dance a tarantella, Cossacks, two dogs, a king, queen, and other figures from a pack of cards, a melon-seller and, best of all, a pair of cancan dancers. Several dolls are sold, the cancan dancer and her partner being bought by two separate purchasers. The customers pay and go home, leaving the shop-keeper to pack the parcels to be fetched the next day, and to close his shop. During the night the toys come to life and grieve for the fate of the parted lovers. It is more than they can bear. In no time the cancan dancers are freed from their boxes, which are filled up with card-board, and the dolls dance to their hearts' content. In the morning the clients come to fetch their purchases, but the dolls are not in their boxes. Thinking they have been swindled, the purchasers begin to turn the shop upside down. At that the Cossacks and other dolls come to the aid of the proprietor and chase out the astonished intruders, after which the little world of automatons gathers happily around the goodhearted craftsman.

■ It is little wonder that the theme of dolls coming to life, so attuned to mime, dance, fantasy, and symbolism, should have inspired numerous works of theatrical dance. *Coppelia, Petrouchka,* and *La Boutique Fantasque* itself are the best known and of most historical importance. The immediate ancestor of Massine's ballet, however, was Hassreiter's *Puppenfee (The Fairy Doll)* of 1888, with music by Joseph Bayer, or, more precisely, the version of it staged by Sergei and Nicholas Legat at the Maryinsky Theater of St. Petersburg in 1907. It was from this production that Massine, apparently at Bakst's suggestion, took his subject for *La Boutique Fantasque,* which Diaghilev described as "*avant tout plus fantasque que boutique.*" It overflowed with a wealth and variety of ideas, comic, parodical, pathetic, and lyrical, which the still youthful artist was able to express in a highly personal, inventive choreography, sustained by a lively and elegant pantomimic style and a masterly command of classical technique. The music was a medley of Rossini's piano pieces from the collection *Peccati di Vecchiaia (Sins of Old Age)* arranged for orchestra by Respighi, but the resulting score was more than a simple orchestration. It was a new creation in which the spirit of Rossini's *Vecchiaia* had been totally absorbed by the taste and compositional methods of Respighi. Léonide Massine also took the part of the cancan dancer during the ballet's first and subsequent seasons with Diaghilev's Russian Ballet and supervised the production of various revivals: in New York on March 20, 1935, for the Monte Carlo Russian Ballet, at Covent Garden, London, on February 27, 1947, for Sadler's Wells Ballet, and at Rotterdam in 1958 for the Nederlands Dans Theater. *La Boutique Fantasque,* in various reconstructions and new versions, has become part of the repertory of numerous international ballet companies.   A.A.

THE THREE-CORNERED HAT *(El Sombrero de Tres Picos or Le Tricorne)*
A one-act ballet. Choreography by Léonide Massine. Scenario by Gregorio Martinez Sierra. Music by Manuel de Falla. Set and costumes by Pablo Picasso. London, Alhambra Theatre, July 22, 1919. Serge Diaghilev's Russian Ballet. Principal dancers: Léonide Massine (the Miller), Tamara Karsavina (the Miller's Wife), Leon Woizikovsky (Corregidor), Stanislas Idzikovsky (the Dandy).

SYNOPSIS. In a small Spanish village live a miller and his wife. They are young, handsome, and happy, caring little about what others think of them. Their harmony is interrupted, however, by the arrival of the Corregidor, the provincial Governor, who clumsily pays court to the miller's wife. Repulsed and made fun of, the old gentleman with the three-cornered hat (the sign of his rank) has the miller arrested and once more pursues his wife. However, she evades him after having pushed him into the river. The Corregidor, furious, goes off to get his clothes dried and comes back dressed in a nightshirt he has found in the miller's house. This gives rise to misunderstandings, for the soldiers arrest their commander, believing him to be the miller, while the miller, escaped from prison, thinks he has been betrayed and threatens to pay the old gentleman back. Finally, a happy conclusion is brought about by the village folk, who drive away the Governor and his soldiers and join the young couple in general rejoicing.

■ This famous ballet, inspired by Pedro de Alarcón's novel, first saw the light as a mime play in Madrid in 1917. But it did not come into its own until it was taken up by the *Ballets Russes* and transformed by Léonide Massine into a choreographic work of unequalled vitality and authenticity, with a memorable part for himself. The confluence of Diaghilev's company and the culture of Spain was remarkably fruitful, bringing together, as it did, the music of de Falla, Picasso's designs, and the brilliant scenario, with all its comedy and satire. Massine adapted the Spanish dances to wonderful effect, producing the *fandango* of the miller's wife, the miller's famous *farruca*, and grand finale *jota*. *The Three-Cornered Hat* is admittedly less dramatic and inventive than *El Amor Brujo*, but it remains one of the most genuine tributes that ballet has paid to Spanish culture. Its continued survival in world repertory proves as much. Massine reproduced the ballet all over the world and his daughter Tania revived it with the Joffrey Ballet at the New York City Center in 1969, using Picasso's original designs.   M.P.

THE MUSIC. *El Sombrero de Tres Picos* is among de Falla's most brilliant works and one that first brought him fame abroad. Complete and perfectly balanced as the score now appears to us, its genesis was not without complications. The first idea was to make the story into an opera, but Pedro de Alarcón the author of the original *El Corregidor y la Molinera (The Governor and the Miller's Wife)* had explicitly forbidden that in his will. There was nothing to stop it being turned into a

ballet, however. Wartime difficulties prevented Diaghilev from doing so, and the music was first used in 1917 to accompany a mime play named after the novel and was played by a skeleton orchestra under Joaquin Turina. When it came to transforming the mime play into a ballet, a great many alterations had to be made. To begin with, the composition of the orchestra had to be enlarged; secondly, while the music of the first part was left unchanged, there were many interpolations and additions to that of the second part. Among these were the splendid closing *jota* and the enormously popular Miller's Dance, which the composer had to create in little more than a day, spurred on by Diaghilev. The definitive score is notably different from that of *El Amor Brujo* in that it uses frankly tonal modes, whereas in the latter more archaic and exotic modes are preferred. Nevertheless, no work of de Falla's is so fresh in its approach or so extraordinarily rich in rhythm and colour.   A.F.

THE CHINESE NIGHTINGALE *(Le Chant du Rossignol)*
One-act ballet. Choreography by Léonide Massine. Music by Igor Stravinsky. Scenario by Mitussov (after Hans Andersen). Sets and costumes by Henri Matisse. Paris, Opéra, February 2, 1920. Serge Diaghilev's Russian Ballet Company. Principal dancers: Tamara Karsavina (the Nightingale), Stanislas Idzikovsky (the Mechanical Nightingale), Lydia Sokolova (Death).

SYNOPSIS. At the splendid court of the Emperor of China a procession of courtiers enlivens the palace precincts with charming and playful dances. The monarch himself often listens with pleasure to the song of his favourite Nightingale, but now the Emperor of Japan has presented him with an amazing mechanical songbird that quite eclipses the first in the magnificence of its jewel-studded plumage. There is debate as to which of the two creatures can trill the more prettily. The Emperor, dazzled with its wealth of precious stones, chooses the twittering automaton and sends the real bird away. The Nightingale flies off, singing its heart out in sorrow. Some time later the Emperor falls gravely ill. There seems to be no cure – or could it be that the birdsong he loves so well could restore him to health? Alas, the mechanical bird remains silent and the true Nightingale cannot be found anywhere. But when Death, clad in his grim red-black, skull-embroidered cloak, comes to claim the Imperial life, the little Nightingale flies in. Its mellifluous notes bring the Emperor back to life and lure Death away, forcing him to return to his sad realm with empty arms. Its master safe, the Nightingale departs again, but promises to come back every night to delight the penitent monarch with its golden voice and so prolong his life.

■ The ballet was arranged by Massine to the symphonic *suite* from Stravinsky's opera *Le Rossignol*, which had been staged by Diaghilev at the Paris Opéra as early as May 26, 1914 (with choreography by B. Romanov, sets and costumes by A. Benois with A.

Scene design by Michael Larionov for Le Chout, *choreographed by Larionov himself and T. Slavinsky.*

Sanin) – when the danced part of the entertainment had not been a success. In the beginning Diaghilev had commissioned the futurist painter Fortunato Depero to design the scenery, but later he substituted Henri Matisse, who replaced Depero's Euclidean and floral geometry with his own delicate scheme of white and turquoise-blue setting off the straw-coloured costumes of the courtiers. Unfortunately, Massine's rather cryptic choreography with its syncopated rhythms failed to please the public, who merely thought the dancers had no ear for music. A curious episode occurred in 1925 in Paris when the fifteen-year-old Alicia Markova was unable to dance the Nightingale's part because of illness. Nobody knew the part except the young Balanchine, who was deputed to dance it, but, either because the costume looked absurd on him or because he momentarily forgot the steps, the audience began to laugh and the performance had to be stopped.

OTHER VERSIONS. 1) Balanchine. Music by Igor Stravinsky. Sets and costumes by Henri Matisse. Paris, Gaîté-Lyrique, June 17, 1925. Danced by A. Markova. 2) Mandrik. Music by I. Stravinsky. Berlin, State Opera House, 1929. 3) Gsovsky. *The Chinese Nightingale.*

Music by W. Egk. Munich, State Opera House, 1953. 4) Cranko. Music by I. Stravinsky. Munich, 1968. 5) John Taras. New York City Ballet. 1972.   G.S.

PUNCHINELLO *(Pulcinella)*

Ballet in one act with sung interlude. Choreography by Léonide Massine. Music by Igor Stravinsky, after Giambattista Pergolesi. Scenario by Diaghilev and Massine. Drop curtain, set, and costumes by Pablo Picasso. Paris, Opéra, May 15, 1920. Principal dancers: Léonide Massine (Pulcinella), Tamara Karsavina (Pimpinella), Lubov Tchernicheva (Prudenza), Vera Nemchinova (Rosetta), Sigmund Novak (Furbo), Stanislas Idzikovsky (Coviello), Nicholas Zverev (Florindo), Enrico Cecchetti (Dottore), Stanislas Kostetsky (Tartaglia).

SYNOPSIS. In a little square overlooking the Bay of Naples, two young gallants stand before the windows of the ladies of their choice, whose houses stand on each side of the street. Coviello and Florindo are courting – with scant success – Rosetta, the doctor's daughter, and Prudenza, daughter of old Tartaglia. Leaning out of

Irène Lagut's sketch for the backcloth of Les Mariés de la Tour Eiffel, *choreographed by Jean Börlin.*

their windows, the two girls see the foolish young men and with half amused, half disdainful smiles, empty two jugs of water over them. Then the infuriated doctor enters with his stick and chases them off. Pulcinella now comes in, draws a small fiddle from his voluminous shirt, and begins to play and dance with frantic glee. Prudenza enters from her house and, advancing on tiptoe, tries to embrace him. Pulcinella, however, disentangles himself and gives her to understand that his heart is engaged elsewhere and finally shoos her away with his cap and drives her back into the house. Now Rosetta appears and tries to charm Pulcinella in her turn. At first indifferent, he ends up giving her a kiss. Pimpinella, his promised bride, comes out, sees him, and is highly indignant. Pulcinella soon wins her round. Coviello and Florindo return and, springing out of the shadows upon their successful rival, load him with blows. The horrified Pimpinella calls for help. Rosetta and Prudenza come running to the rescue, chase the gallants away, lift their victim to his feet, and do their best

to console him. He soon recovers, but each jealous lady claims him for her own. The doctor and Tartaglia, hearing the hullabaloo, hurry out and take their daughters indoors. Freed from their clutches, Pulcinella, exhausted with events, now has to propitiate the resentful Pimpinella again. No sooner has he done so than Coviello and Florindo creep back, disguised in long cloaks. Pulcinella recognizes them and tries to escape with his sweetheart, but before he can quite get away he is felled by a mighty sword blow. He pretends to be dead. The two gallants go off, highly satisfied at their just revenge. Left alone, Pulcinella gets up and goes, happy that his trick has deceived them. Now four little Pulcinellas come in, bearing on their shoulders a double of the full-size Pulcinella. They deposit the apparently lifeless body on the ground with sobs and a touching display of grief. Soon Tartaglia and the doctor arrive, accompanied by their weeping daughters. After a brief inspection the doctor confirms that the corpse is indeed dead. A mysterious stranger dressed as a magician appears and announces that he can bring the apparently dead man back to life. With an imperious gesture, he orders the supine figure to arise. To everyone's amazement and delight, Pulcinella shakes himself and stands up. The magician then removes his wig and gown, revealing himself as the true Pulcinella; his friend Furbo had played the part of the corpse. Unaware of what has occurred, Florindo and Coviello come in disguised as Pulcinella, hoping in that way to win the hearts of Prudenza and Rosetta, while Furbo begins to pay court to Pimpinella. Back comes the furious Pulcinella who kicks everyone in sight. Furbo puts on the discarded magician's cloak and persuades the doctor and Tartaglia to consent to their daughters' marriages to Florindo and Coviello, with whom they are now reconciled. Pulcinella rejoins his Pimpinella, together with the four midget Pulcinellas briskly waving their caps, and all ends in a general dance of rejoicing.

■ The ballet owed its origin to Diaghilev's discovery in the National Library of Naples of an unpublished eighteenth-century manuscript containing various sketches and comedies all relating the adventures of the celebrated Neapolitan mask and entitled *I Quattro Pulcinella (The Four Punchinellos)*. The finding of some music scores – also unpublished – by Pergolesi, or attributed to him, prompted Diaghilev to suggest to Massine that he should arrange a ballet along the lines of the traditional Italian *Commedia dell'Arte*, employing Stravinsky to orchestrate the music and Picasso to design the set and costumes. He hoped with this venture to follow up his previous successes of *The Good-Humoured Ladies*, with music by Scarlatti arranged by Tommasini and *La Boutique Fantasque*, to Rossini's music arranged by Respighi. Collaboration between the ballet's creators went anything but smoothly. Storms blew up that were probably unavoidable in view of their touchy temperaments. Stravinsky left his unmistakable, imprint on the music of Pergolesi, reinforced by a liberal use of brass, wind instruments, and violin *pizzicati*. In the grotesque Neapolitan "mask," Pulcinella, lively, inventive, deceitful opportunist, Massine, a natural character actor and brilliant comic mime, found a role after his own heart. Around this character, in his white shirt, red trousers, and sugar-loaf cap, Massine composed a type of dancing that combined strictly classical means (*entrechats, fouettés, double tour en l'air*) with all the whimsical flourish of folk dancing. Indeed, the critic André Levinson described it as "ironical classicism." It can be observed in the contrast between Pimpinella's dances, with their peasant overtones, the more sophisticated dancing of Prudenza and Rosetta, and the parts of the doctor and Tartaglia, which are largely mime. The fiercest differences of opinion were between Diaghilev and Picasso. Contrary to the former's wishes, Picasso's first sketches were very different from the traditional image of the *Commedia dell'Arte*. The main colour scheme of the set was black, white, and blue, with the houses of the rival ladies converging in angular perspective towards a distant seascape with ship, the whole made by means of a rostrum and false proscenium to look like a stage within a stage, as if reality and make-

Costumes for the Cat, the Cock, and the Goat invented by Michael Larionov, who designed scenery and costumes for Bronislava Nijinska's ballet Renard.

believe were meeting in a typical Italian piazza, center of disputes and serenades. Stravinsky writes in his memoirs that the costume designs, with their exposed faces and large moustaches in place of the traditional masks, were more reminiscent of the Offenbach period than the *Commedia dell'Arte*. When Picasso showed Diaghilev his designs, the latter behaved extremely tactlessly. "These are no good at all!" he cried, flinging the sketches to the floor, and stamped out of the room, slamming the door behind him. Next day, he used all his charm and diplomacy to soothe the painter's ruffled feelings, and persuaded him to give his designs more of the Mediterranean atmosphere we all associate with Pulcinella.

OTHER VERSIONS. 1) Lopokov. Leningrad, Kirov Theater, 1926. 2) Georgy. Hanover, 1926. 3) Jooss. Essen, Opera House, 1932. 4) Woizikovsky. London, Coliseum, *Les Deux Polichinelles*, 1935. 5) West. Western Ballet Theater, 1957. 6) Béjart. Liège, September 10, 1957. Sets and costumes by B. Daydé. 7) Massine. Milan, Scala, December 10, 1971. 8) Balanchine-Robbins. New York, Stravinsky Festival, New York City Ballet, June 23, 1972. Sets and costumes by E. Berman. Danced by E. Villella and V. Verdy. 9) Bolinder. *Commedia Ballettica* (a different plot to the same Stravinsky score). New York, Ballet Russe de Monte Carlo, 1945. 10) Smuin. *Pulcinella Variations* (a different plot to the same score). New York, American Ballet Theater, 1968.   G.S.

THE TOYBOX (La Boîte à Joujoux)

Ballet in one act and four scenes. Choreography by Jean Börlin. Music by Claude Debussy. Scenario, sets, and costumes by André Hellé, Paris, Théâtre des Champs Elysées, February 15, 1921. Ballets Suédois.

SYNOPSIS. In a toyshop Punchinellos, Harlequins, Columbines, dolls, and tin soldiers are dancing. One little soldier falls in love with a beautiful doll, but she has already given her heart to a lazy and quarrelsome Punchinello. This episode is followed by the misadventures of the various characters, each of whom asks for help from his supporters. In the battle that ensues the miniature army opposes an equal number of Punchinellos and the little soldier falls gravely wounded on the field. The doll, now cast aside by the wicked Punchinello, picks him up and gently tends him; at last the tin warrior finds his love returned. Now, healed in body and soul, he can happily wed his sweetheart. Time passes, but in the animated toyshop life goes on. After many years the loving couple, who have been sheepfarming, have made their fortune, while the arrogant Punchinello has become a gamekeeper.

■ The first performance of this children's ballet, with music by Debussy and the same scenario, sets, and costumes by André Hellé, had already been given in Paris at the Théâtre Lyrique du Vaudeville on December 10, 1919, and had met with a favourable reception. In 1921 Jean Börlin decided to revive the entertainment, but with a far more sardonic choreography, turning it into a pointed fable for adults in which, in ironic mime, the toys were perceived as behaving like real people. As Divoire wrote in *Découvertes de la Danse*, in *La Boîte à Joujoux* the dancing became the gesticulations of marionettes, but so intensely studied that each toy, doll, soldier, and Punchinello walked with its own individual movement fitting its character. It was Jean Börlin's task to train the dancers' bodies so that they could with natural simplicity assume the desired rigidity: the doll standing upright on her points, the Punchinello displaying a puppet's insolence, the tin soldier making great play of his heart overflowing, perhaps not so much with sentiment as with sentimentality. Thus the ballet had neither stars, nor soloists in the usual meaning of the words, nor solos to vary the rather mechanical whole, nor contrived aestheticism, to complicate what was intended only as a poignant commentary on Debussy's score. The ballet was very successful everywhere, as can be seen from the fact that out of the 2,766 performances given by the Swedish Ballet in their fifty years of existence, 280 were of *La Boîte à Joujoux*, while *Relâche* and *Le Création du Monde*, far more important to the history of dance, had only twelve and eleven apiece.   G.S.

THE FOOL (Le Chout)

Ballet in six scenes. Choreography by M. Larionov and T. Slavinsky. Music by Sergei Prokofiev. Scenario by Serge Diaghilev, taken from a Russian folk tale. Paris, Théâtre de la Gaîté-Lyrique, March 17, 1921. Diaghilev's Russian Ballet. Principal dancers: T. Slavinsky (the Fool), L. Sokolova (his Wife).

SYNOPSIS. This is the story, greatly to the popular Russian taste, of a fool (the Russian title is *Skazka pro Shuta*) who sells to his friends, the other seven fools of the village, a magic whip which has the power of bringing the dead back to life. His credulous friends buy the whip and then kill their wives to test its powers. Naturally all their attempts at resuscitation are in vain. They go to look for the trickster, who disguises himself in his younger sister's clothes. Unsuccessful in their quest, the seven decide to take the supposed girl back and make her their cook. As soon as they get "her" home, a rich merchant arrives to look for a wife and picks on the supposed cook. The Fool runs away, leaving a goat in his place. The merchant has it killed, upon which the Fool returns with seven soldiers and claims compensation in money for his murdered sister.

■ Although this evocation of a certain type of Russian folklore may seem like a natural sequel to the Stravinskian specimens that preceded it, the ballet was, in fact, a brave attempt to escape from certain obligatory grooves in which balletic literature had become set during recent years. *Le Chout* thus represented a sort of rebellion against current tastes, and a choreographic exploration outside the confines of the dominant Tchaikovskian influence. It brings us a formidable picture of a grotesque world where everything incredible is believed and the folly of superstition replaces reality.

OTHER VERSIONS. A series of unlucky coincidences – the contemporary predominance of Stravinsky, the crises afflicting the *Ballets Russes* on Massine's departure, the scenic design veering towards cubism – all had a bearing on this ballet's relative failure, and hence its fall into oblivion. However, it was revived on April 16, 1932, at the Monte Carlo Opera House, with new choreography by Boris Romanoff. In Italy it was seen for the first time on May 16, 1950 (Teatro Comunale, Florence), with A. M. Milloss as choreographer, sets and costumes by Renato Guttuso, and Ettore

Natalia Goncharova's design for Les Noces *to choreography by Bronislava Nijinska.*

A scene from Les Noces *developed from the sketch on the opposite page.*

Gracis as director of the orchestra. Principal dancers were Vladimir Skuratov and Maria Dalba.   P.C.

THE WEDDING BREAKFAST AT THE EIFFEL TOWER (*Les Mariés de la Tour Eiffel*)

Imaginative burlesque ballet in one act. Choreography by Jean Börlin. Music by Georges Auric, Arthur Honegger, Darius Milhaud, François Poulenc, Germaine Tailleferre. Scenario by Jean Cocteau. Set by Irène Lagut. Costumes and masks by Jean Hugo. Paris, Théâtre des Champs Elysées. June 18, 1921. Principal dancers: Margit Vahlander (the Bride), Paul Eltorp (the Bridegroom), Axel Witzansky (the Photographer), Carina Ari (the Bathing Beauty), Greta Kaer (the Ostrich), Eric Viber (the Lion), Astrid Lindgren (the Cyclist), Yolanda Figoni (the Child), Paul Witzansky (the General).

SYNOPSIS. The scene is a restaurant terrace on the second floor of the Eiffel Tower on the French national holiday of Bastille Day, as we gather from the overture, a military march called "The Fourteenth of July." Two of the great metal trellises supporting the tower form the sides of the proscenium, from which sprout two enormous human gramophone horns functioning as a sort of chorus to comment satirically on everything that happens. Preceded by a huntsman who shoots at an enormous poster announcing the marriage, the wedding procession files in and seats itself at the banquet table. A hunchbacked photographer is approaching to take their portraits, when an ostrich comes out of the camera and struts across the stage while a shower of telegrams falls on the bridal pair. A ridiculous and breathless cyclist, trying in vain to set a new sporting record, pedals onto the stage. Just as the photographer is posing the wedding group a girl in a swimsuit springs out of his swathed tripod and parodies the attitudes of a bathing beauty as depicted on seaside postcards of the early 1900s. The satire on the lower middle class in its Sunday best continues with a general addressing a speech to the happy pair while the guests listen with absurdly deferential attention. He is interrupted, however, by the Awful Child, a spoilt brat who pelts the guests with tennis balls, and by a lion bouncing out of the camera and devouring the general.

■ *Les Mariés de la Tour Eiffel*, together with *Parade* and *Le Boeuf sur le Toit*, makes up Cocteau's trilogy, a sort of antibourgeois manifesto, combining the characteristics of Greek tragedy, drawing room comedy, circus, and music hall. Under the cover of surrealist and grotesque events, it described the ethics and ambitions of a society whose idols, respectability, knowing one's place, hierarchy, ostentation, receptions, class distinctions, social climbing – so typical of the *Belle Époque* – must be destroyed. Nothing was spared in attacking bourgeois institutions, and the music of "The Six" was equally iconoclastic. The same feeling was present in some of the more outstanding numbers in the ballet: the Overture, the Wedding March, the Funeral March, the Dance of the Telegrams, the Dance of the Bathing Beauty, and the Quadrille. There were several innovations that contributed not a little to the satirical buffoonery, including the gramophones, the hideous clothes, and cumbersome cardboard masks designed by Jean Hugo, which made it difficult for the wearers to hear the loudspeaker commentary or even the music (several weeks of exhausting rehearsal were necessary before the dancers could synchronize movement and music), the bold perspectives of Irène Lagut's scenery, which added to the larger-than-life effect already suggested by the heavy masks, and last but not least Jean Cocteau himself at the megaphone, acting as commentator. The ballet was not understood by the audience, who were more stupefied and irritated than indignant, and the evening ended in tumult. There were slating criticisms, to which Cocteau replied, "Mystery inspires the public with a kind of terror. Henceforth I renounce mystery. I will burn it all." G.S.

based on classic academic dance but strongly permeated by "modernism" and characterized by movements derived from Dalcrozian eurythmics, which were converted into an almost parody version of abstract expressionism. Nijinska became the principal choreographer to the *Ballets Russes* until 1926, creating eight new ballets for that renowned company. In 1929 Diaghilev commissioned Serge Lifar to produce a new version of *Renard*, its first creator now being far away and forgotten. It was Lifar's only work for the *Ballets Russes*, appearing in the year of Diaghilev's death, and the first of Lifar's long and distinguished career as a choreographer.

OTHER VERSIONS. 1) Feodor Lopokov. Leningrad, Academic State Theatre, January 2, 1927. 2) Serge Lifar. Paris, Théâtre Sarah Bernhardt, May 21, 1929. Diaghilev's Russian Ballet. 3) George Balanchine. New York, Hunter College Playhouse, January 13, 1947. Ballet Society. 4) Aurel Milloss. Florence, Pergola Theater, Maggio Musicale, 1958. 5) Heinz Rosen. Munich, Bavarian State Opera House, November 17, 1962. 6) Maurice Béjart. Paris, Opéra, 1965; revived at the New York City Centre, November 24, 1971. Ballet du XXme Siècle. 7) David Drew. London, Queen Elizabeth Hall, January 10, 1969. Choreographic Group of the Royal Ballet. A.A.

RENARD

A burlesque ballet with song, words, and music in one act. Choreography by Bronislava Nijinska. Music and scenario by Igor Stravinsky (French version by C. F. Ramuz). Set and costumes by Mikhail Larionov. Paris, Opéra, March 18, 1922. Serge Diaghilev's Russian Ballet. Principal dancers: Bronislava Nijinska, Stanislas Idzikovsky.

SYNOPSIS. A burlesque story in which a fox flatters a cock in order to catch and eat him, but his friends, the cat and the goat, come to the rescue. When they leave, the fox tries again. This time the cat and the goat manage to strangle the fox, who already has the cock between his teeth.

■ Stravinsky used this old folk tale as the basis for a text he wrote to go with one of his scores for small orchestra with cymbals, *guzla*, and four voices. Diaghilev first heard it in 1915, but it was not until seven years later that he thought of staging it. Given the title *Renard*, it was put into the hands of Bronislava Nijinska, Mikhail Larionov (after Diaghilev's first choice, Serge Soudeikine, had refused the commission), and, of course, Igor Stravinsky, though little attention was paid to his ideas about the staging. The vocal quartet was placed in the orchestra pit instead of on the stage, upon which the four dancers interpreted the actions described in the sung text.

Although it was Bronislava Nijinska's first work for the Diaghilev Ballet, *Renard* already showed the imagination and originality of her choreographic style,

Fernand Léger's costume design for La Création du Monde, *a ballet by Jean Börlin to music by Darius Milhaud.*

WEDDING (*Les Noces* or *Svadebka*)

Ballet, or cantata with dances. Choreography by Bronislava Nijinska. Music by Igor Stravinsky. Sets and costumes by Natalia Goncharova. Paris, Gaîté-Lyrique, June 14, 1923. Diaghilev's Russian Ballet. Principal dancers: Felia Dubrovska (the Bride), Leon Woizikovsky (the Bridegroom).

SYNOPSIS. The ballet, originally divided into four scenes, illustrates the rituals related to the preparation and solemnization of a wedding in old peasant Russia. Scene I: blessing the bride, her fears and hopes, her robing and the braiding of her hair. Scene II: blessing and preparation of the bridegroom to the laments of his parents and the congratulations of his friends. Scene III: the bride leaves for the church ceremony, the wedding, and the festivities. Scene IV: the wedding feast, the duties of bride and bridegroom, dancing and drinking, the rite of warming the bridal bed by an older couple, the final song of happiness and love.

■ This unusual ballet, in which, more than in any other, the music acts as a guide, brings ancient folk customs to life, setting them in a musical context of enormous dramatic force expressed in diametrically opposite terms. Stravinsky's symmetries and powerful rhythms endow the ballet with an irresistible strength. The rustic world becomes modern, almost abstract, yet in Nijinska's choreographical interpretation keeps a grassroots authenticity, a natural understanding of peasant feeling. A technically difficult work, *Les Noces* has a musical and balletic vitality that, in one form or another, continues to win praise.

OTHER VERSIONS. Variations on the theme have been numerous, largely in the direction of lightening its load of folklore or of analyzing the psyches of the chief characters, the bride and bridegroom. Without a shadow of doubt, the most significant versions after that of Nijinska have been the two by Jerome Robbins and Maurice Béjart respectively. Robbins presented his *Wedding* at the New York State Theater with the American Ballet on March 30, 1965 (danced by Erin Martin and William Glassman; sets by Oliver Smith, costumes by Patricia Zipprodt, lighting by Jean Rosenthal). Divided into four parts, the ballet begins with the preparation of the bride (the singers and musicians are on stage between two huge figures of saints), her nervousness, and her being carried off the stage as if she were a baby. Next we see the preparation of the bridegroom, also with a reference to childhood. The departure of the bride is seen as a triumph; during the wedding ceremony the bridal pair are placed on a platform to consummate their act of love. The relationship between them and the rest is still that between children and adults. In the *Ballet du XXme Siècle* version by Béjart the emphasis is on the duplication of the bride's and groom's personalities, and their elevation as a symbol. Presented in Paris in 1966, *Les Noces* appeared as yet another affirmation of Béjart's philosophy, nourished an optimism and an awareness of the victory of feeling. M.P.

Sketch by Marie Laurencin for Les Biches, *choreographed by Bronislava Nijinska in 1924.*

THE MUSIC. Although the orchestration was not finished until 1923, *Les Noces* had already been sketched out during the time Stravinsky was working on *Rite of Spring*. From the "pagan Russia" so violently depicted there to the peasant marriage rituals of *Les Noces* was a shorter step than one might suppose. The composer's Russian heart warmed to the idea of a countryside in which daily life was forever in the balance between good humour and the hard struggle with nature. The subtitle, *Russian Choreographic Scenes with Songs and Music*, says more about the musician's intentions than any other words. If in *Rite of Spring* attention was focused on the awe experienced by mankind in face of the higher forces governing nature, the subject dealt with in this theatrical cantata was of the same kind, though on a smaller scale. One has only to think of the awe that seizes the young couple after the wedding feast at the thought of the new life they will transmit from their ancestors to a still nonexistent being. Certainly the original draft was long enough, but not as full of problems as the orchestration, which was not ready until three months before the first night. After *Rite* the composer decided not to put his faith in large orchestras again, and the quest for instrumental colour suited to the new ballet was far from easy. The initial plan of supporting the vocalists by two opposing instrumental masses (strings on one side, wind instruments on the other) was soon dropped in favour of a chamber orchestra like the one used in *Renard*. In a subsequent revision a harmonium replaced the wind, while a piano and two cymbals replaced the strings, but still the problems of the ensemble appeared insurmountable. Only at the last moment did *Les Noces* acquire the instrumental makeup that we know, accompanying the solo voices and chorus with four pianos and percussion. Clearly this orchestration underlines the rhythmic and percussive nature of the score even more strongly.   A.F.

THE CREATION OF THE WORLD (La Création du Monde)

Ballet in one act and five scenes. Choreography by Jean Börlin. Music by Darius Milhaud. Scenario by Blaise Cendras. Sets and costumes by Fernand Léger. Paris, Théâtre des Champs Elysées, October 25, 1923. Ballets Suédois. Principal dancers: Jean Börlin, Ebon Strandin.

SYNOPSIS. From the confused mass of entangled bodies, symbol of primordial chaos, that lies center stage, three divinities emerge: Ngama, Medere, and N'kva, lords of creation. They consult together and weave magic spells which will summon the world to life. Stirred by the divine breath, the chaotic pile gradually begins to live; forms emerge and define themselves as gigantic animals, multicoloured birds, monstrous insects, totemic gods, and dance in homage around the three creators. A luxuriant, teeming vegetation spreads upwards, its leaves giving birth to elephants, giant crabs, tortoises, and monkeys. From the quivering mass, half seen in the darkness that still veils the dawn of life on the planet, the ancient and barbarous triad now calls forth the first human couple in their vulnerable nakedness. With instinctive dignity the first man and the first woman perform the Dance of Desire, imitated by the animals, the witch-doctors and fetish-worshippers, who, with savage longing, each choose their own companions. As the general exaltation grows calmer, the human pair draw aside lovingly to exchange a long embrace that represents the first act of procreation. Meanwhile the living forest grows lighter with the rays of the rising sun and the first spring blossoms on earth.

■ During its brief but intense life (1920–1925), the Ballets Suédois, founded by that enlightened Maecenas and disciple of Diaghilev, Rolf de Maré, gathered both wide acclaim and savage criticism. The company set itself the ambitious task of revolutionizing the art of dance, advancing beyond the decorative and exotic aestheticism of the *Ballet Russes*, not undervaluing their artistic content, but availing themselves of the new currents of thought that, through cubism, dadaism, surrealism, and the new music of the school of Paris, called into question all the old values, aesthetic, pragmatic, and metaphysical. Its banner bore the motto *"Pour les Ballets Suédois le but est toujours un point de départ"* ("For the Ballets Suédois the end is always a new beginning"). *La Création du Monde*, the next-to-last important ballet in the company's repertory, had been in Börlin's mind for several years. Having long taken an interest in the native dances of Africa and all forms of primitive dance, he arranged for himself in 1919 a solo

called *Sculpture Nègre*. His new ballet integrated perfectly with Milhaud's "primitive" music and Fernand Léger's cubist-African stage designs. *La Création du Monde* presented the myth of creation and the origin of man as conceived by the imagination of an African Negro. For the first time black African art entered the theater and, more importantly, the culture of the west. The ballet's influence went far beyond the modest success it achieved, more, such as it was, with the artistic circles of the avant-garde than with lovers of ballet, who were not yet ready for its aggressive iconoclasm. In fact, the fiercest criticisms were levelled at the incongruity of the modernistic treatment of the subject in relation to the traditional forms of the choreography, in which African gods, totemic fetishes, and newly created beings all danced according to classical academic standards. Nevertheless, *La Création du Monde* remains a milestone in the history of dancing by virtue of its happy combination of design, choreography, and music.

OTHER VERSIONS. 1) Ninette de Valois. Sets by E. Wolfe. London, Cambridge Theatre, April 26, 1931; Sadler's Wells Theatre, October 30, 1933. Danced by French, Tudor, Moreton. 2) MacMillan. Sets by Goddard. Stratford-on-Avon, Memorial Theatre, February 12, 1964. Danced by Wells, Anderton, Farley, Royal Ballet. 3) Todd Bolender. New York City Ballet, 1964. 4) N. Kasatkina, V. Vasiliov. Music by A. Petrov. Sets by E. Steinberg. Leningrad, Kirov Theater, March 23, 1971. Danced by Soloviev, Baryshnikov, Panov, Kolpakova. 5) Taylor (*Almost an Echo*). London, Ballet Rambert, 1974.   G.S.

THE MUSIC. The ballet *La Création du Monde* was one of the first works in which Milhaud used compositional elements clearly derived from jazz and Afro-American music to give the aural material the particular "primitive" feeling required by the scenario. The score is written for an unusual combination of instruments, reminiscent of a jazz band, and marks the first use of the saxophone in the "cultured" symphonic field. The other instruments were two flutes, an oboe, two clarinets, a bassoon, a horn, two trumpets, a trombone, a piano, percussion, and four solo string instruments. The resulting music is particularly brilliant and recalls the blues, not merely as a passing reference, but as the true framework of the composition. The central theme bears a remarkable resemblance to Gershwin's *Rhapsody in Blue*, while another melody seems to be related to the famous *St. Louis Blues* by Handy. These themes are, of course, developed and adapted, continually changing from the minor key to the major and vice versa. In regard to rhythm, *La Création du Monde* is, on the whole, fairly simple. Except for one or two short changes the whole work is written in the 2/2 time most typical of jazz. After the prelude we find fairly "classical" syncopated forms, but with the fugue (constructed on a rather rigid thematic plan) we enter fully into the world of jazz. During the composer's many visits to America he became familiar with Afro-American musical criteria, and the impression of dislocation and improvisation in this score is clearly part of its plan. Milhaud's score is extraordinarily skillful: it gives immediate pleasure and is finally overwhelming in effect. A.F.

THE HOUSE PARTY (Les Biches)

Ballet in one act with singing. Choreography by Bronislava Nijinska. Music by François Poulenc. Sets and costumes by Marie Laurencin. Monte Carlo Opera House, January 6, 1924. Diaghilev's Ballet Company. Principal dancers: Vera Nemchinova, Lubov Tchernicheva, Bronislava Nijinska, Lydia Sokolova, Felia Dubrovska, Anatole Vilzak, Leon Woizikovsky, Nicholas Zverev.

SYNOPSIS. There is no definite plot. At a party in a drawing room during the 1920s several girls are lightheartedly dancing (*Rondeau*) around a big divan. The young men in swimsuits come in (*Chanson dansée*) and, after them, a sophisticated lady in a close-fitting blue tunic, who dances first a solo (*Adagietto*) and then with the young men and the other girls (*Jeu*). One of the latter joins two of the youths in a *Rag-mazurka*, while the lady in blue dances with the other one (*Andantino*). After the *Chanson dansée* repeated by two girls, everyone takes part in the gay *Finale*.

■ The subject of *Les Biches*, first conceived by Poulenc, and further defined during close collaboration between himself, Diaghilev, Nijinska, and Marie Laurencin, is little more than an atmosphere halfway between sentimentality and satire, inspired by certain "bright young people" of the immediate postwar years. On this tenuous theatrical thread, so different from the forceful imagination and dramatic content of her earlier "Russian" works, Bronislava Nijinska created a ballet, based on a new, inventive sort of pure dance, which was immediately recognized as her masterpiece. Called the modern *Sylphides* for its vitality and choreographic density, *Les Biches* also resembled Fokine's work in being a suite of abstract dances. Indeed, it constituted a sort of summary of the academic dance of its time both in its internal development and in the integration of external elements derived directly from the sort of ballroom dancing then in vogue. With this composite dance vocabulary, firmly founded on classical techniques, Nijinska created a fanciful and very personal ballet of surprising theatrical effectiveness. While attending a rehearsal, Poulenc wrote enthusiastically to Diaghilev, "Nemchinova's solo (the *Adagietto*) has just finished – what a marvel! – and now they are starting on *Jeu*. I must say that for sheer craziness it surpasses anything you could imagine. Nijinska is a genius. Now listen carefully: rating the sofa to be as much a 'star' as herself, she makes it dance during the whole of *Jeu*! . . . I won't even try to describe what happens next. In one 'presto' movement the girls sit down, spring in the air, land on the upholstery again and turn round on their backs, while two of the boys ride on the back of the sofa, after which they drag that poor couch – which must be extraordinarily strong – in all directions. . . ." (letter quoted by Kochno in *Diaghilev et les Ballets*

Serge Lifar dressed as Pulcinella in Salade. *He devised new choreography for this work in 1935.*

Russes). Apart from these extravagances there were moments of pure dance. Above all, the movement adhered closely to the spirit and structure of Poulenc's music, which in its turn was always mindful of the "dance dimension" for which the score was intended. The delicate colouring of the scenery and costumes designed by Marie Laurencin perfectly matched the atmosphere of the ballet, which met with resounding success on its first night and all its subsequent performances by Diaghilev's Ballet. In 1937 Nijinska revived the ballet under the name of *The House Party* for the Markova-Dolin Company (with those two dancers in the leading parts); then for the Marquis de Cuevas Ballet in 1947 (danced by Marjorie Tallchief and George Skibine); finally for the Royal Ballet on December 2, 1964, with Georgina Parkinson, Svetlana Beriosova, David Blair, Keith Rosson, and Robert Mead in the principal roles. A.A.

CIMAROSIANA

One-act ballet. Idea and choreography by Léonide Massine. Music by Domenico Cimarosa, reorchestrated by Ottorino Respighi. Sets and costumes by José-Maria Sert. Théâtre de Monte Carlo, January 8, 1924. Serge Diaghilev's Russian Ballet. Principal dancers: Lydia Sokolova, Stanislas Idzikovsky.

■ A suite of dances held together by a slender thread of amorous burlesque, *Cimarosiana* is in fact the second-act ballet from the comic *opéra-ballet Le Astuzie Femminili (Feminine Wiles)* by Cimarosa after Goldoni, which was presented by the Diaghilev Company at the Paris Opéra on May 27, 1920. The music was re-orchestrated by Ottorino Respighi; Tamara Karsavina, Lubov Tchernicheva, Vera Nemchinova, Lydia Sokolova, Stanislas Idzikovsky, and Leon Woizikovsky were the dancers; Mafalda de Voltri, Angelo Masni Pierali, and Aurelio Anglada the singers. Massine's penultimate work of his first period with the *Ballets Russes*, it was used as a curtain-raiser for *Rite of Spring* in December 1920. The work was imbued with the spirit of the Italian eighteenth century and, according to Diaghilev, intended to convey the "ironical classicism" of the choreographer.   A.A.

THE BORES *(Les Fâcheux)*

One-act ballet. Choreography by Bronislava Nijinska. Music by Georges Auric. Scenario by Boris Kochno (from Molière's ballet-comedy). Drop curtain, set, and costumes by Georges Braque. Monte Carlo, January 19, 1924. Diaghilev's Russian Ballet. Principal dancers: Lubov Tchernicheva (Orphise), Schollar and Nikitina (two Chatterboxes), Lydia Krasovska (Naiad), Anatole Wilzak (Eraste), Nicholas Zverev (La Montagne), Bronislava Nijinska (Lysandre, the dancing master), Leon Woizikovsky (the Cardplayer), Anton Dolin (the Dandy), Jean Jazvinsky (the Tutor).

SYNOPSIS. Eraste is in love with Orphise, whom he sees passing by in the company of an elegant young gentleman. Jealous, he orders his valet La Montagne to follow them and bring her back. Enter a dance maniac, who insists on showing Eraste a new step of his own invention and forces him to learn it. La Montagne returns to announce that Orphis will soon be there. The dancing master departs, but now two badminton players arrive, pestering Eraste until he is obliged to join in their game. They ask him to help them find their lost shuttlecock and all go off together. Orphise enters and performs a dance. Eraste comes to find her, but two chatterboxes waylay him, while Orphise runs off to take refuge in her guardian's house and observe the scene from his window. No sooner has Eraste rid himself of his two talkative friends than a ballplayer and a cardplayer arrive to bore him. When he manages to get away from them he is joined by Orphise with whom he may be alone at last. It is not long before their secluded talk is interrupted by the arrival of the guardian and his valet, who plan to punish Eraste. Orphise makes off. La Montagne, who has been watching the guardian, calls on his friends for help, and they all set on the old man and his valet. The police intervene, then Eraste comes to rescue the guardian and chase away his attackers. Everyone rushes to the scene, alarmed by the brawling. Orphise appears at the window with a lantern in her hand. When she sees what is happening, she runs to Eraste and throws herself in his arms. Her grateful guardian blesses the young couple (from *Les Fâcheux*, Paris, Quatre Chemins, 1924).

■ The ballet, commissioned from Georges Auric by Diaghilev in the spring of 1922, was produced at the Monte Carlo Theater during the seventeenth season of his ballet company. It first appeared only thirteen days after the Nijinska–Poulenc–Laurencin ballet, *Les Biches*, but was not nearly so successful. This was because the unfolding of the plot lacked spontaneity and the choreography was not of very high quality in spite of its famous literary ancestry (it was derived from Molière's ballet-comedy of the same name), and notwithstanding the distinguished artists who collaborated in its creation. *Les Fâcheux*, in fact, achieved no more than a *succès d'estime* for the following reasons: Kochno's adaptation of Molière's original was not well enough done; the courtly and bourgeois dances lacked authenticity because Nijinska, who arranged them, was not very familiar with the dance vocabulary of the seventeenth century; and finally, there was too sharp a contrast between the mainly mimed action that formed part of Nijinska's choreography, and the dance on point with *entrechats cinq* ("like a ballerina") executed by Anton Dolin in the *Nocturne*, which Diaghilev had insisted on including. Moreover, Auric had agreed to rewrite the music previously composed for Molière's comedy, adapting old French folk songs to a more violent and impudent vein, while Braque had designed imposing architectural sets with dramatic masses of ochre, green, and black. All this tended to suffocate the light comedy of the original work. Other unfortunate incidents also occurred while *Les Fâcheux* was in rehearsal. None of the dancers would consent to appear in the prologue "seminude" as a nymph standing in a niche of verdure; Braque was forced to paint one on the backcloth. Lysandre's skin-tight costume was Stanislas Idzikovsky's excuse for not accepting the part which, in fact, he felt to be below his dignity. In the end Nijinska took the part of the dancing master herself. Lastly, the women dancers' costumes, designed to be double-faced, that is seventeenth-century style in front and uniformly brown at the back so that the dancers could melt into the background when the plot required it, were not used to advantage by Nijinska. While the ballplayers' movements may have lacked sporting energy, the same could not be said of the cardplayers, and certainly not of the badminton dance, in which the players flapped their crossed racquets behind their shoulders almost as if they had been parody wings. The finale somewhat raised the ballet's tone. It was designed to resemble the "coda" which the Milanese masters of the baroque period used to tack on the end of their "*grand ballets*" in the seventeenth century.

OTHER VERSIONS. Massine. Sets and costumes by Braque. Diaghilev's Russian Ballet. Paris, Théâtre Sarah Bernhardt, May 28, 1927.   G.S.

SALADE

Choreographic counterpoint in two acts. Choreography by Léonide Massine. Music by Darius Milhaud. Scenario by Albert Flament. Sets and costumes by Georges Braque. Paris, Théâtre de la Cigale, May 17,

Lydia Sokolova and Anton Dolin in Le Train Bleu, *choreographed by Bronislava Nijinska in 1924.*

1924. Soirées de Paris du Comte Etienne de Beaumont. Principal dancers: Léonide Massine (Pulcinella), Eleonora Marra (Isabella), Allan (Rosetta), Witzansky (Tartaglia), Baikov (Coviello), Streletsky (Cinzio), Ignatov (the Doctor), Sergiev (the Captain).

SYNOPSIS. Act I: old Tartaglia wants to wed his daughter Rosetta to Captain Cartuccia. She weeps and is in depair because she loves Pulcinella and confides this to him. Tartaglia himself wishes to marry Isabella, ward of the Doctor, but the latter's son, Cinzio, also loves Isabella, who returns his affection. Isabella asks Pulcinella to carry a love letter to Cinzio. Coviello, Tartaglia's servant, persuades Pulcinella, who has read the letter, to help the young couple. Pulcinella will disguise himself as the Doctor and make such a noisy nuisance of himself that, once he has disappeared, the real Doctor will be put in prison. This will give Cinzio the chance to pay court to Isabella more freely. Meanwhile Tartaglia is wooing Isabella, who first makes fun of him and then thinks better of it and allows him to understand that, if he gives the Doctor a good thrashing she will marry him. Tartaglia, fooled by this, complies, and it is, of course, Pulcinella, in the guise of the Doctor, who gets the beating. Act II: Captain Cartuccia enters with his soldiers. Tartaglia presents his daughter to the officer, not realizing that it is really Pulcinella, disguised this time as Rosetta, so cleverly dressed and veiled that Cartuccia is quite deceived and pays his court. Suddenly the trickster throws handfuls of flour in the faces of the gullible little squad and runs laughing off with Coviello. Cinzio sings a sad serenade to Isabella, believing she prefers the old man. Now Pulcinella and his friends come back dressed as Cartuccia and his men, all delighted at the idea of going to the wedding. However, the real Captain now arrives in a fury. Everyone runs

away, including Tartaglia, who carries off his daughter. Pulcinella and Coviella reappear in the guise of slave merchants, leading Isabella in chains. The Doctor buys the veiled slave for his son, hoping thus to make Cinzio forget Isabella. Once in possession of the supposed slave, Cinzio flies with her. The Doctor sees he has been made a fool of, but becomes resigned, pardons the culprits, and gives his consent to the marriage, while Rosetta, happy at last, marries the rascally Pulcinella.

■ Massine drew his inspiration for this ballet, as he had done with Stravinsky's *Pulcinella*, from the well-known and complicated plots of the *Commedia dell'Arte*, splendid pretexts for lively pantomime and a rich variety of dances. It is strange that while, as an actor, he excelled at portraying the vivacious, uninhibited Pulcinella, continually changing in and out of disguises and giving life to that most typical of Neopolitan characters, he was in real life introverted, thoughtful, and sparing of words. His quiet temperament became transfigured as soon as he stepped on the stage, embodying the Neapolitan folk hero with all his clown's agility, histrionic gifts, and low-life vivacity, but always faithfully interpreting Milhaud's score, limpid and pungent, ranging from clowning to nobility, and including four songs sung from the orchestra pit.

OTHER VERSIONS. 1) Terpis. Berlin, State Opera House, 1929. 2) Lifar. Paris, Opéra, 1935. Sets and costumes by André Derain. Principal dancers: Serge Lifar (Pulcinella), Suzanne Lorcia (Rosetta), Jacquline Simoni (Isabella), Serge Peretti (Cinzio), Jean Serry (Tartaglia). 3) Gyula Harangozo. Budapest, Royal Hungarian Opera House, 1938. Sets and costumes by Guzztav Oláh. 4) Darrell. Western Theater Ballet, 1961. 5) Milloss. Vienna, State Opera House, 1963.   G.S.

MERCURY *(Mercure)*
Plastic poses in three scenes. Choreography and subject by Léonide Massine. Music by Erik Satie. Drop scene, sets, and costumes by Pablo Picasso. Paris, Théâtre de la Cigale, June 15, 1924. Soirées de Paris du Comte Etienne de Beaumont. Principal dancers: Léonide Massine, Vera Petrova, Nicholas Lissanevich.

SYNOPSIS. There is no real plot. It is more an ironical evocation of certain special aspects of the Graeco-Roman mythological character of Mercury, seen successively in the guise of divine messenger of Olympus, exuberant fertility god, cunning and tricky intriguer, expert but unruly magician, and swift companion of souls on their journey to the Underworld. The very words "plastic poses" tell us that these scenes from literary mythology, whimsically reworked from a satirical angle and not without a whiff of eroticism unusual in those days, were no more than a peg on which to hang a succession of boldly composed tableaux which had little in common with traditional ballet and in which dancing played only a secondary role. Finally, it drew an ironical contrast between the ballet's spirit of avant-garde sacrilege and the melancholy drop curtain in pastel shades depicting a Punchinello with a guitar and a Pierrot with a violin under a white-clouded sky, reminiscent of the dreamy atmosphere of Picasso's "blue" period.

■ During the course of their short season (May 17–June 30, 1924) the *Soirées de Paris*, created under the patronage of the Comte Etienne de Beaumont, quickly won the support of the sophisticated Parisian bourgeoisie, now prepared to accept almost any artistic snobbery or daring innovation in tune with the current trends of art and thought that the cubists, dadaists, and surrealists were imbuing with so much boldness and originality. In any case, the success of these *Soirées* was certainly assisted by Diaghilev's amazing ballet company and by the artistic and musical imagination of Rolf de Maré's Swedish Ballet, which, drawing into their orbit poets such as Cocteau, painters such as Picasso, and composers such as Milhaud and Satie, had prepared the ground for them. So one can well imagine how the public looked forward to the new Picasso/Satie partnership. Alas, the first night proved too much for them. Confusion was total and the cleverness of the production was quite overlooked in the flood of indignant surprise, with the result that the work was a failure. Massine's dynamic choreography, far removed though it was from the romantic imagination, and in spite of its cleverly stylized gesture, was quite overshadowed by the automatically movable architectural scenery designed by Picasso. Being mobile, it often took the place of the performers, who were forced to enter or be masked behind images of themselves constructed of cardboard and steel wire, so that they were depersonalized in a game of superimposition and confusion between reality and illusion that was positively Pirandellian. The double-jointed metal models that dominated the stage, the swinging outline of a woman in the scene entitled *Night*, the three-dimensional brass stars standing out in cold luminescence on the backcloth, became more important than the physical and spiritual human presence. Equally distracting was Satie's clever score, somewhat ironical when not intentionally absurd, and characterized by distorted and parodistic motifs. One could not help thinking of *Parade*, with its grotesque, gigantic managers, or of the impudently provocative *Relâche*. Amid the shouting and fisticuffs of general condemnation, the only one to applaud with enthusiasm was the uninvited spectator Diaghilev, although he considered Etienne de Beaumont a dangerous rival, since he had borrowed so many of his best ideas. Diaghilev once exclaimed *à propos* of the *Soirées de Paris*, "It's a season of Russian Ballet with only our name missing from the posters!" (Kochno). In 1926, when friendly relations were re-established, de Beaumont placed all the scenery and music of *Mercure* at Diaghilev's disposal. The latter presented it with his company on June 2, 1927 at the Sarah Bernhardt Theater in Paris, but once again without success.   G.S.

THE BLUE TRAIN (Le Train Bleu)
A danced operetta in one act. Choreography by Bronis- *lava Nijinska. Music by Darius Milhaud. Scenario by Jean Cocteau. Set by Henri Laurens. Costumes by Coco Chanel. Drop-curtain design by Pablo Picasso. Paris, Théâtre des Champs Elysées, June 20, 1924. Serge Diaghilev's Russian Ballet. Principal dancers: Bronislava Nijinska (the Tennis Champion), Lydia Sokolova (Perlouse), Anton Dolin (le Beau Gosse), Leon Woizikovsky (the Golfer).*

SYNOPSIS. The ballet, set in a fashionable French seaside resort of 1924, and without any definite plot, is a sort of danced musical comedy in which Cocteau, Nijinska, and Milhaud, guided by Diaghilev, amused themselves by painting a satirical portrait of the aristocratic, cosmopolitan, or merely snobbish environment of fashionable seaside resorts.

■ Among the most stylistically effective and expressive moments of the choreography, which was entirely based on movements typical of swimming, golf, tennis, and beach games in general, were the waltz by Sokolova and Woizikovsky and the virtuoso acrobatic dancing of Anton Dolin. The ballet, a perfect example of the French artistic avant-garde (*l'esprit nouveau*) of the immediate postwar era, had a mild success, but was not revived after its original run. The drop curtain designed by Picasso and executed of Prince Shervashidze, depicting two large ladies against a blue background (*La Course*), gained a certain celebrity.   M.B.

THE JAR (La Giara)
One-act ballet. Choreography by Jean Börlin. Music by Alfredo Casella. Scenario by Luigi Pirandello. Sets and costumes by Giorgio De Chirico. Paris, Théâtre des Champs Elysées, November 19, 1924. Swedish Ballet Company. Principal dancers: Axel Witzansky (Don Lollò), Inger Friis (Nela), Eric Viber (Uncle Dima), Jean Börlin (a Young Man).

SYNOPSIS. The peasants on Don Lollò's estate are enjoying a lively dance after the fatigues of the day when three girls in a great state of agitation arrive on the scene. They are followed by a small group of men transporting – with extreme care – a huge jar of oil. Unfortunately, a clumsy movement has broken quite a large fragment from the jar, and it was a new one recently acquired by the miserly Don Lollò. Now they are all afraid, for he is sure to be angry. Sure enough, no sooner does he hear of the accident than he comes storming down to them, and it is only with difficulty that his daughter Nela is able to calm him down. The careless people responsible will have to make good the damage. The best plan, the peasants decide, is to fetch Uncle Dima, the hunchbacked tinker who lives nearby, and ask him to put the matter right. He arrives, climbs inside the jar, and with consummate skill repairs the fracture. When he tries to get out again, however, he finds that now the rim is mended, his hump cannot get through. The onlookers are immensely amused, but the mean Don Lollò gets into a new fury and warns the potmender against trying to get out, because if he breaks

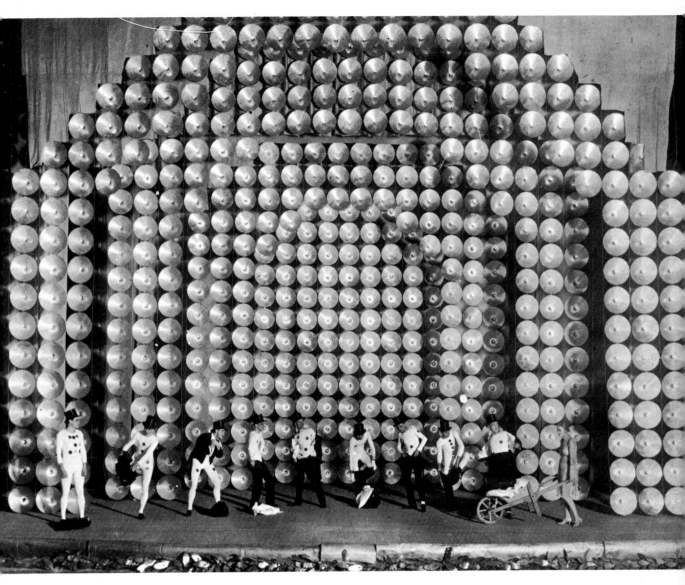

The Swedish Ballet Company in Relâche, *with choreography by Jean Börlin and music by Erik Satie.*
René Clair was responsible for the filmed interlude Entr'acte. *The sets were by Picabia.*

the jar in so doing, he will have to pay for a whole new rim. But the patient – and shrewd – Uncle Dima is in no hurry. He huddles down, pulls out his pipe and prepares to pass the night there with philosophical resignation. His friends laughingly banter him and one by one leave him to himself. The moon comes up, and in the semi-darkness we can see puffs of tobacco smoke rising from the jar with maddening regularity. Now a handsome young man enters to serenade Nela, who comes out of the house to meet her lover. The peasants, attracted by the song, return to drink to the freeing of the dear old man, who joins in the singing at the top of his voice. Excited by the wine, they all break into a frenzied tarantella around the jar, creating an indescribable hubbub, until Don Lollò, furious at being woken up by the din, rushes out of the house and, losing all self-control, gives the pot a mighty kick, thus breaking it himself and

setting the old man free. Shrewd Uncle Dima thus becomes the hero of a lively dance of triumph, while the humiliated Don Lollò returns sulkily to his house, leaving Nela in her lover's arms.

■ This work by Jean Börlin, full of the colourful, slightly coarse good humour of Sicily, drew its inspiration from a short story by Luigi Pirandello. It was certainly the most successful item of the program of four ballets presented in Paris by Rolf de Maré in November 1924. The other three works were: *Le Roseau*, an old Persian legend, *Le Porcher*, from a Hans Andersen fairy tale, and *Le Tournoi Singulier*, a dadaist Japanesery on love and madness. The public greeted *The Jar* with enthusiasm, partly for the flowing stage designs of De Chirico and Casella's tuneful music, a wonder of balance, ingenuity, and witty fantasy, which went so well with the sunny aura of spontaneous vitality created by Börlin's choreography. He had absorbed the atmosphere during his Italian holiday of the preceding year, when he had studied Sicilian folk dances in the company of Pirandello himself. The ballet has passed into the repertory of numerous companies and never fails to please its audience. There was an important revival at the Scala in Milan in March 1943, with choreography by Bianca Gallizia and sets by Veniero Colasanti, the chief dancers being Edda Martignoni, Savaré, Dino Cavallo, and Tony Corcione. After World War II, also at the Scala, new versions were presented by Margherita Wallman (1949, 1953, 1959) and by Luciana Novaro in 1962 with sets and costumes by Aligi Sassu. Another version of historical importance was performed at the Teatro Massimo in Palermo in April 1958, with choreography by Aurel Milloss, sets and costumes by Renato Guttuso, and with Alberto Testa (Uncle Dima), Ludwig Dürst (Don Lollò), Olga Amati (Nela), and Walter Zappolini (the Young Man) dancing the principal parts.

OTHER VERSIONS. 1) R. Galli. New York, Metropolitan Opera House, 1927. 2) B. Nijinska. Buenos Aires, Colon Theater, 1927. 3) N. de Valois. London, Sadler's Wells Ballet and Theatre, October 9, 1934. Sets and costumes by William Chappell. Danced by Appleyard, Helpmann, Gore. This version included two solos, one by Nela, the other a comic one for Uncle Dima constituting the prelude, first danced by Walter Gore. 4) Milloss. Rome, Opera House, 1939, and Palermo at the Teatro Massimo, 1958.   G.S.

THE MUSIC. Leading spirit of early twentieth-century artistic life in Italy, the tireless Alfredo Casella was one of the first composers to realize the need for a radical regeneration of instrumental music. His years in Paris, when he was in contact with the lively artistic life there, led him to become one of the innovators of Italian music during the postwar years. On the one hand he gained strength from the study of composers from earlier centuries, on the other he sought to restore Italy to a level less provincial and more in touch with the movements that inspired the rest of Europe. In *The Jar* Casella used Sicilian folk music not as a pretext for agreeable interludes but as a structural foundation and unifier of work drawn from Pirandello's sunny Mediterranean comedy of the same name. More than twenty years ago Gianandrea Gavazzeni, writing on the work, said, "Ethnic character is first expressed in music, which gives rise to movement and finally to the plastic and painterly qualities of the scene." He added further, "In *La Giara* these entities for the first time find their complete theatrical form together with their associated imagination and style. But the amalgam of European harmony, rhythm, and counterpoint is filtered and transformed through the composer's own personality." Today we might have our doubts about the score's "Italian" characteristics, which to the modern ear seem little more than a series of festive Sicilian dances. Yet we should not underrate the happy touch of the orchestrator, nor the composer's skill in blending his folk

music material to form a most effective and colourful whole.   A.F.

RELÂCHE
Instantaneous ballet in two acts with a cinematographic interlude. Choreography and production by Jean Börlin and Francis Picabia. Music by Erik Satie. Scenario by Francis Picabia (after Cendras). Cinematographic production by René Clair. Paris, Théâtre des Champs Elysées, December 4, 1924. Swedish Ballet. Principal dancers: Edith Bonsdorff (a woman), Jean Börlin (a man), Kaj Smith (another man); principal film actors: Francis Picabia, Erik Satie, Marcel Duchamp, Man Ray, Jean Börlin.

SYNOPSIS. The curtain rises to disclose an act drop on which the names of all those who collaborated in the production are written in transparent letters, rhythmically illuminated like the lighted signs of a modern city. Then a number of car lamps are pointed at the audience and shine with a light that varies in intensity according to the rhythm of the music and of the prologue, which shows on a cinema screen the fleeting images of dancers, joined by a grotesque paralytic, all without any apparent rhyme or reason. A fireman patrols the stage incessantly. A woman in evening dress enters through the audience and mounts the stage, smoking a cigarette. She dances in turn with eight men dressed in tailcoats before going off with one of them. The first act ends with a striptease by the male dancers, who open their evening coats to display rowing vests ornamented with dazzling sequins of mirror glass. During the interval *Entr'acte*, a film made by René Clair from a script by Picabia is shown. It is made up of all sorts of extraordinary pictures: unusual views of feet, a game of chess between Duchamp and Man Ray interrupted by a hose played on them by Picabia, a dance by a bearded ballerina, Jean Börlin in sporting attire killed by a gunshot. His coffin is carried in a hearse decorated with hams and drawn by a dromedary. Mourners are eating the ham and funeral wreaths when the hearse becomes unhooked from the dromedary and rolls away gathering speed as it goes. The mourners pursue it. The hearse overturns on a stretch of grass, and the smiling Jean Börlin jumps out of the coffin dressed in a tailcoat; with the gesture of a conjuror he makes everything disappear, including himself. A screen bearing the word "End" comes up and is promptly punctured by a man jumping through it as if it were a circus hoop and landing in the stalls. The second act returns to "live theater." Dancers parade with notices insulting to the audience, such as, "Anyone who doesn't like this can go to the devil!" or "Fancy! There are some people who prefer the ballets at the Opéra, poor fools!" In the finale the dancers take off their stage clothes and put on their own, while the fireman, still smoking, continuously pours water from one bucket to another and then back again. Erik Satie, who was resposible for the score with its motifs of jazz and palm court music, and the accompaniment to the prelude, based on a student song, *Le Marchand de Navets (The Turnip Seller)*, came to

André Derain's design for the ballet Jack-in-the-Box, *created in 1926 by George Balanchine to music by Erik Satie.*

take his bow in a little Citroën saloon car and drove around the stage waving at the audience with his large melon-coloured cap.

■ Picabia, inspired by a scenario by Cendras, published in *Dada à Paris*, was seized with the idea of rewriting it, and, encouraged by Erik Satie, turned it into a ballet in which, for the first time, cinema was combined with dance spectacle, thus creating a style in tune with the spirit of the work: making reality fantastic and fantasy real. Preparation and staging were left almost entirely to Picabia, the company being away on an American tour, so that Jean Börlin, on his return, had time for only a modest contribution of choreography. *Relâche* was one of the first dadaist manifestos: "It is life, life as I like it," wrote Picabia, "life without a morrow, life today, everything for today, nothing for yesterday, nothing for tomorrow . . . and perpetual motion, the fleeting moment, light, richness, luxury, love, the optimism of happy people, the joy of laughter. Why reflect, why keep to a conventional idea of beauty and happiness?" One can easily imagine the mixed whistles, boos, and applause that greeted this iconoclastic production, though Massine must certainly have had it in mind when he was creating *Ode* in 1928. The ballet's success was too slight for survival and it was the last production put on by

Rolf de Maré's Swedish Ballet Company, launched five years earlier and first presented to the Parisian public on October 25, 1920. The company's very last performance took place in Epernay on March 17, 1925. Only after its disappearance from the cultural and balletic scene did people realize what an aesthetic revolution the Swedish Ballet had brought about. In their magnificent and generous attempt to be the standard bearers of the future, however, they had overstepped their own ideological boundaries and lost their public, who were bewildered by the ultramodern and, for the times, scandalous and sacreligious formula. To have gone further would have been pointless, even for the leaders.   G.S.

THE SAILORS *(Les Matelots)*

Ballet in one act and five scenes. Choreography by Léonide Massine. Music by Georges Auric. Scenario by Boris Kochno. Drop curtain, set, and costumes by Pedro Pruna. Paris, Théâtre de la Gaité-Lyrique, June 17, 1925. Diaghilev's Russian Ballet. Principal dancers: Vera Nemchinova (the Fiancée), Lydia Sokolova (the Friend), Leon Woizikovsky (the Spanish Sailor), Serge Lifar (the French Sailor), Tadeo Slavinsky (the American Sailor).

SYNOPSIS. During their shore leave between voyages, three lively sailors amuse themselves by visiting the dockside bars, making friends with all the pretty girls they meet. One of these forms a serious attachment to the most carefree of the sailors, who promises to marry her on his return. However, he then decides to test her fidelity with the help of his friends. Left alone, the girl gives herself up to a lyrical dance in which sadness at the recent parting and the romanticism of a hope-filled solitude express the sincerity of her love. Her friends try in vain to make her forget the affair and meet other sailors, but she firmly refuses. Meanwhile the three sailors have gone back to their ships to disguise themselves. They return to the bar and try one after the other to seduce the young girl. She steadfastly resists the advances of all three of them, thus convincing her fiancé that she is true to him. The mariners now discard their disguises and the girl throws herself happily into the arms of her beloved sailor.

■ This was the first ballet Massine produced on rejoining Diaghilev's company after five years of absence. Leaving behind him the *Commedia dell'Arte* tradition, the influence of Goldoni and the marionettes of *La Boutique Fantasque*, he now turned to a simple, farcical plot in which a caricatured drollery expressed a new and more modern conception of life. The scene depicted the nightlife of a Mediterranean port and was accused by some of vulgarity, laid as it was in dockside streets and bars with more than a hint of the brothel, and accompanied by tavern songs and licentious choruses. That was more than made up for, however, by the youthful exuberance of the protagonists, for whom Massine composed dances with syncopated steps, sometimes evocative of the music hall, such as the game of cards at which the sailors sit in perilous balance on tilted chairs. In the 1925 London production, Massine even introduced an extra attraction in the person of the street musician G. P. Dines, an ex-sailor who entertained people waiting to enter the theater with his musical spoons. Contrast was provided by the romantic variation of the engaged girl in the moonlit street, an almost moralistic antithesis between virtue and vice. The brilliant personal success of Serge Lifar in his first important role, Pruna's attractive set, and the lively inventiveness of Georges Auric's musical score based on French popular songs, all combined to ensure the ballet an enthusiastic reception by the audience, who at the end of the spectacle wittily presented the dancers with a life belt, a judgment that was not, however, entirely shared by the more perceptive critics.   G.S.

BARABAU

Ballet with choral singing in one act. Choreography and story (from an idea of Diaghilev's) by George Balan-

A scene from The Red Poppy *by Tikhomiroff and Lashchelin. In the foreground is Galina Ulanova in the part of Tao-Hoa.*

Rudolf Nureyev, Noella Pontois, Nanan Thibon, and Wilfride Piollet in Apollon Musagète.

chine. *Music by Vittorio Rieti. Set and costumes by Maurice Utrillo. London, Coliseum, December 11, 1925. Diaghilev's Russian Ballet Company. Principal dancers: Leon Woizikovsky (Barabau), Lydia Sokolova (a peasant woman), Serge Lifar (an officer).*

SYNOPSIS. While Barabau is having a party in his garden with his fellow-villagers, a company of soldiers with an officer comes by and treats the host with unbearable arrogance, looting and dragging the women into an unwilling dance. The ill-used Barabau pretends to fall dead, upon which the soldiers hastily retreat while the villagers mournfully prepare for the funeral. Suddenly Barabau comes to life again and is borne in triumph by his friends.

■ This sunny, light-hearted ballet was suggested to Diaghilev by an Italian children's rhyme called *Barabau* for which the young composer Vittorio Rieti had written an accompaniment later extended into the score for the ballet. *Barabau* is to be remembered not only for Utrillo's stage designs (carried out by Prince Shervashidze, for the painter himself was never in direct contact with the Diaghilev company), but because it marked the beginning of Balanchine's immense achievement as a choreographer. The ballet, revived by Diaghilev in Paris and Monte Carlo in 1926, also appeared in 1935 in a new version danced by Sadler's Wells Ballet in London. A.A.

ROMEO AND JULIET

Ballet ("rehearsal without scenery") in two parts. Choreography by Bronislava Nijinska. Music by Constant Lambert. Paintings by Max Ernst and Joan Miró. Monte Carlo, Opéra, May 4, 1926. Diaghilev's Russian Ballet. Principal dancers: Tamara Karsavina, Serge Lifar, Tadeo Slavinsky, Lydia Sokolova, Leon Woizikovsky, Alexandra Danilova, Felia Dubrovska, Constantin Tcherkas.

SYNOPSIS. A ballet company is rehearsing *Romeo and Juliet* on a bare stage. The dancers of the two title roles arrive. While the ballet master teaches them a *pas de deux*, they make it plain that they are in love. Reproved, they start to rehearse the whole work, continuing up to the deaths of Romeo and Juliet and the fall of the curtain. The other dancers applaud their colleagues, but when the curtain rises again the two have vanished. Soon afterwards we catch a glimpse of them flying off in an airplane.

■ This curious plot was thought up by Diaghilev and Boris Kochno for a ballet that would afford an occasion to present the young English composer Constant Lambert, and at the same time to welcome Bronislava Nijinska back to the company after an absence of two years. It was her last ballet for Diaghilev and, while not without her usual rich classical dance vocabulary or incisive inventiveness in mime, it lacked originality and movement of real interest. Thus the ballet's success was mainly dependent on the dancers: Lifar, radiating youthful charm, and Karsavina, re-creating, as always, the enchantment of her absolute expressive purity. Alice Nikitina took Karsavina's place as Juliet in the Paris production at the Sarah Bernhardt Theater on May 18, 1926. The ballet, for which Joan Miró and Max Ernst had painted two small backcloths for the last scene, purposely devoid of any figurative reference to the action, was calmly received on its first night in Monte Carlo, but when it was presented in Paris it created a quite unexpected scandal. As Boris Kochno recalls: "Because they disapproved of Miró and Max Ernst, members of the surrealist movement, taking part in Diaghilev's capitalist enterprise, André Breton and Louis Aragon, leaders of the movement, tried to sabotage the performance of *Romeo and Juliet*. They planted their disciples throughout the auditorium, mostly young followers of surrealism, who, when the house curtains went up to reveal Miró's painting, raised an indescribable uproar and showered the spectators with pamphlets. . . ." These protesting manifestos declared, among other things, "It may have seemed to Ernst and Miró that their collaboration with Monsieur de Diaghilev, justified by Picasso's example, does not matter very much. Therefore we, who take every care to keep the advance posts of the mind far from any taint of slave-dealing, are under an obligation to denounce, without consideration of persons, an attitude that provides weapons for the worst partisans of doubtful morality." While the leaflets were raining down on the audience, Aragon himself, up in the gallery, harangued the crowd, who were reacting angrily against the agitators. "The ballet," Kochno concludes, "could not continue till the police were called in to expel the demonstrators. The surrealist scandal aroused the Parisians' interest in *Romeo and Juliet* and caused advance bookings for the Diaghilev productions to soar."   A.A.

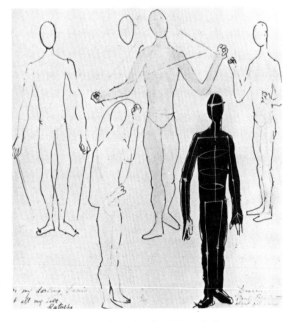

Design by Pavel Tchelitchev for Ode, *a ballet choreographed by Léonide Massine in 1928.*

JACK-IN-THE-BOX
Suite of three dances. Choreography by George Balanchine. Music by Erik Satie, orchestrated by Darius Milhaud. Sets and costumes by André Derain. Paris, Théâtre Sarah Bernhardt, July 3, 1926. Principal dancers: Stanislas Idzikovsky, Alexandra Danilova.

■ The ballet, or rather suite, was an excuse for presenting the unruly Idzikovsky, a *sauteur* with an elevation comparable to Nijinsky's. (Polish by birth, he joined Diaghilev in 1914 and Balanchine in 1926. He also studied under Cecchetti, whose method he helped to codify.) In *Jack-in-the-Box* Idzikovsky played the part of a comic puppet with whom three dancers, one of them Danilova disguised as a black girl, played as if it were a ball. The back of the stage was occupied by large cardboard clouds moved by mimes. Conceived under the influence of "The Six" and developed in the so-called *Ecole d'Arcueil*, the score adopted the typical ironical attitude of that school, inventive, imaginative, free in form, but always bearing the unmistakeable stamp of its French musical origin.   C.M.C.

THE CAT *(La Chatte)*
One-act ballet. Choreography by George Balanchine. Music by Henri Sauguet. Scenario by Sobeka (pseudonym of Boris Kochno). Set and costumes by Gabo and Pevsner. Monte Carlo, Monte Carlo Theater, April 30, 1927. Principal dancers: Olga Spessivtzeva, Serge Lifar.

SYNOPSIS. The story is taken from one of Aesop's fables. A young man falls in love with a cat and begs Venus to turn her into a woman. The goddess consents, but later decides to test the girl's constancy by introducing a mouse into the bridal chamber. The girl immediately leaves her husband's embrace to chase the mouse, and is turned back into her animal form to the despair of her lover, who dies of sorrow.

■ The ballet, created by Balanchine for the Diaghilev company, appeared one year earlier than *Apollon Musagète*. It was immensely successful. Sauguet, the twenty-six-year-old composer, whose first essay in ballet music it was, became so interested in the language of mime that he decided henceforth to make it one of his chief compositional forms. (In 1965 he also composed the score for a television ballet, *The Prince and the Beggar*.) From a theatrical point of view the originality of *La Chatte* lay in the novelty of the set constructed in transparent plastic material against a background of black oilcloth, all of which was sprinkled with talcum powder. The dancers' costumes were likewise made of plastic. The cast of the ballet was also unusual: seven men and one woman. The choreography had little relation to the story, but was designed especially to demonstrate the masculine dancing and perfect beauty of Serge Lifar, then in the flower of his youth, whose feline grace and dexterity were the ballet's principal attraction. His almost gymnastic movements and variations were contrasted and set in high relief by the amorous *pas de deux*

A scene from Bolero *in the version choreographed by Serge Lifar.*

with Spessivtzeva that followed them. On the first night in Paris Spessivtzeva sprained her ankle and had to be replaced by Alice Nikitina, who learned the part in one day. It later became one of Markova's showpieces.

C.M.C.

DANCE OF STEEL *(Pas d'Acier* or *Stalnoi Skok)*
Ballet in four scenes. Choreography by Léonide Massine. Music by Sergei Prokoviev and G. Yakulov. Sets and costumes by G. Yakulov. Paris, Théâtre Sarah Bernhardt, June 8, 1927. Diaghilev's Russian Ballet. Principal dancers: Felia Dubrovska, Lubov Tchernicheva, Alice Nikitina, Léonide Massine, Serge Lifar.

SYNOPSIS. In a very simple setting on two levels framed in metal scaffolding, we watch everyday work in a factory.

■ In the wake of avant-guard experiments in post-revolutionary Russia, and influenced by the teaching of Meyerhold, this ballet is intended as a glorification and apotheosis of machines and labour. The movements and evolutions of the dancers seem to be in counterpoint with the mobile structures that form the scenery. P.C.

THE RED POPPY *(Krasni Mak)*
Ballet in three acts. Choreography by Tikhomirov and Lashchilin. Music by Reinhold M. Glier. Scenario and sets by M. Kurilko and V. Tikhomirov. Moscow, Bolshoi Theater, June 14, 1927.

SYNOPSIS. The plot, laid in China during the 1920s, tells of the arrival of a Soviet ship in a Chinese port and of the immediate feeling of brotherhood between the Russian sailors and the local population. The people rise against their oppressors, while a tender idyll grows up between a pretty Chinese girl and the Soviet captain, whose life she subsequently saves at the cost of her own.

■ The ballet, which abandoned the habitual subject-matter of fairy tales and national history to deal with contemporary events (it was during the Kuomintang regime) was a resounding success in the USSR and was repeated for three hundred successive evenings, a genuine record. Although it was the first ballet based on the new Soviet realism and propaganda, the musical style and the construction of the whole work were clearly reminiscent of the romantic tradition and entirely Tchaikovskian in conception. Frequent use was made of popular songs, among which were the incisive, dramatic notes of the *International* and other revolutionary tunes. In 1949, when the ballet was revived at the Bolshoi Theater in Moscow, the composer produced a revised version, while in 1957, on the thirtieth anniversary of its first performance, a new version with choreography by L. Lavrovsky was presented at the Bolshoi.   P.C.

APOLLO OF THE MUSES (Apollon Musagète)

Ballet in four scenes. Choreography by Adolph Bolm. Music by Igor Stravinsky. Washington, Library of Congress, April 27, 1928. Principal dancers: Adolph Bolm (Apollo), Ruth Page, Elise Reiman, Berenice Holmes (the Muses). Immediately revived by Diaghilev's Russian Ballet in Paris, Théâtre Sarah Bernhardt, June 12, 1928, with choreography by George Balanchine, sets and costumes by André Bauchant, and danced by Serge Lifar (Apollo), Alice Nikitina (Terpsichore), Lubov Tchernicheva (Polyhymnia) and Felia Dubrovska (Calliope).

SYNOPSIS. Scene I: on a high rock in Delos, an Aegean island, on a starry night, Leto gives birth to Apollo. The boy god, at the foot of the rock (represented in later versions by steps leading up to a platform), frees himself from his swaddling clothes and begins to live and communicate with the world. Women bring him a lute. Scene II: Apollo, at the center of the stage with his lute, in a regal variation. The three Muses, Calliope, Polyhymnia, and Terpsichore, approach and do him homage. Apollo assumes their leadership, asking each one of them to name the symbol of her art. To Calliope, muse of poetry, he gives a tablet, to Polyhymnia, muse of acting, he gives a mask, and to Terpsichore, muse of singing and dancing, a lyre. The three Muses dance with their gifts, then Apollo performs another "ideal" variation. He is joined by Terpsichore and later by the other two, and leads them towards Mount Parnassus, ascending the rock at Zeus's summons and severing the last tie with his mother Leto.

■ Stravinsky was commissioned to write the score of *Apollon Musagète* for a festival devoted to contemporary music in 1928, run by the Washington Chamber Music Society and backed by the patroness Elizabeth Sprague Coolidge. It had to be a short ballet (lasting no more than half an hour) with a score composed for a very limited number of players. Stravinsky seized the occasion to realize an idea that had long been close to his heart – a ballet in classical style inspired by Greek mythology. But there was more to it than that: with *Apollon* Stravinsky left behind his past, nourished by violent themes, iconoclasm, and artistic provocation, to draw into the haven of order and harmony, and the cult of beauty freed from any material logic. Stravinsky looked towards the past, to a reign of reason, a world that strove to free itself from chaos and sought justice, not from below, from the primitive strength of the masses, but from the superior wisdom of a prince. Thus *Apollon* takes on the aspect of a turning point, a change of heart: the past brings comfort to the present, for the future holds out no hope of further liberation. It is also a return to Petipa in a dynamic form strongly affected by the anything but mild choreography of Balanchine, and yet closely concerned with classicism. *Apollon Musagète*

thus combines traditional balletic style, the past in the manner of Lully, with the geometrical austerity of modernism, and so becomes an illustrious example of the art that was to be known as neoclassical – an example that was abundantly followed and imitated. The partnership of Stravinsky and Balanchine, which was to produce a long series of important ballets, marked the transition from the era of Diaghilev to that of abstract ballet. After its initial performance in America, the composer offered *Apollon* to Diaghilev, who very naturally entrusted the choreography to Balanchine. Apollo, as seen by the choreographer, is a young man who begins life in primitive, uncivilized conditions and eventually acquires nobility through art. That agreed perfectly with Stravinsky's idea of the ballet, which was basically the restoration of formal, classical beauty through the victory of purity in a world finally ruled by intelligence. The novelty of the idea left the Parisian critics bewildered, while the public may well have been antagonized by the audacity of the choreography (based on the classical tradition, but introducing all kinds of different steps, variations, and attitudes in the dance composition for one male dancer and three ballerinas, with completely new lifts, syncopations, elevations, and *terre à terre* movements, athleticism and remarkable plastic poses). Greek culture is indirectly redefined in terms of absolute vitalism, with little stressing of character. Everything is contrived with great simplicity and immediacy. The symbolic place of Apollo in Stravinsky's aesthetic philosophy and in twentieth-century ballet as a whole is tellingly expressed by the composer himself: "It is good that Dionysius is tamed at last and subjected to the law: now it is the reign of Apollo." Against the Dionysiac spirit of *Rite of Spring* he sets the spirit of Apollo.

THE MUSIC. The score of *Apollon Musagète* is written for strings only and is consistently classical in style: dry harmonies, an abundance of perfect chords, rare polytonal superimposition. Those are borrowed from the past (from Lully and Delibes), but divested of all historical reference to achieve an abstract purity, as in some sterilized Arcadia. The instrumental colour, the violence, the extravagance of the early Stravinsky have no place in this marble vision of static perfection.   M.P.

ODE

Choreographic spectacle in three acts. Choreography by Léonide Massine. Music by Nicholas Nabokov (from a text by Lomonossov). Scenic scheme by Boris Kochno. Decorative contribution by Pavel Tchelitchev and Pierre Charbonnier. Paris, Théâtre Sarah Bernhardt, June 6, 1928. Diaghilev's Russian Ballet. Principal dancers: Irina Beliankina, Felia Dubrovska, Alice Nikitina, Léonide Massine, Serge Lifar.

SYNOPSIS. "An evening meditation on the Glory of God on the occasion of the Aurora Borealis." The statue of Nature descends from her pedestal and displays her charms and her powers. The student enters to pay homage to her, interrupting the dance of the

Above: Paolo Bortoluzzi and Carla Fracci in Le Baiser de la Fée, *produced at the Scala during the 1974–1975 season, with choreography by Loris Gai. Below: The New York City Ballet in a scene from* The Prodigal Son.

spirits that she has evoked. Nature reassumes her super-human aspect.

■ Serge Diaghilev, who had always been a fervent student of Russian history and art, was carried away by the composer Nicholas Nabokov's idea of writing a musical accompaniment to an ode by the eighteenth-century Russian poet Lomonossov. To go with this song, so evocative of the Russia of Empress Elizabeth, Diaghilev planned to produce a ballet which, in its scenic and decorative aspects, would be based on the court festivities of her reign as seen in contemporary Russian painting. The script writer Boris Kochno and the stage designer Pavel Tchelitchev, however, did not adhere closely to the original idea. They conceived a brand of "total theater" with modern scenic techniques involving abstract, geometrical movements in space onto which were projected strange lighting effects and patterns, as well as cinematic film, designed by Pierre Charbonnier. In his choreography, Massine, back with the Diaghilev company for the last time and already inclined towards symbolic abstraction, stressed the mime and gestural content in a balletic composition of bizarre and angular movements and groupings. In spite of the enthusiasm invested by all concerned in both its planning and realization, this curious ballet was coldly received at its first appearance in Paris, and fared no better when repeated at His Majesty's Theatre in London the following month. A.A.

THE GODS GO A-BEGGING (Les Dieux Mendiants)
Pastoral ballet in one act. Choreography by George Balanchine. Scenario by Sobeka (Boris Kochno). Music by Georg Friedrich Händel, adapted by Sir Thomas Beecham. Set by Léon Bakst. Costumes by Juan Gris. London, His Majesty's Theatre, July 16, 1928. Diaghilev's Russian Ballet. Principal dancers: Alexandra Danilova, Lubov Tchernicheva, Felia Dubrovska, Leon Woizikovsky, Constantin Tcherkass.

SYNOPSIS. Into a glade where an aristocratic picnic is in progress a poor shepherd wanders as if he were lost. As a jest the ladies try to seduce him, but he approaches a humble serving-maid instead. The noble guests watch their idyllic dance with scorn until the two cast off their rags and reveal themselves as divinities.

■ Conceived in a stylized rococo taste, the scene being an early seventeenth-century *fête galante*, this ingenious "pastoral" ballet was created at the last moment to fill a gap in the 1928 London season of Diaghilev's Ballet. Such was the haste that Diaghilev decided to make use of Bakst's scenery for *Daphnis and Chloë* (1912) and the costumes designed by Juan Gris for *Les Tentations de la Bergère* (1924). The graceful classicism of Balanchine's choreography, with hardly a hint of his abstract ironical modernity, and the splendid account of it given by Danilova and Woizikovsky, earned the ballet a veritable triumph. Among other versions, the most important was by Ninette de Valois, with sets and costumes by Hugh Stevenson recalling the paintings of Watteau.

OTHER VERSIONS. 1) Ninette de Valois. London, Sadler's Wells Theatre, February 21, 1936. Danced by Elizabeth Miller, William Chappell, Vic-Wells Ballet. 2) David Lichine. Monte Carlo Opera House, 1937. Scenery by Gris, after Bakst. Colonel de Basil's Russian Ballet. A.A.

BOLERO
One-act ballet. Choreography by Bronislava Nijinska. Music by Maurice Ravel. Sets and costumes by Alexandre Benois. Paris, Opéra, November 22, 1928. Principal dancer: Ida Rubinstein.

SYNOPSIS. A gypsy dancer is the center of attraction in an Andalusian tavern. Her sensual dancing and her beauty intoxicate the men who crowd around the table on which she performs. The gypsies join her in a violent crescendo of dance that ends in the flashing of knives.

■ The ballet arose from an idea by the famous ballerina Ida Rubinstein, who asked Maurice Ravel to compose music to accompany a Spanish dance. Ravel first thought of orchestrating a piece of piano music by Albéniz, but changed his mind and wrote an original score that soon became the rage of the concert halls. The bolero was a Spanish dance of the late seventeenth century in ternary form. In Ravel's hands it evolved into an unchanging motif obsessively reiterated, with little relation to authentic folk music, but carrying tremendous emotional impact. The music, original and marvellously written, has proved far more long-lived than the ballet, although that has had a large number of new interpretations. The most interesting was undoubtedly Aurel Milloss's version (Rome, Opera House, June 20, 1944; sets and costumes by Dario Cecchi; danced by Ugo Dell'Ara and Attilia Radice) which stressed the witchcraft aspect of gypsy life, casting a demon as the *deus ex machina* of a story of perdition involving various groups of men and women, and thus a long way from the original idea with its tavern and table. Maurice Béjart went back to Rubinstein's idea (*Ballet du XXme Siècle*, 1961), but, abandoning any suggestion of folk dance, worked the dancing up to a violent finale in which the men overwhelm and submerge the ballerina in a sort of collective orgasm. Other versions have been arranged by Lander, Lifar, Lavrovsky, Tatiana Gsovsky, Pilar Lopez, and Argentinita. M.P.

THE FAIRY'S KISS (Le Baiser de la Fée)
Ballet in four scenes. Choreography by Bronislava Nijinska. Music and scenario (after Hans Andersen) by Igor Stravinsky. Sets and costumes by Alexandre Benois. Paris, Opéra, November 27, 1928. Ida Rubinstein's Ballet Company. Principal dancers: Ida Rubinstein, Ludmilla Schollar, Anatole Vilzak.

SYNOPSIS. In a remote wintry countryside, a woman drags herself through the snow, clasping a baby to her breast. She dies of fatigue and cold, upon which the Ice

Fairy appears, draws near the tiny boy, places a chain bearing a talisman around his neck, kisses him on the forehead, and departs. Guided by the fairy's spell, people come from the nearby village to save the little orphan. They bring him up, and we next seen him a fine young man, betrothed to the miller's daughter and soon to marry her. On the wedding eve the two young people are joining in the village dancing and festivity when a mysterious gypsy woman appears. She reads the hands of some of the merrymakers and finally comes to that of the young man, who is seized with a strange dismay, as if some memory were stirring, and by a bewitched attraction to the woman. The next day the miller's daughter is at home, dressing for the wedding surrounded by her friends. The young man arrives and has a tender interlude with his betrothed, whose face is covered by her wedding veil. Hardly has she left him when he perceives another veiled figure. He approaches her as if drawn by a magic power, lifts the veil, and recognizes the woman of the previous night, now glittering with icy jewels and radiating queenly fascination. It is the Ice Fairy come to claim the youth, fated to preserve single and inviolate the kiss that marked him as her own twenty years before. Spellbound, he follows his fatal mistress, who lures him to her glacial world between life and death while the deserted bride waits anxiously for the bridegroom who will never return.

■ This is one of the rare cases in which the subject, spirit, and general scheme of a ballet depended more on the composer than on the choreographer. Indeed, Stravinsky wrote in his *Chronicle of My Life*, "I received from Mme. Ida Rubinstein a proposal to compose a ballet for her repertory. The painter Alexander Benois, who did some work for her, submitted two plans, one of which seemed very likely to attract me. The idea was that I should compose something inspired by the music of Tchaikovsky. My well-known fondness for this composer, and, still more, the fact that November, the time fixed for the performance, would mark the thirty-fifth anniversary of his death, induced me to accept the offer. It would give me an opportunity of paying my heartfelt homage to Tchaikovsky's wonderful talent.

"As I was free to choose both the subject and scenario of the ballet, I began to search for them, in view of the characteristic trend of Tchaikovsky's music, in the literature of the nineteenth century. With that aim, I turned to a great poet with a gentle, sensitive soul whose imaginative mind was wonderfully akin to that of the musician. I refer to Hans Christian Andersen . . .

"In turning over the pages of Andersen, with which I was fairly familiar, I came across a story which I had completely forgotten that struck me as being the very thing for the idea which I wanted to express. It was the very beautiful story known to us as *The Ice Maiden*."

So it was that Stravinsky came to write a score for *Le Baiser de la Fée* which miraculously absorbed into its Stravinskian classicism the character of Tchaikovsky's music and, more particularly, Tchaikovsky's themes, around which it was almost entirely constructed. Bronislava Nijinska, for her part, fully grasped the feeling of the re-creation, composing a choreography inspired by the ballets of Petipa, that is to say, an academic *ballet d'action* with mime in the late nineteenth-century romantic manner, but stylized, and enriched with all the experience gained from the era of Diaghilev. The Rubinstein company presented the ballet a number of times with success due to the delicate poetry of the idea and to the quality of the music, which have ensured its revival in various guises up to the present day, the most remarkable for its adherence to Stravinsky's original ideas being the purely classical version by George Balanchine (see below).

OTHER VERSIONS. 1) Frederick Ashton. London, Sadler's Wells Theatre, November 26, 1935. Danced by Pearl Argyle, Margot Fonteyn, Harold Turner, Sadler's Wells Ballet. 2) George Balanchine. New York, Metropolitan Opera House, April 27, 1937. Danced by Kathryn Mullowney, Gisella Caccialanza, William Dollar, American Ballet; then idem, April 10, 1940. Danced by Mia Slavenska, Alexandra Danilova, André Eglevsky, Ballets Russes de Monte Carlo; then at the Paris Opéra, July 2, 1947. Danced by Maria Tallchief, Tamara Toumanova, Alexandre Kalioujny; then New York, City Center, November 28, 1950. Danced by Maria Tallchief, Tanaquil Le Clercq, Nicholas Magallanes, New York City Ballet. 3) Nicholas Beriosov. Stuttgart State Theater, July 5, 1958. Stuttgart Ballet. 4) Kenneth MacMillan. London, Covent Garden, April 12, 1960. Danced by Lynn Seymour, Svetlana Beriosova, Donald MacLeary, Royal Ballet. 5) Ronald Hynd. Amsterdam, Stadtsschouwburg, October 16, 1968. Danced by Olga de Haas, Maria Bovet, Sylvester Campbell, Het Nationale Ballet. 6) John Neumeier (his own scenario). Music by Igor Stravinsky with two added fragments by Piotr Ilich Tchaikovsky. Frankfurt-am-Main, Städtische Bühnen, January 2, 1972. Frankfurt Ballet.   A.A.

THE BALL *(Le Bal)*
Ballet in two scenes. Choreography by George Balanchine. Music by Vittorio Rieti. Scenario by Boris Kochno. Sets and costumes by Giorgio De Chirico. Monte Carlo, Opera House, May 7, 1929. Diaghilev's Russian Ballet. Principal dancers: Alexandra Danilova (the Lady), Anton Dolin (the Young Man), André Bobrov (the Astrologist), Felia Dubrovska, Leon Woizikovsky, George Balanchine, Eugénie Lipkovska, Serge Lifar.

SYNOPSIS. Amid a crowd of guests at a ball, a young man, struck by the beauty of a lady in the company of an old astrologer, follows the pair. After an anxious search while the festivities are at their height, the youth finds the lady and begs her to remove her mask. She does so, to reveal the face of a hideous old woman, who, in her turn, follows the horror-stricken young man. The other guests having gone, he is left alone in the empty ballroom; as he is about to depart he sees the lady with the astrologer again. She takes off her first mask, and then the second one of the old crone, to reveal her true face, that of a young and lovely woman, while the astrologer throws off his disguise and appears as a handsome cavalier. They go together towards the door, through which can be seen a horse. The poor young man falls into a swoon.

■ The curious mixture of irony, parody, and mysterious symbolism that made up this ballet found its true artistic expression less in Balanchine's choreography, Rieti's music, or the theatrical ideas of Boris Kochno than in the marvellous scenic design of Giorgio De Chirico. The products of his strange imagination dominated the ballet, the synthesis *a priori* of its other elements. Perhaps just because no three-dimensional pattern could emerge that was not already present in the intense and self-sufficient pertified world of De Chirico's vision, Balanchine's choreography seemed devoid of true invention. Be that as it may, Balanchine's creative personality, central to the ballet of our time, did not emerge until well after his youthful apprenticeship with the Russian Ballet Company in its final phase, ending with the death of its creator, Serge Diaghilev, little more than three months after the first performance of *Le Bal*. A.A.

THE PRODIGAL SON *(Le Fils Prodigue)*
Ballet in three scenes. Choreography by George Balanchine. Music by Sergei Prokoviev. Sets and costumes by Georges Renault. Paris, Théâtre Sarah Bernhardt, May 21, 1929. Diaghilev's Russian Ballet. Principal dancers: Serge Lifar (the Prodigal Son), Felia Dubrovska, Michael Fedorov, Leon Woizikovsky, Anton Dolin.

SYNOPSIS. Scene I: the departure of the Prodigal Son. We are in biblical times. The young man prepares to leave home. Two friends wait for him, while his two sisters look sadly on. The young man is cheerful, happy in the expectation of great adventures. His father tries to detain him, but is met with an attitude of defiance. Once he and his friends have left, the father and his two daughters return to their tent. Scene II: a distant land. A decked table stands beneath a spreading canopy, and around it sits a group of strange bald revellers who play at fantastic games of chance. The son enters with his companions and tries to make friends with the strange men, who at first seem unwilling. Spurred on by his two companions, the youth offers them wine, and the situation suddenly changes. Now they all make much of him and all is merry comradeship. At that moment the Siren enters dressed in a red tunic, a tall hat, and velvet coat. The young man is attracted to her and she – in a scene of increasing debauchery – uses all her subtle powers of seduction. In the end the false friends, the gamblers, and the Siren rob him of all he has. Despairing, he leaves them. The Siren rejoins the others, the table is transformed into a boat, and they all sail off into the darkness. Scene III: the return. The scene is the same as the first. The Prodigal Son, ragged and exhausted, drags himself to the tent and there falls unconscious. His sisters pick him up. He asks forgiveness of his father, who wraps him in his cloak as if he were a baby.

■ Inspired by the Old Testament, *The Prodigal Son* turned out to be a ballet of the expressionist type, loaded with the symbolism of Russian myth. The grotesque element, to which the Prokoviev music is marvellously suited, prevails over the sacred: while the beginning and end keep fairly closely to the biblical story, the middle part is essentially a magical *divertissement* tinged with exoticism. The Siren and the gamblers, who form a sinister, brutish world like a creature that disintegrates and reassembles itself and reveals primitive instincts, are part of a fantasy that has its roots in folklore (the gluttony, the bald, clownish beings, the thefts and seductions of the Siren, the suggestion of a sea voyage). That world interlocks seamlessly with the parable of sin and pardon, because the theme of the repentant son is seen in a dramatic light as an adventure story. The spirit of the ballet – which is one of the most expressionistic Balanchine ever devised – is provocatively violent and sensational. It is also a typically masculine ballet, assembled round the *grand pas de deux* by the young man and the Siren, far removed from any classical model. Prokoviev's vitality contributed a grand musical dynamism, translated by Balanchine into a choreography which, seen again after many years and very different experiences, still communicates its original power. A modernized version in a contemporary setting was presented at the Scala by Mario Pistoni on December 21, 1962, with sets and costumes by Emanuele Luzzati.
M.P.

Musafar Burkanov and Malika Sabirova (in the background) in The Flames of Paris, *Rome, October 13, 1967.*

A scene from the ballet Persephone, *here with choreography by Margherita Wallmann.*

THE WALTZ *(La Valse)*

Ballet (choreographic poem) in one scene. Choreography by Bronislava Nijinska. Music by Maurice Ravel. Set and costumes by Alexandre Benois. Paris, Opéra, May 23, 1929. Ida Rubinstein's Ballet Company. Principal dancers: Ida Rubinstein (a lady), Anatole Vilzak (a gentleman).

SYNOPSIS. The scene represents a sumptuous ballroom of the Second Empire. In the background, behind the parted draperies, a second ballroom can be seen. The first is almost deserted except for two or three ladies sitting on a divan, and another seated opposite them with the master of ceremonies bowing before her. The ladies rise and begin to waltz with their military escorts. Other magnificently crinolined ladies with their attendant officers in dress uniform enter from a side door. All together or in small groups they dance in various formations, creating an effective and original counterpoint with the dancers in the further ballroom, attempting to produce in effect a homage to the Viennese waltz.

■ "Maurice Ravel originally intended the score of *La Valse*, a symphonic celebration of that dance, for Diaghilev's company. The impresario having abandoned the idea of any such ballet, a long dissension arose between him and the distinguished French composer, who had himself written a scenario for the projected work. When *La Valse* was finally produced in Paris for Ida Rubinstein, with choreography by Nijinska, the action followed the composer's scenario quite closely. ... Many years later choreographers have tried to interpret the music of *La Valse* in terms of dance, but have never succeeded in producing a completely satisfactory work. Perhaps Diaghilev was right after all." (Ferdinando Reyna, *Ballets*.)

OTHER VERSIONS. 1) Michael Fokine. Paris, Opéra, June 25, 1931. Ida Rubenstein Ballet Company. 2) Léonide Massine (his creation). Paris, Opéra-Comique, May 17, 1950. 3) Balanchine. New York, City Center, February 20, 1951. Principal dancers: Tanquil Le Clercq, Nicholas Magallanes, Francisco Moncion. New York City Ballet. 4) Janine Charrat. Festival of Santander, August 13, 1955. Janine Charrat's Ballet de France. 5) Harald Lander. Paris, Opéra, January 24, 1958. Principal dancers: Claire Motte, Alexandre Kalioujnj. 6) Frederick Ashton. Milan, Scala, February 1, 1958. Principal dancers: Vera Colombo, Mario Pistoni; repeated London, Covent Garden, March 10, 1959, with Norman Dixon, C. Beckley, J. Daryl, G. Burne. Royal Ballet.　　M.B.

CAPRIOL SUITE

One-act ballet. Choreography by Frederick Ashton. Music by Peter Warlock. Set and costumes by William Chappell. London, Lyric Theatre, February 25, 1930. Marie Rambert Dancers.

SYNOPSIS. In his book *Orchésographie* (1588), Arbeau, the first theorist of ballet, imagined a dialogue with a young beginner called Capriol. The subject was *contemporary* dance forms and the music that accompanied them. That was the starting point of Ashton's ballet, a review of sixteenth-century dances to music of the time, orchestrated by Peter Warlock as a *suite*. It begins with two couples performing a *basse danse*, followed by a pavane for two young men who offer gifts to a girl but are repulsed. The ballet comes to life with a brilliant court dance (*tordion*), then a lively quartet of young people in mock rivalry. The final ensemble elaborates various versions of the *branle* and ends in a gay mood with the company dancing around the principal couples.

■ This graceful resurrection of the past in typically English taste and inspired by Ashton's fastidious imagination is part of the current of thought that goes beyond the neoclassical to the sources of ballet and its courtly and popular components. Ashton's witty creation remained in the Sadler's Wells repertory until after World War II.   M.P.

THE FOOTBALLER *(Futbolist)*

Choreography by Lew Lashchilin. Music by V. Oransky. Scenario by V. Kurdiumov. Moscow, Bolshoi Theater, March 30, 1930.

SYNOPSIS. The ballet contrasts a footballer and his girl friend, two negative characters with subversive intentions, with two noble revolutionary characters. The contrast between the two worlds, in the period when modern art was still in favour in the Soviet Union, although politics and the idea of the "new man" predominated, was expressed even in the choice of music. Socialist (or revolutionary) music for the goodies, jazz and western light music for the baddies.

■ The ballet was very unfavourably received on its first appearance. Years later, on the same subject of football, Igor Moisseiev of the USSR Popular Dance Company created a brilliant and acrobatic sketch characterized by early 1930s modernity comically translated into the movements and spirit of the world of soccer. This entertainment remained in the repertory for many years and was always greeted with enthusiasm for its satirical spirit and concentration on fast and skillful dancing.   M.P.

THE SHAKERS

One-act ballet. Choreography by Doris Humphrey. Traditional American music. Costumes by Pauline Lawrence. New York, Broadway Theater, February 1, 1931. Humphrey Weidman Group.

SYNOPSIS. Ballet without a plot.

■ Inspired by the activity of an early nineteenth-century sect called the "Shakers," the ballet – one of Doris Humphrey's most successful – is a "folk" work representing the religious service in which men and women, on separate sides of the room, sought to exorcise the sins of the body by shaking dances.   M.P.

PRIMITIVE MYSTERIES

Ballet in three parts. Choreography by Martha Graham. Music by Louis Horst. Costumes and lighting by Martha Graham. New York, Craig Theater, February 2, 1931. Principal dancer: Martha Graham.

SYNOPSIS. It is a symbolic, sacred dance. The three parts are called *Hymn to the Virgin, Crucifixion, Hosanna*. In the first part twelve female dancers dressed in blue perform a series of movements, converging to form a sort of halo with their arms around the head of the Virgin, a central figure in white. In the second part a group of three plays the dominant role. In the third part the dancers advance in horizontal lines, finishing in a composition of ritual worship, prostrate around the Virgin, still represented by the leading dancer, who maintains her central position during all three parts. At the beginning all is done in silence, merging into a gradual crescendo of sound from the musical accompaniment consisting of flute, oboe, and piano.

■ *Primitive Mysteries* can be considered one of the masterpieces of modern dance. Here the qualities of innocence and reserve, first displayed in *Adolescence* (1929), reach their peak. It was the last work of Martha Graham devoted to an exclusively religious – Christian theme, showing the influence the cult exercised on the development of her artistic personality. The dancers who took part in these "mysteries" expressed themselves in a form of ritual so intense it might have been deemed pagan, but also surprisingly ingenuous in the clarity and simplicity with which it approached the mystery of the Virgin Birth, the Crucifixion, and the Resurrection. A striking instance of Martha Graham's genius was her success in conveying the rending grief of the Crucifixion without the help of sound or movement, merely by pressing her hands to the sides of her face. *Primitive Mysteries* was revived in 1964 after more than twenty-five years of oblivion.   C.M.C.

FAÇADE

One-act ballet. Choreography by Frederick Ashton. Music by William Walton. Sets and costumes by John Armstrong. London, Cambridge Theatre, April 26, 1931. Camargo Society. Principal dancers: Lydia Lopokova, Alicia Markova, Frederick Ashton.

SYNOPSIS. The ballet consists of nine *divertissements* of a more or less comic nature in a set representing a big

Victorian house. The numbers are as follows: *Scotch Rhapsody* for two ballerinas and one male dancer; *Yodelling Song* (later called *Tyrolienne*) with a milkmaid and three local suitors competing for her favours; a *Polka* solo for a ballerina; *Foxtrot* for two couples; *Waltz*, danced by four girls; *Popular Song* in music-hall style for two male dancers; *Country Dance* for a rather stupid country girl, a village boy, and a dandy; a *Tango* for a gigolo and a naive young girl; and a *Tarantella* as a finale for the whole cast.

■ Walton originally wrote the music used in this work as an accompaniment to verses composed and read by the poetess Edith Sitwell. Frederick Ashton, however, adopted it, without any reference to the poetry except the title, for his brilliantly clever ballet guying themes and types from tradition or the "Roaring Twenties" with a typically English ironic wit.   M.P.

THE GREEN TABLE *(Der grüne Tisch)*
Expressionist ballet (Dance of Death) in eight scenes. Choreography and scenario by Kurt Jooss. Music by Fritz Cohen. Costumes by Hein Heckroth. Paris, Théâtre des Champs Elysées, July 3, 1932. Jooss Ballet.

SYNOPSIS. A group of oldish men in ceremonial dress sits around a long green table: they are attending an international conference. Grotesquely masked, they argue and negotiate about political questions. The two factions at the table cannot agree on the subject under discussion. After a series of meaningless bows and compliments, the diplomats, who have known from the first moment how things would end, shoot each other across the table, and war breaks out, bringing with it all its attendant evils. Death, a character present throughout the ballet, claims his toll of victims; families are divided, soldiers leave for the war, there are scenes of battle, refugees, exile, brothels, then the return of the survivors, all in bitter counterpoint to the cynical peace conference. Once again the diplomats meet over the green table after having shot their revolvers threatingly into the air.

■ Created in the early 1930s from memories of the war and the Depression, presented just before Hitler came into power in Germany, Jooss's ballet proved all too prophetic. The plot, couched in expressionist terms according to the best German traditions, was bloodcurdling, and reopened wounds that were barely healed. Like Alban Berg with *Wozzeck*, Kurt Jooss showed himself to be sensitive to the suffering of ordinary people, and launched a violent indictment against the cynicism and violence of power. The deceit of discussions between the powers, the cruelty derived from it, indifference to the feelings of the individual, resulted in disasters that would forever be repeated – at least until the people developed a greater awareness and seized the revolver from the hands of the diplomats. Jooss, following in the footsteps of Laban as an exponent of free dance, was forced into exile and set up his headquarters at Dartington Hall in England. After World War II he was still able to present his most famous ballet, which had lost nothing of the punch it carried in the 1930s. The choreography is naturally hard-edged and typified by brutally expressive movement. The Jooss school of dance was probably no stranger to the experiments of the German political theater, nourished by antiwar polemics; the opposite pole to Teutonic power-hunger. *The Green Table* enjoyed enormous success in the west and brought the choreographer renown and a success never quite repeated by his later works. Kurt Jooss's German career, cut short by Nazism and the war, never got completely back into its stride, either because of the decadence of expressionism, or because new movements arose capable of representing the suffering and sorrow of new generations.   M.P.

THE FLAMES OF PARIS *(Plamya Paricha)*
Ballet in four acts and five scenes. Choreography by Vassili Vainonen. Music by Boris Asafiev. Scenario N. Volkov and D. Dmitriev. Leningrad, Kirov Theater, November 7, 1932. Principal dancers: Vaktang Chabukiani, Nina Anisimova, Olga Jordan, and Galina Ulanova.

SYNOPSIS. The ballet presents a huge historical panorama bringing to life some episodes in the French Revolution, especially the explosion of popular indignation at social injustices, and the taking of the Bastille. The protagonist is the People, an anonymous crowd of revolutionaries, but within that framework two contrasting female characters stand out, that of Jeanne, the heroine of the people, and the actress, Mireille de Poitiers, who takes pride in her individuality.

■ The ballet, made to celebrate the fifteenth anniversary of the October Revolution, is recognized today as of historical significance because it started a new trend in Soviet ballet. That is to say, *The Flames of Paris* was the first of the heroic ballets glorifying the people, put forward as an alternative to Tchaikovsky's fairy tales. The repertory of such works was later enriched with other important ballets, such as *The Fountain of Bakhchisaray* by the same Asafiev, *Laurentia* by Alexander Krein, and finally *Spartacus*.   P.C.

THE PORTENTS *(Les Présages)*
Choreographic symphony in four parts. Subject and choreography by Léonide Massine. Music by Piotr Ilych Tchaikovsky. Sets and costumes by André Masson. Monte Carlo, Opera House, April 13, 1933. Ballets Russes de Monte Carlo. Principal dancers: Nina Verchinina (Action), Natalia Branitska and Nina Tarakanova (the Temptations), Irina Baronova (Passion), David Lichine (the Hero), Leon Woizikovsky (Fate), Tatiana Riabouchinska (Frivolity).

SYNOPSIS. The ballet portrays man's struggle with his fate. In the backcloth painted with an abstract design of red, green, yellow, mauve, and brown, one can vaguely discern a sinister mask among shooting stars and

A moment in the ballet Serenade *danced by The American Ballet.*

tongues of flame. Part I: *Action*: life with its temptations, desires, and distractions. Part II: *Passion*: torn between Sacred and Profane Love, two lovers finally drive away the sinister, batlike figure of Fate. Part III: *Frivolity*: a party dominated by joyous Frivolity. Part IV: *War:* Fate inspires men with a thirst for battle and glory; peace returns at last, celebrated by men and women in a joyful and triumphal dance around the Hero.

■ This was the first example of a symphonic ballet in Léonide Massine's versatile creative career. Influenced by the central European type of modern dance, which in some of its less strictly expressionist work aimed at the interpretation in movement of great music not originally intended for dancing, Massine sought to express symphonic scores in choreography for soloists and *corps de ballet*, with results generally judged to be masterly but too cerebral and schematic. Nevertheless, the plastic and dynamic composition of his work was often brilliant, and sufficient in itself without any need for narrative or allegorical meaning. So it was with *Les Présages*, a choreographic symphony to parallel Tchaikovsky's *Fifth*, in which not only the philosophical and poetic content and the success of the stage presentation were recognized, but also the purely balletic values of Massine's new departure and the importance of an experiment, favourably regarded by Bruno Walter among others, intended to gauge the possibilities of matching "great" music with ballet.   A.A.

THE SEVEN DEADLY SINS (*Die sieben Todsünden der Kleinbürger*)
One-act ballet with singing. Choreography by George Balanchine. Music by Kurt Weill. Scenario by Bertolt Brecht. Paris, Théâtre des Champs Elysées, June 7, 1933. George Balanchine's Ballets 1933. Principal performers: Lotte Lenya, Tilly Losch.

SYNOPSIS. The action takes place in the United States and starts in Louisiana. The leading character is duplicated: Anna I, reasonable and practical; Anna II, beautiful and a bit crazy. She (or they) tours the States with the object of making money to build a house for herself and her family. Anna I sings (the narrator's voice); Anna II, who dances, is the mirror image of the former. They are sisters, but they are also two aspects of the same personality. The ballet begins with a prologue in which Anna I explains the why and wherefore of the journey on which she is setting out, and describes the characters of the sisters I and II. The Relations, a vocal quartet (two tenors, one baritone, one bass) are gathered on a part of the stage, where they lament Anna's laziness. Scene I: *Sloth*: Anna I photographs Anna II. The latter compromises various men, who pay her blackmail money. Scene II: *Pride*: Anna II works as a dancer in a Memphis cabaret. Anna I warns her not to believe in her act and to renounce pride. Scene III: *Anger*: Anna II is now working as a film extra in Los Angeles, and is indignant at the cruelty that goes on. Anna I tells her that open disapproval of injustice will be met with disapproval. Anna II must put up with it. Scene IV: *Greed*: Anna II is an acrobatic dancer in Philadelphia. She has to keep to a strict diet or she will lose her job, while the others can eat as much as they like. Scene V: *Lust*: in Boston Anna II is loved by a rich man, but she is in love with a young one. Anna I convinces her that what counts is only pleasure and the money that comes from it. Scene VI: *Avarice*: in Baltimore Anna II avoids all generous actions in order to pile up money. Scene VII: *Envy*: Anna II, now in San Francisco, is consumed with envy of other women, but Anna I restates her principles regarding beauty that passes and the price the others will have to pay for possessing it. Epilogue: after seven years' absence, having seen seven cities and succumbed to all the seven deadly sins, Anna I and II go home to Louisiana with money for the house. The hypocritical relations are pleased, even though, for Anna II, the moral cost of the venture has been heavy indeed.

■ *The Seven Deadly Sins* was the last work of the Brecht–Weill collaboration and, after *The Threepenny Opera* (*Dreigröschen Oper*), the most popular. Balanchine met Weill in 1933 in Paris, where the composer, like so many other democratically minded artists, had taken refuge from national socialism, and commissioned him to write the music for a work to be produced by his very new company, *Ballets 1933*. Weill succeeded in bringing Brecht into the venture, and the strange ballet was a success, running for several weeks. Balanchine revived *The Seven Deadly Sins* at the New York City Center in 1958, still employing Lotte Lenya as the singer but with the dancer Allegra Kent in place of Tilly

Scene from the fourth act of The Fountain of Bakhchisaray, *danced by the Bolshoi Ballet Company.*

Losch, and stage designs by Rouben Ter-Arutunian. The choreographer adhered to the original production in many respects, but gave it new life. It is not a simple ballet. It proceeds along different artistic levels, song and dance following their parallel but distinct ways. As Brecht intended, it contained a moral: "to make money one has to sell oneself as merchandise" was the text with which the author wanted to castigate capitalist society typified by its most outstanding example, the United States. It is a cruel story, in which the woman is seen as an object for pleasure and money, and in which the faults of the middle class are mercilessly attacked. The world that the various scenes depict is hard and acquisitive; the only thing that counts is money-power, in the face of which any compromise is acceptable. The clear-sighted toughness of Anna I stifles all Anna II's attempts to escape, calling to mind the conditions of the 1930s with their terrible implications. A typical product of expressionism, the ballet was underpinned by an extremely clever score, adapting itself to suit each situation without losing its quality. Ballroom tunes, choral music, fugues, songs are Weill at his most incisive and inspired. The story and atmosphere are basically Germanic, in spite of the ballet's American background. America is represented as the forerunner of an immoral Europe to come, the mirror of our sins. Yet, a bitter moral can be retrieved from its corruptness — that of redemption. **M.P.**

LES RENDEZ-VOUS

Divertissement *in one act. Choreography by Frederick Ashton. Music by François Auber arranged by Constant Lambert. Set and costumes by William Chappell. London, Sadler's Wells Theatre, December 5, 1933. Principal dancers: Alicia Markova, Stanislas Idzikovsky, Ninette de Valois, Robert Helpmann.*

SYNOPSIS. In a park various couples meet, dance, and express their feelings and their joy. A ballet without a plot.

■ It is a brilliant ballet in Ashton's individual style and very much in the English taste that delights in assembling diverse couples in a striking series of meetings, ceremonies, combinations of dances for two, three, or four, and virtuoso variations. With his acute visual sense, Ashton reproduces the spirit of the 1930s, with the dancers dressed in white, and not without a little irony. He offered his amazing company every technical opportunity of using their skill, agility, and happy inspiration to express this modern *divertissement*. The music he selected was Auber's *Enfant prodigue*, a choice that betrayed his fundamental romanticism. **M.P.**

PERSEPHONE

Balletic opera in three parts. Choreography by Kurt Jooss. Music by Igor Stravinsky. Scenario by André Gide. Set and costumes by André Barsacq. Paris, Opéra, April 30, 1934. Ida Rubinstein Ballet Company. Principal dancer: Ida Rubinstein.

SYNOPSIS. Part I. *The Rape of Persephone*: the goddess of fertility is destined for Pluto, god of the Underworld. The nymphs warn her not to pick the narcissus, sacred to Pluto. Thoughtlessly she does so, and is seized by the King of Hades. Part II: *Persephone in the Underworld*: she is now the Queen of shades and slumbers with a narcissus on her breast. Waking, she asks where she is, longs for the spring, and remembers her earthly husband, Demophöon. Life returns to her. Part III: *Persephone Reborn*: the young goddess is restored to her mother Demeter and to Demophöon. Spring returns to the world. But she knows that her fate lies in her empire of shadows, which suffers without her. One mission done, she must perform another. Mercury shows her the way. So that the spring can be born again – Gide puts the words into Eumolpus's mouth – the seed sown must consent to die in the earth, to reappear like blades of gold flashing in tomorrow's sun.

■ Described by Stravinsky as an opera, *Persephone* is in fact a mixed entertainment, blending song, narration, and dance. It was commissioned by Ida Rubinstein in 1933 and presented together with two ballets by Fokine, *La Valse* and *Diane de Poitiers*. While the title role is usually played by a dancer or actress, the part of the "historical" Eumolpus is sung, there are sung chorals, and the dancing is assigned to emblematic or human characters drawn from imagination or memory.

OTHER VERSIONS. 1) Frederick Ashton. London, Covent Garden, December 12, 1961. The part of Persephone danced by Svetlana Beriosova. 2) Margherita Wallmann (director). Rome, Opera House, April 1956. Principal dancer; Ludmilla Tcherina. The same director-choreographer, to whom we owe the revival of opera at Salzburg, put on *Persephone* again at the Scala on March 10, 1965, with the French actress Annie Girardot as the protagonist and sets and costumes designed by Enrico d'Assia. **M.P.**

THE FOUNTAIN OF BAKHCHISARAY (Bakhcisarajsky Fontan)

Ballet in four acts. Choreography by Rotislav Zakharov. Music by Boris Asafiev. Scenario by Volkov from a poem by Pushkin. Sets by Kodasevic. Leningrad, Kirov Theater, September 28, 1934. Galina Ulanova danced the leading part at the Bolshoi Theater, Moscow, in the same year.

SYNOPSIS. Act I: in a Polish castle Prince Pototsky is celebrating the birthday of his daughter Maria, who is in love with the young noble, Vaslav. The ball is interrupted by invading Tartars, who overcome the Poles. Vaslav springs to the defense of Maria, but the Tartar chief, Gierey, takes him by surprise and strikes him dead. Gierey falls in love with the girl and bears her off. Act II: at Bakhchisaray, in the Khan's harem. Gierey's wives, including his favourite Zarema, await their husband's return. He arrives with poor Maria, whose thoughts are all for Vaslav. Gierey rejects the embrace of Zarema, who is mocked by the other women. Act III:

in the room which she has been granted, Maria plays the harp given her by Vaslav. Gierey enters and offers her his love, but is given to understand that she can never return it, and goes away. Maria dreams of the past. Zarema now enters and begs Maria to give her back her husband. Surprised by Gierey's return, Zarema stabs her rival to death. The Khan threatens to kill her, but sees she is happy to die at his hand and orders her to be taken away by the guard. Act IV: in spite of the continued victories reported by his troops, the Khan is sad. Zarema is sentenced to die. In front of the fountain he has had built in memory of his hopeless love, the Tartar chief waits for death.

■ Like *The Flames of Paris*, this work takes an important place among modern Soviet ballets, because it created an absolutely new type, that is to say, a drama that was at once lyrical and psychological, although based on a classic subject.

OTHER VERSIONS. *The Fountain of Bakhchisaray*, so well known in the Soviet Union, has seldom been attempted outside its boundaries. In its own country it has been performed by some of the greatest Russian dancers. Apart from the brilliant interpretation by Ulanova, Maia Plisetskaia danced the leading part very successfully in Moscow's Bolshoi Theater version, which opened on March 9, 1948, and was reproduced in a Soviet film devoted to ballet and called *Masterpieces of Russian Dance*.   P.C.

SERENADE

Classical ballet in four parts. Choreography by George Balanchine. Music by P. I. Tchaikovsky. Costumes by Jean Lurçat. First public performance: Hartford, Connecticut, Avery Memorial Theater, December 6, 1934. American Ballet Company School. Principal dancers: Kathryn Mullowney, Heidi Vossler, Charles Laskey.

SYNOPSIS. An abstract ballet which "tells its story musically and choreographically without any extraneous narrative," but suggesting "various human emotions and situations." First movement: dancers posed in intersecting rows remain still in the semidarkness. As the lights brighten they dance, following a soloist, only to return to their original positions. One dancer arrives late and moves to her place among the others, but they move away, leaving her alone. A boy enters and approaches her. Second movement: a waltz danced by the pair, later joined by the rest of the dancers. Third movement (the fourth of the music score): five dancers left on the stage perform a lively measure to a Russian theme. Enter a boy, who dances with one of them. She falls to the ground and remains there while the rest of the group leave. Fourth movement (the third of the original score): the girl abandoned on the ground is approached by a second boy, guided by another ballerina, who propels

Robert Helpmann in the leading role in The Rake's Progress, *a ballet by Ninette de Valois.*

him forward, holding her hands over his eyes. He helps the first dancer to rise and dances with both of them, as if uncertain which to choose. At last the one who led him there takes him for herself, while the other girl is left alone again. The rest of the dancers return with three boys who lift the sad heroine straight up above their shoulders and carry her off in a slow procession, her arms open wide.

■ In addition to the poetic magic and classical lucidity of the choreography that make *Serenade* one of the masterpieces of modern dance, it has a historical interest as the first stone in the great edifice of American ballet, founded as it is on the creative and organizational work of George Balanchine. The choreographer himself writes with admirable simplicity in his *Complete Stories of the Great Ballets*, "*Serenade* was the first ballet I made in the United States. A little while after my arrival in America, Lincoln Kirstein, Edward M. Warburg, and I opened the School of American Ballet in New York. Among the courses there was an evening class for theatrical ballet technique. ... *Serenade* grew from those lessons. It seemed to me best for the students to dance something new, something unfamiliar to them. I chose Tchaikovsky's *Serenade*. On the first evening the class consisted of seventeen girls and no boys. I arranged them in diagonal lines and decided to begin with arm movements only, as if doing exercises. That was the start of *Serenade*. At the second lesson there were only nine girls, at the third six. I interpreted the music bit by bit with whatever pupils I had at my disposal at the moment. Boys began to come to the class and I added them to the dance scheme. Once, when the girls were running off the area we used as a stage, one of them fell and began to cry. I told the pianist to carry on and include the incident in the ballet. Another day a girl arrived late for class and I kept that in too." He followed the line of Tchaikovsky's *Serenade for Strings in C major*, op.48, a romantic tribute to Mozart's classical universe, and adhered to the vague thematic progression typical of such "romantic abstractions," producing a work without narrative but with a certain content of pure sentiment. Unimpeachable in style and technique, Balanchine's choreography nevertheless expressed the poetry inherent in his very personal brand of classicism. The rarefied atmosphere of *Serenade* extended to the austerity of the stage design: dancers in simple blue costumes against a blue cyclorama. After being privately performed in White Plains on June 9, 1934, the ballet was shown to the public, and later had its official opening on March 1, 1935, at the Adelphi Theater, New York, with the American Ballet Company, to which Balanchine's school had finally given birth. *Serenade* was gradually perfected by its choreographer until it was definitively transferred to the repertory of the New York City Ballet on October 18, 1948, with costumes designed by Barbara Karinska. Since then it has been constantly performed up to the present day in New York and the rest of the world, and revived by, among others, the Monte Carlo Ballet (1940), the Paris Opéra (1947), the Royal Danish Ballet (1957), the Scala, Milan (1960), and the Royal Ballet (1964), etc.   A.A.

THE RAKE'S PROGRESS

Dramatic ballet in six scenes. Choreography by Ninette de Valois. Music and scenario by Gavin Gordon. Scenery and costumes by Rex Whistler. London, Sadler's Wells Theatre, May 20, 1935. Principal dancers: Walter Gore, Alicia Markova.

SYNOPSIS. Scene I: London in the eighteenth century. An elegant apartment. The Rake, who has newly inherited a fortune, is trying on a suit, receiving news of his horses, practicing with his fencing-master, and taking a dancing lesson. An elderly woman comes in and accuses him of having seduced her daughter while in his service. He gives the mother some money, while the girl stands by in deep embarrassment. Scene II: a room with a bed and card table, where the Rake and his friends amuse themselves with ladies of the town. A friend of the Rake enters, followed by the Rake himself. Amid general merrymaking there is a hint of striptease, a song, heavy drinking, and a general air of vice and luxury. Scene III: the Rake is pursued by his creditors but is saved by the girl he has betrayed, who pays his debts with her savings. Scene IV: the Rake, now impoverished, is in a shady gaming house where he hopes to retrieve his fortune. Instead, he loses everything and finds himself facing a miserable reality. Scene V: the betrayed girl dances alone before the act drop, hoping the Rake will be freed from the debtor's prison. Scene VI: the Rake's end approaches inexorably. He is now in the madhouse among dangerous lunatics. He tries in vain to escape, and repulses the girl who comes to find him. At last, having been laughed at by some elegant visitors, he dies in an attack of hysteria. The girl weeps for him.

■ Ninette de Valois's ballet is based on the series of paintings by William Hogarth entitled *The Rake's Progress* (which was later to inspire an opera by Stravinsky). With cruel realism, Hogarth traced the course of a character symbolically named Rakewell from riches to ruin and madness. The romantic presence of the betrayed girl relieves the dark outlook and stands out against the cynicism of the society in which the protagonist strives in vain to survive. The choreographer, with her excellent moments of humour and satire, owes something to Jooss and Börlin, and has a feeling for eighteenth-century England (especially in relation to the novels and social criticism of the period). The production was a great success and is still occasionally revived at Sadler's Wells. Ninette de Valois, whose best ballet this is, has contributed enormously to the rebirth of British ballet, using her experience with the school of Diaghilev-Fokine and the European modern dance movement to great advantage. She was also a great organizer who has fostered many new talents in the world of ballet. The music is composed in eighteenth-century style in harmony with the period in which the story is set.   M.P.

Serge Lifar during a rehearsal of Icare, *revived in 1962 with Attilio Labis. The backcloth is by Picasso.*

ICARUS (Icare)

Ballet (choreographic legend) in one act. Choreography and subject by Serge Lifar. Rhythms by Serge Lifar, orchestrated by J. E. Szyfer. Set and costumes by Paul R. Larthe. Paris, Opéra, July 9, 1935. Principal dancers: Serge Lifar (Icarus), Lucien Legrand (Daedalus), Hughetti, Barban Didion, Grellier, Efimov, Domansky, Bozzoni, Guylaine.

SYNOPSIS. Amid the jeers and curiosity of a group of young men, Icarus attaches to his arms the wings contrived by his father Daedalus, who urges him to attempt to fly. After several unsuccessful attempts, the youth rises into the air. Intoxicated by the joy of flight, he mounts towards the sun, while his father and the others follow him anxiously with their eyes. Then the wings fall off and he crashes to the ground.

■ As well as being an outstanding dancer and choreographer, Serge Lifar was a passionate theorist and experimenter who had been trained in the forward-looking artistic atmosphere of Diaghilev's Ballet Company. His appointment as director of dancing at the Paris Opéra came at a time when for over thirty years its ballet had been in a state of decadence, considered by Lifar to be due to the subordination of choreography to the other arts, especially music. The idea of the creative independence of dance as an art with its own internal structural and expressive laws was upheld by him in theory in his *Manifeste du Chorégraphe* of 1935, and in practice in his ballet *Icare* of the same year. Lifar put his view very clearly in *La Danse*: "In my *Manifeste du Chorégraphe* I said that ballet *can* exist without music. I never maintained that it *should*, but in *Icare* I did in fact prove it, for the percussion orchestra that accompanies the ballet does not produce music but rhythm in an almost pure state, a rhythm that belongs equally to music and dance, because it is their basis, their first and common basis. . . . Music, which makes my whole being vibrate, inspires me with ideas and feelings of dance, yet strangles my creativeness in dance, forces me to cut short movements in full flight or unduly stretch out an idea that has already been fully expressed from the dance point of view. Our two musics (for dancing, too, is a form of music) are not in unison. I admit to a decided preference for musical ballet, but that did not prevent me from making *Icare* without music. In short, I wanted to emphasize the internal melodic possibilities of the dance." To rhythms invented by himself, the work's sole creator, the simple story of the myth was narrated in purely choreographic terms, which rendered in a clearly articulated language of classical dance all its dramatic and symbolic content. The manner in which Lifar designed a moving, three-dimensional equivalent of that content was typical of his art. As a dancer the character of Icarus became one of his favourite parts, performed by him for nearly twenty years.   A.A.

THE LILAC GARDEN

One-act ballet. Choreography by Antony Tudor. Music by Ernest Chausson. Set and costumes by Hugh Steven-son. London, Mercury Theatre, January 26, 1936. Ballet Rambert. Principal dancers: Antony Tudor, Maude Lloyd, Hugh Laing, Peggy van Praagh.

SYNOPSIS. In late Victorian days, Caroline, a young woman, gives a party for her friends and relations on the eve of marrying a man she does not love. When she meets her fiancé in the lilac garden, it is clear that they are almost strangers to one another. The alternating appearances of the man she really loves and of her future husband's ex-mistress give life to the complicated interplay of the ballet, which ends with Caroline's acceptance of her destiny as a married woman.

■ *The Lilac Garden* ranks as a very beautiful psychological ballet and has won great popularity in Europe and America. Vaguely suggested by Proust's *Recherche*, its romanticism underlined by Chausson's *Poème* for violin and orchestra, the ballet conveys an atmosphere of high intensity, mixing up reality with the characters' memories. Tudor took particular pains with the ambience and lighting of this purely choreographic yet dramatic ballet. He was praised especially for his understanding of feminine psychology and feeling. The choreographic style is mainly classical, but Tudor was perpetually torn between the traditional and the new. In this ballet he broke away from tradition, expressing a desire to contravene the rules of good society and its conventions by means of unusual lifts and attitudes. The story, frank for the period portrayed, is unfolded with perfect clarity, in spite of the intricate feelings of the four characters involved. The impossibility of free choice for Caroline is explained by the situation in which her environment has placed her, with its dizzying round of events and the interruptions by the party guests.   M.P.

THE LOVE OF THE THREE ORANGES (L'Amore delle Tre Melarance)

Ballet in nine scenes. Choreography by Michael Fokine. Music by Giulio Cesare Sonzogno. Scenario by Renato Simoni (from Carlo Gozzi). Sets and costumes by Nicola Benois. Milan, Scala, February 1, 1936. Principal dancers: Nives Poli (Ninetta), Gennaro Corbo (the Prince), Regina Colombo (the girls in the other two oranges), Carletto Thieben (the Witch).

SYNOPSIS. Surrounded by the King and his court stands the sad Prince, to whose face the magician Celio is trying in vain to bring a smile. In a dream the Prince sees a lovely girl, abducted by a wicked witch and made to live in an orange. He falls in love with the dream girl and sets off to look for her. Armed with a magic sword, the Prince succeeds in climbing over an enormously high fence inside which he finds three oranges growing. Out of them step three girls, but only the last of them, his beloved Princess Ninetta, is saved from dying of thirst by the water that springs up at the touch of his magic sword. Left alone while waiting for her loved one, Ninetta is turned into a dove by the Witch, who takes her place, so that when the Prince comes back he is forced to honour his promise by marrying her. While the

A dancer from the Royal Ballet, Covent Garden, in
Jeu de Cartes *at Nervi, 1976.*

Liszt. Scenario by Constant Lambert. Sets and costumes by Cecil Beaton. London, Sadler's Wells Theatre, February 11, 1936. Principal dancers: Margot Fonteyn, Robert Helpmann.

SYNOPSIS. Prologue: the poet's large and mysterious study late at night. The poet is unhappy because the poem he is writing does not go well; he needs some fresh stimulus. The windows light up and in each one he perceives a vision . . . a beautiful woman in a balldress, a hussar, a monk. He is at once attracted to the woman and she returns his sentiments. The apparitions vanish. The poet has found his inspiration but is too disturbed to concentrate. He takes a sleeping draught and falls asleep. Scene I: a ballroom. The poet weaves his way among the dancing couples but they seem unaware of his presence. The lady of the vision enters and the others all dance with her. Suddenly he finds her in his arms, but she leaves him to follow the hussar. Left in the empty ballroom, the poet is in despair. Scene II: a snow-clad forest. The poet, dreaming of his lady, sees a funeral procession approach, led by the monk he saw in the window. Uncovering the figure on the bier, he finds it is his visionary love. The procession winds on, while he sinks weeping to the ground. Scene III: in a cavern, magic rites are in progress. The poet enters and is struck with horror when the lady reappears, now become monstrously ugly. She pursues him; he faints with terror. At that moment the apparition's face grows beautiful again. Epilogue: once more in his study, the poet awakes, disturbed by his dream. Convinced that happiness is forever beyond his reach, he kills himself. The imaginary woman enters and mourns for him. Hooded figures bear the body away.

■ Based on the progammatic scheme of Berlioz's *Symphonie Fantastique*, the ballet (which actually uses music from Liszt's last period) is clearly romantic. Ashton is fascinated by the illusions of the imagination and uses them to construct a stylistically polished drama, but one without a true hero.   M.P.

wedding feast is being prepared in the enormous and chaotic royal kitchen, the dove flies in and hinders the cooks at their work. Then the Witch appears and chases the dove right to the top of the bell tower. Fortunately the Prince has recognized Ninetta even in her bird form and follows in hot pursuit, thus breaking the spell. At last the wedding is celebrated with great pomp.

■ Based on Carlo Gozzi's well-known fairy tale, as was also the far more famous opera by Prokofiev performed fifteen years earlier (although neither Simoni nor Sonzogno could yet have known of it directly), *The Love of the Three Oranges* marks an isolated reappearance at La Scala, twenty years later, of Michael Fokine, the truly great reformer of modern ballet. Although keeping in part to a staging made as unprovocative as possible because of the now hardened arteries of balletic tradition at the Scala – and in Italy as a whole – this late work of Fokine's was one of the few significant ballets performed at the Scala during those years. Fokine was seeking a compromise between that tradition and the new discoveries of the Diaghilev era.   A.A.

APPARITIONS
Ballet in three scenes with prologue and epilogue. Choreography by Frederick Ashton. Music by Franz

SYMPHONIE FANTASTIQUE
Choreographic symphony in five scenes. Choreography by Léonide Massine. Music and story line by Hector Berlioz. Sets and costumes by Christian Bérard. London, Covent Garden Opera House, July 24, 1936. Colonel de Basil's Russian Ballet. Principal dancers: Tamara Toumanova, Léonide Massine, Nina Verchinina, George Sorich.

SYNOPSIS. Having taken opium in a fit of despair, the Young Musician imagines he sees fleeting glimpses of the woman he loves, representing his image of the ideal. During a ball she eludes him. The scene changes to a lonely landscape of the Roman *campagna* where for a moment he tastes happiness among the beauties and simplicities of nature. He is transported to a witches' sabbath and goes through many vicissitudes, from which he emerges regenerated, bathed in the light of a mystic hope.

■ The subject of this celebrated ballet is almost exactly the same as the plot imagined by Berlioz for his *Symphonie Fantastique*, op. 14 (*"épisodes de la vie d'un artiste"*), of which the subdivision into five movements, each with its separate title, was faithfully followed by Massine when he divided his ballet into five scenes. Made at the height of Massine's creative career with the Monte Carlo Ballet, *Symphonie Fantastique* is generally considered his masterpiece in the category of symphonic ballet which he himself had invented (see *Les Présages*, page 215). Though there has been no lack of authoritative criticism of similar attempts at translating symphonic music into dance, it has been acknowledged that in this case there is a remarkable correspondence between Massine's ballet, in spite of its satirical spirit, and the fantastic romanticism of Berlioz's music, to say nothing of the richness of Massine's choreography in this masterly classical composition.   A.A.

DARK ELEGIES

*Ballet in two scenes. Choreography by Antony Tudor. Music by Gustav Mahler (*Kindertotenlieder*). Sets and costumes by Nadia Benois. London, Duchess Theatre, February 19, 1937. Ballet Rambert. Principal dancers: Dame Peggy van Praagh, Agnes de Mille, Maude Loyd, Antony Tudor.*

SYNOPSIS. To the music of Rückert's *Kindertotenlieder* (*Songs for Dead Children*), composed by Gustav Mahler. In the ballet we see a village, destroyed in some huge natural but unexplained disaster, where the inhabitants are mourning their dead, singly or in groups. In a tragic, devastated landscape a couple express their sorrow at the loss of their son.

■ The solo parts are composed in classical style, but the group choreography is influenced by folk dancing. The use of the human voice was, for the period, bold and innovatory. It was no late romantic ballet, but a work of psychological depth which has remained in the Rambert repertory to this day and is considered one of Tudor's masterpieces. According to Marie Rambert, the two scenes could be called Grief and Resignation. M.P.

THE CARD PARTY (Jeu de Cartes)

Ballet in "three hands." Choreography by George Balanchine. Music by Igor Stravinsky. Scenario by Igor Stravinsky and Malaieff. Sets and costumes by Irene Sharoff. New York, Metropolitan Opera House, April 27, 1937. American Ballet. Principal dancer: William Dollar.

SYNOPSIS. The first hand: the stage looks like a huge card table, on which fifteen dancers represent large poker cards. Among them is the Jolly Joker, who directs the game, thus showing up the powerlessness of the Kings and Queens. The second hand: with the help of the four Aces, the Joker vanquishes the Queens and makes fun of their appearance and behaviour. The third hand: a royal straight in hearts beats the Joker, who dis-

appears to make way for a triumph – followed, of course by a new game.

■ Some have claimed to find in this ballet a basic opposition to the idea of the devil as portrayed in *The Soldier's Story*. The Joker, unlike his folk-hero predecessor, is finally defeated, and the end at least appears to be a happy one. But by 1937 Stravinsky had long left the passions and the torments of youth behind him. And on the musical level, too, *Card Party* is nothing but a pleasant *divertissement* or even a market stall for secondhand goods. The occasion for this ballet was an enterprise of Balanchine, who wanted to devote a festival to his old friend Stravinsky, and felt that the festival should be distinguished by an absolutely new work. Stravinsky and Malaieff, a friend of his son, invented this poker ballet, with the intention, says Balanchine, "of showing how the highest cards can be defeated by the low ones. They seem all-powerful, but are in reality mere figureheads." However, a certain surrealist element in this clever and very novel ballet, with its musical quotations (a very clear one from Rossini's *Barber of Seville*), tells us of the state of existential disengagement – the phrase is Roman Vlad's – at which the Russian composer had arrived. The ballet's scheme of poker hands and play was expressed by Balanchine in virtuoso and noble dances. The leading part is obviously the Joker, and very similar characters can be found in some Russian ballets. Stravinsky's attempt to escape from his Russian roots was, perhaps, not so complete after all in this first American collaboration with the great choreographer and his organizing partner, Lincoln Kirstein.

OTHER VERSIONS. 1) Janine Charrat. Théâtre des Champs Elysées, Paris, 1945. Danced by Jean Babilée. 2) Luciana Novaro. Milan, Scala, March 7, 1959. Sets and costumes by Dino Buzzati. Scenario altered with the author's consent to award the final victory to the Joker. 3) John Cranko. Württemberg, State Theater, January 22, 1965. Sets and costumes by Dorothea Zippel.   M.P.

CHECKMATE

Ballet in prologue and one scene. Choreography by Ninette de Valois. Music by Arthur Bliss. Set and costumes by McKnight Kauffer. Paris, Théâtre des Champs Elysées, June 15, 1937. Sadler's Wells Ballet. Principal dancers: June Brae, Robert Helpmann, Pamela May, Harold Turner, William Chappell, Richard Ellis, Michael Somes, Frederick Ashton, Alan Carter, Margot Fonteyn.

SYNOPSIS. The stage is a chessboard on which the forces of Love and Death, represented by the red and black pieces, face each other in enmity. In the prologue we watch the moves of two armoured players seated at a small chess table. They personify Love and Death. Various pieces enter and stand on their squares. The all-powerful Black Queen penetrates the enemy lines. The Red Queen is captured by the Black Knights. A Red

A moment in the ballet Filling Station, *created and danced by Lew Christensen in 1938.*

Knight, torn between love for the Black Queen and loyalty to his King, is slain. Death leads the procession of victors and vanquished. Now the Red King is alone, trapped, facing the Black Queen. Black pieces block every avenue of escape. In spite of a proud and desperate last stand, the wretched King is defeated. Checkmate.

■ Ninette de Valois's tragic allegory of the eternal struggle between love and death is based on the game of chess. The violently rhythmic music by Arthur Bliss adds greatly to the effect. The ballet is broken up into various episodes, not all of great distinction. Its strong points lie in the finale and in the very powerful parts of the Red King and the Black Queen. In these the sense of desperation and inexorable fate rises to the level of epic drama. *Checkmate* was almost the last important ballet created by de Valois before the outbreak of war scattered so many of the company's dancers. The central idea (the game an allegory for death) was new; also, the cast contained many of the greatest English dancers, as can be seen from the program of the first performance. *Checkmate* was successfully revived after the war. M.P.

ALEXANDER THE GREAT (*Alexandre le Grande*)
Ballet in a prologue, three scenes, and an epilogue. Choreography and scenario by Serge Lifar. Music by Philippe Gaubert. Sets and costumes by Paul R. Larthe.

Paris, Opéra, June 21, 1937. Principal dancers: Serge Lifar (Alexander), Yvette Chauviré (a Jewess), Suzanne Lorcia (Queen of Babylon), Solange Schwarz (an Egyptian).

SYNOPSIS. Episodes in the life and legend of Alexander the Great. The hero sets out to conquer the world after having untied the Gordian knot to which an oracle had directed him. Having taken Jerusalem, Alexander treats the Jews in the Temple of Solomon with magnanimity, and takes as his wife the most beautiful daughter of Israel. Arriving in Egypt he is deified and carried in triumph by his troops. When he reaches Babylon he is welcomed to the palace of the Queen, who poisons him. Finally, Zeus appears to claim the hero as his son.

■ This "epic ballet" was among the most successful of Serge Lifar's experimental period, in the early years of his creative career, when he was full of enthusiasm for the choreographic theories he first applied in *Icarus* (see page 222) and included — at least in their explicit demonstrative function — *Song of Songs* (*Cantique des Cantiques*) of 1938. As he wrote in his *La Danse* (1965), "The ballet cycle of *Icarus, David Triumphant,* and *Alexander the Great* is the one to which I attribute the most importance and significance. Would Petipa have recognized the essential classical technique, albeit enriched and renovated, or would he have condemned it? ... What would certainly have surprised him is the

Veronica Tennant as Juliet in Cranko's version of
Romeo and Juliet.

total absence of mime in *any* of my ballets: the question of mime has simply not arisen for me. I have deliberately omitted it as a separate element and used it only as an integral part of the dancing." Indeed, the merit of *Alexander the Great* was a symphonic *suite* by Philippe its best in the variations composed by Lifar for himself in the title role, and in the three *pas de deux*, one in each scene, in which Solange Schwarz, Suzanne Lorcia, and above all the admirable Yvette Chauviré proved themselves to be, at Lifar's side, stars of the first magnitude. Another remarkable asset was the re-creation in classical form of the various ancient and exotic dances. It was this ballet that Lifar referred to especially in the chapter of his *Traité de Chorégraphie* that dealt with the stylization of historical dances. The music used for *Alexander the Great* was a symphonic *suite* by Philippe Gaubert entitled *Inscriptions pour les Portes de la Ville*.   A.A.

FRANCESCA DA RIMINI
Ballet in two scenes. Choreography by David Lichine. Music by Piotr Ilych Tchaikovsky. Scenario by David Lichine and Henry Clifford. Sets and costumes by Oliver Messel, London, Covent Garden Opera House, July 15, 1937. Principal dancers: Lubov Tchernicheva

(Francesca), Marc Platov (Gianciotto Malatesta), Paul Petrov (Paolo Malatesta), Chiara (Eleonora Marra), Tatiana Riabouchinska (Angelic Apparition), Alexandra Danilova (Guinevere), Roman Jasinsky (Lancelot).

SYNOPSIS. Scene I: the lords of Ravenna and Rimini, desirous of ending the conflict that has divided their realms for many years, ratify the peace treaty by arranging a marriage between the son of the first, Gianciotto, and the daughter of the second, Francesca. However, because he is physically so deformed, Gianciotto sends his handsome brother, Paolo, to wed her by proxy. Unfortunately, Francesca falls in love with the younger son, and when unexpectedly, she sees her legal husband she cannot conceal her horror. Told by Girolamo, the Malatesta's spy, of the love between Paolo and Francesca, Gianciotto, blind with fury, first threatens his wife, then drags her away in spite of a devoted attempt by her nurse Chiara to protect her charge by holding a crucifix between Francesca and the crippled husband, and notwithstanding the arrival of Paolo, who is held back by armed guards. Scene II: seated side by side beneath a pergola, Paolo and Francesca are reading the love story of Lancelot and Guinevere (conveyed by two dancers). The tale so affects them that they kiss passionately and abandon themselves to the ecstasy of their love, represented by the dancing figures of angelic musicians. Trumpets announce the return of Gianciotto. Seized by terror, Francesca persuades Paolo to hide on the terrace. Malatesta arrives and his evil dwarfs scamper about until they discover Paolo. In the duel between the brothers that ensues Paolo is killed and Francesca, crazed with grief, throws herself on the sword that killed her lover, falling dead at his side.

■ David Lichine (earlier Lichtenstein) studied under Lubov Egorova and Bronislava Nijinska before becoming *premier danseur* with Colonel de Basil's Russian Ballet Company. In 1933 Lichine began to establish himself as a choreographer, his greatest success being *Graduation Ball* (1940). *Francesca da Rimini* is based on the Fifth Canto of Dante's *Inferno*, depicting the Second Circle, in which carnal lovers are forever blown to and fro by pitiless winds. The accompanying music was Tchaikovsky's symphonic poem *Francesca da Rimini*, which had already inspired Fokine to compose a ballet of the same name for the Maryinsky Theater in St. Petersburg in 1915. The first scene is extremely dramatic, with the mimed parts beautifully in tune with the dancing, which faithfully reflects the emotions evoked by the music. Less happy, perhaps, is the beginning of the second scene, in which the love scenes are threatened by the grating, almost ridiculous, contrast between the angelic vision suggestive of fourteenth-century Sienese paintings and the dancing on point of those improbable angels who were ridiculous rather than celestial. In the finale mimed drama once more prevails, stressed by a group of dancers in the background, whose danced comments were intended to parallel the alternate chanting of the chorus in a Greek tragedy.

A duelling scene from Romeo and Juliet *performed by the Cullberg Ballet. Leonid Lavrovsky's ballet is here seen in a version by Birgit Cullberg.*

OTHER VERSIONS. Mario Pistoni. Sets by Luisa Spinatelli. Costumes by Enrico Job. Milan, Scala, May 13, 1965. Danced by Carla Fracchi and Mario Pistoni. G.S.

FILLING STATION

One-act ballet. Choreography by Lew Christensen. Music by Virgil Thompson. Scenario by Lincoln Kirstein. Sets and costumes by Paul Cadmus. Hartford, Connecticut, Avery Memorial Theater, January 6, 1938. Ballet Caravan. Principal dancers: Lew Christensen, Marie-Jeanne, Eric Hawkins, Michael Kidd, Todd Bolender, Eugene Loring.

SYNOPSIS. The scene is a filling station. Mac, who works there, is reading a book to relieve the boredom of the night. A motorist asks the way. Two truck drivers greet Mac and dance with him until they are interrupted by a policeman who reprimands them for having exceeded the speed limit. The motorist returns with his tiresome wife and complaining daughter. Then comes a tipsy couple from a nightclub. Everyone joins in a lively dance with the girl. The motorist comes back again and the girl from the club throws herself into his arms just as his wife reenters. At this point a gangster bursts into the gas station and takes all their money and jewels. Mac puts out the light; confusion reigns. Blinded by the beam of a flashlight, the gangster makes off. The nightclub girl dies. The policeman arrests the robber and the corpse is carried away. But, surprise, surprise, the girl is not dead after all. She says "Hello" to Mac, everyone leaves, and our young man goes back to his book.

■ A typically American ballet in its music, characters, and background, *Filling Station* unwinds like an adventure film, portraying situations familiar in the news reports of the New World. Its heroes are ordinary people of the working or middle classes: the contrast with classical European ballet is plain. Although the choreography is full of vitality and athleticism, it does not lack farcical interludes, or even moments of pathos, such as the dance for the young couple from the nightclub. *Filling Station* was successfully revived after World War II, by the New York City Ballet in 1953. M.P.

THE SEVENTH SYMPHONY (La Septième Symphonie)

One-act ballet. Subject and choreography by Léonide Massine. Music by Ludwig von Beethoven. Sets and costumes by Christian Bérard. Monte Carlo, Opera House, May 5, 1938. René Blum's Monte Carlo Ballet.

Above: The last scene of Romeo and Juliet *as danced by the Bolshoi Ballet. Opposite: Anneli Alhanko of the Royal Swedish Opera in* Romeo and Juliet.

Principal dancers: Frederick Franklin, Alicia Markova, Igor Youskevich, Nini Theilade, Natalia Krasovska.

SYNOPSIS. In the first movement the Spirit of Creation gives life to the water, the plants, the animals, and Man and Woman, who commit the first sin. The second reveals a scene of human sorrow, represented by the first dead youth, borne by a chorus of men and mourned by a chorus of women. The third movement leads us through the ethereal spaces to the serene bliss of Olympus. The fourth brings us down to earth, where a bacchanale ends in the destruction of humanity.

■ Wagner's opinion that Beethoven's *Seventh Symphony* should be an aoptheosis of the dance inspired Léonide Massine with the idea of creating his next symphonic ballet to that score (see *Les Présages*, page 215, and *Symphonie Fantastique*, page 223). *The Seventh Symphony* was one of the most mature and successful ventures of its kind. In it Massine rose above the abstract intellectual symbolism of his first "danced symphonies," giving the ballet a richer theatrical dimension free of the unyielding structural parallelism of choreo-

graphy and score typical of his earlier attempts; free also of the remaining traces of mime and a certain discontinuity of style that had persisted in them. The classical vocabulary on which his new ballet was firmly based revealed Massine's command of composition for *corps de ballet* and his creative imagination even in the purest academic dance.   A.A.

NOBILISSIMA VISIONE
Choreographic legend in six scenes. Choreography and scenario by Léonide Massine. Music by Paul Hindemith. Sets and costumes by Pavel Tchelitchev. London, Drury Lane Theatre, July 21, 1938. René Blum's Monte Carlo Ballet. Principal dancers: Léonide Massine, Nini Theilade, Jeannette Lauret, Frederick Franklin.

SYNOPSIS. The ballet tells the legend of St. Francis of Assisi from his youth in the paternal home to his conversion, and the traditional episodes of his dedicated life up to his mystic marriage with the lady Poverty.

■ This was Massine's first venture into religious ballet that was to lead to the committed mysticism of *Laudes*

Evangelii of 1952. After the narrative introduction it culminates in the "choreographic mysteries" of the final scenes, in which the mystic symbolism of the solo and group dancing, devoid of the emphasis on content of Massine's earlier works, is achieved with high imagination by the extremely advanced use of gesticulation with the hands and arms. *Nobilissima Visione* was revived several times by the René Blum Company, of which Massine was the principal choreographer and artistic consultant until 1942.   A.A.

LAURENTIA

Ballet in three acts. Choreography by Vaktang Chabukiani. Music by Aleksander Krein. Scenario by Eugen Mandelberg from the play Fuente Ovejuna *by Lope de Vega. Leningrad, Kirov Theater, March 22, 1939.*

SYNOPSIS. The background of the story is the struggle of the Spanish peasants against feudal tyranny and cruelty. Through the vicissitudes that befall the two leading characters, Laurentia and Frondoso, the ballet seizes on the drama of the moment when the peasants' discontent turns to insurrection.

OTHER VERSIONS. L. Lavrovsky. Moscow, Bolshoi Theater, February 19, 1956. Danced by Maia Plisetskaia.   P.C.

PAGANINI

Ballet in one act and three scenes. Choreography by Michael Fokine. Music by Sergei Rachmaninov. Subject by M. Fokine and S. Rachmaninov. Sets and costumes by Serge Sudeikine. London, Covent Garden, June 30, 1939. Principal dancers: Dmitri Rostov, Irina Baronova, Tatiana Riabouchinska.

SYNOPSIS. Scenes from the life of the legendary "satanic" violinist, Paganini.

■ This was one of Fokine's last creations, and not one of his best, although the London audience received it with a certain good will. The subject is treated in the manner of Massine's *Symphonie Fantastique*, or Ashton's *Apparitions*, in which a host of allegorical characters surround a hero living in the real world. Fokine's choreography is showy, sometimes to grotesque effect, as in Paganini's duel with his rivals, when he fences with his violin bow. Moreover, the music (*Rhapsody on a Theme by Paganini*) is too much in the style of Rachmaninov and does not blend well with the events.

OTHER VERSIONS. Leonid M. Lavrovsky. Sets by Ryndin. Moscow, Bolshoi Theater, April 7, 1960. Danced by Yaroslav Sekn as Paganini and Marina Kondratieva as the woman he loves.   C.M.C.

EVERY SOUL IS A CIRCUS

One-act ballet. Choreography by Martha Graham. Music by Paul Nordhoff. Set and lighting by Phillip Stapp. Costumes by Edythe Gilfond. New York, St. James Theater, December 27, 1939. Princiapl dancers: Martha Graham (the Woman), Eric Hawkins (the Ringmaster), Merce Cunningham (the Acrobat).

SYNOPSIS. In a circus are the Ringmaster, and Acrobat, and a frivolous little Woman who is flirting with the Acrobat until the Ringmaster intervenes to save her from the dangerous consequences of her behaviour. With piercing imagination, Martha Graham creates a split personality: the other half is a severely dressed woman who sits apart observing events. Here is an obvious analogy with the choreographer's private life in her dilemma of choice between two men (the Ringmaster and the Acrobat) and in showing herself weak enough to need someone to take care of her. Significant, too, is her final choice (the Ringmaster), evidence of the value she places on the position of head of a hierarchy (the Woman stops, curious, to consider the whip).

■ The title of *Every Soul is a Circus* is taken directly from a poem by Vachel Lindsay. It was the first ballet in which Graham tackled the form of typical American comedy, demonstrating that she was capable of working in a light vein. That is not to say that it was a frivolous work, for in it she showed a warmth that she had not hitherto possessed, and that allowed her to express herself freely, to act, and to enjoy herself. *Every Soul is a Circus* was Merce Cunningham's first appearance with the dance company.   C.M.C.

ROMEO AND JULIET

Ballet in four acts. Choreography by Leonid Lavrovsky. Music by Sergei Prokofiev. Scenario by Radlov, Piotrkovsky, Lavrovsky, and Prokofiev, after Shakespeare's tragedy. Sets and costumes by Peter Williams. Leningrad, Kirov Theater, January 11, 1940. Kirov Ballet. Principal dancers: Galina Ulanova (Juliet), Konstantin Sergeyev (Romeo), A. Lopukov (Mercutio), S. Karen (Tybalt). The "true" first night of this ballet took place on December 30, 1938 at Brno, danced by Vanja Psota and Zora Semberova to choreography by Psota, but it is more realistic to record the premiere of the Kirov version in Leningrad.

SYNOPSIS. Act I. Scene I: it is dawn and Romeo Montague is walking through the streets of Verona. The city awakens; a first skirmish between the feuding households of Montague and Capulet begins to spread but is interrupted by the arrival of the Prince. The hatred between the two families does not grow less, however. Scene II: Young Juliet Capulet is joking with her nurse, who is helping her dress for the ball. The magnificently dressed guests begin to arrive. Romeo with his friends Mercutio and Benvolio come to the ball uninvited, disguised by masks. There is a grand ceremonial dance. Juliet's parents arrange that a young gentleman, Paris, shall be her partner. As she dances, Romeo is enchanted with her grace, while she in turn is not indifferent to his attraction. Tybalt, Juliet's cousin, recognizes Romeo and wants to drive him out with violence, but Capulet intervenes to avoid a clash. The ball ends and everyone leaves. After a little while Juliet returns to look for something she has lost. Romeo reappears and love springs up between the two. There follow the balcony scene, promises, and farewells. Act II. Scene I: in the town square a popular festival is in progress. Amid the general merriment, Romeo, with Juliet in his thoughts, is teased by Mercutio. The nurse brings him a message and a ring from Juliet. Scene II: Romeo goes to Friar Lawrence's cell, where Juliet meets him. The friar unites them in matrimony. In front of a drop curtain a carnival procession goes by. Scene III: once more in the town square. In the midst of the festivities the opposing factions meet. Tybalt and Mercutio challenge one another, but Romeo parts them. Then Tybalt turns on Romeo, who does not accept his challenge. Tybalt, enraged, accuses Romeo of cowardice, upon which Mercutio attacks him and is basely run through with Tybalt's sword. Mercutio dies in his friend's arms, still jesting about life and the futility of power. At last Romeo attacks Tybalt and kills him. While the Capulets mourn for Tybalt, Benvolio drags Romeo from the scene. The young husband is exiled by the Prince. Act III. Scene I: Romeo has joined Juliet in her room for one night of love before his departure. In the morning the nurse comes to warn Juliet that her parents are coming to see her, accompanied by Count Paris. The Capulets tell Juliet that she is to marry him. In vain the girl pleads with them to change their minds. Desperate, she leaves for Friar Lawrence's cell. Scene II: the friar gives Juliet a potion that will make her appear dead: Romeo will come to her in the tomb and take her away. Scene III: Juliet pretends to accept marriage with Paris; preparations are made for the ceremony. Juliet drinks the potion and loses consciousness. Her mother and nurse try to wake her without success. General grief and consternation. Act IV: a funeral procession carries Juliet's body to the family tomb. Romeo, who has heard of her death, is in despair. Arriving at the tomb, he kills himself. She awakens and, finding him dead at her side, drives his dagger into her heart and is united with him in one last dying kiss.

■ Such was the original scenario of this famous ballet, which was subsequently enriched with various details and situations, almost always faithfully derived from the Shakespearian text. Strangely enough, this masterpiece of the twentieth century has not always had a smooth passage. It was commissioned from Prokofiev by the Moscow Bolshoi Theater in 1934, only a short while after the composer's return to his country. Gone were the days of bold experiment and avant-garde art. Now the aim was to enrich the Soviet ballet with a dramatic work that would bring back the splendours of the past and the golden age of Tchaikovsky. Prokofiev worked on the first draft of the scenario with Sergei Radlov, a scholar of English drama. It is known that the two considered changing the end so that the two lovers did not have to die, but the idea was dropped because the faithful Shakespearians of Moscow would not countenance any such betrayal of the original. The score was completed in the autumn of 1935, but various difficulties arose and the ballet was postponed, partly because the Bolshoi dancers found the acting too difficult. The truth was that they were no longer accustomed to the type of work that required them to think in terms of drama and psychology. Was the music too exacting then, or too beautiful? The fact is that, after its first and successful performance as a concerto in Moscow in October 1935, it made the rounds of concert halls in the usual disguise of a *suite*. Prokofiev's score crossed the frontier and became a ballet for the first time at Brno in Czechoslovakia, which was curious, to say the least, when one thinks of the political situation at that time. At last, in 1941, the Soviet authorities decided to let the ballet open at the Kirov, with results that were sensational. Lavrovsky's choreography and Galina Ulanova's interpretation of Juliet were to remain the exemplary pattern for many years. Lavrovsky combined dance and mime in a form characterized by intense romanticism and forceful dramatization of the events. Ulanova, for her part, gave Juliet an image of maturity, ignoring the girl's extreme youth to make her the personification of love, an interpretation enormously admired in the revival at the Bolshoi on December 28, 1946, when the war was over. Moreover, the tragedy was now interwoven with brilliant passages derived from folklore, while many of the minor parts were strongly characterized (Mercutio's death was a favourite instance) to a degree that might seem melodramatic, even caricatured, to a modern audience. As Lavrovsky said, dance must arise naturally from the mimed drama. In short, the word should become physical movement and the emotions of the characters be translated into dance. In this ballet the old Russian love of Shakespeare is expressed with enormous force, while the spirit of the classic drama is faithfully maintained. In any case, the dream of counterbalancing the three Tchaikovsky ballets with three parallel works of equal merit became reality when *Romeo and Juliet* was followed by *Cinderella* and *The Stone Flower*. During the next few years *Romeo and Juliet* carried all before it and was included in the repertories of all, or nearly all, the Soviet companies from the Baltic to central Asia. Still more impressive was the ballet's success abroad, helped, of course, by the triumph of the Bolshoi company's first European tours and by a colour film version of Lavrovsky's work with Galina Ulanova as Juliet. It must be remembered that *Romeo and Juliet* has also been arranged as a ballet to music other than by Prokofiev – by Maurice Béjart to a score by Berlioz, for example, and by Antony Tudor to music by Delius. But it is the Prokofiev version that has predominated as one of the great theatrical productions of our century both by its splendour and by the quality of the music, with its inexhaustible imagination and inimitable style.

OTHER VERSIONS. Many famous choreographers have arranged Prokofiev's ballet. The best-known are: 1) Frederick Ashton. Eleven scenes and a prologue. Copenhagen, Theater Royal, May 19, 1955. Danced by Mona Vangsaae and Henning Kronstamm, Royal

Danish Ballet. 2) John Cranko. Three acts. Venice, Teatro Verde, July 26, 1958. Scala Ballet of Milan. Carla Fracci as Juliet. The brilliant Cranko version is considered one of the best up to the present. In a revised form, it was presented at Stuttgart on November 2, 1962, and has remained in the repertory and been used by other groups. The *grand pas de deux* of the balcony scene has also been performed as a separate item on various occasions in different places, particularly in Italy. In Stuttgart the leading parts were danced by Marcia Haydée and Richard Cragun. 3) Kenneth Mac-Millan. Three acts. Sets and costumes by Nicholas Georgiadis. London, Covent Garden, February 9, 1965. Danced by Margot Fonteyn and Rudolf Nureyev, Royal Ballet. This was a very luxurious and important production, differing from its predecessors in details, and very English in conception. The interpretation of Nureyev and Fonteyn was a model of strength and grace, the gifts of the celebrated pair being raised to an unprecedented level by MacMillan's demanding and meaningful choreography. 4) Rudi von Dantzig. Amsterdam. February 22, 1967. Het Nationale Ballet. 5) Birgit Cullberg. Sets and costumes by Eva Schaeffer. Stockholm, Dramatic Theater, September 28, 1969. Danced by Niklas Ek as Romeo and Lena Wennergren as Juliet. Here the Prokofiev ballet was reduced to one

act. Though still based on Shakespeare's text, this *Romeo and Juliet* was divested of everything that could be considered inessential to the play's main theme of young love torn apart by the relentless fight for power between two rival families. The balletic invention is continuous and, although the ensemble dancing is reduced to essentials, nothing of the dramatic force or visual beauty is lost. In the absence of scenery, Montagues and Capulets are distinguished only by the colour of their very beautiful costumes. As in the Renaissance, the clash of arms and banners is between the Reds and the Blues. The ballet lasts only fifty minutes and is divided into six scenes: Power, Street, Festival, Love, Battle, and Escape. 6) Oleg Vinogradov. Three acts. Costumes by Nina Filimonova. Leningrad, Little Theater, 1973. Malegot Ballet. This interesting version breaks with Soviet tradition and approaches that of Béjart in some of its structural elements. At the beginning of the ballet the company is standing in the center of the stage, dressed in plain leotards. Then each dancer puts on the clothes and assumes the part of one of the characters in the play, which follows the text on broad lines but ends happily in repentance and regeneration. After having symbolically killed the symbols of hatred and social conflict, the dancers return to their original position. The ballet is conceived in a spirit of youth and the choreo-

Solange Schwarz and Serge Lifar in The Knight and the Lady, *created by Lifar in 1941.*

A scene from Concerto Barocco *danced by the New York City Ballet.*

graphy is very different from that of Lavrovsky. Vinogradov, while yeilding some concessions to sentiment, offers an interpretation of Prokofiev's masterpiece that is new, especially to the Soviet Union. 7) John Neumeier. Three acts. Copenhagen, Theater Royal, December 20, 1974. Royal Danish Ballet. A celebration of love and hatred expressed in highly dynamic and dramatic terms.   M.P.

PETER AND THE WOLF *(Petia i Volk)*
Story for speaking voice and orchestra. Choreography by Adolf Bolm. Music and scenario by Sergei Prokofiev. Sets and costumes by Lucinda Ballard. New York, Center Theater, January 13, 1940. Ballet Theater. Principal dancers: Eugene Loring (Peter), William Dollar (the Wolf), Viola Essen (the Little Bird), Karen Conrad (the Duck), Nina Stroganova (the Cat).

SYNOPSIS. Peter and his friends, the Cat and the Little Bird, go off to hunt the Wolf, in spite of the warnings of Peter's grandfather, and finally succeed in catching him.

■ The original purpose of this entertainment was purely educational, since it was designed to teach children to identify the sounds of different musical instruments (and was first performed in Moscow on May 2, 1936, during an entertainment for young people). Only later did it enter the ballet repertory. In that ambience the didactic element was naturally put in the shade by the comic and storybook aspects. The narrator's voice, which was still indispensable to the piece, was adjusted to the overall

rhythm; in other words, it was dependent on the choreographic action.

THE MUSIC. This was one of Prokofiev's first and happiest compositions after returning to his homeland in 1933. Its didactic purpose was made clear by a note at the head of the score, saying, "Each character in the story is represented by a different instrument: the little bird by the flute, the duck by the oboe, the cat by the clarinet, the grandfather by the bassoon, the wolf by the three horns, Peter by the four string instruments, and the gunshots by the kettledrum and bass drum." The educational aspect did not inhibit the composer's inspiration, which produced a delightful score very near to formal perfection, in fact, a mini-masterpiece.   P.C..

LA FETE ETRANGE
Ballet in two scenes. Choreography by Andrée Howard. Music by Gabriel Fauré. Scenario and choice of music by Ronald Crichton. Sets and costumes by Sophie Fedorovich. London, Arts Theatre, May 23, 1940. London Ballet. Principal dancers: Maude Lloyd, Frank Staff, David Paltenghi.

SYNOPSIS. Scene I: near a strange castle, a country boy meets a girl who mistakes him for her fiancé, a nobleman with whom she has an appointment. When the latter arrives, the boy is about to go, but finds himself surrounded by the wedding guests. Scene II: following the wedding party onto the castle terrace, the boy once more meets the young woman. Everything appears to go well and the boy is happy; but the fiancé becomes aware of the tenderness with which his betrothed regards our young hero and leaves. In vain the boy tries to console the despairing girl. He returns to his home alone.

■ A charming ballet which the English choreographer has coloured in vaguely romantic half-tones to the gentle music of Fauré, it traces the fading of happiness into sorrow. According to contemporary critics, the lyrical passages were far richer in invention that the dramatic ones. Andrée Howard's style was influenced by the work of Ashton. M.P.

THE PROSPECT BEFORE US
Ballet in seven scenes. Choreography by Ninette de Valois. Music by William Boyce, arranged by Constant Lambert. Sets and costumes by Roger Furse. London, Sadler's Wells Theatre, July 4, 1940. Sadler's Wells Ballet. Principal dancers: Pamela May, Frederick Ashton, Robert Helpmann.

SYNOPSIS. Scene I: at the King's Theatre in the eighteenth century. Five female dancers are under direction from the great ballet master Noverre, while the chief dancer, Didelot, waits to hear what he is to do. Prima ballerina Theodora begins to dance with Didelot, who mistreats her. Taylor, the manager of the King's Theatre, enters with some guests. The manager of the rival Pantheon Theatre, O'Reilly, wanders about, envious. Vestris, the great dancer, known for his disagreeable character, does not hide his dislike of the visitors. The two managers discuss matters in a somewhat fraught atmosphere. Scene II: on June 17, 1789, the King's Theatre is burned down and the whole company goes over to Taylor's rival, O'Reilly. Scene III: in a poverty-stricken London street a file of dancers wait to be paid by O'Reilly. Scene IV: opening night at the Pantheon. A great success for O'Reilly, despair for Taylor. The triumphant O'Reilly is so exhilarated he joins clumsily in the dancing. Scene V: a year later. Taylor, who has now rebuilt his theater, is discussing with his lawyers as to whether Noverre can be made to return to him. The lawyers pronounce O'Reilly to be in the right, but the latter is now tired of ballets and dancers. Scene VI: this time it is the Pantheon that catches fire, and O'Reilly is not displeased. Taylor gets his dancers back. Scene VII: at the King's Theatre, Noverre is rehearsing the cast and Vestris resents him. The lawyers assure Taylor that he is within his rights now that the Pantheon is burnt, but O'Reilly comes in again, tipsy and envious. Once more he joins the dancers, but soon falls down. Meanwhile the indignant dancers have left the stage. Taylor offers his rival drink. Now the tables are turned: Taylor is highly pleased and O'Reilly completely drunk.

■ With a few comic episodes added, this ballet gives a true account of a situation that occurred in the English theater of the eighteenth century and courageously represents some real dance celebrities of that age. The source of inspiration was an engraving by Thomas Rowlandson and Eber's history of the King's Theatre. The plot is very complicated and perhaps overrich in characterizations. Boyce's music, which suits the work perfectly, was adapted by that versatile genius of the English ballet scene, Constant Lambert. M.P.

LETTER TO THE WORLD
Ballet in five scenes. Choreography by Martha Graham. Subject drawn from a poem by Emily Dickinson. Music by Hunter Johnson. Set by Arch Lauterer. Costumes by Edythe Gilfond. Vermont, Bennington College Theater, August 11, 1940. Principal dancers: Martha Graham (One Who Dances), Merce Cunningham (March), Jane Dudley (Grandmother), Eric Hawkins (the Lover), Sophie Maslow (a Girl), Jean Erdman (One Who Speaks), also David Campbell, Sascha Liebich, David Zellmer.

SYNOPSIS. The story is set in Protestant New England. Dream and reality melt into one another and occupy the same space. The heroine is immersed in memories and the consciousness of her duty. The matriarchal old Grandmother rises before her, snatching away all her emotions of love to bring her back to the sense of the old family tradition. The loss of love, "a pain so deep it consumes my life," as Emily Dickinson's heroine says through the poem, is expressed by Graham in *Letter to the World* through dance.

■ Graham introduced the human voice into this ballet as she had done in *American Document*. This time it was to recite Emily Dickinson's verses. However, she had great difficulty in combining the text with the choreography and spent a great deal of time rehearsing the group, so that there was little left for her own part and on the first night she was forced to improvise. For that reason both *Letter* and *El Penitente* (presented on the same evening) were judged by the critics to be "inadequate" and "not properly worked out." At the end of the season Graham prepared a revised edition. C.M.C.

CONCERTO BAROCCO
Classical ballet in three movements. Choreography by George Balanchine. Music by Johann Sebastian Bach. Sets and costumes by Eugene Berman. New York, Hunter College Playhouse, May 29, 1940. American Ballet. Principal dancers: Marie-Jeanne, Mary Jane Shea, William Dollar.

SYNOPSIS. A concerto ballet, abstract and without plot. First movement: *Vivace*: one group of eight girl dancers is permanently on stage and is joined by two soloists who pursue a choreographic dialogue parallel to the music of the two concerted violins. Second movement: *Largo ma non tanto*: one of the two ballerinas returns carried by a male dancer, with whom she performs an aerial *pas de deux* which intertwines with the less animated movements of the eight members of the *corps de ballet*. Third movement: *Allegro*: a finale with all ten ballerinas in a brilliant counterpoint of lines, steps, light elevations, and fluid regroupings.

■ *Concerto Barocco* is a ballet conceived in Balanchine's purest and most abstract vein, in which dance is seen as arising directly from the musical score, and that in its turn as a realization in sound of lines, rhythms, and relationships of which the choreography is the plastic, moving expression. The choreography is thus not a mere illustration of the music – in this case Bach's *Concerto in D minor for two violins and orchestra* – but its interpretation by Balanchine into a visible counterpoint which involves us in just the same way as does baroque art, not in the subject treated but in the formal means employed. The essence of this type of ballet is thus the elimination of everything extraneous to the brilliant purity of the choreography itself, of which alone it consists. No conceptual narrative or directly dramatic content is to be detected, nor any information conveyed except the plastic and dynamic content of the dancing itself. Thus, although the first production of *Concerto Barocco* was adorned with set and costumes, the eleven dancers in the final version wore simple black and white practice clothes and appeared on a completely bare stage bounded only by a light-coloured cyclorama. Balanchine revived the ballet several times, producing a definitive version for his company, the New York City Ballet, on September 13, 1951, at the New York City Center, with Marie Tallchief, Diana Adams, and Nicholas Magallanes in the principal parts. *Concerto Barocco* has remained in the company's repertory, as well as in that of several other companies.   A.A.

BALLET IMPERIAL

Classical ballet in three movements. Choreography by George Balanchine. Music by Piotr I. Tchaikovsky. Sets and costumes by Mitislav Dobuzhinsky. New York, Hunter College Playhouse, May 27, 1941. American Ballet. Principal dancers: Marie-Jeanne, Gisella Caccialanza, William Dollar.

SYNOPSIS. Concerted ballet without a subject. *Allegro brillante*: a celebration of the ballerina surrounded by the whole *corps de ballet*. *Andante non troppo*: the *premier danseur* finds and then loses among the others his "imperial ballerina." *Allegro con fuoco*: final act, brilliant and rich in movements for the ensemble, the leading pair, and the *corps de ballet*.

■ This work in a frank tribute to the classical style of Marius Petipa as practiced before the Russian Revolution (and to a great degree after it) by the Imperial Ballet of the Maryinsky Theater in St. Petersburg, the school in which Balanchine was trained. Classical dance constitutes the technical basis of Balanchine's style and whole choreographic vocabulary, especially in the *concertanti* ballets (see *Concerto Barocco*, page 234). In *Ballet Imperial*, unlike the others, the relationship with the Maryinsky tradition is proclaimed by the sets and costumes as well. Of this Aurel Milloss wrote (in an eulogy which says much from a choreographer of such

Gayle Young and Sallie Wilson in Pillar of Fire *by Antony Tudor to music by Arnold Schönberg.*

a different provenance), "In declaring that *Ballet Imperial* is a musical paraphrase and not simply a re-creation of the ballets of that Russian court, we have underlined that the visual, structural, and stylistic conception as a whole makes up an image that Balanchine has fashioned by his own highly personal method of transformation. He knows how to 'clothe' reality, and for him 'the medium is the message,' since it implies all that lies within. Yet to this wish to reduce everything to utter objectivity must be added his at first sight inexplicable choice of presenting a 'choreographical concerto' in theatrical form. With theatrical effects, such as the use of scenery, he renders the abstract concrete, so that his abstract choreography in its material frame becomes a superior sort of game in which even mystery acquires a true and precise objectivity." The music used for *Ballet Imperial* is Tchaikovsky's *Second Concerto in G major for piano and orchestra*. Various companies have included *Ballet Imperial* in their repertory. Sadler's Wells Ballet presented it at Covent Garden Opera House in London on April 5, 1950, with Margot Fonteyn, Michael Somes, and Beryl Grey in the principal parts; the Scala in Milan on March 25, 1952, with Olga Amati, Gilda Majocchi, and Giulio Perugini. The New York City Ballet, which revived the work on March 19, 1964, has now acquired a new version called *Tchaikovsky Concerto No. 2*, first presented by Balanchine at the State Theater of New York on January 12, 1973, with Patricia McBride, Peter Martins, and Coleen Neary as the principal dancers.   A.A.

THE KNIGHT AND THE LADY (*Le Chevalier et la Damoiselle*)
Ballet in two acts. Choreography and scenario by Serge Lifar. Music by Philippe Gaubert. Sets by A. M. Cassandre. Paris, Opéra, July 2, 1941. Principal dancers: Solange Schwarz (the Lady), Serge Lifar (the Knight Errant), Serge Peretti (the Blue Knight), Yvette Chauviré.

SYNOPSIS. A Princess of Burgundy in the Middle Ages is the victim of a spell which transforms her every night into a young hind: only he who can make her feel sorrow can set her free. Three Knights swear love and fealty to her and follow her on her nocturnal journeys to the woods. One night the hind with the white antlers strikes a Knight Errant in the chest. He returns the blow and wounds her in the heart, upon which she turns back into a woman. Between them a sudden and ecstatic love is born, but the three other Knights bear the wounded Princess away, after throwing the glove of challenge before the Knight Errant. The Princess arranges a great tourney in the hope of seeing her love, and sure enough he comes, encased in armour and bearing on his coat of arms the emblem of a hind. She recognizes the Knight Errant, who then makes himself known to the three challenging Knights, beats them in fair fight, and so wins the Princess's hand.

■ Counted among Lifar's best creations, *The Knight and the Lady* draws its inspiration from a lay by Marie of France, telling a legend of medieval Brittany – altered to Burgundy in the scenario to avoid the appearance of a reference to *Tristan*, although its atmosphere dominates the ballet. Lifar arranged the choreography after painstaking study of popular and courtly dances of the thirteenth century as recorded in French literary, musical, and iconographical sources of the period. Far from wishing to produce a historical reconstruction, however, his aim was to translate the dances into the typical neoclassical idiom of his choreography in a

Sketch by Jean-Pierre Ponnelle for The Miraculous Mandarin *with choreography by J. J. Etchevery.*

Luciana Savignano in The Miraculous Mandarin.

stylized presentation. In this he was greatly helped by the music of Philippe Gaubert and the scenic designs of Cassandre. A characteristic of *The Knight and the Lady* was that each character had its own recurring choreographic leitmotiv involving the attitude and movement of the whole body, but particularly the free play of the arms and hands which added dramatic expressiveness to the traditional academic technique.   A.A.

BLUEBEARD *(Barbe-bleue)*

Ballet in four acts, two prologues, and three interludes. Choreography by Michael Fokine. Music by Jacques Offenbach. Subject by Fokine. Sets and costumes by Marcel Vertès. Mexico City, Palace of the Fine Arts, October 27, 1941. Ballet Theater. Principal dancers: Anton Dolin (Bluebeard), Alicia Markova, Irina Baronova, Ian Gibson, Antony Tudor, Lucia Chase, Nora Kaye, Rosella Hightower, Jerome Robbins, and others.

SYNOPSIS. First prologue: Old King Bobiche has had a daughter, Ermilia, instead of the expected male heir. After putting a necklace whereby she can be recognized around the baby's neck, he shuts her in a chest and sets it adrift on the river. Second prologue: Bluebeard feasts with his wives. The fifth wife, poisoned by his counsellor Popoloni, dies in his arms. Act I: frivolous Queen Clementina is philandering with her page. Her husband, King Bobiche, surprises them and orders the page to be hanged. But suddenly two Spaniards arrive and the Queen flirts with them, too, until Bobiche has them taken prisoner prior to the usual execution. Two other lovers of the Queen come to the same end. Bobiche now regrets the loss of his daughter and orders his counsellors to look for her. First interlude: Count Oscar, the King's Chancellor, frees the Queen's lovers for a handsome bribe. Act II: in the country, amid the merrymaking rustics, the beautiful Fioretta (who is, of course, poor Ermilia) is courted by a handsome shepherd (really Prince Zaffiro), thus arousing the jealousy of blonde

Boulotte. The alchemist Popoloni arrives in search of a new wife for Bluebeard. Then the terrible Bluebeard himself arrives on the scene. Boulotte has no idea who he is, and consents to become his wife. Meanwhile Oscar discovers Ermilia by means of the necklace. She mistakenly thinks that the shepherd will no longer love her as a Princess. Second interlude: Bluebeard, already tired of Boulotte, sees Oscar and Ermilia pass by and determines that she must be his. Act III: Bluebeard orders Popoloni to poison Boulotte and it is done. But while Bluebeard goes off to capture Ermilia, the alchemist brings all the dead wives back to life. Third interlude: Bluebeard is oppressed by the ghosts of his murdered spouses. Act IV: Bobiche is preparing a grand feast to celebrate the return of his daughter, who he intends shall marry Prince Zaffiro. The girl is obviously thinking of her lost shepherd and when the Prince enters she recognizes him with joy. At this moment the fearsome Bluebeard arrives with drawn sword. Zaffiro fights a duel with him but loses: Bluebeard fells him with a violent blow on the back. But amidst the general despair, Popoloni comes in with five masked ladies who reveal themselves to be the wives of Bluebeard. Happy ending: Popoloni resuscitates the Prince, Bluebeard takes back Boulotte, and everyone, nobles and peasants, joins in final dance.

■ This comic ballet was one of the last works of the great Fokine, who died in 1942. His point of departure was Offenbach's operetta of the same name, and between them they quite demythologized Perrault's

sinister character. Reunited to dance in this production on its first night, which took place in Mexico City, was a veritable galaxy of English and American stars.   M.P.

PILLAR OF FIRE
One-act ballet. Choreography by Antony Tudor. Music by Arnold Schönberg. Scenario by Antony Tudor. Sets and costumes Jo Milziner. New York, Metropolitan Opera House, April 8, 1942. Principal dancers: Nora Kaye, Hugh Laing, Lucia Chase, Annabelle Lyon, Antony Tudor.

SYNOPSIS. The heroine, Hagar, lives with her two sisters. At the beginning we see her seated before her house watching the passers-by. The arrival of the man she loves gladdens her, but he finds himself attracted to the younger sister. Hagar is angry, feeling herself alone and unhappy while the other couples love one another. Convinced she cannot recapture the man she loves, she is overcome by an urge to be embraced by an unknown. A stranger appears and consents to follow her into the house. Afterwards, gnawed by remorse and bitterness, she feels defiled and at everyone's mercy. Considered guilty and rejected, Hagar seeks in vain a solution to her plight, either with her seducer or the others. But in the end the stranger shows understanding and offers her his love. Together and happy, they leave the street where she has known so much sorrow.

■ The source of inspiration of this psychological ballet

Noella Pontois and Charles Jude in Suite en Blanc, *a ballet by Serge Lifar.*

(which has an improbably romantic ending) is the same as that of Schönberg's *Resplendent Night*, a poem entitled "The Woman and the World." Tudor has expanded its narrative core (a man and a woman who redeem a sin through the strength of their mutual love) by adding the characters of the sisters and the local inhabitants and replacing vague nineteenth-century mystery with an exact theatrical background. As on other occasions, the story has been moved to the twentieth century to make certain attitudes more plausible.   M.P.

JINX

One-act ballet. Choreography by Lew Christensen. Music by Benjamin Britten. Set by James Stewart Morcom. Costumes by Felipe Fiocca. New York, National Theater, April 24, 1942. Principal dancers: Janet Reed, Lew Christensen, Conrad Linden.

SYNOPSIS. The story is set in a small circus inhabited with the usual characters: the ballerina, the bareback riders, the clowns, the acrobats, and the bearded lady. Gradually, through a series of episodes, one of the clowns, who has been bullied, takes on the character of the Jinx, a bringer of misfortune, terror, and superstition. He is a sort of *deus ex machina* in reverse; the circus people are threatened by some inexorable disaster they are powerless to prevent. The fatal game begins. Like a cruel ringmaster he makes the others dance to the crack of his whip. Superstition, anger, and fear assume grotesque proportions as the preposterous story draws to its end in the victory of the beaten clown, who takes his final revenge. The brilliant youthful music of Benjamin Britten (*Variations on a theme by Frank Bridge*) contrasts with this tale of superstition and death.   M.P.

THE MIRACULOUS MANDARIN (*Il Mandarino Meraviglioso*)

Choreographic drama in one act. Choreography by Aurel Milloss. Music by Béla Bartòk. Subject by Menyhért Langyel. Set and costumes by Enrico Prampolini. Milan, Scala, October 12, 1942. Principal dancers: Aurel Milloss (the Mandarin), Attilia Radice (the Girl), Filippo Morucci (the old Gallant), Guido Lauri (the Student), Giovanni Brinati, Teofilo Giglio, Adriano Vitale (the three Rogues).

SYNOPSIS. At night, on the outskirts of a big town, three shady-looking characters compel a girl to decoy passers-by with the intention of robbing them. The first victim is a shabby old gallant who makes absurd, amorous advances to her, but is soon chased away by the rogues when they find he has no money. Then comes a shy young man who is sincerely attracted to the girl, but he, too, is poor and the three eliminate him brutally. Now a repulsive figure makes his appearance: it is a Mandarin, a man who has cared for nothing but accumulating wealth, and to that end has always repressed his feelings. The woman begins to dance with a forced eroticism until the Mandarin, at first still and indifferent, is aroused and joins in the savage dance. Finally

he throws himself lecherously on the astonished woman. The three villains attack him, rob him of his gold, and try to suffocate him with a blanket. But he does not die; he gazes at the girl with ever more burning eyes. Not even their daggers can put an end to his desperate sensual vitality. They strangle him but still he continues to move until the girl understands and frees him, allowing him to possess her. Only now that he has achieved his first true moment of life do the amazing man's wounds begin to bleed. And so at last he dies.

■ A short story by the Hungarian playright Menyhért Lengyel gave Béla Bartòk the idea for a score composed in 1919 with the title *A csodálatos mandarin* and intended, in agreement with Lengyel, to accompany a mime-drama. Its first theatrical production was in that form and was directed by Hans Strobach on November 28, 1926, at the Cologne Opera House. The brutal subject, with the crudely realistic presentation the form entailed, created a notorious scandal which led to the banning of the play by order of Konrad Adenauer, then mayor of Cologne. After a similar failure in Prague, Bartòk no longer knew how to put his creation into theatrical form. According to Massimo Mila, the work was among those in which he had advanced furthest towards "the magic of expressionism, without ever abandoning a hard consistency of rhythmic structure, nor a tonal ordering of notes, if only within the range of a modally arbitrary scale.... Expressionism is evident in the immediacy with which the sensual urgency of the plot is transferred without any intermediaries to the violence of sound and wealth of tone colour which renders acceptable this grim sublimation of sexual arousal, or rather raises it to the level of a force of nature." It was Aurel Milloss, ten years later, who convinced Bartòk that the sublimation of the obscene and macabre he had achieved in his music could not be adequately interpreted in purely pantomimic action, and that only the abstract quality and expressive range of dance could portray the internal motive forces of the drama and the plenitude of its spiritual significance, ennobling it and endowing it with an authentic moral dimension. Reworked in this way, *Mandarin* had its first and definitive production in the form of a ballet, or rather a choreographed drama, during the 1942 season of contemporary works at the Scala in Milan. It met with a success, confirmed by numerous revivals up to the present day, that has ranked it as the masterpiece of Milloss and late expressionism. In Aurel Milloss's rigorous choreography the immediacy of the expressionist "scream" is subdued by his personal style, derived partly from the so-called "free dance" of central Europe, and partly from the formal discipline of classical ballet, producing a synthesis in which the "subterranean forces of being" undergo an artistic transformation without which the dramatic edge would be blunted. Milloss has directed numerous revivals of the ballet from its first performance to the present day, always remaining faithful to his original conception: at the Rome Opera House in 1945, in Río di Janeiro in 1954, at the May Festival in Florence in 1957, 1964, and 1974, in Cologne, where it met with a triumphant

Costume design by Christian Bérard for Les Forains, *created by Roland Petit in 1945.*

Sketch by Peter Williams, designer of Cinderella, the ballet by Rostislav Zakharov to music by Sergei Prokofiev.

reception in 1962 (at the same Opera House where the unfortunate mime version of *Mandarin* was played in 1926), at the Vienna State Opera in 1972, and at the Fenice Theater in Venice in 1977. The production is the same except that Enrico Prampolini's set, costumes, and futurist drop scene have been changed in favour of new stage designs; since 1964 by those of Emanuele Luzzati.

OTHER VERSIONS. 1) Gyula Harangozo. Budapest, Opera House, December 9, 1945. Hungarian State Opera Ballet. 2) Todd Bolender. New York, City Center, September 6, 1951. Danced by Todd Bolender and Melissa Hayden, New York City Ballet. 3) Jean Jacques Etchevery. Venice, Fenice Theater, September 13, 1955, and at the Théâtre de la Monnaie, Brussels, on December 2, 1955. 4) Alfred Rodrigues. Edinburgh, Empire Theatre, August 27, 1956. Danced by Michael Somes, Elaine Fifield, Sadler's Wells Ballet; then London, Covent Garden, September 4, 1956. 5) Dimitrije Parlic. Belgrade, National Theater, February 10, 1957. 6) Erika Hanka. Vienna, State Opera House, November 16, 1957. 7) Ernö Vashegyi. Paris, Théâtre des Champs Elysées, October 3, 1958. Danced by Ernö Vashegyi, V. Pasztor, Ballet de France de Janine Charrat. 8) Alan Carter. Munich, Bavarian State Opera

Patricia McBride and Nicholas Magallanes in Night Shadow, *a ballet by George Balanchine, with music by Vittorio Rieti from Vincenzo Bellini.*

House, November 22, 1960. 9) Leonid Lavrovsky. Moscow, Bolshoi Theater, May 21, 1961. Danced by Maris Liepa, Nina Timofeyeva. 10) Joseph Lazzini. New York, Metropolitan Opera House, April 11, 1965. 11) Flemming Flindt. Copenhagen, Theater Royal, January 28, 1967. Danced by Flemming Flindt, Vivi Gelker, Royal Danish Ballet.   A.A.

THE MUSIC. Bartòk still seems to be the most stylistically uneven of all this century's composers. Particularly influenced during his formative years by the great waves of central European music, from Brahms to Wagner, and by impending impressionism, Bartòk's own original musicality was for ever torn between his "native wood-notes wild" and the decadent intellectualism of his day. His compositions always showed the effects of this dualism, this split between an authentic, innate musical manner and an inclination to follow the prevailing trends of the avant-garde. For that reason Bartòk first fell under the sway of Debussy's impressionism and the sumptuous music of Strauss. It was only in the early years of this century – anecdotes suggest 1905 – that the composer discovered the rich vein of folk music and

began to immerse himself in its study, drawing from it new strength for his composition. This interest soon led him into a taste for the primitive and archaic which profoundly affected his later work, while, on the other hand, modern literary and artistic influences were still strong enough in him to produce a realism that one could fairly label German expressionism, learned mostly from Schönberg. The clearest example of this musical contagion is *The Miraculous Mandarin*, which was composed in the years immediately after World War I. The ethnic references, the folk theme fertilize the roots of the work, but all the musical material, so violent in its instrumental and rhythmic stresses, is already soaked in the atonal and polytonal atmosphere that remains the hallmark of that school of composition. Equally personal and original is his use of disturbing, persistent rhythmics and the distribution of tone-colour areas, new in conception and far removed from those of Stravinsky's *Rite* of the same years (though certain aspects of the barbaric rhythms seem related), while his use of chromatic chords – not frozen within the rigid framework of dodecaphony – is clearly derived from the Viennese school.   A.F.

Robert Helpmann, David Blair, Margot Fonteyn, and Frederick Ashton in Cinderella. *Choreography by Ashton. Music by Sergei Prokofiev.*

GAYANÉ

Ballet in four acts and six scenes. Choreography by Nina Aleksandrovna Anisimova. Music by Aram Khachaturian. Scenario by Konstantin Derzhavin. Sets by Natan Altman. Perm, Opera House, December 9, 1942. Principal dancer: N. A. Anisimova.

SYNOPSIS. The ballet tells the story of a young woman, Gayané, who works in a cotton cooperative in Armenia. Her brutal and unfaithful husband is the head of a gang of robbers and outlaws. Tired of so much cruel treatment, Gayané denounces her husband before all his comrades. For revenge, he kidnaps the child of the unhappy marriage as a hostage. There seems no way out of the unhappy situation, but it is finally relieved by the tempestuous arrival of the Red Brigade, whose commander is also the cooperative chairman. After sending the wicked husband, Giko, away to imprisonment, he marries the young Armenian mother, whom he has long loved.

■ *Gayané* is filled with a poetic feeling for nature, conveyed by a great wealth of colour. It is, in reality, a new version of a previous ballet, *Shastje*, presented at Erevan in 1939. The individual characters are well portrayed, but the ensemble scenes are also excellent. The score contains passages of delicate charm and sad orientalized melodies such as those accompanying the cotton-picking scene, Aikha's dance, Gayané's lullaby, and the dance of the old people, but there are also moments of great rhythmic vivacity. Particularly famous for the instrumental virtuosity it inspires is the Saber Dance, which introduces themes from Armenian folk music.   P.C.

SUITE EN BLANC

One-act ballet. Choreography by Serge Lifar. Music by Edouard Lalo (from the ballet Namouna*). Stage design by Dignimant. Zurich, Grand Théâtre, June 19, 1943. Paris Opéra Ballet. Principal dancers: Lycette Darsonval, Solange Schwarz, Yvette Chauviré, Micheline Bardin, Marianne Ivanov, Paulette Dynalix, Serge Lifar, Roger Fenonjois, Roger Ritz.*

SYNOPSIS. A ballet without a theme in a suite of ten

choreographic studies without a dramatic link, danced by numerous soloists and the *corps de ballet* in various formations (*solos, pas de deux, de trois, de cinq*, and ensembles). The costumes are classical white tutus for the girls, tights and full shirts, also in white, for the men. The stage is bare except for a rostrum with two flights of steps on which the *corps de ballet* stand during the solo numbers.

■ One month after its opening in Zurich, *Suite en Blanc* was presented at the Opéra in Paris. Among the seventy ballets created by Serge Lifar during his thirty-year-long career as director of dance and chief dancer at the Opéra, this was the one that was performed most often in the great theater.   M.B.

DANSES CONCERTANTES
Ballet in five parts. Choreography by George Balanchine. Music by Igor Stravinsky. Set and costumes by Eugene Berman. New York, New York City Center, September 10, 1944. Ballets Russes de Monte Carlo. Principal dancers: Alexandra Danilova and Leon Danielian (pas de deux), Maria Tallchief, Ruthanne Boris, Mary Ellen Moylan.

SYNOPSIS. It is a suite of dances.

■ Although it was performed for the first time as a concert piece (1942), *Danses Concertantes* was composed by Stravinsky specifically as a ballet score. The *tempi* were designed for dancing: *Introduction and March, Pas d'Action, Four Variations on a Theme, Pas de Deux, Closing March.* From it Balanchine fashioned an exquisite, strictly classical ballet, its cornerstone, the *pas de deux*, reserved for the star dancers. In 1972, for the occasion of the Stravinsky Festival held by the New York City Ballet to celebrate the composer's ninetieth birthday, Balanchine worked out a new version of *Danses Concertantes*, not only, as he freely admitted, because he could not remember the original choreography, but also because he wanted to create something new for his company of the moment.   C.M.C.

APPALACHIAN SPRING
One-act ballet. Choreography by Martha Graham. Music by Aaron Copland. Set by Isamu Noguchi. Costumes by Edythe Gilfond. Washington, Library of Congress, October 30, 1944. Principal dancers: Martha Graham (the Bride), Eric Hawkins (the Bridegroom), Merce Cunningham (the Revivalist), May O'Donnell (the Pioneer Woman).

SYNOPSIS. This is the story of a young pioneer in nineteenth-century America and his timid bride on their wedding day. During the ceremony, after the preacher has given a hellfire sermon on the wickedness of mankind, the stage goes dark and the congregation kneel, bending their heads at the thought of death and the last judgment. But the little bride finds she cannot bow herself in penitence because happiness is bursting out of her heart. She tries to control it, but breaks into a dance, reverent but unrestrainable, physically rejecting a god that cannot accept love and human happiness.

■ *Appalachian Spring* was Martha Graham's 108th work. It was commissioned by Elizabeth Sprague Coolidge, an intrepid octogenarian (originator of the eponymous foundation). Hawkins had suggested to her that she might give an evening reception in Graham's honour. Mrs. Coolidge commissioned three new ballets to be set to music by Darius Milhaud, Paul Hindemith, and Aaron Copland. It was this score for *Appalachian Spring* that won Copland the Pulitzer Prize. With this ballet Graham concluded her series devoted to America and its history. It is a last affirmative statement. Arrived in her promised land, her ancestress, the key figure of the ballet, became the archetype of the pioneer woman. She is young America emerging into a world of light unclouded by any shadow of the past, living only in the joyous present from the moment she and her bridegroom assume control of their lives and go together on their way. Such an affirmation – we read in her biography by McDonagh – would not have been possible for Martha Graham, either in her work or her life, before she met Eric Hawkins, promoted to being her partner since 1938 (*American Document*) and later, for a brief and stormy period, her husband. *Appalachian Spring* (together with *Night Journey*, the only two ballets by Graham that were entirely filmed for professional use) marked the beginning of the long and uninterrupted collaboration of her dance company with Isamu Noguchi, a sculptor of strong personality, who had already designed sets for some of her youthful works. He followed Lauterer, who had refused *Appalachian Spring* for economic reasons.   C.M.C.

STROLLING PLAYERS (Les Forains)
One-act ballet. Choreography by Roland Petit. Music by Henri Sauguet. Scenario by Boris Kochno. Set and costumes by Christian Bérard. Paris, Théâtre des Champs Elysées, March 2, 1945. Principal dancers: Nina Verubova, Roland Petit, Ethéry Pagava, Christian Foye, Marina de Berg, Hélène Sadovska.

SYNOPSIS. The ballet depicts the working day of a company of acrobats. They arrive on the outskirts of a town and stop to put up their tent and give their performance. A show within the show is provided by the audience watching the troupe's various acts.

■ Presented at a dance recital a little while after Roland Petit had left the Paris Opéra, this ballet was a revelation and marked the true beginning of the choreographer's career. Sauguet vividly describes the ballet's inspiration: "I put into my music all my passion for the fun of the fair, and all my sympathy and pity for the life of those strolling players who carry dream and fantasy beneath their worn and faded garments; in whom the gold and purple still survive. I never thought the ballet would have a future. I composed it as a diversion for

A moment from The Four Temperaments *danced by the New York City Ballet.*

a single evening." Actually it was created in a sort of delirium. While Petit translated the music and action suggested by Sauguet into movement, Bérard rushed off to the Flea Market to find rags and remnants in which to dress the characters. The ballet was not ready until the day of opening. Even the actors portraying the audience had to be recruited from among the friends of the authors and principal dancers.   M.S.M.

CINDERELLA *(Zolushka)*

Ballet in three acts. Choreography by Rostislav Zakharov. Music by Sergei Prokofiev. Sets by Peter Williams. Moscow, Bolshoi Theater, November 21, 1945. Principal dancer: Olga Lepeschinskaia.

SYNOPSIS. Act I: in Cinderella's house her two stepsisters are embroidering a silk scarf. They are their mother's darlings, while Cinderella is treated as a servant. Only her father, now old and weak, is on her side. Cinderella is sad and weeps for her dead mother. When an old beggarwoman comes to the door she is the only one to take pity on her and give her a crust of bread. Then the family set off for the ball and she is left alone. As she sits dreaming of going to the royal reception, the beggarwoman reappears, revealing herself to be the girl's fairy godmother. Cinderella finds her dream coming true. Dressed like a Princess, she will be driven to the palace in a golden coach, but she must leave before the clock has struck midnight. A pair of glass slippers, a magnificent cloak, and exquisite dress, flowers, and jewels make her look more beautiful than ever. Act II: at the grand ball in the Prince's palace the stepmother and her two daughters try to get themselves noticed, but with scant success. Cinderella's appearance, however, creates a sensation; the Prince cannot take his eyes off her. The two fall in love at first sight, but as they dance together their happiness is interrupted by the clock striking twelve. Cinderella flies from the palace, losing one of her slippers on the way. The Prince picks it up. Act III: the Prince travels the world in search of the mysterious lady of the shoe, but in vain. Meanwhile Cinderella at home begins to believe she dreamed it all. Only the slipper still in her possession reassures her. At last the Prince arrives, desperate to find his beloved. The stepsisters and even the stepmother try on the magic shoe, but it will not fit at all. Cinderella sits in the corner, the Prince notices her, and in her confusion, she drops the missing slipper. Now all is clear to the young man, and the fairy godmother reappears to bless the marriage.

■ Even though less important than *Romeo and Juliet*, this second classical ballet by Prokofiev has enjoyed a well-merited popularity ever since its first appearance. Because of the war, its gestation was lengthy – from 1940 to 1944. *Cinderella*, to a much greater extent than *Romeo and Juliet*, was constructed on typically Tchaikovskian lines, with its variations, *adagios*, and *pas de deux*. The composer, however, did not want his chief character to be a mere fairy-tale figure, but "a real person who thinks, moves, suffers, and rejoices like one of ourselves." Musically the ballet was brilliant, but the "light" subject-matter failed to inspire a truly important score, although the vigour, polish, and irony typical of the composer were all present, especially when passages from his past works were recalled; such as, for instance, the gavotte from the *Classical Symphony* or the march from *The Love of Three Oranges*, or when the dramatic strokes of midnight ring out. Cinderella's theme is as graceful as one would expect, while the stepmother and her daughters are characterized by comic touches.

OTHER VERSIONS. 1) Konstantin Sergeyev. Leningrad, Kirov Theater, April 8, 1946. Danced by Natalia Dudinskaia, Kirov Ballet. New staging at the Kirov on July 13, 1964 (with Irina Kolpakova). Sets by Tatiana Bruni. 2) Frederick Ashton. London, Covent Garden, December 23, 1948. Sets and costumes by Jean Denis Malclès. Danced by Moira Shearer, Michael Somes, Robert Helpmann and Frederick Ashton, Sadler's Wells Ballet. It was a brilliant production that became a widespread tradition, with the novelty of the "ugly sisters" being danced by men. The following year the part of Cinderella was taken by Margot Fonteyn. 3) Alfred Rodrigues. Milan, Scala, December 15, 1955. Danced first by Violetta Verdy, then by Carla Fracci. 4) Vaslav Orlikovsky. Paris, Théâtre des Champs Elysées, December 4, 1963. 5) Celia Franca. Toronto, O'Keefe Center, April 15, 1968, National Ballet of Canada. 6) Paolo Bortoluzzi. Milan, Scala, March 16, 1977. Sets and costumes by Germinal Casado. Danced by Luciana Savignano. Here the story is seen as a child's dream and the characters enter from a book of fairy tales. M.P.

NIGHT SHADOW *(La Sonnambula)*

One-act ballet. Choreography by George Balanchine. Music by Vittorio Rieti (after Bellini). Set and costumes by Dorothea Tanning. New York, New York City Center, February 27, 1946. Monte Carlo Russian Ballet. Principal dancers: Alexandra Danilova, Nicholas Magallanes, Maria Tallchief.

SYNOPSIS. A party is in progress in the garden of a big house. The host receives his masked guests; at his side is a beautiful young woman (the Coquette), whose vivacity is in contrast to the solemnity of the guests. Enter the handsome Poet, who is introduced to the young woman. Dancing begins – shepherds, Moors, Harlequin. The Poet and Coquette find each other attractive and dance together. Then everyone goes, leaving the Poet alone. As he sits sadly in the garden a mysterious figure appears and advances towards him. It is a woman in a white dress who seems to be walking in her sleep, always on point, without noticing his presence. The Poet falls in love with her and tries in vain to stop or wake her. When she leaves he follows. The Coquette returns and sees the Poet, her erstwhile admirer, following the somnambulist. The master of the house comes back with his guests, upon which the jealous Coquette tells her lover of what she has seen. The guests begin to dance again, but the host slips away unseen. After a short while the

Poet reenters, bloodstained and mortally wounded by the host. The sleepwalker crosses the stage, the guests follow her. Love has ended in a tragedy of jealousy, for she is the wife of the master of the house (or castle).

■ Bellini's opera of the same name was only a pretext for this dramatic ballet, wrapped in its air of mystery, yet rich in amusing moments such as the *pas de deux* between the poet and the somnambulist who does not see him. Balanchine used the demoniacal atmosphere as a basis for his penetrating, intelligent choreography, harking back to his classical past – in the *divertissements* particularly. *Night Shadow* has been described as a "black" ballet, in the style of Edgar Allan Poe. The music includes themes from Bellini's *La Sonnambula* and *I Puritani*. The ballet is widely diffused and, under the direction of John Taras, has found a place in the repertory of nearly all the important companies.   M.P.

FACSIMILE

Ballet in one scene. Choreography and scenario by Jerome Robbins. Music by Leonard Bernstein. Set by Oliver Smith. Costumes by Irene Sharaff. New York, Broadway Theater, October 24, 1946. Ballet Theater. Principal dancers: Nora Kaye, Jerome Robbins, John Kriza.

SYNOPSIS. Two men and one woman on a beach are pursuing a flirtation for three, the eternal triangle raised to the nth power, but in which love plays no part; sexual attraction is all, or rather, it is a game with life. The two men begin a sort of rivalry for the woman, but it ends in nothing and finally, on various pretexts, they both leave her. She could not care less.

■ The ballet's theme urges us to think: on what values do we base our everyday lives? to what do we devote the greater part of our time? Robbins's answer is, on the whole, pessimistic and disheartening, if what we read in a program note is true: "What interior poverty is revealed by those who can feel alive only if they have perpetual noise, theatrical emotions, and society gossip!" An antiromantic sentiment underlines the boredom and emptiness of three people incapable of happiness.   M.B.

THE FOUR TEMPERAMENTS

Ballet in five parts. Choreography by George Balanchine. Music by Paul Hindemith. Sets and costumes by Kurt Seligmann. Lighting by Jean Rosenthal. New York, Central High School of Needle Trades, November 20, 1946. Ballet Society. Principal dancers: Gisella Caccialanza, Tanaquil Le Clercq, Mary Ellen Moylan, Elise Reiman, Beatrice Tompkins, Todd Bolender, Lew Christensen, Fred Danieli, William Dollar, José Martinez, Francisco Moncion.

SYNOPSIS. An abstract portrayal of the four temperaments into which, according to medieval medical philosophy, the human organism is divided. Theme:

three couples dance three *pas de deux*. First variation (*Melancholy*): a male dancer performs a solo and is then joined by two ballerinas; later four other "mysterious women" make a stately entrance to a vibrant march. Second variation (*Sanguin*): a ballerina and her partner dance in waltz time, accompanied by a secondary group of four men. Third variation (*Phlegmatic*): after a while a solitary male dancer is joined by four girls. Fourth variation (*Choleric*): solo by one ballerina, followed by the whole cast in a summary of all the ballet's dance themes.

■ Paul Hindemith's interest in ancient and medieval philosophy set him off on various compositions, among them the *Theme with Four Variations for piano and string orchestra* of 1940. Six years later Balanchine used this score, with its vaguely programmatic scheme, for his ballet *The Four Temperaments*. He knew that the music referred to the theory of the four temperaments of "humours" of medieval medicine, corresponding to the four elements of physics and, with them, determining the characters of human individuals. In the ballet, however, this philosophical idea was not used as material for a descriptive or narrative drama, but at most only as an abstract scheme relating four choreographic – not conceptual – themes in a composition of pure classical dance. In some ways it had a distinct similarity to Hindemith's *Neue Sachlichkeit* in music. The modern dance influence which some have professed to see in this work has, if it ever existed, been completely integrated in Balanchine's balletic neoclassicism, of which *The Four Temperaments* is one of the most complete and significant examples. The ballet is now in the permanent repertory of the New York City Ballet in a definitive version in which the original sets and costumes have been abandoned in favour of a neutral background and practice clothes. It has been revived by numerous other companies all over the world.   A.A.

ORLANDO'S MADNESS (La Follia di Orlando)

Ballet in three scenes. Choreography by Aurel Milloss. Scenario (after Ariosto) and music by Goffredo Petrassi. Sets and costumes by Felice Casorati. Milan, Scala, April 12, 1947. Principal dancers: Ugo Dell'Ara (Orlando), Wanda Sciaccaluga (Angelica), Carlo Faraboni (Rinaldo), Ennio Sammartino (Medoro), Ladislao Lesnievsky (Astolfo).

SYNOPSIS. Episodes taken from Ariosto's *Orlando Furioso*. Scene I: Orlando and Rinaldo are rivals for the love of Angelica. Scene II: the love between Angelica and Medoro is discovered after Orlando has long searched for his beloved. Orlando falls into madness. Scene III: Astolfo restores him to sanity. The army celebrates the paladin's return and the triumph of reason.

■ This was one of Aurel Milloss's most important works during his time as choreographer and ballet director at the Scala in Milan. Recommended by Arturo Toscanini, he had taken up the post in 1946, the year when the rebuilt theater was reopened. In this production the collaboration of a composer and a stage designer of the caliber of Goffredo Petrassi and Felice Casorati, to say nothing of a group of first-class dancers trained by Milloss himself, bears witness to the Hungarian choreographer's endeavours during his career of over thirty years to raise Italian ballet to its former glory. The epic subject-matter and scenic splendour of *La Follia di Orlando* might seem to place it in the category of grand heroic-romantic ballet. However, the narrative and mimic content is almost entirely dispensed with because Petrassi's score contains a baritone recitative which tells the story, thus freeing the choreography to develop its independent dramatic and lyrical dimension and create a composition in Milloss's most airy and classical style.

OTHER VERSIONS. Tatiana Gsovsky. Milan, Scala, 1964. Principal dancers: Mario Pistoni, Carla Fracci, Bruno Telloli, Roberto Fascilla, Walter Venditti.   A.A.

CRYSTAL PALACE (Palais de Cristal)
(Later called Symphony in C)
Choreography by George Balanchine. Music by Georges Bizet. Set and costumes by Léonor Fini. Paris, Opéra, July 28, 1947. Principal dancers: Lycette Darsonval and Alexandre Kalioujni, Tamara Toumanova and Roger Ritz, Micheline Bardin and Michel Renault, Madeleine Lafon and Max Bozzoni.

SYNOPSIS. A ballet without a plot.

■ Summoned to Paris by the administrator Hirsch for a short period in 1947, Balanchine enriched the Opéra's repertory with several classical works, including *Serenade*, *Apollon Musagète* and *Le Baiser de la Feé*, and also produced this fascinating novelty which was to become famous throughout the world. Provided at first with a sumptuous decor by Léonor Fini, the ballet was later made more completely abstract by being danced in classical costume before a plain blue background. The choreography followed the four movements of Bizet's symphony according to consistent rules, each of the movements having a different pair of soloists and a different deployment of groups in the *corps de ballet*. Balanchine, with his perfect style, interpreted the musical directions in depth: naturally there was a particular composition to match each movement, lively for the opening *allegro*, slow and gentle in the *adagio*, sparkling again for the *allegro vivace*, then rising to a virtuoso level in the final *allegro* and ending with a transcending ensemble, and extraordinary effective final picture. Under the title *Symphony in C*, the work has remained in the repertory of the New York City Ballet, where it has been performed on numerous occasions from 1948 onwards. It has also been danced by the companies of other nations. Its success stems not only from the rich and inventive choreography, but also from its ability to bring out the best in soloists, and *corps de ballet* by means of classical tradition moulded by a modern mind.   M.P.

PORTRAIT OF DON QUIXOTE (Le Portrait de Don Quichotte)
One-act ballet. Subject and choreography by Aurel Milloss. Music by Goffredo Petrassi. Set and costumes by Tom Keogh. Paris, Théâtre des Champs Elysées, November 21, 1947. Les Ballets des Champs Elysées. Principal dancers: Jean Babileé (Don Quixote), Nathalie Philippart (Dulcinea), Christian Foye (Sancho).

SYNOPSIS. A man, obsessed by the character of Don Quixote, wants to repeat his hero's adventures. His servants play along with him, understanding his aberration, and helping him to dress as the new Don Quixote. But the imitation Knight runs into the same troubles as the original. His burning vision urges him towards knightly feats in which he fails; he undergoes ascetic hardships to make him worthy of his ideal incarnated in Dulcinea; he throws himself enthusiastically into hopeless ventures to better the lot of his fellowmen. The crowd only laughs at him and shuts him up in a cage. In trying to escape from it he wounds himself mortally. At that moment he comes to his senses, although his servants still keep up the pious pretence and the faithful Sancho brings him the book of his hero to put him in good heart. He knows now that all is illusion, and dies beneath a shower of leaves from the book scattered from above. Dulcinea reappears, and with her the real Don Quixote, who takes from her hands a bunch of violets and lays it on the body of his would-be imitator.

■ The chivalrous and pathetic figure of Cervantes's hero has inspired numerous works in the history of ballet (see page 132), especially the imaginative narrative elements of the story. Milloss, on the contrary, wanted to make the fullest use of Don Quixote's symbolic dimension and express the ideals that motivated him, reducing the external happenings of Cervantes's plot to a minimum. The ballet shares the characteristics of all Milloss's theatrical work, with its concentrated stylistic austerity and clarity of dramatic expression on the one hand, and on the other its density of poetic content never conceived in merely descriptive or narrative terms but conveyed by myth and symbol rich in cultural, philosophical, and literary implications, yet clear in its abstract idealism and universality. Thus, we have Don Quixote, the sad protagonist of unattainable ideals, in the center of the stage, while the phantasms of his hallucinated imagination gather about him one by one, ranging between the poles of pure spirituality and earthy realism, personified by Dulcinea and Sancho respectively, placed in two little booths, one each side of the set. Everything is expressed in terms of dance in whose essential composition the abstract conceptual scheme finds an artistic reality. The score by Goffredo Petrassi, one of the composers closest to Milloss, was of high inspirational quality. *The Portrait of Don Quixote*, after opening in Paris with great acclaim, was performed by the Ballets des Champs Elysées Company in theaters all over the world. In Italy the ballet was produced at the Opera House in Rome in 1957.   A.A.

Erik Bruhn and Jill Gregory in The Moor's Pavane *by Jose Limon.*

LES MIRAGES

One-act ballet. Choreography by Serge Lifar. Music by Henri Sauguet. Scenario by A. M. Cassandre and Serge Lifar. Sets and costumes by A. M. Cassandre. Paris, Opéra, December 15, 1947. Principal dancers: Yvette Chauviré (the Shadow), Michel Renault (the Young Man), Micheline Bardin (the Woman), Paulette Dynalix (the Moon), Madeleine Lafon (the Chimera), Max Bozzoni (the Merchant).

SYNOPSIS. "In her palace the Moon awakes. The Queen of the Night, still heavy with dreams, rises from her bed of clouds and, preceded by the Shepherd who guides her on her nocturnal pilgrimage, leaves her empty home behind. Unseen, a Young Man creeps inside. His Shadow, who dogs his footsteps, begs him to continue on his way, but he repulses the importunate shade, for on the Moon's abandoned couch he has found the key of dreams. He rushes into the palace, turns the key in a lock, and unintentionally releases the Daughters of the Night. For him they open the gate of illusions: the dream, riches, love. Yet always the object of his desire eludes him. He remains alone with his Shadow. The Chimera vanishes, the Merchants cheat him, the Woman dies in his arms. He is alone with his Shadow. As the day dawns he leaves and she follows him, the only companion he recognizes at last, his solitude" (A. M. Cassandre-S. Lifar).

■ The theme of solitude dominates *Les Mirages*, one of Serge Lifar's best-known ballets. The brilliant melodic invention of Henri Sauguet's score and the fantastic, stylized baroque of Cassandre's stage design, perfectly match the dreaming melancholy of the choreographic enchantment that Lifar weaves into a diaphanous yet rich tissue of dance. The symbolic action unfolds in an orderly flow that reveals the rich variety of the evolutions, steps, and longer passages of dance in the best Lifar tradition, combining classical purity of form with dramatic coherence and density. *Les Mirages* was ready in 1944, but was not performed until 1947, when "King Lifar" returned from an exile to which political and personal passions had forced him. Many years later he wrote of his ballet, ". . . Life is nothing but a succession of illusions which dissolve, leaving Man alone in the face of an indifferent Nature. . . . The final crescendo of Sauguet's music, which soars to the sky like the rising sun while the Palace of the Moon evaporates into thin air, accentuates the loneliness of mankind, lost, with its shadow, in immensity." The ballet was highly thought of on its first appearance and afterwards, some of the credit going to Yvette Chauviré, with her excellent technique and elegant, noble stage presence, who took the part of the Shadow, partnered by the first-rate classical dancer Michel Renault. *Les Mirages* was revived at the Paris Opéra, directed by the choreographer, on October 18, 1977, on the occasion of a *Hommage à Serge Lifar*. A.A.

ETUDE (or *Études*)

One-act ballet. Choreography by Harald Lander. Music by Carl Czerny (Études), arranged by Knudage Riisager. Set by Nordgren. Copenhagen, Theater Royal, January 15, 1948. Principal dancers: Margot Lander, Hans Brenaa, Svend Erik Jensen.

SYNOPSIS. Ballet without a plot. It consists of eighteen parts and simply shows the development of dance steps.

■ Under the title *Études*, the ballet was revived at the Paris Opéra on November 19, 1952, danced by Bardin, Michel Renault, and Alexandre Kalioujny, and was considered to be one of the most beautiful ballets in the Opéra's repertory. It lasts half an hour and was arranged by Lander, bearing in mind the special skills of the Danish Ballet (his first wife, Margot, was in the cast). His second wife, Toni Lander, danced in the production of *Études* in London in 1955 and in New York in 1961. C.M.C.

ORPHEUS

Ballet in three scenes. Choreography by George Balanchine. Music by Igor Stravinsky. Sets and costumes by Isamu Noguchi. Lighting by Jean Rosenthal. New York, New York City Center, April 28, 1948. Ballet Society. Principal dancers: Nicholas Magallanes (Orpheus), Maria Tallchief (Eurydice), Francisco Moncion (Black Angel), Beatrice Tompkins (Queen of the Furies), Tanaquil Leclercq (Queen of the Bacchantes), Herbert Bliss (Apollo).

SYNOPSIS. Scene I: Orpheus is standing, with his back to the audience, before the tomb of his wife Eurydice. After a long dance of mourning he tries in vain to elicit a note from his lyre, but no sound will come. He implores the gods for succour and at last the Black Angel of Death appears and leads him over the Styx towards his lost love. Over his eyes Orpheus wears a golden mask which he must not remove until the end of his journey. Scene II: in Hades, Orpheus and the Angel enter the realm of the Furies, who bar their way. The Angel urges Orpheus to play his lyre and, since the singer cannot see because he is blindfolded, moves his fingers on the strings. At the heavenly sound of the music the Furies grow calm and the tormented souls come out to listen. Finally, Pluto himself appears and pushes Eurydice towards Orpheus until their hands are joined. The two lovers set off on their journey to the land of the living. The way is hard, especially for the man. Eurydice falls and, contact once lost, Orpheus can no longer find her hand. At last, tormented by the desire to see his wife, he takes off his golden mask. Instantly Eurydice sinks lifeless to the ground. Orpheus finds himself back in the world, alone; his arms clutch desperately at the void. He turns to pick up his lyre, but at that moment it disappears. The Bacchantes enter and surround Orpheus, whose eyes are once more masked. They try to seize the mask, then attack him with violence. The music accentuates the singer's terror as the Bacchantes tear him apart piece by piece before beheading him. Scene

A scene from The Age of Anxiety *performed by the New York City Ballet. The work is by Jerome Robbins.*

III: Apollo approaches the remains of Orpheus, raises the golden mask to the skies, calling upon the dead singer's spirit as the god of music. But the sounds that emerge are but a pale imitation of Orpheus's heavenly song. Apollo stays irresolute in front of the tomb. From that monument a flower-garlanded lyre raises heavenwards, symbol of the tenderness and power of music.

■ This modern version of the Orpheus myth was beautifully adapted for the stage by the Japanese sculptor Noguchi, who was among the chief agents of the ballet's success. The choreography is simple, adhering faithfully to the music and the dramatic action.

OTHER VERSIONS. John Cranko. Stuttgart, June 6, 1970. Stuttgart Ballet. Principal dancers: Birgit Keil and Heinz Clauss.   C.M.C.

MARSYAS
Dramatic ballet in one act. Scenario and choreography by Aurel Milloss. Music by Luigi Dallapiccola. Set and costumes by Toti Scialoja. Venice, Fenice Theater, September 9, 1948. Rome Opera Ballet. Principal dancers: E. Foggiolti (Marsyas), Walter Zappolini (Apollo).

SYNOPSIS. The satyr Marsyas discovers a flute discarded by Athene, and with it the gift of music. With enthusiasm he learns to play it skillfully, and dances with frantic joy. Apollo appears; Marsyas, possessed by a reckless spirit, challenges him to a musical contest. The indignant god accepts the challenge and asks the Muses to judge. They come, accompanied by Scythian warriors. Marsyas plays his flute, performing a Dyonisiac dance with wood nymphs. Then Apollo dances to

Tamara Toumanova (Phaedra) and Serge Lifar (Hippolytus) at the first performance of Phèdre *by Cocteau, Lifar, and Auric, 1950.*

the sound of his divine lyre, and, not content with being judged the winner, reverses his instrument and continues to play. Marsyas tries in vain to do the same with his flute, his despairing dance revealing the enormity of attempting to vie with the gods. Apollo and the Muses now feel some pity for him, but the sentence is irreversible. Marsyas is flayed by the Scythians and dies surrounded by the nymphs. The tears that run from their eyes join with the blood of the dead satyr to give rise to a river, the symbol of the immortality that Apollo bestows upon his defeated rival.

■ Luigi Dallapiccola composed the score of *Marsyas* in 1942–1943 at the peak of his creative career, when he was working in close collaboration with Milloss and deeply involved with the choreographer's theories of drama. The myth of Marsyas, symbolizing the tragic defeat of human genius, nourished by Dionysiac fervour, in the face of the inflexible Apollonian perfection of a distant deity, has been endowed by Milloss with a universality of meaning expressed in strictly choreographical terms that makes this ballet a masterpiece among his "classical" works. Thus, the dualism between the human and divine, the Dionysiac and the Apollonian, is expressed not by any allegorical or narrative pantomime, but in terms of pure dance, contrasting the lively, emotional group of nymphs encircling Marsyas with the static mass of Scythians, instruments of divine power. In the case of the two protagonists, the opposition is represented by a difference in style between the

dancing of Apollo, essentially classical, and that of Marsyas, contorted and dynamic. The ballet has often been revived in Italy and other countries. For the productions at the Rome Opera in 1969 and the Scala, Milan, in 1975, the original stage designs of Toti Scialoja were replaced those of Corrado Cagli.   A.A.

THE FOUR SEASONS
Ballet in four scenes. Choreography by Léonide Massine. Music by Antonio Vivaldi. Sets and costumes by Pierre Roy. Scala, Milan, February 19, 1949. Principal dancers: Olga Amati, Walter Venditti, Gilda Majocchi, Attilio Veneri, Vera Colombo, Luciana Novaro, Ugo Dell'Ara.

SYNOPSIS. The ballet, divided into four scenes, begins with "Winter," a classical *ballet blanc*: dances by various characters typify the season. The scene ends with a *pas de deux* by two poor people in the rain. The second scene, "Spring," opens with a shepherd dreaming of a refined girl, a figment of his imagination. His rude awakening among his fellows is a sad disappointment. "Summer," the third scene, follows the pattern of a *ballet de cour*, with dances and variations on the theme of cuckoo, turtle dove, and goldfinch. The fourth and last scene, "Autumn," is also the most complicated and filled with fantastic episodes (such as the drunkard's dream). The season of singing and dancing the harvest in, it ends with a bacchanale.

A scene in Revelations, *a ballet by Alvin Ailey to traditional Afro—American music, a significant example of the eclecticism of modern dance.*

■ Massine's choreography, designed for the Scala, follows the scheme laid down by Vivaldi. The ballet consists of four fanciful scenes, each lasting about ten minutes. In the choreography, imaginative, noble, and comic scenes alternate with one another.　　M.B.

CARMEN

Dramatic ballet in five scenes. Choreography by Roland Petit. Music by George Bizet. Subject inspired by the opera of the same name written by Meilhac and Halévy, and in its turn drawn from Prosper Mérimée's novel. Sets and costumes by Antoni Clavé. London, Prince's Theatre, February 21, 1949. Ballets de Paris. Principal dancers: Renée Jeanmaire and Roland Petit.

SYNOPSIS. Scene I: a street in Seville. Cries are heard from the third story of a building. Two girls come running down a staircase: one of them is Carmen. They are fighting. Don Jose approaches with the intention of separating them, but remains fascinated and completely dominated by Carmen's provocative attitude. Already enslaved by passion, he asks her to meet him again. Scene II: in a tavern. Don Jose dances to the well-known tune of the *Habanera*. Suddenly Carmen appears at the top of the stairs. An admirer begins a campaign of seduction and tries in vain to pester her as she flings herself into a whirling dance. Carmen stops in front of Don Jose, who picks her up and carries her out of the door. Scene III: Carmen's bedroom. It is morning and Don Jose draws the curtains to wake Carmen, who is still asleep. When she wakes the girl tries to rearouse his passion. He is about to yield when three of Carmen's friends enter and persuade the two to follow them. Scene IV: a street in Seville at night. Carmen, her friends, and Don Jose plan to commit a robbery. The latter, completely dominated by Carmen, lies in wait for a passer-by. A man appears and the infatuated lover first stabs him and then takes his money. Carmen and the others draw near, seize the booty, and run away, dragging Don Jose after them. Scene V: entrance of the bull ring in Seville. When the toreador arrives he has eyes for no one but Carmen. Don Jose is also there, and suddenly realizes that the same hypnotic power the girl has exercised on him will now serve to ensnare the toreador. Overcome by a fit of violent jealousy, he throws himself on Carmen as if to strangle her. The girl tries to free herself from his grasp and the two begin a furious duel. Carmen dies, killed by the knife of the man who loves her.　　M.S.M.

THE BRONZE HORSEMAN (*Mednij Vsadnik*)

Ballet in four acts and nine scenes. Choreography by R. Zakharov. Music by Reinhold Glier. Sets and costumes by Bibishov. Leningrad, Kirov Theater, June 6, 1949. Principal dancers: N. Dudinskaia (Parasa) and K. Sergeyev (Evghenij).

SYNOPSIS. The bronze horseman of the title is the statue of Peter the Great, which dominates Petersburg and represents the inflexible and indifferent processes of state. In the shadow of this historic statue, love is born between Parasa and Evghenij. It is 1824, the year of the terrible inundation, during which Parasa is drowned in the invading waters. In despair, Evghenij tries to escape the rising flood. He dies exhausted, cursing the monument of Peter the Great. and his indifference to the suffering of mankind.

■ Made in honour of the 150th anniversary of Pushkin's birth, this production was one of the first Soviet ballets to give the principal role to a male dancer. On such an occasion Zakharov knew how to make full use of virile movement, not neglecting, of course, the athleticism that is one of the essential components of the masculine side of the Russian school.　　P.C.

THE MOOR'S PAVANE

One-act ballet. Choreography by Jose Limon. Music by Henry Purcell. Costumes by Pauline Lawrence. New London, Connecticut College, August 17, 1949. Jose Limon Company. Principal dancers: Jose Limon, Betty Jones, Lucas Hoving, Pauline Koner.

SYNOPSIS. Variations on the theme of *Othello* for four characters: the Moor, his wife, the friend, the friend's wife, in whom we recognize Othello, Desdemona, Iago, and Emilia. The famous story is reduced to its essential ingredients and resembles a grand minuet of love, betrayal, jealousy, death, and retribution. The conflict is played out as if in some fearful inferno in the violence of its passions and the fatal spiral descent from which there is no way out. The ballet portrays the destruction of life and happiness through the unreason of jealousy.

■ *The Moor's Pavane* is unanimously classed as a masterpiece of modern dance and was one of the greatest choreographic achievements of the late Jose Limon, a most interesting figure in American dance. The noble attitude, the strength of passion, and the plastic richness of the choreography are the basic elements which guarantee *Pavane* an honoured place in contemporary ballet.　　M.P.

THE AGE OF ANXIETY

Dramatic ballet in six scenes. Choreography by Jerome Robbins. Music by Leonard Bernstein. Scenario by Jerome Robbins, drawn from The Age of Anxiety *by Wystan Hugh Auden. Sets by Oliver Smith. Costumes by Irene Sharaff. New York, New York City Center of Music and Drama, February 26, 1950. New York City Ballet. Principal dancers: Tanaquil Le Clercq, Francisco Moncion, Todd Bolender, Jerome Robbins, Melissa Hayden, Patricia McBride, Yvonne Mounsey, Beatrice Tompkins, Edward Bigelow, Herbert Bliss.*

SYNOPSIS. Following the scheme of Auden's poem on which the ballet is based, Robbins has divided the work into six parts: *The Prologue, The Seven Ages, The Seven Stages, The Dirge, The Masque, The Epilogue.* Three men and one woman (one of the men is danced by Robbins himself) meet each other for the first time. In their relationship to the others (whether of love or friendship) all are searching for a deep security, something in which to place their hope, or simply a justification for their own existence. Around these four leading characters move various groups of dancers personifying the indifference and violence of society, servility to the bosses, the frenzied pursuit of pleasure, youth, vain desires, and ambition. Some are anonymous figures of mystery, others ordinary, everyday people. In the end, disillusioned, the four characters accept the inevitable loneliness of the human condition and separate, each going his own way.

■ Robbins himself said of this ballet, "It is an attempt to understand the meaning of life." In this work, as in many of his others, which tend to deal with big and complex themes or to portray a rich variety of states of mind and feeling, Robbins has used a wide range of choreographical images, making thorough use of the technical and stylistic vocabularies of classical and modern dance, seizing on every rhythmic or melodic shade of Bernstein's *Second Symphony*, to which this ballet is danced.   M.P.

MISS JULIE *(Fröken Julia)*
Ballet in one act and four scenes. Choreography by Birgit Cullberg. Music by Ture Rangström. Scenario by Allan Fridericia (from the play by August Strindberg). Sets and costumes from the original sketches by Sven Erikson. Västeras, Swedish State Theater, Cullberg Ballets, March 1, 1950. Principal dancers: Elsa Marianne von Rosen (Miss Julie), Julius Mengarelli (Jean), Birgit Cullberg (Kristine).

SYNOPSIS. On a summer evening in 1880 the Count presents to his daughter Julie the fiancé he has chosen for her. Dissatisfied with the forced engagement, she teases her suitor and makes fun of him. Left to herself, the girl goes to the servants' hall of the castle, where a party is in progress. She persuades the valet, Jean, to dance with her, then follows him into the kitchen quarters and finally to his room. When she leaves it at dawn she is surprised by the cook, Kristine. Feeling that she can no longer look her father in the eye, Julie determines to run away with Jean. Before leaving home she plans to take possession of the family jewels, but when she reaches the portrait gallery it seems to her that the ancestral portraits are regarding her with disapproving eyes and that the founder of the family is handing her his sword so that she can kill herself and save her honour. Julie faints. When she regains consciousness, the sword is in her hands. It is pointed at her breast when Jean enters the room for his usual morning inspection. He tries to take the weapon from her, but she uses his hands to kill herself.   C.M.C.

PHAEDRA *(Phèdre)*
One-act ballet. Choreography by Serge Lifar. Music by Georges Auric. Scenario, set, and costumes by Jean

Cocteau. Paris, Opéra, June 14, 1950. Principal dancers: Tamara Toumanova (Phaedra), Serge Lifar (Hippolytus), Liane Daydé (Aricia), Lycette Darsonval (Oenone), Roger Ritz (Theseus).*

SYNOPSIS. Phaedra (Phèdre) nourishes a fatal passion for her stepson, Hippolytus. Suffering from her love as if it were a malady, she reveals it to no one until the nurse cunningly wrings the secret from her with false news of the death of Theseus, her husband, and Hippolytus's father. When the nurse, Oenone, tells Hippolytus of the Queen's infatuation, he, who loves the Princess Aricia, responds with proud disdain. Phaedra kills herself, and the nurse sends a slanderous message to Theseus, throwing the blame for her death on Hippolytus. Theseus curses his son and sends him into exile. Chariot horses trample Hippolytus to death. Only now do the gods explain the tragic sequence of errors, predestined by themselves, and promise Hippolytus divine honours.

■ *Phèdre*, a tragic ballet by Jean Cocteau to interesting music by Georges Auric, contains some of the most dramatically expressive passages of dance created by Lifar in his versatile career. Nevertheless, the flavour of the whole work is dominated by the overwhelming artistic personality of Cocteau, who reconstituted the *Phèdre et Hippolyte* of Racine, inspired in his turn by Euripides's tragedy. Although the story is presented in its barest essence, it is conveyed with a hallucinatory dramatic intensity. Amid dazzling colour, and in front of a scene of brilliant simplicity, somewhere between a temple and a puppet theater, the legend of inexorable fate is unfolded by means of symbols, and the immediate drama of the characters played out. Lifar was able to give his exclusively choreographic invention free rein in the brief lyrical passages, while in the terse dramatic episodes he deliberately limited himself to the tragic intensity of pure gesture, in a mood that was almost expressionist. *Phèdre*, removed from the repertory of the Paris Opéra during Lifar's fifteen-year absence, was reinstated on the occasion of the *Hommage à Serge Lifar* on October 18, 1977, in which the leading roles of Phaedra and Hippolytus were danced by Claire Motte and Michaël Denard.   A.A.

THE DIAMOND-MUNCHER *(La Croqueuse de Diamants)*
Ballet in four parts. Choreography by Roland Petit. Music by Jean-Michel Damase. Scenario by Roland Petit and Alfred Adam. Sets and costumes by Georges Wakhevich. Paris, Théâtre Marigny, September 25, 1950. Principal dancers: Renée Jeanmaire, Roland Petit, Gordon Hamilton.

SYNOPSIS. A beautiful woman has a most unusual peculiarity. She is greedy for diamonds – not to wear but to eat. The ballet follows her adventures in shops and bars, among thieves and people of all sorts. Her hand creeps into other people's pockets; there are sentimental episodes, interventions by the police, escapes, songs both doubtful and delightful.

A ballet rehearsal conducted by the French choreographer, Jean Babilée.

■ *La Croqueuse de Diamants* is more of a "musical" than a traditional ballet. Cleverly contrived by Roland Petit in his most brilliant vein, the piece was made to measure for Renée ("Zizi") Jeanmaire, who showed in it all her qualities as a singing, dancing star with elegant, irresistible verve.   M.S.M.

MEDEA

Ballet in five scenes. Choreography and scenario by Birgit Cullberg. Music by Béla Bartòk; orchestration by Herbert Sandberg. London, Prince's Theatre, February 12, 1951, Royal Swedish Ballet.

SYNOPSIS. Scene I: the happiness of Medea and Jason is destroyed by Creusa, daughter of Creon, King of Corinth. Jason falls in love with her and leaves Medea in order to follow her. Scene II: Creon approves the union of Jason and Creusa. Scene III: Medea cannot forgive the repentant Jason his infidelity. Scene IV: Jason marries Creusa. Medea takes part in the ceremony, offering poisoned gifts to her rival, who dies. Scene V: Jason returns home to claim his children, but Medea kills them.

■ The ballet (actually first danced on October 31, 1950, at the State Theater of Gaevle in Sweden with Maurice Béjart as Jason) was based on the tragedy by Euripides, which it followed fairly closely, supported by various of Bartòk's piano pieces orchestrated. In one version or another, it was quite successful in the English-speaking world.   M.P.

THE CAGE

One-act ballet. Choreography by Jerome Robbins. Music by Igor Stravinsky. Scenario by Jerome Robbins. Set by Jean Rosenthal. Costumes by Ruth Sobotka. New York, New York City Center, June 14, 1951. New York City Ballet. Principal dancers: Nora Kaye (the Novice), Yvonne Mounsey (the Queen), Michael Maule (the First Intruder), Nicholas Magallanes (the Second Intruder).

SYNOPSIS. In a society ruled by women only, a female, the daughter of the Queen, is to pass through a macabre rite of initiation. Left alone, the Novice receives the attentions of a masculine intruder whom she kills. The women begin a dance of victory, but are interrupted by the arrival of a second stranger. Alone again, the Novice this time yields to the man's attraction and the appeal of love. When the Queen and her companions return, she tries at first to defend her lover, then catches the homicidal fury of the group. The male is killed and devoured; the women celebrate their triumph.

■ The costumes, the vaguely cellular patterns of the set, and even the dancers' movements effectively suggest, without making explicit, the ballet's point of departure: in certain insect species the female devours the male after using him for reproductive purposes. Robbins's idea was to stage an allegory of the modern woman seen as a queen bee, and the general atmosphere has something savage and demoniacal about it. The dancing is based partly on the classical style and partly on original invention so as to produce the most effective dramatic vocabulary available. Harsh symbols, absence of beauty, claws, spider's webs accentuate the horrendous rite imagined by Robbins in a mood of misogyny. The music is the *Concerto Grosso for strings in D* by Stravinsky in his neoclassical period.   M.B.

REVENGE *(Vendetta or Revanche)*

Ballet in four scenes and a prologue. Choreography by Ruth Page. Music by Giuseppe Verdi. Scenario by Ruth Page and Nicholas Remisov. Sets and costumes by Antoni Clavé. Paris, Théâtre de l'Empire, October 17, 1951. Ballets des Champs Elysées. Principal dancers: Sonia Arova (Azucena), Vladimir Skuratov (Manrico), Jacqueline Moreau (Leonora), Gérard Ohn (Count di Luna).

SYNOPSIS. Prologue: Count di Luna discovers an old gypsy woman hovering around his son's cradle. The gypsy is accused of witchcraft and condemned to be burned at the stake. For revenge, her daughter Azucena kidnaps one of the Count's other sons and disappears. Scene I: twenty years later. The old Count is dying and asks his other son to continue the search for his lost brother. This brother, brought up by Azucena, alive and now called Manrico, is in love with Leonora, maid of honour to the Queen. The new Count di Luna is jealous and wants to separate them. Leonora and Manrico take refuge in the gypsies' camp. Scene II: following the two lovers, the Count arrives in the camp and challenges

Rosella Hightower in Piège de Lumière, *a ballet by John Taras to music by Jean-Michel Damase.*

Manrico. The Count loses, but his life is spared. He then seizes Leonora and Manrico and imprisons them. Scene III: under torture Leonora promises to marry the Count if he will free Manrico. Scene IV: the wedding is being prepared. Manrico accuses Leonora of infidelity, but the girl, having taken poison to avoid marrying the Count, dies in his arms. The Count orders Manrico to be killed. Upon that Azucena reveals that the two are brothers.

■ The ballet is based on Verdi's *Il Trovatore.* The story is greatly condensed, rising to a dramatic – even melodramatic – climax with perhaps an excess of realism. It is one of the rare examples of a ballet sharing the sentiments that people have grown used to in opera and, unfortunately, retaining the dramatic defects of opera (singing being excluded) while losing its delights.   M.P.

A scene from Deuil en 24 Heures, *devised by Roland Petit to music by Maurice Thiriet.*

LE MASSACRE DES AMAZONES

One-act ballet. Choreography by Janine Charrat. Music by Ivan K. Semenoff. Subject by Janine Cherrat and Maurice Sarrazin. Sets and costumes by Jean Bazaine. Grenoble, Municipal Theater, December 24, 1951. The Janine Charrat Ballet Company. Principal dancers: Janine Charrat (Queen of the Amazons), René Bon (White Horse).

SYNOPSIS. There is a battle between the Amazons and the horses they are trying to tame. The Queen falls victim to the White Horse who massacres the warriors and carries away the body of the dead Queen.

■ This is a personal version of the classical contrast between human intelligence (the Amazons) and animal instinct (the horses). The action is laid in ancient Greece, represented by a set consisting of very few pieces in a very modern style. Janine Charrat created this ballet for the company she founded in the same year, 1951. Ten years later her career as a dancer (she was at the height of her powers and distinguished by a blend of sensitivity and violence) was cut tragically short when she was seriously injured in a fire while rehearsing her ballet *Les Algues* for Parisian television. Later Charrat returned to the stage for a few sporadic appearances, after which she devoted herself to teaching, opening her own

ballet school in Paris in 1969. In 1956 she produced *The Seven Deadly Sins* at the Scala.   C.M.C.

PICNIC AT TINTAGEL

Dramatic ballet in three scenes. Choreography and scenario by Frederick Ashton. Music by Arnold Bax. Sets and costumes by Cecil Beaton. New York, New York City Center, February 28, 1952. New York City Ballet. Principal dancers: Francisco Moncion, Diana Adams, Jacques d'Amboise, Robert Barnett.

SYNOPSIS. The ballet is a transposition of the famous legend of Tristan and Isolde into a period centuries later (1916). The setting is Tintagel, a rocky promontory in Cornwall, where there are ruins supposed to be those of the castle of King Arthur and his knights of the Round Table. Tristan brought the beautiful Isolde there to be the bride of King Mark. The story takes place in the ancient castle. Scene I: the custodian moves about the stage as if only he understood the building's magic. A group of tourists enters, among them a man, his wife, and another man. The husband approaches the caretaker, turning his back on the other two, who unseen take one another tenderly by the hand. The caretaker opens a bottle and pours out a magic potion, and suddenly there is a vortex of people with picnic baskets. The

The New York City Ballet in George Balanchine's Western Symphony.

wine is offered to the woman and her lover. As they put the glass to their lips, the music burst into stormy sound. The other tourists are terrified and take flight. Scene II: the custodian turns and turns about the stage, which at his orders undergoes a magical change. The ruins disappear and we see a room in the castle of King Mark. The caretaker's dream has come true: he has become the magician Merlin, while the man and woman who drank the potion are Tristan and Isolde. The situation repeats itself; two men love the same woman. Tristan and Isolde, left alone, embrace one another tenderly, not knowing that they are observed by one of the King's knights. They dance, and finally sink to the floor in a passionate embrace. But the idyllic atmosphere is suddenly interrupted by King Mark, who accuses Tristan of betraying him. The two men cross swords. Isolde tries to separate them but is wounded and falls to the ground. Tristan is also struck by the king and falls. Scene III: the actors in the tragedy disappear, darkness falls on the stage, the castle vanishes, leaving ruins in its place. In their modern clothes the wife and her lover look into each other's eyes and seem not to have ceased to be Tristan and Isolde. However, the husband enters and pushes his friend to one side, the friend looking at him without understanding. The caretaker comes in as the light fades. Once more alone in the castle, he holds in his hands the crossed swords of the fatal duel. The musical motif of the beginning is heard again, conveying the impression that the story will be repeated *ad infinitum*.

■ The ballet was very favourably received and might have been the start of a longer collaboration between the English choreographer and the New York City Ballet after the success of *Illuminations*. The production was very carefully researched. Ashton (with Beaton) not only worked on the site of the legend, but reread the Arthurian texts and chose music that would suggest both the ancient and the modern. In *Picnic* Ashton's brilliant narrative style reached a high dramatic and emotional level. M.P.

LAUDES EVANGELII
Choreographical mystery in two parts. Choreography by Léonide Massine. Medieval Umbrian sources researched by Giorgio Signorini. Music by Valentino Bucchi (from ancient Laudi *– hymns of praise). Sets and costumes by Ezio Rossi. Perugia, Chiesa di San Domenico, September 26, 1952. Principal dancers: Angelo Pietri (Christ), Geneviève Lespagnol (Mary), Carlo Faraboni (Joseph), Alberto Moro (St. John), Bianca Lampideccia (Veronica), Alberto Testa (Judas). Singers: Antonietta Stella, Rina Corsi, Renato Cappecchi, Silvio Maionica.*

SYNOPSIS. The eight scenes represent the same number of episodes from the Christian gospels: the Annunciation, the Nativity, the Massacre of the Innocents, the Flight into Egypt, the Garden of Gethsemane, the Way of the Cross, The Deposition, the Resurrection.

■ The Umbrian and Tuscan *Laudari* of the fourteenth century provided the textual basis of this moving and visually splendid "choreographic mystery" in which Léonide Massine carried to its logical conclusion the reduction of dance to pure symbolic gesture, and of choreographic composition to massive crowd scenes, as he had already done in *Nobilissma Visione* (see page 228), in an inverse ratio to the classical style of his other works of the same period. From the balletic, literary, and musical points of view, *Laudes Evangelii* was, however, not an archeological reconstruction, but the literally faithful use of single episodes in a very new and vital dramatic form. As Giorgio Signorini, special adviser on the literary sources, wrote, "the *Laudes*, in fact, is not a miracle play or a sequence of dramatized hymns of praise; nor does it imitate the original Umbrian and Tuscan theatrical productions of the fourteenth century. But while it is no 'imitation' as far as faithfulness to those dramatic forms is concerned, it nevertheless aims at a close correspondence with their narrative content, in which 'narration' is indeed both chronicle and drama, a vein of pure, profoundly popular, poetry. The intention behind *Laudes Evangelii* was to translate a story reconstructed from old manuscripts into a new form of theater; to create a contemporary version of that language." Valentino Bucchi, the composer, elucidated further: "Regarding the musical text of this work, we followed, with very few exceptions, the old *Laudi*, remaining faithful, as far as language went, to the original harmonized melody according to the canons of the *ars antiqua*. Having made this musical language our base, however, we felt we could use the utmost freedom in the arrangement of the individual components, the instrumentation, and the tonality." A.A.

LIGHT TRAP *(Piège de Lumière)*
Ballet in three acts. Choreography by John Taras. Scenario by Philippe Hériat. Music by Jean-Michel Damase. Scenery by Felix Labisse. Costumes by André Levasseur. Insect masks by Marie Molotkov. Paris, Théâtre de l'Empire, December 23, 1952. Marquis de Cuevas Ballet. Principal dancers: Rosella Hightower, Vladimir Skuratoff, Serge Golovine.

SYNOPSIS. This unusual story takes place in a virgin forest where a group of escaped convicts live on what they can hunt. The equatorial surroundings are wild and violent. In the heat of the night the fugitives light dazzling beacons to attract insects. At once exotic moths and strange beetles converge on the beam of light and, after fluttering desperately round it, fall at the foot of the trap. Two winged insects, in love with one another, perform a fascinating dance. The male sacrifices himself in vain to save the female from capture, but the young convict who has picked her up by the wings finds nothing left in his hand but a luminous trail.

■ This is one of the most original ballets in the modern repertory. A particularly striking choreographic passage is the procession of escaped prisoners carrying in their arms the inert forms of the moths and butterflies. The robust strength of the bare-chested hunters makes a moving contrast with the fragility of their prey. The staging was enormously imaginative, evoking a haunting and enchanted world outside of time. C.M.C.

Left: A scene from Spartacus *with choreography by Yuri Grigorovich. Opposite page: Another moment from the same ballet, danced by the Bolshoi Company.*

THE WOLF (*Le Loup*)
One-act ballet. Choreography by Roland Petit. Music by Henri Dutilleux. Scenario by Jean Anouilh and Georges Neveux. Set and costumes by Jean Carzou. Paris, Théâtre de l'Empire, March 17, 1953. Ballets de Paris Company. Principal dancers: Violette Verdy, Claire Sombert, Roland Petit, George Reich, J. B. Lemoine.

SYNOPSIS. An itinerant conjurer sets up his stand in front of a village church in which the wedding of a young couple is being celebrated. The Vagabond's specialty is to change people into animals. To attract his audience he makes use of the charms of a gypsy girl. The bridegroom has hardly come out of the church when he becomes fascinated by the beautiful girl and runs away with her. With the complicity of the magician, he has caused his abandoned bride to believe that he has been turned into a wolf. She goes away at the side of a real wolf, thinking him to be her husband. Little by little she realizes her companion's true identity, but she is not afraid. In fact, the animal possesses all the virtues lacking in men: he is strong, loyal, brave, and above all he loves as men will never know how to love. When the villagers discover that a real wolf is living in their midst, they set off to hunt him, armed with hayforks and sickles. The woman will not leave his side, she remains faithful to him, defending him as best she can. Both then die together. M.S.M.

BLACK TIGHTS (*Deuil en 24 Heures*)
Ballet in one act and five scenes. Choreography and scenario by Roland Petit. Music by Maurice Thiriet. Sets and costumes by Antoni Clavé. Paris, Théâtre de l'Empire, March 17, 1953. Ballets de Paris. Principal dancers: Colette Marchand, Serge Perrault, Helène Constantine, George Reich.

SYNOPSIS. With a great deal of irony, the ballet tells the story of a young and attractive woman of the *Belle Époque* who loves dressing in black. She loses her husband as the result of a freakish duel. Quite casually she carries his body out of her room, the walls of which are decorated with the portraits of her former husbands, all dead and buried, and takes it to a salon at *Chez Maxim*'s where professional dancing girls are performing a frenzied cancan.

■ In this piece, as in the *La Croqueuse de Diamants*, Roland Petit has produced a work of theatrical dance much nearer in spirit to music hall or revue than to ballet. M.S.M.

THE STONE FLOWER (*Kamenni Zvetok*)
Ballet in a prologue and four acts. Choreography by Léonid Lavrovsky. Music by Sergei Prokofiev. Scenario by Mira Mendelsohn-Prokofieva and L. Lavrosky, drawn from The Malachite Casket, *a short story of the Urals by Pavel Bazhov. Sets and costumes by T. Starzhentsky. Moscow, Bolshoi Theater, February 12, 1954. Principal dancers: G. Ulanova, M. Plisetskaia, V. Preobrazhensky, A. Yermolayev.*

SYNOPSIS. Prologue: a forest in the Ural Mountains. The Queen of the Copper Mountain, possessor of immense riches, appears. Act I. Scene I: a wood. Caterina, accompanied by her parents, prepares to meet her promised husband, Danilo. Scene II: a miners' cabin. While some of the men are working on stone, Danilo is carving a malachite vase which he plans to decorate with a flower wrought in precious stones. Caterina arrives with her parents and talks to him. Scene III: a dismal heath at the foot of the Urals. The wealthy Severyan, watching the stone being transported, gets into a quarrel with Danilo and tries to take by force the jar he has promised to Caterina. Scene IV: the interior of the cabin again. Danilo, seeking perfection in his craft and tormented by the desire to possess the Stone Flower, is persuaded by his old grandfather, Procopius, to go to the Queen of the Copper Mountain, its owner. Scene V: as in the prologue. The Copper Queen, impressed by Danilo's enthusiasm, invites him to follow her. Act II. Scene I: the Queen's magnificent underground palace. She submits Danilo to a series of tests, all of which he passes brilliantly. As a result he is allowed to see the Stone Flower but, through a magic spell, has no sooner seen it than he is turned to stone. Scene II: the miner's cabin again. While Caterina pines for Danilo, Severyan comes in and declares his passion, but is firmly rebuffed. Afterwards the Queen enters and advises her to go in search of her lover. Act III. Scene I: the outskirts of a prosperous town. Caterina arrives in the middle of an uproarious fair. Severyan is there too, and tries to seize her, but the other women gather to protect her. Finally the Queen herself comes to her aid and, disguised as a gypsy, casts a spell over Severyan, compelling him to follow her. Scene II: a dreadful precipice. After forcing Severyan to perform a frenzied dance, the enchantress has him crushed between two huge rocks. Act IV. Scene I: a forest. While Caterina is resting in a tumbledown shack she is approached by the Spirit of Fire, who promises to take her to Danilo. Scene II: the Queen's underground palace again. Caterina, having been allowed to see Danilo, begs the Queen to release him from the spell. The enchantress consents, and Danilo, waking as if from a long dream, understands that in future he must pursue very different goals and follow very different ideals. Scene III: the heath at the foot of the Urals again. Accompanied by the Queen of the Copper Mountain, Caterina and Danilo are heartily welcomed by the countryfolk, who are eager to celebrate the marriage of the two young people.

■ The first complete production of this ballet was planned for March 1953, but on the 5th of that very month Prokofiev died of a heart attack. Naturally, the opening, although rehearsals were already in progress, had to be postponed, especially as two fragments of the score were still incomplete (the two "numbers" were eventually orchestrated by Dmitri Kabalievsky). The ballet's length and the complexity of the scenic arrangements have limited the world's familiarity with this work, which is, nevertheless, one of the masterpieces of the modern ballet repertory.

OTHER VERSIONS. 1) Yuri Grigorovich. Sets and costumes by Virsaladze. Leningrad, Kirov Theater, April 27, 1957. 2) Loris Gai. Sets and costumes by Anna Anni, directed by Beppo Menegatti. Bologna, Teatro Comunale, March 8, 1973. Danced by Anita Cardus, Carla Fracci, James Urbain, Roberto Fascilla.   P.C.

WESTERN SYMPHONY
Ballet in three movements. Choreography and subject by George Balanchine. Music by Hersky Kay. Set by John Boyt. Costumes by Barbara Karinska. New York, New York City Center, September 7, 1954. New York City Ballet. Principal dancers: Diana Adams, Herbert Bliss, Janet Reed, Nicholas Magallanes, Patricia Wilde, André Eglevsky, Tanaquil Le Clercq, Jacques d'Amboise.

SYNOPSIS. Plotless ballet.

■ Balanchine wanted to create a typically American ballet along the lines of the well-known *Billy the Kid* and *Rodeo* but without a narrative plot. The work was carried out in close collaboration with the young composer Kay, from whom the choreographer commissioned a "symphonic score based on old, indigenous melodies." Above all, Balanchine wanted to give his work a feeling of the wide, open spaces. For reasons of economy, when *Western Symphony* was first performed, the dancers were dressed in simple body stockings and there was no scenery. It was not until the following season that the company was able to afford sets and costumes. The original four scenes were reduced to three, the third scene being omitted.   C.M.C.

BALANCE A TROIS
One-act ballet. Choreography by Jean Babilée. Music by Jean Michel Damase. Set and costumes by Tom Keogh. Monte Carlo, April 25, 1955. Principal dancers: Jean Babilée, Yvette Chauviré, Alexandre Kalioujny.

SYNOPSIS. A girl and two boys are in a gymnasium, practicing their exercises. The two young athletes vie with one another in skill and daring to win the approval of the girl. It is she, however, who does best in the competition which, after it has begun to look threatening, comes to a peaceful and happy end. A combination of muscle and poetry.   M.P.

SYMPHONY FOR A LONELY MAN *(Symphonie pour un Homme Seul)*
One-act ballet. Choreography by Maurice Béjart. Music by Pierre Schaeffer and Pierre Henry. Paris, Théâtre de l'Etoile, July 26, 1955. Ballets de l'Etoile. Principal dancers: Maurice Béjart and Michèle Seigneuret.

SYNOPSIS. A man is alone, as if in prison. Ropes are lowered from above. A woman appears. She is there but she cannot enter into his life. When the man tries to detain her she vanishes. He is in despair, but the search continues.

■ This was Maurice Béjart's first important ballet, made before he established his *Ballet du XXme Siècle*. It was also probably the first to be danced to electronic music, produced in this case by Schaeffer and Henry, two masters of that genre known as "concrete" because it used sounds from real life. The problem that Béjart was tackling in this work was that of loneliness, alienation, the difficulty of communicating with others. In 1953 the choreographer was very aware of the intellectual movements of his day and reflected their anxiety. *Symphony for a Lonely Man* contains not only the feelings of the man, his "heart," the sounds of his life, but also the external elements, good or bad, that accompany them: steps, voices, tunes, bombs, weaknesses, vices, virtues. Without either scenery or stage costumes, modern dancers no longer express fairy tales but the true self. The ballet has become a world classic.   M.P.

THE STILL POINT

One-act ballet. Choreography by Todd Bolender. Music by Claude Debussy. Lee, Massachusetts, Jacob's Pillow Dance Festival, August 3, 1955. Dance Drama Company. Principal dancers: Emily Frankel and Mark Ryder.

SYNOPSIS. A girl feels herself rebuffed and excluded from the joys of others. She takes refuge in dreams and is oppressed by ancestral fears, but at last finds happiness with a young man who understands her feelings.

■ Modern dance with a lingering memory of classicism. *The Still Point* is a ballet that succeeds in creating a romantic atmosphere without being romantic, and in expressing complex feelings with simplicity. Considered one of Bolender's best choreographic works, it is performed often and by a number of different companies. The music is Debussy's *Quartet for strings*, op. 10 (the first three movements), orchestrated by Frank Black. The title comes from T. S. Eliot's *Four Quartets*.   M.P.

MARIO AND THE MAGICIAN *(Mario e il Mago)*

Choreography drama in two acts by Luchino Visconti (after Thomas Mann). Choreography by Léonide Massine. Music by Franco Mannino. Sets and costumes by Lila de Nobili. Milan, Scala, February 25, 1956. Principal dancers: Jean Babilée (Mario), Luciana Novaro (Silvestra), Ugo Dell'Ara (Renato), Salvo Randone (Cipolla, the magician).

SYNOPSIS. Mario, a young waiter at a bar in a seaside resort, loves the provocative Silvestra, girl friend of the ice cream-seller, Renato. After some unlucky attempts to approach the girl, Mario is dismissed by the overbearing owner of the restuarant. The peace of the beach where Mario is sitting, alone and disconsolate, is disturbed by the noise of preparations for the show to be given by the magician, Cipolla. In the evening Mario goes to the little square where, on an improvised stage, Cipolla is entertaining the crowd with experiments in hypnotism at the expense of people picked by chance from the audience. Now Mario is called onto the platform by the magician and hypnotized. He is made to

George Balanchine directs a rehearsal of Agon, *revived at the Paris Opéra in 1960.*

believe that his dreams are coming true: Silvestra loves him and her smiling face appears in every window of a passing train, while the owner of the restaurant seats him on a throne and polishes his shoes. Silvestra draws near him and he kisses her. At this point Mario wakes up to find himself embracing the magician amid general laughter. Humiliated and beside himself with disappointment, he takes a pistol out of his pocket, aims it at Cipolla and kills him. Two policemen take him away.

■ Luchino Visconti's great interest and admiration for the works of Thomas Mann is once more evident in this ballet, the distinguished director's only work for the theater of dance. Although the dance content was the work of the great choreographer Léonide Massine, who splendidly characterized the story and its personages in movement, the real author of *Mario and the Magician* was Visconti, in that he inspired and coordinated the diverse components of this hybrid work made up of dance, mime, music, song, and speech (note among the list of dancers the name of the actor Salvo Randone as the magician). Naturally, Visconti wrote the scenario, drawn from Thomas Mann's novel *Mario und der Zauberer*, freely adapted so as to make Mario the true protagonist of the ballet and the sad hero of the existential oppression which is its theme. Jean Babilée's interpretation of the part was remarkable for its psychological penetration, telling mime, and outstanding vigorous dancing.   A.A.

SPARTACUS (Spartak)

Ballet in three acts and ten scenes. Choreography by Leonid Jakobson. Scenario by Nicolai Volkov. Music by Aram Khachaturian. Leningrad, Kirov Theater, December 27, 1956. Principal dancers: Askold Makarov, Inna Zubkovskaia, Alla Shelest.

SYNOPSIS. Act I: we see a procession of crosses advancing along the Appian Way; beneath one of them is the dying Spartacus. The chief events of his life seem to pass in front of his eyes: his carefree childhood, his capture, slavery, and finally revolt and flight after his fellow-prisoner, Africanus, has been brutally killed. Act II: Spartacus and his companions (it is now just after the revolt of the slaves) assail the villa of the Roman captain Crassus, where a veritable orgy is in progress, and scatter the inhabitants. Act III: at first, fate seems to smile on the rebellious slaves who are threatening the capital itself, but in the end the Roman troops have the best of it. Spartacus bids his last farewell to his wife Phrygia. The battle between the slaves and the Roman army rages; all the rebels perish except Phrygia, who flees. The final scene returns to the Via Appia. Phrygia grieves for her husband, now dead, and for freedom henceforth irremediably lost.

■ This ballet departs from the fairy-tale vein of the earlier *Gayané* and still further from the prevailing Tchaikovsky tradition, to adopt the ideological and patriotic content of the new Soviet ballet to which Boris

Asafiev and Alexander Krein subscribed. Nevertheless, although it partook of the old Franco-Italian tradition (from which, after all, nineteenth-century Russian ballet was derived), *Spartacus* laid stress on masculine athleticism, one of the basic components of the new Russian school, and one that brought out the epic character of the story and its hero particularly well. In that respect, Khachaturian's ballet is a prime example of Soviet dance theater.

OTHER VERSIONS. In 1958 *Spartacus* was presented for the first time at the Bolshoi Theater in Moscow, with choreography by Igor Moisseiev, and Maia Plisetskaia in the feminine lead. The ballet was performed at the same theater on April 4, 1962, with the original choreography by Leonid Jakobson. Still at the Bolshoi, *Spartacus* was produced in 1968 with choreography by Yuri Grigorovich and stage designs by Simon Virsaladze. This new version reduced the slightly grandiloquent heroics and made it look less like a Victorian oleograph of an idealized "Romanity." Credit for the improvement also goes to the principal dancers, Vladimir Vassiliev and Ekaterina Maximova. The same version was later presented at the Scala, Milan, and at the Rome Opera House on September 24, 1970, during the Bolshoi Ballet's tour of Italy. It is worth noting that an important production of this ballet was shown at the Budapest Opera House in 1968, this time with choreography by Laszlo Seregy.   P.C.

THE PRINCE OF THE PAGODAS

Ballet in three acts. Choreography by John Cranko. Music by Benjamin Britten. Sets by John Piper. Costumes by Desmond Healey. London, Covent Garden, January 1, 1957. Royal Ballet. Principal dancers: Svetlana Beriosova, Julia Farron, David Blair, Leslie Edwards, Pirmin Trecu, Ray Powell.

SYNOPSIS. Act I: at the Emperor's court the wrangling jester and dwarf are preparing the room to which four Kings are to come from the four quarters of the globe to compete by means of character dances for the hand of the heiress to the throne, Belle Epine, who has a rival, however, in the person of Princess Belle Rose. To the extreme annoyance of the Emperor, it becomes clear that the Kings prefer the latter Princess. Belle Rose has seen a vision of a handsome Prince to whom her heart goes out. Now all is put into confusion by the arrival of four frogs bearing an emerald jewel box. Belle Epine tries in vain to open it, but Belle Rose does so easily and is magically transported to the land of the Pagodas. Act II: Belle Rose's fantastic journey takes her through the three natural elements: air, water, and fire. Having arrived in the Pagoda kingdom, she is blindfolded, yet finds her Prince and dances with him. However, when curiosity incites her to lift the bandage, the Prince has taken on the appearance of a salamander. Act III: meanwhile Belle Epine has become Empress and the Emperor is shut up in a cage. He is let out, but made to dance in front of the jeering courtiers, pitied only by the clown. At this moment Belle Rose arrives back with her

An example of Balanchine's choreography for the ballet Episodes.

salamander. Belle Epine orders them both to be arrested. Now a wonder occurs: by means of the usual kiss, the salamander recovers his princely form and the palace vanishes. We are back in the land of the Pagodas, where a grand *divertissement* takes place, ending with the wedding celebration of Belle Rose and her handsome Prince, whose hands are joined by the goodhearted jester.

■ This is a modern fairy tale, completely English in music and choreography, but drawing on the themes of classical ballet, with emphasis on the exotic. It was Britten's first direct contribution to ballet. For Cranko it was an opportunity to expand on the famous balletic works of the nineteenth century.   M.P.

THE UNICORN, THE GORGON, AND THE MANTICORE

A madrigalesque ballet in one act. Choreography by John Butler. Music and scenario by Gian Carlo Menotti. Sets by Jean Rosenthal. Costumes by Robert Fletcher, carried out by Karinska. New York, New York City Center, January 15, 1957. Principal dancers: Nicholas Magallanes, Arthur Mitchell, Janet Reed.

SYNOPSIS. This is an ironical fable. For three succes-

sive Sundays a poet has taken his three mythical monsters for a walk through the town. At first he is thought to be mad, but after a while he is followed by all the inhabitants. Only when the poet dies do they realize that the creatures represent youth, manhood, and old age.

■ Described by the composer as a "madrigal-opera for chorus, ten dancers, and nine instruments," its first official performance (like that of several other works by Menotti) was reserved for a limited audience. It took place in the Library of Congress in Washington on October 21, 1956. Butler, who collaborated closely with Menotti, also arranged the choreography for the composer's ballet *Sebastian* in 1963 for the Nederlands Dans Theater.   C.M.C.

AGON

One-act ballet. Choreography by George Balanchine. Music by Igor Stravinsky. Lighting by Nananne Porcher. New York, New York City Center, November 27, 1957. New York City Ballet. Principal dancers: Diana Adams, Melissa Hayden, Barbara Walczak, Barbara Millberg, Todd Bolender, Roy Tobias, Jonathan Watts, Arthur Mitchell, Roberta Lubell, Francia Russell, Dido Sayers, and Ruth Sobotka.

Martha Graham in Acrobats of God, *created by her to Carlos Surinach's music. The ballet illustrates the miseries and glories of the theater world.*

repertory, and also performed elsewhere by various companies, including London's Royal Ballet, which presented it at Covent Garden Opera House on January 25, 1973, with Vergie Derman, Laura Connor, Anthony Dowell, and David Wall in the solo parts.

OTHER VERSIONS. 1) Tatiana Gsovsky. Berlin, Deutsche Oper, May 1958. 2) Kenneth MacMillan. London, Covent Garden, August 20, 1958. Danced by Anya Linden and David Blair. 3) Eske Holm. Copenhagen, Royal Opera House, January 28, 1967.   A.A.

THE MUSIC. In 1957, after nearly a decade of silence in the field of ballet music, Stravinsky presented *Agon*, a score on which he had been working since 1953. During the previous few years the composer had gradually completed his conversion to the twelve-note system – his opera *The Rake's Progress* being the sole exception – so that this work was the first official link between ballet and serial technique. Thus, *Agon* is in no way a continuation of the preceding ballets inspired by ancient Greek mythology (*Apollo Musagète* and *Orpheus*); the title refers to a "combat" or competition, with no particular geographical connotation. Nevertheless, a slender thread connects this production with his more popular neoclassical works, since it is characteristic of Stravinsky never to turn his back definitively on the past, but to recover and preserve that which can still serve a useful expressive purpose. One has the impression, listening to this score, that it forms a sort of musical synthesis of the composer's whole artistic development. The alternation of tonal and modal passages with others that are strictly dodecaphonic finally presents a coherent portrait of his many-sided personality.   A.F.

SYNOPSIS. Plotless abstract ballet danced by eight ballerinas and four male dancers dressed in plain practice clothes on a bare stage. Divided, like the music, into three parts, it runs without interruption, and consists of a suite of dances in various formations, ranging from solos to a triple *pas de quatre*, using all twelve dancers.

■ Of all the many ballets arising from the collaboration of Stravinsky and Balanchine, *Agon* is perhaps that in which the objectivity of form and abstract expression typical of Balanchine's choreography have been carried to their furthest point. The original idea came from Stravinsky, who, in his own serial technique composed a dance suite inspired by some dances described in a French manual of the seventeenth century: single and double *sarabandes*, *gaillardes*, and *branles* in a succession of rhythms called *combat* (literally *agon*). The density, quality, metric insistence, variety, and asymmetrical symmetry of Stravinsky's rhythms have been translated by Balanchine into an austere choreographical composition based on the rules of classical grammar, but with a modern syntax. According to Lincoln Kirstein, "*Agon* is not pure ballet, consisting of dance alone. It is an existential metaphor of tension and anxiety. . . ." Balanchine's original version of *Agon* has been kept continuously in the New York City Ballet's

EMBATTLED GARDEN

One-act ballet. Choreography by Martha Graham. Music by Carlos Surinach. Set by Isamu Noguchi. Costumes by Martha Graham. Lighting by Jean Rosenthal. New York, Adelphi Theater, April 3, 1958. Principal dancers: Yuriko (Eve), Bertram Ross (Adam), Glen Tetley (Stranger), Matt Turney.

SYNOPSIS. This is a satire on the Garden of Eden, in which the figures of Adam and Eve are represented by two characters from everyday life, dominated now as then by a tempter curled around the branches of a tree.

■ The existentialist theories that underlie all Martha Graham's works (she was the daughter of a psychiatrist) define in *Embattled Garden* the path that leads from innocence to knowledge. The characters are Wry and Lilith (Adam and Eve) and a stranger (the serpent). It is a stifling day and the woman is combing her long hair in the shade of a little wood. She is depressed by day after day of boredom; anyone who comes into the garden to dispel it will be welcome, no matter what the consequence. The stranger leaps into the gap of lethargy to relieve the monotony of virtue. The man, her companion, triumphs over him, and he and his woman reaffirm their past love and go back to the wood. The whole episode is repeated day after day; nothing changes except that every time the lovers venture outside the garden of romantic love they accumulate more trespasses to forgive one another. The set consists of a circular rail holding thick posts representing trees. Deliberately, the effect is that of a cage in which the characters seem to be trapped. C.M.C.

SUMMERSPACE

One-act ballet. Choreography by Merce Cunningham. Music by Morton Feldman. Set and costumes by Robert Rauschenberg. Lighting by Nicholas Cernovich. New London, Connecticut College, August 17, 1958. Merce Cunningham and his Dance Company.

SYNOPSIS. Plotless ballet.

■ With Merce Cunningham, American dance made its boldest advances into futurity, with novel, not to say provocative, music and configurations. *Summerspace* was organized around Feldman's graphic sound effects and the magical relations between set and costumes designed by Rauschenberg to break up every spatial division. At the end of the 1950s this was undoubtedly new; but today, alas, the ease with which certain effects can be imitated has lessened the impact of ballets of this kind, unless they are sustained by some idea that extends beyond its moment of conception. In this work four women and two men occupy the stage continuously. The modern dance methods employed, technically demanding and enjoying the advantage of horizontal positions on the floor, have been used as a model, studied and applied by many other choreographers,

even in very different contexts. Cunningham, a friend of John Cage, the grand old man of the American musical advance guard, is a believer in the idea that ballet should be lean, objective, and reduced to its essence. He has been very prolific, as his numerous works testify, e.g., *Torso* (1976), *Rebus* (1975), *Squaregame* (1976), *Travelogue* (1977), *Signals* (1970), and best known of all, *Landrover* (1972). His search for truth has carried his work to the edge of dissolution and to a physical concentration outside the cult of beauty or any proclaimed rules of harmony. M.P.

EPISODES

Ballet in two parts. First episode: choreography by Martha Graham, subject by Stefan Zweig. Principal dancers: Martha Graham, Sallie Wilson, Bertram Ross. Second episode: choreography by George Balanchine. Principal dancers: Violetta Verdy, Diana Adams, Allegra Kent, Melissa Hayden, Jonathan Watts, Nicholas Magallanes, Francisco Moncion, and Paul Taylor. For both episodes: Music by Anton Webern. Set and lighting by David Hays. Costumes by Barbara Karinska and Cecil Beaton. New York, New York City Center, May 14, 1959.

SYNOPSIS. The first part concerns episodes in the life of Mary, Queen of Scots. The second part has no plot.

■ *Episodes*, a homage to the music of Anton Webern, was the first and only collaboration between the two great American representatives of classical and modern dance in the 1950s: George Balanchine and Martha Graham. The collaboration was proposed by Lincoln

Sighilt Pahl and Mats Ek in Adam och Eve *by Birgit Cullberg.*

Right: Ninth Symphony *interpreted by the Ballet du XXme Siècle.*

Kerstein as a combined operation for the New York City Ballet group and the Dance Company. In the event, the two disciplines were too far apart and there was no fusion. Another handicap was the lack of real willingness to cooperate on the part of the two leading spirits. The combined companies performed for two seasons only, after which Graham took her "episode" out of the Dance Company's repertory, while Balanchine inserted his own in the City Ballet's program, excluding the solo variations designed for Paul Taylor, a member of the other group. The first idea had been to produce a ballet that would make as much use as possible of the New York City Ballet dancers, but Graham worked out her choreography with her own group, only demonstrating it to Balanchine when it was too late for his company to learn it, since the classical dancers would have needed a great many rehearsals to get used to the quite different methods of modern dance. Thus, the interchange of members originally planned was reduced to Sallie Wilson (who played the part of Elizabeth I in Graham's episode) and Paul Taylor, who danced solo to Webern's *Variations*, op. 30, in Balanchine's episode. The compromise was too slight to establish the connection between the two works, and the result was a hybrid.   C.M.C.

MOVES
A ballet without music. Choreography by Jerome Robbins. Spoleto, Festival of Two Worlds, Teatro Nuovo, July 3, 1959. The Jerome Robbins USA Ballet Company.

SYNOPSIS. An abstract ballet where the dance narrative explores relationships between the dancers, who each establish their own rhythm.

■ In this work by Jerome Robbins, silence assumes a positive, symbolically allusive meaning: silence and lack of communication or, paradoxically, a vehicle and opportunity for a wider and different communication. In its creator's own words, "I wanted to do a ballet about relationships between people – man and woman, one another, the individual and the group," expressed solely by the movements of bodies, the sound of footfalls, the rustling of clothes, and the rhythms of the dancers' breathing.   M.B.

GHOSTS AT THE GRAND HOTEL *(Fantasmi al Grand Hotel)*
One-act ballet by Luciana Novaro from a subject by Dino Buzzati. Adaptation and choreography by Léonide Massine. Music by Luciano Chailly. Sets and costumes by Dino Buzzati. Milan, Scala, February 11, 1960. Principal dancers: Carla Fracci (She), Carmen Puthod (the Star), Mario Pistoni (the Lover), Amedeo Amodio (the Gangster Boss).

SYNOPSIS. This is the story of a girl who comes to the big city in search of fame and fortune. Fate throws her into the hands of a gang whose headquarters are in the hotel. An unknown man wants to protect her from them. She is apparently transformed into a smart, sophisticated woman. There is a fight in which the gangsters are put to flight and their leader killed. The girl, found beside the body, is suspected, tried, and condemned to death. But the stranger succeeds in saving her. The two turn back to the hotel, but find it in ruins. They decide to follow another way that opens out in front of them, fresh, happy, serene, and, above all, free of the machinations of the underworld.

■ The ballet was a happy event in the collaboration of the writer Buzzati and the composer Chailly. The latter embellished the somewhat surreal and cinematic text with lively music containing elements of jazz and electronic sound.   M.B.

THE LITTLE HUMPBACKED HORSE
Ballet in three acts. Choreography by Alexander Radunsky. Music by Rodion Scedrin. Scenario by Vaisonen and Maliarevsky. Sets by Boris Volkov. Moscow, Bolshoi Theater, March 4, 1960. Bolshoi Ballet.

■ This was a revival of an old ballet very popular with the Russians because it was one of the first with a national and folklore subject. It was put on in St. Petersburg in 1864, music by Pugni, choreography by Saint-Léon, and remained in the repertory for a long time. There was a previous revival, arranged by Gorsky, in

the early years of the new century. Now it has been given a new musical score by Rodion Scedrin, husband of Maia Plisetskaia, who danced the part of the girl, while Valdimir Vassiliev played Ivan. The subject was taken from a story by Piotr Yershov, a specialist in the literature of old Russian folk tales of magic and adventure. Here the magic element predominated with all its traditional wonders. The moral is clearly pointed out: the power of the Czar (or the Khan, in more distant times) was helpless against young Ivan, the common man protected by higher forces.　　　　　　M.P.

ACROBATS OF GOD

One-act ballet. Choreography by Martha Graham. Music by Carlos Surinach. Set by Isamu Noguchi. Costumes by Martha Graham. New York, Adelphi Theater, April 27, 1960. Principal dancers: Martha Graham, Helen McGhee, Paul Taylor, Bertram Ross, Stuart Hodes, Ethel Winter, David Wood.

SYNOPSIS. A celebration of the miseries and grandeurs of theatrical life.

■ The title is a translation of the name *athletae Dei* applied to themselves by the early fathers of the Church (the anchorites) who austerely followed their laws in the solitude of the desert. In *Acrobats* Graham was comparing the valorous spirituality of these ascetics with the severe physical training endured by dancers. The director is transformed into a ringmaster with a whip, who goads the dancers and acrobats as if they were animals to be tamed or domesticated. Martha is the

"artist," stands apart, observes, and makes aloof comments, sometimes correcting her colleagues. But instead of taking part in the activity she becomes alienated and contemplates her image in a mirror as if she were some inaccessible, superior creature. She, too, finishes, however, by being tamed, joining the group, and sharing their pains and their triumphs.　　　　　　C.M.C.

THE HUMAN COMEDY (*La Commedia Umana*)

Ballet in three acts. Choreography by Léonide Massine. Music of the fourteenth century arranged and orchestrated by Claude Arrieu. Scenario by Vittore Branca and Francesco Siciliani (after Boccaccio). Sets and costumes by Alfred Manessier. Nervi, Fifth International Festival of Ballet, July 7, 1960. Balletto Europeo di Nervi. Principal dancers: Carla Fracci, Yvonne Meyer, Duska Sifnios, Tatiana Massine, Vassilli Sulich, Milorad Miskovitch.

■ Taking as his subject various episodes from the *Decameron* by Giovanni Boccaccio, Massine wanted to make a ballet like a vast fresco of dance. Visually it was inspired by the Italian fourteenth century, lively and populated by ordinary people. But he was mindful, too, of the symbolic and ideal content of Boccaccio's stories, applying to the universal human condition. Massine's choreography was now as far removed from the brilliant historical and folk characterizations of his youthful works as from the severe classicism of his symphonic ballets or the dense gestural symbolism of his mystical creations. In this late work it achieved a perfect balance between dance and mime, classical style and modern influences, choreographic substance and narrative clarity. *La Commedia Umana* was Léonide Massine's first production for the European Ballet, a company formed in connection with the Nervi Festival of 1960, and directed during its brief existence by the choreographer himself.   A.A.

LIEBESLIEDER WALTZ

Ballet in one act and two scenes. Choreography by George Balanchine. Music by Johannes Brahms. Sets by David Hays. Costumes by Karinska. New York, New York City Center, November 22, 1960. New York City Ballet. Principal dancers: Diana Adams, Melissa Hayden, Jillana Zimmermann, Violette Verdy, Bill Carter, Conrad Ludlow, Nicholas Magallanes, Jonathan Watts.

SYNOPSIS. As the title indicates, the ballet is devoted to the waltz and the love song. Dancing alternates with singing. The curtain rises on a ballroom of the last century: small tables with candles, a piano at which is seated a couple in clothes of the romantic era, and, gathered around them, four singers. When the music begins, four couples take the floor (dancing a waltz, of course). There follows a song that speaks of love. Thus, turn and turn about, or overlapping, eighteen Brahms waltzes are presented, followed by another fourteen in the second part. For that the scene changes. In place of the ballroom there is a great empty starlit space without walls, and the dancers wear traditional ballet costumes. After the last waltz the performers leave the stage, then come back and stand immobile to hear the echo of the words of the concluding *lied*. The text is by Goethe and says, "And now, Muse, enough! In vain you seek to tell us how misery and joy alternate in the heart that loves."   C.M.C.

BALLET SCHOOL

One-act ballet. Choreography by Asaf Messerer. Music by Glazunov, Liapunov, Liadov, and Shostakovich, arranged by A. Zseitlin. Moscow, Bolshoi Theater, May 6, 1961. Bolshoi Theater Ballet.

SYNOPSIS. Plotless ballet.

■ *Ballet School* is the Bolshoi, or the training at any great school of classical dance, from the first exercises (positions, bar work) to the virtuoso feats of the leading dancers. It was intended by the distinguished ballet master Messerer as the demonstration of a very exact style, formed during years of work and enthusiasm. Not only the great names of the Moscow company were employed in this ballet, but also — and especially — the young and the very young aspirants. *Ballet School* is one of the most successful examples of this kind of work: high academic attainment treated with intelligence and taste.   M.S.M.

ADAM AND EVE (*Adam och Eve*)

One-act ballet. Choreography and subject by Birgit Cullberg. Music by Hilding Rosenbergen. Set by Jan Brazda. Costumes by Per Falk. New York, American Ballet Theater, October 4, 1961. Principal dancers: Marianne Orlando (Eve), Kay Selling (Adam).

SYNOPSIS. The mood is satirical. The first man and woman, alone in the earthly paradise, believe the thunder is the voice of God condemning their love.

■ First presented under the title *Eden*, this short ballet (sixteen minutes) is one of Cullberg's classics, together with *Fröken Julia*, *Red Wine in Green Glasses*, and *Romeo and Juliet*, and is an example of modern dance reducing the old type of *pas de deux* to its essentials. As in other of her works, there is a certain erotic content, demythologized by a delicate touch of comedy. C.M.C.

A MIDSUMMER NIGHT'S DREAM

Ballet in two acts and six scenes. Choreography and scenario (after Shakespeare) by George Balanchine. Music by Felix Mendelssohn. Set and lighting by David Hays. Costumes by Karinska. New York, New York City Center, January 17, 1962. New York City Ballet. Principal dancers: Arthur Mitchell (Puck), Jillana Zimmermann (Helena), Edward Villella (Oberon), Melissa Hayden (Titania), Roland Vasquez (Bottom), Francisco Moncion (Theseus), Patricia McBride (Hermia), Nicholas Magallanes (Lysander), Bill Carter (Demetrius), Gloria Govrin (Hippolyta), Violette Verdy, Conrad Ludlow.

SYNOPSIS. The plot is that of Shakespeare's comedy of the same name, dealing with the fortunes and misfortunes of a group of mortals and immortals, all occurring in a borderland between dream and reality. Two pairs of young lovers alternate with Oberon and Titania, King and Queen of the Fairies, and the rough country clown Bottom. They are all embroiled in a strange and complicated chain of events hatched up by the mischievous sprite Puck, a sort of perverse Cupid. There are amorous entanglements, quarrels without cause, pursuits in the forest, and magical tricks galore, ending with a double wedding in the palace of Oberon and Titania, now reconciled.

■ In *A Midsummer Night's Dream*, the choreographer George Balanchine offers us one of the best examples of how traditional narrative can be combined with his pure and abstract classical style into a whole in which the precision and complexity of the choreography become the raw material of true dramatic action. Only in the last scene does Balanchine abandon the narrative aspect to pay affectionate homage to classical ballet with a long *divertissement* arranged to show off the brilliant academic technique of all soloists and the *corps de ballet*. A ballet on the same subject, also to Mendelssohn's music, but with the title shortened to *The Dream*, was produced by Frederick Ashton on the occasion of the 400th anniversary of Shakespeare's birth.

■ This classic of Spanish literature has been transformed into a ballet by Ailey in terms of modern dance. With the help of Surinach's music, which is a stylization of typical Spanish themes, secular and religious, the choreography has penetrated to the play's essential content, turning it into dance by way of natural gestures as used in realistic theater. In the same manner he has tried to suggest and comment on Spanish life in the spirit of Lorca rather than to imitate him. Thence he has expanded the drama of the matriarchy into a universal dimension, developing the very contemporary subject of the relations between mother and daughter. *The House of Bernarda Alba* also inspired Mats Ek to create a ballet of the same name, which was staged in Stockholm on May 31, 1978, by the Cullberg Ballet with Luc Bouy in the leading part.   C.M.C.

LIEUTENANT KIJÉ (*Podporuchik Kizhe*)
One-act ballet. Choreography by Alexander Lapauri and Olga Tarasova. Music by Sergei Prokofiev. Scenario by Andrei Vejzler and Alexander Miscjarin from the story of the same name by Yuri Tinjanov. Moscow, Bolshoi Theater, February 10, 1963.

SYNOPSIS. The Czar has an idea that in some report he has read of the bravery of an officer called Kijé. In reality, no such person exists. So as not to contradict their Emperor, the courtiers and generals continue to invent heroic acts performed by the phantom lieutenant. When the Czar expresses a desire to have him at court, the only thing to do is to credit the hero with a glorious death. The courtiers' pens finally overwhelm the Emperor.

■ *Lieutenant Kijé* first saw the light in 1943 as a satirical film with a Gogolian flavour. The musical accompaniment by Prokofiev, who had only recently returned to the Soviet Union, won immediate success as a suite. Later the story of the nonexistent hero was made into a ballet, without losing its sacrilegious power. It is a comic ballet, making fun of both the servility of the courtiers and the stupidity of the ruling authority.   P.C.

THE NINTH SYMPHONY (*Neuvième Symphonie*)
Ballet in four movements. Choreography by Maurice Béjart. Music by Ludwig von Beethoven. Brussels, Royal Circus, October 28, 1964. Ballet du XXme Siècle.

SYNOPSIS. The ballet follows the four movements of Beethoven's symphony. First movement: the man sleeps, curled up in a hollow of the earth as if in his mother's womb. First there is fear of birth and awakening. When the man comes to the full consciousness of his powers, he expresses the joy of life, work, struggle, and action. Second movement: the instinctive elation and the awareness of liberty are expressed in a great festival of nature (*Scherzo*) and the people, a tangible symbol of mass energy. Third movement: the rule of love comes into its own (*Adagio*) with the clear luminescence of youth, and the world's couples find the

Rudolf Nureyev and Margot Fonteyn in Paradise Lost, *a modern version of the story of Adam and Eve.*

Put on by the Royal Ballet, it was presented at Covent Garden on April 2, 1964. *The Dream* was revived in August 1973, by John Hart for the Joffrey Ballet.   C.M.C.

FEAST OF ASHES
One-act ballet. Choreography by Alvin Ailey. Music by Carlos Surinach. Subject by Garcia Lorca. Costumes by Jack Venza. New York, Fashion Institute of Technology, September 30, 1962. Robert Joffrey Ballet. Principal dancers: Françoise Martinet, Lisa Bradley, Paul Sutherland.

SYNOPSIS. Taken from Garcia Lorca's play *The House of Bernarda Alba*, the ballet tells of the tragic situation of a girl, Adella, who tries to escape from the fatal demands of her matriarchal family. Her love for the fiancé of one of her elder sisters is the cause of the tragedy.

wonder of happiness. Fourth movement: love becomes a universal force, and in a Dionysiac circle humanity finds the perfect apotheosis of joy, redemption, and complete unity in a better world, where all contradictions are smoothed away and all plurality becomes one.

■ This philosophical ballet, deeply committed on the intellectual level, has been one of the major successes of the past decade. Planned for a very big stage to match the imposing structure of Beethoven's choral symphony, it has been seen by more than half a million people, television apart. In sports stadia, great halls, the tents of vast circuses, *Ninth Symphony* has enthralled the audiences of all nations. Yet the traditional critics have completely failed to appreciate the ballet's true value. In spite of that, Béjart's *Ninth Symphony* remains the most successful attempt so far to involve the masses in dance by way of culture and politics. As has already been stressed in the introduction to this book, we find in *The Ninth Symphony* a fundamental truth of contemporary culture, seen, as always with Béjart, with prophetic perception. The romanticism of Schiller's *Ode to Joy* is interpreted through Nietzsche's fervour, and Beethoven himself acts as a mediator here, the *Ninth Symphony* being the highest point of universal enlightenment in all his work. Béjart said that the dancing followed the composer's path from anger to joy and from darkness to light. He also maintains that his interpretation was not a ballet in the ordinary sense of the word, but a deep human participation in a work that belongs to all mankind. But these words must be interpreted more widely precisely because by taking Beethoven's grandeur as his starting point, Béjart offers a vision of the world as a whole. This vision is worked out by means of the definite symbol of a spiritual collectivism which is transformed into the absolute in the style of Beethoven. A great wind of liberty blows through this ballet, which is unusually eclectic in its choreography. Béjart's polyphonic style – if the term may be applied to dance – takes on a special spatial depth as it flows in harmonious fusion and as if inevitably into the choral conclusion of the symphony with faithfulness and high imagination. The vocabulary, too, ranges wide: from the primitive to classical elegance, from elements of folk dancing to plastic configurations. Striking visual effect is achieved even by the chorus when at the beginning the singers' brown cloaks are opened to reveal an explosion of gold. The human body is brilliantly exploited, not so much in abstract design as with complete vitality. The presence on the stage of dancers of different races adds a further touch to the universality of Béjart's message, which preaches the Nietzschean idea of reconciliation between man and nature "under the spell of Dionysus," and in the Schillerian ecstasy of supreme joy, celestial genius, humanity's evergreen aspirations, freed of all oppression and all conditioning. Dancing, the instrument of liberty and the conquest of the primitive, serves Béjart on this occasion as the miraculous instrument bringing us together. As Nietzsche said, "In singing and dancing man expresses himself as a member of a higher order."   M.P.

ONEGIN

Ballet in three acts, based on Alexander Pushkin's poem. Choreography by John Cranko. Music by Piotr I. Tchaikovsky, arranged and orchestrated by Kurt Heinz Stolze. Sets and costumes by Jürgen Rose. Stuttgart, Württemberg Municipal Theater, April 13, 1965. Principal dancers: Marcia Haydée and Heinz Clauss.

SYNOPSIS. Act I. Scene I: in a country house preparations for a celebration are in progress. It is the birthday of the young and romantic Tatiana. The mistress of the house, Larina, her daughter Olga, the nurse, and some other girls are busy with their dresses, when a gunshot interrupts their chatter. Lensky, the young poet engaged to Olga, comes in and explains that he has been out shooting with his friend from the city. He presents Eugene Onegin, a young nobleman bored with town life and in search of new emotions. Tatiana falls in love with Onegin at once, but he thinks of her only as a girl who has read too many romantic novels. Scene II: Tatiana decides to write to him and charges the nurse to deliver her letter to the man she loves and by whom she hopes to be loved. Act II. Scene I: it is Tatiana's birthday party. Onegin, more irritated than moved by her note, says he cannot love her and tears it up. Tatiana is in despair; she does not even notice the gentle courtship of an elderly admirer, Prince Gremin. Onegin, more bored than ever, teases Lensky by paying court to Olga, who foolishly encourages him. Lensky takes the matter very seriously and challenges Onegin to a duel. Scene II: in vain Tatiana and Olga implore Lensky to avoid the duel. The poet feels that he has been betrayed by his best friend in what lies nearest to his heart, and will not listen to reason. The duel takes place and, as foreseen, Onegin kills Lensky. For the first time the cynical man about town feels horror at himself. Tatiana, broken-hearted, realizes that she was mistaken in her love. Act III. Scene I: some years later Onegin, back in St. Petersburg, is invited to a ball by Prince Gremin, who meanwhile has married Tatiana. Onegin recognizes the woman who loved him in vain and is profoundly disturbed. Scene II: Tatiana receives a letter from Onegin declaring his love for her. The man presents himself to receive an answer. But now Tatiana has grown up, she is a woman, and has forsaken the illusions of youth, even if she still feels her passionate love of girlhood for him. She sends Onegin away, telling him she could never find happiness with him, and tears up his letter. He leaves in despair.

■ *Onegin* is considered not only one of John Cranko's best choreographic works, but also a brilliant example of dramatic ballet. Cranko has adhered to Pushkin's poem with faithfulness and discretion, but he has not used Tchaikovsky's score for the famous opera on the same subject. Instead, he commissioned Stolze to assemble and arrange several of the Russian composer's minor compositions for chamber or full orchestra. In this way he avoided the danger of merely turning the opera into a ballet, and allowed himself greater room for maneuver. A very cultured man, with a great sense of theater, Cranko created a work of rare intensity and unusual choreographic richness. His

The New York City Ballet in Jewels, *an abstract ballet by George Balanchine to music by Gabriel Fauré, Igor Stravinsky, and Piotr I. Tchaikovsky.*

characters were strongly delineated and he was not afraid to run the risk of sometimes appearing melodramatic. The contrast between the indolent little world of the country and the cynicism of the aristocrat from the capital, and the tragedy stemming from the meeting of the two, survive almost intact from poem to ballet. Watching it, one must forget the musical beauty of Tchaikovsky's opera, especially the great, incomparable "letter scene." The music becomes the weakest aspect of the ballet, for Stolze was not a particularly gifted transcriber or orchestrator and, after all, the best music for the story of *Onegin* remains that written for the opera. Cranko did not invest the plot with new symbols or extraneous interpretations, but sought to make the characters live for us through the drama, through recognition of their feelings and by a flow of luminous balletic ideas, always externalized on the highest professional level. Cranko's premature death can never be sufficiently mourned by the world of dance.   M.P.

NOTRE DAME DE PARIS

Ballet in two acts. Choreography and scenario (from the homonymous novel by Victor Hugo) by Roland Peiti. Music by Maurice Jarre. Sets by René Aglio. Costumes by Yves Saint-Laurent. Paris, Opéra, December 11, 1965. Principal dancers: Claire Motte (Esmeralda), Roland Petit (Quasimodo), Cyril Atanassov, Jean-Pierre Bonnefous.

SYNOPSIS. Act I: Archdeacon Frollo of the Cathedral of Notre Dame in Paris plans to abduct the beautiful gypsy girl, Esmeralda, with whom he is infatuated. He enlists the aid of the poor, crushed bellringer, Quasimodo, who is hunchbacked and hideously deformed. The plot fails through the providential intervention of Captain Phoebus, who rescues the girl. Quasimodo is severely punished, and only Esmeralda, who meanwhile has fallen in love with the Captain, shows any tenderness or pity for the poor hunchback. From that day on Quasimodo nurtures a devotion and humble love for the beautiful gypsy. During a meeting with Esmeralda, Phoebus is stabbed by Archdeacon Frollo, mad with jealousy. The gypsy is accused of the crime and the Captain does nothing to exonerate her. Act II: Quasimodo saves Esmeralda from torture and carries her to Notre Dame, where there is right of sanctuary, but the right is revoked and, in spite of Quasimodo's desperate defense, the girl is seized and taken back to be tortured. From the cathedral tower, Frollo watches unmoved, but the hunchback avenges Esmeralda by strangling the wicked priest and then leaving with Esmeralda's body.

■ Victor Hugo's novel inspired Roland Petit with a dramatic ballet which achieved a considerable success. The character drawing is traditional and strongly emphasized, perhaps in the case of Quasimodo a little too near to caricature. On the other hand, the crowd scenes, played in symbolic settings, are very convincing and effective. Petit uses geometrical dance patterns, often in horizontal lines. The leading parts are difficult, demanding real virtuosity. At present the ballet is in the repertory of the Bolshoi Ballet of Moscow. M.B.

THE STREET (La Strada)

One-act ballet. Choreography by Mario Pistoni. Music by Nino Rota. Subject by Federico Fellini and Tullio Pinelli from the film of the same name by F. Fellini. Sets and costumes by Luciano Damiani. Milan, Scala, September 2, 1966. Principal dancers: Carla Fracci (Gelsomina), Aldo Santambrogio (Zampano), Mario Pistoni (the Madman).

SYNOPSIS. Based on Fellini's film of 1954, the ballet retells in a poetic key a story of alienation in the modern era. It is the drama of Gelsomina, a girl sold by her mother to the charlatan Zampano.

■ A ballet in which man's violence and oppression are portrayed in a poetic vision in which dreams of happiness are shattered in the glare of hard reality. Pistoni's choreography, strongly oriented towards modern themes, plainly shows the influence of the cinema. M.B.

ROMEO AND JULIET

Ballet in a prologue, two acts, and an epilogue. Choreography by Maurice Béjart. Music by Hector Berlioz.

Luciana Savignano and Daniel Lommel in Bhakti *by Maurice Béjart.*

Costumes by Germinal Casado. Brussels, Royal Circus, November 17, 1966. Ballet du XXme Siècle.

SYNOPSIS. Prologue: the dancers enter the empty stage for a rehearsal. A quarrel breaks out and develops into a fight. The *maître-de-ballet* intervenes, pacifies them, and explains the moral by telling them a story on the theme of love and hate, *Romeo and Juliet*. Act I: Verona. The Montagues and Capulets, facing one another menacingly in the town square, are separated by Friar Lawrence. Romeo, a melancholy young man, goes with his friend Mercutio to the masked ball at the Capulets' house, and suddenly finds himself in front of their daughter Juliet. Tybalt separates them, but later that night the two young people meet again and play their first great love scene. Then Queen Mab provokes a new quarrel, which brings about the death of Mercutio and Tybalt. Act II: Juliet, in despair at Romeo's exile, seeks advice from Friar Lawrence, who gives her the sleep potion that counterfeits death. Thought to have perished, the girl is carried to the family tomb. Romeo arrives there and, in the fatal misunderstanding that follows, both lovers kill themselves. Epilogue: as at the beginning, the dancers return to the stage for a rehearsal. In the happy atmosphere that prevails, sad thoughts of Romeo and Juliet dissolve in the slogan "Make love, not war."

■ With his acute sensitivity to the problems of living, and faithful to his philosophy of the world's redemption through love, Béjart in 1966 understood the attitude of the young, which so soon afterwards was to produce the riots of 1968. Pacifism, the communal spirit, youth, the message of "make love, not war" sent out by the American universities, lie at the base of this return to the story of Romeo and Juliet, eternal example of the conflicts and blindness of power. Béjart framed his tragedy in a modern society as a model of behaviour not to be followed and a way of telling us that these young artists are, unlike the doomed pair, destined for love and mutual comprehension. Thus it is that Romeo and Juliet represent theater (Oleg Vinagradov was to make the same choice seven years later) while the dancers stand for life, a life full of hope that could easily be imagined in the optimistic awakening of freedom in the 1960s. Shakespeare's tragedy was rearranged, with interludes in the Elizabethan style, and confusion piled on confusion by the magical intervention of Queen Mab, enigmatic messenger of beauty and death. In Béjart's version the courtly background is missing; the Capulet and Montague families, the characters of Paris and Benvolio, have all disappeared. Béjart depicts himself as father to this huge, young family, taking the part of the ballet master. His extraordinary intuition, which ends the spectacle with a "hymn of joy," creates a magical fusion of past fiction and modern reality. This prophetic vision of a better world, as the choreographer himself remarked, unites "the tousled romanticism of the young Berlioz, whose warmth and generosity were not without a certain artlessness, with the magic and cruelty of Shakespeare." The grand Berlioz tapestry gives romantically violent stimulus to the choreographer's

The ballet Embrace Tiger and Return to Mountain. *Choreography by Glen Tetley to music by Subotnick.*

imagination, which enriches the love-destruction-reconstruction theme with powerful crowd scenes, moments of lyrical abandon, and modern theatrical solutions. Various members of the company have danced the principal roles at different times, from Paolo Bortoluzzi to Jorge Donn and from Suzanne Farrell to Rita Poelvoorde.   M.P.

PARADISE LOST

One-act ballet. Choreography by Roland Petit. Music by Marius Constant. Scenario by Jean Cau. Set by Martial Raysse. London, Covent Garden, February 23, 1967. Principal dancers: Margot Fonteyn and Rudolf Nureyev.

SYNOPSIS. The plot of the ballet is borrowed from a poem by Jean Cau, "Every paradise is found only to be lost," and thus does not refer to Milton's famous work. On the stage stands a large egg delineated by neon lights. There is a countdown as for space missiles, at the end of which man is hatched: Adam. He explores his own nature and powers. There is his first sorrow and the birth of Eve. The initial resentment between man and woman slowly dissolves into harmony. Then comes the serpent bringing temptation, seduction, and Adam's aggressive sexuality. Finally the hero flings himself into a hugely magnified mouth of Eve. Innocence is destroyed by an attacking mob, while God's wrath descends on the guilty.

■ The Garden of Eden myth is interpreted with intensity through a long sequence of solos and dances for two. The symbols are enlarged to underline the message of a modern, even scientific, vision.   M.B.

JEWELS

Ballet in three parts. Choreography by George Balanchine. Music by Gabriel Fauré, Igor Stravinsky, and Piotr I. Tchaikovsky. Set by Peter Harvey. Costumes by Karinska. New York, New York State Theater, April 13, 1967. New York City Ballet. Principal dancers: Violette Verdy and Conrad Ludlow, Mimi Paul and Francisco Moncion, Patricia McBride, Edward Villella and Patricia Neary, Suzanne Farell and Jacques d'Amboise.

SYNOPSIS. An abstract ballet.

■ This is a grand classical ballet inspired by jewels. The idea came to Balanchine after a visit to the famous jewellers, Arpels, where he had been entranced by the collection of gems. The choreographer decided to dress the dancers as if they were precious stones. In the same line of thought the emeralds would be accompanied by the music of Fauré (*Pelléas et Mélisande, Shylock*), the rubies by Stravinsky (*Capriccio for piano and orchestra*), and the diamonds by Tchaikovsky (*Third Symphony*). The ballet, like the music, is strongly contrasted. The emeralds are danced in the traditional French style by two couples, three soloists, and ten girls; the rubies, in the more modern and American tone Stravinsky suggests, by one couple, one soloist, and a mixed *corps de ballet*; finally, the diamonds, more exalted and romantic (the *Symphony*'s first movement is omitted) consist, as before, of one couple, a group of soloists, and the full *corps de ballet*. Balanchine's choreography, like the jewels themselves, is glittering, a marvellous display of classical erudition and a backward glance at the glories of ballet's past. Clearly we are no longer in the time of Petipa, for the high academic style is transformed into something much more dynamic and geometrical, far from the romantic languors of that era. It is a stunning parade of *pas de deux*, variations, ensembles, and national dances (such as the final Polonaise) which give the *corps de ballet* the chance to exhibit at the highest level all the academic skill and intelligence that Balanchine has carried into his American achievement.   M.P.

CARMEN SUITE

One-act ballet. Choreography by Alberto Alonso. Music by Georges Bizet arranged by Rodion Scedrin. Moscow, Bolshoi Theater, April 20, 1967. Principal dancers: Maia Plisetskaia, Nikolai Fadeyechev, Radchenko.

SYNOPSIS. This is the story of *Carmen* by Merimée, envisaged as a mortal combat fought in an arena between the gypsy and Don Jose and dominated by inevitable fate symbolized in the stylized head of a bull. The ballet's interpretative key is that Carmen is a free woman, honest and sincere, whereas Don Jose is a liar and destined to lose her. The bull represents fate. Carmen and the bull die at the same moment because their destiny is the same. Even the duel between Carmen and her lover is seen as a bullfight.

■ Made to measure for the great Soviet ballerina Maia Plisetskaia by the Cuban choreographer Alonso, *Carmen Suite* is an intensely dramatic ballet. The Latin spirit is emphasized by the partly Spanish choreography consisting of forceful, rhythmic steps with a high degree of tension. Only the music connects the ballet with Bizet's opera.   M.P.

AFTER EDEN

One-act ballet. Choreography by John Butler. Music by Lee Hoiby. Set by Rouben Ter-Arutunian. New York, Broadway Theater, November 9, 1967. Harkness Ballet. Principal dancers: Lone Isaksen and Lowrence Rhodes.

SYNOPSIS. This is the story of Adam and Eve after their original sin and expulsion from Paradise. Through their psychology, fears, sorrows, repentance, and ecstasy, they find themselves united anew to face the future together.

■ The theme has been used all too much in the world of ballet, but in employing it yet again John Butler has produced a work of high imagination, told with so much harmony of expression and intelligent understanding of psychology that the story becomes the story of all humanity.   M.P.

CIRCLES

One-act ballet. Choreography by Glen Tetley. Music by Luciano Berio. Set and costumes by Nadine Baylis. The Hague, Theater Royal, March 5, 1968. Nederlands Dans Theater.

SYNOPSIS. The interpretation of three poems by E. E. Cummings.

■ A modern ballet for six dancers, each of whom begins with some movements executed in silence. In the first two movements there are two *pas de deux*, while the whole cast takes part in the third. Berio's music, bearing the same title, for female voice, harp, and percussion, is a good example of an avant-garde composition suitable for avant-garde dance.   M.P.

BHAKTI

Ballet in three parts. Choreography by Maurice Béjart. Traditional Hindu music with some by Ravi Shankar. Costumes by Germinal Casado. Avignon, July 26, 1968. Ballet du XXme Siècle.

SYNOPSIS. Ballet without a plot.

■ The ballet *Bhakti* is clearly inspired by Indian religion and philosophy. It is a meeting of two civilizations, of the east and the west, fashioned by Béjart into a kind of love poem, which he defines thus: "Through love we identify with divinity. Whenever we seek to revive an old legend of a god, it reveals one of the aspects of supreme reality." The myth is rediscovered through intellect and, beyond that, the understanding of a culture and the apprehension of far-off and infinite worlds. The choreographic basis of *Bhakti* is the *pas de deux*. The first part is devoted to Rama, incarnation of Vishnu, and to his love for Sita, symbol of purity, as told in the *Ramayana*. In the second part the protagonist is Krishna, another incarnation of Vishnu. He is the god of youth and beauty, the divine fluteplayer, whose amorous adventures with shepherdesses and the beautiful Radha are described in the *Gita Govinda*. Krishna is also, and above all, the teacher. Finally, the third part shows Shiva, third person of the Hindu trinity, the god of destruction, in so far as it relates to illusion and personality. He is also the god of dance, and his wife Shakti is nothing other than the vital energy that comes from him and returns to him, still yet eternally in movement. The ballet uses a whole range of Indian gestures and positions, with their symbolic meanings, and, as often occurs with Béjart, the dance is sometimes slowed down to obtain plastic effects in movement. Naturally, even in this case, the oriental movements never decline into folk-dance effects, but are interpreted in a European spirit to form a flow of technique and a precise style of rhythm and gesture closely related to the fascinating music used for the occasion.   M.P.

EMBRACE TIGER AND RETURN TO MOUNTAIN

One-act ballet. Choreography by Glen Tetley. Music by Morton Subotnick. Set and costumes by Nadine Baylis. London, Jeanette Cochrane Theatre, November 21, 1968. Ballet Rambert. Principal dancers: Sandra Craig, Peter Curtis, Christopher Bruce, Gayrie McSween, Mary Willis.

SYNOPSIS. Abstract ballet.

■ The ballet was inspired by a form of Chinese martial art, T'ai-chi, based on thirty-seven movements, of which the one giving this work its name is the seventeenth. The dance movements are derived from the rules governing this kind of contest, excluding any form of aggression and founded on concentration and static balance, using the force and attack of one's opponent to overbalance him and bring him to the ground. Subotnick's electronic music is called *Silver Apple of the Moon*. Here Tetley

Dances at a Gathering *by Jerome Robbins, danced by the New York City Ballet.*

realizes a point of choreographic contact between the western style and the eastern. The use of a mirrored floor underlines the symbolic deployment of the dancers. Many modern dance companies keep this ballet in their repertory.　　　　　　　　　　　　　　　　M.B.

THE TAMING OF THE SHREW

Ballet in two acts. Choreography by John Cranko. Music by Domenico Scarlatti, arranged by Kurt Heinz Stolze. Sets and costumes by Elizabeth Dalton. Stuttgart, Württemberg State Theater, March 16, 1969. Stuttgart Ballet. Principal dancers: Marcia Haydeé and Richard Cragun.

SYNOPSIS. Act I: Baptista, a rich gentleman, has two daughters, Bianca and Katharina. The former is courted by three men, but Baptista explains that Katharina, the elder, must be married first. The suitors having been dismissed, young Petruchio arrives. He has been robbed by two women of the street so, needing the money, decides to pay court to Katharina, who has an unmanagable character. He is introduced to the Shrew, who at first treats him ferociously, but finally consents to marry him. Meanwhile Bianca has made it plain that of all her suitors she prefers the student Lucentio. Act II: Katharina's wedding approaches, but the bridegroom behaves atrociously. He takes his bride away before the marriage feast, keeps her without food, in the cold, and without even a bed. Finally he tames her so that she becomes mild and obedient. Bianca, too, weds her Lucentio, while the other two suitors are tricked into marrying the two ladies of the street. There is a change of roles. Bianca shows herself to be far from angelic, while Katharina, the former Shrew, astounds everybody with her gentleness and docility.

■ This brilliant ballet, based on Shakespeare's famous comedy, is an amusing piece of theater in which dancing takes the place of words with rare perfection. Cranko displays extraordinary liveliness, great balletic imagination, and a wonderful gift for characterization. The middle section of the ballet, in particular where Petruchio makes his shrewish wife see reason, is a masterpiece of irony and energetic, articulate dance. As a duet, it stands at the opposite pole to the romantic tradition. Cranko here shows himself faithful to the spirit of Shakespeare. It is a pity that the music does not come up to the same level of exuberance and wit.　　M.P.

NOMOS ALPHA

One-act ballet. Choreography by Maurice Béjart. Music by Iannis Xenakis. Royan, Festival of Royan, April 2, 1969. Ballet du XXme Siècle. Principal dancer: Paolo Bortoluzzi.

SYNOPSIS. Abstract ballet.

The Ballet de Lyon in Alexander Nevsky; *choreography by Vittorio Biagi, music by Prokofiev.*

■ The work is an extraordinary choreographic composition for a single male dancer following the music of Xenakis according to an interpretive, imitative process of incredible purity and freshness. The dancer, dressed in red, stands in a cone of light, then expresses a whole range of sensations, gestures, and attitudes in continuous relation to the music, written for 'cello and recorded on tape. In *Nomos Alpha* Béjart, in a mood of gay amusement, displays the whole range of his dance vocabulary, placing in a mainly modern context elements of classical, modern, and character dance, stretching to the utmost the technical and expressive capabilities of the human body and matching the virtuosity of Xenakis's music. The ballet is also worthy of study for Bortoluzzi's qualities as a dancer, his smoothly flowing agility, his sense of humour, and his sensitivity to every nuance of the music, which he transforms into pure dance.   M.P.

DANCES AT A GATHERING

One-act ballet. Choreography by Jerome Robbins. Music by Frédéric Chopin. Costumes by Joe Eula. Lighting by Thomas Skelton. New York, New York State Theater, May 8, 1969. New York City Ballet. Principal dancers: Allegra Kent, Sara Leland, Kay Mazzo, Patricia McBride, Violette Verdy, Anthony Blum, John Clifford, Robert Maiorano, John Prinz, Edward Villella.

SYNOPSIS. A suite of dances without a definite subject, although there is the suggestion of a prolonged amorous skirmish, vaguely rustic and innocent, with various couples forming, parting, and reforming in an interplay at once tender and ironical. The musicians and a piano are visible on the left side of the bare stage, on which ten dancers perform, interconnected by the delicate shades of their simple costumes.

■ Dedicated to the memory of Jean Rosenthal, the technical adviser to the New York City Ballet, who died in 1969, *Dances at a Gathering* is, in style, one of Jerome Robbins's most explicitly classical ballets. Some have professed to see this phase in Robbins's work as simply the result of Balanchine's influence. In reality, Jerome Robbins, artistic codirector with Balanchine of the New York City Ballet, is the leading exponent of American modern dance and a choreographer of unique personality. What he has drawn from Balanchine is the enriched and stylized groundwork of classical dance, which he has in turn moulded and elaborated in his own very personal style, characterized by a certain all-American light and sparkling humour, into which he has integrated contributions from diverse sources such as jazz, folk dance, and even the exuberant acrobatics of the circus. *Dances at a Gathering* reveals the most limpidly classical aspect of that style. The dance pattern is linear but rich in steps, dashing evolutions, and feats of virtuosity, treated with a cool irony that removes from them any hint of mere showiness, and always keeping the unity of the whole. It is a pure form of choreography in which everything is expressed in terms of

dance and uninterrupted movements. The music to which the ballet is danced endows it with a certain romantic atmosphere. It consists of eighteen piano pieces by Chopin: Mazurkas, Waltzes, Studies, a Scherzo, and a Nocturne. Permanently in the repertory of the New York City Ballet, *Dances at a Gathering* has also been presented by the British Royal Ballet at Covent Garden Opera House in London on October 19, 1970, with Laura Connor, Ann Jenner, Monica Mason, Lynn Seymour, Antoinette Sibley, Michael Coleman, Anthony Dowell, Desmond Kelly, Rudolf Nureyev, and David Wall.   A.A.

THE ROPES OF TIME

One-act ballet. Choreography by Rudi van Dantzig. Music by Jan Boerman. Set and costumes by Toer van Schayk. London, Royal Opera House, Covent Garden, March 2, 1970. Royal Ballet. Principal dancers: Rudolf Nureyev (the Traveller), Diana Vere, Monica Mason.

SYNOPSIS. There are three characters in the ballet, the Traveller, Life, and Death. On the darkened stage a man stands balanced on a hemisphere, which is, in fact, part of a great egg. Suddenly he falls off. The egg hatches, giving birth to the Traveller who, dancing with ten other youths, sets off on the long journey of life. Life and Death make their entrances and join in the dance, then, one after the other, come to the Traveller's side and go with him on his way. For the pilgrim his two companions are a constant recall to reality and a reminder of the transience of earthly values.   M.B.

EARLY SONGS

One-act ballet. Choreography by Eliot Feld. Music by Richard Strauss. Costumes by Stanley Simmons. New York, Brooklyn Academy of Music, April 2, 1970. American Ballet Company. Principal dancers: Eliot Feld, Christine Sarry, John Sowinsky, Elizabeth Lee, Christina Stirling, Richard Munro.

SYNOPSIS. Ballet without a plot.

■ In this ballet, through the use of solos, *pas de deux*, and ensembles, Feld at times identifies with or forms a dialectic counterpoint to the atmosphere, melody, and rhythmic structure of Strauss's *Lieder* (fourteen youthful works by the Bavarian composer). Thus the dancers stress certain passages with significant movements, freely interpreting and commenting on them, while at other moments the steps and configurations are intended to correspond exactly to the musical texture and faithfully to recreate its spirit. The ballet is profoundly romantic.   M.B.

COULD THIS BE DEATH? *(Serait-ce la Mort?)*

One-act ballet. Choreography by Maurice Béjart. Music by Richard Strauss (Vier letzte Lieder, Four Last Songs), sung by Elizabeth Schwarzkopf. Marseilles, Opera House, April 4, 1970. Principal dancers: Jorge

The Ballet du XXme Siècle in Firebird *by Maurice Béjart, a new version in which he sets the fairy tale aside and adopts a political interpretation.*

Donn, Maina Gielgud, Menia Martinez, Laura Proença, Kristina Schubert.

SYNOPSIS. Ballet without a plot, directly inspired by the *Lieder* of Richard Strauss.

■ With *Serait-ce la Mort?* Béjart advances still further in his exploration of the German romantic and late romantic world, which has always been one of his chief creative influences, from Goethe to Mahler, from Nietzsche to Wagner, from Beethoven to Novalis. After his Wagnerian works (*Bacchanale* from *Tannhäuser* in 1961; *Mathilde* in 1965; and *Les Vainqueurs* in 1969), his encounter with Richard Strauss came through a lyrical meditation on death. Conceived as an all-devouring being in *Reine Verte* (1962), but defeated in *Notre Faust* (1975) by the perennial return of youth in the child Faust reborn, death is here seen as the disquieting last companion. The title is taken from the final verse (*Ist dies etwa der Tod?* Can this be death?) of the fourth and last *Lied, Im Abendrot* (At sunset), to the words of Josef von Eichendorff (the other three are to verses by Hermann Hesse) summarizing the work's theme. A man

(Jorge Donn), near his end, sees once more the three women he has loved and who have helped him on his passage through life. But there is a fourth female figure, enigmatic and mysterious, obsessive yet elusive, barely identifiable, who will go with him to the threshold of death. To the first song (*Frühling*, Spring) the hero and the four loved women hold hands, forming a chain, their movements infused with a sweet, sad enchantment, interspersed with arabesques and attitudes. The three adagios that follow, performed by the three women in perfect harmony with the Straussian melody, are unsurpassable for the linear composition and stylistic purity with which they sum up the tragic lyricism and melting tenderness of the words. During the intervals between the *Lieder*, Death (Kristina Schubert), white-clad, implacable, expresses the tolling of Destiny in frigid arabesques. But the innermost significance of the work lies in the hero's sorrowful recall of time past. A slow arching of the back, a fleeting dance in *plié*, a submissive gesture of the hand, are enough – perfect tribute to the depth of feeling intrinsic in Strauss's score – to illuminate the loving encounter and the endurance of grief.   S.B.

The American Ballet in Theater *by Eliot Feld, a ballet based on the* Commedia dell'Arte.

Right: The Ballet du XXme Siècle in Nijinsky Clown of God *by Maurice Béjart.*

ALEXANDER NEVSKY

One-act ballet. Choreography by Vittorio Biagi. Music by Sergei Prokofiev. Set and costumes by Roger Bernard and Joëlle Roustan. Lyons, Opera House, May 21, 1970. Ballet de Lyons. Principal dancer: Vittorio Biagi.

SYNOPSIS. The ballet has no plot, its point of departure being Prokofiev's famous *Cantata* composed for the film *Alexander Nevsky* by Eisenstein, telling of the fight of the Russian people against the Teutonic knights. Eisenstein's masterpiece and Prokofiev's stupendous score are respected, although the ballet does not follow the narrative. Its aim is to evoke the spirit of liberty in an abstract rather than a figurative way. Composed for the ensemble divided into massive blocks, Biagi's *Nevsky* forcefully interprets the spirit of the drama and music: without telling a story, he makes the imagination work. In the choreographer's own words, "the intention is to express the ideology of the Russian people as a symbol of the struggle against every kind of oppression." In this way the ballet is both epic and abstract, and figures among the best choreographic works of the Italian dancer, trained at the Scala and grown to artistic maturity at the side of Maurice Béjart.   M.P.

THE RIVER

One-act ballet. Choreography by Alvin Ailey. Music by Duke Ellington. Costumes by Frank Thompson. New York, State Theater, Lincoln Center, June 25, 1970. American Ballet Theater. Principal dancers: John Prinz, Alexandra Radius, Han Ebbelaar, Marcos Paredes, Ivan Nagy. Reconstructed and included in the repertory of the Harkness Ballet and later that of the Ballet International de Caracas.

SYNOPSIS. *The River* portrays the relationship between water, nature, and man, but is otherwise without plot.

■ The ballet is composed around Duke Ellington's beautiful score and follows its program of sweetness, irony, joy, and sense of community. Different parts are entitled *The Spring, Meandering Stream, The Rapids, The Lake, The Waterfall, The Whirlpool, The Banks, The Two Cities,* but various numbers can be integrated in others, such as *The Sea,* or else repeated with the addition of a prologue and epilogue. The construction, with some solos, *pas de deux,* and group movements, is mainly modern, with a few classical passages for the ensemble. Ailey, among the most intelligent of American choreographers, sometimes has his tongue in his cheek, making fun of certain celebrated personalities. He can draw character strongly and with empathy. The meaning of the ballet is that the river represents life, its course is that of mankind; the two banks are separated, but people can cross from one to the other to overcome divisions and loneliness.   M.P.

MUTATIONS

Ballet in one movement. Choreography by Glen Tetley. Cinematic choreography by Hans van Manen. Music by Karlheinz Stockhausen. Set by Nadine Baylis. Costumes by Emmy van Leersum and Gijis Bakker. Lighting by John B. Read. Visualization by Jean-Paul Vroom. Scheveningen, Circus Theater, July 3, 1970. Nederlands Dans Theater. Principal dancers: Anja Licher and Gérard Lemaitre.

SYNOPSIS. An abstract ballet.

■ When *Mutations* first appeared in America (New York, Brooklyn Academy of Music, March 29, 1972) having already been well received in London, it was a historic occasion for the New York theater. It was the first "nude ballet' to be staged in an important theater by a major company. Apart from the nudity, there was the novelty of three cinema screens in the background, onto which films were projected at the same time as the stage action by live dancers. Furthermore, the stage was extended by a gangway that reached into the middle of the stalls. It was, in fact, not a completely nude ballet.

Clothes played an important symbolical role. The fully-clothed dancers performed restricted, encumbered movements, the seminaked used their freedom aggressively, while the completely naked experienced the joy of unfettered movement without any constriction. Van Manen first got the idea for this ballet when he was commissioned to create a work to celebrate the twenty-fifth anniversary of the liberation of the Netherlands from the Nazis. It seemed to him possible to speak of liberty only in language that was free and even visually denuded — "If the ballet has to be about freedom, we should make it completely *free*" (Van Manen). Later he collaborated with Tetley, who arranged the live part of the ballet together with the Nederlands Dans Theater. C.M.C.

FIREBIRD

*One-act ballet. Choreography and scenario by Maurice Béjart. Music by Igor Stravinsky (*Suite for Orchestra, 1919*). Set and costumes by Joëlle Roustan and Roger Bernard. Paris, Palais des Sports, October 31, 1970. Ballet du XXme Siècle. Principal dancer: Michael Denard.*

SYNOPSIS. In spite of Stravinsky's music being used, this is not a version of Fokine's ballet. The old Russian fairy tale has been replaced by a fable on the theme of liberty and revolution. According to Béjart the Firebird is the Phoenix who rises anew from its own ashes. Thus, it tells of a partisan hero who, with his soldiers, fights and dies in a battle against invisible enemies. From defeat and death, however, new Phoenixes arise in a red apotheosis of the people. The final scene shows the triumphant meeting of the partisans in uniform and the people of the future in red leotards. They form a united group, expressing their belief in the invincibility of revolution. The poet, like the revolutionary, comments Béjart, is a bird of fire.

■ This version of the famous ballet has enjoyed worldwide success because of the novelty of its assumptions and the violence and concentration of its choreographic action. Apart from the leading dancer's virtuosity, there are choral passages, classically interpreted to the music and themes of Stravinsky. In the finale the composition of the ensemble movements conveys the impression of great harmony and strength. Béjart's version of *Fire-*

bird has passed into the repertory of several other companies, and is a happy example of the reworking of Stravinsky ballets that culminated in the recent psychoanalytical interpretation of *Petrouchka*.   M.P.

THEATER
One-act ballet. Choreography by Eliot Feld. Music by Richard Strauss. Costumes by Frank Thompson. Lighting by Jennifer Tipton. New York, Brooklyn Academy of Music, January 6, 1971. American Ballet Company. Principal dancers: Eliot Feld (Pierrot), Elizabeth Lee, Edward Verso.

SYNOPSIS. The ballet hinges on the tragic personality of Pierrot and is based on the masks of the *Commedia dell'Arte*. Snubbed, left out, made fun of, poor Pierrot is mixed up in the merriment and tricks of Harlequin, Colombine, and Punchinello. The tears of Pierrot — of whom Feld himself gives an interpretation of great power and expressiveness — are swept away at the end in a shower of coloured balloons. Now the dancers return and Pierrot leaves the scene.

■ The opening of the ballet, with Pierrot intent on his makeup, immediately conveys the impression of a tragic soul, but for the others, thanks partly to the splendour of the lighting and costumes, we know that the glittering world of feasting and fun is open wide. The accompanying music, *Burlesque for piano and orchestra* by Richard Strauss, is admirably suited to the subject. M.B.

CHOREOGRAPHIC OFFERING *(Offrande Choréographique)*
Ballet by Maurice Béjart. Choreography in collaboration with the dancers of the Ballet du XXme Siècle. Music by Johann Sebastian Bach (Musical Offering). Percussion improvised by Fernand Schirren. Iguanophones devised and made by Simon Lewie. Brussels, Théâtre de la Monnaie, January 13, 1971. First presentation abroad, January 25, 1971, at the Brooklyn Academy of Music in New York.

SYNOPSIS. This is not a dramatic ballet, but a dialectic interpretation of the Bach masterwork, meant as a presentation (hence the "Offering" of the title) by the ballet company. It is a most elaborate construction, in which the classical style is transposed into a modern key, playing on the contrasts between theme and countertheme. The ballet's structure is built up on the following lines: development of the royal theme (of Frederick the Great of Prussia) and a dance theme of the great ballet master Cecchetti, taken from his *adagio* exercises; the use of eight central canons from the *Musical Offering*, with an analogous development of the compositional construction. The countertheme, represented by dancers and percussion, modifies and parodies the classical theme in a modern spirit. A contrast, or, as Béjart puts it, a contest, emerges. Which of the two forces will win? Life itself supplies the answer. Theme and counter-theme are danced by two young men, one in classical, the other in free, style. At the end a girl offers the audience a rose.

Peter Martins and Kay Mazzo in Duo Concertante, *with choreography by Balanchine and music by Stravinsky.*

Maia Plisetskaia (center front) and the Bolshoi corps de ballet *in* Anna Karenina.

■ On several occasions Maurice Béjart has experimented with a kind of collective effort, allotting choreographic tasks to his dancers. He has worked in this way with his dance school, Mudra, creating a sort of guided workshop, with sometimes surprising results. In *Offrande Choréographique* the reins of the enterprise have been very tightly held by Béjart, who has imposed the inflexible logic of reason. In other cases results have been less satisfactory, as with *Acqua Alta (High Water)*, created at Venice for "Dance 1975," or even disastrous, as in the second part of *Heliogabalus*, which was unrestrained to the point of bad taste.   M.P.

SONG OF THE WAYFARER *(Chant du Compagnon Errant)*
*One-act ballet. Choreography by Maurice Béjart. Music by Gustav Mahler (*Lieder eines fahrenden Gesellen*). Brussels, Forêt National (Palais des Sports), March 11, 1971. Principal dancers: Rudolf Nureyev and Paolo Bortoluzzi.*

SYNOPSIS. Nonnarrative ballet directly inspired by the *Lieder* of Gustav Mahler.

■ To these songs by the youthful Mahler, Béjart has devised a small jewel of a ballet in which his creativity has attained the heights of stylistic austerity and the depths of emotion and pathos. At the age of twenty-four, Mahler wrote the words and music of *Lieder eines fahrenden Gesellen* (some of its themes were used again in his *First Symphony*), which to some extent reflected his own unhappiness at an unrequited love. The wandering youth, the hero (whose journeys faintly echo Schubert's *Winterreise*), is one of the "itinerant clerks" of the Middle Ages, who travelled from city to city in search of learning. In this *pas de deux* for two men (in fact, a true ballet in itself), Béjart returns to an idea that haunts him – the split personality. Without any decor, this meeting – or clash – is developed in action dense with emotion, deeply felt, yet pared to the bone. A young man (Nureyev or Jorge Donn), full of perplexity about his life, finds himself faced with his other self (Bortoluzzi or Daniel Lommel), the symbolic figure of fate, conscience, and death, but also the companion, friend, and loved one. In this danced counterpoint the two performers move sometimes in parallel, sometimes parting ways, sometimes forming contrasting patterns in space, but always expressing the composer's intentions with the utmost sensitivity – either the sad, lyrical nostalgia of the first *Lied*, changing in the second to a quick and joyous exaltation of nature, or the tragic accents and dark death wish of the third song imperceptibly merging into the last, in which the distressed and exhausted youth sets off towards an unknown, frightening destination. The choreography (in which the second position predominates) demands great interpretive dancing. In the ballet's aspect of music made visible, the literal understanding of the score, note for note, is perfectly fused with its deepest, most arcane, inner significance.   S.B.

STAGES

Multimedium ballet. Produced and choreographed by Robert Cohan. Music by Arne Nordheim and Bob Downes. Designs by Peter Farmer. Lighting by John B. Read. Film sequences and projections by Anthony McCall. London, The Place, April 22, 1971. The London Contemporary Dance Theatre. Principal dancers: William Louther and Naomi Lapzeson.

SYNOPSIS. A multimedium morality in two stages, this "heromyth" is an allegory of man on a lonely quest for reality and his true self. In Stage I he descends to a Bosch-like Underworld which, in fact, represents our own world of reality and illusion. He meets the Furies, who torment him and lash him to a cross, then the mysterious Goddess of Illusion, who tantalizes and eludes him. Yet, contemplating his image in a mirror, he persists in his quest. Stage II suggests that the myths which once supported us have now been reduced to the level of strip cartoon and the mass-media exploitation of the hero cult. The Furies become the Kings Road cuties of the time, many-tentacled monsters attack the Hero, sirens lure him; there is a suggestion of the Theseus legend, with bull-dancing athletes. The questor, with growing despair, watches the degeneration of all that was heroic and finally, climbing to the summit of the multitiered set, where the gateway to the Underworld is placed, overturns its pillars and, like Samson, brings the whole scene to utter destruction. Alone, he must pursue his quest.

■ This was the first large-scale spectacular work put on by the London Contemporary Dance Theatre and marked its turning point from a brave, precarious venture to its present position as one of the foremost modern dance companies in Europe. The American Robert Cohan, its artistic director and chief choreographer, saw his first ballet, *Murder in the Gorbals* by Robert Helpmann, at Sadler's Wells in 1944, and was inspired by it to devote his life to dance. He joined Martha Graham's company and was soon dancing major roles. The London Contemporary Dance Theatre has toured all over the world and possesses its own flourishing school. Growing from its American roots, it has developed its own distinctive style. Prerecorded tapes of Arne Nordheim's electronic music accompany Stage I. The music for Stage II is Bob Downes's extended jazz. *Stages* was presented at Sadler's Wells in

1973, toured widely in Britain, and was seen in Paris and Berlin in 1974.   O.O.

THE GOLDBERG VARIATIONS

Ballet in two parts. Choreography by Jerome Robbins. Music by Johann Sebastian Bach. Costumes by Joe Eula. Lighting by Thomas Skelton. New York, New York State Theater, May 27, 1971. New York City Ballet. Principal dancers: Gesley Kirkland, Sara Leland, John Clifford, Robert Maiorano, Karin von Aroldingen, Anthony Blum, Patricia McBride, Helgi Tomasson, Peter Martins, Bruce Wells.

SYNOPSIS. Ballet without a plot.

■ This is a complex series of choreographic annotations based on the whole of Bach's famous *Goldberg Variations* (played on the piano and, in later performances of the same ballet, on a harpsichord by Gordon Boelzner), it is one of Jerome Robbins's most classical and – in the unanimous opinion of the critics – most successful works.   M.B.

ANASTASIA

Ballet in three acts. Scenario and choreography by Kenneth MacMillan. Music by Piotr Ilyich Tchaikovsky and Bohuslav Martinu. Electronic music by Fritz Winckel and Rüdiger Rüfer. Sets and costumes by Barry Kay. Lighting by Robert Ornbo. London, Covent Garden, July 22, 1971. Royal Ballet. Principal dancers: Lynn Seymour, Svetlana Beriosova, Antoinette Sibley, Anthony Dowell, Derek Rencher.

SYNOPSIS. Act I: August 1914. The Imperial family are enjoying a picnic with their friends, a group of naval officers, and Rasputin. The party is interrupted when news arrives of the outbreak of war. A front scene shows growing social unrest in the city. Act II: Petrograd, March 1917. In spite of increasing tension, the Czar gives a ball for his youngest daughter, Anastasia. The famous ballerina who was his mistress before he married has been invited to entertain the guests. Anastasia is puzzled by the relationships at court. A revolutionary group enters the ballroom and stops the festivities. Another front scene shows incidents of the October Revolution. Act III: some years later. A woman in a Berlin hospital believes she is Anastasia. For her, past and present, dream and reality, intermingle. She relives incidents since the murder of the Imperial family: her rescue by two brothers, the birth of her child, her marriage, the loss of husband and child, her attempted suicide, and finally the meetings with relatives of the Imperial family who deny that she is the Grand Duchess Anastasia.

■ The first act is set to Tchaikovsky's *First Symphony*, the second act to his *Third Symphony*. A complete change is signalled in Act III by the electronic music (produced by Fritz Winckel and Rüdiger Rüfer) and Martinu's *Fantasies Symphoniques*. The spectacular

Maia Plisetskaia and Anatoli Berdichev in La Rose Malade *by Roland Petit.*

and ingenious scenery changes in the same way from the splendour of the Imperial court to the starkness of the revolutionary and hospital scenes, while the dancing, which in the first two acts is classical in style, becomes modern dance in the last act. Some critics have found this marked dichotomy disconcerting. Lynn Seymour's performance, however, was extremely moving in both techniques. The sharp difference between the two parts is accounted for by the last section having originally been presented as a one-act ballet at the Deutsche Oper in West Berlin on June 25, 1967, when MacMillan was director of the ballet company there. He extended it for Covent Garden, although he revived the original version for the Stuttgart Ballet in 1976.   O.O.

NIJINSKY – CLOWN OF GOD (*Nijinski, Clown de Dieu*)

Ballet in two parts. Choreography and subject by Maurice Béjart. Music by Pierre Henri. Sets and costumes by Joëlle Roustan and Roger Bernard. Brussels, Forêt National, October 8, 1971. Ballet du XXme Siècle. Principal dancers: Jorge Dann (Clown of God), Paolo Bortoluzzi, Daniel Lommel, Mischa van Hoecke, Jorg Lanner, Suzanne Farrell, Angèle

Albrecht, Pierre Dobrievic (Diaghilev).

SYNOPSIS. Part I: the creation of the world. Lying about on the stage are naked, faceless bodies. Little by little they come to life until one of them detaches itself from the rest, who have formed the Circle of Life. God gives him a face and he begins to live and dance. It is Man, the Clown of God. God gives man heaven on earth, and with that we are magically transported to the period of Diaghilev's Russian Ballet. To the Clown, the Eternal Spirit gives the Dance, that is the Ballerina, for company, and as guardians and friends the Rose, the Faun, Petrouchka and the Golden Slave, symbols of air, water, and fire. Then comes the vision, at first unreal, then with a real face, of the Woman, the Wife, Love. During God's absence Nijinsky is tempted by the woman and marries her. The anger of Diaghilev erupts like the anger of God, and Nijinsky is expelled from the paradise of the *Ballets Russes*. 1914 is the year of the Fall, the end of an era. Part II: Diaghilev is no longer God, and Nijinsky continues his search for love and divinity, without help from his wife. He endures his Calvary until worn out in 1919 by the horrors of war and overwhelmed by the madness of the times. His existence ends, but his ballet lives to follow the way he

A moment from the ballet Le Marteau sans Maître, *created by Béjart to music by Boulez.*

started, that must finally lead to the service of God and the love of all.

■ This was one of the great spectacles worked out by Béjart in the years before his search for the *ballet-comédie* formula. It was obvious from the beginning that it would need a huge cast and great open spaces such as the Forêt National in Brussels, the Palais des Sports in Paris, or Madison Square Garden in New York. It is based on the diary of the great Russian dancer, Vaslav Nijinsky, and particularly on a passage contained in it, "I am a clown of God. ... I mean that a clown is all right when he expresses love. A clown without love is not from God." From which Béjart gets his idea of equating God with Diaghilev and Paradise with his Russian Ballet. He is not presenting a biography of the great artist who died mad, but a parable of his unhappiness. Nijinsky is portrayed as a fallen angel searching in vain for salvation through love, one who dies mad but leaves behind a message to be passed on by his doubles, that is to say, by the characters in his ballets. It is an ingenious idea, enabling us to perceive the protagonist as a mythical character, a generator of visions, feeling, and psychological interpretation. The great ballets of the period, *Le Spectre de la Rose, Scheherezade, L'Après-midi d'un Faune,* and *Petrouchka,* are aspects of the soul and art of Nijinsky the man. Perhaps here the reader should be reminded that Nijinsky, whom Diaghilev succeeded in intellectually dominating, tried to get out of his power by marrying, but was then expelled from the company with fury. After having given proof of a genius for choreography, now fully reinstated, he lost his reason and vegetated, shut away from the world in a state of complete alienation. Scenically the ballet is impressive. The stage is dominated by a black background with a great cross; enormous dummy figures, one of them representing Diaghilev, are used, and there are many interesting lighting effects. The cast is very large and the choreography luxuriant, complex, and virtuoso. Notes from Tchaikovsky's *Pathétique* are mingled with the avant-garde score of Pierre Henri, recorded on magnetic tape. Enthusiastically received by the audience, it met with mixed opinions from the critics. *Nijinsky Clown of God* was one of Béjart's magical all-star ballets, and dancing in it Jorge Dann and Suzanne Farrell made one of the biggest successes of their careers. The ballet's weight of symbolism, the choice of the anti-Diaghilev side, the provocative boldness of the duplication and multiplication of characters, lead into an irresistible flow of emotion, which may at first seem disturbing, but which arises from an iron interpretative logic and an extremely subtle psychological analysis. M.P.

THE TRIUMPH OF DEATH
Ballet in ten scenes. Choreography by Flemming Flindt. Music by Thomas Koppel. Sets and costumes by Paul Arnt Thomsen. Copenhagen, Theater Royal, February 19, 1972. Royal Danish Ballet.

SYNOPSIS. Based on a play by Eugène Ionesco, the ballet shows the endless ways in which the destructive forces of corruption, tyranny, and pollution act upon modern humanity and on the materialistic society in which we live.

■ Rock music, the sins of the consumer society, protest, and violence are the soil from which this ballet springs. It is intended as a brutal message of salvation, exposing with crude images and considerable eroticism the moral decadence, the pursuit of fashion, and the play of negative forces. In Flindt's usual style, it goes against or beyond the limits of current morality, attacking the evils of both today and yesterday. M.P.

ANNA KARENINA

Ballet in three acts. Choreography by Maia Plisetskaia, Natalia Ryzhenko, Victor Smirnov-Golovanov. Music by Rodion K. Scedrin. Scenario by Boris Lvov-Anokhin, drawn from Leo Tolstoy's novel of the same name. Moscow, Bolshoi Theater, June 10, 1972. Principal dancer: Maia Plisetskaia.

SYNOPSIS. Act I: Anna and Vronsky meet quite by chance at the St. Petersburg railway station. A sequence of events leads fatally to the two falling in love, and Anna's husband, Karenin, cannot prevent the passionate affair. Act II: at this point Anna's choice seems unalterable, while the husband's concern is now to save appearances and with them his position in the eyes of good society, of which he feels himself to be a part. But the two lovers will accept no compromise that could diminish their individuality, and run away abroad together. Anna leaves her son with his father. Act III: overcome with desire to see her son, Anna returns to her own country, but finds her old circles openly hostile. Society's moral condemnation seems to Anna final and without appeal. At St. Petersburg station she remembers her first meeting with Vronsky, and in despair commits suicide by throwing herself under a train.

■ The ballet's instant success was not a matter of chance, nor entirely due to the pathetic figure of the heroine. Plisetskaia's choreography was able to bring the other characters to life as well, not dwelling only on the eternal triangle beloved of drawing-room comedy, but counterbalancing it with conservative society and its false morality. In her own part Plisetskaia created a romantic, heroic figure fighting desperately for her love and her dignity. P.C.

SYMPHONY IN THREE MOVEMENTS

One-act ballet. Choreography by George Balanchine. Music by Igor Stravinsky. Lighting by Ronald Bates. New York, New York State Theater, Lincoln Center, June 18, 1972. New York City Ballet. Principal dancers: Helgi Tomasson, Sara Leland, Edward Villella.

SYNOPSIS. Ballet without a plot.

■ Returning to an old project of his, Balanchine produced this ballet as part of the festival organized by the New York City Ballet to honour Stravinsky on his ninetieth birthday. Stravinsky's symphony (lasting some twenty minutes) plays on various contrasts in tone colour, including that of the two chief instruments, the harp and the piano. The dance design follows the musical suggestions without attaching them to any plot. The middle movement, *Andante*, is a *pas de deux* described as "a mysterious, sensual, and mediative interlude with shades of exoticism." Balanchine says the symphony's first movement was composed as a possible accompaniment to a cinema film, while the second was intended (but never used) for a scene where the Virgin Mary appears in the film version of Werfel's novel *Bernadette*. The same symphony also formed the musical basis of an earlier ballet presented at the Empire Theatre in Sunderland, England, on November 7, 1963, with choreography by Hans van Manen. C.M.C.

TWILIGHT

One-act ballet. Choreography by Hans van Manen. Music by John Cage. Sets and costumes by Jean Paul Vroon. Amsterdam, Stadsschouwburg, June 20, 1972. Netherlands National Ballet. Principal dancers: Alexandra Radius and Han Ebbelaar.

SYNOPSIS. Ballet without a plot.

■ This is a dance for one man and one woman to advanced music by John Cage. An unusual feature of this ballet is that the girl wears shoes with heels, which she discards at a certain point to join her partner in a freer and more affectionate finale. *Twilight*, like other short works of this type – which could be called chamber ballets – is often performed. The title comes from the dimming of the lights at the end, when the two dancers gently merge into the night. M.P.

DUO CONCERTANTE

Choreographic duet in five movements. Choreography by George Balanchine. Music by Igor Stravinsky. Lighting by Ronald Bates. New York, New York State Theater, June 22, 1972. New York City Ballet. Dancers: Kay Mazzo and Peter Martins.

■ To the music of Igor Stravinsky's *Duo Concertante* for violin and piano (1932), George Balanchine has composed this ballet for two solo dancers, which is numbered among his quintessential works. The ballerina and her partner listen motionless to the first movement of *Duo*, standing beside the two musical instruments, which are situated on the left of the stage. They then move center stage, and to the next four movements (*Eclogues I and II, Gigue, Dithyramb*) perform a *pas de deux* that is a marvel of choreographic density, in which the sensitive, abstract response to the instrumental dialogue is nothing short of perfection. In contrast to this richness, the theatrical effects are austere. There is no scenery, the lighting is elementary, the dancers wear the usual simple practice outfits and perform without any mimic action an uninterrupted series of classical steps and figures conceived in Balanchine's most ascetic yet most polished style. The movement is an end in itself, devoid of all ordinary expressiveness, signifying only the idea of absolute harmony manifesting itself simultaneously in the two different languages of music and dance.   A.A.

CONTRE
One-act ballet. Choreography by Felix Blaska. Music by Luciano Berio. Grenoble, Maison de la Culture, December 12, 1972. Principal dancers: Vera Falatoff, Aliocha Gorki, Vlado Pilinger.

SYNOPSIS. Abstract ballet with no plot.

■ Produced after seven years of intensive choreographic experiment, inspired and sustained largely by the music of Stravinsky, Prokofiev, and Béla Bartòk, Contre is the result of the first meeting between Felix Blaska and Luciano Berio, a meeting that proved of fundamental importance to his career. In this work Blaska temporarily cast aside his usual modes of expression, made up of humour, liveliness, and a rivetting, amused dynamism, to adopt instead a more compact, restrained style, expressing itself more in volume than in line, with marked plastic values and strong attack. Two violently opposed groups (echoes of Béjart's Le Sacre du Printemps) appear to confront each other for the conquest of power, symbolized by a woman (Vera Falatoff). Without relating any story, Blaska translates the disturbing violence of Berio's score in strictly gestural terms, inviting the audience to "open themselves to the choreography completely" (Blaska). The collaboration between Blaska and the composer has continued and given rise to at least fifteen ballets, including Folk Songs (1973), a scintillating entertainment of masks, directed by Sylvie Guy, Agnus (1974), a first attempt at a mystic ballet, and Memory (1975), an evocative, atmospheric work.   S.B.

O ROSE, THOU ART SICK (La Rose Malade)
Ballet in three parts. Choreography by Roland Petit. Music by Gustav Mahler Second and Fifth Symphonies. Costumes by Yves St. Laurent. Paris, Palais des Sports, January 10, 1973. Ballets de Marseille. Principal dancer: Maia Plisetskaia.

SYNOPSIS. Ballet without a plot, interpreting a state of mind inspired by William Blake's poem ("O Rose, thou art sick/The invisible worm ... Has found out thy bed/Of crimson joy/And his dark secret love/Does thy life destroy").

■ This ballet was created for the Bolshoi prima donna Maia Plisetskaia. The final pas de deux is constructed in modern dance style combined with classical adagio forms. La Rose Malade gave Plisetskaia an opportunity to reveal her gifts as actress and dancer and to demonstrate the grace of her arm movements.   M.B.

VOLUNTARIES
One-act ballet. Choreography by Glen Tetley. Music by François Poulenc. Sets and costumes by Rouben Ter-Arutunian. Stuttgart, Württemberg State Theater, December 22, 1973. Stuttgart Ballet. Principal dancers: Marcia Haydée, Richard Cragun, Birgit Keil.

SYNOPSIS. Ballet without a plot.

■ This was Tetley's first work for the Stuttgart Ballet Company, of which he later became director. It was set to the score of the Concerto in G minor for organ, strings and kettledrums by Francis Poulenc, conceived as a composition of "linked solos (Voluntaries)." Embellished by the virtuoso dancing of Haydée and Cragun, the ballet reproduced in choreographic form the structure of Poulenc's work, inspired by the free improvisations for organ and drum which often preceded, accompanied, or followed religious functions. The ballet, which was enormously successful, was made in honour of the great choreographer John Cranko, who was director of the German company and died in August 1973. It was a combination of classical choreography in Cranko's style and modern dance, resulting in a happy and harmonious blend.   M.B.

SCENES OF CHILDHOOD (Kinderszenen)
One-act ballet. Choreography by John Neumeier. Music by Robert Schumann. Hamburg, State Opera House, season of 1974. Hamburg Ballet.

SYNOPSIS. A dancer introduces us to the world of Robert Schumann and the mental hospital at Endenich where the mentally sick composer relives his memories: the tie with his mother, the struggle for Clara's love, the meeting with Clara and Brahms. The point of reference is the piano, situated on the stage, through which Schumann tries to communicate with others.

■ This was a romantic interlude among the productions for the Hamburg Ballet directed by Neumeier. Here the American choreographer's work is clear and delicate, yet conceived in the ultramodern manner derived from the American school and, in particular, Balanchine. While at Hamburg, the young Neumeier also created a number of more abstract works such as Dämmern, Die Stille (Silence), Rondo, and Desiderio, in which the study of the body and its expressive potentiality predominates. These short ballets are counterparts in miniature of the massive constructions in which the corps de ballet plays a major part and is used en bloc. There is something surprising about the lasting relationship between modern choreographers and romantic, or even late romantic music.   M.P.

RODIN BROUGHT TO LIFE (Rodin mis en Vie)
One-act ballet. Choreography by Margo Sappington. Music by Michael Kamen. Costumes by Willa Kim. New York, April 17, 1974. Harkness Ballet. Principal dancers: Zane Wilson, Chris Jensen, Jeanette Vondersaar.

SYNOPSIS. The ballet consists of eleven numbers inspired by the sculpture of Auguste Rodin, presenting dance compositions of strong, plastic configurations and evolutions, concluding with an impressive, Dantesque vision of the *Gates of Hell*. Sometimes ironical, sometimes baroque, the ballet includes *The Age of Bronze*, *The Bust of Adèle*, *The Crouching Woman*, *The American Athlete*, *One of the Danaïdes*, *The Robber*, *The Eternal Idol*, *Eternal Spring*, *The Kiss*, *The Burghers of Calais*. Variations alternate with group movements, using various interpretative techniques, with the aim of ennobling the language of the body and its expressive potentialities.

■ Margo Sappington's ideas have worked well, and *Rodin mis en Vie*, in spite of the banality of Kamen's music, stands out for its originality and imagination. It remains one of the bulwarks of the Caracas National Ballet, who inherited it from the Harkness Ballet, a group now extinct. The dances for men are particularly interesting.   M.P.

DON JUAN

Ballet in five scenes. Choreography and subject by John Neumeier. Music by Christoph W. Gluck and Tomas Luis de Victoria. Sets and costumes by Filippo Sanjust. Text by Max Frisch. Speaking voice, Ralph Richardson. New York, Metropolitan Opera House, April 26, 1974. National Ballet of Canada. Principal dancer: Rudolph Nureyev.

SYNOPSIS. On All Souls' Day a funeral passes by. It is that of the Commendatore, killed by Don Juan, who now plans to ensnare the lady in white following the procession, the Commendatore's daughter, Anna. In the next scene Don Juan's servant is organizing a grand feast, engaging dancers who are to present his master's amorous adventures in the form of a *divertissement*. Thus we witness in flashback Don Juan's seduction of Doña Anna and the murder of her father. Anna appears to Don Juan as a vision, but he cannot retain her and is left alone in contemplation of his own soul. There is another entertainment, this time a rustic one, arranged by the servant, at which the Don tries to seduce a country girl. Anna's arrival sets the women against each other. A third banquet "of damnation" is prepared, and develops into an orgy. Don Juan follows Anna, but meets a procession carrying an empty coffin. He realizes that the coffin is for him, and that Doña Anna has become his Angel of Death.

■ This is a dramatic ballet with psychological implications, a celebration of strong emotions. Neumeier has reduced the story to its basic elements. The action moves with cinematographical rhythm around the trio Juan-Anna-servant, the last assuming the role of *deux ex machina*. Through Neumeier's energetic choreography, using massive group movements and classical passages of genuine power, Rudolph Nureyev was able to give a memorable portrayal of the defeated seducer's neurosis.   M.P.

DYBBUK VARIATIONS

Ballet in eleven parts. Choreography by Jerome Robbins. Music by Leonard Bernstein. Scenery by Reuben Ter-Arutunian. Costumes by Patricia Zipprodt. New York, New York State Theater, May 15, 1974. New York City Ballet. Principal dancers: Patricia McBride and Helgi Tomasson.

SYNOPSIS. An abstract interpretation of Shalom Ansky's play *The Dybbuk*, arranged by the choreographer in the following order: 1) Dance of seven men in the Holy Place. 2) Male duo, two couples, three couples. 3) Angelic messengers, variations for three men. 4) The dream, a *pas de deux*. 5) Evocation of the Cabbala and variations. 6) Passage. 7) Dance of the Girls. 8) Transition. 9) *Pas de deux*. 10) Exorcism. 11) Reprise and coda.

■ The ballet arose from an idea that had interested Bernstein and Robbins since 1954. Both Jewish, they were fascinated by the concept of the *dybbuk*, imbedded in the Hebrew folklore of central Europe. A *dybbuk* is a restless spirit of the dead that enters and possesses the body of a living person, who finally comes to behave and speak like the deceased. The subject was popularized by Ansky's play, which had been reappraised in the new Israeli culture. On the basis of that text Robbins constructed a ballet which shared the play's rites and hallucinatory spirituality. Summarized, the story is as follows: two friends agree that if one of them has a son and the other a daughter, the two young people will marry. The two children are duly born to them. Thus Leah and Chanon meet and fall in love, although unaware of their parents' pact. But Leah is rich and Chanon poor, which makes the marriage impossible. Chanon then turns to the Cabbala, a book of mysticism and black magic, to win Leah. He is, however, overcome by the dark forces he has released, and dies. Returning as a *dybbuk* to Leah's wedding, he is driven out by exorcism. Leah chooses to die in order to be reunited with her promised husband. A stern product of Hebrew culture, Robbins's and Bernstein's ballet is also an act of faith and an examination of the spiritual moving forces of an ancient civilization. A Hebrew Romeo and Juliet destroy themselves in a theocratic society by striving for a forbidden love through spells and magic powers reaching into the dark areas of the unconscious. The *pas de deux* of the "possessed" (part 9) is of such potency as to give the audience an authentic shiver. Bernstein's music often refers to traditional Jewish themes.   M.P.

JAROSLAVNA

Ballet in three acts. Choreography by Oleg Vinogradov. Music by Boris Tichenko. Scenario drawn from The Song of Igor's Army. *Set and costumes by Oleg Vinogradov. Direction by Yuri Liubimov. Leningrad, Maly Theater, June 30, 1974. Ballet Malegot.*

SYNOPSIS. Act I. First episode: *The enemy*: the Russian people are threatened with a Tartar invasion. They live oppressed while the Princes fight among themselves and think only of their own interests. Scenes of toil and terror. Second episode: *Mobilization*: in face of danger the army prepares for defense and, dogged by disagreements, Igor goes to war. Third episode: *The departure*: the army sets off for the battlefield. Fourth episode: *The Russian women*: their men away at the war, the women take on responsibility for work and the countryside. Act II. First episode: *The expedition*: amid a thousand difficulties the army marches to battle. Second episode: *Darkness*: at night beside the river Don, Igor encourages his troops. Third episode: *The first encounter*: in the morning battle with the barbarous Polovstian hordes begins. Fourth episode: *An interval of rest*: Igor's followers take cover. Fifth episode: *Encirclement*: the Russian army is pressed on all sides by the Polovstians of Konchak. Act III. First episode: *The second encounter*: during a fierce battle Igor is taken prisoner. Second episode: *Igor's imprisonment and state of slavery*. Third episode: *At Putivl*: Jaroslavna weeps for the loss of her husband Igor. Fourth episode: *Escape*: Igor succeeds in breaking out of prison and returns to his own country. Fifth episode: *Putivl again*: Igor returns and is welcomed with joy, but he knows he has to muster a new defending army. Sixth episode: *The summons*: all dissension over, the Russians can at last defend themselves against the hordes of unbelievers and hope to live in peace.

■ The ballet has no direct connection with Borodin's opera *Prince Igor*, but stems rather from old chronicles and a twelfth-century poem about the Russian hero. Thus there are no concessions to folklore or the nineteenth-century love for colourful romance. On the contrary, it is a return to certain archaic forms of the past

and an intense and very Christian spirituality. This was a new departure for Soviet theater and culture, which are only very hesitantly advancing towards renewal and a different set of values. *Jaroslavna* – it was remarked at its first showing in the west – is on the same ideological lines as the film *Rublev* by Tarkovsky (Rublev was an icon painter). It is certainly not by chance that in this ballet the Russian people, always the real protagonist in the operatic theater of Russia, as can be observed in the original *Boris*, should be seen with all their feeling for religion, firmly attached to its patriotic and orthodox roots. Above the tunics of Igor's soldiers shines the face of Christ, and that vision is not without a certain significance. The ballet is also important in that to the traditional mysticism of the Russian people it adds a clear political gloss, representing the danger that forever threatens under different guises, and the inexhaustible strength of a people that survives all the betrayals of its leaders. Another obvious reference is to innocence and redemption, as in *Boris Godunov*, based on the solidity of a peasant civilization capable of enormous suffering and legendary courage – Tichenko's music also fits perfectly into this vision, which has supreme moments of emotional tension. Indeed, although the score is modern to the point of destroying all tonality, it contains virile Orthodox chorales in the ancient ecclesiastical tradition. Sets and costumes, too, are far from the hallowed formulae of Soviet spectacle. There is a simple backcloth with phrases from the Igorian epic written on it in Cyrillic script; there are simple leotards suggesting poverty and bearing indications of the peasant world for the women, with naked torsos in modern dance style for the men. This trend towards symbolism, so prevalent in the west today, should not be interpreted as mere imitation, but as an authentic revival of dramatic values that

For the Sweet Memory of that Day *or* The Triumphs of Petrarch. *Choreography by Maurice Béjart. Scenery and costumes designed by Joëlle Roustan and Roger Bernard.*

Another scene from For the Sweet Memory of that Day. *The ballet, here shown on a conventional stage, was first performed in the open air against the splendid background of the Boboli Gardens in Florence.*

can be most easily expressed in a free choreography and a multifaceted composition in which stylistic experiments of various kinds have their place. The beginning of *Jaroslavna* can be considered almost abstract, even if the harshness of the movements suggests the toil and exhaustion undergone by the populace. In contrast, the scenes of conflict and battle have a brutal violence, relived only by the extreme gentleness of the women's dances. The women are, when all is said and done, the force on which society depends for survival, and so it is right that the ballet should be named after Jaroslavna and not Prince Igor, and should celebrate not war but love. A surprising feature is the casting of the barbarians, who are seen against the light performing very fast dances on point, with a striking use of the arm and leg movements suggestive of lances. Later we discover that these Polovstians are women dancers, whose travesty is carried off without the faintest touch of bad taste. As in the choreographer's production of *La Fille Mal Gardée*, distinctly similar to the English version, and in Prokofiev's powerful version of *Romeo and Juliet*, one detects in *Jaroslavna* a yearning for regeneration that may be the portent of deeply innovatory things to come. M.P.

FOR THE SWEET MEMORY OF THAT DAY or THE TRIUMPHS OF PETRARCH *(Per la Dolce Memoria di Quel Giorno* or *I Trionfi di Petrarca)*
Ballet in six parts. Choreography and subject by Maurice Béjart. Music by Luciano Berio. Interludes by Maurice Béjart and Mischa van Hoecke. Sets and costumes by Joëlle Roustan and Roger Bernard. Florence, Boboli Gardens, July 7, 1974. Ballet du XXme Siècle and the Mudra Group of Brussels. Principal dancers: Jorge Dann (the Poet), Suzanne Farrell (Laura), Rita Poelvoorde, and all the company's soloists.

SYNOPSIS. Part I: *The Triumph of Love*: the poet dreams of a tragic procession and sees the Triumph of Love it celebrates. From the crowd of prisoners a friend emerges to tell him of the troubles and torments lovers bear. Part II: *The Triumph of Chastity*: the virginal Laura appears leading a leashed unicorn, symbol of purity. Cupid has no power against her, and his arrows splinter. Chastity wins while Love is taken prisoner and isolated. Part III: *The Triumph of Death*: youth and purity are helpless against Death, who makes all humanity his slaves. Even Laura is conquered. Part IV: *The Triumph of Fame*: rebirth through memory. The Poet identifies himself with Fame and is raised to glory.

Above: Luciana Savignano and Jorge Donn in What love tells me *by Maurice Béjart.*
Opposite: A pose from Fold on Fold, *another of Maurice Béjart's ballets.*

In a fierce duel Fame conquers Death. Part V: *The Triumph of Time*: Time advances with its train, covering everything and bringing forgetfulness. Time gathers up Laura and the Poet forever, stripped of every vestige of the world. Part VI: *The Triumph of Eternity*: a mystic, universal vision in which all mankind exists in purity, couple after couple, young and sinless, to achieve an ecstatic immobility.

■ It should be noted in passing that, in addition to its usual meaning, Triumph denotes the decorated pageant cart used in medieval plays and processions. This ballet was first presented in the wonderful surroundings of the Boboli Gardens in a space much larger than any ordinary theatrical setting. An immense stage of uneven shape was conconstructed between the trees and classical statues scattered among the encircling lawns like relics of an ancient civilization. Beyond the platform, groups of dancer-mimes from the Mudra School represented a woodland people, acting as a commentary on the action. From the lateral avenues, the great allegorical carts, the various Triumphs, entered the acting area. The effect was stupendous. Perhaps no such spectacle has ever been seen on the modern stage. The ballet was commissioned by Italian Radiotelevision through the director, Francesco Siciliani. It grew into a splendid homage to the civilization and great poetry of Italy's fourteenth century, not so much from an academic angle as from continual visual references and the way in which it was presented. Béjart read and deeply studied Petrarch's text. He was greatly helped in creating the atmosphere by Roustan and Bernard, who devised a sumptuous setting and exceedingly beautiful costumes. The plot, summarized under headings above, must be explained further. All at once the Poet (Petrarch) is shown to us as a beautiful young man dressed like a modern dancer with bare torso and brown trousers. He is, however, not meant to be the historical poet but a symbol of amorous youth. The entry of the first triumphal cart (Love) bearing a youth (the "cruel boy") armed with a bow brings with it a desperate chain gang of captives (the sentenced lovers) and conveys an idea of how irresistible passion is. The *pas de trois* by the friend, Cupid, and the woman, the challenge to high-flown emotions, the folly, and the generosity, all suggest the ruthlessness of fate. The Chastity scene is a triumph of white. Laura, contrasted with Love, brings with her the unicorn of virginity and purity. The white-veiled virgins and the assexual angels in their modest robes are, however, the instruments of Love's condemnation. He falls, disarmed and agonized, amid the apotheosis of universal purity. Equally effective in its symbolism is the black and silver cart of Death. Death itself, white-masked and also clad in black and silver, with a Samurai-like stubbed breastplate, is a mysterious figure arising from the oriental bedrock of Béjart's mythology. The women following in the Shadow's train are Fates in flying black gowns, emblems of an endless night. Colour is of psychological importance throughout. Thus Fame is a splendid, vigorous young man in red facing a futuristic flayed Phoenix, like some character in a magical strip-cartoon. At that point in the ballet, marked by a triumphal *pas de quatre*, the young hero is transformed into the laurel-wreathed poet and borne aloft in the blazing chariot after Death itself has shared the fate of Love and been defeated. The following scene is also carried along on magical invention. Time, like a god divided in two, tramples with high heals on the multitude, a tangle of heads and hands beneath a great sea-green stretch of canvas. Petrarch and Laura appear to us in the reign of Time and the expectation of eternity. Almost naked and so free, they join the other couples who have been undulating beneath the white trampled cloth and now return to occupy the stage in a joyous day of judgment, the pagan beauty of which gradually subsides into that universal unity that has been one of Béjart's constant preoccupations from *The Ninth Symphony* onwards. The final tableau, too, demonstrates the acceptance of a pacific, oriental philosophy of approach to the absolute. It leaves no doubt that Béjart propounds a close link between fourteenth-century poetry and contemporary culture, rejecting once more the crude facts of biography to introduce in their place a bringing together of the two far-distanced epochs. Petrarch's intentions are replaced by Béjart's, the poet's mysticism by that of the choreographer. And yet, miraculously, the text is not betrayed. On the level of dance, the multiplicity and contemporaneity of events, it is like an immense fresco that proceeds in ever-shifting compositions and transferences. Classical steps, Asiatic gestures, plastic poses, brilliantly controlled mime, and mass movement are rationally interpolated in a great poetic rite that takes place in an epoch where time and space have ceased to exist. The ballet's title is derived word for word from the second verse of *The Triumph of Love*, and tells us that this is indeed a ballet of memory,

a recovery of the past, an imaginative and intellectual evocation. A masterpiece of harmony, and the complex creation of a cultured man who is not satisfied with the merely episodic, *Trionfi* is visually linked to the place where it was created, and, alas, loses some of its fascination when performed in a theater. M.P.

VAGARIES OF THE HUMAN HEART (*Les Intermittences du Coeur*)

Ballet in two acts and thirteen scenes. Choreography by Roland Petit. Music by Ludwig van Beethoven, Debussy, Fauré, Franck, Hahn, Saint-Saëns, Wagner. Scenery by René Allio. Costumes by Christine Laurent. Monte Carlo, Opera House, August 24, 1974. Ballets de Marseille. Principal dancers: Loipa Araujo, Rudy Bryans, Denys Ganio, Richard Duquenoy, Karen Kain, Michael Denard.

SYNOPSIS. Act I: some pictures of a Proustian paradise. Scene I: the Verdurin clan and its *patronne*. Snobbery of the newly rich and bored worldliness. The Duchesse de Guermantes and her salon. Madame Verdurin's career crowned by marriage to the Duc de Guermantes. Scene II: the *petite phrase de Vinteuil*, some bars from a sonata on the love of Swann for Odette. Scene III: the hawthorn or the magic words. Farewell to the country and a meeting with the *fillette d'un blond roux*: Gilberte. Scene IV: the metaphors of passion. How Odette becomes Swann's mistress. Scene V: *les jeunes filles en fleur* or the enchanted holiday. Pictures of the sea with the novelist and the girls dressed in white, the symbol of purity. Scene VI: Albertine and Andrée, or the Prison of Doubt. The discovery, behind the symbols of purity, of lies, tricks, immodesty, and equivocal desires. Scene VII: to see her asleep, or hostile reality. Albertine, Proust's prisoner. Because of irrational jealousy, he can love her only when she sleeps. Act II: some pictures of the Proustian hell. Scene VIII: Baron de Charlus and his idol, the violinist Morel. Dreams and longings of the Baron, who idealizes the artist but cannot conquer him. Scene IX: Monsieur de Charlus defeated by the impossible. Terrible visions of Morel's freedom through vice; discovery of Morel among the women in a brothel. Scene X: the Underworlds of de Charlus. The baron, in search of forbidden adventures, follows some soldiers into a hotel of ill-fame and is flogged by an employee of the house. Scene XI: casual meeting with an unknown. In a dark city, secret and forbidden rites in search of unholy pleasures. Scene XII: Morel and Saint-Loup challenged by the angels. With diabolical cunning, Morel introduces Saint-Loup to the world of vice. He is killed as soon as he returns to the front. Scene XIII: this idea of death. The world of the Guermantes founders on the rocks of war. In its disappearance the narrator sees his own end. The festivities for him are now but "black" dances of mourning.

■ In this ballet Roland Petit has tackled the almost impossible task of condensing the immense universe of Marcel Proust's *A la Recherche du Temps Perdu* into the short span of a single evening. His aim was to con-

trast the world of happiness with that of perversion, heaven with hell, renouncing clearly and rightly any literary content. This procedure resulted in a large number of independent scenes strung together by the thread of memory, enabling Petit to pinpoint tender and dramatic moments and reconstruct a distant world with expressive fidelity. The first part "in white" and the second "in black" both revolve around the constant of malicious cunning, initially in relation to love and later to disintegration and death. Petit's usual irony and charm are replaced by a morbid sense of evil and an ambiguous fatalism. Not all the pitfalls of bad taste are avoided in the second act, in which the homosexual relationship is explicit and concessions made to erotic suggestion are, for the period, rather too coarse (the display of men and women in the nude, for instance). It is decidedly not one of Roland Petit's best ballets. He may well have been overawed by the complexity of the plot, but it cannot be denied that it was a work of cultural boldness and not without an iconoclastic spirit. The music was selected with care and conveys the exact period atmosphere, apart from the questionable choice of Wagner's overture to *Rienzi* for the finale. M.P.

FOLD ON FOLD (*Pli selon Pli*)

Ballet in five parts. Choreography by Maurice Béjart. Music by Pierre Boulez. Brussels, Théâtre de la Monnaie, October 22, 1974. Ballet du XXme Siècle.

SYNOPSIS. Abstract ballet.

■ *Fold on Fold (Pli selon Pli)* is the result of several years' work, which came to an end when Béjart's choreographical ideas materialized in the five parts of this danced poem: in a close relationship between Mallarmé's poetry and the music of Boulez, that is to say, between a poet of the most brilliant daring and symbolism and a composer of the more discriminating avant-garde. The outcome is a ballet that even the most feared critics from the American press (with Clive Barnes at their head) could not do other than praise. The title comes from a poem not used in his earlier work, *Remémoration d'Amis Belges*, the final underlining of an intellectual-emotional relationship with Mother France by the exiled Béjart, a Marseillais who never attained his rightful place in Paris. The five parts are called *Don, Mallarmé I, II, III*, and *Tombeau*. The first three were made in 1975 for Europelia/France at Brussels. *Mallarmé III* was presented in Shiraz in 1973, and *Tombeau* a few months later, in the autumn, in Brussels. It is, according to Béjart, a nonfigurative work based exclusively on the relationship between music and gesture. The choreography consists of classical style and modern dance with some features derived from the east, fused into an arc that stretches from birth (*Don*) to death. The three improvisations on Mallarmé refer respectively to

Natalia Bessmertnova and Vladimir Vassiliev in Ivan the Terrible *by Yuri Grigorovich.*

the harmonious freedom of adolescence, the world of the clown, and an atmosphere that is at once lyrical and grotesque, as demonstrated in a double *pas de deux*.   M.P.

WHAT LOVE TELLS ME (Ce que l'Amour me dit)
Ballet in three movements by Maurice Béjart. Choreography by Maurice Béjart. Music by Gustav Mahler (fourth, fifth, and sixth movements of his Third Symphony*). Costumes by Judith Gombar. Monte Carlo, Opera House, December 24, 1974. Ballet du XXme Siècle. Principal dancers: Jean Michel Bouvron, Angèle Albrecht, Luciana Savignano, Catherine Verneuil, Michel Gascard, Dyane Gray-Cullert, Ivan Marko, Patrice Touron.*

SYNOPSIS. There is no real plot, but rather an interpretation in dance of Mahler's art in relation to the philosophy of Nietzsche, one of the key points in Béjart's intellectual history. The two spiritual components of the ballet are nature and love, with their mysteries and liberations. The first movement, *What the man tells me*, is a nocturne constructed around *Thus Spake Zarathusthra(O Mensch, gib Acht!)* and gives the feeling of a world waking and reaching out towards the light. The second movement is the discovery of innocence and the joy of loving: a passage from the *Knaben Wunderhorn* (another of Mahler's passions was the collection of nursery songs), *Es singen drei Engel einem süssen Gesang (Three angels sing a pleasant song)*, is also used in the ballet to bestow purity. The last part, corresponding to Mahler's title *What love tells me*, is a multiplication of the emotions which gradually accumulate a general happiness and offer mankind a hope that will never be dispelled.

■ A sort of balletic symphony, *What love tells me* — which enjoyed considerable success — belongs in Béjart's philosophical vein and develops a line of thought started with Beethoven's *Ninth Symphony*. The connection with Nietzsche was not in this case the Dionysiac aspect but love of nature and between people. The great force of love that Mahler expended on this symphony corresponds to the vital impulse of youth in search of itself that Béjart, in the early 1970s, interpreted in so many ways, but always with a coherent confidence. The choreography was composed with the young members of the *Ballet du XXme Siècle* in mind, and exploited all their athletic and expressive talents. Special care was bestowed on the leading part danced by Luciana Savignano from the Scala in Milan, who was subsequently a frequent guest star with the Belgian company.   M.P.

BLOOD WEDDING (Bodas de Sangre)
Ballet in six scenes by Federico Garcia Lorca. Choreography by Antonio Gades. Music by Emilio de Diego. Production in 1974 by Antonio Gades's Spanish Ballet Company (Compañia de Baile Español). Principal dancers: Antonio Gades, Cristina Hoyos, Pilar Cardenas, Carmen, Juan Antonio.

SYNOPSIS. Scene I: it is the wedding morning, and the bridegroom, helped by his mother, is putting on his dress coat. The mother sees to her horror that he is carrying a knife. He reassures her, but the sound of galloping hooves seems to her a presage of evil. Scene II: a guest, Leonardo, and his wife are ready for the wedding feast. He lags behind, while she dandles the child. A dance of jealousy between the two, after which she leaves with their little boy. Scene III: left alone, Leonardo dreams. He sees the bride in her wedding gown and dances a love dance with her. At the same time the bride is overcome with desire for him and expresses it in imagination. A sensual dance by the pair. Scene IV: Leonardo arrives at the bride's house. The feast begins and everyone dances. Leonardo kisses the bride; the wife is jealous and separates them. At the end of the wedding feast Leonardo's wife announces in despair that her husband and the bride have eloped on horseback. The bridegroom's mother hands her son the knife and incites him to vengeance. Scene V: Leonardo appears with the bride and runs away. The bridegroom and his men intervene and the hunt continues. The bridegroom overtakes Leonardo and challenges him to a duel to the death. The two men kill each other at the same moment in the sight of the bride, who unites them in a tender embrace.

■ The ballet combines elements of drama and folklore to present us with an accurate picture of the Spanish world and a tragedy of love and jealousy. The use of folk dance, the traditional precision of the movement, and the drama of the story open the way to a new type of Spanish ballet that is not pure folk dance. In particular, the long duel scene, performed in slow motion as if every movement was to be prolonged into infinity, strikes us by its irresistible tragic force and the supreme elegance of the gestures. As in flamenco dancing, the ballet uses dancers, guitarists, and singers. The play of ancient symbols, the knife, the horse, the wedding clothes, belong directly to the literary tradition of which Garcia Lorca was one of the greatest exponents. For Gades, Spanish dance is the incomparable expression of the sorrow, joy, suffering, and hope of the people. His work was never properly appreciated under the Franco regime.   M.P.

FOUR SCHUMANN PIECES
Ballet in four movements. Choreography by Hans van Manen. Music by Robert Schumann (Quartet for strings, op. 141, no. 3). Sets and costumes by Jean Paul Vroom. London, Covent Garden, January 31, 1975. Royal Ballet. Principal dancer: Anthony Dowell; in later versions, Rudolph Nureyev.

SYNOPSIS. This is a ballet without plot, based on an abstract interpretation of Schumann's music. We see human relationships developing as the movements of the quartet progress. There are eleven dancers: five couples and one soloist. *Four Schumann Pieces* speaks of loneliness and the need to communicate. Sometimes the solo dancer approaches the couples, at other times he draws away, but in the end he chooses to join them.   M.P.

Carolyn Carlson in L'Or des Fous. *Carlson was also the choreographer.*

IVAN THE TERRIBLE *(Ivan Grosnji)*
Ballet in two acts. Choreography by Yuri Grigorovich. Music by Sergei Prokofiev, arranged by Mikhail Chulaki. Sets and costumes by Simon Virsaladze. Moscow, Bolshoi Theater, February 20, 1975. Principal dancers: Yuri Vladimirov and Natalia Bessmertnova.

SYNOPSIS. Act I: we are told of Ivan, his power, his falling in love with Anastasia, the courtiers' jealous intrigues, Ivan's departure for the war and his victory over the invaders, Anastasia's long wait, the Czar's victorious return, and his illness. A revolt of the boyars is put down. Act II: Ivan's happiness is threatened by conspirators. After Anastasia's death from poisoning, amidst plots and rebellions, Ivan destroys his enemies, emerging once more relentlessly pursuing the triumph of the Russian people.

■ Conceived as a great mass spectacle by Grigorovich in his usual complicated but craftsmanlike style, the ballet is not intended to be historically accurate, but the picture of a period when Russia was racked by violence, treachery, and rebellion. It is related to nineteenth-century opera and a theatrical tradition derived from Mussorgsky's *Boris*. Ivan emerges as a remarkable character, a dual personality of sentimental and cruel

aspects. The drama is expressed in intense and massive choreography, now lyrical, now dramatic, now grotesque. The Prokofiev music used comes from the sound track of Eisenstein's film, combined with other compositions such as the *Russian Overture*, a part of *The Third Symphony*, and the cantata *Alexander Nevsky*. The great Bolshoi dancer Vladimir Vassiliev shone in the part of Ivan.   M.P.

FOOL'S GOLD *(L'Or des Fous)*
*One-act ballet. Choreography by Carolyn Carlson. Music by Girolamo Arrigo (*Sonata dell'Evocazione*). Pianist: Anne-Marie Fijal. Electro-acoustics and sound by Philippe Besombes. Text by John Davis and Henry Smith. Scenery and lighting by John Davis. Paris, Théâtre de la Ville, March 18, 1975. Principal dancers: Carolyn Carlson, Henry Smith, Odile Azagury, Larrio Ekson, Patrick Fort, Caroline Marcadé, Peter Morin, Dominique Petit, Anne-Marie Reynand, Quentin Rouillier, Christine Varjan, Anna Weil.*

SYNOPSIS. An abstract ballet.

■ *Fool's Gold*, created about a year after Carolyn Carlson was appointed *étoile choréographe* at the Paris

Above and opposite: Two scenes from Notre Faust, *devised by Maurice Béjart to music by Johann Sebastian Bach and Argentine tangos. This work breaks definitively with the traditional type of ballet by creating a spectacle in which dance is mixed with advanced theatrical techniques.*

Opéra (1974), is one of the ballets most expressive of the American dancer-choreographer's aesthetic canons. A member of Alwyn Nikolais's company from 1966, she received the best dancer prize at the International Festival of Dance in Paris in 1968. In 1971 she left the Nikolais Dance Theater after having arranged some twenty ballets there. She then worked as soloist, teacher, and choreographer for various schools and companies: the Anne Béranger Company (1971–1972), the London School of Contemporary Dance (September–December 1972), and Maurice Béjart's Mudra School, Brussels (1973). Her chief creations prior to *L'Or des Fous* were *Densité 21·5* (in 1973 for *Hommage à Varèse* at the Paris Opéra), *Verfangen* (December 1973 at the Piccola Scala, Milan), *Sablier-Prison*, and *Il y a juste un Instant* for the Opéra, where on November 13 of the same year she danced at the side of Rudolph Nureyev in Glen Tetley's *Tristan*. *L'Or des Fous*, Carlson's first work after the founding of GRTOP (Groupe de Recher-

ches Théâtrales de l'Opéra de Paris, January 1975), directed by herself, was a theatrically effective ballet in which many different elements were blended: dance (directly descended from the most recent forms of American modern dance), music (mostly vibrations and electro-acoustic effects), the human voice (reduced to inarticulate sounds and stammering, sadly mocking itself and the power of words to communicate), lighting and projection (in which the influence of Nikolais is more perceptible). The dancers move over the stage like people in a dream, poetic emanations escaping from reality, while Carlson herself in her solo uses her body as "potentiality," as a variable source of energy, and an object of geometric-anatomical analysis.   S.B.

THE GOLDEN FOOLS *(Les Fous d'Or)*
One-act ballet. Choreography by Carolyn Carlson. Music by Igor Wakhevitch sung by Eve Brenner. Text

by John Davis and Henry Smith. Set, lighting, and costumes by John Davis. Paris, Théâtre de la Ville, March 25, 1975. Principal dancers: Carolyn Carlson, Henry Smith, Odile Azagury, Larrio Ekson, Patrick Fort, Caroline Marcadé, Peter Morin, Dominique Petit, Anne-Marie Reynand, Quentin Rouillier, Christian Varjan, Anna Weil. This work forms the second part of a diptych, the first half of which, L'Or des Fous, was originally performed seven days earlier. The two ballets are generally shown together.

SYNOPSIS. An abstract ballet.

■ In *Les Fous d'Or* Carolyn Carlson once more creates her dreamlike, surreal world inhibited by illusory phantoms, creatures of unreality who help the American dancer to weave her web of choreography. The dancers' costumes, long, narrow, white tunics, fairly obviously refer to the sad condition of madness. The characters express themselves in oscillating or broken movements with the jerky distortions of marionettes, as if to demonstrate the incurability of the cuts and fractures of a life which has lost unity forever. The atmosphere is emotionally dense, vibrant with dramatic tension, yet every now and again relieved by comic or grotesque interruptions arising from the voice of Eve Brenner, the ironic gags of Larrio Ekson, and the miming of Anna Weil, who recites a monologue destined never to be finished. Among these images and evocations, Carolyn Carlson appears as an estranged enigmatic figure, white-masked, with a mop of red hair, quite unable to understand what is going on.   S.B.

ORIENT-OCCIDENT
One-act ballet. Choreography by Ronald Hynd. Music by Iannis Xenakis. Venice, Fenice Theater, June 29, 1975 (for the Festival of Dance 1975). Tokyo Ballet Company. Principal dancers: Makato Fukuyama, Lee San Chong, Hiroshi Sato.

SYNOPSIS. Marco Polo, the famous Venetian merchant traveller, leaves for the Orient, following the Silk Road and reaching the court of the Great Khan of China. He faces countless risks and perils and even an attempt at seduction by his host. After many years and other journeys he returns home loaded with riches.

■ The ballet treats the adventures of Marco Polo with utter lack of respect, but very amusingly. The figure of the famous traveller is made fun of, but without ever lapsing into bad taste. Hynd deals with the historical material intelligently, but with freedom and fantasy, quite untroubled by the question of authenticity. It is a malicious entertainment in which Asiatic figures, oriental symbols, artifices derived from the Japanese theater, and the classical dance techniques of Europe appear side by side. The music of Xenakis is well suited to this fantastic ballet, which also enjoys the advantages of delightful colour and effective lighting. *Orient-Occident* was one of the liveliest successes of "Dance 75," the only work on the program, in fact, possessing a

high degree of originality in either ideas or choreography. There are all too few funny ballets: this is one of the best. An extremely interesting feature from the scenic point of view was the use of long strips of silk at different times to represent a landscape or convey its changing character.   M.P.

X LAND

One-act ballet. Collective choreographic creation by the Groupe de Recherches Théâtrales de l'Opéra de Paris, directed by Carolyn Carlson. Music by Barre Phillips, John Surman, and Dieter Feichtner. Sets and lighting by John Davis. Festival of Avignon, August 1975. Principal dancers: Carolyn Carlson, Odile Azagury, Patrick Fort, Dominique Petit, Anne-Marie Reynaud, Caroline Marcadé, Peter Morin, Quentin Rouillier, Fritz Tummers, Christine Varjan.

SYNOPSIS. An abstract ballet.

■ Immediately after creating *Spar* on June 24, 1975, a solo for Paolo Bortoluzzi, Carlson presented this "collective choreography" (dedicated to the memory of Anna Weil) based on improvisations arranged and produced by herself. The ballet, only outlined choreographically, acquired new aesthetic and plastic qualities at each performance. Constructed technically by the dovetailing, juxtaposition, and breaking down of images, *X Land* described the development of everyday gestures in a sharp, disjointed style devoid of all narrative and capable of expressing no more than fragmented scenes. The work is based on contrasts between the sudden speeding up of gesture, and movement so slow as to resemble slow-motion film, producing surprising effects, as when Carlson's barely perceptible pulsebeats progressively transfer their rhythm to her whole body. By such devices, time is made to stretch out of all proportion, creating the impression of a dream rather than of reality.   S.B.

NOTRE FAUST

Balletic play in two parts. Choreography by Maurice Béjart. Music by J. S. Bach and Argentine tangos. Subject by Maurice Béjart. Sets and costumes by Thierry Bousquet. Brussels, Théâtre Royale de la Monnaie, December 12, 1975. Ballet de XXme Siècle. Principal dancers: Yan Le Gac and Maurice Béjart (Faust and Mephistopheles respectively, old and young), Jorge Donn, Bertrand Pie, Patrice Touron, Monet Robier, Catherine Verneuil, Maguy Marin.

SYNOPSIS. Part I: Doctor Faust in his study considers the emptiness of a life devoted to book-learning. He calls up spirits from heaven; then Mephistopheles appears to him dressed as a student. Mephistopheles promises Faust happiness. He will be the Doctor's servant in this world, but after death the roles will be reversed. Faust accepts, and the two sign a pact in blood. A transformation takes place: Faust enters the body of the young student, Mephistopheles that of the elderly scholar. Together they leave to conquer the world. At this point Mephistopheles introduces Faust to his masters, Lucifer, Satan, and Beelzebub, who offer him pleasures and wealth. But Faust sees the reflection of Margaret in a mirror and chooses love. The girl appears, but then Mephistopheles takes on her aspect and in the end Faust is left alone and disappointed. His demon guide then takes him to the Walpurgis Night witches' sabbath. In the middle of the black magic rites a vision of Margaret returns to trouble him. Finally the scene changes to the prison where Margaret, who has lost her reason, waits for death, having been accused of murdering her mother and child. Faust cannot persuade her to follow him. "She is damned," cries Mephistopheles. "She is saved," a voice replies. Part II: Faust, oppressed with sorrow, lies in a meadow. Ariel, accompanied by nature spirits, awakens him and gives him back his faith. Mephistopheles, however, returns to persuade him to continue his journey through the world. They reach the Emperor's court and offer him their services. Mephistopheles is employed as jester, while Faust is charged with magically resuscitating Helen of Troy. Faust succeeds in the task, but immediately falls in love with "the most beautiful woman in the world." Once more Mephistopheles intervenes between Faust and Helen. They wish to have a son who will be the symbolic embodiment of German genius and Greek beauty. So Euphorione is born and attempts to fly, but like Icarus falls headlong and is killed. Helen returns to the kingdom of the shades, leaving Faust alone once more. Keep on going, his demon tells him: they ascend to the land of mothers, where Faust finds his own, remembers his childhood, and pictures himself as a boy. His heart is filled with joy; he dies of happiness. All is finished, cries Mephistopheles. But no, everything begins anew, answers the young Faust. He is another explorer of life, for the story of Faust is eternal and is still going on. A fallen angel, a rope, and Faust-Mephistopheles soars upwards.

■ After the great fresco of *For the Sweet Memory of that Day*, *Notre Faust* was a milestone on the way to that perfect example of the *ballet-comédie* that was to be *Le Molière Imaginaire*. On its first appearance it was greeted as a most important event in the development of modern ballet both for its bold insights and the significance of the argument that sustains it. Subtitled *Variations on a theme of Goethe*, Béjart's *Faust* breaks definitively with the traditional patterns of ballet in attempting to construct a multifaceted spectacle in which speech is used and classical dance forms are spiced with avant-garde theatrical effects. Béjart's thought proceeded on two intellectual levels. "Hell," he said, "is heaven in reverse. In Christian tradition Lucifer is he who carries light and the devils are fallen angels. Thus they are not terrifying monsters but subtle tempters and seducers. The infernal subversion should, then, be represented by a certain use of the Christian liturgy, with the Black Mass in place of the sacrificial Mass." As to Faust's character, Béjart maintains that the most obvious problem is that of solitude. Mephistopheles separates him from the things he loves. Another aspect of the work is the "doubling," inasmuch as Faust and Mephistopheles are two opposing states of the same person. Man is nearly always a dual being who "often wishes to do evil but often does good." The exchange of personalities between the two protagonists is the key to the ballet's interpretation: from it arises a dialectical confrontation between reality and magic caused by the inexhaustibility, and hence the continuation, of the myth. There is also a multiplicity of pictorial effects in the ballet, especially at the witches' sabbath, and great beauty, most of all, perhaps, in the magnificent costumes worn by Béjart's splendid dancers in the Satanic parts. The spoken sections are either short dialogues in verse or vocal and gestural passages interpolated in some great ceremony set in an imaginary world of incredible fantasy and richness. The old desire to astonish, so dear to Béjart in his earlier days, is here supported on a solid logical foundation. There is a moving moment when the devil appears to Faust in student attire, looking very much like some modern pop idol (one is reminded of Tommy in Ken Russell's film of that name). Another exciting scene that occurs soon afterwards is the transformation of the old Faust (played by Béjart himself) into a humble and waggish Mephistopheles, a sort of employee in the pay of the highest authority. An interchange of masks, derived from ancient Greek or oriental drama, characterizes the scene with the fallen angles, while the sabbath becomes a sort of party at which the young guests, so many doubles of young Faust, dance with unrestrained abandon. The second part is, if anything, even richer in fantastic devices. In the evocation of Helen, the flight of the new Icarus, and still more in the touching scene with the mother, the ballet grows less metaphysical and more autobiographical. The stupendous *Agnus Dei* from Bach's *Mass* brings the finale to the level of classical perfection and sustained emotion. The recitation of some verses from Goethe introduced into the balletic "program," expresses Béjart's philosophy, in which death is set against an everlasting quest: "Only he deserves life and liberty who has to conquer them anew every day. . . . To be in a free world among free people. To the passing moment I could then say 'Stop, and be beautiful.'" It was a bold move to set the *Mass in B minor* side by side with Argentine tangos, some of them well known: it underlines the contrast between the spirituality of the liturgy and the violence of a fierce, sometimes brutal, popular dance. Two other musical items are also present in *Notre Faust*: a fragment in the American style for the witches' sabbath and a nineteenth-century piece by Minkus for the meeting with his mother. The choreographer was thus faced with a wide range of music on which to base his mixed, theatrically effective, and coldly comic choreography.   M.P.

THIRD SYMPHONY

Ballet in six movements. Choreography by John Neumeier. Music by Gustav Mahler. Hamburg, State Opera House, 1975. Principal dancers: Zhandra Rodriguez, Magali Messac, Salvatori Aiello, Truman Finney.

SYNOPSIS. Ballet without a plot.

■ To Mahler's *Third Symphony* John Neumeier, an American choreographer of German descent, has here constructed a powerful panorama rich in impressive sculptural grouping and mass movement that in some way symbolizes the tragic history of the German people during this century. The choreographer's style is characterized by vehement gesture and very muscular and plastically correlated attitudes. His work while in Hamburg seems to be a blend of the American school with the German taste for the absolute. Neumeier's ballets are never spiritual nor at all romantic, but abundantly rhythmic and dynamic. The tremendous music of Mahler has allowed Neumeier to create an earthy ballet at the opposite pole to Béjart's *Ninth Symphony*. The titles he has given to the different movements are: *Yesterday, Summer, Autumn, Night, Angel, What Love has told me*. As we have already seen, Béjart composed his delightful *What Love tells me (Ce que l'Amour me dit)* to the music of one of those parts, but the two choreographers have absolutely nothing in common intellectually, so different are their cultural points of departure. Whereas Béjart's goal is the universal, the sublimation of love, Neumeier aims at a climate of night and tragedy, as with this work, in which the masculine roles are very important (*Yesterday*). With the release from the unhappiness of generations, an idea of love is born which is violent and more heavily charged with Eros. His interest in Mahler was subsequently expressed in other works, such as *Rückerlieder* (1976) and *Fourth Symphony* (1977).   M.P.

PUSH COMES TO SHOVE

*(Ballet in a prelude and four movements. Choreography by Twyla Tharp. Music by Haydn and Lamb (*Symphony in C, *op. 82, and* Boema Rag 1919 *respectively), arranged by David Bourne. Costumes by Santo Loquasto. Lighting by Jennifer Tipton. New York, Uris Theater, January 9, 1976. American Ballet. Principal dancers: Mikhail Baryshnikov, Martine van Hamel, Marianne Cherkassky, Christopher Aponte.*

SYNOPSIS. Comic ballet without a real plot.

■ *Push Comes to Shove* is an amusing specimen of modern ballet based on contradictions with plenty of surrealist humour. The hero is launched on a hilarious, schizophrenic adventure to the double musical track consisting now of Lamb's music and now of the Haydn symphony. Ranging from vaudeville to *danseur noble* – to quote George Balanchine – the hero expresses a rich variety of emotions from which elements of comic (and silent) films and echoes of music hall (or circus) are not excluded. The ballet was built on the personality of Baryshnikov, from whom it demands not only his usual dancing and acrobatic virtuosity but also a more than usual sense of humour. Tharp intermingles past and present with great skill, while, on the choreographic plane, we have the happiest mixture of invention and intellectual provocation.   M.P.

Heliogabalus *by Béjart, danced by his Ballet du XXme Siècle.*

A MONTH IN THE COUNTRY

One-act ballet freely adapted from Turgenev's play. Choreography by Frederick Ashton. Music by Frédéric Chopin, arranged by John Lanchbery. Set and costumes by Julia Trevelyan Oman. Lighting by William Bundy. London, Covent Garden, February 12, 1976. Royal Ballet. Principal dancers: Lynn Seymour (Natalia), David Drew (Yslaev, her husband), Wayne Sleep (Kolia, their son), Denise Nunn (Vera), Derek Rencher (Rakitin), Marguerite Porter (Katia), Anthony Conway (Matvei), Anthony Dowell (Beliaev).

SYNOPSIS. The action takes place at Yslaev's country house in 1850. Beliaev, a young student engaged as tutor for Kolia, disrupts the emotional stability of the household. Finally, Rakitin, Natalia's admirer, insists that he and the tutor must both leave in order to restore a semblance of calm to Yslaev's family life. (Program note by F. Ashton.)

■ While the action of the play has of necessity been condensed and adapted to form the subject-matter of a one-act ballet, the spirit of the original Turgenev play, with its subtle yet turbulent emotions, has been wonderfully preserved. Contributing greatly to that atmosphere is the music to which the ballet is set: *"La ci darem" Variations, Fantasia on Polish Airs, Andante spionato*, and *Grand Polonaise in E flat* for piano and orchestra, all among Chopin's earlier and less familiar works. O.O.

BLACK ANGELS

Ballet in one act. Choreography by Christopher Bruce. Music by George Crumb. Set and costumes by Nadine Baylis. Lighting by John B. Reid. First performed in the Arts Centre, Horsham, England, on May 11, 1976; London premiere: Sadler's Wells Theatre, June 16, 1976. Rambert Ballet. Principal dancers: Lucy Burge, Zoltan Imre, Bob Smith, Leigh Warren, Catherine Becque, Sylvia Yamada.

SYNOPSIS. Lucifer and his angels fall from heaven. They suffer but try despairingly and in vain to defy their punishment. A Christ figure, Mary, and two bright angels intervene. The Crucifixion brings redemption to the world, but not to "Hell's derelicts." The devil still stalks the earth.

■ Marie Rambert, born in Warsaw in 1888, inspired by both Isadora Duncan and Anna Pavlova, finished her training in music and dance with three years' study at the Dalcroze School of Eurythmics in Geneva. From there she was summoned by Diaghilev to help Nijinsky with the musical side of *Rite of Spring* and remained with his company. She settled in London in 1914 and in 1930 founded her first small ballet company, the seed from which the entire spreading tree of British ballet grew. Ballet Rambert, of which both Frederick Ashton and Anthony Tudor were once members, was at first completely devoted to classical ballet, but in 1966 went over to modern dance.

Black Angels is a deeply serious work dealing with the eternal struggle between good and evil. Six dancers interpret the torment and defiance of these "derelicts of Hell." At times in the ballet they also represent Christ, his Cross, and the bright angels. Christopher Bruce is one of the finest and most highly regarded choreographers of our time, as well as being a distinguished dancer. In the balletic line of descent, he has learned much from Glen Tetley who, in his turn, was influenced primarily by Martha Graham, but also by the English choreographer Anthony Tudor. Bruce works with great creative vitality and intensity, drawing from the unconscious self an inspiration that grows and changes "as it meets the air." Thus he prefers to work with his dancers, composer, designer, and lighting expert from the inception of a new ballet. In this case, however, the music came first (*Black Angels* by George Crumb, 1970). As Christopher Bruce said, "It gave everything to me: every movement arose out of it, the form and design were conditioned by it." George Crumb is a composer of elemental power. As in his *Vox Balaenae* (1970), there is a sense of lonely space and mysterious sonorities echoing through the abyss. He uses conventional instruments in an unconventional way, even the ghostly effect of a violin bow drawn across partly filled glasses of water, or voices whispering and murmuring in a medly of tongues. Deeply interested in numerology, he has based his work on a complex formula of 7 and 13, which naturally affects the choreography. The music is divided into thirteen sections: I *Departure*: (1) Threnody I: Night of the Electric Insects, (2) Sounds of bones and flutes, (3) Lost Bells, (4) Devil-music, (5) Danse Macabre; II *Absence*: (6) Pavane Lachrymae (*Der Tod und das Mädchen*), (7) Threnody II: Black Angels, (8) Sarabanda de la Muerte Oscura, (9) Lost Bells (Echo); III *Return*: (10) God-music, (11) Ancient Voices, (12) Ancient Voices (Echo), (13) Threnody III: Night of the Electric Insects. Another source of inspiration that may have lain in the choreographer's subconscious is English poetry such as Milton's, or Marlow's lines "Oh, I'll leap up to my God! Who pulls me down?/See, see, where Christ's blood streams in the firmament!" The great curves and hollows of Nadine Baylis's impressive scenery bear vague suggestions of William Blake's watercolours, or engraved illustrations for Dante's Inferno. "Yet it was her vision . . . giving the sense of an enclosed world set in the cold and empty spaces beyond the stars" (Richard Austin). To all this the dancers gave an interpretation of emotional intensity. After its first performance at Horsham on May 11, 1976, the ballet was presented at the Théâtre de la Ville in Paris a week later, before the London premiere on June 16th. O.O.

STABAT MATER

One-act ballet. Choreography by Conrad Drzewiecki. Music by Krzysztof Penderecki. Poznan, Polski Teatr Tanca, June 12, 1976. Poznan Ballet.

SYNOPSIS. The ballet is based on the traditional religious theme of the Seven Sorrows of Our Lady, which has inspired so many paintings and religious works over the centuries.

■ One of the most interesting among the dance companies of Poland is the Poznan Ballet, of which Conrad Drzewiecki is artistic director and chief choreographer. It seems to foreshadow the predominant aesthetic developments in that country. Without wishing to detract in any way from the activities of the Warsaw Opera (devoted chiefly to preserving the great classical repertory), or the opera companies of Bytom and Gdansk, it can be said that the Poznan Ballet stands at the side of the famous Pantomime Theater at Wroclaw directed by Tomaszewsky, and the Lodz Opera Company, which, with its periodical Congresses of International Ballet (in which choreographers such as Tetley, Béjart, and Tudor have taken part), has become the meeting point and exchange between Polish choreographic-aesthetic activities and trends, and those of the west. For *Stabat Mater*, set to a composition for three unaccompanied choirs by Penderecki, Conrad Drzewiecki has arranged choreography of high religious inspiration, showing a remarkable ability to express himself in the style, new to him, of modern dance. In this creation, full of plastic strength, movement evolves in fugal form, or by a counterpoint of linear and circular forms, or consolidates to form massive groups, or grows vertically into a human cathedral, a choral symbol of religion and piety. The modern language employed, for all its complicated and sometimes even overloaded character, is uncommonly effective (it must not be forgotten that Drzewiecki's multifaceted experience ranges from a long immersion in the great nineteenth-century classics with the Marquis de Cuevas Company to a period as Jose Limon's assistant at the Juilliard School of Music in New York). Dramatic physical tension (as in the lament for the dead Christ, visually reminiscent of the ascetic mysticism of Cosmé Tura) is countered by extremely stylized hieratic gestures in profile as seen in ancient Egyptian art.   S.B.

HELIOGABALUS *(Héliogabale)*
Ballet in two parts. Choreography by Maurice Béjart, with creative interpolations by the dancers. Music by various composers from Bach to Rota. Scenic and costume design by the Yantra Group. Milan, Scala, September 24, 1976. Ballet du XXme Siècle at Brussels. Principal dancers: Pierre Clementi, Luciana Savignano, Patrice Touron, Maguy Marin.

SYNOPSIS. Part I: we are told, as in a dream, of the career of Heliogabalus, a Roman Emperor who reigned at the beginning of the third century A.D. His life was very short, for he was born in Syria in 204 A.D. and killed in Rome eighteen years later. At the age of five, he was made priest of the sun in the temple of Baal, the reason he is called Heliogabalus. Under the influence of four women, his mother, grandmother, aunt, and great-aunt, all called Julia, he was raised to the highest office in the Empire. His reign was a mixture of superstition and licentiousness while he tried to impose the monotheistic worship of the sun on Rome. Excesses and sexual unrestraint were rife at his court. He was assassinated by a guard, possibly at the instigation of his

grandmother. Part II: everything has been turned upside down, the moon has replaced the sun, and, now in the modern age, uniting Antonin Artaud's novel with his real life-story, climax is reached in the alienation of a hospital scene.

■ The first part of the ballet, which had its world premiere at Persepolis in the summer of 1976, was splendidly spectacular and full of daring choreographic devices inspired by the surrounding Asiatic scene. Unfortunately, the addition of a second act in the definitive version presented at the Scala in Milan completely debased the quality of the whole work (except for the Moon variation performed by Savignano), turning it into a pantomimic bag of tricks in the worst possible taste. It became very clear that collective work in ballet is usually doomed to failure, because the different contributions tend to be aesthetically incompatible. However, the first part remains valid. Luxurious fantasy blends with voluptuous eroticism to evoke a pagan world, the whole based on a philosophy of Indian provenance that sees a state of primal sexual unity as surmounting the division between male and female. Heliogabalus, much in fashion at the time, thus became a special symbol and the reflection of an ambiguous ideology. Absorbed in the writings of Antonin Artaud, Béjart delved into magic and the esoteric, producing a ritual of dance with roots that went down into a primitive soil where love and cruelty become confused in a wild delirium, where, as the choreographer says, east and west meet, the sexes merge, and religions revive. The music is important only in the first part, in which we hear traditional African pieces, the first great aria from Verdi's *Macbeth* (with the voice of Callas), and the chanting of names and words from Artaud's book. M.P.

LE MOLIÈRE IMAGINAIRE
Ballet-play in two parts. Choreography and subject by Maurice Béjart. Music by Nino Rota. Sets and costumes by Joëlle Roustan and Roger Bernard. Paris, Comédie Française, December 3, 1976. Ballet du XXme Siècle. Principal dancers: Robert Hirsch, Bertrand Pie, Maurice Béjart, Jorge Donn, Rita Poelvoorde, Jan Nuyts, Catherine Verneuil. Elizabeth Cooper, and the entire company.

SYNOPSIS. Part I: the curtain rises to reveal an armchair set center stage. It is to be occupied by the *Malade Imaginaire* of Molière's play. On one side a woman in black, with a chalk-white face, is playing the piano: she is Death. An actor dressed in modern clothes sits in the armchair, when suddenly the master of his craft, Scaramouche, bursts in and, using trick effects with mirrors, acts as if he were his instructor in the art of acting. And now the stage begins to fill up with theater people — acrobats and masks from the *Commedia dell'Arte* among them. The child Molière comes in with his grandfather, the good upholsterer Cressé, and wanders among the actors in enchantment. Scapine takes the child and pops him into his sack, in spite of his grandfather's protests. Soon afterwards Molière emerges from the sack as

Luc Bouy in Saint George and the Dragon, *a ballet by Mats Ek with allegorical, political overtones.*

Luc Bouy, Norio Yoshida, and Yngve Horn in Soweto. *Choreography and subject by Mats Ek.*

a young man with moustache and long hair, as seen in his best-known portraits. And so Molière becomes an actor and begins his roving life with the comedians' wagon that does double service as the stage of the Théâtre Illustre. He is arrested for debt, then freed, and progressing from part to part, eventually arrives at success. The Molière family is at court; extracts of plays, historical personages, flash by before us. He is there to see King Louis XIV dance his famous solo as the absolute Sun King, accompanied by drums and kettledrums in an extended variation. Young Molière has now become Molière the man, and we recognize in him the actor of the opening scene. Part II: Molière grows old in glory, but his company of actors, penned in the frivolity of the court, has lost its former joy in living. Betrayed in his affections, broken-hearted at the death of Armande's son, Molière is overwhelmed by the characters in his plays. Lully intrigues against him to gain the King's favour; Tartuffe infuriates him with his censoriousness and underhand priests. Then the actor identifies himself with his own "imaginary invalid" and, sinking into the fateful armchair, dies. But no, that must not be! The actors rush onto the stage, the Sun King appears in triumph. Molière recovers, the actors enter in a great sack and return him his property. When the King exclaims, "This is the century of Louis XIV!," Molière replies "It is the century of Molière!"

■ Presented in the temple of French theater, the Comédie Française, with one of its most famous actors, Robert Hirsch, in the leading part, *Le Molière Imaginaire* showed itself to be an epoch-making event in the history of modern ballet, and was greeted as a masterpiece. In Molière's own "house" a prodigy had occured: the acceptance of a new form of entertainment, the ballet-play, a reversal in name of Molière's special genre, the *comédie-ballet*. A definite step forward had been taken in the direction of a total experience, joining song and speech to dance and music in a context of exceptional professionalism, worthy of the old play-actors and faithful to the French style that it was everyone's aim to achieve. Béjart's "Life of Molière" also impresses one as a cultural event, an interpretation of an eternal being and becoming; art, life, happiness, sorrow, power. Humanly speaking, it was a realization of an old dream of Béjart's, in that he was identifying with the man who inspired his youthful ambition, that is to say Jean-Baptiste Poquelin, otherwise Molière. It is significant that the choreographer from Marseilles, when he left his paternal roof (he was the son of an intellectual) to devote himself to the art of ballet, changed his name of Berger to Béjart. And Béjart was the surname of the family of actors whom Poquelin joined in 1643 when he decided to work in the theatre. The choice was not a chance one. For years Berger-Béjart had cherished the idea of working in parallel with Poquelin-Molière and standing at his side. But to achieve the work of art he dreamt of in the ballet-play, he needed a company that knew how to dance, recite, sing and make music, and that company had yet to be born. For that very purpose the Mudra school was founded, a school where a new generation of dancers could be taught, but not only in

terms of dance. The first important appearance of the young people from Mudra occurred at Florence on the first night of *For the Sweet Memory of that Day* or *The Triumphs of Petrarch*. In *Le Molière Imaginaire* the products of Mudra were used to the full, while other dancers in the group then at Béjart's side were able to learn how to be actors, too. In the ballet-play the play is the guest of the ballet, whereas in Molière's time it was the other way round. The formula is simple: the dances are interpolated with spoken passages, the characters in the play are directed choreographically, the spiritual themes are interpreted in a socially modern key. If, in the end, Molière triumphs over power, that is a further proof of Béjart's belief in the man and his intelligence. The only thing that is not conquered is death, personified in the beautiful lady in black who has remained on the stage since the beginning. But even death cannot defeat genius, which is the real, true master of life. With amazing speed and complete mastery of stage effects, Béjart transforms Molière from child to old man, meanwhile telling the story of France, art, and society. He expects the audience to know everything about the theater of Molière, but he also expounds with typical clarity and French *esprit*. "Every shade of feeling and satire, every moment of indignation," wrote the Parisian critics, "is matched by dancing that elucidates and extends it, conjuring up the style of the seventeenth century to achieve a total, complete and polyvalent result." If Molière's theater was the critical conscience of its era, Béjart's ballet is a reflection of it, extending it to our own day and resolving conflicts in an anarchistic way. Here stands Molière with his actors, his women, his passions; there stand the King, his nobles, the priests, the malicious corporations, the ridiculous ladies, the misers, misanthropes, social climbers, new middle class, and the aged, full of envious spite. For Béjart it is youth that counts, and for him Molière is ever young because he is immortal. The comic and the tragic are eternally young. Entrusting the dual leading role of the playwright and the eternal actor to the actor laureate Robert Hirsch (for whom Béjart substituted when the former had an accident on the set), Béjart did not want to abolish the *premier/danseur* but to reestablish the complete man of the theater, able to use both leg and voice with equal skill. Not without a certain disingenuousness, the choreographer reserved the small part of the grandfather for himself, as if to identify with the one member of the family who helped little Jean-Baptiste to understand the theater. Naturally we find in this ballet the masks of the *Commedia dell'Arte*, the tumblers, the wandering players, and all the free-roving world from which the masterpieces and joy of the most liberated theatrical creativity could be born. To these Béjart gives all his sympathy, while their counterparts at court are painted with acid irony. He gives the Sun King an important variation, comparing him to an oriental divinity, but at the same time revealing his weaknesses and fatuity. The tenderness underlying the playwright's family life is emphasized by the presence on the stage of a little girl, Menou, who is Armande as a child, and there is also an Arcadian picture of nature seen as a protective mother. The actors' shabby clothes are contrasted to the feathers and brocades of the nobles; real people and stage characters intermingle, fuse, and change roles. In something like an Argentine tango, the malignant shades dance a sarabande around Tartuffe; still more violent is the sarabande of the physicians around the Imaginary Invalid. Amid realistic bouts of coughing, Molière becomes a poor actor without power, an empty vessal, but it is Béjart who saves him by driving him back onto the stage as an eternal symbol who humbles the King and recovers all his old possessions. The symbolic sack, a magic element from the past and a sign of property, is used to represent a world no one can steal from us. The tragedy turns to festivity again, and it seems that the moment is eternal and not left behind in the past. It will be easier to understand the reasoning behind *Molière*, which some have unjustly criticized as lacking in choreographic quantity, if we note what Maurice Béjart has to say, namely that two words are often spoken in *Le Molière Imaginaire*: "nature" and "deception," and that he is fighting to impose a feeling for the natural, his love of nature, liberty, youth, and happiness. They are not abstract concepts or fuzzy generalizations but the tangible signs of a total awareness that questions belief in accepted codes and breaks up the world of reassuring habits. Nino Rota's music, without being very significant, serves the ballet well, conveying with only a few references to the past the world of today's theater. M.P.

SAINT GEORGE AND THE DRAGON (S:t Göran och Draken)

One-act ballet. Choreography, subject, and lighting by Mats Ek. Music: a collage of pop and folk music. Costumes by Marie Louise De Geer Bergensträhle. Stockholm, Dramatic Theater, December 20, 1976. Principal dancers: Mats Ek (St. George), Ana Laguna (the Princess), Łuc Bouy (the Dragon).

SYNOPSIS. The ballet is a political allegory based on the legend of the hero who saves the Princess from the dragon.

■ Here, in a quite anticonformist and comic-satirical mood (so often displayed in the work of Mats Ek's mother, Birgit Cullberg), Saint George is seen as a western hero — a kind of "marine" simpleton — who meets his match in foreign cultures (represented by the Dragon and the Princess) and goes in search of something he can win for himself, something apart from the noble enterprises of other knights, without strain or fear. Two other characters are an old woman and a child, personifying the past and the future of humanity. Perhaps the most interesting character is the Dragon, bristling with lances like a warrior in a Japanese picture, who is depicted both sympathetically and dramatically. C.M.C.

THIS, THAT, AND THE OTHER

A ballet in three parts. Choreography by Carolyn Carlson. Music by Igor Wakhevich. Stage design and lighting by John Davis. First performance of This and That, Paris, Théâtre de la Ville, February 8, 1977; first performance of The Other, Paris, Opéra, April 30, 1977, an occasion on which the whole trilogy was staged. Principal dancers: Carolyn Carlson, Larrio Ekson, Caroline Marcadé, Jorma Ustinen, Dominique Petit, Peter Morin, Michèle Collison (of Peter Brook's International Centre of Theatrical Research), and Philippe Hottier (of Ariane Mnouchkine's company).

SYNOPSIS. Abstract ballet with no plot.

■.In this trilogy Carolyn Carlson appears to have mitigated the usual bare dryness of her style to allow the dancing some breathing-space, freer and more generous movement, and a more unified and coherent choreographic construction. Her universe is poetic, symbolic, allusive, as if pulsating to the restless beat of the wings of memory and dreams. Here it is cadenced by the creatures of her imagination, who appear at intervals as a sort of leitmotif weaving the ballet into unity. A young woman dressed in a long, white robe crosses the stage, holding some dry branches in her arms as if they were a baby. Then come a clown with a magic wand, an improbable shepherd without sheep, and some ghostly extras from the music hall. They are all travellers on the same journey: in search of their own identities (as the title indicates). In this interior voyage from birth to death by way of solitude, Carolyn Carlson is dealing with the basic theme of her quest: a redefinition of space and time. S.B.

SOWETO

One-act ballet. Choreography, subject, lighting, and costumes by Mats Ek. Musical accompaniment: a collage of contemporary classical, light, and jazz music. Stockholm, Opera House, June 12, 1977. Cullberg Ballet.

SYNOPSIS. The story is inspired by the revolt of the young people of Johannesburg's black quarter against apartheid. In the spring of 1976 the police suppressed student manifestations with violence. Many paid with their lives for the rebellion against poverty and oppression.

■ In Mats Ek's ballet, white power is represented by a mechanical doll dressed in a white crinoline and carrying a parasol. After having watched the insurrection quite immobile, she moves ineffectively along a fixed oval track, shaking her head in a negative way. Against her unyielding inaccessibility the dreams and illusions of black society batter in vain. Although taking sides, Ek does not fall into the trap of propaganda tract, and because of that the ballet retains its validity. The musical collage is purely functional, serving to mark the successive phases of growing awareness in an oppressed community which redeems itself after having touched the depths of degradation. The character of the revolutionary mother who invites her people to revolt was repeated by Cullberg in 1978. C.M.C.

Lorca Massine (left) in his Esoterik Satie, *a ballet set to Erik Satie's music.*

REQUIEM *(Malédictions et Lumières)*
Ballet in two acts and four scenes. Idea and choreography by Joseph Russillo. Music by Fauré, Verdi, Sciortino. Costumes by Russillo, de Livry, Vergez. Lighting by Pierre Saveron, properties by Pierre Simona. Nervi, Teatro dei Parchi, July 15, 1977. The Joseph Russillo Ballet Theater. Principal dancers: Joseph Russillo and Daniel Agésilas.

SYNOPSIS. Based mainly on the Old Testament, particularly the Book of Genesis, the ballet deals symbolically with the destiny of humankind in the struggle between good and evil. It is a neoimpressionist interpretation that starts with the creation of the world: the plot is conducted by a "tempter" in a tuxedo and is divided into scenes that follow a narrative, but symbolical, sequence. The first act begins with the creation of the heavens and the earth and continues with the expulsion from Eden to end with the reestablishment of men and women after Noah's flood. But this new world of happiness and light is swept away – as the second act demonstrates – by human sin and divine wrath, always in reference to the Christian story and the New Testament, until purification comes through the Resurrection of Jesus Christ, and equilibrium is once more achieved.

■ Russillo uses lighting to dramatic ends and evolves a very eclectic style of choreography, using the human body plastically (and often in chaste nudity) in movements that are sometimes extremely slowed down and extended into space. The choreographer, Italian in origin, grew up and perfected his art in New York, finally establishing himself in Paris. He offers a synthesis of disparate themes, setting himself hard problems and solving them perhaps a little too elaborately. *Requiem* is a dramatic ballet, orchestrated down to the finest detail, slightly too long maybe, but always stimulating. The choice of music, such as Fauré's *Requiem* and Verdi's *Requiem Mass*, reveals a mystical sense pervaded with an existential pessimism. M.P.

GAITE PARISIENNE
One-act ballet. Choreography by Maurice Béjart. Music by Jacques Offenbach, adapted and orchestrated by Manuel Rosenthal. Sets and costumes by Thierry Bosquet. Lighting by Allan Burret. Brussels, Théâtre Royal de la Monnaie, January 27, 1978. Principal dancers: Victor Ullate, Rita Poelvoorde, Jorge Donn, Catherine Verneuil, Jean-Michel Bouvron, Mathé Souverbie, Micha van Hoecke, Yvan Marko, Luciana Savignano, Daniel Lommel.

SYNOPSIS. A youth arrives in Paris to study dancing. He spends his time with dreams and fantasies, thanks to which he feels himself to be living in the gay and brilliant days of the Second Empire.

■ In *Gaîté Parisienne*, a largely autobiographical work, Béjart (who among other things danced in Massine's ballet of the same name when he was twenty-one, and made his first venture into theatrical production with Offenbach's *Tales of Hoffman*) tells of the French capital's first impact on him. Directly based on the most deeply felt pages of his book *L'Autre Chant de la Danse*, the ballet is lively, joyful, light, and translucent, like most of his works. It is a humorous, nostalgic meditation on the dance by means of dancing, conducted in the spirit of comedy and strung together on the thread of memory. Bim (the young Béjart, danced by Ullate), small, youthfully slender, rather plain, but bright-eyed and bushy-tailed, arrives in Paris to devote himself to dancing. He begins study with his teacher, Madame (Mathé Souverbie). Dressed in black, her eyes encircled with kohl, her hair shiny black and arranged like that of Olga Spessivtzeva, with dead-white face, blood-red lips and fingernails, Madame is portrayed with irony but affection. She teaches him hard lessons in a strong Russian accent, regrets the glories of St. Petersburg, tortures but loves her pupil, even tortures him because she loves him, according to the iron discipline of ballet. Bim-Béjart continually escapes into dreams, imagining himself in a brilliant, luxurious city, the Paris of the Second Empire, the only one he recognizes in the streets of the capital where the traces of the *grand siècle* are no more. In front of Bim's fascinated eyes pass visions of the past, transfigured into myth, burlesque, and fantasy. He beholds the Opéra with its great diva (Catherine Ver-

neuil) and the tailcoated patrons; then his father, romanticized into a heroic hussar (with a suggestion of Victor Hugo's "my father, that hero with the sweet smile"); then Napoleon III, conceited and ridiculous (Jean-Michel Bouvron), followed by the lightly tripping, hedge-sitting Offenbach (Micha van Hoecke), Ludwig II of Bavaria lost in dreams of grandeur (Yvan Marko), and the Empress Eugénie. Then comes the explosion of the Commune. In spite of the difficulty of constructing a ballet on two levels, real and imaginary, Béjart has succeeded in keeping the multiplicity and waywardness of this dream world under control, without slipping into bad taste. On the contrary, because of the contrasts, he has created a beautifully balanced work. Whenever the emotions of the remembered scene begin to predominate, a Chaplinesque touch of humour intervenes to bring us back to earth. The dominant chord of this brief, danced autobiography is the feeling of time which deeply relates this ballet to all the choreographer's other works. Time is a measure of existence, historical time, time reviewed in memory. Once again a gleam of the Proustian world shines through the web of Béjart's choreography. S.B.

MAYERLING
Ballet in a prologue, three acts, and an epilogue. Music by Franz Liszt, arranged and orchestrated by John Lanchbery. Scenario by Gillian Freeman. Stage designs by Nicholas Georgiadis. London, Covent Garden, February 14, 1978. The Royal Ballet. Principal dancers: Stephen Jefferies (the Crown Prince), Alfreda Thorogood (Baroness Vetsera), Denis Dunn, Michael Somes, Monica Mason, Jennifer Penney.

SYNOPSIS. Prologue: the cemetery at Heiligenkreuz before dawn. Act I: Vienna, the Hofburg. Scene I: the ballroom. At the ball celebrating his wedding to the Princess Stephanie of Belgium, whom he does not love, the Crown Prince flirts openly with other women, to the indignation of his wife and parents. Mary Vetsera is introduced to him by her mother. Four Hungarian officers enter. They are friends of the Prince and plead with him to aid them in their separatist cause. Scene II: the Empress's apartments. Elizabeth is with her ladies-in-waiting. Rudolf visits her before going to his bride. He seeks to gain her sympathy for his unhappiness. Scene III: Rudolf's apartments. Stephanie is prepared for her wedding night. Rudolf, finding her alone, terrifies her with a revolver before making love to her. Act II. Scene I: a notorious tavern. Rudolf has insisted that the unhappy Stephanie comes with him in disguise. They are accompanied by the Prince's faithful cab driver, Bratfisch. The whores are resentful. Stephanie leaves in disgust. Rudolf remains behind with his mistress, Mitzi Caspar, and his Hungarian friends. There is a police raid during which they hide. Overtaken by despair, Rudolf suggests a suicide pact, but Mitzi will have none of it. Scene II: outside the tavern. Mary Vetsera is again introduced to the Prince, this time by Countess Larisch, a former mistress. Scene III: the Vetsera house. Mary is absorbed in a portrait of Rudolf when Countess Larisch calls. She tells Mary's fortune with cards, assuring her that her dream of romance will come true. Mary gives her a letter for Rudolf. Scene IV: the Hofburg. Emperor Franz Josef's birthday celebration, a strange occasion on which the Emperor's mistress, the Empress, her lover, and the Prime Minister are present, exchange facetious gifts, and watch a firework display. Rudolf looks on with bitter feelings. Countess Larisch hands him Mary's letter. Scene V: Mary and the Prince meet for the first time. Act III. Scene I: the countryside. A royal shoot. A pleasant day until suddenly and un-accountably Rudolf fires wildly, killing a member of the court and narrowly missing the Emperor. Scene II: Rudolf's apartments at the Hofburg. The Empress finds Countess Larisch with the Prince and dismisses her, not knowing that Mary is waiting outside. Rudolf asks Mary to die with him. Scene III: the hunting lodge at Mayerling. Rudolf is drinking with his friends, but sends them away, before Bratfisch arrives with Mary. The Prince makes love to her, then, after calming her nerves with morphine, shoots her. His friends, disturbed by the shot, come back, but are reassured. When they are gone, Rudolf shoots himself. Epilogue: the cemetery at Heiligenkreuz before dawn.

■ MacMillan's interest was not only in the strange story of the double suicide and the characters involved, but also in the decadent state of the Austrian Empire, with so much glitter and ceremony covering so much squalor and corruption. Each act ends with an important *pas de deux* signalling a further stage in the degeneration of Rudolf's character, the one in the third act leading directly into the murder and suicide. In contrast to the usual practice in modern dance of interpreting music in movement inspired by it, MacMillan looked for music that would interpret his ideas, although, of course, the individual passages and movements followed the suggestions of the score. John Lanchbery, the orchestrator, felt that Liszt would be the right composer for place, period, and feeling. The choreographer concurred. The music used was carefully chosen to express the emotions involved in each scene, and to avoid pieces that were already too familiar. The selection that was finally chosen was the *Faust Symphony*, one of the *Mephisto Waltzes, Soirée de Vienne* and *Twelve Transcendental Studies*.   O.O.

GENESIS
One-act ballet. Choreography by Alicia Alonso. Music by Luigi Nono. Set by Jesus Soto. Cuba, National Ballet, April 1978. Principal dancers: Maria Elena Llorente, Jorge Esquivel.

SYNOPSIS. An abstract ballet.

■ To electronic music by Nono (*A Floresta*) and in Soto's ravishing set (a forest of ribbons played on by extraordinarily effective lighting), the great Alicia Alonso, choreographer, ballerina, and director of the Cuban Ballet, tells the story of humanity's liberation from violence, war, constraints, and slavery in a modern

and vital style, almost always influenced by modern dance methods. The lighting shifts and changes with the movements of the dancers as they pass among the components of the set, which at different points represents a forest, a prison, or a plantation. When the new life comes into being and all chains are broken, the bells, which have been suspended above the stage, appear to peal in celebration and descend among the dancers.

M.P.

ESOTERIK SATIE
Ballet in two movements and an illustrated interval. Choreography and scenario by Lorca Massine. Music by Erik Satie. Set and costumes by Raimonda Gaetani. Milan, Teatro Lirico, May 5, 1978. Corps de ballet of the Scala, Milan. Principal dancers: Lorca Massine, Anna Razzi, Paolo Podini, Bruno Vescovo, Maurizio Bellezza, Oriella Dorella, Gabriele Tenneriello.

SYNOPSIS. The ballet evokes the world and cultural background of Erik Satie, the antiromantic composer and personality who moved in the forefront of the twentieth-century avant-garde, through a sequence of scenes interpreting his major compositions. From his anti-Wagnerian polemics to the cabaret turns for the intelligentsia, from his early mysticism to the deeply ironical state of mind that followed, we pass to the Satie works which influenced modern ballet, such as the Léonide Massine–Cocteau–Picasso production *Parade*. The film *Entr'acte* by René Clair, interpolated in the ballet *Relâche* (with score by Satie), is also used in the finale, which shows the resurrection of Erik into a white paradise inhabited by bearded angels in white tutus. *Esoterik Satie* is completed with some of the composer's phrases on film, some advertising drop scenes by Satie himself, and comments broadcast in the foyer by loudspeakers during the interval, together with *In Praise of Critics*, from one of his more disrespectful lectures.

■ Lorca Massine composed this ballet after careful historical research. His design – largely successful – was to restore the flavour of a distant time to a modern audience. The choreography is not particularly inventive. While the language is classical, there are frequent ironical overtones and various cabaret turns. Some costumes and visual elements from *Parade* are included. When not recorded, the music is performed on two pianos; in the prologue we hear the overture to Wagner's *Tannhäuser* played with tongue in cheek.

M.P.

ECUATORIAL
One-act ballet. Choreography by Martha Graham. Music by Edgar Varèse. New York, Metropolitan Opera House, June 26, 1978. Martha Graham Dance Company. Principal dancers: Yuriko Kibura and Mario Delamo.

SYNOPSIS. A comedy of love and courtship between the priestess of the Moon and the celebrant of the Sun.

■ This most recent creation of Martha Graham, now in her eighties, returns to the theme of relationships between men and women, the rejections, passions, frustrations, and the poetry of mythical love. The ballet was danced on the same evening as two other new productions, *The Owl and the Pussycat*, in which Liza Minelli, appearing at the Metropolitan for the first time, recited Edward Lear's verse, and *Pan's Flute*, a musical pastoral in song and sound, a loving fable that was almost a homage to the period of modern dance associated with the style of Denishawn.   M.P.

THE QUEEN OF SPADES
One-act ballet. Choreography by Roland Petit. Music by Piotr I. Tchaikovsky. Sets by André Beaurepaire. Costumes by Jacques Schmidt and Emmanuel Peduzzi. Paris, Théâtre des Champs Elysées, October 17, 1978. Ballets de Marseille. Principal dancers: Mikhail Baryshnikov (Hermann), Evelyne Desutter, Jacqueline Rayet.

SYNOPSIS. Scene I: Hermann, a young cavalry officer, enters and takes stock of his situation. His poverty oppresses him. Scene II: in a gaming room men and women are seated around a table, looking as if they had emerged from some shadowy past. Hermann watches them as if bewitched. The aged Countess Anna Fedorovna sits at one corner. It is said that she possesses a cabalistic secret, three cards that cannot fail to win. The old lady is accompanied by her young ward, Lisa. Hermann pays court to Lisa to ingratiate himself with the Countess. Scene III: at a ball Hermann continues his seduction of Lisa, who finally gives him the key to her room. Scene IV: the Countess has returned home and her maid is getting her ready for bed. Hermann bursts in and implores the old lady in vain to reveal the secret of the cards to him. She dies of fright. Lisa is horrified, but Hermann, instead of consoling her, leaves abruptly. Scene V: Hermann dreams that the dead Countess appears and tells him the secret of the three cards. Scene VI: the gaming room again. Hermann tries his luck. The first two cards seen in his dream turn up and he wins; but the third card is the Queen of Spades. When he sees that she has the face of the dead Countess he becomes insane.   M.P.

■ The ballet, which draws its inspiration more from the story by Pushkin than from Tchaikovsky's eponymous work, was built around the prodigious personality of the Russian dancer Baryshnikov, and existed only in relation to his presence on stage. The rest is mere decoration and rarely assumes any dramatic significance. The characters of Lisa and the Countess in particular are not very finely drawn. Petit devised a difficult and demanding part for Baryshnikov, which the dancer tackled with extraordinary balletic exploits and with great tragic presence. The music was arranged by Laurent Petitgirard on themes from Tchaikovsky's work.

LOVE AND THE POET*(Amor di Poeta)*
Ballet in four parts. Choreography by Maurice Béjart. Music by Robert Schumann and Nino Rota. Brussels, Palais des Beaux Arts, December 5, 1978. Ballet du XXme Siècle. Principal dancers: Jorge Donn (the Poet), Shonach Mirk, Martine Detournay, Katalin Csarnoy, André Ziemsky, Jan Nuyts, Bertrand Pie, Yann Le Gac.

SYNOPSIS. A poetic and surreal fantasy on the theme of poetry, love, and myth. Part I: the friends. In this scene there appear the Muses, a cat who is the magical friend of poets, and the present but inaccessible lady of whom the bride is only a caricature. Part II: the force of death. A strange trio, the man in black who directs the circus of anguish and derision, the woman in white, who change disguises, and the motorcyclist, who is mechanized death, a modern version of Pegasus. Part III: mythological characters. Pegasus, symbol of ancient poetry, Dionysus, and Zarathushtra introduce us to theater and dance. Part IV: the poetry of mockery. Here is the circus with clowns, Pierrot, and George Sand, the devourer of poets. The poet is something of a mixture between the great romantics and Fellini the film director. A final fusion of the arts takes place to poetic words and music.

■ Like *Gaîté Parisienne*, this fantastic ballet of Béjart's follows the path of entertainment and, to some extent, detachment. There is a vague connection, however, with some very contemporary themes, references to various past experiments, motorcycling, and transvestism. In *Love and the Poet* (set to the *Lieder* of Schumann and to Rota's music, mostly from Fellini film scores), some familiar symbols emerge from Béjart's "property store": Pegasus and Zarathushtra, George Sand and Baudelaire, the *blousons noirs*, and the Muses, Pierrot, and surreal monsters. It is a vast pastiche on the subjects of love, happiness, and folly in which the most diverse components are sewn together with white thread. Choreographically mathematical, *Love and the Poet* is fascinating in its lively, vital way, but perhaps marks a pause in Béjart's creativity in anticipation of more demanding ventures.   M.P.

THE FOUR SEASONS
One-act ballet in four sections. Choreography by Jerome Robbins. Music by Giuseppe Verdi. Sets and costumes by Santo Loquasto. Lighting by Jennifer Tipton. New York. Lincoln Center, New York State Theater. New York City Ballet. January 18, 1979. Principal dancers: Heather Watts, Kyra Nichols, Daniel Duell, Stephanie Saland, Bart Cook, Patricia McBride, Mikhail Baryshnikov.

SYNOPSIS. Plotless ballet in four scenes. The god Janus introduces personifications of the four seasons and commands a dance for each one.

■ Jerome Robbins has used selections from the ballet scores in Verdi's operas *I Vespri Siciliani*, *I Lombardi* and *Il Trovatore* for this work, which lasts over half an hour. It is an elegant, light-hearted, lucid piece which catches the spirit of Verdi's music. Winter beckons and snowflakes rush in, chased by gusts of wind: Joseph Duell and Peter Frame. Heather Watts, a latecomer, conquers the wind with a flick of her wand and leads the shivering corps as they warm up by dancing. The Spring section has as its pivotal point a waltz for Kyra Nichols and Daniel Duell and a *divertissement* for four dancers costumed as peapods. Bart Cook and Stephanie Saland dance the rather thin Summer section, which conveys an oriental torpor. Fall is a bacchanal in the Bolshoi style, thrillingly danced by Baryshnikov and Patricia McBride, in which Robbins makes use of Baryshnikov's leaps and turns, as well as his sense of humour. Peter Martins and Suzanne Farrell alternated in this section, with different choreography for both.   M.H.

THE TILLER IN THE FIELDS

One-act ballet. Choreography by Antony Tudor. Music by Antonin Dvorak. Sets by Ming Cho Lee. Costumes by Willa Kim. Lighting by Thomas Skelton. New York. Lincoln Center, Metropolitan Opera House. American Ballet Theater, April 5, 1979. Principal dancers: Gelsey Kirkland, Patrick Bissell.

SYNOPSIS. The ballet opens in an airy, pastoral setting. Slavic peasants linking arms cavort in rural celebration. A happy, innocent youth is dancing among them. A gypsy girl, obviously an outsider, appears. He ignores her at first, but is disturbed by her presence and attracted to her. The lights dim. They dance together in a romantic *pas de deux*. He runs off after her, carrying his jacket. The youth and some village boys return to play athletic games. The exuberant mood continues. Then the gypsy girl returns, wearing the youth's jacket. She opens it to disclose that she is pregnant. He is astonished, but chooses to remain with her.

■ Antony Tudor is a master of psychological dance-drama but his output is small and any new work from him automatically draws attention. He has always been interested in sexual themes, particularly sexual repression (*Pillar of Fire, Dim Lustre, Jardin aux Lilas*). But audiences were left mystified by this work. The choreography is formal, subtle and lyrical, the music (Dvorak's *Symphonies No. 2 and No. 6* and *In Nature's Realm*) exuberant. But the sudden introduction of naturalism (in the form of a pregnant belly) into a classical work was jarring.   M.H.

LE BOURGEOIS GENTILHOMME

One-act ballet. Choreography by George Balanchine and Jerome Robbins. Music by Richard Strauss. Sets and costumes by Rouben Ter-Arutunian. Lighting by Gilbert V. Hemsley, Jr. New York. Lincoln Center, New York State Theater. Dancers of the New York City Ballet Company and students of the School of American Ballet in a production by the New York City Opera Company. April 8, 1979. Principal dancers: Rudolf Nureyev, Patricia McBride, Jean-Pierre Bonnefous.

SYNOPSIS. This ballet is based on the Molière play of the same name. M. Jourdain, a nouveau-riche bourgeois, wants to become an aristocrat. He forbids his daughter Lucile to marry her lover Cléonte because he is not of noble birth. Cléonte appears in various disguises as dancing master, fencing teacher, tailor, and a rich Turk who wants to marry Lucile. A classical *pas de sept* is danced for the entertainment of the Turk, Lucille, and M. Jourdain. Lucile performs a sad solo and leaves. Cléonte and his helpers dress Jourdain as a Turk in beard, turban, robe and saber. Six lackeys disappear under a cloth to form an elephant and M. Jourdain sits on top. As Cléonte still disguised as the Turk dances a solo, Lucile reappears. She rejects him, unaware of his identity. He takes off his moustache and she recognizes him. M. Jourdain responds to their pleading and gives them his blessing.

■ The production shared a double bill with New York City Opera's *Dido and Aeneas* and provided Rudolf Nureyev with his first opportunity to dance a role choreographed for him by George Balanchine. After starting work, Balanchine became ill and Jerome Robbins took over. Balanchine returned and made the final revisions. He had first created a ballet on this theme in 1932 for René Blum's Ballet Théâtre du Monte Carlo and again in 1944 for the Ballets Russes de Monte Carlo. None of his former choreography was retained in this version. The neoclassical *pas de sept*, danced by students from the School of American Ballet, is charming and pretty. The choreography for the rest of the ballet is fast and witty, with Jean-Pierre Bonnefous supremely funny as the buffoon, M. Jourdain.   M.H.

THE TEMPEST

A full-length ballet. Choreography by Glen Tetley, based on William Shakespeare's play. Music by Arne Nordheim. Stage design by Nadine Baylis. Lighting by John B. Read. Projection design by Malcolm Hoare. Commissioned for the Schwetzingen Festival, it was first performed there at the Rokoko Theater by the Rambert Ballet Company on May 3, 1979. First performance in Britain: July 3, 1979. Principal dancers: Christopher Bruce, Gianfranco Paoluzi, Thomas Yang, Mark Wraith, Lucy Burge.

SYNOPSIS. The plot of *The Tempest* will be well known to most readers. It concerns the magician-duke Prospero, whose duchy has been usurped by his brother Antonio. Some fifteen years earlier the usurper cast Prospero and his baby daughter Miranda adrift in a frail boat, certain they would perish. However, they landed safely on an island inhabited only by the earthy, half-human Caliban and the airy spirit Ariel, imprisoned in a tree by Caliban's dead witch-mother. Prospero freed Ariel, who became his servant, and tried in vain to reform Caliban, finally making him his slave. Now Miranda has grown to lovely young womanhood. The usurping Duke with Alonso, King of Naples, and the latter's son, Ferdinand, have been wrecked on the island by Prospero's spell. Ferdinand meets Miranda and they fall in love. With the help of his magic powers and his airy spirit, Prospero teases and misleads Antonio, Alonso, and their crew, but finally forgives them, renounces future magic, and all return to his regained dukedom.

■ This, Glen Tetley's first full-length work, is one of the most important developments in modern dance, and the most ambitious production to date of the London-based Ballet Rambert. For over four years *The Tempest* simmered in Tetley's imagination. "Through this long period," says the choreographer, "I returned again and again to the play until it seemed to enter my subconscious, and, like Caliban, 'when I waked I cried to sleep again.'" From the beginning of practical work on the ballet it has been a collaboration between the choreograher, the composer Arne Nordheim, the designer Nadine Baylis, and John B. Read, the lighting expert, so that movement, sound, and colour blend together with a perfection that makes the whole a masterpiece of poetry and imagination. The set is a fantasy of curved and overlapping shapes in sailcloth transformed by projection into sails, cliffs, vortices and caverns. On the stage lie sixteen square yards of silk which, moving with the dancers, irresistibly suggests the rippling of surf. The whole decor is visually ravishing and creates a climate redolent of sea and enchantment. To quote Glen Tetley's own words on *The Tempest*, "Each theme has a countertheme, and the countertheme has its own countertheme. . . . The atmosphere is magical and the language is metaphor; Ariel and Caliban are powerful dream figures. The sleeping and awakening dream flux, the sea changes, the tempest that resides within, the very structure of Shakespeare's world, speak as powerfully as his words." *The Tempest* has been used before as a balletic subject, notably at the King's Theatre, London, on April 4, 1774; by Jean Coralli in 1834, with music by Jean Schneitzhöffer, and Fanny Elssler in the leading female role, at the Paris Théâtre de l'Académie Royale de Musique; in London in 1838 by Filippo Taglioni in a version considerably adapted for Maria Taglioni; in 1869 in Turin; and in 1889, once more in Paris. In June 1964 Andrée Howard created a version of *The Tempest* to music by Michael Tippett for the London Dance Theatre. It was first performed at the Theatre Royal, Nottingham. Except in regard to subject, none of these is related to Tetley's version.   O.O.

THE IDIOT

Three-act ballet. Choreography by Valery Panov. Music by Dimitri Shostakovich. Sets and projections by Gunther Schneider-Siemssen. Costumes by Bernd Muller. Berlin. Deutsche Oper. Ballet of the Deutsche Oper. June 25, 1979. Principal dancers: Vladimir Gelvan, Eva Evdokimova, Reda Sheta, Galina Panova.

SYNOPSIS. A three-and-a-half hour ballet based on Dostoyevsky's novel, with its theme of love, destruction and death in Czarist Russia. The plot centers around four main characters, Prince Myshkin, his friend/antagonist Rogozhin, the young Aglaya (who loves Myshkin) and the beautiful Nastasya whose wiles lead to destruction. The first scene opens with Prince Myshkin and Rogozhin meeting each other in the corridor of a train. Their strange friendship begins. Myshkin arrives in St. Petersburg and makes his way to General Yepanshin's house. Inside, he frolics with the general's daughters, in particular with his youngest, Aglaya, a bit of a tomboy. The general and his secretary Totksy plot to marry Nastasya, Totsky's protegée, to Ganya Ivolgin. Myshkin knocks off a cloth which covers her picture and is struck by her beauty. Scene II is at the Ivolgins' house. Ganya's drunken father cavorts with a couple of slatterns and attracts the other lodgers who join in. Myshkin (who is living there) sees Nastasya. She mistakes him for a servant at first. Ganya and his mother and sister argue about Nastasya. Rogozhin appears (he wants to marry her, too) and the scene draws to a climax when Ganya slaps Myshkin and then begs him to forgive him. Scene III takes place at Nastasya's birthday party. She dances with Myshkin, then Rogozhin arrives with money he has promised her. She throws it on the fire and challenges Ganya to retrieve it. Ganya is left in despair. Nastasya and Rogozhin leave and Myshkin follows them. Act II opens with a gypsy dance. Rogozhin is waiting for Nastasya in a café. He hopes to marry her but she rejects him. Scene II in Rogozhin's house finds him angry and despairing. Myshkin visits him and they declare their allegiance to each other and exchange crosses. In Scene III Myshkin is in the street and events build up to his epileptic fit. Act III begins with Myshkin convalescing at Pavlovsk. Aglaya (the youngest of the three girls introduced in the first act) visits him. He meets her parents in the park and feelings begin to develop between him and Aglaya. Nastasya arrives at the resort. Aglaya attacks her, Myshkin tries to protect Natasya out of pity, and ends up losing Aglaya. The scene shifts to a church door. Myshkin is leading Nastasya to their wedding when she leaves him again, going off with Rogozhin. But Rogozhin realizes that she will never truly belong to him and he kills her. Myshkin finds him and commiserates. Myshkin goes mad, and the ballet ends with an apocalyptic vision.

■ It is not the first time an attempt has been made to put *The Idiot* onstage. In 1952 a production was mounted in Berlin with choreography by Tatiana Gsovsky to music by Henze, and a revised version was staged in 1959 in which Myshkin's role was shared by an actor and dancer. Panov's version was enthusiastically received, with half-hour ovations for the production and the many dancers (over 100) who took part. It is Panov's third full-length ballet for the company (following *Cinderella* and *Rite of Spring*). Panov adapted the epic story to dance by using classical ballet, pageants of Russian life, folklore and scenes of society. Thirty pieces of Shostakovich's music make up the score, most of them presented in their entirety. Panov's choreography is often brilliant, particularly for the two leading women, as are some of the sequences for the two men. He keeps the action moving and skilfully delineates his characters so that they project with drama and intensity. He has studied both male roles himself and alternates in the two parts.   M.H.

SONGS, LAMENTATIONS, AND PRAISES

Ballet in three parts. Choreography by Robert Cohan. Music by Geoffrey Burgon. Design by Norberto Chiesa. Lighting by John B. Read. First performed in Israel at the Jerusalem Theater, August 7, 1979. London Contemporary Dance Theatre. London premiere: November 27, 1979, Sadler's Wells. Danced by the entire company.

SYNOPSIS. The ballet interprets three verses from the Bible. Each section begins with a figure in black, the Painter of the Soul, who by his invocatory circling movements seems to conjure visions. In the first part, *Songs* ("Take me with you and we will run together; bring me into your chamber, O King"), the atmosphere is one of sexual love as successive couples in leotards dance together. *Lamentations* ("The joy of our heart has ceased; our dance is turned into mourning") is illustrated by strange batrachian springing expressive of harsh pain; then, to a humming music, representing the women's laments, the female dancers turn and revolve, alternating with thundrous sounds accompanying the men's anguished leaps. The *Praises* section ("Praise ye the Lord. Praise God in his sanctuary; praise him with timbrel and dance") envisages praise as exhilarated joy. Entering singly at first, the company, dressed in graded colours of red, gradually fills the stage with rapturous gyrations. A great jumping finale by the men brings the ballet to a conclusion of high excitement.

■ The work was specially commissioned for the International Seminar on the Bible in Dance. To Cohan, who was at that time devoting his energies entirely to abstract choreography concerned with forms and movements as an autonomous, all-embracing element, the composition of a ballet on a definite subject presented problems. These he solved by interpreting the verses in purely abstract terms expressive of their spirit and mood. The work has, nevertheless, a strong emotional content, enhanced by Burgon's stirring, especially commissioned music, and the design and lighting by Chiesa and Read respectively.   O.O.

MANFRED

One-act ballet in four scenes. Choreography by Rudolf Nureyev. Music by Tchaikovsky. Sets by Radu Boruzescu. Costumes by Miruna Boruzescu. Lighting by Serge Peyrat. Paris. Palais des Sports. Ballet de l'Opéra de Paris. November 20, 1979. Principal dancers: Jean Guizerix, Wilfride Piollet, Dominique Khalfouni, Sylvia Clavier, Stephane Prince.

SYNOPSIS. The poet (Byron) enters to sombre music, limping down a steep flight of stairs. Characters of his life are introduced as in a waking dream: Astarte, the poet's muse and consolation, who also represents his sister and lover; his mother and his wife. He dances with a young man but their relationship is suddenly broken off by the beloved's death. These duets are shown against a background of an ensemble representing monks drinking from human skulls, changing to innocent choirboys, then to Byron's society friends. From time to time Sin, a menacing figure in black, watches the poet. Figures obstruct the poet's path and block the way of his companion. His solo ends in despair, and he rushes away. Scene II takes place in the Alps, in a lighter and more cheerful vein. Mountain spirits enter. The poet joins them. A trio, Mary Shelley, Shelley and Mary's half-sister Claire, appears. But their friendship with the poet is interrupted by the death of Shelley. Scene III is in Italy. The poet is in love with a Countess but he is distracted by thoughts of the fighting between Turks and Greek patriots. Astarte appears to him in a vision as a captive whom he tries to rescue in hand-to-hand combat. He is tormented by thoughts of the drowned Shelley. After each episode he returns to the Countess but is obsessed by the urge for adventure, and takes off. Scene IV begins in an orgiastic frenzy in which the poet summons up devilish apparitions from the grave. He rushes from woman to woman; he rescues Astarte (who symbolizes the liberty of Greece) from the Turks. He joins the war. Figures in black return and their past relationships with the poet are briefly recapitulated. An enormous wave pours over the stage and sweeps them aside. The poet is left clinging to a piece of wreckage. He is at peace, freed by death. Astarte comes in and joins him as the light fades.

■ Nureyev has based his ballet on the life of the hero of Byron's poem *Manfred*, themes from other poems, and Byron's life. He had hoped to dance the role himself, but was prevented from appearing at its premiere because of an injury. The hero is constantly on stage for nearly an hour and a quarter, and the role demands strong dramatic presence and technique. The emotional tension runs high and the ballet moves with no letup. The choreography is abundant, fast and energetic. Nureyev has tried to capture the romantic agony of Byron's life, and his ballet is full of drama and colour.   M.H.

List of Ballets

Ballets are entered under their English title where this exists. Foreign-language titles for these English titles are included only where their alphabetical order does not immediately precede or follow the English entry.

List of Choreographers

PICTURE SOURCES

Libraries, Collections, Societies, Museums, Theaters

Bibliothèque de l'Arsenal, Paris: 63, 104, 118b. Bibliothèque de l'Institut, Paris: 57, 61. Bibliothèque de l'Opéra, Paris: 64, 65, 66, 69, 72, 73r, 73l, 76r, 76l, 93, 98, 99, 102r, 126, 162a, 162b, 171, 195. Bibliothèque Nationale, Paris: 42, 43, 50r, 50l, 51, 52–3, 55, 56, 181. Biblioteca Nazionale, Florence: 44, 45. Civica Raccolta Stampe Achille Bertarelli: 79, 108, 113, 118a, 122. Collection Larionov: 189. Collection Milon: 111, 121b and l. The Cullberg Ballet: 227, 267, 307, 308. Dansmuseet, Stockholm: 201. State Tretyakov Gallery, Moscow: 163. International Color Library: 134. Boris Kochno Collection: 161, 193. Det Kongelige Teater: 109, 119l, 119r, 120, 125. Library of Congress: 153r. Lincoln Center Library: 216, 251. Musée d'Art Moderne, Paris: 182. Musée des Arts Décoratifs, Paris: 48–9, 94. Museo Teatro alla Scala: 71, 78, 80, 81a and r, 81b and l, 83, 85, 86, 87, 88–9, 90, 91, 92, 97, 102l, 110, 116, 117, 135, 147a, 190. Museum and Library of the Performing Arts, New York: 206. Opéra de Paris: 221. San Francisco Ballet: 225. Teatro La Fenice, Venice: 236. Victoria and Albert Museum, London: 103, 114.

Photographic Agencies and Photographers

AP Laser Photo: 175. Mondadori Photographic Archive: 33, 55, 56, 60, 61, 63, 95, 97, 101, 115, 127, 137, 141, 167, 174, 175, 176, 177, 181, 183, 186, 187, 191, 192, 193, 194, 197, 203, 204, 206, 223, 226, 238, 240, 253, 259, 261, 295. Raoul Barba: 156, 166, 172. Alain Bejart: 294. Henri Cartier-Bresson: 263. Giancarlo Costa: 64, 65, 195. Carlo Dani: 80, 88–9, 110, 116, 147a, 147b, 173. Mike Davis: 77, 169b, 199, 219, 243, 260, 266. Del Grande: 268–9. Drouet: 159, 160. Kenn Duncan: 11, 116, 281. Farabola: 212, 271, 282–3, 288. Fratelli Fabbri Editori, Milan: 189, 190, 236. Gerschel: 153l. Giraudon: 94. Marek Habdas: 229. Harcourt: 207. Jacqueline Hyde: 182. International Foto Service: 204. John R. Johnsen: 109, 119l, 119r, 125. Lalance: 42, 43, 48–9, 50r, 50l, 51, 52–3, 57, 66, 69, 72, 73r, 73l, 76r, 76l, 93, 98, 99, 102r, 118b, 162a, 162b, 171. Leone: 33. Erich Lessing (Magnum): 256. Serge Lido: 169a, 179, 205, 232, 257, 258, 265, 278, 299. Lipnitzki: 197, 252. Liverani: 102l. Giorgio Lotti: 6, 15, 20, 21, 29, 37, 68, 121a and r, 131, 138–9, 146, 237, 280, 285, 292, 293, 300, 301, 304. Colette Masson: 238. Rigmor Mydtskov: 120. Planeta, Moscow: 106–7, 142, 143, 150, 151, 152, 154–5, 217, 228, 241, 297. Photos Match: 259. Roger Pic: 221. Piccagliani: 209a, 213, 274, 287, 311. Pucciarelli: 103, 114. Laura Rizzi: 183. Enar Merkel Rydberg: 275. Saporetti: 101, 108, 118a, 122. Scala: 44, 45. Seth-Eastman-Mochs: 129. Leslie-Spinks: 227, 267, 307, 308. Martha Swope: 209b, 233, 235, 242, 245, 249, 273, 277, 284.
© S.P.A.D.E.M.: 162a, 162b, 167, 171, 181, 182, 186, 187, 190, 194, 221, 240.
© A.D.A.G.P.: 177, 189, 203.